HARCOURT
· TROPHIES ·
A HARCOURT READING/LANGUAGE ARTS PROGRAM

GATHER AROUND

TEACHER'S EDITION

SENIOR AUTHORS
Isabel L. Beck ◆ Roger C. Farr ◆ Dorothy S. Strickland

AUTHORS
Alma Flor Ada ◆ Marcia Brechtel ◆ Margaret McKeown
Nancy Roser ◆ Hallie Kay Yopp

SENIOR CONSULTANT
Asa G. Hilliard III

CONSULTANTS
F. Isabel Campoy ◆ David A. Monti

Orlando   Boston   Dallas   Chicago   San Diego

Visit *The Learning Site!*

www.harcourtschool.com

Acknowledgments appear in the back of this book.

Printed in the United States of America

ISBN 0-15-339740-3

8 9 10   030   10 09 08 07 06

Program Authors

SENIOR AUTHORS

Isabel L. Beck
Professor of Education and Senior Scientist at the Learning Research and Development Center, University of Pittsburgh

Research Contributions: Reading Comprehension, Beginning Reading, Phonics, Vocabulary

Roger C. Farr
Chancellor's Professor of Education and Director of the Center for Innovation in Assessment, Indiana University, Bloomington

Research Contributions: Instructional Assessment, Reading Strategies, Staff Development

Dorothy S. Strickland
Samuel DeWitt Proctor Professor of Education, Rutgers University

Research Contributions: Early Literacy, Elementary Reading/Language Arts, Writing, Intervention

AUTHORS

Alma Flor Ada
Director of Doctoral Studies in the International Multicultural Program, University of San Francisco

Research Contributions: English as a Second Language, Bilingual Education, Family Involvement

Marcia Brechtel
Director of Training, Project GLAD, Fountain Valley School District, Fountain Valley, California

Research Contributions: English as a Second Language, Bilingual Education

Margaret McKeown
Research Scientist at the Learning Research and Development Center, University of Pittsburgh

Research Contributions: Reading Comprehension, Vocabulary

Nancy Roser
Professor, Language and Literacy Studies, University of Texas, Austin

Research Contributions: Early Literacy, Phonics, Comprehension, Fluency

Hallie Kay Yopp
Professor, Department of Elementary Bilingual and Reading Education, California State University, Fullerton

Research Contributions: Phonemic Awareness, Early Childhood

SENIOR CONSULTANT

Asa G. Hilliard III
Fuller E. Callaway Professor of Urban Education, Department of Educational Foundations, Georgia State University, Atlanta

Research Contributions: Multicultural Literature and Education

CONSULTANTS

F. Isabel Campoy
Former President, Association of Spanish Professionals in the USA

Research Contributions: English as a Second Language, Family Involvement

David A. Monti
Professor, Reading/Language Arts Department, Central Connecticut State University

Research Contributions: Classroom Management, Technology, Family Involvement

PROFESSIONAL DEVELOPMENT FOR READING
Supports Research-Based Instruction

Professional Development for Reading *guides teachers through the process of delivering research-based instruction in phonemic awareness, phonics, fluency, vocabulary, and text comprehension.*

COURSES

■ **Teaching Phonemic Awareness, Grades K–1** The role of phonemic awareness in learning to read and strategies for teaching

■ **Teaching Phonics, Kindergarten** Systematic, explicit phonics instruction including special attention to letter-sound relationships

■ **Teaching Phonics, Grade 1** Teaching letter-sound relationships, word blending and word building, and reading decodable texts

■ **Teaching Phonics, Grade 2, and Strategies for Intervention, Grades 3–6** Principles of decoding and research-based intervention strategies for older students

■ **Teaching Fluency, Grades 1–6** The progression from efficient decoding to text comprehension

■ **Teaching Vocabulary, Grades K–2** The progression of vocabulary through primary grades, including its role as a bridge between phonics and comprehension

■ **Teaching Vocabulary, Grades 3–6** The role of vocabulary learning strategies in improving reading in older students

■ **Teaching Text Comprehension, Grades K–1** The role of listening comprehension in learning to read and the transition from listening to reading comprehension

■ **Teaching Text Comprehension, Grades 2–6** Techniques for teaching reading strategies for students to use

■ **Assessment to Inform Instruction, Grades K–6** Entry-level, monitoring, and summative assessments

■ **An Overview of Reading Instruction for Teachers, Administrators, and Parents, Grades K–6** The building blocks of research-based reading instruction: phonemic awareness, phonics, fluency, vocabulary, and text comprehension

COMPONENTS FOR EACH COURSE

Participant Guide contains copies of transparencies, activity pages, and summaries of articles for professional reading

Trainer Guide provides step-by-step instructions for presenting teaching strategies and materials, supported by research

TRANSPARENCY IG

Research Says
Teach Phonics Systematically and Explicity

Systematic and **explicit** phonics instructions:

- Is more effective than non-systematic or no phonics instruction.

- Significantly improves kindergartners' and first-graders' word recogniotion and spelling.

- Significantly improves children's reading comprehension.

- Is effective for children from all socioeconomic levels.

- Is most effective when introduced in kindergarten or first grade.

(Put Reading First, pp. 13–I5)

Session 1 • **Teaching Phonics: Grade I**   Transparency IG

Transparencies present key points in a visual format

Video shows models of research-based instruction

Interactive Instructional Resources from *Trophies* demonstrate principles taught in the courses (varies per course)

PHONEMIC AWARENESS

Research clearly shows that phonemic awareness is one of the primary predictors of success in learning to read and instruction in phonemic awareness significantly supports students' reading and writing achievement.

Phonemic awareness is the awareness of sounds in spoken language. It is recognizing and understanding that speech is made up of a series of individual sounds, or phonemes, and that the individual sounds can be manipulated. A phonemically aware child can segment and blend strings of isolated sounds to form words. Phonemic awareness falls under the umbrella of phonological awareness, which also includes recognizing and manipulating larger units of sound, such as syllables and words. Phonemic awareness can be difficult for young children to attain because it demands a shift in attention from the *content* of speech to the *form* of speech. It requires individuals to attend to the sounds of speech separate from their meanings. Primary grade teachers will find that a handful of children enter school with well-developed phonemic awareness. Other children have only a rudimentary sense of the sound structure of speech. With extended exposure to a language-rich environment, most children develop phonemic awareness over time.

Research has shown that phonemic awareness is significantly related to success in learning to read and spell. The relationship is one of reciprocal causation or mutual facilitation. That is, phonemic awareness supports reading and spelling acquisition, and instruction in reading and spelling, in turn, supports further understanding of the phonemic basis of our speech. The relationship is so powerful that researchers have concluded the following:

- Phonemic awareness is the most potent predictor of success in learning to read (Stanovich, 1986, 1994).
- The lack of phonemic awareness is the most powerful determinant of the likelihood of failure to learn to read (Adams, 1990).
- Phonemic awareness is the most important core and causal factor separating normal and disabled readers (Adams, 1990).

Phonemic awareness is central in learning to read and spell because English and other alphabetic languages map speech to print at the level of phonemes. Our written language is a representation of the *sounds* of our spoken language. It is critical to understand that our speech is made up of sounds. Without this insight, written language makes little sense.

Direct instruction in phonemic awareness helps children decode new words and remember how to read familiar words. Growth and improvement in phonemic awareness can be facilitated through instruction and practice in phonemic awareness tasks such as these:

- **Phoneme isolation,** which requires students to recognize individual sounds in words. For example, "What is the last sound in *hop*?" (/p/)
- **Phoneme matching,** which requires students to recognize the same sound in different words. For example, "Which two words begin with the same sound—*bed, bike, cat*?" (*bed, bike*)
- **Phoneme blending,** which asks students to form a recognizable word after listening to separately spoken sounds. For example, "What word is /a/ -/p/ -/l/?" (*apple*)
- **Phoneme segmentation,** which has students break a word into its individual sounds. For example, "What sounds do you hear in the word *dog*?" (/d/-/ô/-/g/)
- **Phoneme deletion,** which requires students to identify what word remains when a specific phoneme has been removed. For example, "Say *spin* without /s/." (*pin*)
- **Phoneme addition,** which requires the identification of a word when a phoneme is added. For example, "Say *row* with /g/ at the beginning." (*grow*)

Q **What types of phonemic awareness activities or tasks are children exposed to in the program?**

A Phonemic awareness instruction in *Trophies* is strongly supported by the finding that phonemic awareness is one of the most potent predictors of success in learning to read. Activities for stimulating phonemic awareness are incorporated throughout the program. There are two types of phonemic awareness instruction in *Trophies.* The first is word-play activities that draw attention to sounds in spoken language, recited poems, and read-aloud literature. The second type is more formal instruction that focuses on single phonemes to prepare students for studying the letter-sound correspondences for those phonemes.

Q **What phonemic awareness skills are taught in kindergarten and grade 1?**

A Phonemic awareness instruction in *Trophies* follows a systematic, developmental sequence progressing in difficulty from an awareness of words, syllables, and onset/rimes to isolating medial phonemes, substituting phonemes, and other manipulating tasks.

> **"** A growing number of studies indicate that phonemic awareness is not simply a strong predictor, but that it is a necessary prerequisite for success in learning to read. **"**
>
> **— Hallie Kay Yopp**
> Professor
> Department of Elementary
> Bilingual and Reading Education,
> California State University,
> Fullerton

Phonemic Awareness Skills Sequence

- Word Segmentation
- Rhyme Recognition and Production
- Syllable Blending
- Syllable Segmentation
- Syllable Deletion
- Onset and Rime Blending
- Initial Phoneme Isolation

- Final Phoneme Isolation
- Medial Phoneme Isolation
- Phoneme Blending
- Phoneme Segmentation
- Phoneme Substitution
- Phoneme Addition
- Phoneme Deletion

Q **How do the phonemic awareness lessons relate to the phonics lessons in *Trophies*?**

A In kindergarten and grade 1, each phonemic awareness lesson is tied to a phonics lesson. A phonemic awareness lesson, for example, could focus on blending phonemes in words with the /i/ sound, featuring such words as *sit, lip,* and *if.* The subsequent phonics lesson would be the short sound of the letter *i.*

Look for

- ✔ Daily phonemic awareness lessons in Kindergarten and Grade 1
- ✔ Additional Support Activities to Reteach and Extend
- ✔ Point-of-use suggestions for Reaching All Learners

WHAT RESEARCH SAYS ABOUT
EXPLICIT, SYSTEMATIC PHONICS

Decoding is the process of translating written words into speech. Phonics instruction gives students the knowledge of letter-sound correspondences and strategies they need to make the translations and to be successful readers.

Explicit, systematic phonics instruction can help children learn to read more effectively. Current and confirmed research shows that systematic phonics instruction has a significant effect on reading achievement. Research findings clearly indicate that phonics instruction in kindergarten and first grade produces a dramatic impact on reading achievement. In phonics instruction letter-sound correspondences are taught sequentially and cumulatively and are then applied. The individual sounds represented by letters are blended to form words, and those words appear in decodable text. At grade 2, more complex letter patterns are introduced and practiced. This type of instruction allows students to continually build on what they learn.

Word Blending and Word Building are essential aspects of phonics instruction. Word Blending is combining the sounds represented by letter sequences to decode and pronounce words. In phonics instruction beginning in kindergarten or first grade, students are explicitly taught the process of blending individual sounds into words. They begin with VC or CVC words, such as *at* or *man,* and progress to words with consonant blends, as in *tent* and *split*. In contrast to Word Blending, which focuses on decoding a particular word, Word Building allows students to practice making words by using previously taught letter-sound relationships. Word Building activities require children to focus attention on each letter in the sequence of letters that make up words. This helps children develop a sense of the alphabetic system of written English.

As students progress through the grades, they receive direct instruction in decoding multisyllabic words. Direct instruction in recognizing syllables will help students develop effective strategies to read longer, unfamiliar words. Research shows that good readers chunk letter patterns into manageable units in order to read a long, unfamiliar word. Effective strategies include

- identifying syllable boundaries
- identifying syllable types
- isolating affixes
- applying phonics knowledge to blend syllables in sequence

Direct instruction in these strategies helps students recognize word parts so they can apply phonics generalizations to decode unfamiliar words.

> **Decoding is important because this early skill accurately predicts later skill in reading comprehension.**
> — **Isabel L. Beck**
> **Professor of Education and Senior Scientist at the Learning Research and Development Center, University of Pittsburgh**

Q How is Word Blending taught in *Trophies*?

A The purpose of Word Blending instruction is to provide students with practice in combining the sounds represented by letter sequences to decode words. *Trophies* employs the cumulative blending method, which has students blend sounds successively as they are pronounced.

Q How does *Trophies* use Word Building to help students with decoding (reading) and encoding (spelling)?

A In the decoding portion of Word Building, teachers first tell students what letters to put in what place. For example, students are told to put *c* at the beginning, *a* after *c,* and *t* at the end. They are asked to read the word *cat* and then are asked to change *c* to *m* and read the new word, *mat.* In Word Building activities that help encoding, students are asked which letter in the word *cat* needs to change to make the word *mat.* This encoding approach is used to build spelling words throughout the first grade program.

Q How are students taught to decode multisyllabic words?

A Students are taught to see words as patterns of letters, to identify long words by breaking them down into syllable units, and to blend the syllables to form and read long words. Decoding lessons throughout grades 2–6 directly and explicitly provide students with various strategies, including understanding syllable types and patterns and recognizing such word structures as prefixes, suffixes, and root words, to decode multisyllabic words.

Look for

- ✔ Phonics and spelling lessons
- ✔ Word Blending
- ✔ Word Building
- ✔ Decoding/Phonics lessons in Grades 2–6
- ✔ Additional Support Activities to reteach and extend

READING ALOUD

Reading aloud to students contributes to their motivation, comprehension, vocabulary, fluency, knowledge base, literary understanding, familiarity with academic and literary terms, sense of community, enjoyment, and perhaps to a lifetime love of literature.

Sharing and responding to books during read-aloud time helps develop communication and oral language skills and improves comprehension. Literature that is read aloud to students serves as the vehicle for developing literary insights, including sensitivity to the sounds and structure of language. Students learn how powerful written language can be when fluent readers read aloud, interpreting a text through appropriate intonation, pacing, and phrasing. Comprehension skills are developed as students ask and answer questions and share their personal understandings. More advanced students who are read to and who get to talk with others about the best of written language learn both to discuss texts knowingly and to interpret their meanings expressively.

Reading aloud exposes students to more challenging texts than they may be able to read independently. Vocabulary development is fostered by listening to both familiar and challenging selections read aloud. Texts read aloud that are conceptually challenging for students can effectively improve language and comprehension abilities. Listening to challenging texts also exposes students to text structures and content knowledge that are more sophisticated than they may encounter in their own reading.

Listening skills and strategies are greatly improved during read-aloud activities. When students are encouraged to respond to stories read aloud, they tend to listen intently in order to recall relevant content. When students listen responsively and frequently to literature and expository texts, they hone critical-thinking skills that will serve them in many other contexts. In sum, reading aloud

- models fluent reading behavior
- builds students' vocabularies and concepts
- creates an interest in narrative structures
- builds background knowledge by introducing children to new ideas and concepts and by expanding on what is familiar to them
- exposes students to different text structures and genres, such as stories, alphabet books, poetry, and informational books

❝ Sharing literature with children increases their vocabulary and their understanding of how language works. Sharing stories, informational books, and poetry with children has become increasingly valued for its cognitive contribution to children's literary development. ❞

— Dorothy S. Strickland
Samuel DeWitt Proctor
Professor of Education,
Rutgers University

Q **How does *Trophies* provide opportunities for teachers to read aloud to their students?**

A *Trophies* provides a comprehensive collection of read-aloud selections for all levels of instruction. In kindergarten through grade 2, the program includes read-aloud options for students every day. In grades 3–6, a read-aloud selection accompanies every lesson in the *Teacher's Edition*. Read-aloud selections are available in *Read-Aloud Anthologies* for kindergarten through grade 2, the *Library Books Collections* for kindergarten through grade 6 and in several other formats.

Q **What genres can students meet through read-alouds?**

A Students encounter a wide variety of literary genres and expository texts through read-aloud selections in all grades. Expository nonfiction becomes more prevalent as students move up the grades. Other genres include poetry, finger plays, folktales, myths, and narrative nonfiction. In lessons in grades 3-6 with focus skills, such as narrative elements or text structure, the genre of the read-aloud selection matches the genre of the reading selection.

Q **What kind of instruction accompanies read-aloud selections in *Trophies*?**

A In kindergarten and grade 1, the instruction that accompanies Sharing Literature includes three options:
- Build Concept Vocabulary
- Develop Listening Comprehension
- Listen and Respond

In grade 2, options include Develop Listening Comprehension, Set a Purpose, and Recognize Genre. The instructional focus in kindergarten centers on concepts about print and beginning narrative analysis (characters, setting, important events). As students move up the grades, they are taught more complex literary skills, such as following the structure of stories, recognizing their beginnings, middles, and endings, and even occasionally generating alternative endings. In grades 3–6, read-alouds also serve as a vehicle for exploring expository text structures.

Look for

✔ **Daily "Sharing Literature" activities in Kindergarten through Grade 2**

✔ **Read-aloud selections and instruction with every lesson in Grades 2–6**

✔ *Library Books Collections* **at all grades**

✔ *Read-Aloud Anthologies* **in Kindergarten through Grade 2**

COMPREHENSION

Reading comprehension is the complex process of constructing meaning from texts. Recent comprehension research has been guided by the idea that the process is strategic and interactive.

Comprehension is the construction of meaning through an interactive exchange of ideas between the text and the reader. Comprehension strategies are interactive processes that allow readers to monitor and self-assess how well they understand what they are reading. These processes include determining the purpose or purposes for reading, such as to obtain information or to be entertained. After the purpose is determined, readers activate prior knowledge about the content of the text and its structure. Research has shown that the more readers know about the content of a particular text, the more likely they will understand, integrate, and remember the new information. Familiarity with the genre or text structure also fosters comprehension.

Most students need explicit instruction in comprehension skills and strategies. Research shows that comprehension skills and strategies are necessary for student success and that they do not develop automatically in most students. Without explicit instruction and guidance, many readers fail to acquire automatic use of these skills and strategies and show little flexibility in applying them to understand a variety of texts. Research shows that poor readers who are directly taught a particular strategy do as well as good readers who have used the strategy spontaneously. Typically, direct instruction consists of

- an explanation of what the skill or strategy is and how it aids comprehension
- modeling how to use the skill or strategy
- working directly with students as they apply the skill or strategy, offering assistance as needed
- having students apply the skill or strategy independently and repeatedly

Students need extensive direct instruction, guidance, and cumulative practice until they can independently determine the method of constructing meaning that works for them.

Students need to learn strategies for comprehending a wide variety of texts, including both fiction and nonfiction. In kindergarten, students should be taught to understand narrative structure. They should learn to identify the beginning, middle, and ending of a story and other literary elements, such as characters and setting. Then they can use their knowledge of these elements to retell stories they have listened to. In first through third grade, readers deepen their knowledge of these narrative elements and interact with others as book discussants and literary meaning makers. They learn to use the specific language of literature study, such as *point of view* and *character trait*. By grades 4–6, students must have the skills, strategies, and knowledge of text structures to comprehend complex nonfiction texts, including those in the classroom content areas. Students need to be explicitly and systematically taught the organizational structure of expository text, e.g., compare/contrast, cause/effect, and main idea and details. These organizational structures should be taught systematically and reviewed cumulatively.

" One of the fundamental understandings about the nature of reading is that it is a constructive act. Specifically, a reader does not extract meaning from a page, but constructs meaning from information on the page and information already in his/her mind. "

— **Isabel L. Beck**
Professor of Education and Senior Scientist at the Learning Research and Development Center, University of Pittsburgh

Q How does *Trophies* provide explicit instruction in comprehension?

A *Trophies* features systematic and explicit comprehension instruction grounded in current and confirmed research. Comprehension instruction in kindergarten focuses on helping students construct meaning from stories read to them. From the earliest grades, teachers guide students before, during, and after reading in the use of strategies to monitor comprehension. Guided comprehension questions ask students to apply a variety of comprehension skills and strategies appropriate to particular selections. Each tested skill is introduced, reinforced, assessed informally, retaught as needed, reviewed at least twice, and maintained throughout each grade level.

Q How does comprehension instruction in *Trophies* build through the grades?

A Comprehension instruction in *Trophies* is rigorous, developmental, and spiraled. Students gain increasingly sophisticated skills and strategies to help them understand texts successfully. In the instructional components of the earliest grades, emergent and beginning readers develop use of strategies as they respond to texts read by the teacher, and more advanced students begin to apply skills and strategies to texts they read themselves. Students demonstrate their comprehension through asking and answering questions, retelling stories, discussing characters, comparing stories, and making and confirming predictions. As students progress through the grades, they build upon their existing skills and read a more extensive variety of texts.

Q How is instruction in genres and text structures developed in the program?

A The foundation of *Trophies* is a wide variety of fiction and nonfiction selections, including many paired selections to promote reading across texts. Instruction in both the *Pupil Edition* and *Teacher's Edition* helps students develop a thorough understanding of genre characteristics and text structures. In kindergarten, students explore story elements, such as characters, setting, and important events. As students move up the grades, they analyze both literary elements and devices and expository organizational patterns, such as cause/effect and compare/contrast, to understand increasingly difficult texts.

Look for

- ✔ Focus Strategies and Focus Skills
- ✔ Diagnostic Checks
- ✔ Additional Support Activities
- ✔ Guided Comprehension
- ✔ Strategies Good Readers Use
- ✔ Ongoing Assessment
- ✔ *Comprehension Cards*

VOCABULARY

A large and flexible vocabulary is the hallmark of an educated person. The more words students acquire, the better chance they will have for success in reading, writing, and spelling.

Students acquire vocabulary knowledge through extensive reading in a variety of texts. The amount of reading students do in and out of school is a strong indicator of students' vocabulary acquisition. Research supports exposing students to rich language environments through listening to literature and reading a variety of genres independently. Their vocabulary knowledge grows when they hear stories containing unfamiliar words. As students progress through the grades, their reading of books and other materials contributes more significantly to vocabulary knowledge than viewing television, participating in conversations, or other typical oral language activities. In other words, increasing students' volume of reading is the best way to promote vocabulary growth.

Students need multiple encounters with key vocabulary words in order to improve comprehension. Current and confirmed research has shown that students need to encounter a word several times before it is known well enough to facilitate comprehension. Direct instruction in vocabulary has an important role here because learning words from context is far from automatic. After being introduced to new words, students need opportunities to see those words again in their reading and to develop their own uses for the words in a variety of different contexts, in relationship to other words, and both inside and outside of the classroom. For instruction to enhance comprehension, new words need to become a permanent part of students' repertoires, which means instruction must go well beyond providing information on word meanings.

Students can benefit from direct instruction in vocabulary strategies. Although estimates of vocabulary size and growth vary, children likely learn between 1,000 and 5,000 words per year—and the average child learns about 3,000 words. Since wide reading provides a significant source for increasing word knowledge, it is imperative that students learn key strategies to help them learn new words as they are encountered. Vocabulary strategies students should know by third grade include

- using a dictionary and other reference sources to understand the meanings of unknown words
- using context to determine the meanings of unfamiliar words
- learning about the relationships between words (synonyms, antonyms, and multiple-meaning words)
- exploring shades of meaning of words that are synonyms or near-synonyms
- using morphemic analysis—breaking words into meaning-bearing components, such as prefixes and roots

At grades 3 and above, morphemic analysis becomes an even more valuable dimension of vocabulary instruction. For example, learning just one root, *astro*, can help students unlock the meanings of such words as *astronaut*, *astronomy*, *astrology*, and *astrological*.

❝ Research on vocabulary shows that for learners to come to know words in a meaningful way, they need to engage with word meanings and build habits of attending to words and exploring their uses in thoughtful and lively ways. ❞

— **Margaret C. McKeown**
Research Scientist
Learning Research and Development Center,
University of Pittsburgh

Q How does *Trophies* provide exposure to a wide variety of texts?

A *Trophies* provides students with a wealth of opportunities to read a rich variety of texts. The *Pupil Editions,* the nucleus of the program in grades 1–6, feature a variety of high-quality literature selections that help students build vocabulary. *Trophies* also provides students with extensive reading opportunities through such components as these:

- *Big Books* (kindergarten and grade 1)
- *Read-Aloud Anthologies* (kindergarten through grade 2)
- *Library Books Collections* (kindergarten through grade 6)
- *Books for All Learners* (grades 1–6)
- *Intervention Readers* (grades 2–6)
- *Teacher's Edition* Read-Aloud Selections (grades 2–6)

Q How does the program provide multiple exposures to key vocabulary?

A Students are given many rich exposures to key vocabulary through the following program features:

- Vocabulary in context on *Teaching Transparencies*
- *Pupil Edition* and *Teacher's Edition* Vocabulary Power pages
- *Pupil Edition* main selections
- Word Study pages of the *Teacher's Edition* (grades 3–6)
- Additional Support Activities in the *Teacher's Edition*
- *Practice Books*
- *Books for All Learners*
- *Intervention Readers*

Q How does *Trophies* facilitate the teaching of vocabulary-learning strategies?

A Lessons include explicit teaching and modeling of vocabulary strategies. Specific lessons in both the *Pupil Edition* and *Teacher's Edition* provide direct instruction that helps enable students to increase their vocabulary every time they read. Strategies include using a dictionary, using context to determine word meaning, and understanding word structures and word relationships.

Look for

- ✔ Building Background and Vocabulary
- ✔ *Big Book* lessons
- ✔ Listening Comprehension
- ✔ Word Study (grades 3–6)
- ✔ Lessons on word relationships and word structure (grades 3–6)
- ✔ Additional Support Activities

FLUENCY

Research recognizes fluency as a strong indicator of efficient and proficient reading. A fluent reader reads with accuracy at an appropriate rate, attending to phrasing. When the reading is oral, it reflects a speech-like pace.

Oral fluency is reading with speed, accuracy, and prosody—meaning that the reader uses stress, pitch, and juncture of spoken language. Researchers have repeatedly demonstrated the relationship between fluency and reading comprehension. If a reader must devote most of his or her cognitive attention to pronouncing words, comprehension suffers. It follows then that students who read fluently can devote more attention to meaning and thus increase their comprehension. This is why oral reading fluency is an important goal of reading instruction, especially in the elementary grades. Word recognition must be automatic—freeing cognitive resources for comprehending text. If word recognition is labored, cognitive resources are consumed by decoding, leaving little or no resources for interpretation. In Kindergarten and at the beginning of grade 1, oral reading may sound less like speech because students are still learning to decode and to identify words. Nevertheless, with appropriate support, text that "fits", and time to practice, students soon begin to read simple texts in a natural, more fluent manner. By the beginning of grade 2, many students have come to enjoy the sounds of their own voices reading. They choose to read and reread with the natural sounds of spoken language and have few interruptions due to inadequate word attack or word recognition problems.

Fluent readers can
- recognize words automatically
- group individual words into meaningful phrases
- apply strategies rapidly to identify unknown words
- determine where to place emphasis or pause to make sense of a text

Fluency can be developed through directed reading practice, opportunities for repeated reading, and other instructional strategies. The primary method to improve fluency is directed reading practice in accessible texts. Practice does not replace instruction; it provides the reader opportunity to gain speed and accuracy within manageable text. One form of directed reading practice is repeated reading, which gives a developing reader more time and chances with the same text.

Repeated reading
- provides practice reading words in context
- produces gains in reading rate, accuracy, and comprehension
- helps lower-achieving readers

❝ Children gain reading fluency when they can read at a steady rate, recognizing words accurately and achieving correctness in phrasing and intonation. ❞

— **Nancy Roser**
Professor, Language and Literacy Studies
The University of Texas at Austin

Q How does *Trophies* teach and assess oral reading fluency?

A Toward developing fluent readers, *Trophies* provides explicit, systematic phonics instruction to build word recognition skills that enable students to become efficient decoders. (See the Phonics section of these pages for more information.) *Trophies* also provides the following tools that enable teachers to assess student progress on an ongoing basis:

- Oral reading passages in the back of each *Teacher's Edition (Grades 2-6)*
- Guidelines to help teachers use these passages (Grades 2-6)
- *Oral Reading Fluency Assessment*

Q How does *Trophies* provide intervention for students who are not developing oral reading fluency at an appropriate pace?

A In the grades 2-6 *Intervention Resource Kit,* every day of instruction includes a fluency builder activity. Students are assigned repeated readings with cumulative texts. These readings begin with word lists, expand to include multiple sentences, and eventually become extended self-selected passages. Fluency performance-assessment activities are also provided in the *Intervention Teacher's Guides.*

Q How does *Trophies* provide opportunities for repeated readings?

A In grades 1–6, the Rereading for Fluency features offer a wide variety of engaging activities that have students reread with a focus on expression, pacing, and intonation. These activities include

- **Echo Reading**—Students repeat (echo) what the teacher reads aloud.
- **Choral Reading**—Groups of students read aloud with the teacher simultaneously.
- **Repeated Reading**—The teacher models, and students reread several times until fluency is gained.
- **Readers Theatre**—Students assume roles and read them aloud from the text.
- **Partner Reading**—Students take turns reading aloud with a partner.
- **Tape-Assisted Reading**—Students listen to an audiotext and read along with the recording.
- **Phrase-Cued Text**—Students read texts that have been "chunked" into syntactic phrases.
- **Shared Reading**—Students join in as the teacher reads to the whole group.

Look for

✔ Rereading for Fluency
✔ Oral reading passages in the *Teacher's Edition*
✔ *Oral Reading Fluency Assessment*
✔ Fluency Routine Cards
✔ *Intervention Teacher's Guides*

ASSESSMENT

Assessment is integral to instruction. By choosing the appropriate assessment tools and methods, you can find out where your students are instructionally and plan accordingly.

Assessment is the process of collecting information in order to make instructional decisions about students. Good decisions require good information and to provide this information, assessment of students and their learning must be continuous. Because the reading process is composed of many complex skills, such as comprehension, word attack, and synthesis of information, no one assessment tool can evaluate completely all aspects of reading. Teachers need to gather information about their students in many ways, both formally and informally. Assessment helps them plan instruction, and ongoing assessments throughout the instructional process should guide their decisions and actions.

Assessment must systematically inform instruction and help teachers differentiate instruction. The first tool the classroom teacher requires is an entry-level assessment instrument to identify students' instructional level and potential for participating in grade-level instruction. This diagnostic instrument should be sensitive to gaps and strengths in student learning. After placement, teachers need differentiation strategies that are flexible and that can be easily adapted according to continual monitoring of student progress.

Assessments for monitoring progress should be used to determine ongoing priorities for instruction. The use of both formal and informal tools and strategies, including formative and summative assessments, provides a comprehensive picture of students' achievement as they progress through an instructional program. Informal assessments encourage teachers to observe students as they read, write, and discuss. These assessments provide immediate feedback and allow teachers to quickly determine which students are having difficulty and need additional instruction and practice. Formal assessments provide opportunities for teachers to take a more focused look at how students are progressing. Whether formal or informal, monitoring instruments and activities should be

- frequent
- ongoing
- easy to score and interpret

Teachers should be provided with clear options for monitoring and clear pathways for providing intervention and enrichment as needed. Less frequent summative assessments may be used to gauge long-term growth.

Student progress needs to be communicated to parents and guardians on a regular basis. As students become more accountable for their learning through standards-based testing, teachers are becoming more accountable not only to administrators but also to families. A complete instructional program should offer means for teachers to communicate with families about how their students are progressing and how families can contribute to students' growth.

> **Knowing how well a student can use literacy skills such as reading, writing, listening, and speaking is vital to effective instruction.**
>
> **— Roger Farr**
> Chancellor's Professor and Director of the Center for Innovation in Assessment, Indiana University, Bloomington

Q How does *Trophies* integrate entry-level group and individual assessments with instruction?

A The *Placement and Diagnostic Assessment* provides an overview of specific diagnostic information about prerequisite skills for each grade level. In addition, *Reading and Language Skills Assessment* pretests can be used to determine whether students need additional instruction and practice in phonics, comprehension skills, vocabulary, writing, and writing conventions.

Q What monitoring instruments are included with *Trophies*?

A Formative assessments that facilitate monitoring student progress include

- Diagnostic Checks at point of use for immediate assessment of understanding, with follow-up Additional Support Activities in the *Teacher's Edition*
- Ongoing Assessment to assess and model the use of reading strategies, in the *Teacher's Edition*
- *Intervention Assessment Book*
- Performance Assessment activities in the *Teacher's Edition*
- *End-of-Selection Tests* to monitor students' comprehension of each selection

In each theme's *Teacher's Edition*, the Theme Assessment to Plan Instruction section provides a clear road map for using assessment to adapt instruction to student needs.

Q What other assessment instruments are used in *Trophies*?

A The *Reading and Language Skills Assessment*, which includes posttests for end-of-theme assessment and Mid-Year and End-of-Year Tests, provides information about students' mastery of reading skills. Other assessments instruments in *Trophies* include

- *Holistic Assessment*, which uses authentic, theme-related passages and provides a more global, holistic evaluation of students' reading and writing ability
- *Oral Reading Fluency Assessment*, which monitors accuracy and rate
- *Assessment Handbook* (Kindergarten)

Look for

In the *Teacher's Edition*
✓ Diagnostic Checks
✓ Ongoing Assessment
✓ Performance Assessment
✓ Theme Assessment to Plan Instruction

Other Components
✓ *Placement* and *Diagnostic Assessments*
✓ *Reading and Language Skills Assessment (Pretests and Posttests)*
✓ *Holistic Assessment*
✓ *Oral Reading Fluency Assessment*
✓ *Assessment Handbook* (Kindergarten)

WRITING

Good writing skills are critical both to students' academic achievement and to their future success in society.

Writing instruction should incorporate explicit modeling and practice in the conventions of written English. All students can benefit from systematic instruction and practice in spelling, grammar, usage, mechanics, and presentation skills, such as handwriting and document preparation. Mastering these conventions enables students to communicate their ideas and information clearly and effectively.

- In kindergarten, children should use their growing knowledge of language structure and the conventions of print to begin expressing their ideas through words and pictures and putting these ideas into writing, with words spelled phonetically.

- In grades 1–3, students should continue to transfer their developing reading skills to writing conventions by using their knowledge of word structure and phonics to spell new words. They should learn and apply the fundamentals of grammar, mechanics, and sentence structure.

- In grades 4–6, instruction should build advanced spelling, grammar, and mechanics skills and should apply them in student writing of narratives, descriptions, and other extended compositions. Students should be systematically taught to apply writing conventions in purposeful writing activities.

Students should learn about and practice the process skills that good writers use. Many students do not realize, until they are told, that most stories and articles are not written in one sitting. Good writers plan, revise, rewrite, and rethink during the process of writing. Instruction in writing processes can spring from author features and interviews with the writers whose works students are reading. The teacher's modeling of effective prewriting, drafting, revising, proofreading, and publishing techniques should build upon this understanding. Particular attention should systematically be paid to revision strategies such as adding, deleting, clarifying, and rearranging text. Students

should apply these strategies to their own work repeatedly and should learn new techniques gradually and cumulatively.

Systematic instruction in writer's craft skills should be applied to the process. Students should be taught that, whatever the form of their writing, they must determine a clear focus, organize their ideas, use effective word choice and sentence structures, and express their own viewpoint. These writer's craft skills should be taught through focused exercises and writing tasks and should be reinforced cumulatively in lessons that teach the elements of longer writing forms.

" Effective writing is both an art and a science. The ability to generate interesting ideas and a pleasing style characterizes the art side; mastering the craft and its conventions characterizes the science side. Good instruction judiciously attends to both. "

— Dorothy S. Strickland
Samuel DeWitt Proctor
Professor of Education,
Rutgers University

Q How does *Trophies* provide instruction and practice in the conventions of written English?

A *Trophies* provides systematic, explicit instruction and abundant practice in spelling, grammar, usage, and mechanics in daily, easy-to-use lessons. Transparencies, activities, and practice sheets are provided for modeling and practice. Presentation skills are also formally taught, with an emphasis on handwriting at the lower grades. Spelling instruction, especially at the primary grades, is closely linked to phonics instruction. All skills of conventions are applied in purposeful writing activities.

Q How does *Trophies* teach the process of writing?

A From the earliest grades, students using *Trophies* learn that good writers plan and revise their writing. Students are guided through the prewriting, drafting, revising, and proofreading stages with models, practice activities, graphic organizers, and checklists. Instruction in presentation skills, such as handwriting and speaking, guides the publishing stage. Teacher rubrics for evaluation are provided at point of use, and reproducible student rubrics are provided in the back of the *Teacher's Edition*.

Q How does *Trophies* apply writer's craft instruction to the writing process?

A In kindergarten, students begin to write sentences and brief narratives about familiar experiences. Students also engage in shared and interactive writing in kindergarten through grade 2. In grades 1 and 2, instruction in story grammar and sentence types becomes more sophisticated, with students learning about and applying one component, such as capitalization, at a time. In grades 2–6, explicit writer's craft lessons are built into the writing strand and follow this format:

- Weeks 1 and 2 of the unit present writer's craft skills, such as organizing, choosing words, and writing effective sentences. Students complete targeted exercises and apply the craft in relatively brief writing forms.
- Weeks 3 and 4 present longer writing forms, emphasizing the steps of the writing process. The writer's craft skills learned in Weeks 1 and 2 are applied in longer compositions.
- In grades 3–6, Week 5 presents a timed writing test in which students apply what they have learned.

Look for

- ✔ Writer's Craft lessons
- ✔ Writing Process lessons
- ✔ Timed or Tested Writing lessons
- ✔ 5-day grammar and spelling lessons
- ✔ Traits of good writing

LISTENING AND SPEAKING

Increasingly, young people must comprehend, and are expected to create, messages that are oral and visual rather than strictly written. Listening and speaking skills are essential to achievement in both reading and writing.

Listening to narratives, poetry, and nonfiction texts builds thinking and language skills that students need for success in reading and writing. The domains of the language arts (listening, speaking, reading, and writing) are closely connected. Listening instruction and speaking instruction are critical scaffolds that support reading comprehension, vocabulary knowledge, and oral communication skills. Classroom instruction must be focused on these skills and must also strategically address the needs of students with limited levels of language experience or whose language experiences are primarily in languages other than English.

Listening instruction and speaking instruction should progress developmentally through the grades. In the primary grades, instruction should focus on

- listening to and retelling stories, with an emphasis on story grammar (setting, characters, and important events)
- explicit modeling of standard English structures, with frequent opportunities to repeat sentences and recite rhymes and songs
- brief oral presentations about familiar topics and experiences
- developing familiarity with academic and literary terms

As students move up the grades, they should develop increasingly sophisticated listening and speaking skills, including the more complex production skills. By grades 4–6, students should be increasingly capable of

- delivering both narrative and expository presentations using a range of narrative and rhetorical devices
- modeling their own presentations on effective text structures they have analyzed in their reading
- orally responding to literature in ways that demonstrate advanced understanding and insight
- supporting their interpretations with facts and specific examples
- interpreting and using verbal and nonverbal messages
- analyzing oral and visual messages, purposes, and persuasive techniques

❝ Oral response activities encourage critical thinking and allow students to bring their individuality to the process of responding to literature. ❞

— **Hallie Kay Yopp**
Professor
Department of Elementary Bilingual and Reading Education, California State University, Fullerton

Q **How does _Trophies_ provide rich listening experiences that build understanding of language structures and texts?**

A From the very first day of kindergarten through the end of grade 6, _Trophies_ provides abundant and varied texts, support, and modeling for listening instruction. With resources such as _Big Books, Read-Aloud Anthologies,_ and Audiotext of the reading selections, the teacher has every type of narrative and expository text available. _Trophies_ also provides direct instruction and engaging response activities so that teachers can use each listening selection to its full advantage. The _English-Language Learners Resource Kit_ provides additional opportunities for students with special needs to develop an understanding of English language structure, concept vocabulary and background, and listening comprehension skills.

Q **How does _Trophies_ develop listening through the grades?**

A Listening is developed through the Sharing Literature features in kindergarten through grade 2 with such options as Build Concept Vocabulary, Develop Listening Comprehension, and Listen and Respond and through the _Read-Aloud Anthologies._ In grades 3–6, read-alouds serve as a vehicle for setting a purpose for listening and develop listening comprehension and listening strategies.

Q **How does _Trophies_ provide instruction in speaking and in making presentations?**

A _Trophies_ provides instruction to guide students in making both narrative and expository presentations. In kindergarten, each lesson offers formal and informal speaking opportunities through the Share Time feature. In grades 1 and 2, speaking activities are included in the Rereading for Fluency and in the Wrap-Up sections of the lesson. The Morning Message feature in kindergarten through grade 2 provides additional informal speaking opportunities. In grades 3–6, presentation skills become more sophisticated. Students are asked to make such presentations as extended oral reports, multimedia presentations, debates, and persuasive speeches.

Look for

✓ **Develop Listening Comprehension**
✓ **Daily "Sharing Literature" activities (Kindergarten through Grade 2)**
✓ **Read-Aloud selections and instruction with every lesson (Grades 2–6)**
✓ **Morning Message (Kindergarten–Grade 2)**
✓ **Author's Chair presentations (Kindergarten–Grade 2)**
✓ **Rereading for Fluency**
✓ **Listening and Speaking Lessons (Grades 3–6)**
✓ **Presentation Rubrics (Grades 2–6)**
✓ **_Read-Aloud Anthologies_ (Kindergarten–Grade 2)**

WHAT RESEARCH SAYS ABOUT

REACHING ALL LEARNERS

Students come to school with diverse experiences and language backgrounds. Teachers, who are charged with providing universal access to high-quality instruction, require specially designed plans and materials to help all students meet or exceed grade-level standards.

Curriculum and instruction must be carefully planned to provide for students who need varying levels of intervention and challenge. Students require additional instruction, practice, and extension at different times and in different degrees. Some students need occasional reteaching and slight modifications in pacing, while others are at greater risk and require more intensive intervention. Research shows that students with learning difficulties need more review and practice to perform a new task automatically. Instruction should cumulatively integrate simpler or previously learned tasks with newer, more complex activities. In addition, research shows the following:

- Reading difficulties can stem from inaccuracy in identifying words.
- Intervention should be geared toward a student's level of reading development.
- Diagnostic testing results should show what students know and what they need to know; frequent assessment is critical.
- Instruction should be direct and explicit.

Curriculum and instruction must be structured to meet the needs of English-language learners. The 2000 U.S. Census confirmed what many educators already knew: more and more students do not speak English as their first language. Widely ranging levels of English proficiency in mainstream classrooms present special challenges and opportunities for teachers. Depending on their level of English acquisition and their grade placement, English-language learners need varying degrees of additional support in areas such as oral language, English phonology, vocabulary, background information, and the academic language of school.

Students who already meet or exceed grade-level expectations need opportunities for enrichment or acceleration. They need to be challenged by vocabulary extension study and exposure to sophisticated literature in a variety of genres. Students may also be encouraged to carry out investigations that extend their learning. Such activities should promote sustained investigative skills: raising questions, researching answers, and organizing information. Several research studies have shown the importance of setting high standards for advanced learners. An instructional program that clearly provides for differentiation at a variety of levels can be the tool teachers need to provide universal access to high-level standards.

❝ In the process of helping students learn, we want to support them in discovering that each person is unique and has a unique contribution to make towards creating a better world for all. ❞

— **Alma Flor Ada**
Director of Doctoral Studies in the
International Multicultural Program
University of San Francisco

— **F. Isabel Campoy**
Former President, Association of
Spanish Professionals in the USA

Q How does *Trophies* provide differentiated instruction at a variety of levels?

A *Trophies* was designed to accommodate a diverse student population, with tiers of differentiation for different needs. Diagnostic Checks, with brief activities, are positioned at point of use within each lesson in the *Teacher's Edition* so that specific needs of students can be identified and addressed. Additional Support Activities, tied closely to the lessons, are provided for further differentiation. The three types of activities address below-level readers, advanced students, and English-language learners. In addition, Alternative Teaching Strategies are provided for students who perform below level on the *Reading and Language Skills Assessments.* The *Library Books Collections* and the *Books for All Learners* also provide students at all levels with a wealth of reading opportunities in a variety of genres.

Q What additional support does *Trophies* provide?

A An *Intervention Resource Kit* and an *English-Language Learners Resource Kit* are available for students with greater needs.
Both kits
- align closely with the core program
- provide rigorous daily lessons
- provide abundant cumulative, spiraled practice

For below-level readers, the *Intervention Resource Kit* preteaches and reteaches the same skills and concepts that are taught in the core program. The *English-Language Learners Resource Kit* builds background, vocabulary and concepts, academic language, comprehension, and language arts. Finally, to guide teachers in making instructional decisions, *Trophies* provides a complete assessment program, with instruments for entry-level assessment, monitoring of progress, and summative assessment. (See the Assessment section of these pages for more information.)

Look for

- ✔ **Reaching All Learners**
- ✔ **Diagnostic Checks**
- ✔ **Additional Support Activities**
- ✔ **Practice pages for all levels**
- ✔ ***Books for All Learners***
- ✔ ***Intervention Resource Kit***
- ✔ ***English-Language Learners Resource Kit***
- ✔ ***Library Books Collections***
- ✔ ***Placement and Diagnostic Assessments***

CLASSROOM MANAGEMENT

The task of managing the classroom is becoming increasingly complex. Teachers are seeking to maximize instructional effectiveness for students with a diverse range of skills and backgrounds.

Classroom management is a critical variable related to student achievement. Research shows that the more time teachers spend dealing with student behavior and interruptions in instruction, the more student achievement suffers. A classroom environment that promotes student growth and learning results from making effective decisions about the organization and scheduling of instruction and the physical arrangement of the classroom.

Effective organization includes differentiating instruction to engage all students in instructional-level activities. Grouping strategies are important for addressing diverse needs, but grouping must never be treated as an aim in itself. Flexible grouping can help ensure that all students meet instructional goals, and it can be effective in helping students participate and contribute in a learning environment. Grouping should be fluid and temporary, varying according to individual students' progress and interests and should allow time for students to function independently and be responsible for their own work. The types of instruction that are most successful in the major grouping patterns include

Whole Group
- Sharing literature
- Developing concepts
- Providing modeling
- Presenting new knowledge

Small Group
- Developing skills
- Practicing processes
- Collaborating on projects
- Providing challenge activities

After flexible work groups are established, effective classroom organization should focus on scheduling classroom activities and creating a classroom arrangement that facilitates learning. Initially, teachers might establish one or two learning centers based on tasks that are familiar to students. Then teachers can develop other centers and routines as needed. Before beginning a routine, teachers should introduce students to the procedures for using each area, ensuring that students understand what they are to do and how much time they should spend in each area. A rotation schedule should be established so that students can easily move from one area to another as tasks are completed. Helping students become familiar with schedules and routines enables the teacher to devote more time to individual and small-group instruction.

> **" The organization of the classroom should provide students with many opportunities to share with teachers and other students the things they are reading and writing. "**
>
> — **Roger Farr**
> Chancellor's Professor and Director of the
> Center for Innovation in Assessment,
> Indiana University, Bloomington

Q How can teachers keep other students engaged in meaningful experiences while providing instruction to students with special needs?

A *Trophies* provides an abundance of productive materials and ideas for independent and small-group work

- Managing the Classroom sections in the back of the *Teacher's Editions* that provide clear instructions in arranging the classroom with centers or stations, using a Work Board with center icons to help organize routines and schedules, and tracking student progress.
- Classroom Management and Reading and Writing Routines sections in the *Teacher's Editions* (grades 1–2) that provide suggestions for individual, whole-group, and small-group activities.
- Cross-Curricular Centers and Stations with pacing suggestions to regulate student participation
- Lesson-specific Workboards to help teachers manage groups and individuals simultaneously
- Integration of content from social studies, science, and other content areas
- *Books for All Learners* to allow students to read independently at their own level
- Practice pages for students with diverse skills and language backgrounds
- Theme Projects for extended group work
- Comprehension Cards, *Library Books Collections,* and other resources to facilitate group and independent reading

Q How does *Trophies* help teachers manage its instructional pathways for classrooms with diverse learners?

A *Trophies* provides a clear, manageable system of diagnostic assessment checkpoints, ongoing formal assessment and performance-based opportunities, and instructional pathways for teachers to follow based on results. In addition to easy-to-use lesson planners that include suggested pacing, the system provides

- Diagnostic Checks and customized activities at point of use
- Additional Support Activities to reinforce, reteach, and extend key concepts in every lesson
- *Intervention Resource Kits* and *English-Language Learners Resource Kits* for more intensive instruction
- Alternative Teaching Strategies for additional options to modify instruction

For more information, see Theme Assessment to Plan Instruction in each *Teacher's Edition.*

Look for

✔ **Diagnostic Checks**
✔ **Cross-Curricular Centers or Stations**
✔ **Work Boards**
✔ ***Books for All Learners***
✔ ***Library Books Collections***
✔ **Practice pages**
✔ **Theme Projects**
✔ **Comprehension Cards**
✔ **Managing the Classroom**

Contents

The Story of a Blue Bird   8A

by Tomek Bogacki

Phonics Long Vowel /ī/ *igh*

BIG BOOK **To Market, To Market**

(Focus Skill) **Plot**

Frog and Toad All Year   38A

by Arnold Lobel

Phonics Long Vowels /ā/ *ai*, *ay*

BIG BOOK **I Swam with a Seal**

READING ACROSS TEXTS **Frogs in Trees?** *by Mark Warner*

(Focus Skill) **Cause/Effect**

Fishing Bears   68A

by Ruth Berman/photographed by Lynn M. Stone

Phonics Long Vowel /ī/ *i*

BIG BOOK **To Market, To Market**

(Focus Skill) **Main Idea**

Reference Materials

Additional Support Activities

Theme Resources

Introducing the Book

Discuss the Title and Cover

Read aloud the title, *Gather Around,* and ask children what they think it means. Then ask children to look at the cover illustration and tell who and what they see. Discuss with them how the title of the book fits with the picture of the owl and the other birds. Invite volunteers to tell about times they have "gathered around" to hear a good story and about other things they like to do when they "gather around" with friends and family.

Discuss the Book's Organization

Discuss the letter with children. Direct children's attention to the letter from the authors at the beginning of the *Pupil Edition.* Ask them to think about what the authors might have to say to them and why they would write a letter. Then read the letter aloud to children. Ask volunteers to tell what they think the authors mean by "let the adventure begin."

Examine other parts of the book. Have children turn to each feature. Briefly discuss how each part helps readers use the book and understand the stories.

- Table of Contents—shows titles, authors, and page numbers
- Theme Opener—has theme title and related artwork
- Word Power—introduces selection high-frequency words and vocabulary words
- Genre Notes and Labels—describe the different types of literature
- Making Connections—provides activities related to the stories
- Focus Skill/Phonics Skill—provides instruction in key skills
- Test Preparation—reinforces the Focus Skill or Phonics Skill with sample test questions
- Writer's Handbook—explains the writing process and provides models for writing and words for writing
- Glossary—contains high-frequency words, vocabulary words, and decodable words. Each word has an example sentence and some are illustrated.

HARCOURT
· T R O P H I E S ·

A HARCOURT READING/LANGUAGE ARTS PROGRAM

GATHER AROUND

SENIOR AUTHORS
Isabel L. Beck ◆ Roger C. Farr ◆ Dorothy S. Strickland

AUTHORS
Alma Flor Ada ◆ Marcia Brechtel ◆ Margaret McKeown
Nancy Roser ◆ Hallie Kay Yopp

SENIOR CONSULTANT
Asa G. Hilliard III

CONSULTANTS
F. Isabel Campoy ◆ David A. Monti

Harcourt

Orlando   Boston   Dallas   Chicago   San Diego

Visit *The Learning Site!*

www.harcourtschool.com

HARCOURT
· T R O P H I E S ·

A HARCOURT READING/LANGUAGE ARTS PROGRAM

GATHER AROUND

Dear Reader,

Gather Around for some terrific stories! In this book, you will learn to be a detective. You will also meet a brave little bird, a baby baboon, and a very silly pig. Like some of the characters in these stories, you may be surprised by what you find. So, turn the page and let the adventure begin!

Sincerely,

The Authors

The Authors

THEME 6

Going Places
CONTENTS

Theme Big Books

I Swam with a Seal

To Market, To Market

Decodable Books 27-34

THEME 6

Going Places

The world around us is full of interesting things for us to learn and explore.

Theme Resources

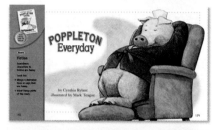

 All the above selections are available on **Audiotext 5.**

INDEND/SELF-SELECTED READING

Library Books

Teaching plans for classroom Library Books can be found on pages 253S–253X.

Little Fox Goes to the End of the World
by Ann Tompert
The Big Dipper
by Franklyn M. Branley
Peeping and Sleeping
by Fran Manushkin

 Reading Outside of Class
20 Minutes
Additional trade book titles can be found on page T47. Have children complete the *"My Reading Log"* form on page R14.

 ### Books for All Learners

BELOW-LEVEL

ON-LEVEL

ADVANCED

ELL

Teaching suggestions for the Books for All Learners can be found on pages 37M–37P, 67O–67R, 97M–97P, 123M–123P, 155M–155P, 185O–185R, 217M–217P, 253M–253P.

TECHNOLOGY RESOURCES

- *Phonics Express™* CD-ROM
  Short Vowel /e/ea
  Long Vowels /ī/igh; /ā/ai, ay; /ī/i; /ō/o;
  /(y)o͞o/u-e
  Consonant /j/g, dge
  Phonograms -ail, -ain
  Vowel Variant /o͞o/oo
- *Writing Express™* CD-ROM
- *Media Literacy and Communication Skills Package* VIDEO
- *Grammar Jingles™* CD
- *Reading and Language Skills Assessment* CD-ROM

Teacher Resources
- Graphic Organizers
- Language Support
- Classroom Management
- Lesson Planner

Resources for Parents
- Helping Your Child Learn to Read
- Helping Your Child Learn to Write

- Helping Your Child Take Tests
- Internet Safety
- Homework Helper

Student Activities
- Author/Illustrator Information
- Skill Activities
- Test Tutor
- Writing Activities
- Grammar Activities

The Learning Site: www.harcourtschool.com

PROFESSIONAL DEVELOPMENT

Professional Development for Reading courses combine scientifically-based research with practical classroom strategies. Topics include:

- Phonemic Awareness
- Phonics
- Vocabulary
- Fluency
- Text Comprehension
- Assessment

	The Story of a Blue Bird pp. 8A–37P	**Frog and Toad All Year** pp. 38A–67R
• **Phonemic Awareness** • **Phonics** • **Spelling**	**Long Vowel** /ī/igh **Contractions** 's, n't, 'll **Inflections** -ed, -ing (drop final e)	**Long Vowels** /ā/ai, ay **Phonograms** -ail, -ain **Inflections** -ed, -ing (drop final e)
• **Reading** • **Comprehension** • **High-Frequency Words** • **Vocabulary**	**Read** Fiction **Plot T** **High-Frequency Words T** *nothing, thought* **Vocabulary T** *afraid, flew, join, learn, wonder*	**Read** Fiction **Read Across Texts** "Frogs in Trees?" MAGAZINE ARTICLE **Cause/Effect** **High-Frequency Words T** *cold, sure* **Vocabulary T** *caught, hurried, near, son*
• **Independent Reading**	**Books for All Learners** **Below-Level:** *Flying High* **On-Level:** *The Bird in the Plum Tree* **Advanced:** *The Wright Brothers* **English-Language Learners:** *What's Your Favorite Color?*	**Books for All Learners** **Below-Level:** *Rainy Day Pals* **On-Level:** *Two Snails* **Advanced:** *Just Around the Corner* **English-Language Learners:** *What Season Is It?*
• **Writing** • **Grammar**	**Theme Writing:** Writing about Journeys **Describing Words:** -er and -est	**Theme Writing:** Writing about the Story **Verbs T**
• **Cross-Curricular Centers**	**Math** Flock of Birds **Science** Observing Birds **Social Studies** Bird's-Eye View **Art** Bird Collage	**Science** Signs of Spring  **Social Studies** Seasons Around the World **Computer** Create a Clip Art Scene **Art** Art Around the Corner

T = tested skill

Fishing Bears
pp. 68A–97P

Long Vowel /ī/i
Inflections -ed, -ing (double final consonant)

Read Nonfiction
Main Idea T
High-Frequency Word T
both
Vocabulary T
during, ready

 Books for All Learners

Below-Level: *Young Animals*
On-Level: *Counting Bears*
Advanced: *The Wild Giant Panda*
English-Language Learners:
   Every Animal Has a Home

Theme Writing: Writing a Poem
Verbs That Tell About Now T

 Math
   Bear Families
 Science
   Life of a River
 Computer
   Kinds of Bears
 Music
   The Bear Went Over the Mountain

How to Be a Nature Detective
pp. 98A–123P

Long Vowel /ō/o
Contractions 've, 'd, 're

Read Nonfiction
Main Idea T
Vocabulary T
clues, detective, floor, nature, piece, pulls

 Books for All Learners

Below-Level: *The Thing that Visited Our Camp*
On-Level: *Girl Detectives*
Advanced: *Looking For Clues*
English-Language Learners: *A Cat Has Four Paws*

Theme Writing: Writing about Animals
Using *Am*, *Is*, and *Are*

 Math
   Measure Footprints
 Science
   Animal Food
 Computer
   Animal Clues
 Art
   Vegetable and Fruit Prints

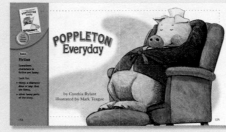

	The Puddle pp. 124A–155P	Poppleton Everyday pp. 156A–185R
• Phonemic Awareness • **Phonics** • Spelling	**Consonants** /j/*g, dge* **Inflections** *-ed, -ing* (drop final e) **Contractions** *'ve, 'd, 're*	**Long Vowel** /(y)o͞o/*u-e* **Contractions** *'ve, 'd, 're* **Inflections** *-ed, -ing* (double final consonant)
• Reading • Comprehension • High-Frequency Words • Vocabulary	**Read** Fiction **Read Across Texts** *"Time to Play"* POEM **Plot T** **Vocabulary T** *angry, okay, nearly, sorry*	**Read** Fiction **Predict Outcomes** **High-Frequency Words T** *boy, head, read* **Vocabulary T** *brought, few*

• Independent Reading	**Books for All Learners**
	Below-Level: *Storm Watch*
	On-Level: *The Edge of the Puddle*
	Advanced: *The World of Water*
	English-Language Learners:
	   All Kinds of Weather
		Books for All Learners
		Below-Level: *Goldy and the Three Bears*
		On-Level: *All About Pigs*
		Advanced: *Little Pig at the State Fair*
		English-Language Learners:
		   The Furniture in My House

• Writing • Grammar	**Theme Writing:** Creative Writing **Verbs that Tell About the Past T**	**Theme Writing:** Writing a Fantasy Story **Using *Was* and *Were***

• Cross-Curricular Centers	**Science**
	   Evaporation Diagram
	Social Studies
	   Puddle Rules
	Computer
	   A Way to Play
	Health
	   All-Weather Wear
		Math
		   How Many Pigs?
		Science
		   Home for Pig
		Social Studies
		   City Life or Farm Life
		Computer
		   Write Fantasy Stories

T = tested skill

Sleep Is for Everyone pp. 186A–217P	**Baboon** pp. 218A–253P
Short Vowel /e/ea **Inflections** -er, -est **Inflections** -ed, -ing (double final consonant)	**Vowel Variant** /o͞o/oo **Phonograms** -oom, -oot

Read Nonfiction
Read Across Texts
  "Pretending" POEM
Main Idea T
Vocabulary T
afternoon, bicycle, carry, hours, parents, words
	Read Informational Fiction
	Read Across Texts
	  "Piggyback Ride" MAGAZINE ARTICLE
	Plot T
	Vocabulary T
	against, careful, fire, quietly, shook

Books for All Learners
Below-Level: An Afternoon Nap
On-Level: Ready, Set, Sleep
Advanced: Jobs at All Hours
English Language Learners:
  Touch Your Nose, Wiggle Your Toes
	Books for All Learners
	Below-Level: Baboon's Park
	On-Level: Around the Zoo with Baboon
	Advanced: Who Is in the Pond?
	English Language Learners:
	  Let's Visit the Zoo

Theme Writing: Writing about Sleep **Using Go and What**	**Theme Writing:** Writing about Animals **Contractions with Not**

Math
  Add Them Up!
 Science
  Observing Animals
 Social Studies
  Night Jobs
 Computer
  Animal Dreams
	Math
	  Animal Groups
	 Science
	  Baboon's Day
	 Computer
	  Publish a Story
	 Art
	  Art Adventure

Theme Assessment
to Plan Instruction

Entry-Level Assessment *Assesses essential prior knowledge and skills*

PLACEMENT AND DIAGNOSTIC ASSESSMENTS
Use to diagnose individual children and to make placement decisions.

• **Reading and Language Skills Assessment: Book 1-5 Pretest**

Administer the Pretest	
Diagnosis	**Prescription**
IF performance is	**THEN** use these available resources
BELOW-LEVEL	• Core Instruction in the Teacher's Edition • Below-Level Reaching All Learners notes (at point of use in the Teacher's Edition) • Extra-Support Copying Masters • Intervention Resource Kit
ON-LEVEL	• Core Instruction in the Teacher's Edition • Cross-Curricular Centers • Practice Book
ADVANCED	• Core Instruction in the Teacher's Edition • Advanced Reaching All Learners notes (at point of use in the Teacher's Edition) • Challenge Copying Masters

Monitoring of Progress *Lesson resources and assessment instruments*

REACHING ALL LEARNERS

Diagnostic Check: Sequence

If... children have difficulty telling the sequence of events in the story,

Then... have children look back through the illustrations to help figure out what has happened and when.

ADDITIONAL SUPPORT ACTIVITIES

BELOW-LEVEL	Reteach, p. S6
ADVANCED	Extend, p. S7
ENGLISH-LANGUAGE LEARNER	Reteach, p. S7

• **End-of-Selection Tests (in Practice Book)**

• **Oral Reading Fluency Assessment**

Assess progress and customize instruction	
Diagnosis	**Prescription**
IF children do not perform well on the • Diagnostic Checks (at point of use in the Teacher's Edition) • End-of-Selection Tests (in Practice Book) • Oral Reading Fluency Assessment	**THEN** choose from these available resources • Additional Support Activities pp. S2–S49 • Books for All Learners • Intervention Resource Kit • Extra Support Copying Masters
IF children do perform well on the • Diagnostic Checks (at point of use in the Teacher's Edition) • End-of-Selection Tests (in Practice Book) • Oral Reading Fluency Assessment	**THEN** choose from these lesson resources • Additional Support Activities (Advanced) pp. S2–S49 • Books for All Learners • Challenge Copying Masters • Chart their progress. See pages R19–R21.

Summative Assessment *Assesses mastery of theme objectives*

- **Holistic Assessment Book 1-5**
- **Reading and Language Skills Assessment: Book 1-5 Posttest**
- **Reading and Language Skills Assessment: End-of-Year Test**

Administer End-of-Book tests	
Diagnosis	**Prescription**
IF performance is	**THEN** use these available resources
BELOW-LEVEL	• Alternative Teaching Strategies, pp. T2–T12. • Intervention Resource Kit • Chart their progress. See pp. R19–R21.
ON-LEVEL	• Chart their progress. See pp. R19–R21.
ADVANCED	• Provide accelerated instruction in higher-grade-level materials. • Chart their progress. See pages R19–R21.

Technology *Reading and Language Skills CD-ROM*

Use this CD-ROM to
- administer assessments electronically.
- customize assessments to focus on specific standards.
- track children's progress.

Reaching All Learners

■ BELOW-LEVEL

Levels of Support

Point-of-use Diagnostic Checks in the Teacher's Edition

pp. 8P, 14–15, 24–25, 33G, 35I, 38P, 42–43, 52–53, 59G, 67B, 68P, 82–83, 86–87, 93G, 95I, 98P, 102–103, 112–113, 119G, 121I, 124P, 136–137, 153I, 156P, 160–161, 168–169, 181G, 185B, 186P, 194–195, 200–201, 211G, 215I, 218P, 224–225, 242–243, 247G, 251I

See also point-of-use Notes throughout the lessons.

For additional point-of-use support, use the Extra Support Copying Masters, pp. 3–63.

Additional Support Activities

Phonemic Awareness, pp. S2, S8, S14, S20, S26, S32, S38, S44

Phonics, pp. S4, S10, S16, S22, S28, S34, S40, S46

Comprehension, pp. S6, S18, S24, S30, S42, S48

High-Frequency and Vocabulary Words, pp. S12, S36

Intervention Resource Kit

■ ENGLISH-LANGUAGE LEARNERS

Levels of Support

Point-of-use Diagnostic Checks in the Teacher's Edition

pp. 8P, 14–15, 24–25, 33G, 35I, 38P, 42–43, 52–53, 59G, 67B, 68P, 82–83, 86–87, 93G, 95I, 98P, 102–103, 112–113, 119G, 121I, 124P, 136–137, 153I, 156P, 160–161, 168–169, 181G, 185B, 186P, 194–195, 200–201, 211G, 215I, 218P, 224–225, 242–243, 247G, 251I

See also point-of-use Notes throughout the lessons.

For additional point-of-use support, use the English-Language Learners Copying Masters, pp. 3–63.

Additional Support Activities

Phonemic Awareness, pp. S3, S9, S15, S21, S27, S33, S39, S45

Phonics, pp. S5, S11, S17, S23, S29, S35, S41, S47

Comprehension, pp. S7, S19, S25, S31, S43, S49

High-Frequency and Vocabulary Words, pp. S13, S37

 Visit *The Learning Site:* www.harcourtschool.com

See Language Support

English-Language Learners Resource Kit

■ **ADVANCED**

Levels of Support

Point-of-use Diagnostic Checks in the Teacher's Edition

pp. 8P, 14–15, 24–25, 33G, 35I, 38P, 42–43, 52–53, 59G, 67B, 68P, 82–83, 86–87, 93G, 95I, 98P, 102–103, 112–113, 119G, 121I, 124P, 136–137, 153I, 156P, 160–161, 168–169, 181G, 185B, 186P, 194–195, 200–201, 211G, 215I, 218P, 224–225, 242–243, 247G, 251I

See also point-of-use Notes throughout the lessons.

For additional point-of-use enrichment, use the Challenge Copying Masters, pp. 3–63.

Additional Support Activities

Phonemic Awareness: pp. S3, S9, S15, S21, S27, S33, S39, S45

Phonics: pp. S5, S11, S17, S23, S29, S35, S41, S47

Comprehension: pp. S7, S19, S25, S31, S43, S49

High-Frequency and Vocabulary Words: pp. S13, S37

Accelerated Instruction

Use higher-grade-level materials for accelerated instruction.

Theme Project: 7B

COMBINATION CLASSROOMS

Individualizing Instruction

Providing developmentally appropriate instruction to all children is the primary goal in any classroom. Strategies for individualizing instruction in a combination classroom include:

- providing a variety of tasks at each center—to challenge advanced learners and to support children who need reinforcement for some skills.

- developing learning contracts with children and parents outlining specific goals to be met.

- using small flexible groups for phonics instruction and reading Decodable Books, the *Pupil's Edition*, Books for All Learners, and trade books.

- grouping children according to how they learn best. Provide kinesthetic and visual learners time to work with *Alphabet Cards, Word Builders*, and *Letter Cards*. Auditory learners can do the same while listening to the teacher modeling word building on tape.

STUDENTS WITH SPECIAL NEEDS

Physical Disabilities

Some children have certain physical needs that require special modifications to instruction. These children have *physical disabilities*. Strategies for working with these children include:

- providing visually-impaired children opportunities to read large print books and big books and engaging them in auditory learning experiences.

- presenting hearing-impaired children with visual-learning opportunities and additional time for listening to repeated readings on tape.

- placing classroom and center materials within easy grasp of children with gross motor difficulties and providing open workspace for children with adaptive equipment such as wheelchairs or walkers.

Additional Homework Ideas

Visit *The Learning Site*: www.harcourtschool.com • See Resources for Parents and Teachers: Homework Helper.

	Reading	Phonics	Writing	Theme	Cross-Curricular
WEEK 1	**Retell** "The Story of a Blue Bird" to a family member from the point of view of one of the other birds in the story.	**Draw and label a mural** of things that have *igh* in their name.	**Write a letter** telling the blue bird about a time when you learned something new.	**Ask a family member** to tell about a time he or she went exploring at your age. **Write a sentence** and **draw a picture** about it.	**MATH** With a family member, draw and cut out several bird shapes from blue, red, and yellow construction paper. **Make a pattern** with the shapes.
WEEK 2	**Draw or cut** out pictures from magazines to go with the high-frequency word *cold*. [Cold]	**List words** that rhyme with *sail* and *pay*. **sail mail pail**	**Make a bookmark** that shows your favorite part of the story. **Write sentences** that tell why it is your favorite part.	**Write a paragraph** explaining how the story "Frog and Toad All Year" fits with the theme "Going Places."	**SOCIAL STUDIES** Have a family member help you **draw and label a map** of your backyard. Then use the map to go exploring.
WEEK 3	**Tell a few facts** to a family member from the story "Fishing Bears."	**Write rhyming words** for *grind* and *child*. [grind child rind wild]	**Write a poem** for a friend or family member about an animal.	**Create a greeting card** to celebrate the arrival of spring.	**ART Draw or Paint** a realistic picture of a bear. **Tell** a family member facts about the bear.
WEEK 4	**Take turns reading** a book with a family member by alternating the pages read. 	**Look in books or magazines** for long vowel *o* words that do not end with e. **Make a list** and choose two words to **write in a sentence.**	**Write** down the title of your **favorite story** and explain why you like it.	**Write** about a time when you watched an animal explore its surroundings.	**SCIENCE** With a family member, **observe** a plant or animal. **Write an entry** in an observation log to describe what you see.

Additional Homework Ideas

Visit *The Learning Site:* **www.harcourtschool.com • See Resources for Parents and Teachers: Homework Helper.**

	Reading	Phonics	Writing	Theme	Cross-Curricular
WEEK 5	Take turns **reading dialogue** from "The Puddle" with a family member.	**Find words** that end with *dge* in a book or a magazine. ledge pledge	**Write a song or rhyme** about playing in a puddle on a rainy day.	**Draw a picture** of a character in a story who was looking for something. **Write a sentence** about your picture.	**SCIENCE Estimate** how many drops of water will fill a teaspoon. Then use an eyedropper with water to fill the teaspoon. **Record the number.**
WEEK 6	**Tell the story** "Poppleton Everyday" to a family member.	**Make a collage** of things that have a long vowel *u* and end with an e. **Label** each thing in your collage.	**Make a story web** for a fantasy story about a talking animal. **Jot down** your ideas.	**Make a list** of new things you have discovered or learned about in the past few weeks.	**SCIENCE Estimate** the number of hours you sleep in one week. Record the number of hours and **compare the data** to your estimate.
WEEK 7	**Compare yourself to a character** from a favorite story. Explain to a family member why you think the character thinks and acts as you do.	**Write words** that rhyme with *bread.* **Draw pictures** of three of the words.	**List reasons** why sleep is for everyone. Pick one reason and **draw a picture** about it.	**Send an e-mail** or write a letter to a friend telling him or her about something you found or discovered.	**MATH Measure** the length of your hand using your hand as the unit of measurement.
WEEK 8	**Retell** a story from this unit to a family member. Use the sequence words *first, next,* and *last.*	**Draw pictures** of four things that rhyme with *boot* and **label** each picture. root	**Write** three questions you would ask a baboon. ? ? ?	**Create a paper mask** of a character you have read about in this theme. **Write words** that describe the character.	**MATH Write** addition and subtraction **word problems** about baboons. Make the sums and differences no more than 20.

Setting the Stage with Big Books

To Market, To Market
Anne Miranda
ILLUSTRATED BY
Janet Stevens

Modeling Fluency

- Stimulate by reading rich literature
- Develop vocabulary
- Model reading strategies

Theme Connection

To Market, To Market tells the story of a woman who goes to market to buy a pig. In subsequent trips to the market, she acquires a growing number of animals and a growing number of problems as the animals all get loose and misbehave. A last trip to the market solves the problem, however, when the woman buys all sorts of delicious vegetables and makes hot soup for everyone. The selection invites children to think about how exploring even the most common places can be an adventure.

Ideas for Sharing Literature

RHYMING WORDS As children become familiar with the rhyming format of this story, pause to allow them to predict or join in on the words that complete the rhymes. Encourage children to use the illustrations as well as their knowledge of rhyming words to help them say the correct words.

CHORAL RECITING As you reread *To Market, To Market*, have children join in on the repeated phrase "To market, to market."

OPPORTUNITIES TO SHARE

To Market, To Market

- Lesson 27, p. 8H
- Lesson 27, p. 8M
- Lesson 27, p. 37D
- Lesson 29, p. 68H
- Lesson 29, p. 97D
- Lesson 32, p. 156H
- Lesson 32, p. 185F
- Lesson 33, p. 186H
- Lesson 33, p. 186M
- Lesson 33, p. 217D

THIS IS
THE
LAST
STRAW!

I'm a shopping disgrace.

Everything's running all over the place!

The LAMB's on the bed.

The PIG's in the kitchen.

The COW's on the couch.

There's a DUCK on my head!

The HEN's in the cupboard.

The GOOSE is there, too.

The GOAT's in the closet— it's chewing my shoe!

The TROUT's in the bathtub. This place is a zoo!

I'm hungry, I'm cranky— now what will I do?

To market, to market,

to buy some POTATOES, CELERY, BEETS.

and some ripe red TOMATOES.

some PEA PODS and PEPPERS,

and GARLIC and SPICE.

a round head of CABBAGE.

a sack of BROWN RICE.

Add OKRA

and ONIONS

and one CARROT bunch.

Home again, home again—

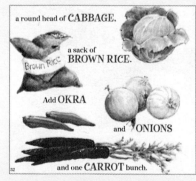

hot SOUP

for lunch!

Setting the Stage with Big Books

CHARLOTTE AGELL

Modeling Fluency

- Stimulate by reading rich literature
- Develop vocabulary
- Model reading strategies

Theme Connection

In *I Swam with a Seal*, a sister and brother tell about going to different places and seeing various animals in their habitats. The children imitate the animals' way of moving or the sounds they make, and the animals wonder why the children don't have flippers or floppy ears or other features that the animals have. The book invites children to think about the people, places, or things they might see while exploring and their relationship to what they see.

Ideas for Sharing Literature

ECHO RECITING Pause after you read aloud the question that each animal asks. Have children echo you by reciting the same question aloud.

APPRECIATING LANGUAGE As you reread *I Swam with a Seal*, call attention to some of the colorful action words in the story, such as *slithered, flickering, pranced, whinnied, stalked,* and *meandered*. Encourage children to talk about and act out the meaning of each word.

OPPORTUNITIES TO SHARE

I Swam with a Seal

- Lesson 28, p. 38H
- Lesson 28, p. 38M
- Lesson 28, p. 67F

- Lesson 30, p. 98H
- Lesson 30, p. 98P
- Lesson 30, p. 123D

- Lesson 31, p. 124H
- Lesson 31, p. 124M
- Lesson 31, p. 155D

- Lesson 34, p. 218H
- Lesson 34, p. 253D

CHARLOTTE AGELL

I Swam with a Seal

I swam with a seal
in the calm blue sea.
The seal took a good, long
look at me.

4

*Where are your shiny flippers,
you funny seal?*

5

I hopped with a hare
in the tall, tall grass.
The hare glanced at me
as if to ask . . .

6

*Where are your floppy ears,
you funny hare?*

7

I flew with a falcon
with my feet on the ground.
The falcon sailed by
with hardly a sound.

8

*Where are your broad wings,
you funny falcon?*

9

I slithered with a snake
near the old stone wall.
The snake didn't look
at me at all.

10

*Where is your flickering tongue,
you funny snake?*

11

I pranced with a pony
in the meadow by the hill.
The pony whinnied
and then was still.

12

*Where is your wild mane,
you funny pony?*

13

I bothered a beaver
who was building a dam.
She slapped the water,
and away she swam.

14

*Where is your strong tail,
you funny beaver?*

15

I trailed a turtle
by the potting shed.
He spied me,
and in went his head.

16

*Where is your hard shell,
you funny turtle?*

17

I giggled with a gull
on the fishing dock.
He was louder,
but we both could squawk.

18

*Where is your gaping beak,
you funny gull?*

19

I peeked at a porcupine
in a tall pine tree.
I was hiding,
but he could see.

20

*Where are your sharp quills,
you funny porcupine?*

21

I danced with a dog
in the busy park.
She licked my face
and taught me to bark.

22

*Where is your furry coat,
you funny dog?*

23

I happened on a heron
fishing in the stream.
She stalked by me,
quiet as a dream.

24

*Where are your long, skinny legs,
you funny heron?*

25

I meandered with a moose
in the evening fog.
He hardly looked up
from his meal in the bog.

26

*Where are your proud antlers,
you funny moose?*

27

I cuddled with a cat
as the moon shone in.
She purred and purred
and kissed me on the chin.

28

*Where are your tickling whiskers,
you funny cat?*

29

We snuggled with our grandpa
in our beds by the light.
He read us a story,
then said, "Good night."

30

*Sleep well and sweet dreams,
you funny, funny honeys!*

31

Introduce the Theme

Read aloud the theme title and discuss the illustration. Ask what "Going Places" means and how the picture shows this. Discuss where the animals in the boat might be going.

Preview the Theme

Have children page through the stories in the theme. Talk about the characters and what is happening in various illustrations. Discuss what the stories might be about and the places the characters in each story might go.

Build Theme Connections

Relate to Personal Experience

Have children tell about a time when they went exploring with a friend
or family member. Ask them how they felt about the experience. You
may wish to use the following poem to help children explore and elaborate on feelings associated with making new discoveries.

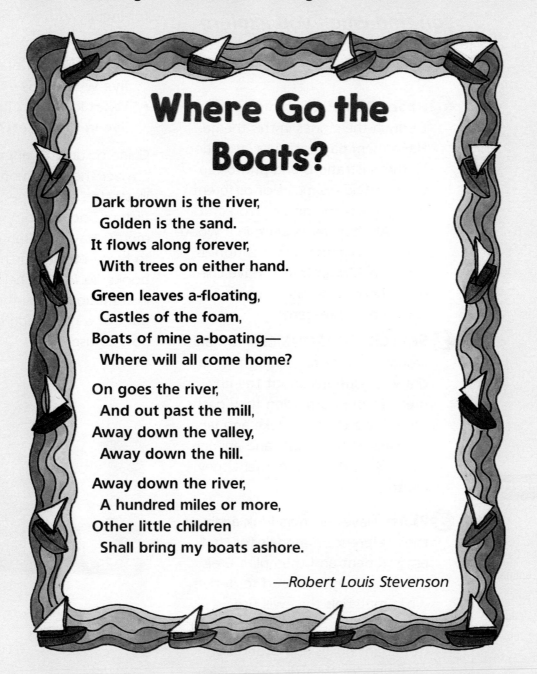

Where Go the Boats?

Dark brown is the river,
  Golden is the sand.
It flows along forever,
  With trees on either hand.

Green leaves a-floating,
  Castles of the foam,
Boats of mine a-boating—
  Where will all come home?

On goes the river,
  And out past the mill,
Away down the valley,
  Away down the hill.

Away down the river,
  A hundred miles or more,
Other little children
  Shall bring my boats ashore.

—Robert Louis Stevenson

Dioramas

Children can work together as a group and then in pairs to create a *Diorama*. Their purpose will be to show what a certain environment looks like.

OBJECTIVE:

To create a diorama that shows what a certain environment looks like.

30-45 Minutes

Materials

- nonfiction picture books
- illustrated encyclopedias
- paper, pencils, cardboard
- cardboard boxes, scissors, glue
- poster paints, brushes
- markers, crayons

School-Home Connection

Invite family members to visit the classroom to see the dioramas. Besides pointing out and naming the animals, plants, and other items, children can tell family members how they learned about the place and how they constructed their diorama.

Visit *The Learning Site:*
www.harcourtschool.com

PROJECT QUESTION

What kinds of things can you find when you explore a place?

1 RESEARCH Have children page through the stories in this theme. Have them pay particular attention to the illustrations and photo captions to find examples of different types of environments. "Frog and Toad All Year" takes place in a woodland environment and "Baboon" is set in an African forest. Have children choose one environment to focus on and research.

2 SKETCH ENVIRONMENT Organize children into pairs. Guide them to draw conclusions about the environment from information they gathered. Have children make and label sketches of the plants and animals that live in the environment they chose.

3 PLAN Have partners look again at their reference materials for that environment and then plan their diorama. They will need to decide what materials they will use.

4 CONSTRUCT Have children use cardboard boxes and other art materials for their dioramas. Each pair of children should also create a display card for the diorama.

Suggestions for Inquiry

The Theme Project can be a springboard for inquiry into a variety of topics. Use prompts such as:

- **What kinds of plants and animals live where it is very cold?**
- **What kinds of plants and animals live in the desert?**

Guide children to appropriate sources to answer their questions. Help them locate illustrated encyclopedias and nonfiction picture books about various environments. Have children use chapter titles to help in their search for information in books. To further help children find information, show them an index in the back of a nonfiction book and explain how to use it.

Classroom Management

Managing Your Time to Meet with Small Groups

Whole Group
40 Minutes

- **MORNING MESSAGE**

- **Sharing Literature**
- **Phonemic Awareness**
- **Phonics**
- **Spelling**
- **High-Frequency Words**
- **Vocabulary**

Small Group
60-90 Minutes

With Teacher
- **Reading Support**
  DECODABLE BOOK
  PUPIL EDITION SELECTIONS

Independent
- **Reading and Writing Routines**
- **Practice Pages**
- **Cross-Curricular Centers**

Whole Group
30 Minutes

- **Writing**
- **Grammar**
  DAILY LANGUAGE PRACTICE

Reading and Writing Routines

Rereading for Fluency

Add books that children can read to the ongoing collections in their **Browsing Boxes.** Children can read the books independently or with a partner.

Words to Remember

Post high-frequency and vocabulary words on a wall, write them on a chart, or display them in a pocket chart. Have children work with the words, sorting them, using them in sentences or illustrating them.

Independent Reading

Gather books related to the lesson's *Pupil Edition* selection. Children can self-select books to read. See the Self-Selected Reading page within each week's lesson.

Journal Writing

Have children write and draw in their **Journal** on self-selected topics or from suggested prompts.

Teacher Notes

Reading Selections

BIG BOOK

To Market, To Market

Anne Miranda

ILLUSTRATED BY
Janet Stevens

DECODABLE BOOK

Applies Long Vowel /ī/igh

Seeing the Sights

by
Susan Blackaby
Illustrated by
Tracy Sabin

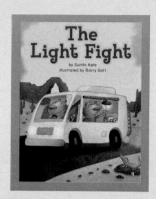

The Light Fight

by Sunita Apte
illustrated by Barry Gott

▲ Decodable Book 27
"Seeing the Sights"
"The Light Fight"

PUPIL EDITION

Genre

Fiction

In fiction for children, animals sometimes act like people.

Look for:

• Ways the birds in the story act like people.

• Ways the birds are like real birds.

The Story of a Blue Bird

by Tomek Bogacki

10

11

SUMMARY: *A young bird explores the world outside his nest.*

 "The Story of a Blue Bird" is available on *Audiotext 5.*

8A **Gather Around**

Books for All Learners

Lesson Plans on pages 37M–37P

BELOW-LEVEL

- **Phonics:** Long Vowel /ī/*igh*
- **Vocabulary:** *afraid, join, learn*
- **High-Frequency Word:** *nothing*

ON-LEVEL

- **Phonics:** Long Vowel /ī/*igh*
- **Vocabulary:** *afraid, flew, join, learn, wonder*
- **High-Frequency Words:** *nothing, thought*

ADVANCED

- **Phonics:** Long Vowel /ī/*igh*
- **Vocabulary:** *afraid, flew, join, learn, wonder*
- **High-Frequency Words:** *nothing, thought*

ELL

- *Strong Picture Support*
- *Concept Vocabulary*

MULTI-LEVELED PRACTICE

Practice Book, pp. 2–9

Extra Support, pp. 3–9

Challenge, pp. 3–9

English-Language Learners, pp. 3–9

Technology

- *Phonics Express™* CD-ROM, Level B
- *Writing Express™* CD-ROM
- *Grammar Jingles™* CD, Primary
- *Reading and Language Skills Assessment* CD-ROM
- *The Learning Site:* www.harcourtschool.com

ADDITIONAL RESOURCES

Phonics Practice Book, pp. 224–225, 308–311

Spelling Practice Book, pp. 67–68

Language Handbook, pp. 114–117

Read-Aloud Literature
- Read-Aloud Anthology, pp. 137, 144

Teaching Transparencies 79–81, 106

Word Builders/Word Builder Cards

Letter Cards

Intervention Resource Kit, Lesson 27

English-Language Learners Resource Kit, Lesson 27

ORAL LANGUAGE — 30 Minutes

• **Sharing Literature**

• **Phonemic Awareness**

WORD WORK — 30 Minutes

• **Phonics**

• **Spelling**

• **High-Frequency Words**

• **Vocabulary**

READING — 45 Minutes

• **Comprehension**
• **Fluency**

Daily Routines
• Morning Message
• Daily Language Practice
• Writing Prompt

• **Independent Reading**

LANGUAGE ARTS — 45 Minutes

• **Writing**

• **Grammar**

Daily Language Practice
Spiral Review

Day 1

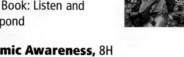

Sharing Literature, 8H
Big Book: Listen and Respond

Phonemic Awareness, 8H
Phoneme Substitution; Focus on /ī/

 Phonics, 8I
Introduce: Long Vowel /ī/*igh*

Spelling, 8K
Pretest; Word Sort **T**

Vocabulary, 8K
Review: *touch, twelve* **T**

 Read
Apply Phonics, 8L

DECODABLE BOOK 27
"Seeing the Sights"

 Independent Reading
Books for All Learners

 Shared Writing, 8M
Theme Word Chart

Writing Prompt
Have children write about how they would travel to their favorite place.

Grammar, 8N
Introduce: Describing Words: *-er* and *-est* **T**

Daily Language Practice
I mit take a trip? (might, trip.)

Day 2

Sharing Literature, 8P
Song: Listen and Respond

Phonemic Awareness, 8P
Phoneme Isolation; Focus on /ī/

 **Phonics,** 8Q
Review: Long Vowel /ī/*igh*

Spelling, 8Q
Word Building **T**

High-Frequency Words, 8S
Introduce: *nothing, thought* **T**

Vocabulary, 8S
Introduce: *afraid, flew, join, learn, wonder*

Word Power, pp. 8–9

Read
Read the Selection, 9A

PUPIL EDITION
"The Story of a Blue Bird," pp. 8–33

Comprehension

(Focus Skill) Plot **T**

(Focus Strategy) Look for Word Bits and Parts

 Independent Reading
Books for All Learners

 Independent Writing, 33B
Story Response

Writing Prompt
Have children write about something new they tried to do, and how they felt.

Grammar, 33C
Review: Describing Words: *-er* and *-est* **T**

Daily Language Practice
flew everywhere together (The birds,.)

8C **Gather Around** **T**=tested skill

Focus Skill
Plot

Phonics
Long Vowel /ī/*igh*

Focus of the Week:
- HIGH-FREQUENCY WORDS: *nothing, thought*
- VOCABULARY: *afraid, flew, join, learn, wonder*
- COMPREHENSION: Plot
- WRITING: Describing Words: *-er* and *-est*

Day 3

Sharing Literature, 33E
Poem: Listen and Respond

Phonemic Awareness, 33E
Rhyming Words; Focus on /ī/

Phonics, 33F
Review: Long Vowel /ī/*igh*

Spelling, 33H
State the Generalization **T**

High-Frequency Words, 33I
Review: *nothing, thought* **T**

Vocabulary, 33I
Review: *afraid, flew, join, learn, wonder*

Read
Rereading for Fluency, 33J

Making Connections, 34–35

Apply Phonics, 33G
DECODABLE BOOK 27
"The Light Fight"

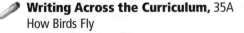 **Independent Reading**
Books for All Learners

✏ **Writing Across the Curriculum,** 35A
How Birds Fly

Writing Prompt
Have children write about a place they would fly to if they could fly.

Grammar, 35B
Review: Describing Words: *-er* and *-est* **T**

Daily Language Practice
The highest of the two birds is the **blue bird** (higher, bird.)

Day 4

Sharing Literature, 35D
Poem: Listen and Respond

Phonemic Awareness, 35D
Phoneme Substitution; Focus on /ī/ and /ē/

Phonics, 35E
Build Words

Spelling, 35G
Review **T**

High-Frequency Words, 35H
Review: *nothing, thought* **T**

Vocabulary, 35H
Review: *afraid, flew, join, learn, wonder*

Read
Comprehension, 35I

 Plot, pp. 36–37

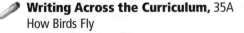 **Independent Reading**
Books for All Learners

✏ **Shared Writing,** 37A
Story About a Problem

Writing Prompt
Have children draw and write about a bird in flight.

Grammar, 37B
Review: Describing Words: *-er* and *-est* **T**

Daily Language Practice
The blue bird couldn't sleep at nite?
(night.)

Day 5

Sharing Literature, 37D
Big Book: Build Concept Vocabulary

Phonemic Awareness, 37D
Phoneme Isolation; Focus on Inflections *-ed, -ing*

Phonics, 37E
Review: Contractions *'s, n't, 'll*
Introduce: Inflections *-ed, -ing*

Spelling, 37G
Posttest; Writing Application **T**

High-Frequency Words, 35H
Review: *nothing, thought* **T**

Vocabulary, 37H
Review: *afraid, flew, join, learn, wonder*

Read
Rereading for Fluency, 37I

Self-Selected Reading, 37J

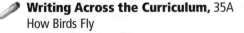 **Independent Reading**
Books for All Learners

✏ **Interactive Writing,** 37K
Postcards

Self-Selected Writing
Have children write about a topic of their choice.

Grammar, 37L
Review: Describing Words: *-er* and *-est* **T**

Daily Language Practice
i am tallest than my friend. (I, taller)

Cross-Curricular Centers

ART CENTER

Bird Collage

Have children cut pictures of birds, leaves, clouds, and trees from magazines and use them to create a bird collage. Display their collages on the bulletin board.

30 Minutes

Materials
- old magazines
- poster board or construction paper
- glue

MATH CENTER

Flocks of Birds

Cut 10–20 simple bird shapes from three different colors of paper and put them into a paper bag. Cut three cloud shapes from white paper. One group member reaches in the bag and pulls out a handful of birds. Then the children work to sort birds of each color onto a different cloud. When the birds are sorted, group members can make up math questions, such as: *How many blue birds are there? How many red birds are there? How many blue and red birds are there?* The other group members answer.

30 Minutes

Materials
- colored paper bird shapes
- white paper clouds
- paper bag

LETTER AND WORD CENTER

Anagrams

Place plastic consonant letters in one paper bag and vowels in another. Each child pulls out two or three vowels and four or five consonants (for a total of seven letters each). Each child creates as many words as he or she can in five minutes and then writes them on a sheet of paper. They can then switch letters and repeat the activity. When they are finished, they can compare word lists to see if they made the same words or different ones.

**doll
dog
down**

15 Minutes

Materials
- plastic letter forms
- paper bags
- pencil and paper

SCIENCE CENTER

Observing Birds

If possible, allow children to observe the behavior of birds outside a convenient window. If no viewing place is available, show a video of birds. Children should observe bird behavior and then discuss their observations with their partner. Then have them write a few sentences describing what they noticed and illustrate their work.

I saw a bird eating seeds.

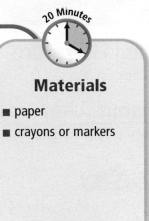

20 Minutes

Materials

- paper
- crayons or markers

SOCIAL STUDIES CENTER

Bird's-Eye View

Suggest to children that they create a bird's-eye view of the school, their home, or neighborhood. Provide examples of simple maps as models. Display their maps on the board.

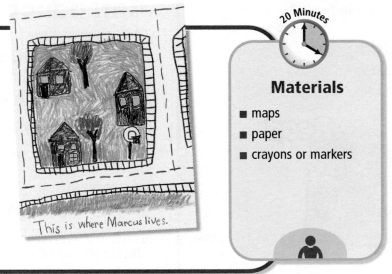

This is where Marcus lives.

20 Minutes

Materials

- maps
- paper
- crayons or markers

HOMEWORK FOR THE WEEK

The Homework Copying Master provides activities to complete for each day of the week.

Visit *The Learning Site:* www.harcourtschool.com

See Resources for Parents and Teachers: Homework Helper.

Homework, p. T39 ▶

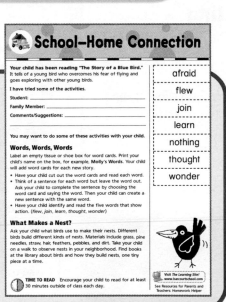

School–Home Connection

Your child has been reading "The Story of a Blue Bird." It tells of a young bird who overcomes his fear of flying and goes exploring with other young birds.

I have tried some of the activities.

Student: _____

Family Member: _____

Comments/Suggestions: _____

You may want to do some of these activities with your child.

Words, Words, Words

Label an empty tissue or shoe box for word cards. Print your child's name on the box, for example, **Molly's Words.** Your child will add word cards for each new story.

- Have your child cut out the word cards and read each word.
- Think of a sentence for each word but leave the word out. Ask your child to complete the sentence by choosing the word card and saying the word. Then your child can create a new sentence using the same word.
- Have your child identify and read the five words that show action. *(flew, join, learn, thought, wonder)*

What Makes a Nest?

Ask your child what birds use to make their nests. Different birds build different kinds of nests. Materials include grass, pine needles, straw, hair, feathers, pebbles, and dirt. Take your child on a walk to observe nests in your neighborhood. Find books at the library about birds and how they build nests, one tiny piece at a time.

TIME TO READ Encourage your child to read for at least 30 minutes outside of class each day.

Visit The Learning Site! www.harcourtschool.com

See Resources for Parents and Teachers: Homework Helper

| afraid |
| flew |
| join |
| learn |
| nothing |
| thought |
| wonder |

WARM UP

MORNING MESSAGE

Good Morning!

Today is _____.

Let's go to the market.

We can buy _____ and _____.

Then we can _____.

Introduce the Day

Tell children that they will be reading a book with you entitled *To Market, To Market*. Explain that the book is about a woman who shops at a supermarket. Guide children in generating a message about shopping at a supermarket.

• **Have you ever shopped at a supermarket? What was it like?**

• **What things can you buy at a supermarket?**

As you write the message, ask volunteers to write letters, words, and punctuation to reinforce skills. For example, volunteers can add the appropriate punctuation to the end of telling sentences and use letter-sound relationships to help spell the names of items they could buy at a supermarket.

Read the Message

Read the message. Use the message to focus on selected skills that have been previously taught.

Apply Skills

Concepts of Print Ask children how many words are in the sentence *Let's go to the market.* Ask how they can tell. Discuss why it is important to leave space between words in a sentence.	**Phonics** Ask volunteers to frame and read words that have specific vowel sounds such as short *a*, short *e*, long *o*, or long *e*.

Sharing Literature

LISTEN AND RESPOND

Introduce the Big Book Display the cover. Read aloud the title and the names of the author and the illustrator.

Connect to Prior Knowledge Discuss the cover illustration and the illustrations on pages 4–7. Ask children if they have ever visited a supermarket like the one in the illustrations.

Set a Purpose Ask children to predict what else the woman might get at the market and what problems she might have. Suggest that children listen to find out what happens as the woman makes more trips to the market.

Read and Respond Track the print as you read the book aloud. Emphasize the repetitive language pattern, the rhythm, and the rhyme. Allow time for children to react to the humor in the story events and illustrations. Encourage them to share their thoughts and feelings about the story.

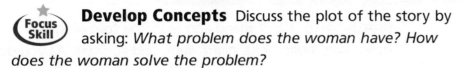 **Develop Concepts** Discuss the plot of the story by asking: *What problem does the woman have? How does the woman solve the problem?*

▲ **Big Book**

 ◄ **"I've a Pair of Fishes,"** *Oo-pples and Boo-noo-noos: Songs and Activities for Phonemic Awareness,* page 71

Phonemic Awareness

PHONEME SUBSTITUTION

Words from the Big Book Say *peg.* Ask children to change the middle sound to name an animal from *To Market, To Market.* (pig) Continue with the following words:

hone (hen)   **gas** (goose)   **limb** (lamb)
deck (duck)   **gate** (goat)   **treat** (trout)

FOCUS ON /ī/

Phoneme Isolation Say *might. I hear /ī/ in the middle of might.* Tell children to say the vowel sound they hear in each of the following words:

high (/ī/)   **light** (/ī/)   **sigh** (/ī/)   **fright** (/ī/)

BELOW-LEVEL

Slowly elongate words so children can more easily hear the vowel sound.

ADVANCED

Ask children to think of words with the /ī/ sound in the middle.

Day 1

OBJECTIVES

- *To generate the long vowel sound of igh*
- *To build words using known letters and sounds*
- *To read simple, regular words*

SKILL TRACE

/ī/igh	
INTRODUCE	**8I–8L**
Reteach	S4–S5, T2
Review	8Q–8R, 33F–33G, 35E–35F
T Test	Bk 1-5
Maintain	Bk 2-1

teaching tip

Vocabulary To ensure that children understand word meanings, have them do the following: *Make a sighing sound. Point to their thigh. Point to what gives them sight. Name something that shines bright. Pantomime a bird in flight.*

15-20 Minutes

Materials

■ blank word cards

Phonics and Spelling
Long Vowel /ī/ *igh*

✔ *Introduce*

TEACH/MODEL

Introduce /ī/*igh* Write these words on the board: *time, try, tried.* Have children read the words and identify the vowel sound. (long *i*) Remind children that the long vowel sound of *i* can be spelled in different ways. Then display *Letter Cards i, g, h* and have children say the letter names. Explain that the letters *igh* together can also stand for the long vowel sound of *i*.

Tell children that the letters *igh* stand for the /ī/ sound in the middle of the words *night, sight,* and *right.* Have children repeat each word after you as you run your hand under the *Letter Cards.*

WORD BLENDING

Words with /ī/*igh* Blend and read the following words: *high, thigh, sigh, sight, right, night, light,* and *sunlight.* As you demonstrate each step using a pocket chart and *Letter Cards,* have children repeat after you using their *Word Builders* and *Word Builder Cards.*

Phonics CENTER

Word Card Chain

Copy the chart shown on the board. Have small groups work together to make word cards with *-ight* words. Children can take turns writing words on cards. Writers should hold up their word cards for the group to read and then place them in a "chain" on a table. When the chain is completed, children can take turns reading the words.

WORD BUILDING

| b | g | h | h | i | l | m | n | r | t |

Build Spelling Words Place the letters *igh* in a pocket chart. Say the letter names and the sound they stand for together. Have children do the same with their *Word Builders* and *Word Builder Cards*. Repeat with the letter *h*. Model how to blend the word *high*. Slide your hand under the letters as you slowly elongate the sounds—/hhī̄ī/. Then read the word naturally—*high*. Have children do the same.

Have children build and read new words by telling them:

- Change the first *h* to *n* and add a *t* at the end. What word did you make?

- Change the *n* to *l*. What word did you make?

- Change the *l* to *r*. What word did you make?

- Change the *r* to *m*. What word did you make?

- Change the *m* to *br*. What word did you make?

Dictate /ī/igh Words Dictate the words *light* and *night* and have children write them in their journal. Suggest that they either draw a picture or write about each word.

5-DAY PHONICS/SPELLING

DAY 1	Introduce /ī/*igh*
DAY 2	Word Building with /ī/*igh*
DAY 3	Word Building with /ī/*igh*
DAY 4	Word Building with /ī/*igh*, /ē/*e, ee, ea*
DAY 5	Contractions *'s, n't, 'll*: Inflections *-ed, -ing* (drop final *e*)

BELOW-LEVEL

To reinforce that *igh* stands for one sound, make and distribute to each child a single *Word Builder Card* for *igh*. Have children use this card to build the Spelling Words.

ENGLISH-LANGUAGE LEARNERS

Some children may have difficulty in distinguishing vowel sounds. Model the /ī/ sound for them, and then have them practice the sound, using a mirror to check for correct tongue and lip placement.

Phonics Resources

Phonics Express™ CD-ROM, **Level B** Roamer/Route 5/Park

Phonics Practice Book, pp. 224–225

Spelling Words

1. high
2. night
3. light
4. right
5. might
6. bright
7. rode
8. those
9. touch
10. twelve

Phonics and Spelling

INTRODUCE THE WORDS

Pretest Read aloud the first word and the Dictation Sentence. Repeat the word as children write it. Write the correct spelling on the board and have children circle the word if they spelled it correctly and write it correctly if they did not. Repeat for words 2–10.

1. **high** The kite is up **high** in the sky.
2. **night** I like to sleep at **night**.
3. **light** It is **light** when the sun is out.
4. **right** This book is the **right** one.
5. **might** I **might** go to the zoo today.
6. **bright** My bike is **bright** blue.

Review

7. **rode** We **rode** on the bus.
8. **those** **Those** books are mine.

Vocabulary

9. **touch** I like to **touch** soft things.
10. **twelve** Max has **twelve** apples.

Word Sort Place the headings "Ends with t" and "Does not end with t" at the top of a pocket chart. Write each Spelling Word on an index card. Display the cards and ask: *Does this word end with a t or does it end with another letter?* Place the words in the correct column as children direct. Then have children read the words aloud.

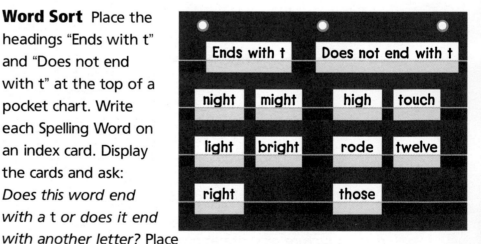

Ends with t		Does not end with t	
night	might	high	touch
light	bright	rode	twelve
right		those	

▲ Practice Book, p. 2

Apply Phonics

Read

APPLY /ī/igh

Write the following sentences on the board or chart paper. Have children read the first sentence as you track the print. Frame the word *night* and have children read it. Continue with the other sentences.

The stars are out at night.
It is high in the sky.
The starlight is bright.

Have children read "Seeing the Sights" in *Decodable Book 27*.

▲ **Decodable Book 27**
"Seeing the Sights"

Managing Small Groups

Read the *Decodable Book* with small groups of children. While you work with small groups, have other children do the following:

- **Self-Selected Reading**
- **Practice Pages**
- **Cross-Curricular Centers**
- **Journal Writing**

Use the suggested Classroom Management outline on page 7C for the whole-group/small-group schedule.

School–Home Connection

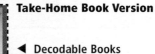

Take-Home Book Version

◄ Decodable Books Take-Home Version

ONGOING ASSESSMENT

Note how well children
- read sentences without modeling.
- decode words in "Seeing the Sights."
- complete long vowel /ī/igh practice pages.

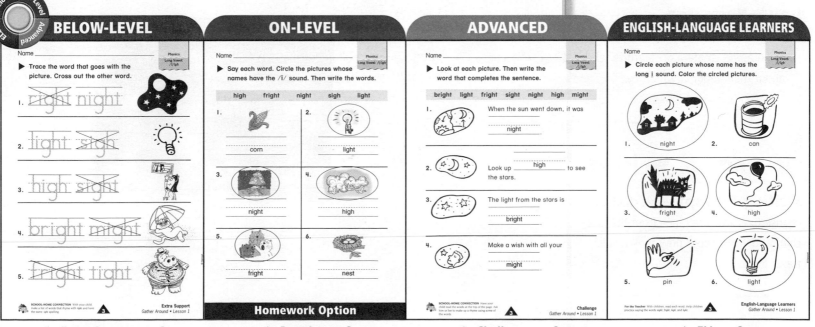

BELOW-LEVEL	ON-LEVEL	ADVANCED	ENGLISH-LANGUAGE LEARNERS
▲ Extra Support, p. 3	▲ Practice, p. 3	▲ Challenge, p. 3	▲ ELL, p. 3

I mit take a trip?

I **might** take a trip.

Writing Every Day

Day 1: Theme Word Chart
Work together to write lists about interesting places and ways to travel.

Day 2: Story Response
Have children write about a learning experience and compare it with the blue bird's experience.

Day 3: How Birds Fly
Have children find information and write about how birds fly.

Day 4: Story About a Problem
Guide children in writing a story in which an animal character solves or overcomes a problem.

Day 5: Postcards
Have children choose a place to explore and create a postcard to tell about their imaginary journey.

journal  writing

Writing Prompt Have children choose their favorite place from the first chart and write about how they would travel there.

Shared Writing
Theme Word Chart

BRAINSTORM

Generate Theme-Related Words Tell children that they will be reading many stories in which characters visit interesting places. Review where the woman in the big book story goes and why it is an interesting place.

Then ask children to think of some places they would like to read about or visit. Record responses on a chart. Discuss ways story characters might travel, and record children's ideas on another chart.

Read and Display the Words Read the words aloud. Then have children read decodable and previously taught words. Display the charts so children can refer to them as they write throughout the upcoming weeks. Have children add to the charts occasionally as they read and think about new places.

Interesting Places	
ocean	mountains
big city	moon
jungle	

Ways to Travel	
fly	walk
drive	daydream
swim	

Grammar

Describing Words: -er and -est

5-DAY	
DAY 1	**Introduce Describing Words: -er, -est**
DAY 2	Make Comparison Cards
DAY 3	Describe How Birds Fly
DAY 4	Illustrate Comparisons
DAY 5	Compare Places

OBJECTIVE

To introduce describing words with -er and -est

SKILL TRACE

DESCRIBING WORDS -er, -est	
INTRODUCE	**8N**
Review	33C, 35B, 37B, 37L
T Test	Bk 1-5

TEACH/MODEL

Introduce Describing Words with *-er* and *-est* Make three cards of different colors: a red card, a longer blue card, and an even longer green card. Display the red card and the blue card. Point to each as you describe them in this manner: *The red card is long. The blue card is longer.* Point to each card and repeat the describing words *long, longer.* Add the green card. Describe the cards as follows: *The red card is long. The blue card is longer. The green card is the longest.* Repeat the describing words as you point to each card: *long, longer, longest.* Write the words on the cards.

Make Comparisons Remind children that when you described two cards, you used the words *long* and *longer* and that when you described three cards, you also used *longest*. Explain that describing words that end with *-er* and *-est* are used to compare things.

PRACTICE/APPLY

Display *Teaching Transparency 79* Have children name the pictures (car, jet, rocket) and then compare how fast each vehicle is. For example: *A car is fast. A jet is faster. A rocket is the fastest.* Then read the first word in the chart and have children supply describing words with *-er* and *-est* as you record them. Ask volunteers to use the words to compare sweet things. Continue with the other words.

▼ **Teaching Transparency 79**

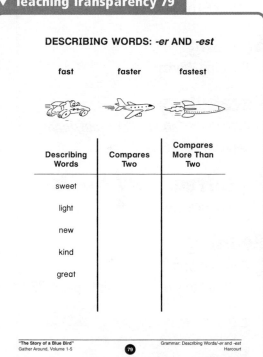

DESCRIBING WORDS: *-er* AND *-est*

	fast	faster	fastest

Describing Words	Compares Two	Compares More Than Two
sweet		
light		
new		
kind		
great		

"The Story of a Blue Bird"
Gather Around, Volume 1-5 — 79 — Grammar: Describing Words/-er and -est
Harcourt

Revisit the Big Book

WRAP UP

Reread Together Track the print as you reread the big book. After reading, ask volunteers to tell which part of the story they liked best.

▲ **Big Book**

S.S.R. Sustained Silent Reading
Have children read silently from a book of their choice. See page 37J for tips on helping children choose books.

Practice Book, p. 4

Name _____

► Add **er** or **est** to the word so that it correctly completes the sentence. Write the word on the line.

bright

1. This bird has ____**brighter**____ colors than that bird.

high

2. The blue bird lands on a ____**higher**____ branch than the green bird.

tight

3. Birds make nests in the ____**tightest**____ places.

TRY THIS With a partner, act out the words light, lighter, lightest and high, higher, highest.

▲ **Practice Book, p. 4**

ORAL LANGUAGE

WARM UP
MORNING MESSAGE

Good Morning!

Today is _____. What animals can fly?

_____ can fly.

_____ fly by using _____.

If I could fly, I would _____.

Introduce the Day

Tell children that they will be reading a story about an animal that learns how to fly. Guide them to think about animals that can fly and what it would be like to be able to fly. Ask:

• **What animals can fly?**

• **What helps these animals fly?**

• **Where would you go if you could fly?**

As you write the message, ask volunteers to spell words they know and to use letter-sounds to help you spell other words. Ask them what punctuation marks should come at the end of sentences.

Read the Message

Read the message. Use the message to focus on selected skills that have been previously taught.

Apply Skills

Phonics Ask volunteers to frame and read words that have the long vowel sound of *i*. Discuss how the spelling pattern in words such as *fly* and *by* can help readers know how to read the words.

Grammar/Mechanics As you point to the punctuation marks in the message, have children name them. Discuss how question marks, commas, and periods help readers understand the meaning of sentences.

Sharing Literature

LISTEN AND RESPOND

Connect to Prior Knowledge Review the animals children discussed for the Morning Message. Then tell children they are going to learn a song about birds.

Sing a Song Teach children the first verse of the song "What Do the Birds See?" Use the tune of "The Old Gray Mare." As children sing, encourage them to imagine what the birds might see.

Add Verses to a Song Ask volunteers to tell what they imagined the birds were seeing. Then lead children in singing new verses, using their ideas in the second verse of the song.

What Do the Birds See?

What do the birds see
When they fly way up high,
When they fly way up high,
When they fly way up high?
What do the birds see
When they fly way up high,
Up in the big, blue sky?
The birds can see _____
When they fly way up high,
When they fly way up high,
When they fly way up high.
The birds can see _____
When they fly way up high,
Up in the big, blue sky!

Phonemic Awareness

PHONEME ISOLATION

Words from "What Do the Birds See?" Ask children to listen for the vowel sound as you say a word. Say the word *see*. Have children say the vowel sound—/ē/. Continue with the following words:

high (/ī/)	**when** (/e/)	**fly** (/ī/)	**way** (/ā/)
up (/u/)	**sky** (/ī/)	**big** (/i/)	**blue** (/o͞o/)

FOCUS ON /ī/

Distinguish Medial Sounds Say the word *flight. I hear the sound /ī/ in the middle of* flight. Say these words and have children repeat each word that has the sound /ī/.

heat (no)	**sight** (yes)	**night** (yes)	**sheet** (no)
mean (no)	**speak** (no)	**right** (yes)	**might** (yes)

REACHING ALL LEARNERS

Diagnostic Check: Phonemic Awareness

If... children cannot distinguish medial vowel sounds...

Then... have them practice identifying the vowel sound at the beginning of words such as *eat, ice, each,* and *I'm.*

ADDITIONAL SUPPORT ACTIVITIES

BELOW-LEVEL	Reteach, p. S2
ADVANCED	Extend, p.S3
ENGLISH-LANGUAGE LEARNERS	Reteach, p. S3

The Story of a Blue Bird   **8P**

OBJECTIVES

- To blend sounds into words
- To read and write Spelling Words

SKILL TRACE

/ī/*igh*		
Introduce	8I–8L	
Reteach	S4–S5, T2	
Review	8Q–8R, 33F–33G, 35E–35F	
T Test	Bk 1-5	
Maintain	Bk 2-1	

Spelling Words

1. **high**
2. **night**
3. **light**
4. **right**
5. **might**
6. **bright**
7. **rode**
8. **those**
9. **touch**
10. **twelve**

Phonics and Spelling
Long Vowel /ī/*igh* ✔ Review

5-DAY SPELLING	
DAY 1	Pretest; Word Sort
DAY 2	**Word Building**
DAY 3	State the Generalization
DAY 4	Review
DAY 5	Posttest; Writing Application

WORD BUILDING

Blend and Read a Spelling Word Display *Letter Cards h, i, g, h.* Ask children to say the sound for *h* and the sound for *igh* as you place the cards in a pocket chart. Slide your hand under the letters as you blend the sounds—/hhīī/. Have children repeat after you. Then read the word naturally—*high*, and have children do the same.

Build Spelling Words Ask children which letters you should change to make *high* become *night*. (change *h* to *n*, add *t* at the end) Have children read the word. Continue building the Spelling Words shown in this manner and having children read them.

BELOW-LEVEL

Some children may have difficulty mastering the *igh* spelling. Have them copy each word, using colored markers. Tell them to use the same color for the *igh* part of every word.

ENGLISH-LANGUAGE LEARNERS

Some children may be confused by the number of ways the long *i* sound can be spelled in English. Write a number of words on the board to show different long *i* spellings (such as *light, fly, tie,* and *bite*).

Apply Phonics

READ WORDS IN CONTEXT

5-DAY PHONICS/SPELLING	
DAY 1	Introduce /ī/*igh*
DAY 2	**Word Building with /ī/*igh***
DAY 3	Word Building with /ī/*igh*
DAY 4	Word Building with /ī/*igh*, /ē/*e*, *ea, ee*
DAY 5	Contractions *'s, n't, 'll* Inflections *-ed, -ing* (drop final *e*)

Write the following sentences on the board or on chart paper and have children read them aloud.

> I like to read **those** books at **night**.
> I need a **light** to read them **right**.
> This **light** is up **high**.
> It is as **bright** as **twelve lights**.
> I **might** read about the horse Bob **rode**.
> I can almost **touch** that horse!

Phonics Resources

Phonics Express™ CD-ROM, **Level B**
Sparkle/Route 3/Fire Station

 Dictate Words Dictate to children several words from the pocket chart, and have them write the words on a dry-erase board or in their journal.

high
night
light
right
might
bright

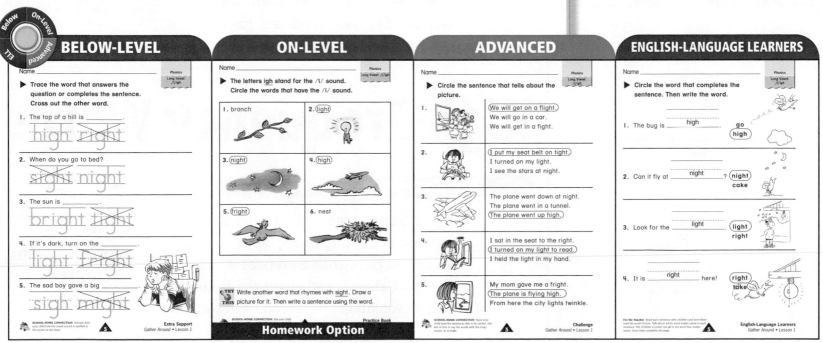

▲ Extra Support, p. 5   ▲ Practice, p. 5   ▲ Challenge, p. 5   ▲ ELL, p. 5

The Story of a Blue Bird   **8R**

Vocabulary

afraid   scared

flew   did fly

join   take part with others

learn   to know something new

wonder   to think about

High-Frequency Words

nothing   not anything

thought   used the mind

▼ Teaching Transparency 80

VOCABULARY

afraid   flew   join   learn   wonder

HIGH-FREQUENCY WORDS

nothing   thought

Mama Bird wanted Little Bird to <u>learn</u> how to fly.

"Come and <u>join</u> me," Mama Bird said.

Little Bird just sat in the nest.

"There's <u>nothing</u> to it," said Mama Bird.

Little Bird just sat in the nest.

"I <u>wonder</u> if Little Bird is <u>afraid</u>," Mama Bird <u>thought</u>.

All of a sudden, Little Bird <u>flew</u> to the next tree.

Then he flew back to the nest.

"You did it!" cried Mama Bird.

"The Story of a Blue Bird"
Gather Around, Volume 1-5   **80**   Vocabulary/High-Frequency Words
Harcourt

Building Background

TALK ABOUT BIRDS

Make a Bird Web Tell children that they are going to read a story about a bird. Use a word web to record information children know about birds.

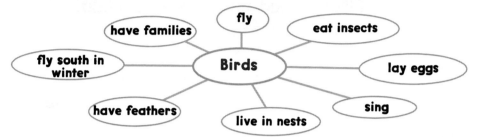

Discuss Story Words Write these words on the board: *answered, colorful, happily, imagining, suddenly,* and *pool.* Read each word aloud to children. Discuss the meaning of each word.

Vocabulary

IDENTIFY WORDS

Echo Read Display *Teaching Transparency 80* or write the words and poem on the board. Point to the words *afraid, flew, join, learn,* and *wonder.* Say each word and have children repeat it.

> **INTRODUCE**
>
> **Vocabulary**
> afraid   learn
> flew   wonder
> join

High-Frequency Words

INTRODUCE WORDS IN CONTEXT

Read Sentences Point to the words *nothing* and *thought.* Say each word and have children repeat it. Track the print as you read aloud the sentences. Call on volunteers to reread each sentence.

> **INTRODUCE**
>
> **High-Frequency Words**
> nothing   thought

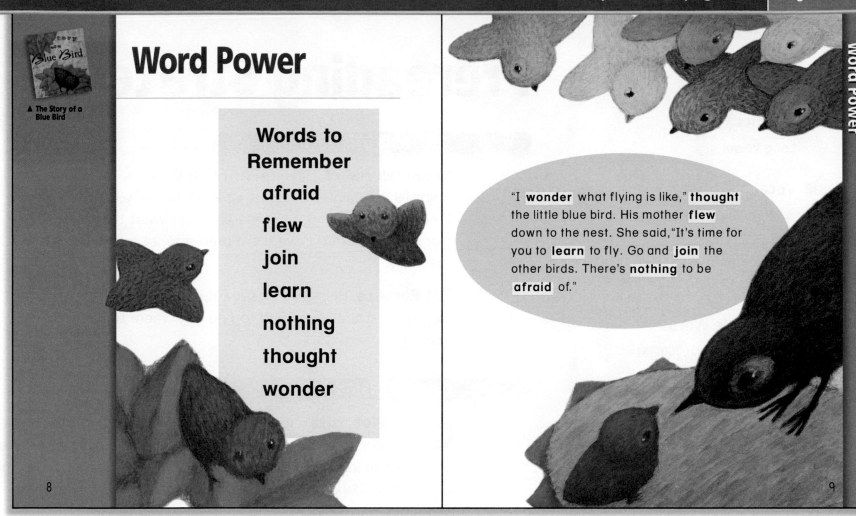

Word Power

Words to Remember

afraid

flew

join

learn

nothing

thought

wonder

▲ The Story of a Blue Bird

"I **wonder** what flying is like," **thought** the little blue bird. His mother **flew** down to the nest. She said, "It's time for you to **learn** to fly. Go and **join** the other birds. There's **nothing** to be **afraid** of."

8

9

Word Power

Pages 8–9 Have children read aloud the Words to Remember. Then have children read the sentences aloud. Have children point to the Words to Remember in the sentences.

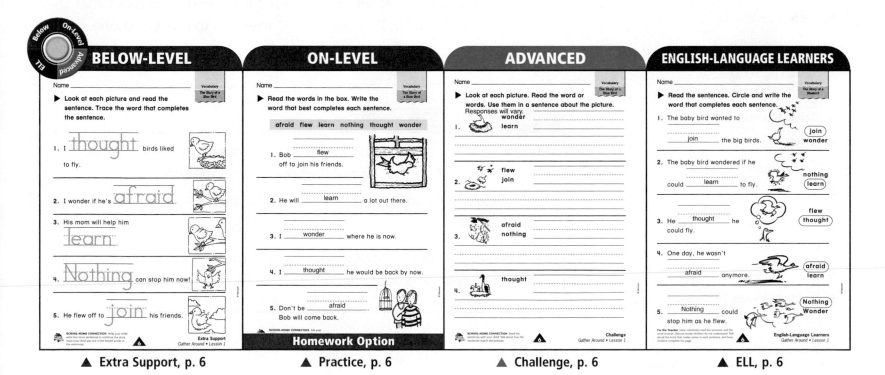

BELOW-LEVEL

Name _____

▶ Look at each picture and read the sentence. Trace the word that completes the sentence.

1. I thought birds liked to fly.

2. I wonder if he's afraid

3. His mom will help him learn

4. Nothing can stop him now!

5. He flew off to join his friends.

▲ Extra Support, p. 6

ON-LEVEL

Name _____

▶ Read the words in the box. Write the word that best completes each sentence.

afraid flew learn nothing thought wonder

1. Bob flew off to join his friends.

2. He will learn a lot out there.

3. I wonder where he is now.

4. I thought he would be back by now.

5. Don't be afraid Bob will come back.

Homework Option

▲ Practice, p. 6

ADVANCED

Name _____

▶ Look at each picture. Read the word or words. Use them in a sentence about the picture. Responses will vary.

1. wonder learn

2. flew join

3. afraid nothing

4. thought

▲ Challenge, p. 6

ENGLISH-LANGUAGE LEARNERS

Name _____

▶ Read the sentences. Circle and write the word that completes each sentence.

1. The baby bird wanted to _____ join the big birds. (join / wonder)

2. The baby bird wondered if he could learn to fly. (nothing / learn)

3. He thought he could fly. (flew / thought)

4. One day, he wasn't afraid anymore. (afraid / learn)

5. Nothing could stop him as he flew. (Nothing / Wonder)

▲ ELL, p. 6

The Story of a Blue Bird **8–9**

■ **Phonics**

Long Vowel /ī/*igh*

■ **Vocabulary**

afraid, flew, join, learn, wonder

■ **High-Frequency Words**

nothing, thought

■ **Decodable Words**

See the list on pp. T50–T51

■ **Comprehension**

 Plot

 Look for Word Bits and Parts

Strategies Good Readers Use

To Recognize Words

• Use Decoding/Phonics

• **Look for Word Bits and Parts**

To Gain Meaning

• Self-Correct

• Read Ahead

• Reread

• Reread Aloud

• Use Picture Clues to Confirm Meaning

• Make and Confirm Predictions

• Sequence Events/Summarize

• Create Mental Images

• Make Inferences

Prereading Strategies

PREPARING TO READ

Preview/Predict Have children read the title. Then have them point to the name of the author/illustrator as you read it aloud. Preview pages 12–15. Ask children to tell what they think the story will be about. Have them predict what might happen in the story.

Set Purpose Help children set a purpose for reading. If necessary, suggest that they read to find out where the blue bird might go.

COMPREHENSION SKILL

 Plot Explain to children that the events that make up a story are called the plot. Point out that story events often tell how a character's problem is solved. Remind children that in the big book *To Market, To Market,* the plot was about the woman's problem with the animals and how she solved the problem.

STRATEGY

Look for Word Bits and Parts Remind children that often they can figure out a long word they don't know by looking at parts of the word. Write the word *everyone* on the board. Ask children to point out any letter combinations that they already know. If necessary, call attention to *every* and *one*.

Managing Small Groups

Read "The Story of a Blue Bird" with small groups of children. While you work with small groups, have other children do the following:

• **Self-Selected Reading**   • **Cross-Curricular Centers**

• **Practice Pages**   • **Journal Writing**

Use the suggested Classroom Management outline on page 7C for the whole-group/small-group schedule.

Genre

Fiction

In fiction for children, animals sometimes act like people.

Look for:

- Ways the birds in the story act like people.
- Ways the birds are like real birds.

10

The Story of a Blue Bird by Tomek Bogacki

11

Guided Comprehension

Pages 10–11 Have children reread the title and review their predictions about the blue bird. Have them confirm their predictions as they read ahead.

GENRE: Fiction

Read aloud the information about fiction stories on page 10. Tell children that fiction includes

- characters who are not real
- events that did not happen

BELOW-LEVEL	ON-LEVEL	ADVANCED	ENGLISH-LANGUAGE LEARNERS
Work in a small group with children. Have each child read pages aloud in turn. If children encounter unfamiliar words, encourage them to look for familiar word parts to help them decode the word. SMALL GROUP	As children read the selection, use the Guided Comprehension questions to direct their reading. WHOLE CLASS/SMALL GROUP	Have children make predictions about the story and then read the selection independently. Have children share why they made the predictions they did and whether or not the story ended the way they expected. SMALL GROUP/INDEPENDENT	Read aloud several nouns from the story, such as *bird, nest, tree, brother,* and *sister.* Let children explain any words they know. Define the others for them before they begin reading. SMALL GROUP
ADDITIONAL SUPPORT See Intervention Resource Kit, Lesson 27. *Intervention Teacher's Guide pp. 262–271.*			**ADDITIONAL SUPPORT** See English-Language Learners Resource Kit, Lesson 27. *English-Language Learners Teacher's Guide pp. 158–159*

A little blue bird was born in the nest of a big tree. He grew fast.

12   13

Guided Comprehension

Pages 12–13 Have children look at the illustration and tell what they notice about the baby birds. Ask them where the baby birds are and how they can tell. Then have children read to find out if they are right.

1 **NOTE DETAILS** Where was the little blue bird born? (in the nest of a big tree)

2 **DRAW CONCLUSIONS** Who do you think will be the main character in this story? (the little blue bird) **What clues can you find to show you are right?** (Possible response: The little blue bird is the only character mentioned on the first two pages.)

3 **MAKE PREDICTIONS** What do you think will happen next? (Possible response: The bird will learn to fly.)

BELOW-LEVEL

Have children listen to "The Story of a Blue Bird" on Audiotext 5. Children can listen and follow along in their books. The cassette provides children with a model for accurate decoding.

ENGLISH-LANGUAGE LEARNERS

Have children identify parts of the pictures that are mentioned in the text. For example, have them read the word *nest* and point to the nest in the illustration.

"Why don't you go and learn how to fly with your brother and sister? Don't you wonder what is out there?" his mother asked. "Oh, yes. But I am still a little bit afraid," the blue bird answered.

So while the other birds tested their wings the little blue bird sat in the nest, watching.

14

15

Guided Comprehension

Pages 14–15 Have children look at the illustration. Then have them read to find out what the birds are saying.

1 (Focus Skill) **PLOT** What problem does the little blue bird have? (He wonders what is off in the distance, but he is afraid to fly.)

2 **VOCABULARY** What does it mean that "the other birds tested their wings"? (They were learning to fly.) **Have you ever "tested your wings" to try to learn something new?** (Possible response: Yes, I learned to ride a bike. Accept responses that describe learning experiences.)

3 **MAKE PREDICTIONS** Do you think the little blue bird will ever learn to fly? Why or why not? (Possible response: Yes, because he will want to join his brother and sister.)

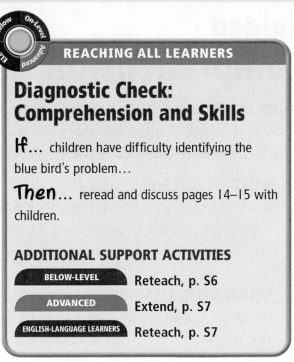

REACHING ALL LEARNERS

Diagnostic Check: Comprehension and Skills

If... children have difficulty identifying the blue bird's problem...

Then... reread and discuss pages 14–15 with children.

ADDITIONAL SUPPORT ACTIVITIES

BELOW-LEVEL	Reteach, p. S6
ADVANCED	Extend, p. S7
ENGLISH-LANGUAGE LEARNERS	Reteach, p. S7

The Story of a Blue Bird **14–15**

At night he couldn't sleep,
imagining what might be
out there beyond the trees.

"Mama, Mama, what is out
there?" he asked.
"Nothing," she said. "Now
go to sleep."

Nothing? he wondered . . .
And he couldn't stop
thinking about it.

16

17

Guided Comprehension

Pages 16–17 Have children use the illustration to tell what time of day it is at this point in the story. Have children read to find out what the little blue bird is thinking about.

1 **NOTE DETAILS/SETTING How does the picture help you tell what time of day it is?** (It shows a dark sky, a moon, and stars.) **How do the words help you tell what time it is?** (They tell us it is night and that the bird couldn't sleep.)

2 **DRAW CONCLUSIONS Why do you think the mother bird tells the little blue bird that there is nothing behind the trees?** (Possible response: She wants him to go to sleep.) **What does she mean by "nothing"?** (She means that there is nothing interesting.)

3 **CHARACTERS' EMOTIONS Do you think the little blue bird believes his mother?** (Possible response: No, he is still curious because he keeps wondering about it.)

Strategies Good Readers Use

 Focus Strategy **Look for Word Bits and Parts**

Have children find and frame the word that comes before *the trees* in the first sentence. Discuss how they can use parts of the word to figure out the whole word. Lead children to understand that they can use the word part *be* and then use letter sounds to figure out the other word part. Have children sweep a finger under the word as they say it—*beyond*.

The next morning the little blue bird was gone, and everyone wondered what had happened.

18

19

Guided Comprehension

Pages 18–19 Have children describe the illustration. Have them read to find out what the feather means.

1 **INTERPRET STORY EVENTS** Are you surprised that the little blue bird is gone? Why or why not? (Possible responses: Yes, because he was afraid. No, because he was curious.)

2 **DRAW CONCLUSIONS** Where you think the little blue bird has gone? (Possible response: to see what is beyond the trees)

3 **DRAW CONCLUSIONS** What did you read in the story that makes you think so? (Possible response: When the other birds were sleeping, the little blue bird wondered what was beyond the trees.)

SCIENCE

Bird Habits Share the following information with children: It is natural for small birds to leave the nest once they have learned to fly, but it takes time to master the task. While the young birds are learning to fly, they will stay with their families and be fed by their parents.

"Nothing, nothing, where is this nothing?" the little blue bird thought as he walked away from his nest in the big tree.

"Is nothing high, or is nothing low?
Is nothing here, or is nothing there?
What does nothing look like?"

There was no one to ask, so he kept on going.

20

21

Guided Comprehension

Pages 20–21 Have children read to find out what the little bird is doing and why he left the nest.

① **CONFIRM PREDICTIONS** Was your prediction correct about where the little blue bird had gone? (Possible response: Yes, because I thought he was going exploring.)

② **DRAW CONCLUSIONS** What do you think the little blue bird thinks "nothing" is? (He thinks "nothing" is something real that can be seen.) What does the little blue bird say to make you think that? (He asks himself where he can find it and what it looks like.)

③ **EXPRESS PERSONAL OPINIONS** Do you think the little blue bird can find "nothing"? Why or why not? (Possible response: No, because it is *no thing*; if he found it, it would have to be something.)

BELOW-LEVEL

Point out the quotation marks. Remind children that quotation marks indicate the exact words that a character is saying or thinking. Model by reading the page aloud, using vocal expression to show how the little bird feels. Then have volunteers read aloud.

He came upon a pool of blue water. It looked like nothing he had ever seen before, but he didn't know if this was the nothing he was looking for.

"What are you looking for?" someone asked him.

22

23

Guided Comprehension

Pages 22–23 Have children look at the illustration and tell what the little blue bird has found. Have them read to find out if it is what he's looking for.

1 **INTERPRET STORY EVENTS** What does the little blue bird find? (a pool of water) Does he think that this is the "nothing" he is looking for? Why or why not? (The little bird doesn't know what he is looking for, so he doesn't know if he's found it.)

2 (Focus Strategy) **USE WORD BITS AND PARTS** Point to the first word in the last line on page 22. What information did you use to read this word? (Possible response: *Someone* is made up of two smaller words, *some* and *one*.)

3 **MAKE PREDICTIONS** Who do you think the "someone" is who asked the question? (Possible response: another bird)

The Story of a Blue Bird **22–23**

"Nothing," he answered, surprised.
"Oh! Come with me," said the green bird.
And the blue bird joined him.

Suddenly a flock of colorful birds came flying by.
"What are you looking for?" they asked.
"Nothing," the green bird answered.
"Oh! Come with us," they called.
And the green bird spread his wings and flew up.

24

25

Guided Comprehension

Pages 24–25 Have children read to confirm predictions.

1 **EVALUATE** Do you think the green bird really knows what the blue bird is looking for? Why or why not? (Possible responses: No, because he is just as young as the blue bird. Yes, because he tells the blue bird to come with him.)

2 **DRAW CONCLUSIONS** Are the other birds as young as the blue bird and the green bird? How can you tell? (They're probably older because they are bigger.)

3 **MAKE PREDICTIONS** Do you think the other birds know what "nothing" is? Why or why not? (Possible response: Yes, because they are older and have been flying for a longer time.)

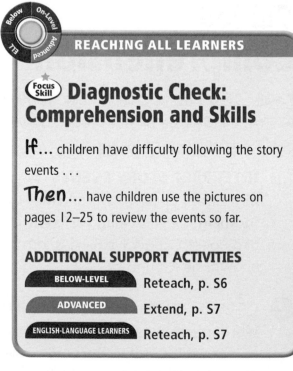

REACHING ALL LEARNERS

(Focus Skill) Diagnostic Check: Comprehension and Skills

If... children have difficulty following the story events . . .

Then... have children use the pictures on pages 12–25 to review the events so far.

ADDITIONAL SUPPORT ACTIVITIES

BELOW-LEVEL	Reteach, p. S6
ADVANCED	Extend, p. S7
ENGLISH-LANGUAGE LEARNERS	Reteach, p. S7

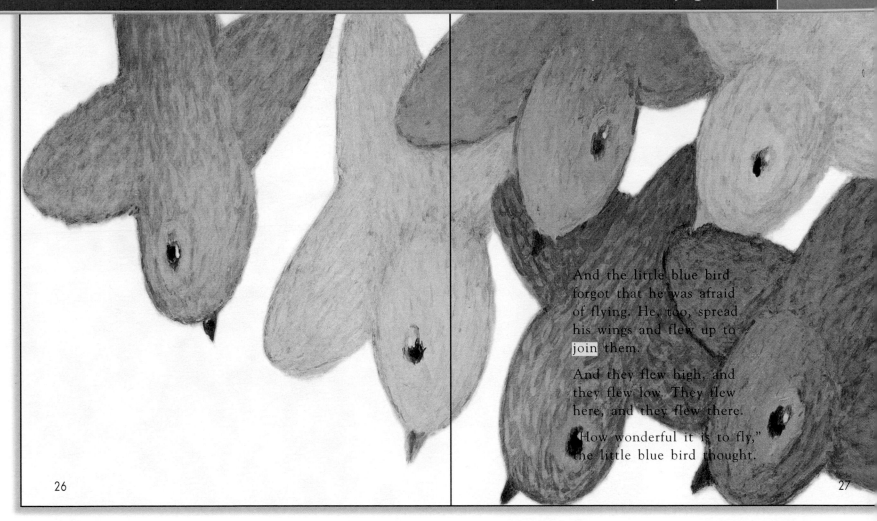

And the little blue bird forgot that he was afraid of flying. He, too, spread his wings and flew up to join them.

And they flew high, and they flew low. They flew here, and they flew there.

"How wonderful it is to fly," the little blue bird thought.

26   27

Guided Comprehension

Pages 26–27 Have children read to find out something surprising about what "nothing" is and about the little blue bird.

1 **DRAW CONCLUSIONS** How does the blue bird learn to fly? (He joins the other birds and forgets about his fear.)

2 *(Focus Skill)* **RECOGNIZE ELEMENTS OF PLOT** Is it surprising that the blue bird finally learns to fly? Why or why not? (Possible response: Yes, because he was so afraid before.)

3 **IDENTIFY WITH CHARACTERS** What do you think the other, older birds think "nothing" is? (nothing special—Help children understand that to the other birds, flying is nothing special.) **Have you ever answered "nothing" when someone asked what you were doing? Were you really doing "nothing"?** (Possible response: Yes; I was watching TV. Encourage children to relate personal experiences.)

Strategies Good Readers Use

(Focus Strategy) **Use Word Bits and Parts**
    Remind children that when they come across a long word that looks unfamiliar, they can often use parts of the word to help them figure it out. Write the words *forgot*, *flying*, and *wonderful* on cards. Cut the cards apart to help children see how the word parts can help them read the entire word: *for/got, fly/ing, won/der/ful*.

"Where have you been? What have you seen?" asked his brother and sister when the blue bird came back home.

"What happened to make you fly so well?" asked his mother.

"Nothing," said the blue bird, happily fluttering his wings.

"Tell us, tell us all about it," said his brother and sister.

"Come with me!" said the blue bird.

28

29

Guided Comprehension

Pages 28–30 Have children use the illustration to tell where the blue bird is now. Then have them read to find out what he tells his family.

1 **DETERMINE CHARACTERS' EMOTIONS** How does the little blue bird's family feel to see him back at the nest? (They are happy he is home and excited to hear about his experiences.)

2 (Focus Skill) **RECOGNIZE ELEMENTS OF PLOT** What do you think the blue bird means when he answers "nothing" to their questions? (He probably means "nothing special.")

3 (Focus Skill) **RECOGNIZE ELEMENTS OF PLOT** Is the story ending what you expected? Why or why not? (Possible response: Yes, because I knew the blue bird would learn how to fly.)

ADVANCED

Use the following questions to conduct a discussion about the plot.

- Would this story have been as enjoyable if the blue bird hadn't learned to fly? Why or why not?

- What stories have you read that have a similar plot—in which a character solves a problem?

- Do you think it's important that problems are solved in stories? Why or why not?

And they flew high, and they flew low.
They flew here, and they flew there. They flew everywhere . . . all together.

30

Think and Respond

1. What was the little blue bird looking for? What does he find?
2. How does the green bird help the blue bird?
3. Why is it easier for the blue bird to fly with his new friends than alone?
4. Tell about the first time you tried to do something. Tell what you did and how you felt.
5. What lesson does the blue bird learn in the story?

31

Think and Respond

1. (Focus Skill) The little blue bird wanted to find out what the "nothing" was beyond the trees. He found out how to overcome his fear of flying. **RECOGNIZE ELEMENTS OF PLOT**

2. Possible response: The green bird joins the little blue bird in looking for "nothing," so the little blue bird isn't alone anymore. **IMPORTANT DETAILS**

3. The little blue bird forgot about being afraid. **DETERMINE CHARACTERS' EMOTIONS**

4. Possible response: The first time I tried to ride my bike I felt scared. Accept reasonable responses. Encourage children to explain their responses. **IDENTIFY WITH CHARACTERS**

5. Possible response: Overcoming a fear can lead to a wonderful new experience. Accept reasonable responses. **INTERPRET THEME**

Meet the Author/Illustrator

Tomek Bogacki

Tomek Bogacki grew up in his grandparents' big house near a river in Poland. He rode his bike to the meadows at the edge of town. He also drew, painted, and wrote stories.

Now Tomek Bogacki illustrates and writes children's books. Children all over the world have enjoyed them, so he keeps making new ones.

Tomek Bogacki

Visit *The Learning Site!*
www.harcourtschool.com

32

33

Meet the Author/Illustrator

Pages 32–33 Review with children that an **author** writes a story, and an **illustrator** creates pictures to go with the writing. Emphasize that Tomek Bogacki both wrote and illustrated "The Story of a Blue Bird." Identify Tomek Bogacki in the photograph. Then read aloud the information on page 32 as children follow along. If possible, use a world map or a globe to show where Poland is.

Visit *The Learning Site:* www.harcourtschool.com

See Resources for Parents and Teachers: Author/Illustrator Features.

Retelling

COMPREHENSION FOCUS

Focus Skill **Plot** Remind children that the plot of a story is what happens as a character tries to solve a problem, and that a plot has a beginning, middle, and end. Display *Teaching Transparency 105* or draw a similar chart on the board.

Work with children to complete the first box of the story chart by having them tell what happens at the beginning of the story. (The little blue bird is afraid to fly.) Follow the same procedure, recording children's responses to complete the chart. Underline the words that tell the blue bird's problem. Have children use the chart to retell the story.

Save the completed transparency or chart for reuse with the Comprehension activity on page 35I.

▲ *End-of-Selection Test*, Practice Book, pp. A33–A35

▼ **Teaching Transparency 105**

> The little blue bird is afraid to fly.
>
> ⬇
>
> The blue bird wonders what is beyond the trees. His mother tells him, "nothing."
>
> ⬇
>
> He leaves the nest to look for "nothing."
>
> ⬇
>
> He meets a green bird and a flock of other birds. He is so busy flying that he forgets to be afraid.
>
> ⬇
>
> The blue bird comes home. His brother and sister fly with him.

"The Story of a Blue Bird"
Gather Around, Volume 1-5   **105**   Comprehension
Harcourt

The Story of a Blue Bird   **33A**

Writing
Story Response

5-DAY WRITING	
DAY 1	SHARED: Theme Word Chart
DAY 2	INDEPENDENT: **Story Response**
DAY 3	CROSS-CURRICULAR: How Birds Fly
DAY 4	SHARED: Story About a Problem
DAY 5	INTERACTIVE: Postcards

DAILY LANGUAGE PRACTICE

flew everywhere
together

The birds flew
everywhere together.

BELOW-LEVEL

Have children draw a picture of themselves trying something new and write a caption to describe the picture.

ADVANCED

Before children begin writing in their journal, have them use a Venn diagram to compare their experiences with those of the little blue bird.

ENGLISH-LANGUAGE LEARNERS

Have children draw a picture of their ideas. Discuss the picture, helping children use English words to describe what is happening. Label parts of the picture with self-stick notes so that children can use the words in their writing.

IDENTIFY WITH A CHARACTER

Connect to Personal Experience Make a chart similar to the one shown. Fill in the first column by reviewing that in "The Story of a Blue Bird," the blue bird was afraid to fly, but once he learned how he enjoyed it. Then ask children to think about something new they tried to do. Talk about how they felt before they attempted the task for the first time and how they felt afterward.

Compare Feelings Complete other columns in the chart to tell about children's feelings. Have children compare their feelings with those of the little blue bird.

	How the bird felt about flying.	How Juan felt about swimming.	How Ali felt about tasting a mango.
before	He was scared.	I was scared.	I didn't think I'd like it.
after	He wasn't scared anymore. He felt wonderful.	I like it. I was proud of myself for trying.	I didn't like it, but was glad I tasted it. I won't have to do it again.

WRITE A JOURNAL ENTRY

 Journal Writing Have children write about and illustrate their experience. Encourage them to compare their experience with that of the little blue bird; remind them that they can tell in what ways their experience and feelings were the same and what ways they were different.

5-DAY GRAMMAR

DAY 1	Introduce Describing Words: *-er, -est*
DAY 2	**Make Comparison Cards**
DAY 3	Describe How Birds Fly
DAY 4	Illustrate Comparisons
DAY 5	Compare Places

Grammar

Describing Words: -er, and -est

REVIEW

Review Concepts Display three relatively small objects. Have children tell you how to arrange the objects in order from *small* to *smallest*. Ask volunteers to say sentences that compare any two or three of the objects, using the describing words *small*, *smaller*, or *smallest*. Repeat the activity, having volunteers use the words *big*, *bigger*, or *biggest*.

Make Comparison Cards

Have children brainstorm other words that can be used to compare things. Write each word, its *-er* form, and its *-est* form on the board. Then give each child three index cards. Have them draw and label pictures to go with one set of words. Children can exchange card sets with a partner, read the labels, and arrange the cards in order.

 Sing a Song

Sing a Summary Remind children that they sang a song called "What Do the Birds See?" (page 8P) Guide children in singing a new verse that summarizes "The Story of a Blue Bird."

**The blue bird met friends when he left the nest,
Saw things when he left the nest,
Learned to fly when he tried his best.
The blue bird went home to his mother's nest
And together they all flew.**

Have children read silently from a book of their choice. See page 37J for tips on helping children choose books.

SKILL TRACE

DESCRIBING WORDS *-er, -est*

Introduce	8N
REVIEW	**33C, 35B, 37B, 37L**
T Test	Bk 1-5

BELOW-LEVEL

Write frames for children. Then give them a list of known words they can use to complete the frames.

_____ + *er* = _____

_____ + *est* = _____

ADVANCED

Have children use forms of the words *high* and *bright* to describe things in the sky.

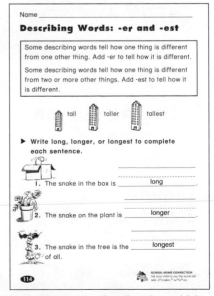

Name _____

Describing Words: -er and -est

Some describing words tell how one thing is different from one other thing. Add -er to tell how it is different.

Some describing words tell how one thing is different from two or more other things. Add -est to tell how it is different.

tall   taller   tallest

▶ Write long, longer, or longest to complete each sentence.

1. The snake in the box is _____ long _____.

2. The snake on the plant is _____ longer _____.

3. The snake in the tree is the _____ longest _____ of all.

▲ Language Handbook, p. 114

The Story of a Blue Bird   **33C**

Day 3

Sharing Literature
Poem: "The Swing"

Phonemic Awareness
Rhyming Words; Focus on /ī/

Phonics

REVIEW: Long Vowel /ī/*igh*

Spelling
State the Generalization

Vocabulary
REVIEW: *afraid, flew, join, learn, wonder*

High-Frequency Words
REVIEW: *nothing, thought*

Reading
Rereading for Fluency
Pupil Edition
"The Story of a Blue Bird,"
pp. 10–30

Making Connections, pp. 34–35

Writing Across the Curriculum ✎
How Birds Fly

Grammar
REVIEW: Describing Words: *-er* and *-est*

WARM UP

MORNING MESSAGE

Good Morning!

Today is _____.
The little bird thought flying was pleasant.
What do you think is a pleasant thing to do?
It's pleasant to _____.
_____ thinks _____ is pleasant.

Introduce the Day

Tell children that today they will listen to a poem about something that is pleasant to do. Guide them in generating a message about pleasant activities. Ask:

• **Think about the little bird in "The Story of a Blue Bird." Did he think flying was pleasant? How do you know?**

• **What things do you think are pleasant to do?**

As you write the message, ask volunteers to write previously taught letters, words, and/or punctuation to reinforce skills. Ask a volunteer to write their name in the last sentence.

Read the Message

Read the message. Use the message to focus on selected skills that have been previously taught.

Apply Skills

| **High-Frequency Words** Ask volunteers to point to and read words they recognize immediately, such as *what, you,* and *thought*. | **Grammar** Have children think of words that mean the same or almost the same as pleasant, such as *fun, nice, wonderful,* and *enjoyable*. |

Sharing Literature

LISTEN AND RESPOND

Connect to Prior Knowledge Remind children that they are going to listen to a poem about something the poet thinks is pleasant. Ask children to listen to find out if they agree with the poet.

Listen to a Poem Read aloud the "The Swing." Then reread the poem as children imagine that they are seeing the sights described in the poem.

Build Language Skills Discuss how the poet describes what can be seen from the swing. Ask: *Where is the swing? What kind of day is it? What can the poet see? Do you agree with the poet that riding high on a swing is the "pleasantest thing" a child can do? Do you think there is something "pleasanter"?*

Connect Ideas Lead children in a discussion of how riding a swing and flying like a bird are similar and different. Ask whether they think the little bird in "The Story of a Blue Bird" would be afraid of flying high on a swing and why.

Phonemic Awareness

RHYMING WORDS

Words from "The Swing" Remind children that many poems use rhyming words. Say the word *swing* and ask volunteers to say words that rhyme. Continue with other words from the poem.

child   air   blue   brown   green   cattle

FOCUS ON /ī/

Segment Sounds Say the word *sight*, and then segment the sounds—/s/ /ī/ /t/. Have children repeat the sounds after you. Say the following words and have children segment the sounds. Ask children what sound they hear in the middle of each word. (/ī/)

night (/n/ /ī/ /t/)   **fight** (/f/ /ī/ /t/)   **light** (/l/ /ī/ /t/)
right (/r/ /ī/ /t/)   **bright** (/b/ /r/ /ī/ /t/)   **flight** (/f/ /l/ /ī/ /t/)

The Swing

How do you like to go
    up in a swing,
Up in the air
    so blue?
Oh, I do
    think it is the
    pleasantest thing
Ever a child can do!

Up in the air and over the wall,
Till I can see so wide,
Rivers and trees and cattle and all
Over the countryside—

Till I look down on the garden
    green,
Down on the roof so brown—
Up in the air I go flying again,
Up in the air and down!

Robert Louis Stevenson

ENGLISH-LANGUAGE LEARNERS

Work with children as they segment sounds. Say each phoneme separately and clearly to help children become familiar with sounds encountered in English.

OBJECTIVES

- *To generate the long vowel sound of* i
- *To blend sounds into words*
- *To read simple, regular words*

SKILL TRACE

/ī/*igh*	
Introduce	8I–8L
Reteach	S4, T2
REVIEW	**8Q–8R, 33F–33G, 35E–35F**
T Test	Bk I-5
Maintain	Bk 2-1

Phonics Resources

Phonics Express™ **CD-ROM,**
Level B Sparkle/Route 4/Park

Phonics
Long Vowel /ī/ *igh* ✔ *Review*

WORD BUILDING

b	e	f	g	h	i	l	m	r	s	t

Guided Practice Place the letters *r, i, g, h, t* in a pocket chart. Have children do the same with their *Word Builders* and *Word Builder Cards*. Remind children that the letters *igh* together stand for the long vowel /ī/ sound. Model how to blend the word *right*. Slide your hand under the letters as you slowly elongate the sounds—/rrīītt/. Then read the word naturally—*right*. Have children do the same.

r	i	g	h	t

r	i	g	h	t

Have children build and read new words by telling them:

- Change the *r* to *l*. What word did you make?

l	i	g	h	t

- Change the *l* to *s*. What word did you make?

s	i	g	h	t

- Take away the *gh*. What word did you make?

s	i	t

- Change the *s* to *f*. What word did you make?

f	i	t

- Add *gh* after the *i*. What word did you make?

f	i	g	h	t

Continue word building with this word sequence: *flight, fright, bright, bit, bite, mite, might.*

Apply Phonics

READ WORDS IN CONTEXT

Display *Teaching Transparency 81* or write the following sentences on the board or on chart paper. Have volunteers read the story one sentence at a time. Call on volunteers to underline or frame words with *igh*. Ask other volunteers to point out other words that have the long *i* sound.

▼ **Teaching Transparency 81**

LONG VOWEL /ī/igh

The birds take flight. They fly high in the bright sky. When night comes, they stop. "It's time to rest," a little bird sighs.

"We all might need a rest," a big bird sighs.

"The Story of a Blue Bird"
Gather Around, Volume 1-5

81

Phonics: Long Vowel /ī/igh
Harcourt

 Write Words Tell children to choose two words with long vowel /ī/*igh* and write them in their journal.

5-DAY PHONICS

DAY 1	Introduce /ī/igh
DAY 2	Word Building with /ī/igh
DAY 3	**Word Building with /ī/igh**
DAY 4	Word Building with /ī/igh, /ē/e, ee, ea
DAY 5	Contractions 's, n't, 'll; Inflections -ed, -ing (drop final e)

REACHING ALL LEARNERS

Diagnostic Check: Phonics

If... children have difficulty reading words with long vowel /ī/igh ...

Then... have them read "The Light Fight" in *Decodable Book 27* to reinforce long vowel /ī/igh.

◀ **Decodable Book 27 "The Light Fight," pp. 9–16**

ADDITIONAL SUPPORT ACTIVITIES

BELOW-LEVEL	Reteach, p. S4
ADVANCED	Extend, p. S5
ENGLISH-LANGUAGE LEARNERS	Reteach, p. S5

 **School-Home Connection**

Take-Home Book Version

◀ **Decodable Books Take-Home Version**

Spelling Words

1. high
2. night
3. light
4. right
5. might
6. bright
7. rode
8. those
9. touch
10. twelve

journal writing

Have children copy the Spelling Words into their journal.

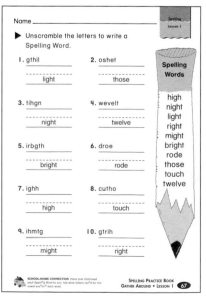

▲ Spelling Practice Book, p. 67

Spelling

5-DAY SPELLING

DAY 1	Pretest; Word Sort
DAY 2	Word Building
DAY 3	**State the Generalization**
DAY 4	Review
DAY 5	Posttest; Writing Application

TEACH/MODEL

State the Generalization for /ī/igh Write the Spelling Words on the board and have children read them aloud. Discuss what is the same about words 1–6. (They all have the /ī/ sound; they all have igh.) Have volunteers circle the letters that stand for /ī/ in each word. Remind children that the letters igh are used to spell the /ī/ sound.

Review the Generalization for /ō/o-e For words 7–8, ask children to identify the spelling pattern. (consonant-vowel-consonant-final e) Remind children that words with this pattern often have a long vowel sound. Have children identify the vowel sound in rode and those. (/ō/)

Review the Vocabulary Words Point out that the words touch and twelve do not follow the same patterns as the other words.

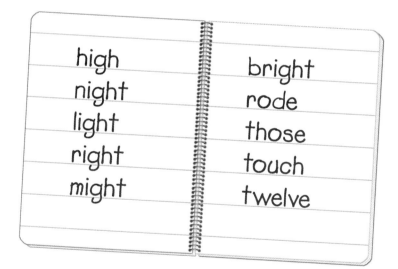

ADVANCED

Have children create a dictionary of igh words. Encourage them to use other words in addition to the Spelling Words.

ENGLISH-LANGUAGE LEARNERS

Help children associate Spelling Words with the ideas they represent by having them draw pictures about the words. They can then exchange their pictures with a partner and identify the words depicted in each.

Vocabulary

REVIEW WORDS IN STORY CONTEXT

Reinforce Word Recognition

Duplicate and distribute the Story Strips for "The Story of a Blue Bird" (page T65). Display *Word Cards* or write the vocabulary words on the board: *afraid, flew, join, learn, wonder.* Have children complete each sentence with a word from the list. Then partners can take turns reading the strips to each other.

> **REVIEW**
>
> **Vocabulary**
>
> afraid   learn
> flew   wonder
> join

> The little blue bird was _____ to fly.

> "I _____ where nothing is," thought the little blue bird.

> A green bird asked the blue bird to _____ him.

> The blue bird and the green bird _____ with a flock of birds.

> The little blue bird forgot he was afraid to _____ how to fly.

High-Frequency Words

Have children continue the Story Strip activity using the high-frequency words *nothing* and *thought.*

> **REVIEW**
>
> **High-Frequency Words**
>
> nothing   thought

> He left the nest to look for _____.

> The little blue bird _____ hard.

After children complete the Story Strips, they can work with a partner to check their work. Then have children arrange the Story Strips in order and read them aloud to retell the story.

ADVANCED

Have children write a story using all the vocabulary words. Suggest that they illustrate their stories.

ENGLISH-LANGUAGE LEARNERS

In many languages, a double negative is grammatically correct. Have children practice using the words *anything* and *nothing* in oral sentences such as: *I can't find anything. I can find nothing. I don't see anything. I see nothing.*

teaching tip

Learned Words Examine the posted words and remove those that children understand, can spell, and can use with mastery.

▲ *Pupil Edition*, pp. 10–30

FLUENCY ROUTINES For support, see Fluency Routine Cards in Theme Resources, pp. T83–T84.

teaching tip

Explain that when partners work together, the listener's job is as important as the reader's. Point out that the listener should follow along, listen carefully, help with words if necessary, and give feedback about how the reader sounds—for example: *Is the reader using good expression?*

Rereading for Fluency

GROUPS

Shared Reading

● BELOW-LEVEL/ENGLISH-LANGUAGE LEARNERS
Remind children that some of the sentences in the story tell what happens and some tell what the characters say. Ask children to track the print and listen to your voice as you read aloud pages 13–14. Point out that on page 14, the quotation marks are a signal that the sentences are dialogue. Reread the pages and invite children to join in. Continue in a similar manner through the rest of the story. TEACHER-DIRECTED

PARTNERS

Partner Reading

● ON-LEVEL/ADVANCED Have partners take turns reading and listening to each other. Remind them that the reader should use quotation marks and other punctuation marks as a guide for expression, and the listener should give feedback about how the reader sounds. Give pairs the option of reading one page or two pages at a time. Encourage them to reread to improve fluency. INDEPENDENT

Managing Small Groups

Reread for fluency with children working individually, with partners, or in small groups. While you work with small groups, have other children do the following:

- **Self-Selected Reading**
- **Practice Pages**
- **Cross-Curricular Centers**
- **Journal Writing**

Use the suggested Classroom Management outline on page 7C for the whole-group/small-group schedule.

Making Connections

▲ The Story of a Blue Bird

If You Could Fly

If you could fly like a bird, where would you go? What would you see from the air? Draw and write your ideas. Share your work.

Writing
CONNECTION

My Flight

I flew over a park.

I saw lots of grass.

I saw a man walking his dog.

34

Birds and Their Nests

The little blue bird hatched from an egg in a nest. Find out more about birds and bird nests. Share what you learn.

Science/ Technology CONNECTION

Nothing = Zero

The little blue bird didn't understand what **nothing** means. Another word for **nothing** is **zero**. Draw and write a number sentence that ends with zero.

Math CONNECTION

$2 - 2 = 0$

35

Making Connections

WRITING

If You Could Fly Have children brainstorm places they might fly over if they were a bird. Encourage them to include details in their drawing and writing. Some children might like to label features such as lakes, mountains, parks, and roads on their drawings. Allow children to post their work in a classroom display titled "If We Could Fly."

SCIENCE

Birds and Their Nests Suggest that children use sources such as books about birds, videos, and Internet sites to find out more about birds. Discuss ways in which children can share what they learn. For example, they could write a report or gather together for small-group discussions.

Information about hatching of birds can be found on *The Learning Site:* www.harcourtschool.com

MATH

Nothing = Zero Reinforce the concept of number sentences with familiar examples, such as $2 + 1 = 3$ and $5 - 3 = 2$. Emphasize that for this activity, children must think of a number sentence for which the answer is 0. Review the example shown. If necessary, explain that there were two carrots until the rabbit ate them, which left no carrots or zero carrots. Encourage children to draw and write similar examples and then share their work with classmates.

$5 - 5 = 0$

$100 - 100 = 0$

The Story of a Blue Bird **34–35**

Writing Across the Curriculum

How Birds Fly

DAILY LANGUAGE PRACTICE

The highest of the two birds is the blue bird

The higher of the two birds is the blue bird.

journal writing

Writing Prompt Have children write in their journal about a place they would fly to if they could fly.

BELOW-LEVEL

To help children write their ideas, have them tell you what they want to say. Then have them record their ideas on a cassette and play it back as they write.

ADVANCED

Suggest that children do additional independent research on birds to extend their report.

ENGLISH-LANGUAGE LEARNERS

Some children may need reinforcement in using and writing English words. Have them draw their ideas first and then think of words that tell what is happening in the pictures.

RESEARCH

Use Science Resources Share resource materials that provide facts about how birds fly. Help children summarize information with an idea web.

WRITE A REPORT

Draft Have children use the information from the idea web, as well as other resource materials if they wish, to write sentences about how birds fly.

Proofread Have partners work together to make suggestions about one another's writing. Suggest that children ask themselves the following questions:

- **Does each sentence begin with a capital letter?**
- **Does each sentence have an end mark?**
- **Does each sentence make sense?**

Have children tell one another what they like best about the other's writing. Then have children evaluate their own writing, thinking about how well they communicate their messages.

Grammar

Describing Words: -er and -est

5-DAY GRAMMAR

DAY 1	Introduce Describing Words: *-er, -est*
DAY 2	Make Comparison Cards
DAY 3	**Describe How Birds Fly**
DAY 4	Illustrate Comparisons
DAY 5	Compare Places

Day 3

REVIEW

Describe How Birds Fly On the board, write a list of words that can be used to describe how birds fly, such as *high, swift, fast, near.* Have children write the *-er* and *-est* forms of each word.

Revisit Writing Have children look for describing words that compare in their writing. If there are none, encourage them to think of a place where a comparison could be added.

WRAP UP Author's Chair

Share Facts About Birds Have children seat themselves around the classroom Author's Chair. Invite volunteers to take turns sitting in the Author's Chair to read their report about birds. Remind children to listen attentively to each speaker. Point out that after a speaker has finished, listeners may politely ask questions to find out more.

S.S.R. *Sustained Silent Reading*
Have children read silently from a book of their choice. See page 37J for tips on helping children choose books.

SKILL TRACE

DESCRIBING WORDS *-er, -est*

Introduce	8N
REVIEW	**33C, 35B, 37B, 37L**
T Test	Bk 1-5

ENGLISH-LANGUAGE LEARNERS
Below / On-Level / Advanced / ELL

Have children arrange objects to demonstrate how adding *-er* and *-est* to describing words changes them by degree. For example, they can line up different shades of crayons or markers to depict *green, greener,* and *greenest.*

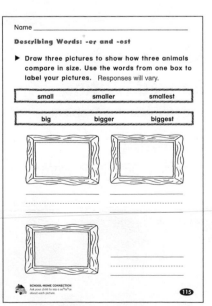

▲ Language Handbook, p. 115

The Story of a Blue Bird　　**35B**

Day at a Glance
Day 4

Sharing Literature
Poem: "Wouldn't You?"

Phonemic Awareness
Phoneme Substitution; Focus on /ī/ and /ē/

Phonics

Build Words

Spelling
Review

Vocabulary
REVIEW: *afraid, flew, join, learn, wonder*

High-Frequency Words
REVIEW: *nothing, thought*

Reading

Comprehension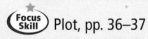

(Focus Skill) Plot, pp. 36–37

Shared Writing ✏
Story About a Problem

Grammar
REVIEW: Describing Words: *-er* and *-est*

WARM UP

MORNING MESSAGE

Good Morning!

Today is _____.

Green is the color of _____ and _____.

_____ is blue.

_____ and _____ are bright colors.

_____'s favorite color is _____.

Introduce the Day

Remind children of the different colors of birds in "The Story of a Blue Bird." Work with children to generate a message about colors. Ask:

• **What kinds of things are colored green? What things are blue?**

• **Which color do you like best? How would you describe that color?**

As you write the message, call on volunteers to help write previously taught letters, words, and/or punctuation to reinforce skills, or to direct you regarding letter or word spacing.

Read the Message

Read the message. Use the message to focus on selected skills that have been previously taught.

Apply Skills

Concept Vocabulary Have children identify words in the message that name colors. Have children name other color words they know, and write those words on the board.

Grammar Have children compare the brightness of various colors. Use the following sentence frames: _____ *is brighter than* _____. _____ *is the brightest color of all.* You may want to add children's responses to the message.

Sharing Literature

LISTEN AND RESPOND

Read "Wouldn't You?" Copy the poem "Wouldn't You?" on chart paper. Call attention to the title and ask children what it might mean. Have them predict what the poem might be about. Then track the print as you read the poem aloud.

Respond Ask children what the title is asking them. (if they would want to go where the wind goes) Then have them answer the question and explain their reasons.

Creative Movement Discuss children's experiences with various kinds of wind—gentle breezes, strong winds, stormy winds. Reread the poem several times while small groups take turns pantomiming how a bird might fly in such winds. Lead children in using their voices to express the strength of the wind.

Wouldn't You?

If I
Could go
As high
And low
As the wind
As the wind
As the wind
Can blow—

I'd go!

John Ciardi

Phonemic Awareness

PHONEME SUBSTITUTION

Words from "Wouldn't You?" Say *wouldn't*. Tell children to listen as you change /w/ to /k/. Then say *couldn't*. Have children repeat the word after you. Continue with the following words:

go: **Change /g/ to /s/.** (so)   *high:* **Change /h/ to /fl/.** (fly)
low: **Change /l/ to /t/.** (tow)   *as:* **Change /z/ to /sk/.** (ask)
and: **Change /a/ to /e/.** (end)   *blow:* **Change /ō/ to /o͞o/.** (blue)

FOCUS ON /ī/ AND /ē/

Blend Segmented Sounds Ask children to listen as you say some sounds and then blend the sounds to say a word. Say: /m/ /ī/ /t/ . . . *might*. Say the following sounds. Have children blend the sounds into words.

/k/ /ē/ /p/ (keep)   /l/ /ī/ /t/ (light)   /t/ /ī/ /t/ (tight)
/l/ /ē/ /n/ (lean)   /r/ /ī/ /t/ (right)   /n/ /ī/ /t/ (night)
/n/ /ē/ /d/ (need)   /t/ /ē/ /m/ (team)   /h/ /ī/ (high)

BELOW-LEVEL

If children have difficulty blending segmented sounds, have them blend the initial sound with the rest of the word—for example, /k/-*eep.*

ENGLISH-LANGUAGE LEARNERS

Use word pairs such as the following to reinforce the difference between the /d/ sound and the /t/ sound in English: *sat—sad, seat—seed, right—ride, wheat—weed, white—wide.* Have children pay attention to the position of their tongue as they pronounce each sound.

The Story of a Blue Bird   **35D**

Day 4

OBJECTIVES

* *To discriminate between the sound-letter relationships /ī/igh and /ē/e, ee, ea*

* *To read and write words with /ī/igh and /ē/e, ee, ea*

SKILL TRACE

	/ī/**igh**	/ē/**e,ee, ea**
Introduce	8I–8L	Bk 1-4, 8I–8L
Reteach	S4–S5, T2	Bk 1-4, S4, T2
REVIEW	8Q–8R, 33F–33G, 35E–35F	Bk 1-4, 8Q–8R, 29F–29G, 33E–33F 35E
T Test	Bk 1-5	Bk 1-5
Maintain	Bk 2-1	Bk 1-5

teaching tip

Homophones Remind students that some words sound the same but are spelled differently and have different meanings. Point out the words *meet/meat* and *feet/feat*. Explain the meaning of each word.

Phonics Resources

Phonics Express™ **CD-ROM, Level B** Sparkle/Route 6/Park

Phonics
Build Words ✔ *Review*

WORD BUILDING

Focus on Patterns List these words on the board: *might, meet, meat*. Point to *might* and have children read it. Underline *igh* and ask what sound the letters stand for. (long *i*) Repeat with *meet* (ee) and *meat* (ea). (long *e*)

Point out the letter patterns: *consonant-igh-consonant* and *consonant-vowel-vowel-consonant*. Have children reread each word and tell how many letters they see and how many sounds they hear. Point out that in each word, the two or three underlined letters stand for only one sound.

Build and Read Words Use a pocket chart and *Letter Cards* to form *right*. Blend the sounds /rrīītt/, then read the word naturally— *right*. Have children repeat after you. Ask volunteers to build new words in the pocket chart.

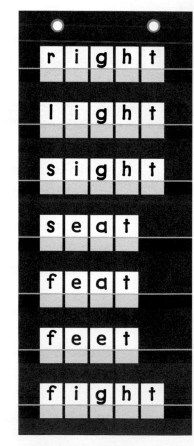

■ Change the *r* to *l*. Read the word.

■ Change the *l* to *s*. Read the word.

■ Replace *igh* with *ea*. Read the word.

■ Change the *s* to *f*. Read the word.

■ Change the *a* to *e*. Read the word.

■ Replace *ee* with *igh*. Read the word.

Continue word building with this word sequence: *meat, might, fright, flight, fleet*.

Write the words *light, sight,* and *seat* on the board and have children read the words aloud.

5-DAY PHONICS	
DAY 1	Introduce /ī/*igh*
DAY 2	Word Building with /ī/*igh*
DAY 3	Word Building with /ī/*igh*
DAY 4	**Word Building with /ī/*igh*, /ē/*e*, *ee*, *ea***
DAY 5	Contractions '*s*, *n't*, '*ll*; Inflections -*ed*, -*ing* (drop final *e*)

Apply Phonics

APPLY PHONICS SKILLS

Dictate Sentences Dictate the following sentences:

> I might meet a friend.
> My seat is in sight.

Have children write the sentences on a dry-erase board or in their journal.

I might meet a friend.

BELOW-LEVEL

Build the following word pairs and guide children in blending the sounds to read each word: *see—sigh*, *sight—seat*, *meet—might*, *night—neat*.

ADVANCED

Write the following words on the board: *sigh*, *might*, *flight*. Have children make new words by substituting the following letters for *igh*: *ee*, *ea*, *oa*, *ow*, *ay*. Help children check spelling; for example, *float* versus *flowt*.

ENGLISH-LANGUAGE LEARNERS

To reinforce that in English, different letter combinations can stand for the same sound, make word cards for the following: *see*, *sea*, *meet*, *meat*, *might*, *mite*. Help children read the words and match those that sound the same.

BELOW-LEVEL

Name _____

▶ Trace the word that goes with the picture. Cross out the other word.

1. boat ~~coat~~
2. tight ~~fight~~
3. high ~~bright~~
4. ~~beach~~ meat
5. night ~~sigh~~

▲ Extra Support, p. 7

ON-LEVEL

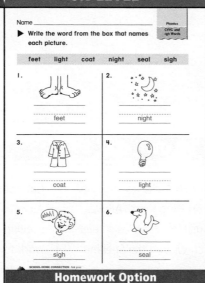

Name _____

▶ Write the word from the box that names each picture.

feet   light   coat   night   seal   sigh

1. feet
2. night
3. coat
4. light
5. sigh
6. seal

Homework Option

▲ Practice, p. 7

ADVANCED

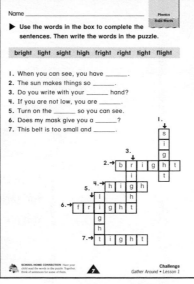

Name _____

▶ Use the words in the box to complete the sentences. Then write the words in the puzzle.

bright   light   sight   high   fright   right   tight   flight

1. When you can see, you have _____.
2. The sun makes things so _____.
3. Do you write with your _____ hand?
4. If you are not low, you are _____.
5. Turn on the _____ so you can see.
6. Does my mask give you a _____?
7. This belt is too small and _____.

▲ Challenge, p. 7

ENGLISH-LANGUAGE LEARNERS

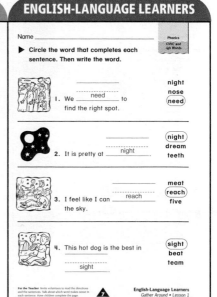

Name _____

▶ Circle the word that completes each sentence. Then write the word.

1. We _____ to find the right spot.   night / nose / **need**
2. It is pretty at _____.   **night** / dream / teeth
3. I feel like I can _____ the sky.   meat / **reach** / five
4. This hot dog is the best in _____.   **sight** / beat / team

▲ ELL, p. 7

Spelling Words

1. high
2. night
3. light
4. right
5. might
6. bright
7. rode
8. those
9. touch
10. twelve

Spelling

5-DAY SPELLING	
DAY 1	Pretest; Word Sort
DAY 2	Word Building
DAY 3	State the Generalization
DAY 4	**Review**
DAY 5	Posttest; Writing Application

REVIEW

Spelling Words Use a pocket chart and *Letter Cards* to form words. Have children listen to your directions and change one letter in each word to spell a Spelling Word. Have them write the Spelling Word on a sheet of paper or in their journal. Then ask a volunteer to change the *Letter Card* in the pocket chart so that children can self-check the word.

- Form *sigh* in the pocket chart and have children read it aloud. **Which Spelling Word is made with one letter changed?** *(high)*

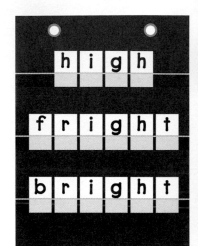

- Form *fright* in the pocket chart and have children read it aloud. **Which Spelling Word is made by changing one letter?** *(bright)*

- Form *flight* in the pocket chart and have children read it aloud. **Which Spelling Word is made by taking away one letter?** *(light)*

- Point to *light*. **Which Spelling Words are made by changing the first letter?** *(night, right, might)*

Follow a similar procedure with *rope (rode)* and *nose (those).*

Vocabulary Words Display *Letter Cards c, e, e, h, l, o, t, t, u, v, w.* Ask volunteers to form the words *touch* and *twelve.*

Name _____

▶ Write the letter or letters that complete each Spelling Word. Then trace the rest of the word.

1. m i **g h t**   2. t w **e l v e**

3. n i **g h t**   4. t h **o s e**

5. t o u **c h**   6. r **i g h t**

7. l **i g h t**   8. b r **i g h t**

Spelling Words
high
night
light
right
might
bright
rode
those
touch
twelve

▶ Unscramble the letters to make a Spelling Word.

9. g h h i   10. e r o d
   high   rode

▲ Spelling Practice Book, p. 68

BELOW-LEVEL

Have children make a word card for each Spelling Word. Allow them to use the cards as a reference when writing the Spelling Words.

ADVANCED

Have children create riddles that serve as clues to words from the spelling list. Partners can then work together to ask and answer the riddles.

Vocabulary

REVIEW WORDS IN CONTEXT

Use Words in Context Give each child one of the following *Word Cards: afraid, flew, join, learn, wonder.* Have each child in turn show his or her card to the group, read the word on the card, and use the word in a sentence about "The Story of a Blue Bird."

Reinforce Word Recognition Provide each child with a set of Individual Word Cards for *afraid, flew, join, learn, wonder* (page T34). To reinforce word recognition, have partners match like cards, read the words aloud, and then use the words in a sentence.

REVIEW

Vocabulary

afraid   learn

flew   wonder

join

High-Frequency Words

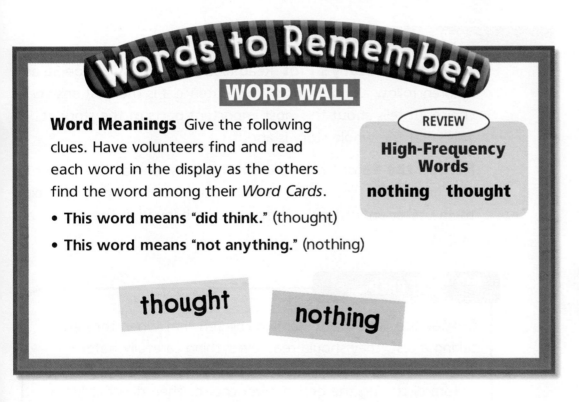

Words to Remember

WORD WALL

Word Meanings Give the following clues. Have volunteers find and read each word in the display as the others find the word among their *Word Cards*.

REVIEW

High-Frequency Words

nothing   thought

- **This word means "did think."** (thought)
- **This word means "not anything."** (nothing)

thought   nothing

▲ *Pupil Edition, pp. 10–30*

OBJECTIVE

To recognize the elements of plot

SKILL TRACE

PLOT	
INTRODUCE	9A, 33A, 35I
Reteach	S6–S7, T11
Review	125A, 149A, 153I, 219A, 247A, 251I
T Test	Bk 1-5

REACHING ALL LEARNERS

Diagnostic Check: Comprehension and Skills

If... children have difficulty identifying story plots...

Then... have them talk about favorite stories—stories they have read or stories they have seen performed on television or at the movies. Use these examples to develop a basic concept of plot.

ADDITIONAL SUPPORT ACTIVITIES

BELOW-LEVEL Reteach, p. S6

ADVANCED Extend, p. S7

ENGLISH-LANGUAGE LEARNERS Reteach, p. S7

⭐ Focus Skill **Comprehension**

Plot

TEACH/MODEL

Develop Concepts Display the chart you made with children about the plot of "The Story of a Blue Bird" (page 33A). Review the chart to illustrate how to distinguish which story events are important when telling a story's plot.

MODEL The little blue bird's problem is a very important part of the plot. The little bird does and sees many things. When I think about the plot, I want to remember the most important things. At the beginning of the story, his mother tells him that "nothing" is beyond the trees. That is why he leaves the nest— to look for "nothing." In the middle, he meets some other birds. This is important because he becomes so busy flying with them that he forgets his fear. At the end, he comes home and gets his sister and brother to fly with him. This is important because it shows that he really has overcome his fear.

PRACTICE/APPLY

Recognize a Story's Plot Read aloud *Pupil Edition* page 36 as children follow along. Discuss why sentence 3 is the best answer choice. (It tells about the most important parts of the story; it tells what the whole story is about.)

Reread the Selection Have small groups reread "The Story of a Blue Bird" aloud. Emphasize that thinking about the plot will help them better understand the events that happen in the story.

TEST PREP

Model the Test Item Remind children that when they are taking a test, they should read everything carefully before they decide on an answer. Read the entire page with children before discussing the best answer choice. Then direct children to place a finger on the circle beside their answer. Discuss why the third answer is the best choice. (It tells about the most important parts of the whole story.)

Plot

▲ The Story of a Blue Bird

The main things that happen in a story make up the **plot** of that story.

Think about "The Story of a Blue Bird." What important things happen? Choose the sentence that best tells the **plot**.

1. A little bird hatches from an egg and grows fast.
2. A little bird walks to a pool of blue water.
3. A little bird is afraid at first, but at last he learns to fly.

Why do you think the sentence you chose best tells the **plot** of the story?

Visit *The Learning Site!*
www.harcourtschool.com
See Skills and Activities

36

Test Prep
Plot

Read this story.

Chuck at Bat
The bases were loaded. Chuck was at bat. "Crack!" went the bat. It was a home run! "We will win!" shouted Chuck's team.

1. Which sentence best tells the plot of the story?
   ○ Chuck did not want to bat.
   ○ Chuck shouted, "We will win!"
   ○ Chuck helped his team win.

Tip
Think about the important things that happen. Then read each answer choice carefully.

37

Focus Skill

Visit *The Learning Site*
www.harcourtschool.com
See Skill Activities and Test Tutors: Plot.

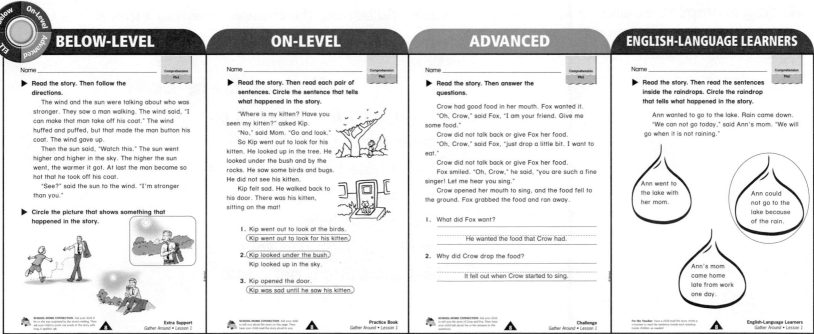

▲ Extra Support, p. 8   ▲ Practice, p. 8   ▲ Challenge, p. 8   ▲ ELL, p. 8

LANGUAGE ARTS

5-DAY WRITING	
DAY 1	SHARED: Theme Word Chart
DAY 2	INDEPENDENT: Story Response
DAY 3	CROSS-CURRICULAR: How Birds Fly
DAY 4	**SHARED: Story About a Problem**
DAY 5	INTERACTIVE: Postcards

Shared Writing

Story About a Problem

FOCUS ON PLOT

Connect Ideas Remind children that "The Story of a Blue Bird" is about a little bird who is afraid to fly; the story events are about how the little bird learns to fly. Tell children that they are going to write a story about how an animal character solves a problem.

Brainstorm Story Ideas Guide children in generating a list of possible problems. Record children's ideas on a chart.

Character's Problems

afraid of the dark	loses something
gets lost	can't do something others can
forgets something	wants to make a new friend

DRAFT

Write Together Have children choose an animal character and a problem. Then work with them to draft a story. Begin by stating the animal's problem. Then prompt children by asking questions such as *What could happen next? Could someone help? What would you do?* Use the example shown as a model.

Hippo Gets Lost

Hippo can't find the path home.
She is lost!
Snake tries to help.
He can't find the path.
Bird tries to help.
He flies up high and sees the path.
Bird helps Hippo get home.

DAILY LANGUAGE PRACTICE

The blue bird couldn't sleep at nite?

The blue bird couldn't sleep at <u>night</u>.

BELOW-LEVEL

Use the example to help children write a story about an animal character who is lost. Have them decide the kind of animal they want to write about.

ADVANCED

Encourage children to write and illustrate their own story about a character who solves a problem.

journal writing

Writing Prompt Have children draw a picture of a bird in flight and write a sentence about their picture.

Grammar

Describing Words: -er and -est

5-DAY GRAMMAR

DAY 1	Introduce Describing Words
DAY 2	Make Comparison Cards
DAY 3	Describe How Birds Fly
DAY 4	**Illustrate Comparisons**
DAY 5	Compare Places

SKILL TRACE

	DESCRIBING WORDS *-er, -est*
Introduce	8N
REVIEW	**33C, 35B, 37B, 37L**
T Test	Bk 1-5

REVIEW

Use Words from the Story Write the following words on the board and have children read them: *fast, high, low.* Explain that these are describing words from "The Story of a Blue Bird." Call on volunteers to write the *-er* and *-est* forms of the words under the base words. Have children read the words, and then ask children to tell what they know about using describing words with *-er* and *-est* to make comparisons. (Use *-er* words to compare two things; use *-est* words to compare three or more things.)

Illustrate Comparisons

Ask children to draw a picture of three birds flying. Have them use a word on the board to label each bird in their drawing. Provide time for children to display and talk about their work.

WRAP UP · Listen to a Poem

Connect Ideas Remind children that in "The Story of a Blue Bird," the little bird wandered away from his home. Invite children to listen to a poem about some toy boats that set off from the safety of the shore and float down a stream to a distant shore. Read aloud "Where Go the Boats?"

Respond Have children respond to the poem by sharing their opinions and expressing their feelings.

▲ **"Where Go the Boats?" p. 144**

S.S.R. Have children read silently from a book of their choice. See page 37J for tips on helping children choose books.

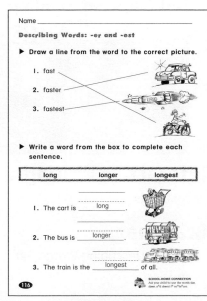

▲ **Language Handbook, p. 116**

The Story of a Blue Bird **37B**

Day at a Glance
Day 5

Sharing Literature
Big Book: *To Market, To Market*

Phonemic Awareness
Phoneme Isolation; Focus on Inflections *-ed*, *-ing*

Phonics
REVIEW: Contractions *'s, n't, 'll*
INTRODUCE: Inflections *-ed*, *-ing* (drop final *e*)

Spelling
Posttest; Writing Application

Vocabulary
REVIEW: *afraid, flew, join, learn, wonder*

High-Frequency Words
REVIEW: *nothing, thought*

Reading
Rereading for Fluency
Pupil Edition
"The Story of a Blue Bird," pp. 10–30

Self-Selected Reading

Read

Interactive Writing
Postcards

Grammar
REVIEW: Describing Words: *-er* and *-est*

WARM UP — MORNING MESSAGE

Good Morning!

Today is _____.

I'm glad that I can _____.

One thing I haven't tried to do is _____.

One thing I'd like to learn to do is _____.

Introduce the Day

Remind children that the little blue bird was scared to fly at first, but soon he came to enjoy it. Guide children to generate a message about exploring new things. Ask questions such as:

- **What is something that you have never tried to do?**
- **What is something new that you could try to do today?**

Remind children to listen attentively and to stay on topic while speaking. When children suggest a word or phrase, have them help you write it, using previously taught letters and/or words.

Read the Message

Read the message. Use the message to focus on selected skills that have been previously taught.

Apply Skills

Word Structure Have children point out words with contractions in the message. Ask them to tell you which two words were put together to make the contraction.

Grammar/Mechanics Ask children to point out the words in the message that start with a capital letter. Have them state the rule that explains why those words are capitalized.

Sharing Literature

BUILD CONCEPT VOCABULARY

Shared Reading Have children read the title of the big book. As you read aloud, encourage children to respond to the humor.

Explore a Word Discuss how children feel about the story. Say: *Many stories are funny. Some stories are very, very funny—they are hilarious.* Have children say *hilarious.* Then discuss whether they think the story is hilarious. Page through the book and ask children to use the word *hilarious* to tell about the funniest events. Ask volunteers to tell about other stories they think are hilarious. Then have children tell what word they have been talking about. Ask: *What does* hilarious *mean?* (very funny)

Focus Skill

Plot Review the plot of *To Market, To Market.* Say the following sentences and ask children to choose the one that best describes the plot: *A woman buys a lamb at the market. A woman solves a problem with animals that misbehave. A goat eats a woman's coat.* Emphasize that the plot tells about the whole story, not just part of it.

▲ **Big Book**

Phonemic Awareness

PHONEME ISOLATION

Words from the Big Book Say the word *trout.* Point out that *trout* begins with two consonant sounds that are blended together—/t/ and /r/. Read the following words, emphasizing the initial sounds. Ask children to raise their hand if they hear a word that begins with two consonant sounds.

swam (yes) **goat** (no) **pig** (no) **stubborn** (yes)
cranky (yes) **brown** (yes) **duck** (no) **spice** (yes)

FOCUS ON INFLECTIONS *-ed, -ing*

Generate Rhymes Say *baking.* The word *taking* rhymes with *baking.* Have children name words that rhyme with the following words:

talking   **liked**   **shared**   **peeling**   **toasted**

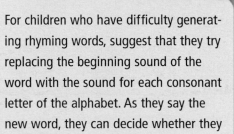

BELOW-LEVEL

For children who have difficulty generating rhyming words, suggest that they try replacing the beginning sound of the word with the sound for each consonant letter of the alphabet. As they say the new word, they can decide whether they recognize it as a word.

ADVANCED

Have children create two-line rhymes, using words from the rhyming activity.

Phonics

Contractions 's, n't, 'll

 Review

OBJECTIVE

To recognize, read, and write contractions with 's, n't, and 'll

SKILL TRACE

CONTRACTIONS 's, n't, 'll	
Introduce	Bk 1-1, 69F, 95F, 141F
	Bk 1-4, 35E–35F
Reteach	Bk 1-4, T3
Review	Bk 1-2, 107F; Bk 1-4, 123F, 215F
T Test	Bk 1-4
MAINTAIN	Bk 1-4, 37E

BELOW-LEVEL

Have children work with partners to create sentences using contractions.

ENGLISH-LANGUAGE LEARNERS

Work with individuals or small groups to review the lesson. Use sentence starters such as the following:

- I can run, but I can't _____.
- I will learn English words. These are the words that I'll learn. . . .

Phonics Resources

Phonics Practice Book, pp. 308–311

REVIEW WORD MEANING

Review Contractions Write the sentence pairs shown below on the board or on chart paper. Track the print as children read aloud the first pair. Ask whether the sentences have the same meaning. Elicit that *She's* is a shorter form of *She is*. Point to the apostrophe and ask what it means. (It takes the place of the *i* in *is*.) Use a similar procedure for the remaining sentence pairs.

She is happy.	I cannot run.	He will write soon.
She's happy.	I can't run.	He'll write soon.

WORK WITH PATTERNS

Demonstrate Understanding Display the following sentence pairs. Have children read the first sentence, and then ask a volunteer to write the contraction for the underlined words. Have children read both sentences aloud. Elicit that the sentences have the same meaning and that the contraction in the second sentence is a shorter way of saying the underlined words in the first sentence.

Bob <u>is not</u> here today.   He <u>is</u> ill.
Bob ____ here today.   ____ ill.
I hope <u>we will</u> see him soon.
I hope ____ see him soon.

Write Sentences with Contractions Write the following on the board: *I'll, haven't, she's*. Have children write a sentence for each contraction. Provide time for children to share their work.

I'll go home now.

Inflections -ed, -ing

 *Review*

WORK WITH PATTERNS

Analyze Inflections A group of first graders is planning a trip to a nature center. Write on the board these sentences: *Jan and Bill hope to see frogs in the pond. Last fall we hoped to go there, but it rained too hard. Everybody is hoping for good weather.*

Have children read aloud the sentences as you track the print. Point to the word *hope* in the first sentence, emphasizing the consonant-vowel-consonant-silent *e* pattern. Help children to recognize the base word *hope* in the second sentence. Ask how the base word was changed when the ending *-ed* was added. (The *e* was dropped.) Explain that in some words, the *e* is dropped before adding *-ed*.

Follow a similar procedure with the third sentence to introduce the concept of dropping *e* before adding *-ing*. Remind children that *hope* and *hoping* tell about what is happening now, and *hoped* tells about past action.

APPLY PHONICS

Write Words with -ed and -ing Copy the following chart on the board. Have children write the words and use them in sentences.

bake + ed = ____   vote + ed = ____   smile + ed = ____

bake + ing = ____   vote + ing = ____   smile + ing = ____

5-DAY PHONICS

DAY 1	Introduce /ī/igh
DAY 2	Word Building with /ī/igh
DAY 3	Word Building with /ī/igh
DAY 4	Word Building with /ī/igh, /ē/e, ee, ea
DAY 5	**Contractions 's, n't, 'll: Inflections -ed, -ing (drop final e)**

OBJECTIVES

• *To discriminate between words with different patterns*

• *To drop final e to add inflections -ed, -ing*

SKILL TRACE

INFLECTIONS -ed, -ing (drop final e)	
INTRODUCE	**Bk 1-4, 65F; Bk 1-5, 37F**
Reteach	T3
Review	67H, 155E
T Test	Bk 1-5
Maintain	Bk 2-1

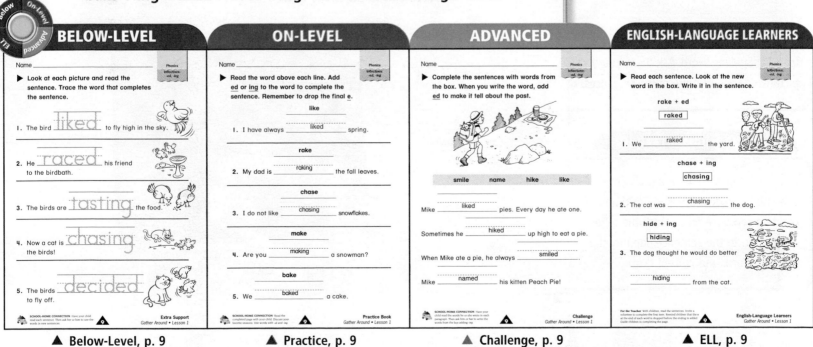

▲ Below-Level, p. 9   ▲ Practice, p. 9   ▲ Challenge, p. 9   ▲ ELL, p. 9

The Story of a Blue Bird   **37F**

Spelling Words

1. high
2. night
3. light
4. right
5. might
6. bright
7. rode
8. those
9. touch
10. twelve

WORD WORK

Spelling

5-DAY SPELLING

DAY 1	Pretest; Word Sort
DAY 2	Word Building
DAY 3	State the Generalization
DAY 4	Review
DAY 5	**Posttest; Writing Application**

ASSESS/APPLY

Posttest Assess children's progress using the words and the Dictation Sentences from Day 1.

1. **high**   The kite is up **high** in the sky.
2. **night**   I like to sleep at **night**.
3. **light**   It is **light** when the sun is out.
4. **right**   This book is the **right** one.
5. **might**   I **might** go to the zoo today.
6. **bright**   My bike is **bright** blue.

Review

7. **rode**   We **rode** on the bus.
8. **those**   **Those** books are mine.

Vocabulary

9. **touch**   I like to **touch** soft things.
10. **twelve**   Max has **twelve** apples.

Writing Application Have children complete and illustrate the following sentence frames.

What are those _____?

At night I might see _____.

The hill is so high that _____.

At night I might see stars.

BELOW-LEVEL

Have pairs of children work with *Word Builder Cards*. One partner reads a Spelling Word and the other partner uses the cards to spell it. Together, the partners check the spelling.

ADVANCED

Have children write their own sentence for each Spelling Word. Ask them to draw pictures for one or more of the sentences.

ENGLISH-LANGUAGE LEARNERS

Have children work with a partner. Have one child choose a Spelling Word and create a sentence for it. Have the other child listen to the sentence, identify the Spelling Word, and write it down.

Vocabulary

REVIEW

Reinforce Words One by one, hold up a *Word Card* for each vocabulary word: *afraid, flew, join, learn, wonder.* Have children read the word, spell it, read it again, and spell it again. Then put down the *Word Card,* but leave your hand up. Ask children to say and spell the word one more time. Repeat this activity for all five words.

> **REVIEW**
> **Vocabulary**
> afraid   learn
> flew   wonder
> join

Provide additional practice using the high-frequency words. Say the following sentence starters and have children complete them:

> **Nothing is more fun than . . . .**
> **The first time I saw my favorite TV show, I thought . . . .**

High-Frequency Words

ENGLISH-LANGUAGE LEARNERS

Help children understand the relationship between *think* and *thought.* Have them complete the following sentences:

> **I thought I wouldn't like to _____.**
> **Now I think _____ is fun.**

Words to Remember
WORD WALL

Identify Words in Sentences Write the following sentences on the board. Display *Word Cards* for *nothing* and *thought*. Have volunteers match one of the *Word Cards* to a word in one of the sentences and then underline the word. Have children read the sentences together in a whisper, raising their voices only to say the underlined words.

> **REVIEW**
> **High-Frequency Words**
> nothing   thought

- **I saw a lump in my bed. I thought it was a bear!** (thought)
- **There was nothing to be afraid of. It was my teddy bear!** (nothing)

▲ *Pupil Edition, pp. 10–30*

FLUENCY ROUTINES For support, see Fluency Routine Cards in Theme Resources, pp. T83–T84.

teaching tip

As children track print and read aloud, note whether they know the difference between a line of text and a sentence. Provide additional fluency practice to develop this understanding.

Rereading for Fluency

PARTNERS

Readers Theatre

ON-LEVEL/ADVANCED Have children use the Character Cutouts (page T17) to make stick puppets. As children read the story aloud, have them use the puppets to dramatize the events. Remind them to read with expression as if they are talking. INDEPENDENT

GROUPS

Echo Reading

BELOW-LEVEL/ENGLISH-LANGUAGE LEARNERS Have children track the print and echo read each sentence on pages 13–19. Point out that when you read dialogue, your voice changes to show how the characters feel. Continue, having children echo read longer and longer passages. Pause occasionally to reread and emphasize appropriate expression and intonation. Encourage children to reread the story on their own. TEACHER-DIRECTED

> What does nothing look like?

> What does nothing look like?

Managing Small Groups

Reread for fluency with children working individually, with partners, or in small groups. While you work with small groups, have other children do the following:

- **Self-Selected Reading**
- **Practice Pages**
- **Cross-Curricular Centers**
- **Journal Writing**

Use the suggested Classroom Management outline on page 7C for the whole-group/small-group schedule.

Self-Selected Reading

INDEPENDENT READING

Have children choose a book from the **Browsing Boxes** or the **Reading Center** to read independently during a sustained silent reading time. Children may also want to reread a story from their *Pupil Edition.* These are some books you may want to gather that relate to "The Story of a Blue Bird."

Decodable Books

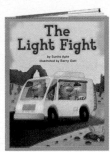

Decodable Book 27
"Seeing the Sights" by Susan Blackaby

"The Light Fight" by Sunita Apte

Cut-Out/Fold-Up Book

The Long Flight
Practice Book, pp. 65–66

Books for All Learners

Flying High
by Roberta Cruz

The Bird in the Plum Tree
by Lucy Floyd

The Wright Brothers
by Lucy Floyd

What's Your Favorite Color?
by Enrique Flores

choosing books

To guide children in selecting books at their independent reading level, suggest that they read one or two pages of the book. If there are at least five words that the child can't read, he or she should try an easier book.

related books

- *Dream Around the World* by Deborah Eaton. Instant Reader, Harcourt, 1997.

  A boy goes to sleep and dreams about traveling all over the world. BELOW-LEVEL

- *Are You My Mother?* by P.D. Eastman. Random House, 1960.

  A newly hatched bird sets out on an adventure looking for his mother. BELOW-LEVEL

- *The Story of Ferdinand* by Munro Leaf. Puffin Books, 1977.

  A classic story about a little Spanish bull who would rather sit and smell the flowers than fight. ON-LEVEL

- *The Little House* by Virginia Lee Burton. Houghton Mifflin, 1969.

  A pretty little house in the country watches the city build up all around her until she is moved back to the country. ADVANCED

Interactive Writing

Postcards

5-DAY WRITING	
DAY 1	SHARED: Theme Word Chart
DAY 2	INDEPENDENT: Story Response
DAY 3	CROSS-CURRICULAR: How Birds Fly
DAY 4	SHARED: Story About a Problem
DAY 5	INTERACTIVE: **Postcards**

DAILY LANGUAGE PRACTICE

i am tallest than my friend.

I am <u>taller</u> than my friend.

journal writing

Self-Selected Writing Have children write in their journal about a topic of their choice. They may want to illustrate their writing.

BELOW-LEVEL

Provide children with a pattern for their postcards. Have them complete the following sentence frames:

I am exploring _____.

I have seen _____.

The best part is _____.

I still want to _____.

ADVANCED

Have children do research about the place they have chosen and include two facts about it in the postcard message.

PREWRITING

Generate Ideas Review the explorations children have read about in *To Market, To Market* and "The Story of a Blue Bird." Then invite children to brainstorm places they would like to explore. Record children's ideas on the board. You may also wish to provide resource materials that include pictures of places children might like to explore, such as mountains, forests, or faraway lands. Have the group choose a place they would like to explore.

SHARE THE PEN

Model a Postcard Message If possible, show examples of picture postcards. Explain that people often send postcards to friends and family when they are visiting another place. Draw a large rectangle on the board to represent a postcard. Work with children to create a postcard message. Ask questions such as the following. Have volunteers write words and insert punctuation.

- **To whom should we write?**

- **How do we begin a message? What mark goes at the end of the greeting?**

- **What should we say about our make-believe adventure?**

- **How should we end the message?**

- **How should we address the postcard?**

Independent Writing Give each child an unlined index card. Have children use the group-made postcard message to create their own postcards. On one side of the card, they can draw a picture of a place they choose. On the other side, they can write a message to a friend or family member about the imaginary exploration. Ask children to share their postcards.

5-DAY GRAMMAR

DAY 1	Introduce Describing Words: -er,-est
DAY 2	Make Comparison Cards
DAY 3	Describe How Birds Fly
DAY 4	Illustrate Comparisons
DAY 5	**Compare Places**

Grammar

Describing Words: -er and -est

REVIEW

Compare Places Guide children in using describing words to compare the places they wrote about in their postcards in the writing activity on page 37K. Write sentences such as the following on the board. Have volunteers tell why the *-er* or *-est* ending is appropriate for the comparisons.

close   The lake is ____ than the seashore.
            The river is the ____ place.

hot   It is ____ at the lake than at the river.
           The seashore is the ____ place.

SKILL TRACE

DESCRIBING WORDS *-er, -est*

Introduce	8N
REVIEW	**33C, 35B, 37B, 37L**
T Test	Bk 1-5

Grammar Resources

Grammar Jingles™ CD, **Primary,** Track 15, "Big and Small"

WRAP UP ## Listen to a Song

Compare Ideas Across Texts Invite children to listen as you read aloud the lyrics to the song "The Baby Chicks Sing" on page 137 of the *Read-Aloud Anthology.* (If you read music or know someone who does, you could teach the song to children.) After reading the song lyrics, ask children to compare and contrast the actions of the mother hen in the song and the little blue bird's mother in "The Story of a Blue Bird."

▲ "The Baby Chicks Sing," p. 137

S.S.R.
Sustained Silent Reading

Have children read silently from a book of their choice. See page 37J for tips on helping children choose books.

Name _____

Describing Words: -er and -est

► Circle the word that completes each sentence about the picture. Then write the word.

(smaller) smallest

1. The hen is _____ smaller _____ than the pig.

(smaller) smallest

2. The pig is _____ smaller _____ than the horse.

(tallest) taller

3. The horse is the _____ tallest _____ of all.

smaller (smallest)

4. The bird is the _____ smallest _____ of all.

117

▲ Language Handbook, p. 117

The Story of a Blue Bird   **37L**

Books for All Learners

Reinforcing Skills and Strategies

■ BELOW-LEVEL

Flying High
by Roberta Cruz

Flying High

✓ **Phonics: Long Vowel /ī/** *igh*

✓ **Vocabulary: *afraid, join, learn***

✓ **High-Frequency Word: *nothing***

✓ **Focus Skill: Plot**

SUMMARY   Three hatchlings venture from the nest for their first flight.

Visit *The Learning Site:*
www.harcourtschool.com
See Resources for Parents and Teachers: Books for All Learners.

BEFORE READING

Build Background Ask children to share what they know about birds, especially baby birds. Encourage them to discuss what birds look like, where they live, and what they eat.

Preview/Set Purpose Have children identify the title and help them read it. Point out the author and illustrator. Then have them look at the first few pages and predict what the book is about. Have children set a purpose for reading, such as *I want to find out who will be flying high.*

READING THE BOOK

Pages 2–4 Where is the tree? (beside the house) Where is the nest? (high up in the tree) How does the picture on page 4 help you know about bird nests? (It is a close-up that shows details.) NOTE DETAILS, RELATE PICTURES TO TEXT

Pages 5–9 How does the mama bird know her babies are hungry? (They cry, "Cheep, cheep, cheep!") What does the mama bird do for her hungry babies? (She finds food for them.) How do you know the small birds want to fly? (They flap their wings and hop.) SUMMARIZE

Pages 10–12 What happens after the first bird flies above the house and tree? (The other birds fly.) What happens at the end of this story? (All the baby birds fly.) SUMMARIZE, RELATE PICTURES TO TEXT, PLOT

RESPONDING

Illustrate Information Have children fold a sheet of drawing paper into quarters and copy onto it four illustrations from the book. They can refer to these to tell partners about the development of young birds.

BELOW-LEVEL

ON-LEVEL

ADVANCED

ELL

Flying High

by Roberta Cruz

The Bird in the Plum Tree

a folktale retold by Lucy Floyd
illustrated by Yu Cha Pak

The Wright Brothers
by Lucy Floyd

What's Your Favorite COLOR?
by Enrique Flores
illustrated by Beth Griffis Johnson

▲ p. 37O   ▲ p. 37P

Oral Reading Fluency

Use Books for All Learners to promote oral reading fluency.

See **Fluency Routine Cards**, pp. T83–T84.

■ ON-LEVEL

The Bird in the Plum Tree

a folktale retold by Lucy Floyd
illustrated by Yu Cha Pak

The Bird in the Plum Tree

 Phonics: Long Vowel /ī/*igh*

 Vocabulary: *afraid, flew, join, learn, wonder*

 High-Frequency Words: *nothing, thought*

 Focus Skill: Plot

SUMMARY In this Japanese folktale, a mighty ruler learns from the values of a small boy.

 Visit *The Learning Site:*
www.harcourtschool.com
See Resources for Parents and Teachers: Books for All Learners.

BEFORE READING

Build Background Have children tell about objects and events that are especially meaningful to them. Invite them to tell what makes them so important.

Preview/Set Purpose Have children identify the title and help them read it. Point out the author and illustrator. Then have children look at the first few pages of the book and predict what the story is about. Have children set a purpose for reading, such as *I want to find out what kind of bird lives in the plum tree.*

READING THE BOOK

Pages 2–7 What happens at the beginning of this story? (The Mighty One's plum tree dies.) What happens next? (The Mighty One wants to replace it with Tim-Tim's plum tree.) PLOT, SEQUENCE

Pages 8–10 What do the Mighty One's men do when they find the tree? (They dig it up and take it away.) What does Tim-Tim tie to the tree? (a note) What happens to the bird? (It flies away with the tree.) ANALYZE CHARACTERS

Pages 11–13 What does the Mighty One find in the tree? (Tim-Tim's note with a picture of the tree and a verse) What does the note tell him? (that Tim-Tim missed his bird) SUMMARIZE

Pages 14–16 What does the Mighty One do with the tree after he reads the note? (He returns it to Tim-Tim.) Why do you think he does this? (Possible response: He learns that friendship is more important than possessions.) SUMMARIZE, DRAW CONCLUSIONS

RESPONDING

Retell the Story Have children draw pictures of key story events on small cards. They can use the picture cards to retell the story. Guide them in using proper phrasing, pitch, and modulation.

Books for
All Learners
Reinforcing Skills and Strategies

■ ADVANCED

The Wright Brothers

☑ **Phonics: Long Vowel /ī/igh**

☑ **Vocabulary:** *afraid, flew, join, learn, wonder*

☑ **High-Frequency Words:** *nothing, thought*

☑ **Focus Skill: Plot**

SUMMARY Readers learn about the Wright brothers: their childhood, first flight, and contributions to modern life.

Visit *The Learning Site:*
www.harcourtschool.com
See Resources for Parents and
Teachers: Books for All Learners.

BEFORE READING

Build Background Ask volunteers to tell how things fly, such as airplanes, helicopters, birds, and kites. Prompt them to discuss what keeps each in the air and how it changes direction.

Preview/Set Purpose Have children identify the title and help them read it. Point out the author and illustrator. Then have children look at the first few pages of the nonfiction book and predict what it is about. Have children set a purpose for reading, such as *I want to find out how the Wright brothers learned about flying.*

READING THE BOOK

Pages 2–5 Who invented the first airplane? (Wilbur and Orville Wright) What did they call it? (*The Flyer*) How did the Wright boys feel about learning? (They were eager to learn.) ANALYZE CHARACTERS, DETERMINE CHARACTERS' TRAITS

Pages 6–12 What did they do in their shop? (They put bikes together and sold them.) What problem with airplanes did the Wright Brothers try to solve? (how to steer an airplane) How did they solve it? (They found a way to twist the wing tips.) What did they do next? (They built *The Flyer*.) PLOT, SEQUENCE

Pages 13–16 What happened to airplanes after the flight of *The Flyer?* (The Wright brothers and others learned more and made more advanced airplanes.) How did the Wright brothers change the world? (Many people now fly. Boats and spacecraft work better.) SUMMARIZE

RESPONDING

Make Fact Cards Have children use index cards to make fact cards about the Wright brothers and their scientific contributions. Ask them to draw a picture of an event on one side of a card and to write a sentence about it on the other side.

BELOW-LEVEL

Flying High

by Roberta Cruz

ON-LEVEL

The Bird in the Plum Tree

a folktale retold by Lucy Floyd
illustrated by Yu Cha Pak

ADVANCED

The **Wright Brothers**
by Lucy Floyd

ELL

What's Your Favorite **COLOR?**
by Enrique Flores
illustrated by Beth Griffs Johnson

▲ p. 37M   ▲ p. 37N

Managing Small Groups

While you work with small groups, have other children do the following:

- Self-Selected Reading
- Practice Pages
- Cross-Curricular Centers
- Journal Writing

■ ENGLISH-LANGUAGE LEARNERS

What's Your Favorite **COLOR?**
by Enrique Flores
illustrated by Beth Griffs Johnson

What's Your Favorite Color?

 Strong Picture Support

 Concept Vocabulary

✓ Theme Related

SUMMARY   Nine colorful characters tell readers their favorite colors.

 Visit *The Learning Site:*
www.harcourtschool.com
See Resources for Parents and Teachers: Books for All Learners.

BEFORE READING

Build Background Play a question-and-answer game so children practice naming colors. For example, point to a few red objects and say, *Red, red. What do you see that's red?* Continue with other colors.

Preview/Set Purpose Have children identify the title and help them read it. Point out the author and illustrator. Then have children look at the first few pages and predict what the story is about. Have children set a purpose for reading, such as *I want to find out if anyone likes my favorite color.*

READING THE BOOK

Pages 2–6 What question do the children ask? (*What's your favorite color?*) What color does the girl like? (yellow) Who likes brown basketballs and brown bears? (the boy) What colors do the children on pages 5 and 6 like? (green and orange) SUMMARIZE

Pages 7–10 How do you know the girl on page 7 likes purple? (She wears a purple dress, holds purple flowers, and says she does.) Who likes black and blue? (two boys) RELATE PICTURES TO TEXT; SUMMARIZE

Pages 11–12 What color does the girl on page 11 like? (white) What colors do all the children together like? (yellow, brown, green, orange, purple, black, blue, red, white) What's your favorite color? (Possible response: Blue, because the sky is blue. Accept reasonable responses. Encourage children to explain their responses.) SUMMARIZE; EXPRESS PERSONAL OPINIONS

RESPONDING

Draw Color Portraits Have children use the book pages as a model for drawing pictures of themselves surrounded by objects of their favorite color. Guide them to label their pictures and then describe them to classmates.

The Story of a Blue Bird   **37P**

Teacher Notes

Teacher Notes

Reading Selections

BIG BOOK

DECODABLE BOOK

Applies /ā/ ai, ay

▲ Decodable Book 28
"Daisy"
"A Gray Day"
"One Rainy Day"
"Rain, I Say"

PUPIL EDITION

ALA Notable Book

Genre

Fiction

Sometimes in fiction there is a "story within a story."

Look for:

• the parts of the story that are happening in the story present— or now.

• the story that one character tells about the past.

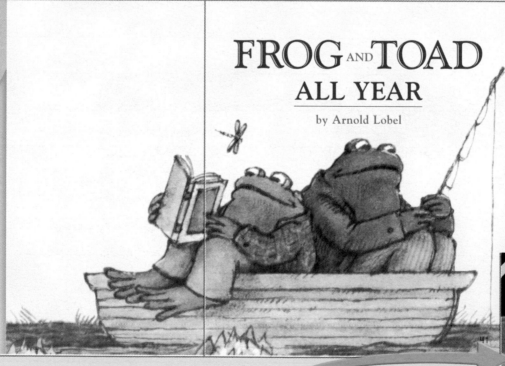

FROG AND TOAD ALL YEAR

by Arnold Lobel

40

41

▼ **READING ACROSS TEXTS:**
"Frogs in Trees?"
GENRE: Nonfiction

Comparing Fiction and Nonfiction

SUMMARY: *Frog tells Toad about the time he went looking for spring.*

"Frog and Toad All Year" is available on *Audiotext 5*.

Books for All Learners

Lesson Plans on pages 67O–67R

BELOW-LEVEL

- **Phonics:** Long Vowel /ā/*ai, ay*
- **Vocabulary:** *caught, hurried*
- **High-Frequency Words:** *cold, sure*

ON-LEVEL

- **Phonics:** Long Vowel /ā/*ai, ay*
- **Vocabulary:** *caught, hurried, near, son*
- **High-Frequency Words:** *cold, sure*

ADVANCED

- **Phonics:** Long Vowel /ā/*ai, ay*
- **Vocabulary:** *caught, hurried, near, son*
- **High-Frequency Words:** *cold, sure*

ELL

- *Strong Picture Support*
- *Concept Vocabulary*

MULTI-LEVELED PRACTICE

Practice Book, pp. 10–16, 67–68

Extra Support, pp. 11–16

Challenge, pp. 11–16

English-Language Learners, pp. 11–16

Technology

- *Phonics Express™ CD-ROM, Level B*
- *Writing Express™ CD-ROM*
- *Grammar Jingles™ CD, Primary*
- *Reading and Language Skills Assessment CD-ROM*
- *The Learning Site:* www.harcourtschool.com

ADDITIONAL RESOURCES

Phonics Practice Book, pp. 226–233, 240–241, 308–311

Spelling Practice Book, pp. 69–70

Language Handbook, pp. 118–121

Read-Aloud Literature
- Big Book of Rhymes, p. 21
- Read-Aloud Anthology, pp. 134–135

Teaching Transparencies 82–84, 109

Cross-Curricular Activity Cards, p. T13

Word Builders/Word Builder Cards

Letter Cards

Intervention Resource Kit, Lesson 28

English-Language Learners Resource Kit, Lesson 28

30 Minutes

ORAL LANGUAGE

- **Sharing Literature**

- **Phonemic Awareness**

30 Minutes

WORD WORK

- **Phonics**

- **Spelling**

- **Vocabulary**

- **High-Frequency Words**

45 Minutes

READING

- **Comprehension**

- **Fluency**

Daily Routines
- Morning Message
- Daily Language Practice
- Writing Prompt

45 Minutes

- **Independent Reading**

LANGUAGE ARTS

- **Writing**

- **Grammar**

Daily Language Practice
Spiral Review

Day 1

Sharing Literature, 38H
Big Book: Listen and Respond

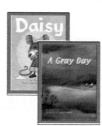

Phonemic Awareness, 38H
Phoneme Segmentation; Focus on /ā/

Phonics, 38I
Introduce: Long Vowels /ā/ai, ay **T**

Spelling, 38K
Pretest; Word Sort **T**

High-Frequency Words, 38K
Review: *learn, join* **T**

Read
Apply Phonics, 38L

DECODABLE BOOK 28
"Daisy"
"A Gray Day"

 Independent Reading
Books for All Learners

 Shared Writing, 38M
"I Learned" List

Writing Prompt
Have children write their own "I Learned" list.

Grammar, 38N
Introduce: Verbs **T**

Daily Language Practice
the ran will stop. (The, rain)

Day 2

Sharing Literature, 38P
Rhyme: Listen and Respond

Phonemic Awareness, 38P
Phoneme Counting; Focus on /ā/

Phonics, 38Q
Review: Long Vowels /ā/ai, ay **T**

Spelling, 38Q
Word Building **T**

Vocabulary, 38S
Introduce: *caught, hurried, near, son* **T**

High-Frequency Words, 38S
Introduce: *cold, sure* **T**

Word Power, pp. 38–39

Read
Read the Selection, 39A

PUPIL EDITION:
"Frog and Toad All Year,"
pp. 38–59

 Comprehension
Cause/Effect

 Reread

Independent Reading
Books for All Learners

Interactive Writing, 59B
Story Response

Writing Prompt
Have children illustrate one of the story ideas the group did not write about; then write a sentence about the picture.

Grammar, 59C
Review: Verbs **T**

Daily Language Practice
Will you plai with me (play,?)

Focus Skill
Cause/Effect

Phonics
Long Vowel /ā/
ai, ay

Focus of the Week:
- HIGH-FREQUENCY WORDS: *cold, sure*
- VOCABULARY WORDS: *caught, hurried, near, son*
- COMPREHENSION: Cause/Effect
- WRITING: Verbs

Day 3

Sharing Literature, 59E
Poem: Build Concept Vocabulary

Phonemic Awareness, 59E
Initial Phoneme Deletion/Substitution;
Focus on /ā/

 Phonics, 59F
Review: Long Vowels /ā/*ai, ay* **T**

Spelling, 59H
State the Generalization **T**

Vocabulary, 59I
Review: *caught, hurried, near, son*

High-Frequency Words, 59I
Review: *cold, sure* **T**

 Read
Rereading for Fluency, 59J

Reading Across Texts, 60–63
"Frogs in Trees?"

Making Connections, pp. 64–65

Apply Phonics, 59G
DECODABLE BOOK 28
"One Rainy Day"
"Rain, I Say"

⚫ **Independent Reading**
Books for All Learners

✏️ **Independent Writing,** 65B
Dialogue

Writing Prompt
Have children write a sentence about something they might say to a friend.

Grammar, 65C
Review: Verbs **T**

Daily Language Practice
Mom and i sayl away. (I, sail)

Day 4

Sharing Literature, 65E
Poem: Build Concept Vocabulary

Phonemic Awareness, 65E
Phoneme Substitution/Deletion; Focus on /ā/

 Phonics, 65F
Build Words **T**

Spelling, 67A
Review **T**

Vocabulary, 67B
Review: *caught, hurried, near, son*

High-Frequency Words, 67B
Review: *cold, sure* **T**

Read
Reread the Selection, 67B

⚫ **Independent Reading**
Books for All Learners

✏️ **Writing Across the Curriculum,** 67C
Report

Self-Selected Writing
Have children write in their journal about a topic of their choice.

Grammar, 67D
Review: Verbs **T**

Daily Language Practice
Today the Sky is grae. (sky, gray)

Day 5

Sharing Literature, 67F
Big Book: Listen and Respond

Phonemic Awareness, 67F
Final Phoneme Deletion; Focus on /ā/, /l/, /n/

Phonics, 67G
Review: Inflections *-ed, ing* Phonograms *-ail, -ain* **T**

Spelling, 67I
Posttest; Writing Application **T**

Vocabulary, 67J
Review: *caught, hurried, near, son*

High-Frequency Words, 67J
Review: *cold, sure* **T**

Read
Rereading for Fluency, 67K

Self-Selected Reading, 67L

⚫ **Independent Reading**
Books for All Learners

✏️ **Independent Writing,** 67M
Lists

Writing Prompt
Have children write a sentence about an idea from their list.

Grammar, 67N
Review: Verbs **T**

Daily Language Practice
We play with the tran (train.)

Cross-Curricular Centers

COMPUTER CENTER

Create a Clip Art Scene

Tell children to think about what they would do if they went exploring. Have them cut and paste clip art images or use a draw or paint program to create an action scene. Have them type a sentence that tells about something that is happening in the picture.

The cat chases the dog.

Materials

- computer
- software for creating pictures

LETTER AND WORD CENTER

Long Vowel /ā/ Words

Provide index cards on which you have written the letter pair *ay* and the phonograms *ail*, *ain*, and *ate*, beginning as far to the left as possible. Have children take turns with a partner adding *Letter Cards* before one index card to form a word and read it aloud. Encourage them to see how many words they can make with each letter pattern.

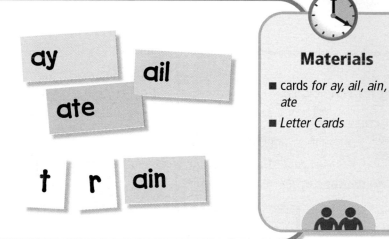

Materials

- cards *for ay, ail, ain, ate*
- *Letter Cards*

SCIENCE CENTER

Signs of Spring

Have children go "looking for spring." Children in small groups can exchange ideas about signs that spring is coming or has arrived. Then they can work together to create a list of "Signs of Spring." The list should have words, phrases, and pictures about spring. Have groups display their charts in the classroom.

Materials

- chart paper
- markers or other writing materials
- crayons or colored pencils

ART CENTER

Art Around the Corner

As an extension of the Making Connections writing activity (pages 64–65), have children think of more things they might find "just around the corner" and make a stand-up card display. Have children fold a sheet of drawing paper in half. Then, on one side of the fold, they can copy this sentence, filling in the blank: _____ *is just around the corner*. On the other side, they can draw a picture to illustrate it.

30 Minutes

Materials

■ drawing paper labeled
_____ *is just around the corner.*
■ crayons or colored pencils

SOCIAL STUDIES CENTER

Seasons Around the World

Briefly explain that when it's spring in the United States, countries in another part of the world are having fall weather. Put masking tape around the equator on the globe and point out that every place below the tape has fall when we have spring. Have children work in pairs to study the globe and choose a country in the part of the globe below the tape. Have children write on the chart paper the name of the country they chose.

When it's spring here, it's fall in
Brazil.

15 Minutes

Materials

■ globe
■ masking tape
■ chart paper with the words *When it's spring here, it's fall in*
■ markers

HOMEWORK FOR THE WEEK

The Homework Copying Master provides activities to complete for each day of the week.

    Visit *The Learning Site:* www.harcourtschool.com

See Resources for Parents and Teachers: Homework Helper.

Homework, p. T40 ▶

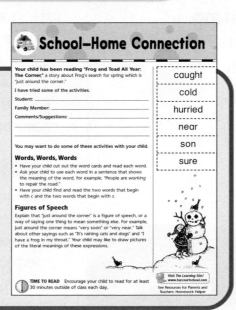

🚌 School–Home Connection

Your child has been reading "Frog and Toad All Year: The Corner," a story about Frog's search for spring which is "just around the corner."

I have tried some of the activities.

Student: _____
Family Member: _____
Comments/Suggestions: _____

You may want to do some of these activities with your child.

Words, Words, Words
• Have your child cut out the word cards and read each word.
• Ask your child to use each word in a sentence that shows the meaning of the word, for example, "People are working to repair the road."
• Have your child find and read the two words that begin with *c* and the two words that begin with *s*.

Figures of Speech
Explain that "just around the corner" is a figure of speech, or a way of saying one thing to mean something else. For example, *just around the corner* means "very soon" or "very near." Talk about other sayings such as "It's raining cats and dogs" and "I have a frog in my throat." Your child may like to draw pictures of the literal meanings of these expressions.

🕐 **TIME TO READ** Encourage your child to read for at least 30 minutes outside of class each day.

Visit *The Learning Site!* www.harcourtschool.com
See Resources for Parents and Teachers: Homework Helper

| caught |
| cold |
| hurried |
| near |
| son |
| sure |

Sharing Literature
Big Book: *I Swam with a Seal*

Phonemic Awareness
Phoneme Segmentation; Focus on /ā/

Phonics
INTRODUCE: Long Vowels /ā/*ai, ay*

Spelling
Pretest; Word Sort

High-Frequency Words
REVIEW: *learn, join*

Reading
Decodable Book 28
"Daisy"
"A Gray Day"

Shared Writing ✏
"I Learned" List

Grammar
INTRODUCE: Verbs

WARM UP

MORNING MESSAGE

Good Morning!

Today is _____. It's fun to go to new places and see new sights.

I like to go to _____. You can see _____ there.

We wonder what it's like to be a _____.

Introduce the Day

Tell children that today they will listen to a story about a brother and sister who go exploring and see animals in different places. Guide children in generating a message about going places and seeing things. Ask:

• **What are some places you visit?**

• **What do you see there?**

• **Do you ever wonder what it's like to be an animal? What animals do you wonder about?**

As you write the message, ask volunteers to write previously taught letters, words, and/or punctuation. For example, have volunteers write the words *new* and *places*. Remind children that they learned the word *wonder* last week. Have them find the word *wonder* in the message.

Read the Message

Read the message. Use the message to focus on selected skills that have been previously taught.

Apply Skills

Grammar/Mechanics Help children distinguish between kinds of places and special names of specific places. Have volunteers tell which words for places need to begin with capital letters.

Phonics Remind children that the letters *igh* often have the long vowel sound of *i*. Have a volunteer point to and read a word with *igh* in the message. (sights)

Sharing Literature

LISTEN AND RESPOND

Connect to Prior Knowledge Ask children to name animals they have seen. Ask children to share details about each animal, such as where they saw it, what it looked like, what it sounded like, and how it moved.

Discuss Author/Illustrator Display the big book cover. Have a volunteer point to the name of the author/illustrator. Ask children why there is only one name on this book cover.

Set a Purpose/Read Have children set a purpose for listening. If necessary, suggest that children think about what is unusual about the animals.

Return to the Purpose Ask volunteers to tell what their favorite part of the story was and why. Remind children of their purpose for listening to the story. Ask: *What is unusual about these animals? Why do the animals think the children are "funny"?*

▲ **Big Book**

Phonemic Awareness

PHONEME SEGMENTATION

Words from the Big Book Remind children of the seal in *I Swam with a Seal*. Say *seal* slowly, emphasizing each sound, and ask children which sounds they hear in *seal*. (/s/ /ē/ /l/) Then say *The seal swam*. Ask which sounds children hear in *swam*. (/s/ /w/ /a/ /m/) Repeat, using various animal names and motions from the big book.

dog (/d/ /o/ /g/) **licked** (/l/ /i/ /k/ /t/) **moose** (/m/ /o͞o/ /s/)
looked (/l/ /o͞o/ /k/ /t/) **cat** (/k/ /a/ /t/) **purred** (/p/ /ûr/ /d/)

FOCUS ON /ā/

Identify Initial Phonemes Tell children that you will say a word slowly and they will tell what sound is heard at the beginning. Model by saying *aid. I hear the sound /ā/ at the beginning of* aid. Ask children what sound they hear at the beginning of these words:

ate (/ā/)   **aim** (/ā/)   **ape** (/ā/)   **age** (/ā/)   **ace** (/ā/)

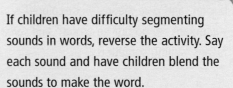
BELOW-LEVEL

If children have difficulty segmenting sounds in words, reverse the activity. Say each sound and have children blend the sounds to make the word.

ADVANCED

Have children segment more complex words from the big book, such as *falcon* (/f/ /a/ /l/ /k/ /ə/ /n/), *sailed* (/s/ /ā /l/ /d/), *slithered* (/s/ /l/ /i/ /th/ /ûr/ /d/), *pranced* (/p/ /r/ /a/ /n/ /s/ /t/), *beaver* (/b/ /ē/ /v/ /ûr/), and *bothered* (/b/ /o/ /th/ /ûr/ /d/).

OBJECTIVES

- *To generate the long vowel sound of a*
- *To build words using known letters and sounds*
- *To read simple, regular words*

SKILL TRACE

/ā/ai, ay	
INTRODUCE	38I–38L
Reteach	S10, T4
Review	38Q–38R, 59F–59G
Review	65F
T Test	Bk 1-5

teaching tip

Build Vocabulary As you model blending the words *pail* and *sail*, explain that other words sound like *pail* (*pale*) and *sail* (*sale*). Explain that *pail* means "a bucket" and *pale* means "light-colored"; *sail* means "to go out on a boat" and *sale* means "selling something."

 and Spelling
Long Vowels /ā/ ai, ay

✔ *Introduce*

TEACH/MODEL

Introduce /ā/ai, ay Display *Alphabet Cards Aa* and *Ii*. Say the name of each letter. Point out that the letters *a* and *i* together can stand for one sound—/ā/, the long vowel sound of *a* in words such as *aim* and *aid*.

Hold up *Letter Cards a* and *i* together and say /ā/. Tell children that the sound /ā/ appears in the middle of the words *chain*, *sail*, and *pail*. Have children repeat the sound several times as you touch the cards. Explain that *ai* is usually at the beginning or in the middle of a word.

Next, display *Alphabet Cards Aa* and *Yy*. Explain that the letters *a* and *y* together can also stand for the long vowel sound of *a*. Hold up *Letter Cards a* and *y* together and tell children that the sound /ā/ appears at the end of the words *day*, *say*, and *pay*. Have children repeat the sound. Explain that *ay* is usually at the end of a word.

WORD BLENDING

Words with /ā/ai, ay Blend and read the words *day*, *say*, *sail*, and *pail*. As you demonstrate each step using a pocket chart and *Letter Cards*, have children repeat after you, using *Word Builders* and *Word Builder Cards*.

WORD BUILDING

5-DAY PHONICS

DAY 1	**Introduce /ā/ai, ay**
DAY 2	Word Building with /ā/ai, ay
DAY 3	Word Building with /ā/ai, ay
DAY 4	Word Building with /ā/ai, ay, and a-e
DAY 5	Phonograms -ail, -ain Inflections -ed, -ing

Build Spelling Words Place the letter *d* in a pocket chart. Have children do the same with their *Word Builders* and *Word Builder Cards*. Repeat with the letters *a* and *y*. Model how to blend the word *day*. Slide your hand under the letters as you slowly elongate the sounds—/ddāā/. Then read the word naturally—*day*. Have children do the same.

Have children build and read new words by telling them:

■ Change the *d* to *s*. What word did you make?

■ Change the *y* to *i*. Add *l*. What word did you make?

■ Change the *s* to *p*. What word did you make?

■ Take away the *l*. Change the *i* to *y*. What word did you make?

■ Add *l* after the *p*. What word did you make?

 Dictate Long /ā/ai, ay Words Dictate the words *pay*, *say*, *pail*, and *sail* and have children write them in their journal. Suggest that they either draw a picture or write about each word.

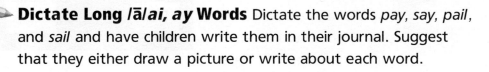

BELOW-LEVEL

If children have trouble with the words in the lesson, focus on words with *ay*. Review the short *a* words *sad*, *pad*, and *dad*. Then change the *d* at the end of each word to *y* and have children practice saying the sound /ā/. Working with familiar words and sounds can bolster children's confidence.

ADVANCED

Have children build more complex words with *ay* and *ai*, such as *tray*, *gray*, and *away*, or *snail*, *trail*, and *claim*.

Phonics Resources

Phonics Express™ CD-ROM, **Level B** Roamer/Route 6/Train Station

Phonics Practice Book, pp. 226–233

Spelling Words

1. day
2. say
3. sail
4. pail
5. pay
6. play
7. right
8. high
9. learn
10. join

Phonics and Spelling

5-DAY SPELLING	
DAY 1	**Pretest; Word Sort**
DAY 2	Word Building
DAY 3	State the Generalization
DAY 4	Review
DAY 5	Posttest; Writing Application

INTRODUCE THE WORDS

Pretest Read aloud the first word and the Dictation Sentence. Repeat the word as children write it. Write the correct spelling on the board. Have children circle the word if they spelled it correctly or write it correctly if they did not. Repeat for words 2–10.

1. **day**   This is a rainy **day**.
2. **say**   I want to **say** something.
3. **sail**   We will **sail** on the boat.
4. **pail**   Jane put sand in her **pail**.
5. **pay**   I want to **pay** for this book.
6. **play**   After school, you can **play**.

Review

7. **right**   We always try to do what is **right**.
8. **high**   The airplane flew very **high**.

High-Frequency

9. **learn**   Our class will **learn** a lot.
10. **join**   Ray is going to **join** the Math Club.

Word Sort Write the words *vowel sound* and *consonant sound* on index cards and place them at the top of a pocket chart. Write the Spelling Words on index cards. Display the cards and ask "Which words end in a vowel sound? Which words end in a consonant sound?" Place

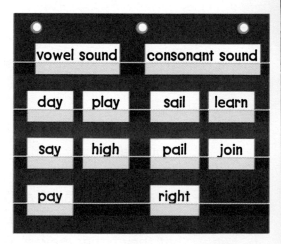

the words in the correct columns as children direct. Then have children read aloud all the words in the chart.

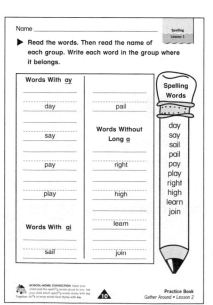

▲ Practice Book, p. 10

38K   Gather Around

Apply Phonics

Read
A Gray Day

Daisy
by Sheila Bizeh
Illustrated by Richard Bernal

▲ **Decodable Book 28**
"Daisy"
"A Gray Day"

APPLY /ā/*ai*, *ay*

Write the following sentences on the board or on chart paper. Have children read the first sentence as you track the print. Frame the words *Jay* and *pail* and have children read them. Continue with the other sentences.

> **Jay** has a **pail**.
> We will **sail** on the **bay** all **day**.
> **Fay may** have some **mail**.

Have children read "Daisy" and "A Gray Day" in *Decodable Book 28*.

Managing Small Groups

Read the *Decodable Book* with small groups of children. While you work with small groups, have other children do the following:

- **Self-Selected Reading**
- **Practice Pages**
- **Cross-Curricular Centers**
- **Journal Writing**

Use the suggested Classroom Management outline on page 7C for the whole-group/small-group schedule.

School-Home Connection

Take-Home Book Version

A Gray Day

Daisy

◄ Decodable Books Take-Home Version

ONGOING ASSESSMENT

Note how well children
- read sentences without modeling.
- decode words in "Daisy" and "A Gray Day."
- complete long vowel /ā/*ai*, *ay* practice pages.

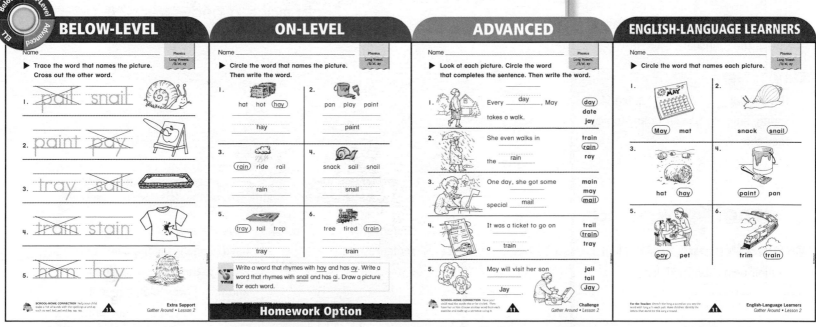

| BELOW-LEVEL | ON-LEVEL | ADVANCED | ENGLISH-LANGUAGE LEARNERS |

▲ Extra Support, p. 11   ▲ Practice, p. 11   ▲ Challenge, p. 11   ▲ ELL, p. 11

Frog and Toad All Year **38L**

LANGUAGE ARTS

Shared Writing

"I Learned" List

DAILY LANGUAGE PRACTICE

the ran will stop.

The <u>rain</u> will stop.

Writing Every Day

Day I: "I Learned" List
Work together to make a list of things children have learned.

Day 2: Story Response
Have children extend the *Pupil Edition* story by writing about what might happen next.

Day 3: Dialogue
Have children write dialogue between Frog and Toad.

Day 4: Report
Have children write a report about one of the four seasons.

Day 5: Lists
Have children create lists related to spring, animals, games, or any topic they choose.

journal writing

Writing Prompt Have children write their own "I Learned" list.

BRAINSTORM

Elicit Learning Experiences Ask children to discuss exploring. Point out that exploring means more than just going on trips filled with adventure. Help children understand that when they learn anything new, they are exploring, too. Write *I Learned* on chart paper and read the words aloud. Ask children to think about things they have recently learned to do. Have them suggest ideas to go on a list. As children respond, record their suggestions on the chart. Encourage children to share details such as where they learned these things and who taught them.

SHARE

Read and Display the List Read the list aloud, having children read decodable and previously taught words with you. Display the list so that children can refer to it throughout the week.

I Learned
Kim: ride a bike
Sam: skate
Ashley: tie a bow
Zack: make a bed

ADVANCED	ENGLISH-LANGUAGE LEARNERS
Have children write "I Want to Learn" sentences.	Have children act out things they have learned. Say the name of it, add it to the list, read it aloud, and then have children repeat the name as you track the print.

Grammar *Verbs*

5-DAY GRAMMAR

DAY 1	Introduce Verbs
DAY 2	Use Verbs in Sentences
DAY 3	Interesting Verbs
DAY 4	Verb Game
DAY 5	Verbs in Sentences

TEACH/MODEL

Introduce Verbs Point out the verbs on the "I Learned" list that children helped write. Explain that words that tell what someone or something does are called *verbs*.

Ask children to make up sentences about what someone or something does, using the list from page 38M for ideas. Write each sentence on a sentence strip and cut the words apart. Point out the verb in each sentence. Remind children that the verb is the word that tells what someone or something does.

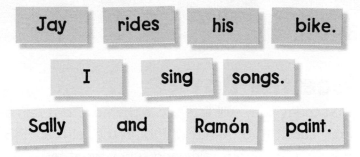

Jay   rides   his   bike.

I   sing   songs.

Sally   and   Ramón   paint.

PRACTICE/APPLY

Display Teaching Transparency 82 Have children read the first sentence aloud and tell which word is the verb. *(read)* Write the word *read* on the board. Continue the same way with the rest of the sentences. Ask children to suggest other verbs that might make sense in each sentence.

WRAP UP **Reread the Big Book**

Link to the Theme Tell children, as they listen again to the big book, to think about all the places the children explore. After rereading *I Swam with a Seal*, ask children where they might want to explore, what animal they might find there, and what they would like to do with the animal.

▲ Big Book

S.S.R.
Sustained Silent Reading

Have children read silently from a book of their choice. See page 67L for tips on helping children choose books.

OBJECTIVE
To define and identify verbs

SKILL TRACE

VERBS	
INTRODUCE	**38N**
Reteach	T5
Review	59C, 65C, 67D, 67N
T Test	Bk 1-5

▼ **Teaching Transparency 82**

VERBS

1. We read at school.
2. I dream at night.
3. Jane skates fast.
4. My pet plays with me.
5. Jack catches the ball.

"Frog and Toad All Year"
Gather Around, Volume 1-5   82   Grammar: Verbs
Harcourt

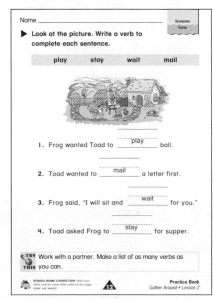

Name _____

▶ Look at the picture. Write a verb to complete each sentence.

play	stay	wait	mail

1. Frog wanted Toad to ___play___ ball.

2. Toad wanted to ___mail___ a letter first.

3. Frog said, "I will sit and ___wait___ for you."

4. Toad asked Frog to ___stay___ for supper.

TRY THIS Work with a partner. Make a list of as many verbs as you can.

Practice Book
Gather Around • Lesson 2

▲ Practice Book, p. 12

Day at a Glance
Day 2

Sharing Literature
Rhyme: "Rain, Rain, Go Away"

Phonemic Awareness
Phoneme Counting; Focus on /ā/

Phonics
REVIEW: Long Vowels /ā/ai, ay

Spelling
Word Building

Vocabulary
INTRODUCE: *caught, hurried, near son*

High-Frequency Words
INTRODUCE: *cold, sure*

Reading
Pupil Edition
"Frog and Toad All Year," pp. 38–59

Interactive Writing ✏
Story Response

Grammar
REVIEW: Verbs

WARM UP
MORNING MESSAGE
Good Morning!

Today is _____.

Today the weather is _____.

We _____ on sunny days.

We _____ on rainy days.

Introduce the Day
Tell children that today they will listen to a rhyme about rain and will also read a story about two friends caught in the rain. Guide them in generating a message about rainy and sunny weather. Ask:

- **What is the weather like today?**
- **What are some things you do when it's sunny?**
- **What are some things you do when it rains?**

As you write the message, ask volunteers to write previously taught letters, words, and/or punctuation to reinforce skills. For example, have volunteers write the words *Today, rainy,* and *days.*

Read the Message
Read the message. Use the message to focus on selected skills that have been previously taught.

Apply Skills

Phonics Ask volunteers to point to and read aloud words that have the long vowel sound of *a.* (*Today, days, rainy*) Review these words, stressing the sound /ā/ in each word.	**Grammar** Once children have helped you complete the last two sentences, ask volunteers to point to the verbs in those sentences. Ask children what a verb tells. (what someone or something does)

Sharing Literature

LISTEN AND RESPOND

Connect to Prior Knowledge Ask children what they do when it rains. Ask them to name their favorite rainy-day activity.

Respond to Literature Read aloud the rhyme "Rain, Rain, Go Away." Ask children why they think the child in the rhyme wants the rain to go away. Then ask why the rain should "come again some other day."

Focus Skill **Cause/Effect** Ask children whether rain is good or bad, and why. Ask what would happen if it did not rain at all. Have children name things that happen because it rains.

Phonemic Awareness

PHONEME COUNTING

Words from "Rain, Rain, Go Away" Tell children to listen carefully as you say words from the rhyme. Say *How many sounds do you hear in the word* rain? (3) Children may use counters to check the number of sounds. Then say each of the following words slowly and clearly and have children tell how many sounds they hear in each.

go (2)	**away** (3)	**come** (3)	**some** (3)
day (2)	**other** (3)	**to** (2)	**play** (3)

FOCUS ON /ā/

Phoneme Addition Tell children that they can add /ā/ before a sound to make a word. Model by saying /m/—*If I add /ā/ before /m/, I get* aim. Continue, having children add /ā/ before these sounds:

/t/ (ate)   /d/ (aid)   /s/ (ace)   /j/ (age)

Then tell children that you will say a sound and they will add the sound /ā/ after that sound to make a word. Model by saying /w/—*If I add /ā/ after /w/, I get* way. Continue with the following:

/d/ (day)   /p/ (pay)   /m/ (may)   /s/ (say)

Rain, Rain, Go Away

Rain, rain, go away.

Come again some other day.

Rain, rain, go away.

Little (Johnny) wants to play.

REACHING ALL LEARNERS

Diagnostic Check: Phonemic Awareness

If... children cannot make words by adding an initial or final phoneme . . .

Then... try a visual approach by using counters. For example, show children a counter and tell them it stands for /d/. Show a second counter and tell children it stands for /ā/. Hold the /ā/ in front of the /d/ counter and the model blending *aid*.

ADDITIONAL SUPPORT ACTIVITIES

BELOW-LEVEL Reteach, p. S8

ADVANCED Extend, p. S9

ENGLISH-LANGUAGE LEARNERS Reteach, p. S9

OBJECTIVES

- *To blend sounds into words*
- *To read and write Spelling Words*

SKILL TRACE

/ā/ai, ay	
Introduce	38I–38L
Reteach	S10, T4
REVIEW	**38Q–38R, 59F–59G**
Review	65F
T Test	Bk 1-5

Spelling Words

1. **day**
2. **say**
3. **sail**
4. **pail**
5. **pay**
6. **play**
7. **right**
8. **high**
9. **learn**
10. **join**

5-DAY SPELLING	
DAY 1	Pretest; Word Sort
DAY 2	**Word Building**
DAY 3	State the Generalization
DAY 4	Review
DAY 5	Posttest; Writing Application

Phonics and Spelling
Long Vowels /ā/ *ai, ay*

 ✔ *Review*

WORD BUILDING

Blend and Read a Spelling Word
Place *Letter Card d* in a pocket chart, followed by the letters *a* and *y* together. Ask children to say the sound of each letter or letter pair as you place it in the chart. Slide your hand under the letters as you blend the sounds /ddāā/. Have children repeat after you. Then read the word naturally—*day*, and have children do the same.

Build Spelling Words Ask children which letter you should change to make *day* become *say*. (change *d* to *s*) Continue building the Spelling Words shown in this manner and having children read them.

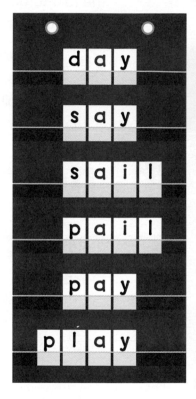

BELOW-LEVEL	**ENGLISH-LANGUAGE LEARNERS**
Children may have difficulty following the activity from a distance. Have them use *Word Builder Cards* and *Word Builders* or a pocket chart to construct each Spelling Word.	Have children use each word in a sentence. Then have them draw a picture for each sentence. Help them write on each picture the Spelling Word it illustrates. Then have children point to the word and spell it aloud as they point to each letter.

Apply Phonics

READ WORDS IN CONTEXT

Write the following sentences on the board or on chart paper and have children read them aloud.

I **say** this is the **right day** to **play**.
May likes to **play** with a **pail**.
We make **high** piles of clay.
Next, I want to **join** the boat club.
I will **pay** to **learn** to **sail**.

 Dictate Words Dictate to children several words from the pocket chart, and have them write the words on a dry-erase board or in their journal.

say
pay
day
play
sail
pail

5-DAY PHONICS/SPELLING	
DAY 1	Introduce /ā/ai, ay
DAY 2	**Word Building with /ā/ai, ay**
DAY 3	Word Building with /ā/ai, ay
DAY 4	Word Building with /ā/ai, ay, and a-e
DAY 5	Phonograms -ail, -ain Inflections -ed, -ing

 Phonics Resources

Phonics Express™ CD-ROM, **Level B** Roamer/Route 6/ Park, Market

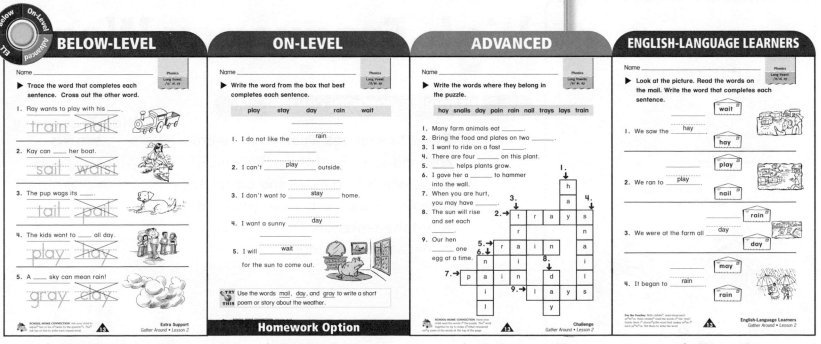

▲ Extra Support, p. 13   ▲ Practice, p. 13   ▲ Challenge, p. 13   ▲ ELL, p. 13

Vocabulary

caught	surprised, trapped
hurried	moved fast
near	close by
son	male child

High-Frequency Words

cold	not warm
sure	certain

VOCABULARY WORDS
caught   hurried   near   son

HIGH-FREQUENCY WORDS
cold   sure

Frog got <u>caught</u> in the rain.
He was wet and <u>cold</u>.
His house was <u>near</u>.
Frog <u>hurried</u> home.
He was <u>sure</u> his house would be warm.
Frog's dad said, "<u>Son</u>, I'm glad you're home."

"Frog and Toad All Year"
Gather Around, Volume 1-5   83   Vocabulary/High-Frequency
                                                Harcourt

READING

Building Background

TALK ABOUT SPRING

Make a Word Web for Spring
Tell children that they are going to read a story about a frog who goes looking for spring. Guide children in completing a concept web about spring.

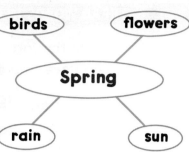

Discuss Story Words List the words *clothes, meadow, polly-wog, spoiled, tired,* and *woods* on the board. Point to each word and read it aloud. Ask volunteers to tell what each word means. Provide help as needed to define each word. Also provide a visual connection wherever possible.

Vocabulary

IDENTIFY WORDS

Echo Read Display *Teaching Transparency 83*. Point to the words *caught, hurried, near,* and *son*. Say each word and have children repeat it.

> INTRODUCE
> **Vocabulary**
> caught   near
> hurried   son

High-Frequency Words

INTRODUCE WORDS IN CONTEXT

Read Sentences Point to the words *cold* and *sure*. Read the definitions of these words to children and discuss their meaning. Track the print as you read aloud the sentences. Call on volunteers to reread each sentence.

> INTRODUCE
> **High-Frequency Words**
> cold   sure

Word Power

▲ Frog and Toad
All Year

Words to Remember

caught

cold

hurried

near

son

sure

It was a very **cold** day.
Frog was standing **near** his father.
"**Son**, it's going to snow," said his father.
"Let's make **sure** that we don't get **caught** in the storm."
Frog and his father **hurried** home.

38   39

Word Power

Pages 38–39 Have children read aloud the Words to Remember. Then have them read the sentences aloud. Have children point to the Words to Remember in the sentences.

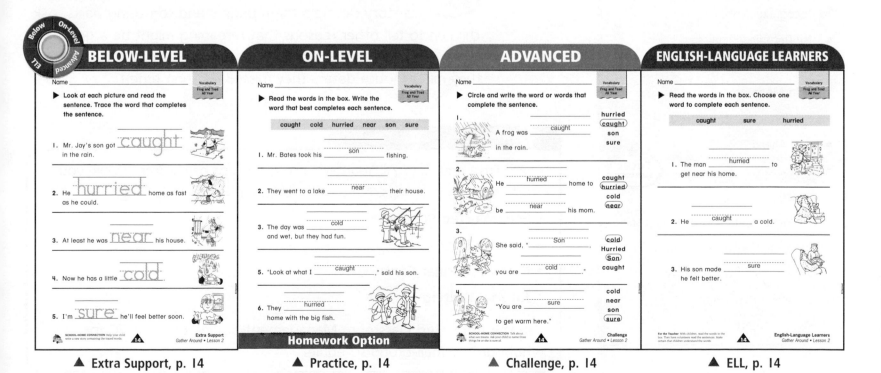

BELOW-LEVEL

Name _____

▶ Look at each picture and read the sentence. Trace the word that completes the sentence.

1. Mr. Jay's son got **caught** in the rain.

2. He **hurried** home as fast as he could.

3. At least he was **near** his house.

4. Now he has a little **cold**.

5. I'm **sure** he'll feel better soon.

▲ Extra Support, p. 14

ON-LEVEL

Name _____

▶ Read the words in the box. Write the word that best completes each sentence.

caught	cold	hurried	near	son	sure

1. Mr. Bates took his _____ **son** _____ fishing.

2. They went to a lake _____ **near** _____ their house.

3. The day was _____ **cold** _____ and wet, but they had fun.

5. "Look at what I _____ **caught** _____," said his son.

6. They _____ **hurried** _____ home with the big fish.

Homework Option

▲ Practice, p. 14

ADVANCED

Name _____

▶ Circle and write the word or words that complete the sentence.

1. A frog was _____ **caught** _____ in the rain.
   hurried / **caught** / son / sure

2. He _____ **hurried** _____ home to be _____ **near** _____ his mom.
   caught / **hurried** / cold / **near**

3. She said, "_____ **Son** _____, you are _____ **cold** _____.
   cold / Hurried / **Son** / caught

4. "You are _____ **sure** _____ to get warm here."
   cold / near / son / **sure**

▲ Challenge, p. 14

ENGLISH-LANGUAGE LEARNERS

Name _____

▶ Read the words in the box. Choose one word to complete each sentence.

caught	sure	hurried

1. The man _____ **hurried** _____ to get near his home.

2. He _____ **caught** _____ a cold.

3. His son made _____ **sure** _____ he felt better.

▲ ELL, p. 14

Phonics

Long Vowels /ā/ *ai, ay*

Vocabulary

caught, hurried, near, son

High-Frequency Words

cold, sure

Decodable Words

See the list on p. T50–T51.

Comprehension

 Cause/Effect

 Reread

Strategies
Good Readers Use

To Recognize Words

- Use Decoding/Phonics
- Look for Word Bits and Parts

To Gain Meaning

- Self-Correct
- Read Ahead
- **Reread**
- Reread Aloud
- Use Picture Clues to Confirm Meaning
- Make and Confirm Predictions
- Sequence Events/Summarize
- Create Mental Images
- Make Inferences

39A   Gather Around

Prereading Strategies

PREPARING TO READ

Preview/Predict Discuss pages 40–41. Ask children to read aloud the title. Then ask children who the author is and how they know. Have children talk about the pictures on pages 43 and 44. Have children predict whether this will be a story about real frogs and toads or a make-believe story. Ask why they think so.

Set Purpose Have children set a purpose for reading. If necessary, suggest that they read to find out if the story will really tell what Frog and Toad do all year long.

COMPREHENSION SKILL

 Cause/Effect Remind children that sometimes one thing that happens in a story makes another thing happen. Tell children to think about "The Story of a Blue Bird." Ask what happened in that story that made the little blue bird begin to fly. (The other birds flew away, and he forgot to be afraid to fly.) Then ask children to look for examples of things that make other things happen as they read "Frog and Toad All Year."

COMPREHENSION STRATEGY

Reread Remind children that rereading a few pages of a story can help them understand confusing parts. Ask children to tell other reasons that rereading might be a good idea. (They might remember parts of the story they had forgotten; they might notice details they missed the first time.)

Managing Small Groups

Read "Frog and Toad All Year" with small groups of children. While you work with small groups, have other children do the following:

- **Self-Selected Reading**
- **Practice Pages**
- **Cross-Curricular Centers**
- **Journal Writing**

Use the suggested Classroom Management outline on page 7C for the whole-group/small-group schedule.

Genre

Fiction

Sometimes in fiction there is a "story within a story."

Look for:

• the parts of the story that are happening in the story present— or now.

• the story that one character tells about the past.

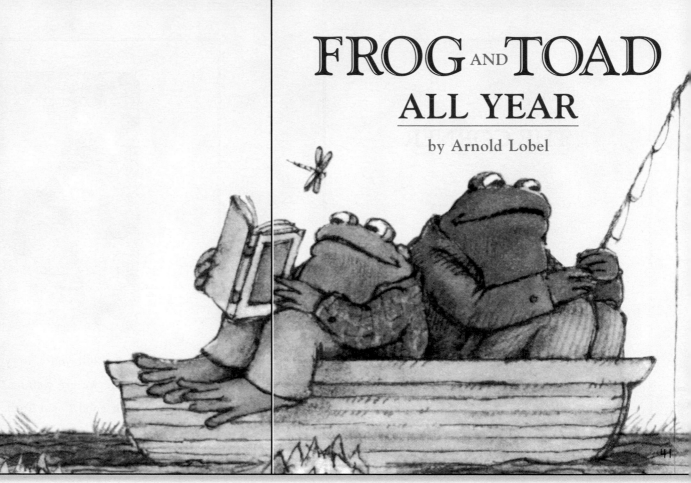

FROG AND TOAD
ALL YEAR
by Arnold Lobel

40

41

Guided Comprehension

Pages 40–41 Have children reread the title and review their predictions about whether this is a story about real frogs and toads or a make-believe story.

GENRE: Fiction

Read aloud the information about fiction on page 40. Tell children that fiction includes

• events that could not really happen.

• characters who are not real.

BELOW-LEVEL	ON-LEVEL	ADVANCED	ENGLISH-LANGUAGE LEARNERS
Read aloud the sentence *Frog and Toad were caught in the rain.* Ask which words tell what happened to Frog and Toad. Then read the rest of the story aloud to children, clarifying unfamiliar words. SMALL GROUP	As children read the selection, use the Guided Comprehension questions to direct their reading. WHOLE GROUP/SMALL GROUP	Encourage children to picture in their minds what is happening as they read the story. Have them share their mental images of parts of the story that are not specifically shown in illustrations. SMALL GROUP/INDEPENDENT	Have children make a clay Frog and a clay Toad. As you read the selection, have children act it out with their clay figures. SMALL GROUP
ADDITIONAL SUPPORT See Intervention Resource Kit, Lesson 28. *Intervention Teacher's Guide* pp. 272–281			**ADDITIONAL SUPPORT** See English-Language Learners Resource Kit, Lesson 28. *English-Language Learners Teacher's Guide* pp. 164–165

THE CORNER

Frog and Toad
were caught in the rain.
They ran to Frog's house.
"I am all wet," said Toad.
"The day is spoiled."
"Have some tea and cake,"
said Frog. "The rain will stop.
If you stand near the stove,
your clothes will soon be dry.

I will tell you a story
while we are waiting," said Frog.
"Oh good," said Toad.

42

43

Guided Comprehension

Pages 42–43 Have children look at the illustration. Call their attention to the drops of water and ask why they think Frog and Toad are dripping. Then have them read to find out.

1 (Focus Skill) **CAUSE/EFFECT** Why are Frog and Toad dripping wet? Which clue words tell you? (They have just been caught in the rain; *rain* and *wet*.)

2 (Focus Strategy) **REREAD** Who says "The day is spoiled"—Frog or Toad? Reread these two pages to figure it out. (Toad says "The day is spoiled." Rereading helps us understand that *The day is spoiled* makes more sense with *I am all wet* than with *Have some tea and cake*.)

REACHING ALL LEARNERS

Diagnostic Check: Vocabulary and High-Frequency Words

If... children have difficulty reading the vocabulary words *caught* or *near* . . .

Then... place a *Word Card* next to that same word on the story page, and have children repeat the word after you.

ADDITIONAL SUPPORT ACTIVITIES

BELOW-LEVEL　　Reteach, p. S12

ADVANCED　　Extend, p. S13

ENGLISH-LANGUAGE LEARNERS　　Reteach, p. S13

44

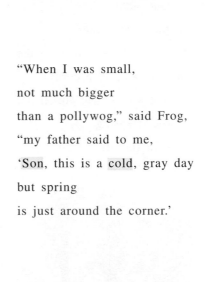

"When I was small,
not much bigger
than a pollywog," said Frog,
"my father said to me,
'Son, this is a cold, gray day
but spring
is just around the corner.'

Guided Comprehension

Pages 44–45 Point out that the two characters in the illustration don't look exactly like Frog and Toad. Ask children who the characters might be. Then have them read to find out.

❶ DRAW CONCLUSIONS Who are the characters in the picture? (Frog and his father a long time ago) **How do you know?** (The text says *When I was small* and *my father said to me.*)

❷ DRAW CONCLUSIONS In what season of the year do you think Frog's story begins? How do you know? (It begins in winter; it is cold, and Frog's father says that spring is just around the corner.)

❸ UNDERSTAND FIGURATIVE LANGUAGE What do you think Frog's father meant when he said "spring is just around the corner"? (Possible response: It is almost spring.)

I wanted spring to come.
I went out
to find that corner.
I walked down a path in the woods
until I came to a corner.
I went around the corner
to see if spring
was on the other side."

"And was it?" asked Toad.
"No," said Frog.
"There was only a pine tree,
three pebbles
and some dry grass.

47

Guided Comprehension

Pages 46–47 Have children look at the illustrations. Ask what Frog is doing. Then have children read to find out.

1 NOTE DETAILS What is Frog doing? (He is looking for a corner; he wants to find spring around the corner.)

2 NOTE DETAILS What does Frog find around the corner in the woods? (a pine tree, three pebbles, and some dry grass)

3 DETERMINE CHARACTERS' EMOTIONS Do you think Frog was disappointed? Why? (Possible response: Yes, because he didn't find spring. Accept reasonable responses. Encourage children to explain their responses.)

STUDENT SELF-ASSESSMENT

Have children ask themselves the following questions to assess how they are reading:

- Do I think about all the words in a sentence to help me understand words I don't know?
- Do I read carefully to understand why events happen the way they do in the story?
- When I don't understand something, do I reread to understand it better?

I walked
in the meadow.
Soon I came to
another corner.
I went around the corner
to see if spring was there."
"Did you find it?" asked Toad.

"No," said Frog.
"There was only
an old worm
asleep on a
tree stump."

48

49

Guided Comprehension

Pages 48–49 Ask children to predict what Frog will do next. Have them read to check their predictions.

1 **CONFIRM PREDICTIONS** **Were you right about what Frog is doing? How did you know?** (Possible response: Yes, I thought Frog was still looking for spring around a corner, and when he told Toad that he walked in the meadow, I knew I was right.)

2 **NOTE DETAILS** **What does Frog find in the meadow?** (an old worm asleep on a tree stump)

3 **MAKE PREDICTIONS** **Do you think Frog finds spring around the next corner? Why?** (Possible response: No, because spring is not really around a corner that you can walk to. Accept reasonable responses. Have children explain their responses.)

BELOW-LEVEL

Some children may be confused about who is speaking because there are no quotation marks at the beginning of this page. Have them look back at page 47. Read aloud the sentence that begins *There was only. . . .* Point out the marks at the beginning of the sentence and say that those marks show that Frog says these words. Help children read ahead to find the marks that show when Frog stops talking. (after *to see if spring was there,* page 48) Remind children that Frog is telling a story, and sometimes he says several sentences before he stops talking, so they have to look for the marks at the beginning and end of what the character says.

"I walked along the river
until I came to
another corner.
I went around the corner
to look for spring."
"Was it there?" asked Toad.

Guided Comprehension

Pages 50–51 Have children look at the illustration. Ask if they think these pages will tell whether Frog will find spring, and why they think as they do. Have them read to find out.

1 NOTE DETAILS Where does Frog go next? (along the river)

2 CONFIRM PREDICTIONS What did we find out about whether Frog finds spring? (He hasn't found it yet; he's still looking.)

3 MAKE PREDICTIONS Do you think Frog will find spring at the river? Why? (Possible responses: Yes, because he's looking hard; no, because he hasn't found it in any of the other places he looked. Accept reasonable responses. Encourage children to explain their responses.)

ENGLISH-LANGUAGE LEARNERS

If children are having difficulty with words such as *woods, pebbles, meadow, worm, stump,* or *river,* have them include these words in their own picture dictionary. Have children illustrate each word and write the word below their picture.

"No," said Frog.
"There was only
some wet mud
and a lizard who was chasing
his tail."
"You must have been tired,"
said Toad.
"I was tired," said Frog,
"and it started
to rain."

52

"I went back home.
When I got there," said Frog,
"I found another corner.
It was the corner of my house."
"Did you go around it?"
asked Toad.
"I went around that corner, too,"
said Frog.
"What did you see?"
asked Toad.

Guided Comprehension

Pages 52–53 Have children look at the illustrations and ask what they think Frog finds. Have them read to find out.

1 **NOTE DETAILS** What does Frog find at the river? (wet mud and a lizard chasing his tail)

2 (Focus Skill) **CAUSE/EFFECT** Why do you think Frog goes home? (Possible response: Frog says that he is tired and wet. He is probably getting discouraged because he has looked around many corners but still hasn't found spring. Accept reasonable responses. Encourage children to explain their responses.)

"I saw the sun coming out,"
said Frog. "I saw birds
sitting and singing in a tree.
I saw my mother and father
working in their garden.
I saw flowers in the garden."

54

"You found it!" cried Toad.
"Yes," said Frog.
"I was very happy.
I had found the corner
that spring was just around."
"Look, Frog," said Toad.
"You were right.
The rain has stopped."
Frog and Toad hurried outside.

55

Guided Comprehension

Pages 54–56 Have children look at page 54. Ask where they think Frog is and what he sees. Then have them read to find out.

1 **NOTE DETAILS** **What does Frog see around the corner of his house?** (the sun coming out, birds, his parents working in the garden, flowers)

2 **INTERPRET STORY EVENTS** **How does Frog know that he has found spring?** (Possible responses: Birds are singing; flowers are blooming; the sun is coming out.)

3 **REREAD** **Why did Frog and Toad hurry outside? Reread to find out.** (Possible response: When I reread this part of the story, I found out that Frog and Toad hurried outside to make sure that spring had really come.)

They ran around the corner
of Frog's house
to make sure
that spring had come again.

Think and Respond

1 What does Frog do to find spring?

2 What signs of spring does Frog find?

3 How does Frog's story help Toad feel better?

4 Tell about a time when a friend did something that made you feel better.

5 What did you like most about this story? Tell why.

57

Think and Respond

1 He looks around every corner. **RECALL DETAILS**

2 Frog finds the sun coming out, birds singing in trees, his parents working in the garden, and flowers in the garden. **RECALL DETAILS**

3 Possible response: It helps Toad forget about being caught in the rain. **IDENTIFY WITH CHARACTERS**

4 Possible response: A friend sending a nice card or sharing a cookie. **IDENTIFY WITH CHARACTERS**

5 Possible response: I liked the end of the story, because Frog really did come around the corner and find spring. Accept reasonable responses. Encourage children to explain their responses. **EXPRESS PERSONAL OPINIONS**

ABOUT THE
AUTHOR/ILLUSTRATOR

ARNOLD LOBEL

Arnold Lobel was both a writer and an illustrator of books for children. Frog and Toad are two of the many wonderful characters he created. He got the idea to write about frogs and toads while sitting on his front porch. He thought about frogs and toads, which look alike but are very different. Then he began writing about the characters we know today.

Visit *The Learning Site!*
www.harcourtschool.com

Meet the Author/Illustrator

Pages 58–59 Explain that these pages tell about the person who wrote and illustrated "Frog and Toad All Year." Identify Arnold Lobel in the photograph on page 58. Remind children that an **author** writes a story and an **illustrator** creates pictures to go with the writing. Read aloud page 59.

Visit *The Learning Site:* www.harcourtschool.com
See Resources for Parents and Teachers: Author/Illustrator Features.

Retelling

COMPREHENSION FOCUS

Focus Skill **Cause/Effect** Remind children that sometimes things that happen in a story cause other things to happen. Help children recall what made Frog go out looking around corners. (Frog's father told him spring was just around the corner, and Frog wanted spring to come.)

RETELL AND SUMMARIZE THE STORY

Summarize with a Story Map Display *Teaching Transparency 109* or draw a similar chart on the board or on chart paper. Work with children to complete a story map to summarize "Frog and Toad All Year." To get children started, prompt them with questions such as these: *Why did Frog and Toad run to Frog's house? Why do you think Frog told Toad a story?*

Point out that "Frog and Toad All Year" is really one story inside another story. Explain that the story begins as Frog and Toad get caught in the rain and ends when they go back outside after the rain stops, but the main story is the one Frog tells Toad in the middle. Have children suggest phrases or sentences that summarize Frog's story. Write their suggestions in the Middle box. Help children use the story map to summarize the story.

COMPREHENSION CHECK

▲ **End-of-Selection Test, Practice Book, pp. A37–A39**

▼ **Teaching Transparency 109**

Beginning
Frog and Toad are caught in the rain. They run to Frog's house. Frog tells a story.

Middle
Frog's father says that spring is just around the corner. Frog looks around several corners for spring. Frog goes home and finds spring.

End
The rain stops. Frog and Toad go back outside.

109

DAILY LANGUAGE PRACTICE

Will you plai with me

Will you <u>play</u> with me?

Interactive Writing *Story Response*

SHARE THE PEN

Generate Ideas Tell children that they will work together to write about what Frog and Toad do next. Brainstorm what might happen after Frog and Toad go back outside. Write children's ideas on the board or on chart paper.

> sailed down the river
> jump in puddles
> look for worms

Help children choose one of the ideas to write a story about. Have children dictate sentences to tell what happens first, next, and last to Frog and Toad. Invite children to take the marker and help write the sentences on chart paper. Ask questions such as the following:

- **What's an interesting verb we can use to make our sentence exciting?**
- **What is the next word in our sentence? How is that word spelled?**
- **What punctuation do we need at the end of this sentence?**

If children can write complete sentences, have them do so. Involve others by having them write short words with known sounds and spellings. Periodically, pause to read what has been written.

Read the Story Have children read the completed story with you. Display the story for children to read independently.

journal  writing

Writing Prompt Have children draw a picture to illustrate one of the story ideas the group did not write about. Then have them write a sentence about the picture.

ENGLISH-LANGUAGE LEARNERS

Help children follow the action of the story by involving the entire group in acting sentences out as they are written. Children can also be encouraged to contribute to the writing by acting out sentences that they have difficulty saying.

Grammar *Verbs*

5-DAY GRAMMAR

DAY 1	Introduce Verbs
DAY 2	**Use Verbs in Sentences**
DAY 3	Interesting Verbs
DAY 4	Verb Game
DAY 5	Identify Verbs

REVIEW

Review Verbs Reread aloud the first two lines of the rhyme "Rain, Rain, Go Away" (page 38P). Ask them to name the words in those lines that tell what someone or something does. *(go, come)* List the words on the board. Point out that these words are opposites. Say the following verbs one at a time, write each one on the board, and ask children to suggest words that name the opposite action: start *(stop, finish)*, open *(shut, close)*, whisper *(shout)*, work *(play)*, wake *(sleep)*. Write children's suggestions on the board. Model writing sentences using the verbs.

MODEL **If I want to write about stopping, I can write the sentence *We stop at the red light*. I make sure the sentence has a verb—*stop*—because every sentence needs a verb to make sense.**

Generate Sentences Remind children that a word that tells what someone or something does is called a verb. Explain that every complete sentence has a verb. Have children suggest sentences using the verbs listed on the board. As you write each sentence, ask volunteers to tell you how to spell words that they have learned or that include previously taught spellings. Have volunteers tell you what punctuation to put at the end of the sentence.

WRAP UP Recite a Rhyme

Walk in Place Have children listen to a rhyme about walking in the rain. Track the print as you read aloud "To Walk in Warm Rain." Read the rhyme several times. Then invite children to stand up and walk in place every time you say the line *To walk in warm rain*. Encourage children to suggest other ways to use actions to show what is happening in the rhyme.

To Walk in Warm Rain

To walk in warm rain
  And get wetter and wetter!
To do it again—
To walk in warm rain
  Till you drip like a drain.
To walk in warm rain
  And get wetter and wetter.
David McCord

▲ **Big Book of Rhymes p. 21**

S.S.R.
Sustained Silent Reading

Have children read silently from a book of their choice. See page 67L for tips on helping children choose books.

SKILL TRACE

VERBS	
Introduce	38N
Reteach	T5
REVIEW	**59C, 65C, 67D, 67N**
T Test	Bk 1-5

Below · On-Level · Advanced · ELL

BELOW-LEVEL

Have children work in groups and select a picture in a magazine. They can say one sentence that tells what is happening in the picture. Help children write the sentence and then have them underline the verb or verbs.

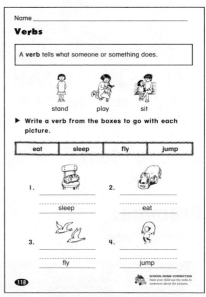

Name _____

Verbs

A **verb** tells what someone or something does.

stand   play   sit

▶ Write a verb from the boxes to go with each picture.

| eat | sleep | fly | jump |

1. _____ sleep
2. _____ eat
3. _____ fly
4. _____ jump

118

▲ **Language Handbook, p. 118**

Frog and Toad All Year   **59C**

Sharing Literature
Poem: "The Tree Frog"

Phonemic Awareness
Initial Phoneme Deletion/
Substitution; Focus on /ā/

Phonics
REVIEW: Long Vowel /ā/ai, ay

Spelling
State the Generalization

Vocabulary
REVIEW: *caught, hurried, near, son*

High-Frequency Words
REVIEW: *cold, sure*

Reading

Rereading for Fluency
Pupil Edition
"Frog and Toad All Year," pp. 40–56

Read

Reading Across Texts
"Frogs in Trees?" pp. 60–63
Making Connections, pp. 64–65

Independent Writing ✏
Dialogue

Grammar
REVIEW: Verbs

WARM UP

MORNING MESSAGE

Good Morning!

Today is _____.

What do you know about frogs?

Frogs can be green, _____, and _____.

Frogs live in _____ or _____.

Introduce the Day

Tell children that today they will hear a poem about tree frogs and will also read an article about them. Guide children in generating a message about frogs. Ask:

• **What are some different kinds of frogs you know about?**

• **What are frogs like?**

• **Where do you think tree frogs live? Where do other kinds of frogs live?**

As you write the message, ask volunteers to write previously taught words and punctuation. Some may be able to write complete sentences. Remind them to leave appropriate space between words.

Read the Message

Read the message. Use the message to focus on selected skills that have been previously taught.

Apply Skills

Concept Vocabulary Direct children's attention to the describing words, such as *green*, in the message. Ask how many other words they can think of to describe frogs. Prompt if necessary by asking for words that tell about size or shape.

Grammar Ask a volunteer to point to and read the verb in the last sentence. *(live)* Then ask children to suggest other words that tell about things that frogs do.

Sharing Literature

BUILD CONCEPT VOCABULARY

Connect to Prior Knowledge Remind children of information they have shared about frogs. Discuss what colors frogs are, where frogs live, and what sounds they make. Ask what children know about tree frogs. Then read "The Tree Frog" aloud.

Sound Words Reread the first two lines of the poem. Ask children what they think the words *creaks* and *croaks* mean. Explain that the poet used these words because they make us think of what a frog sounds like. Encourage children to say *creak* and *croak* in a "froggy" voice. Write the words *creak* and *croak* on the board and ask children to suggest other words for sounds animals make. Have children say the word in the voice of the animal.

Phonemic Awareness

INITIAL PHONEME DELETION/SUBSTITUTION

Words from "The Tree Frog" Tell children that you will say a word and then ask them to change or take away the first sound to make a new word. Model by saying *tree. Change the first sound from /t/ to /f/.* (free) Continue with the following words:

deep: Change /d/ to /ch/. (cheep)   **time: Change /t/ to /d/.** (dime)
stops: Take away the first /s/. (tops)   **till: Take away the /t/.** (ill)

FOCUS ON /ā/

Phoneme Addition and Deletion Tell children that they are going to make new words by adding the sound /n/ to the end of words you say. Model by saying *What word do I make if I add /n/ to the end of* lay? (lane) Continue with the following words:

pay (pain)   **play** (plain)   **may** (main)   **stay** (stain)

Then ask children to make new words by taking away /n/ at the end of words. Model by saying *What word do I make if I take away /n/ from* rain? (ray) Continue with these words:

main (may)   **rain** (ray)   **train** (tray)   **grain** (gray)

The Tree Frog

The tree frog
Creaks and croaks and croaks
And says "Dee deep"
And stops, till when
It's time to say
"Dee deep" again.

John Travers Moor

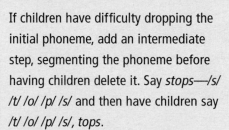

◀ "The Name Game," *Oo-pples and Boo-noo-noos: Songs and Activities for Phonemic Awareness,* pp. 105–111

BELOW-LEVEL

If children have difficulty dropping the initial phoneme, add an intermediate step, segmenting the phoneme before having children delete it. Say *stops—/s/ /t/ /o/ /p/ /s/* and then have children say */t/ /o/ /p/ /s/, tops.*

ENGLISH-LANGUAGE LEARNERS

Visit *The Learning Site:* www.harcourtschool.com See Language Support.

OBJECTIVES

- *To generate the long vowel sound of a*
- *To blend sounds into words*
- *To read simple, regular words*

SKILL TRACE

/ā/ *ai, ay*	
Introduce	38I–38L
Reteach	S10, T4
REVIEW	**38Q–38R, 59F–59G**
Review	65E–65F
T Test	Bk 1-5

Phonics Resources

Phonics Express™ CD-ROM, **Level B** Sparkle/Route 3/Building Site

---

Phonics

Long Vowels /ā/ *ai, ay*

✔ *Review*

WORD BUILDING

s a i l r y p m h w t

Guided Practice Place the letters *s, a, i, l* in a pocket chart. Have children do the same with their *Word Builders* and *Word Builder Cards.* Model how to blend the word *sail.* Slide your hand under the letters as you slowly elongate the sounds—/ssāāll/. Then read the word naturally—*sail.* Have children do the same.

| s | a | i | l |

Have children build and read new words by telling them:

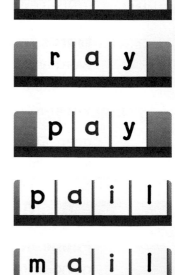

- Change the *s* to *r.* What word did you make?

| r | a | i | l |

- Take away the *l.* Change the *i* to *y.* What word did you make?

| r | a | y |

- Change the *r* to *p.* What word did you make?

| p | a | y |

- Change the *y* to *i.* Add *l.* What word did you make?

| p | a | i | l |

- Change *p* to *m.* What word did you make?

| m | a | i | l |

- Take away the *l.* Change the *i* to *y.* What word did you make?

| m | a | y |

Continue word building with this word sequence: *hay, hail, wail, wait, way.*

Apply Phonics

READ WORDS IN CONTEXT

Display *Teaching Transparency 84* or write the following sentences on the board or on chart paper. Have volunteers read the story one sentence at a time. Call on other volunteers to underline or frame words with the sound /ā/.

▼ **Teaching Transparency 84**

LONG VOWELS /ā/*ai, ay*

Kay has two clay cars. Kay likes to play with her clay cars. She can play with them all day.

Kay puts her cars in a pail. She puts the pail away. She will wait and play another day.

"Frog and Toad All Year"
Gather Around, Volume 1-5   **84**   Phonics: Long Vowels /ā/ai, ay
Harcourt

Write Words Tell children to choose two long *a* words with *ai* and two long *a* words with *ay* and write them in their journal.

5-DAY PHONICS/SPELLING

DAY 1	Introduce /ā/*ai, ay*
DAY 2	Word Building with /ā/*ai, ay*
DAY 3	**Word Building with /ā/*ai, ay***
DAY 4	Word Building with /ā/*ai, ay,* and *a-e*
DAY 5	Phonograms *-ail, -ain* Inflections *-ed, -ing*

REACHING ALL LEARNERS

Diagnostic Check: Phonics

If... children cannot decode words with long vowel /ā/*ai, ay*...

Then... have them read "One Rainy Day" and "Rain, I Say" in *Decodable Book 28* to reinforce long vowel /ā/*ai, ay.*

▲ **Decodable Book 28**
"One Rainy Day"
"Rain, I Say"

ADDITIONAL SUPPORT ACTIVITIES

BELOW-LEVEL	Reteach, p. S10
ADVANCED	Extend, p. S11
ENGLISH-LANGUAGE LEARNERS	Reteach, p. S11

School-Home Connection

Take-Home Book Version

◄ Decodable Books Take-Home Version

Spelling Words

1. day
2. say
3. sail
4. pail
5. pay
6. play
7. right
8. high
9. learn
10. join

journal writing

Have children copy the Spelling Words into their journal.

Word Sorts

Spelling
Lesson 2

▶ Make cards for the Spelling Words. Lay them down and read them.

Spelling Words

1. Put the words with long *a* in one group and those without long *a* in another group. Write the words on the chart.
2. Put the words with long *i* in one group and those without long *i* in another group. Then write the words.

Words With Long a		Words Without Long a	
day	pail		
say	pay	right	learn
sail	play	high	join

Words With Long i		Words Without Long i	
right		day	pay
high		say	play
		sail	learn
		pail	join

Spelling Words
day
say
sail
pail
pay
play
right
high
learn
join
My Own Word

SCHOOL-HOME CONNECTION Point to and read the Spelling Words aloud with your child. Talk about how the words are alike and how they are different.

SPELLING PRACTICE BOOK
GATHER AROUND • LESSON 2 **69**

▲ Spelling Practice Book, p. 69

Spelling

5-DAY SPELLING

DAY 1	Pretest; Word Sort
DAY 2	Word Building
DAY 3	**State the Generalization**
DAY 4	Review
DAY 5	Posttest; Writing Application

TEACH/MODEL

State the Generalization for /ā/ai and ay Write the Spelling Words on the board and have children read them aloud. Discuss what is the same about words 1, 2, 5, and 6. (They all have the sound /ā/; they all have *ay*.) Have volunteers circle the letters that stand for /ā/ in each word. Tell children that the letters *ay* are used to spell the sound /ā/, especially at the end of words.

Repeat the procedure with words 3 and 4. (They both have the sound /ā/; they both have *ai*.) Tell children that the letters *ai* are also used to spell the sound /ā/.

Review the Generalization for /ī/igh Follow a similar procedure for words 7 and 8. Remind children that the letters *igh* are sometimes used to spell the long vowel sound of *i*, /ī/.

Review the High-Frequency Words Point out that the words *learn* and *join* do not follow the same patterns as the other words.

BELOW-LEVEL	ADVANCED
Group the Spelling Words according to the letter patterns *ay*, *ai*, and *igh*, dictate the words one group at a time, and have children write the words. Tell children which group you'll be dictating. Knowing which group each word is in will help children spell the words and reinforce letter pattern recognition.	Have pairs of children dictate sentences with the Spelling Words to each other. Have one partner dictate while the other writes the words. Have children change roles. Then have them self-check.

Vocabulary

REVIEW WORDS IN CONTEXT

Read Words in Context Write the following sentences on tagboard strips. Use different colors either for the print or for the paper. Display the strips and the *Picture Card frog.* Track the print as you read the sentences aloud. Then ask a volunteer to read aloud the first two sentences. Have two other volunteers read the third and fourth sentences. Repeat several times.

> REVIEW
> **Vocabulary**
> caught   near
> hurried   son

Frog's father said, "Son, it's raining outside.

Don't get caught in the rain."

Frog stayed near the house.

When it started to rain, Frog hurried home.

High-Frequency Words

Words to Remember

WORD WALL

Match Words Hold up *Word Cards* with the words *cold* and *sure.* Ask volunteers to find and point to these words posted on the display. Have children read each word aloud and use it in an oral sentence. You also may wish to have children distinguish between two similar-looking words, such as *cold* and *could* or *sure* and *she.*

> REVIEW
> **High-Frequency Words**
> cold   sure

cold

sure

BELOW-LEVEL

Have children work in a small group with the sentence strips. Read each sentence aloud. Then repeat the vocabulary word in the sentence *(Son, caught, near, hurried)* and have children point to that word.

ADVANCED

Have children write their own sentence for each vocabulary word. Then pairs of children can play a game, taking turns reading one of their sentences aloud, but saying *Dee deep* instead of the vocabulary word. The partner responds by telling which word makes sense in the sentence.

ENGLISH-LANGUAGE LEARNERS

Pantomime each sentence as you read it aloud. (You might want to draw a simple outline of a house on the board as a prop for sentences 3 and 4.) Reread the sentences, encouraging children to act them out along with you. Then reread the sentences one more time, this time pausing to let children supply each vocabulary word.

▲ *Pupil Edition,* pp. 40–56

FLUENCY ROUTINES For support, see Fluency Routine Cards in Theme Resources, pp. T83–T84.

Rereading for Fluency

GROUPS

Readers Theatre

● **ADVANCED** Have children work in groups of three. Two children can use the Character Cutouts of Frog and Toad (page T18) as they read the parts of those characters, while the third child can read the rest of the text. Remind children to read with expression. Tell children who are reading the parts of Frog and Toad to think about what the characters' voices might sound like.

INDEPENDENT

Managing Small Groups

Reread for fluency with children working individually, with partners, or in small groups. While you work with small groups, have other children do the following:

• **Self-Selected Reading**

• **Practice Pages**

• **Cross-Curricular Centers**

• **Journal Writing**

Use the suggested Classroom Management outline on page 7C for the whole-group/small-group schedule.

PARTNERS

Partner Reading

⦿ **ON-LEVEL** Have partners take turns reading two-page spreads of "Frog and Toad All Year." Before turning to the next page, the partner who was listening can point out details in the illustrations on that spread that helped him or her understand what the other child was reading. INDEPENDENT

INDIVIDUALS

Tape-Assisted Reading

⦿ **BELOW-LEVEL/ENGLISH-LANGUAGE LEARNERS** Help individual children use *Audiotext 5* to practice reading "Frog and Toad All Year." Play a brief passage as the child follows along, and then have the child read the same passage aloud. If the child reads the passage fairly well, go directly to the next passage. If the child seems to have difficulty understanding what was read, discuss confusing parts of the passage and then have the child reread it before going on to the next passage. If the child has difficulty pronouncing the words or stumbles over many of them, replay the passage and have the child repeat again before going on to the next passage. TEACHER-DIRECTED

Frogs
in Trees?
by Mark Warner

What do you think of when you think of frogs? Things that hop, right? Well how about things that *climb*? Some frogs climb bushes and trees. These frogs are called *tree frogs*.

60

61

Reading Across Texts

READ A SCIENCE ARTICLE

Build Background Find out what children already know about tree frogs. Ask children what they think tree frogs look like. Ask how children think tree frogs might be like frogs that live near water and how they might be different. List their ideas on the board or on chart paper.

Preview/Predict Have children read the title and preview the illustrations. Tell them that "Frogs in Trees?" is an article and elicit information about what an article is. Ask children if they can tell from the pictures what they will learn from this article.

Set Purpose/Read Help children set a purpose for reading, such as to find out why frogs would be in trees. Then read aloud "Frogs in Trees?" while children follow along.

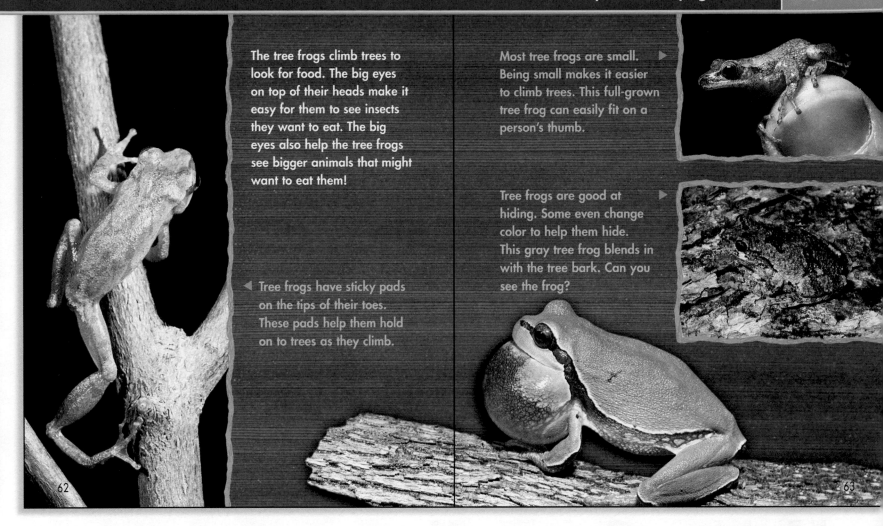

The tree frogs climb trees to look for food. The big eyes on top of their heads make it easy for them to see insects they want to eat. The big eyes also help the tree frogs see bigger animals that might want to eat them!

◀ Tree frogs have sticky pads on the tips of their toes. These pads help them hold on to trees as they climb.

Most tree frogs are small. ▶ Being small makes it easier to climb trees. This full-grown tree frog can easily fit on a person's thumb.

Tree frogs are good at ▶ hiding. Some even change color to help them hide. This gray tree frog blends in with the tree bark. Can you see the frog?

62   63

SUMMARIZE/EXTEND

Check Understanding Find out what children know about tree frogs. Ask children why tree frogs climb trees and what features help tree frogs do different things they need to do. Lead children to summarize the article. Ask what else they would like to know about tree frogs and how they might find out more.

SCIENCE

Make Tree Frog Models Organize children into groups of three or four. Give each group enough modeling clay for each child to make a frog. Identify a surface onto which they can safely press the clay frogs, such as a metal file cabinet. Have children follow the directions on the card. Discuss whether a big or small frog is better suited to be a tree frog.

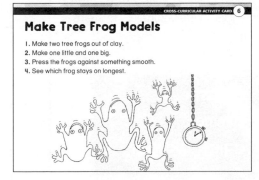

CROSS-CURRICULAR ACTIVITY CARD **6**

Make Tree Frog Models

1. Make two tree frogs out of clay.
2. Make one little and one big.
3. Press the frogs against something smooth.
4. See which frog stays on longest.

▲ Cross-Curricular Activity Card, p. T13

Teacher Read-Aloud

▲ Frog and Toad All Year

Making Connections

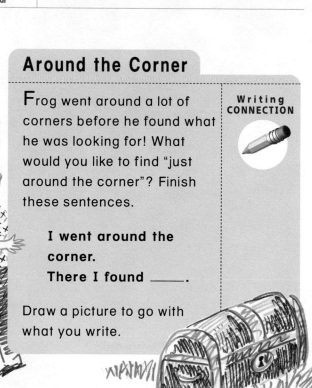

Around the Corner

Writing CONNECTION

Frog went around a lot of corners before he found what he was looking for! What would you like to find "just around the corner"? Finish these sentences.

I went around the corner.
There I found _____.

Draw a picture to go with what you write.

64

Making Connections

A Frog's Life

You have learned some things about real frogs. Find out something else about frogs. Share what you learn.

Science/ Technology CONNECTION

Jump and Measure

Jump like a frog as far as you can. Have two friends measure with yarn how far you jumped. Take turns. Then compare pieces of yarn. Who jumped the farthest?

Math CONNECTION

65

Making Connections

WRITING

Around the Corner Have children brainstorm a list of things they would like to find. Tell them that their idea can be an actual object, or it can be something as unusual as spring—or even more unusual. Read the sentences with children and tell them to choose an idea from the list or another idea of their own to finish the sentences. Invite volunteers to share their writing.

> a castle
> summer
> a new bicycle

SCIENCE/TECHNOLOGY

A Frog's Life Remind children that they learned some things about real frogs in "Where Do Frogs Come From?" and in "Frogs in Trees?" Ask them to use library books or the Internet to find new facts about frogs. They can share their information with classmates orally or in writing.

 Information about frogs can be found on *The Learning Site* at **www.harcourtschool.com.**

MATH

Jump and Measure Organize children in groups of three. Mark a starting line with masking tape and provide each group with yarn. Have one child jump while another holds one end of the yarn at the starting line. Then the third member of the group walks to where the jumper landed and cuts the yarn. Have children tape their name to their piece of yarn. When all have jumped, they can compare their pieces of yarn.

Comprehension

Details

TEACH/MODEL

Develop Concepts Remind children that the details in a story help make the story more interesting. Read aloud pages 42–43 of "Frog and Toad All Year."

MODEL The author could have just told us that Toad is upset and Frog is nice to him, but I thought the details the author gave to let us know those things were much more interesting. How did he let us know that Toad is upset? (Toad says that the day is spoiled.) What details tell us that Frog is nice to Toad? (Frog offers Toad tea and cake; he says that the rain will stop; he tells Toad to stand near the stove to dry his clothes; he tells Toad a story.)

PRACTICE/APPLY

Reread for Details Ask children what Frog looks for in "Frog and Toad All Year." (spring) Tell children to look through the story for details that tell about where Frog goes as he looks for spring and what he finds in each place.

List Story Details Help children complete a chart on the board to list the details they find.

Where Frog Went	What Frog Found
woods	pine tree, three pebbles, dry grass
meadow	worm asleep on a tree stump
river	wet mud, lizard chasing his tail
home	spring—birds singing, mother and father in garden, flowers

▲ *Pupil Edition*, pp. 40–57

OBJECTIVE

To note details in a story

SKILL TRACE

DETAILS	
Introduce	Bk 1-1, 49A, 65A
Reteach	S36, T13
Review	Bk 1-2, 85A, 101A, 105I; 135A, 155A, 159I
MAINTAIN	**65A, 171A**

ENGLISH-LANGUAGE LEARNERS

If children have difficulty naming details from the story, have them point them out in the pictures. Name each detail as it is pointed out. Then write it on the board and read it aloud. Have children repeat the detail as you track the print.

Frog and Toad All Year **65A**

LANGUAGE ARTS

5-DAY WRITING	
DAY 1	SHARED: "I Learned" List
DAY 2	INTERACTIVE: Story Response
DAY 3	**INDEPENDENT: Dialogue**
DAY 4	CROSS-CURRICULAR: Report
DAY 5	INDEPENDENT: Lists

DAILY LANGUAGE PRACTICE

Mom and i sayl away.

Mom and <u>I</u> <u>sail</u> away.

Writing Resources

 Writing Express™ CD-ROM, Post Office, Gizmos and Gadgets

journal writing

Writing Prompt Have children write a sentence about something they might say to a friend they like to do things with.

ADVANCED

Children can extend their dialogue by adding more pages with additional speech balloons.

ENGLISH-LANGUAGE LEARNERS

Children can draw pictures in their speech balloons for words they don't know. Then have them tell you what their characters are saying. Write the words under the pictures to help children make visual associations.

Writing

Dialogue

GENERATE IDEAS

Brainstorm Ask children to listen to what Frog and Toad say to each other as you reread page 55 of "Frog and Toad All Year." After reading the last sentence, *Frog and Toad hurried outside,* ask children to think of things Frog and Toad might do next. List children's ideas on the board. Children might recall some ideas that were suggested, but not used, for the group story on Day 2.

> plant a garden
> have a picnic
> go swimming

Write Dialogue Tell children to choose a topic from the list. Have them draw Frog and Toad, or let them use copies of the Character Cutouts on page T18 to glue onto paper. Then ask children to think of things Frog and Toad could say to each other about their new activity. Have children write in speech balloons what they want Frog and Toad to say.

Handwriting Suggest that children write each sentence on scrap paper first and then copy it neatly onto their paper and draw a speech balloon around it.

Grammar

Verbs

5-DAY GRAMMAR

DAY 1	Introduce Verbs
DAY 2	Use Verbs in Sentences
DAY 3	**Interesting Verbs**
DAY 4	Verb Game
DAY 5	Identify Verbs

Day 3

REVIEW

Interesting Verbs Make word cards for *She, goes, to, the*, and *house* and a punctuation card with a period. Form the following sentence in a pocket chart and have children read it. Ask which word is a verb. *(goes)*

Make word cards for *runs, skips,* and *climbs*. Remove the card for *goes* and replace it with *runs*.

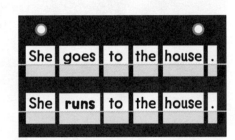

Ask children which sentence is more interesting. Point out that *runs* gives us a clearer idea of how someone goes to the house. Repeat with *skips* and *climbs*. Ask children what kind of house someone might climb to.

Have children suggest other verbs to tell how someone might go somewhere. List the verbs on the board. Then have children use the verbs to make more sentences. Remind them to say who, which verb, and where the person or people are going.

SKILL TRACE

	VERBS	
Introduce	38N	
Reteach	T5	
REVIEW	59C, 65C, 67D, 67N	
T Test	Bk 1-5	

ADVANCED

List the following verbs: *say, eat, take*. Have children write a simple sentence with each of the verbs and then rewrite the sentence using a more interesting verb.

WRAP UP Revisit Literature

Connect Ideas Across Texts Remind children that they read "Frogs in Trees?" and listened to a poem about a tree frog. Review "The Tree Frog" from page 59E, encouraging children to join in on lines they remember. Ask what is different about the poem and "Frogs in Trees?" Discuss what children learned from each. Ask if they think the poem is meant to teach a lot about frogs or if it is just for fun.

Author's Chair Invite children to sit in the Author's Chair and read aloud their sets of Frog and Toad dialogue.

S.S.R.
Sustained Silent Reading

Have children read silently from a book of their choice. See page 67L for tips on helping children choose books.

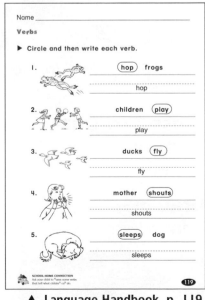

Verbs
► Circle and then write each verb.

1. (hop) frogs
   hop
2. children (play)
   play
3. ducks (fly)
   fly
4. mother (shouts)
   shouts
5. (sleeps) dog
   sleeps

▲ Language Handbook, p. 119

Frog and Toad All Year **65C**

Day at a Glance
Day 4

Sharing Literature
Poem: "River Winding"

Phonemic Awareness
Phoneme Substitution/Deletion;
Focus on /ā/

Phonics
Build Words

Spelling
Review

Vocabulary
REVIEW: *caught, hurried, near, son*

High-Frequency Words
REVIEW: *cold, sure*

Reading

Reread the Selection
Pupil Edition
"Frog and Toad All Year," pp. 40–56

PHONICS: Long Vowel /ā/ *ai, ay,*
pp. 66–67

Cross-Curricular Writing ✎
Report

Grammar
REVIEW: Verbs

WARM UP
MORNING MESSAGE

Good Morning!

Today is _____.

We wonder about _____.

We say, "What _____?"

We say, "Where _____?"

Introduce the Day
Point out to children that a good way to explore new things is to ask questions. Tell children that today they will listen to a poem that asks questions about things the poet wants to know. Guide children in generating a message about wondering and asking questions. Ask:

• **What are some things you wonder about?**

• **What questions might we ask that begin with the word *What*?**

• **What questions might we ask that begin with the word *Where*?**

As you write the message, ask volunteers to write previously taught letters, words, and/or punctuation to reinforce skills. For example, have a volunteer write *We say*. Other volunteers can write the question mark at the end of each question.

Read the Message
Read the message. Use the message to focus on selected skills that have been previously taught.

Apply Skills

Phonics Ask children to point out and read words with the sound /ā/, such as *Today* and *say*. You may want to point out that the *a* in the words *about* and *what* has a different sound.

Grammar/Mechanics Point out the quotation marks and remind children that these marks are used to show what someone is saying.

Sharing Literature

BUILD CONCEPT VOCABULARY

Connect to Prior Knowledge Tell children you are going to read a poem that contains many questions. Read "River Winding."

Word-Learning Strategy Tell children they can use what they know about rivers to understand the meaning of *winding*. Say: *Rivers don't always flow in a straight line. Sometimes rivers turn and twist as they flow around hills or mountains.* Guide children to use this information to tell what *winding* means—"turning and twisting." Draw a winding line to illustrate. Then reread the poem and have children visualize the winding river.

River Winding

Rain falling, what things do
 you grow?
Snow melting, where do
 you go?
Wind blowing, what trees do
 you know?
River winding, where do
 you flow?

Charlotte Zolotow

Phonemic Awareness

PHONEME SUBSTITUTION/DELETION

Words from "River Winding" Say the word *grow* from the poem and ask children to name the final vowel sound. (ō) Then ask children to change the sound /ō/ to /ā/ to make a new word. *(gray)* Follow the same procedure with these words:

mow (may)   **bow** (bay)   **sow** (say)   **dough** (day)

Next, have children repeat the word *grow* and then ask them to take away the beginning sound to make a new word. *(row)* Use the same procedure with the following words:

snow (no)   **go** (oh)   **blow** (low)   **crow** (row)

FOCUS ON /ā/

Distinguish Phonemes Tell children that you will say words that have the long vowel sound of *a*. Ask children to tell whether /ā/ is heard at the beginning, in the middle, or at the end of each word. Model by saying *Where is /ā/ heard in* sail? (middle). Continue with the following words:

mail (middle)   **day** (end)   **way** (end)   **aim** (beginning)
bake (middle)   **age** (beginning)   **late** (middle)   **may** (end)

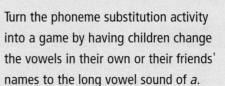

ADVANCED

Turn the phoneme substitution activity into a game by having children change the vowels in their own or their friends' names to the long vowel sound of *a*.

ENGLISH-LANGUAGE LEARNERS

Visit *The Learning Site:*
www.harcourtschool.com
See Language Support.

OBJECTIVES

- *To discriminate among the sound-letter relationships /ā/ai, ay, and a-e*

- *To read and write words with ai, ay, and a-e*

SKILL TRACE

	/ā/ai, ay	/ā/a-e
Introduce	38I–38L	Bk 1-4, 36I–36L
Reteach	S10, T4	Bk 1-4, S10, T4
Review	38Q–38R,	Bk 1-4, 36Q–36R,
	59F–59G	61F–61G, 63E–63F, 151F
REVIEW	**65F**	
MAINTAIN		**Bk 1-5, 65F, 183E**
T Test	Bk 1-5	Bk 1-5

Phonics Resources

Phonics Express™ CD-ROM, Level B Sparkle/Route 5/Harbor

Phonics
Build Words ✔ *Review*

WORD BUILDING

Build and Read Words Use a pocket chart and *Letter Cards a, c, e, i, l, m, n, p,* and *y.* Display the letters *m, a,* and *y* in the pocket chart and ask children which letters stand for the long vowel sound of *a.*

Place the letters close together. Slide your hand slowly under the letters as you blend the sounds—/mmāā/. Then read the word naturally—*may.* Have children repeat after you.

Repeat this procedure for the word *main* and then the word *mane.* Discuss the different meanings of the words *main* and *mane.*

Ask volunteers to build new words in the pocket chart.

- Change the *m* in *mane* to *p.* Read the word.

- Add an *l* between the *p* and the *a.* Read the word.

- Take away the *e.* Add an *i* after the *a.* Read the word.

- Take away the *n.* Take away the *i.* Add *y.* Read the word.

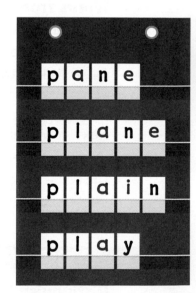

Continue word building with this word sequence: *lay, lane, cane, came, claim, clay.*

Review the Skill Have children turn to pages 66-67 in their *Pupil Edition.* Read to them the information about long vowel /ā/ai, ay and discuss the questions on the page. Then model the test items by reading aloud the questions and discussing the answer choices. Use the tip on the page to help children select the correct answer.

Words with *ai* and *ay* (Phonics Skill)

Teacher Read-Aloud

▲ Frog and Toad All Year

You know the long sound of **a** spelled a-e in words like **cake** and **game**.

The letters **ai** and **ay** can also stand for the long sound of **a**. Here are some words from "Frog and Toad All Year."

rain	waiting	tail
gray	day	

Put these groups of letters in order to make two words with the long sound of **a**.

y t s a	i a n m

You may want to use your Word Builder.

66

Test Prep

Long Vowel: /ā/ *ai, ay*

1. Choose a word that names the picture.

train   tape   tray
○   ○   ○

2. Choose a word that names the picture.

sale   snail   snack
○   ○   ○

Tip
Look at the words carefully. Read each word from beginning to end.

67

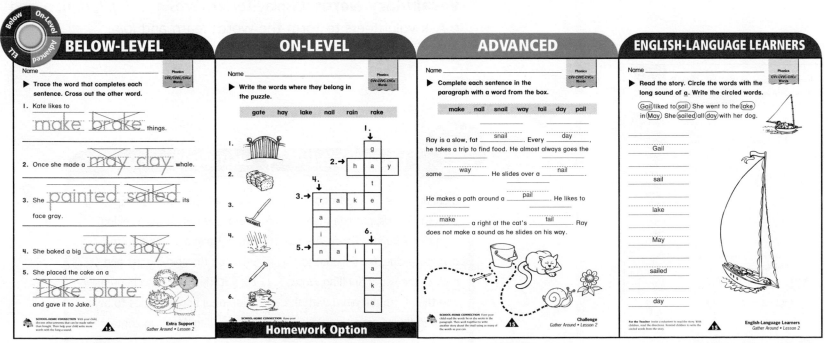

BELOW-LEVEL

▲ Extra Support, p. 15

ON-LEVEL

▲ Practice, p. 15

Homework Option

ADVANCED

▲ Challenge, p. 15

ENGLISH-LANGUAGE LEARNERS

▲ ELL, p. 15

Spelling Words

1. day
2. say
3. sail
4. pail
5. pay
6. play
7. right
8. high
9. learn
10. join

Spelling

5-DAY SPELLING

DAY 1	Pretest; Word Sort
DAY 2	Word Building
DAY 3	State the Generalization
DAY 4	**Review**
DAY 5	Posttest; Writing Application

REVIEW

Spelling Words Use a pocket chart and *Letter Cards* to form words. Have children listen to your directions and change one letter in each word to spell a Spelling Word. Have them write the Spelling Word on a sheet of paper or in their journal. Then have a volunteer change the *Letter Card* in the pocket chart so that children can self-check the word.

- Form *dad* in the pocket chart and have children read it aloud. **Which Spelling Word is made with one letter changed?** *(day)*

- Form *soil* in the pocket chart and have children read it aloud. **Which Spelling Word is made with one letter changed?** *(sail)*

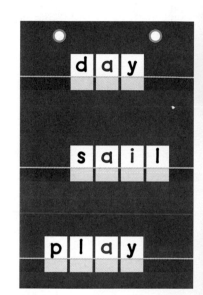

- Form *clay* in the pocket chart and have children read it aloud. **Which Spelling Word is made with one letter changed?** *(play)*

Follow a similar procedure with the following words: *light (right), sigh (high), sat (say), pain (pail), pad (pay).*

Vocabulary Words Display *Letter Cards a, e, i, j, l, n, n, o,* and *r.* Ask volunteers to form the words *learn* and *join.*

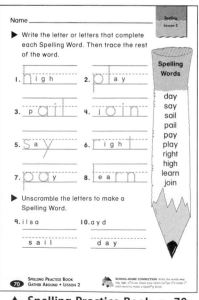

▲ Spelling Practice Book, p. 70

67A **Gather Around**

BELOW-LEVEL

If children are having trouble with the words, provide them with *Word Builder Cards.* As you give each clue, tell children to look at the list of Spelling Words and then form the word with the *Word Builder Cards.*

ENGLISH-LANGUAGE LEARNERS

Say a sentence for each Spelling Word and repeat the Spelling Word. Have children find the word on the spelling list and copy it. This will give children additional opportunities to hear the Spelling Words in context.

Vocabulary

WRITE WORDS IN STORY CONTEXT

Reinforce Word Recognition
Duplicate and distribute the Story Strips
for "Frog and Toad All Year" (page T66).
Display *Word Cards* or write the
vocabulary words on the board: *caught, hurried, near, Son.* Have
children complete the Story Strip sentences and then work with
partners to check their work.

> REVIEW
> **Vocabulary**
> caught   near
> hurried   son

> Frog and Toad were ___ in the rain.

> Frog said, "Stand ___ the stove to get dry."

> One day, Frog's dad said, "___, spring is just around the corner."

> At last, Frog and Toad ___ outside.

High-Frequency Words

WRITE WORDS IN STORY CONTEXT

Reinforce Word Recognition Display
Word Cards or write the high-frequency
words on the board: *cold, sure.* Children
can complete the Story Strip sentences
and work with their partner to check their work. After the Story
Strip sentences are completed, partners can arrange the Story
Strips in order to retell the story.

> REVIEW
> **High-Frequency Words**
> cold   sure

> They got wet and ___.

> They wanted to make ___ spring had come again.

Read

▲ *Pupil Edition,* pp. 40–56

Reread the Selection Have
children reread "Frog and Toad All
Year" after working with Story Strips to
see if they ordered the strips correctly.

REACHING ALL LEARNERS

Diagnostic Check: Vocabulary and High-Frequency Words

If... children have difficulty recognizing and reading certain new vocabulary or high-frequency words . . .

Then... help them write each word within a brief, catchy phrase that might help them remember the word. For example: *got caught, cold as ice.*

ADDITIONAL SUPPORT ACTIVITIES

BELOW-LEVEL	Reteach, p. S12
ADVANCED	Extend, p. S13
ENGLISH-LANGUAGE LEARNERS	Reteach, p. S13

LANGUAGE ARTS

5-DAY WRITING	
DAY 1	SHARED: "I Learned" List
DAY 2	INTERACTIVE: Story Response
DAY 3	INDEPENDENT: Dialogue
DAY 4	CROSS-CURRICULAR: **Report**
DAY 5	INDEPENDENT: Lists

DAILY LANGUAGE PRACTICE

Today the Sky is grae.

Today the <u>s</u>ky is <u>gray</u>.

Writing Across the Curriculum

Report

GENERATE IDEAS

Tap Prior Knowledge Review what children know about the four seasons. For each season, ask: *What is the weather like? What do you like to do in this season? What else do you know about the season?* List children's ideas on the board or on chart paper.

Winter	Spring	Summer	Fall
cold	cool	hot	cool
snowy	rainy	sunny	leaves change colors
ice-skate	splash in puddles	swim	pick apples

teaching tip

Don't assume that all children have the same experience of the seasons. Children new to the area might have lived in places where the climate is quite different. Children may or may not think of winter as snowy and spring as rainy. They may or may not have observed leaves changing color in the fall.

DRAFT

Write a Report Have children use the ideas on the list to write a short report on one of the four seasons. Encourage children to write at least two or three sentences.

journal writing

Self-Selected Writing Have children write in their journal about a topic of their choice.

ADVANCED	ENGLISH-LANGUAGE LEARNERS
Have children write about all four seasons, writing one sentence that lists the seasons and one or two sentences about each season.	Have children tell which season they want to write about. Write at the bottom of a sheet of paper: *In winter (spring, summer, fall),* _____. Have children draw a picture above the sentence or paste a picture from a magazine. Then help them complete the sentence by writing two or three words that go with the picture.

Grammar

Verbs

5-DAY GRAMMAR

DAY 1	Introduce Verbs
DAY 2	Use Verbs in Sentences
DAY 3	Interesting Verbs
DAY 4	**Verb Game**
DAY 5	Identify Verbs

Day 4

REVIEW

Play "Name This Verb" Ask a volunteer to think of a verb and a word that rhymes with it. Then have the volunteer say a clue for the verb and have children try to guess the verb. Model by saying: *This is something you do after school. It rhymes with* clay. *(play)* The child who correctly identifies the verb can go next. If children need help thinking of verbs and rhyming words, you might make the following suggestions: *run-fun; walk-talk, jump-pump, read-need, swim-him.*

WRAP UP — Sing a Song

Create New Verses for a Song Have children join in singing one or two verses of the song "I Wish I Was a Mole in the Ground." Then ask children what they would include in singing verses about a frog or a toad or springtime. You may want to model by singing the following for children:

▲ "I Wish I Was a Mole in the Ground," pp. 134–135

> I wish I was a frog in a bog,
> I wish I was a frog in a bog.
> If I was a frog in a bog,
> I'd leap from log to log,
> And I wish I was a frog in a bog.

After singing the new verse, have children create verses of their own to sing.

S.S.R.
Sustained Silent Reading

Have children read silently from a book of their choice. See page 67L for tips on helping children choose books.

SKILL TRACE

VERBS	
Introduce	38N
Reteach	T5
REVIEW	**59C, 65C, 67D, 67N**
T Test	Bk 1-5

BELOW-LEVEL

Below · On-Level · Advanced · ELL

If children have trouble identifying verbs, have them whisper their word to you or write it down and show it to you before they make up their clue. Ask: *Is this something you do?* If the child can correctly answer *yes*, provide help as needed to create a clue. If not, have the child choose another word and repeat the process.

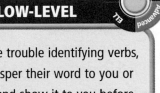

Name _____

Verbs

► Circle the verb in each sentence. Then write the word.

1. We (climb) the hill. ___climb___
2. We (hike) on a path. ___hike___
3. Our dog (runs) up the hill, too. ___runs___
4. We (rest) at the top. ___rest___
5. We (eat) our fruit and cake. ___eat___

120

▲ Language Handbook, p. 120

Sharing Literature
Big Book: *I Swam with a Seal*

Phonemic Awareness
Final Phoneme Deletion; Focus on
/ā/, /l/, /n/

Phonics
Phonograms *-ail,-ain;*
Inflections *-ed, -ing* (drop e)

Spelling
Posttest; Writing Application

Vocabulary
REVIEW: *caught, hurried, near, son*

High-Frequency Words
REVIEW: *cold, sure*

Reading
Rereading for Fluency
Pupil Edition
   "Frog and Toad All Year," pp. 40–56

Self-Selected Reading

Read

FROG and TOAD
ALL YEAR
by Arnold Lobel

Independent Writing ✏
Lists

Grammar
REVIEW: Verbs

WARM UP MORNING MESSAGE
Good Morning!

Today is _____.

We would like to play with _____ and _____.

We might play a game of _____.

To be safe, we should play only with _____.

Introduce the Day

Tell children that today they will revisit the story *I Swam with a Seal.*
Ask children to imagine themselves exploring new places and playing
with animals there. Ask:

• **What kinds of animals do you like to imagine playing with?**

• **What kinds of games could you play with those animals?**

• **What kinds of animals can you really play with?**

As you write the message, ask volunteers to write previously taught
letters, words, and/or punctuation. For example, have volunteers
write the word *play.* Point out that it is not safe to play with wild
animals or animals you aren't familiar with.

Read the Message

Read the message. Use the message to focus on selected skills that
have been previously taught.

Apply Skills

Phonics Point out the words
Today, play, and *safe* and ask children to name the vowel sound in
those words. Then have children
suggest other words with the
sound /ā/. List them in columns
according to their spellings: *ay, ai,*
or *a-e.*

Grammar Ask volunteers to
point to and read the word in
each of the last three sentences
that tells what someone or
something does.

Sharing Literature

LISTEN AND RESPOND

Review the Book Display *I Swam with a Seal*. Ask a volunteer to summarize what the book is about. (Children do different things with different animals.) Reread the big book as children listen to recall what the children do with each animal.

Respond to Literature Ask children which parts of the story they like most and least, and have them explain why.

Visualize Tell children to think about the animals in the story. Then tell them to picture themselves in the story and think about seeing an animal, either one from the story or one of their choice. Ask: *What animal are you seeing? Where are you seeing it? What are you doing? What question does it ask you?*

Phonemic Awareness

FINAL PHONEME DELETION

Words from the Big Book Tell children that you will say some words from *I Swam with a Seal*, and that you want them to say a new word by leaving out the last sound of each word. Model with the word *pine*. Say *pine* without the /n/. (pie) Continue with the following words:

Say *seal* without the /l/. (sea)   **Say *meal* without the /l/.** (me)
Say *stone* without the /n/. (stow) **Say *moose* without the /s/.** (moo)
Say *bark* without the /k/. (bar)   **Say *shone* without the /n/.** (show)

FOCUS ON /ā/, /l/, /n/

Phoneme Substitution Tell children that you will say a word and they will change the ending sound to make a new word. Model the first item by saying *mail*. *If I change /l/ to /n/, I get* main. Continue the procedure with the following words:

Change /l/ to /n/. What is the word?

mail (main)   **rail** (rain)   **pail** (pain)   **trail** (train)

▲ **Big Book**

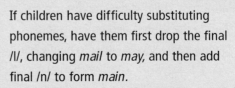

BELOW-LEVEL

If children have difficulty substituting phonemes, have them first drop the final /l/, changing *mail* to *may*, and then add final /n/ to form *main*.

OBJECTIVES

- *To discriminate between words with different patterns*

- *To use common vowel spelling patterns to read words*

SKILL TRACE

Phonograms -ail, -ain	
INTRODUCE	**67G**
Reteach	S10

Phonics Resources

***Phonics Express™* CD-ROM, Level B** Roamer/Route 6/Harbor

Phonics Practice Book, pp. 308–311

BELOW-LEVEL

Write on separate cards words with -*ail* and -*ain*. First read the -*ail* words with children, elongating the sounds. Then do the same with the -*ain* words. Mix the cards and have children take turns picking a card and reading the word.

ENGLISH-LANGUAGE LEARNERS

Slowly say the words *pail, snail, nail, mail, rain, train, stain,* and *drain,* elongating the sounds and pointing to the phonogram. Have children repeat each word. If the word is in the children's picture dictionary, have them look at the picture as they say the word. If not, have children draw a picture and add it to their own picture dictionary.

WORD WORK

Phonics
Phonograms *-ail, -ain*

WORKING WITH PATTERNS

Listen for Rhyming Words Say the words *fail* and *tail*. Ask children how the words are the same. (They both end with /āl/; they rhyme.) Using the words *hail, rain, pail, stain,* and *sail,* have children show "thumbs up" when they hear a word that rhymes with *tail.*

Then say *gain* and *main*. Ask how these words are the same. (They both end with /ā/; they rhyme.) Have children show "thumbs up" when they hear a word that rhymes with *gain*. Say *bail, plain, rail, chain,* and *train*.

Discriminate Sounds As you read the following words, have children say whether each one rhymes with *tail* or *gain*.

    fail   jail   main   pain   mail   rain   rail   brain

Build Words Write -*ail* and -*ain* at the head of two columns on chart paper. Have children suggest words that end with either -*ail* or -*ain* and name the beginning letter or letters. Have children read each word as it is added to the chart. Then have children read both sets of words in the final list. End the activity by playing a game in which you point to words at random and children call out the words you point to.

-ail	-ain
pail	rain
trail	grain
snail	train
nail	Spain
jail	plain
mail	stain

APPLY PHONICS SKILLS

Write Words with *-ail* and *-ain* Have children write in their journal at least one word for each phonogram. Then have them write sentences using their words.

Inflections *-ed, -ing*

5-DAY PHONICS

DAY 1	Introduce /ā/*ai, ay*
DAY 2	Word Building with /ā/*ai, ay*
DAY 3	Word Building with /ā/*ai, ay*
DAY 4	Word Building with /ā/*ai, ay*, and *a-e*
DAY 5	**Phonograms *-ail, -ain* Inflections *-ed, -ing***

REVIEW

Review Inflections *-ed* and *-ing* Write the following words in a column on the board: *chase, skate, hike, close.* Ask children how to change *chase* before adding *-ed* to the word. (Drop the final e.) Write *chased* next to *chase.* Repeat for *-ing*, writing *chasing* next to *chased.* Then have children tell you how to write the other words when you add *-ed* and *-ing.*

chase	chased	chasing
skate		
hike		
close		

Remind children that the ending *-ed* added to a word can stand for the sounds /t/, /d/, or /ed/.

APPLY PHONICS SKILLS

Write Sentences with *-ed* and *-ing* Words Have children write in their journal four sentences with two of the *-ed* words and two of the *-ing* words they made.

OBJECTIVE

To review the inflections -ed *and* -ing

SKILL TRACE

Inflections *-ed, -ing* (drop final e)	
Introduce	Bk 1-4, 65F
REVIEW	**37F, 67H, 155F**
T Test	Bk 1-5

BELOW-LEVEL

If children have trouble with *-ed* and *-ing* inflections, work with them using additional words. *(race, vote, bake, wipe, name)*

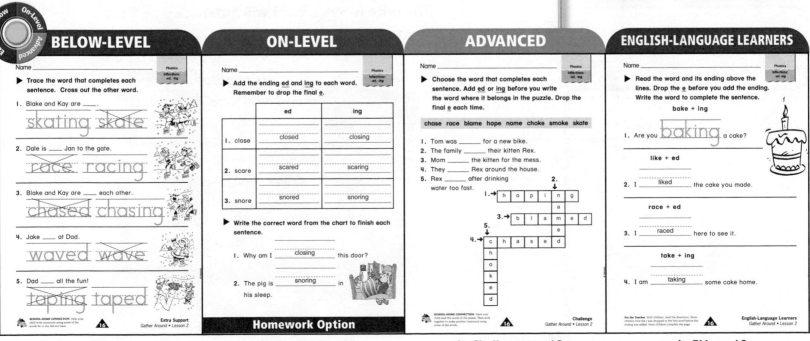

▲ Extra Support, p. 16   ▲ Practice, p. 16   ▲ Challenge, p. 16   ▲ ELL, p. 16

Spelling Words

1. **day**
2. **say**
3. **sail**
4. **pail**
5. **pay**
6. **play**
7. **right**
8. **high**
9. **learn**
10. **join**

BELOW-LEVEL

To help children see the various word patterns, have them write the Spelling Words using different colors: the letters *ai* and *ay* in red, *igh* in blue, and all the other letters in black or pencil.

ADVANCED

Have children write their own sentence for each Spelling Word. Have children share their sentences with a partner.

WORD WORK

Spelling

5-DAY SPELLING	
DAY 1	Pretest; Word Sort
DAY 2	Word Building
DAY 3	State the Generalization
DAY 4	Review
DAY 5	**Posttest; Writing Application**

ASSESS/APPLY

Posttest Assess children's progress using the words and the Dictation Sentences from Day 1.

1. **day**   This is a rainy **day**.
2. **say**   I want to **say** something.
3. **sail**   We will **sail** on the boat.
4. **pail**   Jane put sand in her **pail**.
5. **pay**   I want to **pay** for this book.
6. **play**   After school, you can **play**.

Review

7. **right**   We always try to do what is **right**.
8. **high**   The airplane flew very **high**.

Vocabulary

9. **learn**   Our class will **learn** a lot.
10. **join**   Ray is going to **join** the Math Club.

Writing Application Have children complete and illustrate the following sentence frames:

I will _____ my boat.

I like to _____ in the sand with my _____.

The price is too _____. I will not _____.

Vocabulary

USE WORDS IN SENTENCES

REVIEW
Vocabulary
caught   near
hurried   son

Reinforce Usage Display *Word Cards* or list the following words on the board: *caught, hurried, near, son.* Ask volunteers to use each word in a sentence. Have children create sentences that use the words in a context other than that of "Frog and Toad All Year." Record at least one sentence for each word on the board. Track the print as you read the sentences to children.

caught   hurried   near   son

ADVANCED

Ask children to write sentences that use two or more of the vocabulary words.

ENGLISH-LANGUAGE LEARNERS

Work with children individually. Say each word and have the child pantomime an action or point to something appropriate for each word. This will increase children's familiarity with the words and will help you assess their understanding of the words.

High-Frequency Words

Words to Remember
WORD WALL

Complete Sentences Have children use the displayed words to complete the following sentences. Have volunteers frame the words as children read them aloud.

REVIEW
High-Frequency Words
cold   sure

It is too ___ to stay outside. *(cold)*
Make ___ you put on a coat. *(sure)*

▲ *Pupil Edition,* pp. 40–56

FLUENCY ROUTINES For
support, see Fluency Routine Cards in
Theme Resources, pp. T83–T84.

teaching tip

Fluent readers read quickly, accurately,
and smoothly; they self-correct efficiently.
Keep these characteristics in mind as you
model fluent reading and plan for further
instruction.

Rereading for Fluency

GROUPS

Choral Reading

ON-LEVEL/BELOW-LEVEL Have children form small groups to
choral read "Frog and Toad All Year." Help children decide how to
divide the text among the groups. Assign the pages and have children
practice reading. Then have them reread the selection aloud. As
children practice, help them with words, sentences, or parts of the
story that are giving them trouble. TEACHER-DIRECTED

PARTNERS

Repeated Reading

**ADVANCED/ENGLISH-LANGUAGE
LEARNERS** Have partners practice reading aloud
two consecutive pages from their favorite part of the story.
Explain that readers should practice reading the pages aloud two or
three times, trying to read more smoothly and expressively with each
reading; listeners should follow along and give feedback about how
the readers sound. After practice, bring children together and have
volunteers read for the group. INDEPENDENT

> You found it!

Managing Small Groups

Reread for fluency with children working individually, with partners, or
in small groups. While you work with small groups, have other children
do the following:

- **Self-Selected Reading**
- **Cross-Curricular Centers**
- **Practice Pages**
- **Journal Writing**

Use the suggested Classroom Management outline on page 7C for the
whole-group/small-group schedule.

Self-Selected Reading

INDEPENDENT READING

Have children choose a book from the **Browsing Boxes** or the **Reading Center** to read independently during a sustained silent reading time. Children may also want to reread a story from their *Pupil Edition.* These are some books you may want to gather that relate to "Frog and Toad All Year."

choosing books

To guide children in selecting books at their independent reading level, suggest that they read one or two pages of the book. If there are at least five words that the child can't read, he or she should try an easier book.

Decodable Books

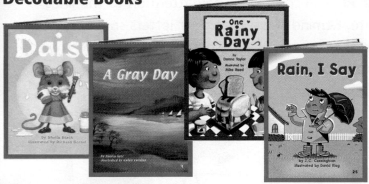

Decodable Book 28
"Daisy" by Sheila Black
"A Gray Day" by Sunita Apte
"One Rainy Day" by Donna Taylor
"Rain, I Say" by J. C. Cunningham

Cut-Out/Fold-Up Book

Frog and Mouse
Practice Book, pp. 67–68

related books

- *Henry* by F. R. Robinson. Instant Reader, Harcourt, 1997. Henry is a little different from the other members of his family. BELOW-LEVEL

- *Who Stole the Cookies?* by Judith Moffatt. Grossett & Dunlap, 1996. A series of animals deny having stolen the cookies until the thief turns up in a cave. BELOW-LEVEL

- *Frog and Toad Together* by Arnold Lobel. HarperCollins, 1972. Classic companion stories in one compilation, including "A List," "Cookies," and "The Dream." ON-LEVEL

- *Frogs* by Gail Gibbons. Holiday House, 1993. An informational book about frogs, from their beginnings as tadpoles to how they differ from toads. ADVANCED

Books for All Learners

Rainy Day Pals
by Robin Cruise

Two Snails
by Sandra Widener

Just Around the Corner
by Sandra Widener

What Season Is It?
by Kathryn E. Lewis

5-DAY WRITING

DAY 1	SHARED: "I Learned" List
DAY 2	INTERACTIVE: Story Response
DAY 3	INDEPENDENT: Dialogue
DAY 4	CROSS-CURRICULAR: Report
DAY 5	INDEPENDENT: **Lists**

DAILY LANGUAGE PRACTICE

We play with the tran

We play with the <u>train</u>.

journal  writing

Writing Prompt Have children write a sentence about an idea from their list.

Writing Resources

 Writing Express™ CD-ROM, Arcade, Gizmos and Gadgets

ENGLISH-LANGUAGE LEARNERS

Children can create a picture list. Help them label the pictures on their list. Then help them say the words aloud.

LANGUAGE ARTS

Writing

Lists

ADD TO "I LEARNED" LIST

Generate Ideas Revisit the "I Learned" list (page 38M) with children. Ask them to add to the list. Tell them to think about new things they have learned just this week as well as other things they have learned before.

Write a List Tell children to write their own list. Tell them that they can choose a topic you provide or think of their own topic. Suggest topics such as *Things to Do in Spring, Ways Animals Move,* and *My Favorite Games.*

Handwriting Remind children to pay attention to the lines when they write. Remind them that their letters should rest right on the line and their capital letters should not go above the top line. Letters such as *g, j, p, q,* and *y* should not go all the way down to the next line.

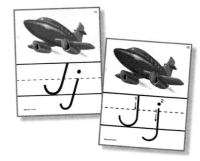
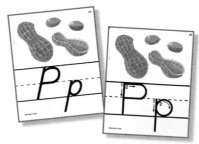

Grammar

Verbs

5-DAY GRAMMAR

DAY 1	Introduce Verbs
DAY 2	Use Verbs in Sentences
DAY 3	Interesting Verbs
DAY 4	Verb Game
DAY 5	**Identify Verbs**

REVIEW

Identify Verbs Tell children that you will write some sentences on the board. For each sentence, ask a volunteer to find the verb and act out what the verb tells.

> Jack naps.
> We read books.
> Jane plays ball.
> I walked home.
> Tom jumped.
> Kim skated.
> Kate smiled.

WRAP UP Share Ideas

Use the Author's Chair Have children share their list. Ask why they chose the topic they did. Remind speakers to read clearly and loudly enough for listeners to understand. Remind listeners to sit quietly and be attentive. After the reading, remind listeners to ask questions about the writing if there is something that they don't understand. Model how to politely ask questions for clarification.

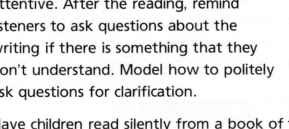

S.S.R. *Sustained Silent Reading*

Have children read silently from a book of their choice. See page 67L for tips on helping children choose books.

SKILL TRACE

VERBS

Introduce	38N
Reteach	T5
REVIEW	**59C, 65C, 67D, 67N**
T Test	Bk 1-5

ENGLISH-LANGUAGE LEARNERS

Below · On-Level · Advanced · ELL

Have children write their own name on a large index card. Have each child pantomime an action. Write the verb for that action on another card. Display both cards as the child pantomimes the action. Touch each card as you read the child's name and the verb. Then have the child repeat after you.

technology

Visit *The Learning Site:*
www.harcourtschool.com
See Go for Grammar Gold, Multimedia Grammar Glossary.

Name _____

Verbs

▶ Write the verb that completes each sentence. Use the words in the boxes.

hatch	plays	sleeps
	walks	eats

1. The chicks ____hatch____ from their eggs.

2. Mandy ____plays____ with her dog.

3. Her dad ____walks____ home.

4. The cat ____sleeps____ on the rug.

5. Her brother ____eats____ a snack.

SCHOOL-HOME CONNECTION
Ask your child to name some verbs about his or her favorite activities, such as play, read, cook.

121

▲ Language Handbook, p. 121

Books for All Learners

Reinforcing Skills and Strategies

■ BELOW-LEVEL

Rainy Day Pals

✓ **Phonics:** Long Vowels /ā/*ai, ay*

✓ **Vocabulary:** *caught, hurried*

✓ **High-Frequency Words:** *cold, sure*

✓ **Focus Skill: Cause/Effect**

SUMMARY Two friends enjoy fishing indoors when rain prevents their outdoor trip.

 Visit *The Learning Site:*
www.harcourtschool.com
See Resources for Parents and Teachers:
Books for All Learners.

BEFORE READING

Build Background Ask children to tell what they enjoy doing on a rainy day. Have them tell whom they like to be with and what activities they like.

Preview/Set Purpose Have children identify the title and help them read it. Point out the author and illustrator. Then have children look at the first few pages of the book and predict what the story is about. Have children set a purpose for reading, such as *I want to find out what the rainy day friends do.*

READING THE BOOK

Pages 2–4 How does Nick look when he arrives at Anna's house? (He is wet, wears a rain slicker, and carries an umbrella.) Why is he sad? (The two friends can't go fishing because of the rain. He thinks there is nothing to do indoors.) RELATE PICTURES TO TEXT, CAUSE/EFFECT

Pages 5–9 Why does Nick suddenly feel happier? (Anna thinks of a way to fish indoors.) What does Anna say after she fishes? ("I caught a big blue one.") What does Nick really catch? (a big red boot) CAUSE/EFFECT, SUMMARIZE

Pages 10–12 How do the two feel at the end of the story? (warm and happy) Why does Nick think rainy day friends are the best? (He knows it's easy to have fun on a sunny day, but only a best friend can make a rainy day fun.) PLOT, ANALYZE CHARACTERS

RESPONDING

Draw Rainy-Day Pictures On one side of a piece of drawing paper, have each child draw a picture of what Anna and Nick did on their rainy day. On the other side, have children draw pictures of something they like to do on a rainy day. Invite children to share their pictures and compare their fun with Anna's and Nick's.

BELOW-LEVEL

ON-LEVEL

ADVANCED

ELL

▲ p. 67Q   ▲ p. 67R

■ ON-LEVEL

Two Snails

 Phonics: Long Vowels /ā/*ai, ay*

 Vocabulary: *caught, hurried, near, son*

 High-Frequency Words: *cold, sure*

 Focus Skill: Cause/Effect

SUMMARY A mother snail and her son take a journey to see the world in a new way.

 Visit *The Learning Site:* www.harcourtschool.com
See Resources for Parents and Teachers: Books for All Learners.

BEFORE READING

Build Background Ask volunteers to tell how things look when they are seen from high up. For example, volunteers can tell what they have seen from a tall building, a tree, a Ferris wheel, or an airplane.

Preview/Set Purpose Have children identify the title and help them read it. Point out the author and illustrator. Then have children look at the first few pages of the book and predict what the story is about. Have children set a purpose for reading, such as *I want to find out if the snails leave their home.*

READING THE BOOK

Pages 2–5 What does Wally want to do? (leave home and have some fun) Why do you think Fay doesn't want to go? (Possible response: She is afraid.) DETERMINE CHARACTERS' TRAITS; DRAW CONCLUSIONS

Pages 6–10 What happens when Wally reaches the top of the drain and looks down? (He feels dizzy.) CAUSE/EFFECT

Pages 11–16 How do you know the snails will go up the drain again? (Fay tells Wally she'd like to go again, and Wally says he'd go any day.) Why do you think the author wrote this story? (Possible response: to let people know that sometimes it's okay to try new things. Accept reasonable responses. Encourage children to explain their responses.)
DRAW CONCLUSIONS, RECOGNIZE AUTHOR'S PURPOSE, EXPRESS PERSONAL OPINIONS

RESPONDING

Draw the Snails' World Have children draw pictures of the location where Fay and Wally live, first from the snails' usual perspective on the ground, and then their view of it from the top of the drain pipe. Ask children to tell partners about the pictures.

Books for All Learners

Reinforcing Skills and Strategies

■ ADVANCED

JUST AROUND THE CORNER

by Sandra Widener
illustrated by Larry Reinhart

Just Around the Corner

✓ **Phonics: Long Vowels /ā/ ai, ay**

✓ **Vocabulary: caught, hurried, near, son**

✓ **High-Frequency Words: cold, sure**

✓ **Focus Skill: Cause/Effect**

SUMMARY In this play, a pair of animals leaves its winter home to look for signs of spring.

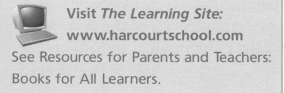

Visit *The Learning Site:*
www.harcourtschool.com

See Resources for Parents and Teachers:
Books for All Learners.

BEFORE READING

Build Background Ask children to describe how the outdoors looks and feels in different seasons. Have them tell about activities they enjoy in each season.

Preview/Set Purpose Have children identify the title and help them read it. Point out the author and illustrator. Then have children look at the first few pages and predict what the play is about. Have children set a purpose for reading, such as *I want to find out what is around the corner.*

READING THE BOOK

Pages 2–5 What does the newspaper mean by "spring is just around the corner"? (Spring is coming soon.) Why does Ray want to stay inside and wait for signs of spring? (It's raining.) What does Grace want to do? (take a trip to look for clues that spring is near) INTERPRET FIGURATIVE LANGUAGE, NOTE DETAILS

Pages 6–10 What clues does Ray notice first? (The snow has melted and the weather is warm.) What clue does Grace notice next? (A flower is blooming.) SEQUENCE

Pages 11–16 Why don't Grace and Ray need coats? (It's warm.) Why do you think Grace says, "Spring is here"? (because all of their clues led them to that conclusion) CAUSE/EFFECT, DRAW CONCLUSIONS

RESPONDING

Perform the Play Have a small group of children work together to make stick puppets of Ray and Grace. They may want to make colorful mural of the characters' springtime world as well. Encourage them to practice reading the play and then to perform it for each other.

▲ p. 67O   ▲ p. 67P

Managing Small Groups

While you work with small groups have other children do the following:

- Self-Selected Reading
- Practice Pages
- Cross-Curricular Centers
- Journal Writing

■ ENGLISH-LANGUAGE LEARNERS

What Season Is It?

 Strong Picture Support

 Concept Vocabulary

 Theme Related

SUMMARY Readers learn about the four seasons from pictures and written descriptions, and then identify them.

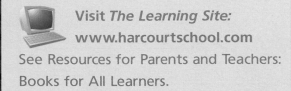

**Visit *The Learning Site:*
www.harcourtschool.com**

See Resources for Parents and Teachers: Books for All Learners.

BEFORE READING

Build Background Remind children of a few activities your class has done during the school year, and invite them to remember others. As the activities are discussed, help children recall what the weather and season were for each one.

Preview/Set Purpose Have children identify the title and help them read it. Point out the author and illustrator. Then have children look at the first few pages and predict what the book is about. Have children set a purpose for reading, such as *I want to find out if the book tells about summer.*

READING THE BOOK

Pages 2–4 Look at the trees. What happens to them? (They change color.) On page 4, what word tells the season? (*fall*) RELATE PICTURES TO TEXT, NOTE DETAILS

Pages 5–7 What season is shown on page 7? (winter) Is this kind of winter like winter in your state? Why or why not? (Possible response: No, because we don't get snow.) RELATE PICTURES TO TEXT, OFFER PERSONAL OPINIONS

Pages 8–10 What happens to flowers in the spring? (They bloom.) CAUSE/EFFECT

Pages 11–12 What is this story mostly about? (the four seasons) MAIN IDEA

RESPONDING

Pantomime the Story Reread the story aloud to the class. As you read each page, have children pantomime the actions of the children in the story. After the rereading, review the different types of weather and have children recall the outdoor activities mentioned in the story for each type of weather.

Reading Selections

BIG BOOK

DECODABLE BOOK

Applies Long Vowel i

▲ Decodable Book 29
"Hi, Green Beans!"
"Wild, Wild Things"

PUPIL EDITION

Genre

Nonfiction

Some nonfiction pieces use photographs to give information.

Look for:

• Ways the photographs add information.

• Facts about bears that may be new to you.

70

71

SUMMARY: *This nonfiction selection tells about how bears fish and prepare for winter.*

 "Fishing Bears" is available on *Audiotext 5.*

Books for
All Learners

Lesson Plans on pages 97M–97P

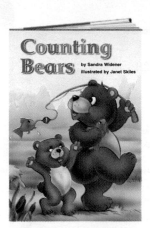

BELOW-LEVEL
- **Phonics: Long Vowel /ī/i**
- **Vocabulary: *during, ready***
- **High-Frequency Word: *both***

ON-LEVEL
- **Phonics: Long Vowel /ī/i**
- **Vocabulary: *during, ready***
- **High-Frequency Word: *both***

ADVANCED
- **Phonics: Long Vowel /ī/i**
- **Vocabulary: *during, ready***
- **High-Frequency Word: *both***

ELL
- ***Strong Picture Support***
- ***Concept Vocabulary***

MULTI-LEVELED PRACTICE

Practice Book, pp. 17–24

Extra Support, pp. 18–24

Challenge, pp. 18–24

English-Language Learners, pp. 18–24

Technology

- *Phonics Express™ CD-ROM, Level B*
- *Writing Express™ CD-ROM*
- *Grammar Jingles™ CD, Primary*
- *The Learning Site:* www.harcourtschool.com
- *Reading and Language Skills Assessment* CD-ROM

ADDITIONAL RESOURCES

Phonics Practice Book, pp. 234–235

Spelling Practice Book, pp. 71–72

Language Handbook, pp. 122–125

Read-Aloud Literature
- Big Book of Rhymes, pp. 6–7, 38–39
- Read-Aloud Anthology, pp. 55–64

Teaching Transparencies 85–87, 108

Word Builders/Word Builder Cards

Letter Cards

Intervention Resource Kit, Lesson 29

English-Language Learners Resource Kit, Lesson 29

ORAL LANGUAGE

- **Sharing Literature**

- **Phonemic Awareness**

WORD WORK

- **Phonics**

- **Spelling**

- **High-Frequency Words**

- **Vocabulary**

READING

- **Comprehension**
- **Fluency**

Daily Routines

- Morning Message
- Daily Language Practice
- Writing Prompt

- **Independent Reading**

LANGUAGE ARTS

- **Writing**

- **Grammar**

Daily Language Practice
Spiral Review

Day 1

Sharing Literature, 68H
Big Book: Listen and Respond

Phonemic Awareness, 68H
Phoneme Isolation; Focus on /ī/

 **Phonics,** 68I
Introduce: Long Vowel /ī/i

Spelling, 68K
Pretest; Word Sort **T**

High-Frequency Words, 68K
Review: *sure* **T**

Vocabulary, 68K
Review: *son* **T**

Read **Apply Phonics,** 68L

DECODABLE BOOK 29
"Hi, Green Beans!"

 Independent Reading
Books for All Learners

Writing Process, 68M
Prewriting

Writing Prompt
Have children write sentences using words from the winter web.

Grammar, 68N
Introduce: Verbs That Tell About Now **T**

Daily Language Practice
I think if is kold outside. (it, cold)

Day 2

Sharing Literature, 68P
Poem: Listen and Respond

Phonemic Awareness, 68P
Phoneme Isolation; Focus on /ī/

Phonics, 68Q
Review: Long Vowel /ī/i

Spelling, 68Q
Word Building **T**

High-Frequency Words, 68S
Introduce: *both* **T**

Vocabulary, 68S
Introduce: *during, ready* **T**

Word Power, pp. 68–69

Read **Read the Selection,** 69A

PUPIL EDITION
"Fishing Bears,"
pp. 68–93

Comprehension

 Main Idea **T**

Self-Correct

 Independent Reading
Books for All Learners

Writing Process, 93B
Drafting

Writing Prompt
Have children make a list of interesting describing words.

Grammar, 93C
Review: Verbs That Tell About Now **T**

Daily Language Practice
May we see th wild Bears? (the, bears)

Focus Skill

Main Idea

Phonics

Long Vowel /ī/i

Focus of the Week:
- HIGH-FREQUENCY WORD: *both*
- VOCABULARY: *during, ready*
- COMPREHENSION: Main Idea
- WRITING PROCESS: Poem

Day 3

Sharing Literature, 93E
Finger Play: Build Concept Vocabulary

Phonemic Awareness, 93E
Phoneme Isolation; Focus on /ĭ/

Phonics, 93F
Review: Long Vowel /ī/i
Spelling, 93H
State the Generalization **T**
High-Frequency Words, 93I
Review: *both* **T**
Vocabulary, 93I
Review: *during, ready* **T**

Read
Rereading for Fluency, 93J

Making Connections, 94–95

Apply Phonics, 93G
DECODABLE BOOK 29
"Wild, Wild Things"

⬤ **Independent Reading**
Books for All Learners

✐ **Writing Process,** 95A
Responding and Revising

Writing Prompt
Have children choose a phrase from their poem and add words to make a complete thought.
Grammar, 95B
Review: Verbs That Tell About Now **T**

Daily Language Practice
I like to pla the in snow. (play, in the)

Day 4

Sharing Literature, 95D
Poem: Build Concept Vocabulary

Phonemic Awareness, 95D
Phoneme Blending; Focus on /ī/

Phonics, 95E
Build Words
Spelling, 95G
Review **T**
High-Frequency Words, 95H
Review: *both* **T**
Vocabulary, 95H
Review: *during, ready* **T**

Read
Comprehension, 95I

Focus Skill Main Idea, **T**
pp. 96–97

⬤ **Independent Reading**
Books for All Learners

✐ **Writing Process,** 97A
Proofreading

Writing Prompt
Have children draw and write about an animal in a winter setting.

Grammar, 97B
Review: Verbs That Tell About Now **T**

Daily Language Practice
Turn the lite on again? (light, again.)

Day 5

Sharing Literature, 97D
Big Book: Listen and Respond

Phonemic Awareness, 97D
Phoneme Isolation; Focus on Inflections *-ed, -ing*

Phonics, 97E
Introduce: Inflections *-ed, -ing*
Spelling, 97G
Posttest; Writing Application **T**
High-Frequency Words, 97H
Review: *both* **T**
Vocabulary, 97H
Review: *during, ready* **T**

Read
Rereading for Fluency, 97I

Self-Selected Reading, 97J

⬤ **Independent Reading**
Books for All Learners

✐ **Writing Process,** 97K
Publishing

Self-Selected Writing
Have children write about a topic of their choice.

Grammar, 97L
Review: Verbs That Tell About Now **T**

Daily Language Practice
Where can we cach a fish. (catch, fish?)

Cross-Curricular Centers

COMPUTER CENTER

Kinds of Bears

Have children use an electronic reference with which they are familiar and search for information on different kinds of bears. If the reference software has a note function, children may use that to make a list of different kinds of bears. Otherwise children can write a list. Children may also want to include facts or illustrations for one or more of the bears on their list. (Though there is still some question of how the giant panda should be classified, allow children to include the panda since it is now often classified as a bear.)

Pandas eat bamboo.

45 Minutes

Materials

- computer; printer
- electronic reference, such as a multimedia encyclopedia or Internet access to a children's search engine

MUSIC CENTER

The Bear Went Over the Mountain

If necessary, teach children to sing "The Bear Went Over the Mountain" to the tune of "For He's a Jolly Good Fellow." Then have children create additional verses. When they are ready, have them record their song. They may want to play instruments as they sing.

30 Minutes

Materials

- tape recorder
- cassette
- musical instruments, optional

SCIENCE CENTER

Life of a River

Have children create a poster showing the fish and plants that live in or near a river. Tell children to label the different plants and animals in the river.

45 Minutes

Materials

- posterboard
- books about rivers and aquatic plants and animals
- crayons or markers

MATH CENTER

Bear Families

For each child, provide several cutouts of adult bears and cubs. Have children paste the cutouts on pieces of paper in family groups of one mother and two or three cubs. Tell children to use the bear families to practice addition and subtraction by putting the families into groups, or separating them.

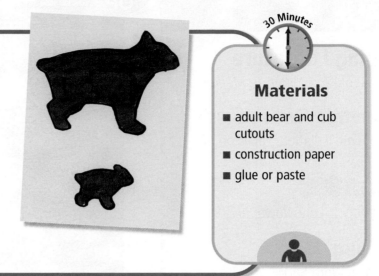

30 Minutes

Materials

■ adult bear and cub cutouts
■ construction paper
■ glue or paste

LETTER AND WORD CENTER

Missing Letters

Write long *i* words on index cards, leaving a blank for one of the letters: *wi__d, m__ne, c__ild, din__, mil__, n__ne, pin__, l__ne, spin__, pi__t.* On the reverse side write the complete word. Have children choose cards and use plastic letters or letter tiles to complete the word. Have children write each word as they form it. Children can check their work by turning over the card.

wi__d

din__

15 Minutes

Materials

■ index cards with words as indicated
■ plastic letters or letter tiles
■ paper
■ pencil

 HOMEWORK FOR THE WEEK

The Homework Copying Master provides activities to complete for each day of the week.

    Visit *The Learning Site:* www.harcourtschool.com

See Resources for Parents and Teachers: Homework Helper.

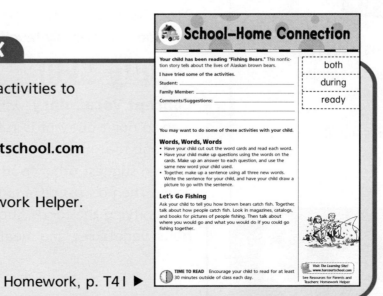

both
during
ready

Homework, p. T41 ▶

Sharing Literature
Big Book: *To Market, To Market*

Phonemic Awareness
Phoneme Isolation; Focus on /ī/

Phonics
INTRODUCE: Long Vowel /ī/*i*

Spelling
Pretest; Word Sort

Vocabulary
REVIEW: *son*

High-Frequency Word
REVIEW: *sure*

Reading
Decodable Book 29
"Hi, Green Beans!"

Read

Independent Writing
Writing Process: Prewriting

Grammar
INTRODUCE: Verbs that Tell
About Now

ORAL LANGUAGE

WARM UP MORNING MESSAGE

Good Morning!

Today is _____.

Grandma likes to make vegetable soup.

She adds _____, _____, and _____.

The soup tastes hot and _____.

Introduce the Day

Tell children that today they will once again listen to a story about a trip to a market that becomes an adventure. Ask children to imagine going to a market to buy things to make soup. Say:

- **What vegetables would you add to a pot of soup?**
- **How would you describe the taste of vegetable soup?**

As you write the message, have children write previously taught letters, words, and/or punctuation to reinforce skills. For instance, have children add the period at the end of each sentence or the words with long *a—Today, make, tastes.*

Read the Message

Read the message. Use the message to focus on selected skills that have been previously taught.

Apply Skills

Concept Vocabulary Ask children to point out words in the message that name foods. Have children suggest other foods they enjoy. Then discuss different ways of classifying the foods, such as fruits, vegetables, and meats.

Grammar/Mechanics Ask children whether there are asking or telling sentences in the message, and how they know. (Telling sentences; each ends with a period.) Then point out the commas in the third sentence; remind children that when several items are listed, they are separated by commas to make the meaning clear.

Sharing Literature

LISTEN AND RESPOND

Review the Big Book Display *To Market, To Market*, and have children recall what the story is about. Reread the big book aloud and have children chime in on sections of patterned text. Stop occasionally for children to comment on the illustrations. Have them name their favorites and tell why. Ask them how the pictures help to tell the story.

Respond to Literature Direct children to take turns acting out the role of the woman as she goes to market or chases the animals around her home. Then reread the story and have children pantomime the actions.

▲ **Big Book**

Phonemic Awareness

PHONEME ISOLATION

Words from the Big Book Tell children that you will say one word, followed by another word in which one sound has been changed. Children will tell whether the sound that changes is at the beginning, in the middle, or at the end of the word. Model by saying *coat-goat. The sound /k/ changes to /g/ at the beginning of the word.* Continue with the following words:

hen-pen (beginning)   **coop-cool** (end)
lamb-swam (beginning)   **home-hole** (end)
duck-dock (middle)   **beet-bean** (end)
goose-loose (beginning) **bad-bed** (middle)

FOCUS ON /ī/

Identify /ī/ in Words Say the word *idea* and tell what sound is heard at the beginning—/ī/ Continue with the following words:

ice (/ī/)   **island** (/ī/)   **iris** (/ī/)   **ivy** (/ī/)

Use a similar procedure with the following words. Have children identify the vowel sound in the middle.

pint (/ī/)   **wild** (/ī/)   **blind** (/ī/)   **child** (/ī/)

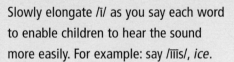

BELOW-LEVEL

Slowly elongate /ī/ as you say each word to enable children to hear the sound more easily. For example: say /īīīs/, *ice.*

ADVANCED

Have children make a new word by replacing the middle sound of a word you say with /ī/. For example, say *mend;* then have children say *mind.* Say these words: *blond (blind), fund (find),* and *paint (pint).*

OBJECTIVES

- *To generate the long vowel sound /ī/, spelled i*

- *To build words using known letters and sounds*

- *To read simple, regular words*

SKILL TRACE

/ī/i	
INTRODUCE	68I–68L
Reteach	S16
Review	68Q–68R, 93F–93G, 95E–95F

Phonics and Spelling
Long Vowel /ī/i *Introduce*

TEACH/MODEL

Introduce /ī/i Display *Alphabet Card Ii* and say the letter and picture names. Remind children that the letter *i* can stand for the long *i* sound— /ī/, as in *ice*.

List these words on the board: *mine, light, fly, pie.* Have children read the words and tell which letters stand for the long *i* sound. Underline *i* and *e* in *mine*, *igh* in *light*, *y* in *fly*, and *ie* in *pie*. Tell children that they are going to learn another spelling pattern for the long *i* sound.

WORD BLENDING

Words with /ī/i Use *Letter Cards* to build *find* in a pocket chart. Have children use their *Word Builders* and *Word Builder Cards*. Point out that many words with this spelling pattern—one vowel with consonants before and after it—have a short vowel sound. Explain that in some words, the *i* can stand for the long *i* sound. Blend the sounds to read *find*. Continue with the following words: *blind, mind, mild.*

Phonics CENTER

15 Minutes

Materials

- teacher-made copying master

Rhyming Word Game

Prepare a copying master that contains word cards for the following: *kind, smiled, dined, find, wild, shined, grind, piled, mind, child, mild, lined.* Distribute a copy to partners. Have them cut the cards apart, read the words, and sort them into two groups of rhyming words. As you review children's work, point out the different spelling patterns.

5-DAY PHONICS/SPELLING

DAY 1	Introduce /ī/i
DAY 2	Word Building with /ī/i
DAY 3	Word Building with /ī/i
DAY 4	Word Building with /ī/i and /ī/i-e
DAY 5	Inflections -ed, -ing

WORD BUILDING

Build Spelling Words Place the letter *r* In a pocket chart and say the sound. Have children do the same with their *Word Builders* and *Word Builder Cards.* Repeat with the letters *i*, *n*, and *d*. Model how to blend the word *rind*. Slide your hand under the letters as you slowly elongate the sounds—*/rrīīnnd/.* Then read the word naturally—*rind*. Have children do the same.

r	i	n	d

Have children build and read new words by telling them:

- Change the *r* to *k*. What word did you make?

k	i	n	d

- Change the *k* to *m*. What word did you make?

m	i	n	d

- Change the *n* to *l*. What word did you make?

m	i	l	d

- Change the *m* to *ch*. What word did you make?

c	h	i	l	d

- Change the *ch* to *w*. What word did you make?

w	i	l	d

Dictate Long /ī/i Words Dictate the words *child* and *find* and have children write them in their journal. Suggest that they either draw a picture or write about each word.

BELOW-LEVEL

Help children distinguish between short *i* and long *i* by modeling and elongating both vowel sounds. As examples use word pairs such as *milled-mild, chilled-child,* and *grinned-grind.*

ENGLISH-LANGUAGE LEARNERS

Have children work with partners. Tell them to take turns watching their partner's mouth and observing the position of the tongue and lips as he or she says the sound /ī/. Continue with partners observing one another as they say words with the sound /ī/.

Phonics Resources

***Phonics Express™ CD-ROM,
Level B*** Roamer/Route 6/
Building Site

Phonics Practice Book, pp. 234–235

Spelling Words

1. find
2. kind
3. mind
4. mild
5. child
6. wild
7. day
8. play
9. sure
10. son

Phonics and Spelling

	5-DAY SPELLING
DAY 1	**Pretest; Word Sort**
DAY 2	Word Building
DAY 3	State the Generalization
DAY 4	Review
DAY 5	Posttest; Writing Application

INTRODUCE THE WORDS

Pretest Read aloud the first word and the Dictation Sentence. Repeat the word as children write it. Write the correct spelling on the board and have children circle the word if they spelled it correctly and write it correctly if they did not. Repeat for words 2–10.

1. **find**   Did you **find** your boots?
2. **kind**   It was **kind** of you to share your toys.
3. **mind**   My **mind** grows as I learn new things.
4. **mild**   I like **mild** spring weather.
5. **child** Did you see the **child** with his mother?
6. **wild**   Bears live in the **wild**.

Review

7. **day**   How many hours are there in one **day?**
8. **play**   It's fun to **play** in the park.

High-Frequency

9. **sure**   I am **sure** that I had my coat.

Vocabulary

10. **son**   Mr. Lopez's **son** looks just like him.

Word Sort Draw a chart with three columns on the board. Label the columns *-nd*, *-ld* and long *a*. Write each Spelling Word on an index card. Display the cards and ask, "Which words have long *i* and end with *nd*? Which words have long *i* and end with *ld*? Which words have the long *a* sound?" Place the words in the correct columns as children direct. For words 9-10, ask children to suggest headings for columns into which those words might fit.

-nd	*-ld*	long *a*
find	mild	day
mind	child	play
kind	wild	

Practice Book page

Name _____

Spelling Lesson 3

▶ Read the words. Then read the name of each group. Write each word in the group where it belongs.

Words With **ind**	Words With **ild**	**Spelling Words**
find	mild	find
kind	child	kind
		mind
mind	wild	mild
Words Without !		child
		wild
		day
day	sure	play
		sure
play	son	son

SCHOOL-HOME CONNECTION: Ask your child to read the Spelling Words aloud to you. Take turns making up sentences using two or three of the spelling words.

Practice Book
Gather Around • Lesson 3

▲ Practice Book, p. 17

Apply Phonics

Read

APPLY /ī/i

Write the following sentences on the board or on chart paper. Have children read the first sentence as you track the print. Frame the words *find* and *wild* and have children read them. Continue with the other sentences.

▲ Decodable Book 29
"Hi, Green Beans!"

Joan wanted to find books about wild bears.
She found all kinds of books.
She found out that bears can stand on their hind legs.

Have children read "Hi, Green Beans!" in *Decodable Book 29*.

Managing Small Groups

Read the *Decodable Book* with small groups of children. While you work with small groups, have other children do the following:

• **Self-Selected Reading**
• **Practice Pages**
• **Cross-Curricular Centers**
• **Journal Writing**

Use the suggested Classroom Management outline on page 7C for the whole-group/small-group schedule.

School–Home Connection

Take-Home Book Version

◀ Decodable Books
Take-Home Version

ONGOING ASSESSMENT

Note how well children
• read sentences without modeling.
• decode words in "Hi, Green Beans!"
• complete long vowel /ī/i practice pages.

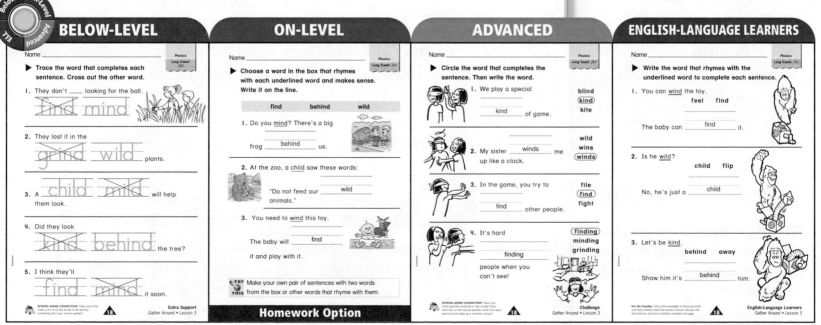

▲ Extra Support, p. 18   ▲ Practice, p. 18   ▲ Challenge, p. 18   ▲ ELL, p. 18

Writing Every Day

Day 1: Prewrite
Have children create a word web about winter.

Day 2: Draft
Have children use words from the web to create a first draft of a poem.

Day 3: Respond and Revise
Have children add describing words and other interesting words to their poem.

Day 4: Proofread
Have children work with partners to proofread their revised draft.

Day 5: Publish
Have children create a finished draft of their poem and illustrate it.

journal writing

Writing Prompt Have children write one or more sentences that contain words or phrases suggested for the winter web.

LANGUAGE ARTS

Writing Process

Poem

PREWRITING

Talk About Poetry Help children recall poems from earlier lessons. If necessary, display pages 6–7 of the *Big Book of Rhymes* and read aloud "There Once Was a Fish." Explain that poems may rhyme, but that they don't have to. Next, remind children that they discussed and wrote reports about seasons of the year when they read "Frog and Toad All Year." Tell children that now they will write a poem about winter.

Explore the Theme Write the word *Winter* on the board or on chart paper. Work with children to create a web of images and words related to winter.

Display the Web Read aloud the web entries. Display the web for children to use as they draft their poems on Day 2.

ADVANCED	**ENGLISH-LANGUAGE LEARNERS**
Have children write their own word web about winter.	Assign children a partner so they can work together to find, draw, or pantomime the words and phrases in the web.

Grammar

Verbs That Tell About Now

5-DAY GRAMMAR

DAY 1	Introduce Verbs That Tell About Now
DAY 2	Verbs That Tell About Now
DAY 3	Verbs That Tell About Now
DAY 4	Action Game
DAY 5	Identify Verbs That Tell About Now

TEACH/MODEL

Introduce Verbs That Tell About Now Display the title page of *To Market, To Market* and have children pantomime what the woman is doing. (pushing a shopping cart) As children pantomime, write the following sentence on the board.

We push a cart.

Read the sentence aloud and ask children to identify the telling part. (push a cart) Ask if children are pushing right now. (yes) Explain that verbs can tell about things that are happening now.

PRACTICE/APPLY

Display *Teaching Transparency 85* Briefly discuss the illustration or talk about ways to feed birds in the winter. Then point to the verbs, or write them and the sentences on the board. Have children read the verbs. Call on volunteers to read a sentence and choose the verb that would best complete it. Children should also read aloud the completed sentence and identify when the action is happening.

WRAP UP Sharing Circle

Discuss Prior Reading Tell children that soon they will read about real bears. Have children name books and stories that they have read about make-believe bears. If necessary, prompt children's memory by suggesting the stories "Jack and Rick" and "Little Bear's Friend," David McPhail's Brown Bear books, or the old tale "Goldilocks and the Three Bears." Have children list clues from these books and stories that show they are make-believe. (Possible answers: Bears wear clothes and live in houses. Bears talk. Bears paint houses and do other things people do. There are drawings instead of photographs.)

S.S.R. Sustained Silent Reading

Have children read silently from a book of their choice. See page 97J for tips on helping children choose books.

OBJECTIVE

To identify verbs that tell what is happening now

SKILL TRACE

VERBS THAT TELL ABOUT NOW	
INTRODUCE	**68N**
Reteach	T7
Review	93C, 95B, 97B, 97L
T Test	Bk 1-5

▼ **Teaching Transparency 85**

VERBS THAT TELL ABOUT NOW

fills   peck   make   fly   scrapes

1. Pam and Kim _____ a bird feeder.
2. Pam _____ out the rind.
3. Kim _____ the rind with peanut butter and seeds.
4. The wild birds _____ to the bird feeder.
5. They _____ at the seeds.

"Fishing Bears"
Gather Around, Volume 1-5   85   Grammar: Verbs That Tell About Now
Harcourt

Name _____

Grammar
Verbs That Tell About Now

► Write the verb that best completes each sentence.

drink   find   help   make   fill

1. I __fill__ the bird bath.
2. Birds __drink__ from it.
3. They come and __find__ seeds in our feeder.
4. We __help__ birds because we like them.
5. I __make__ bird feeders for my friends, too.

TRY THIS Work with a friend to read a news story about a sports team. Together, find the verbs that tell about now.

SCHOOL-HOME CONNECTION Have your child read you the completed page. Together, make up more sentences that use the verbs from this page.

19   Practice Book
Gather Around • Lesson 3

▲ Practice Book, p. 19

Day at a Glance
Day 2

Sharing Literature
Poem: "Wild Beasts"

Phonemic Awareness
Phoneme Isolation; Focus on /ī/

Phonics

REVIEW: Long Vowel /ī/*i*

Spelling
Building Words

Vocabulary
INTRODUCE: *during, ready*

High-Frequency Word
INTRODUCE: *both*

Reading
Pupil Edition
    "Fishing Bears," pp. 68–93

Independent Writing ✏
Writing Process: Drafting

Grammar
REVIEW: Verbs That Tell About Now

680   Gather Around

MORNING MESSAGE

WARM UP

Good Morning!

Today is _____.

Sometimes I pretend that _____.

I can be a wild animal or _____.

Pretending is fun because _____.

Introduce the Day

Tell children that they are going to listen to a poem that explores ways to pretend. Guide them in writing a message about pretending. Ask:

- **What do you like to pretend?**
- **If you could be anyone or anything, what would you choose?**
- **Why do you enjoy playing make-believe?**

As you write the message, invite volunteers to write previously taught or decodable words, and/or punctuation to reinforce skills. For instance, have them write words with short vowels, such as *can* and *fun*. Remind them to pay attention to the spacing between letters and words, and to write letters legibly so that others can easily read them.

Read the Message

Read the message. Use the message to focus on selected skills that have been previously taught.

Apply Skills

Phonics Have children look for words that contain the sound /ī/. (*I, wild*) Have children change the initial sound in *wild* to form other words with the long vowel sound of *i*.

Grammar Have children identify, in the second sentence, an action word that tells about now. (*pretend*) Remind them that the action word is called a verb, and it tells what someone does.

Sharing Literature

LISTEN AND RESPOND

Connect to Prior Knowledge Lead children in a discussion about playing games of "make-believe." Have children listen carefully as you read aloud the poem "Wild Beasts." Elicit that the speaker and a friend are pretending to be wild animals. Ask children to tell what clues helped them figure it out.

Respond to Literature After reading, encourage children to share their thoughts and feelings about the poem. Ask:

• Would you rather be a lion or a bear? Why?

• Do you think "Wild Beasts" is a good title for this poem? Why?

Reread the poem. Have children take turns taking the role of the bear or the lion.

Phonemic Awareness

PHONEME ISOLATION

Words from "Wild Beasts" Remind children of the words *chair* and *bear* from the poem "Wild Beasts." Ask them how the two words are alike. (They rhyme; both end with /r/.) Tell children that you are going to say more words. Ask children to identify the sound at the end of each word.

growl (/l/)	**den** (/n/)	**lion** (/n/)	**roar** (/r/)
shall (/l/)	**tiger** (/r/)	**wild** (/d/)	**cave** (/v/)
bird (/d/)	**fire** (/r/)	**run** (/n/)	**hunt** (/t/)

FOCUS ON /ī/

Phoneme Blending Tell children that you will say each sound in a word slowly and they will blend the sounds to say the word naturally. Segment the word *kind* into phonemes (/k/ /ī/ /n/ /d/). Then say it naturally—*kind*. Continue with the following words:

/w/ /ī/ /l/ /d/ (wild) /p/ /ī/ /n/ /t/ (pint) /f/ /ī/ /n/ /d/ (find)

/m/ /ī/ /l/ /d/ (mild) /b/ /l/ /ī/ /n/ /d/ (blind) /ch/ /ī/ /l/ /d/ (child)

Ask children how all the words are alike. (They all have /ī/.)

Wild Beasts

I will be a lion
　　And you shall be a bear,
And each of us will have a den
　　Beneath a nursery chair:
And you must growl and growl
　　and growl,
　　And I will roar and roar.
And then—why then—you'll
　　growl again,
　　And I will roar some more!

Evaleen Stein

REACHING ALL LEARNERS

Diagnostic Check: Phonemic Awareness

If... children have difficulty blending phonemes in words with /ī/ ...

Then... have them practice isolating phonemes in the following words: *pie, shy, mine, hide.*

ADDITIONAL SUPPORT ACTIVITIES

BELOW-LEVEL Reteach, p. S14

ADVANCED Extend, p. S15

ENGLISH-LANGUAGE LEARNERS Reteach, p. S15

OBJECTIVES

- *To blend sounds into words*

- *To read and write Spelling Words*

SKILL TRACE

/ī/i	
Introduce	68I–68L
Reteach	S16-S17
REVIEW	**68Q–68R, 93F–93G, 95E–95F**

Spelling Words

1. **find**
2. **kind**
3. **mind**
4. **mild**
5. **child**
6. **wild**
7. **day**
8. **play**
9. **sure**
10. **son**

Phonics and Spelling

Long Vowel /ī/i *Review*

5-DAY SPELLING	
DAY 1	Pretest; Word Sort
DAY 2	**Word Building**
DAY 3	State the Generalization
DAY 4	Review
DAY 5	Posttest; Writing Application

WORD BUILDING

Blend and Read a Spelling Word
Place *Letter Cards f, i, n,* and *d* in a pocket chart. Ask children to say the sound of each letter as you place it in the chart. Slide your hand under the letters as you blend the sounds—/ffīīnndd/. Have children repeat after you. Then read the word naturally—*find*, and have children do the same.

Build Spelling Words Ask children what letter you should change to make *find* become *kind*. (change *f* to *k*) Continue building the Spelling Words shown in this manner and having children read them.

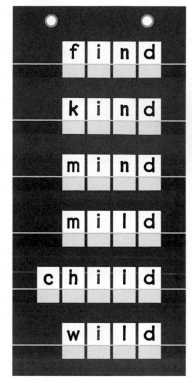

BELOW-LEVEL	ADVANCED
If children have difficulty identifying what letter to change in a word, repeat the word, emphasizing the target sound. Then have children say the word along with you.	Have children create short poems using words from the spelling list.

Apply Phonics

READ WORDS IN CONTEXT

Write the following sentences on the board or on chart paper and have children read them aloud.

> What **kind** of **wild** beasts did you **find**?
> It was a **mild** spring **day**.
> The **child** is **sure** she can write her name.
> Mr. Smith's **son** will **play** with us today.
> Try to see in your **mind** where the story
> takes place.

Dictate Words Dictate to children several words from the pocket chart, and have them write the words on a dry-erase board or in their journal.

kind
find
mind
mild
wild
child

5-DAY PHONICS	
DAY 1	Introduce /ī/i
DAY 2	**Word Building with /ī/i**
DAY 3	Word Building with /ī/i
DAY 4	Word Building with /ī/i and /ī/i-e
DAY 5	Inflections -ed, -ing

Phonics Resources

***Phonics Express™* CD-ROM, Level B** Sparkle/Route 1/Park

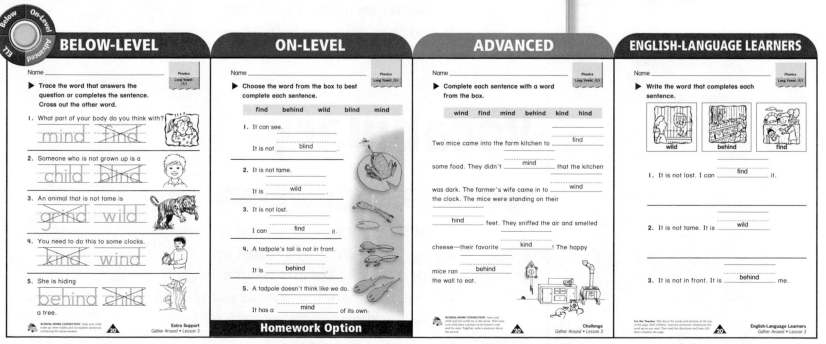

BELOW-LEVEL

▲ Extra Support, p. 20

ON-LEVEL

▲ Practice, p. 20

ADVANCED

▲ Challenge, p. 20

ENGLISH-LANGUAGE LEARNERS

▲ ELL, p. 20

High-Frequency Word

both two things together

Vocabulary

during taking place at the same time

ready all set to do something

Building Background

TALK ABOUT BEARS

Make a Web About Bears Tell children that they are going to read a selection about Alaskan brown bears. Guide children in completing a concept web about bears.

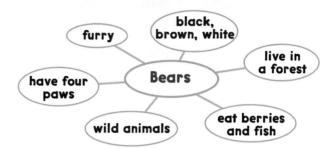

Discuss Story Words Write the words *Alaskan, cozy, enemies, hibernate, salmon,* and *usually* on the board. Point to each word and read it aloud. Talk about word meanings as necessary.

High-Frequency Words

IDENTIFY WORDS

Echo Read Display *Teaching Transparency 86* or write the words and sentences on the board. Point to and read the word *both*. Have children repeat it.

> **INTRODUCE**
> **High-Frequency Word**
> **both**

Vocabulary

INTRODUCE WORDS IN CONTEXT

Read Sentences Point to the words *during* and *ready*. Have children say the words after you. Discuss their meanings as necessary. Track the print as you read aloud the sentences. Call on volunteers to reread each sentence.

> **INTRODUCE**
> **Vocabulary**
> **during   ready**

▼ **Teaching Transparency 86**

HIGH-FREQUENCY WORDS
both

VOCABULARY WORDS
during   ready

During a storm, my sister and I play inside.
We would both like to play out in the sun. Both of
us are ready for the rain to end.

"Fishing Bears"
Gather Around, Volume 1-5   86   High-Frequency Words/Vocabulary
                                                                          Harcourt

▲ Fishing Bears

Word Power

Words to Remember

both

during

ready

Both of these bears need to eat now.
They have to get **ready** for winter.
They will sleep a lot **during** the winter.

68   69

Word Power

Word Power

Pages 68–69 Have children read aloud the Words to Remember. Have them read the sentences aloud. Then have children point to the Words to Remember in the sentences.

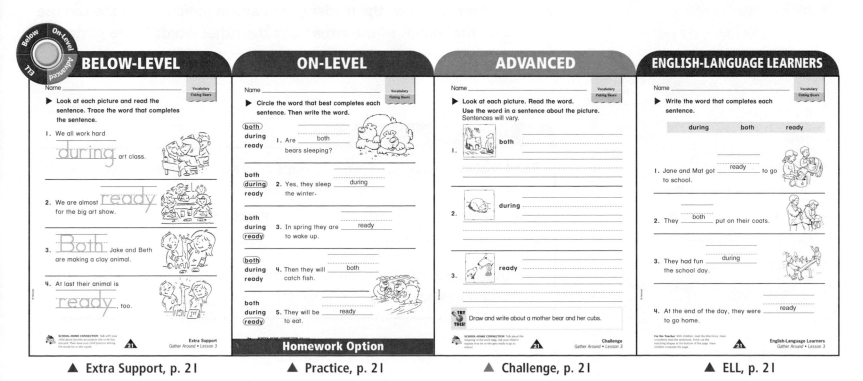

BELOW-LEVEL	ON-LEVEL	ADVANCED	ENGLISH-LANGUAGE LEARNERS

▲ Extra Support, p. 21   ▲ Practice, p. 21   ▲ Challenge, p. 21   ▲ ELL, p. 21

Fishing Bears **68–69**

READING

Prereading Strategies

Phonics

Long Vowel: /ī/*i*

High-Frequency Word

both

Vocabulary

during

ready

Decodable Words

See the lists on pages T50–T51.

Comprehension

 (Focus Skill) Main Idea

(Focus Strategy) Self-Correct

Strategies Good Readers Use

To recognize words

- Use Decoding/Phonics
- Look for Word Bits and Parts

To gain meaning

- **Self-Correct** (Focus Strategy)
- Read Ahead
- Reread
- Reread Aloud
- Use Picture Clues to Confirm Meaning
- Make and Confirm Predictions
- Sequence Events/Summarize
- Create Mental Images
- Make Inferences

PREPARING TO READ

Preview/Predict Discuss pages 70–71. Ask children to read the title aloud. Point out and read the names of the author and photographer. Discuss what a photographer does, and then talk about the pictures on pages 72–75. Help children discuss what they might learn in this selection.

Set Purpose Help children set a purpose for reading. If necessary, suggest that they read to find out why bears fish.

COMPREHENSION SKILL

(Focus Skill) **Main Idea** Tell children that an author often chooses one particular topic to write about. What that author's article, story, or paragraph is mostly about is called the main idea. Point out that an author includes details about the main idea to make the writing interesting and informative. As children read "Fishing Bears," have them think about the main idea and how the details give more information about it.

COMPREHENSION STRATEGY

 (Focus Strategy) **Self-Correct** Explain to children that sometimes a reader misreads a word, so the sentence doesn't make sense. When the reader goes back to reread, he or she can use the sounds of the letters and the other words in the sentence to figure out the word and read it correctly.

Managing Small Groups

Read "Fishing Bears" with small groups of children. While you work with small groups, have other children do the following:

- **Self-Selected Reading**
- **Practice Pages**
- **Cross-Curricular Centers**
- **Journal Writing**

Use the suggested Classroom Management Outline on page 7C for the whole-group/small-group schedule.

Genre

Nonfiction

Some nonfiction pieces use photographs to give information.

Look for:

- Ways the photographs add information.
- Facts about bears that may be new to you.

70

FISHING BEARS

by Ruth Berman

photographs by Lynn M. Stone

71

Guided Comprehension

Pages 70–71 Have children reread the title and review their discussion of what the selection might be about.

GENRE: Nonfiction

Read aloud the information about nonfiction on page 70. Tell children that nonfiction includes

- factual information.
- events that can happen.
- places that exist.

BELOW-LEVEL	ON-LEVEL	ADVANCED	ENGLISH-LANGUAGE LEARNERS
Encourage children to use context clues and letter-sounds to help them decode unfamiliar words. Have children reread certain sentences or sections if they have difficulty comprehending the ideas. SMALL GROUP **ADDITIONAL SUPPORT** Intervention Resource Kit, Lesson 29. *Intervention Teacher's Guide pp. 282–291*	As children read the selection, use the Guided Comprehension questions to direct their reading. WHOLE GROUP/SMALL GROUP	Have children add to the "Bears" concept web any additional facts that they learn about bears as they read the selection independently. After reading, have children work in small groups to discuss main ideas and details from the selection. INDEPENDENT/SMALL GROUP	Read through the selection with children. Discuss the meaning of words such as *napping, trail,* and *sneak.* Allow children to share their own definitions of words. SMALL GROUP **ADDITIONAL SUPPORT** English-Language Learners Resource Kit, Lesson 29. *English-Language Learners Teacher's Guide pp. 170–171*

These are brown bear tracks. How many toe marks can you count?

This is an Alaskan brown bear.
Alaskan brown bears live near water.

They have small ears, small eyes, and a big long nose.

72

73

Guided Comprehension

Pages 72–73 Have children look at the photograph of the bear tracks. Then have them read to find out where Alaskan brown bears live.

1 **SPECULATE** **Why do you think the bears live near water?** (Possible responses: They need water to drink; maybe they catch fish. Accept reasonable responses. Encourage children to explain their responses.)

2 **MAKE COMPARISONS** **How is a bear paw like your foot?** (It has five toes.) **How do you know that?** (The author asks readers to count the toe marks in the tracks.)

3 **NOTE DETAILS/AUTHOR'S CRAFT** **Describe the Alaskan brown bear's face.** (small ears and eyes, big long nose) **Why do you think the author includes this information?** (Accept reasonable responses. Possible response: Maybe other kinds of bears look different.)

BELOW-LEVEL

Encourage children to pay attention to the pictures in this story. Suggest that they look at the pictures to confirm the meaning of the sentences they read and to help them with any words or sentences that seem unclear. Monitor their progress by having them point out pictures and the relevant details that correspond as they read through the text.

Bears can stand up on their hind legs.

This mother bear stands to smell the air for food and for enemies.

Mother bears usually have twins or triplets.

Baby bears are called cubs.

74

75

Guided Comprehension

Pages 74–75 Briefly discuss the illustrations. Then have children read to find out about bear families.

1 **DETAILS** What are baby bears called? *(cubs)* Read the sentence that tells. *(Baby bears are called cubs.)*

2 **DRAW CONCLUSIONS** How many cubs does a mother bear usually have? How did you figure this out? (Two or three; the story says mother bears have twins or triplets—twins means two babies and triplets means three.)

3 **CAUSE-EFFECT/SPECULATE** Why do bears sometimes stand on their hind legs? (to smell food and enemies) What enemies do you think a bear might have? (Possible responses: bigger animals, people who kill bears)

BELOW-LEVEL

Reinforce letter-sound associations by pointing out *hind* on page 74. Emphasize that the word contains the sound /ī/. Tell children to notice other words containing the long *i* sound (spelled various ways) as they read the story.

ENGLISH-LANGUAGE LEARNERS

Some children may be unfamiliar with the term *triplets*. Explain that two babies born on the same day to the same parents are called *twins* and that three babies are called *triplets*. Guide children in a discussion of the number of babies different animals may have in a litter.

Cubs stay with their mothers for one to three years.

This cub is napping on Mom!

76

These cubs are playing.

Brown bears eat both plants and animals.

77

Guided Comprehension

Pages 76–77 Discuss the photographs. Then have children read to find out more about bear families.

1 MAKE JUDGMENTS Why do you think bear cubs stay with their mother so long? (Possible response: Mothers provide protection and food and teach them to survive on their own. Accept reasonable responses.)

2 EXPRESS PERSONAL OPINIONS Does it surprise you that bear cubs like to play? Why or why not? (Possible response: No, my dog likes to play with me, so I think that other animals might like to play too. Accept reasonable responses.)

3 NOTE DETAILS What do brown bears eat? (both plants and animals)

SOCIAL STUDIES

Explain to children that the brown bears in the story live in Alaska. Encourage them to find out more about Alaska by looking for information in an encyclopedia or other reference books. Have them create a poster about Alaska, decorating it with photographs of the animals and people of the state. You may wish to tie this activity with the upcoming Making Connections social studies activity (*Pupil Edition*, p. 94).

Most furry animals walk on their toes.

Bears walk with their feet
flat on the ground.

78

These bears are walking on a trail.

The trail ends at a river. Brown bears look
for fish in rivers.

79

Guided Comprehension

Pages 78–79 Briefly discuss the photographs. Then have children read to find out what is special about how bears walk.

1 **MAKE COMPARISONS** How is a bear's way of walking different from the way most other furry animals walk? (Bears walk with their feet flat on the ground, instead of on their toes.)

2 **DRAW CONCLUSIONS** Why do you think there is a trail to the river? (Accept reasonable responses. Possible response: because bears walk back and forth to the river often)

Strategies Good Readers Use

Self-Correct Read aloud the last two sentences on page 79, substituting the words *rider* and *riders* for *river* and *rivers.* Ask: *Does what I've read make sense? What's wrong? What should I do to correct it?* Have children explain the steps that should be taken; promote assistance as necessary.

Look! These bears are fighting over a good fishing spot.

The bigger bear wins. It is about to catch a salmon!

What do you think this bear is doing?

It is fishing for salmon under the water.

80

81

Guided Comprehension

Pages 80–81 Have children read to find out what the bears are doing.

1 **NOTE DETAILS/SPECULATE** **What are the bears fighting about?** (a good fishing spot) **What would make one fishing spot better than another?** (Possible response: It would be easy to catch fish in some places.)

2 **DRAW CONCLUSIONS/CONTEXT** **What is a salmon?** (a fish) **How do you know?** (The bears are fishing; the words say that one bear is about to catch a salmon.)

3 **EXPRESS PERSONAL OPINIONS** **Are you surprised that bears can swim under water?** (Encourage children to elaborate.) **What other surprising facts have you learned so far?** (Children should point out text and/or pictures.)

Strategies Good Readers Use

Focus Strategy

Self-Correct Remind children to reread words and sentences if they don't make sense. Remind them to use letter-sounds and the meaning of other words to figure out unfamiliar words.

These bears are pouncing on salmon.

82

Can you find a mother and her cubs in this picture?

The mother is keeping her cubs safe from a male bear.

83

Guided Comprehension

Pages 82–83 Have children look at the photographs and read to find out what the bears are doing.

1 (**Focus Skill**) **MAIN IDEA** Think about pages 80–82. **What are these three pages mostly about?** (Children's responses should indicate an understanding that fishing is an important source of food.)

2 **DRAW CONCLUSIONS** Why do you think a mother bear has to protect her cubs from a male bear? (Possible response: Male bears probably hurt cubs.)

REACHING ALL LEARNERS

Diagnostic Check: Comprehension and Skills

If... children have trouble identifying the main idea of pages 80–82 . . .

Then... have them reread the pages and talk about the photographs. Elicit that all the photos show bears in water, and that either the word *fishing* or *salmon* appears on each page.

ADDITIONAL SUPPORT ACTIVITIES

BELOW-LEVEL Reteach, p. S18

ADVANCED Extend, p. S19

ENGLISH-LANGUAGE LEARNERS Reteach, p. S19

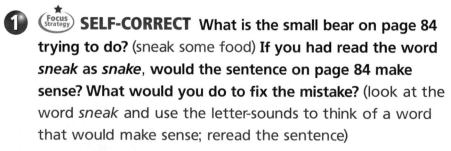

This small bear is trying to sneak some food!

84

Alaskan Brown bears also eat clams.

Bears have to dig for clams.

85

Guided Comprehension

Pages 84–85 Have children read to find out more facts about what bears eat.

1 (Focus Strategy) **SELF-CORRECT** What is the small bear on page 84 trying to do? (sneak some food) If you had read the word *sneak* as *snake*, would the sentence on page 84 make sense? What would you do to fix the mistake? (look at the word *sneak* and use the letter-sounds to think of a word that would make sense; reread the sentence)

2 **NOTE DETAILS** Where do bears get the clams that they eat? (They dig for them.)

ADVANCED

Encourage children to find out more information about bears. Have them look in encyclopedias or other books and add information they find to the web that they created during prereading.

ENGLISH-LANGUAGE LEARNERS

Remind children to point out parts of the pictures that are described in the text. Doing this will help reinforce new vocabulary and concepts.

Alaskan brown bears get ready for winter by eating a lot.

Eating a lot makes them fat.

86

Why do bears need to get fat?

Fat keeps them warm and healthy during the winter.

87

Guided Comprehension

Pages 86–87 Discuss photographs. Then have children read to find out how bears get ready for winter

1 **NOTE DETAILS** What do brown bears do to get ready for winter? (eat a lot)

2 **CAUSE/EFFECT** How does eating a lot help them? (Eating a lot makes them fat, which keeps them warm and healthy during the long winter months.)

3 (Focus Skill) **MAIN IDEA** What are these pages mostly about? (how Alaskan brown bears get ready for winter)

REACHING ALL LEARNERS

Diagnostic Check: Comprehension and Skills

If... children are having difficulty determining a main idea for these pages . . .

Then... give them a choice of three topics: fishing for salmon, getting ready for winter, keeping warm. Help children understand that the second topic best tells the main idea because it tells what all the facts are about.

ADDITIONAL SUPPORT ACTIVITIES

BELOW-LEVEL Reteach, p. S18

ADVANCED Extend, p. S19

ENGLISH-LANGUAGE LEARNERS Reteach, p. S19

Fishing Bears **86–87**

Brown bears stay in dens for most of the winter. A brown bear is hibernating in this cozy den.

When bears hibernate, they are in a deep sleep.

88

In the spring, bears leave their dens to look for food.

89

Guided Comprehension

Pages 88–89 Have children look at the photographs. Ask children what seasons the photographs show and how they know. Then have children read to find out how brown bears spend the winter.

1 **NOTE DETAILS** What is a den? (the place where bears hibernate during the winter)

2 **DRAW CONCLUSIONS** When do bears wake up? Which sentence tells this? (in the spring; *In the spring, bears leave their dens to look for food*.)

3 **INTERPRETING STORY EVENTS** Why do you think that bears hibernate in the winter, instead of in the summer? (They sleep when it's cold; finding food would be difficult.)

Then bears eat and eat.

They will be fat again by next winter.

90

Fishing is hard work!
It is time to rest.

91

Guided Comprehension

Pages 90–91 Have children read to find out what happens when the bears look for food.

1 **(Focus Skill) MAIN IDEA** What do the bears do through the spring and summer? ("eat and eat") **What will happen by next winter?** (They will be fat again.)

2 **EXPRESS PERSONAL OPINIONS** What is happening on page 91? (The bear is taking a rest.) **Do you like the way the author and the photographer ended the selection? Why or why not?** (Possible responses: Yes, because I like the photograph. No, because I want to know more about bears. Accept all reasonable responses.)

Strategies
Good Readers Use

(Focus Strategy) Self-Correct Ask children to leaf through the selection to find any words or sentences that they reread in order to make a correction. Ask volunteers to share the steps they used.

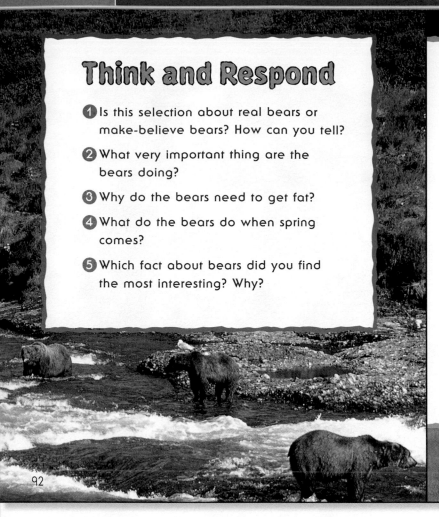

Think and Respond

1. Is this selection about real bears or make-believe bears? How can you tell?

2. What very important thing are the bears doing?

3. Why do the bears need to get fat?

4. What do the bears do when spring comes?

5. Which fact about bears did you find the most interesting? Why?

Meet the Author

Ruth Berman

Ruth Berman lives in California with her husband, her daughter, two dogs, and a cat. She likes writing for children. She says, "I hope my books teach children to love and respect animals."

Meet the Photographer

Lynn M. Stone

Lynn M. Stone took the pictures for *Fishing Bears* in a bear sanctuary in Alaska. Animals are protected there. Only a few people enter the sanctuary each year. "I felt like I had won a prize when I was picked to go into the sanctuary," says Mr. Stone.

Teacher Read-Aloud

92
93

Think and Respond

1. The text tells facts about real bears; the photographs show real bears. **LITERARY RESPONSE**

2. Possible response: hunting for fish and other food; caring for cubs. **SUMMARIZE**

3. The fat keeps them healthy and warm in the winter when they hibernate and don't eat. **CAUSE/EFFECT**

4. They wake up, leave their dens, and look for food again. **IMPORTANT DETAILS**

5. Possible response: Bears eat plants and animals; I thought they ate only plants. Accept reasonable responses. **PERSONAL RESPONSE**

Meet the Author and the Photographer

Page 93 Explain that this page tells about the people who created the story "Fishing Bears." Identify Ruth Berman and Lynn M. Stone in the photographs on page 93. Review the roles of author and photographer. Read aloud page 93 as you track the print.

 Visit *The Learning Site*: www.harcourtschool.com

See Resources for Parents and Teachers: Author/Illustrator Features.

Retelling

COMPREHENSION FOCUS

Focus Skill **Main Idea** Remind children that authors often organize information by starting with a main idea and then adding details to tell about it. Explain that the author of "Fishing Bears" chose one main idea about bears and then added many details to make the book interesting.

RETELL AND SUMMARIZE THE STORY

Use a Main Idea Chart Ask children to recall what "Fishing Bears" is mostly about. Invite children to contribute details they remember. Point out that there is a lot of information but that now you want them to decide on the most important thing that the whole selection is about. Prompt children with questions such as these:

• **What kind of bears does the author tell about?** (Alaskan brown bears)

• **What very important thing do the bears have to do before winter begins?** (eat a lot and get fat)

Use *Teaching Transparency 108* or draw a large box on the board labeled *Main Idea*. Work with children to write one sentence that tells what the selection is mostly about.

Help children suggest details from the selection that relate to the main idea. Consolidate their responses and fill in the Details boxes on the chart. Help children use the chart to summarize "Fishing Bears."

COMPREHENSION CHECK

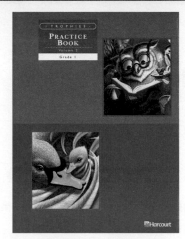

▲ *End-of-Selection Test,*
Practice Book, pp. A41–A43

▼ **Teaching Transparency 108**

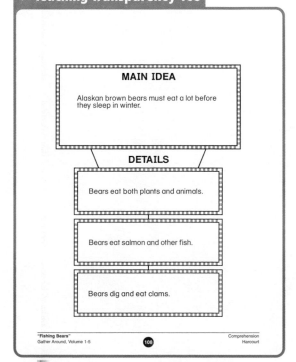

MAIN IDEA

Alaskan brown bears must eat a lot before they sleep in winter.

DETAILS

Bears eat both plants and animals.

Bears eat salmon and other fish.

Bears dig and eat clams.

"Fishing Bears"
Gather Around, Volume 1-5   108   Comprehension
Harcourt

LANGUAGE ARTS

DAILY LANGUAGE PRACTICE

May we see th wild Bears?

May we see <u>the</u> wild <u>bears</u>?

teaching tip

Discuss the differences between a poem and a story: a poem can be shorter; a poem may not have a plot or characters; a poem might not follow the rules for capital letters; a poem might have many rhyming words.

journal writing

Writing Prompt Have children make a list of interesting describing words. They may use these words in poems they write now or refer to the list later during any writing assignment.

LANGUAGE ARTS

5-DAY WRITING	
DAY I	Prewriting
DAY 2	**Drafting**
DAY 3	Responding and Revising
DAY 4	Proofreading
DAY 5	Publishing

Writing Process

Poem

DRAFTING

Review the Topic Have children think again about winter weather, activities, and holidays. Display the web from Day I and call on children to read it aloud. Add to the web as needed.

Model Drafting Engage children in writing sentences or phrases about winter. Remind children that they can look at the web for ideas. Together, devise a poetry frame such as the one shown below that describes early winter. As you write, point out the spaces between the letters and words and have children spell familiar words.

> The grass ____.
> Leaves ____ from trees.
> The wind ____
> And touches my ____.

Write Drafts Have children copy and complete each poetry line with their own words. Encourage them to add more lines as well. Make sure children understand that their work doesn't have to be perfect now. Explain that in this stage—Drafting—the most important thing is to get ideas down on paper. Have children save their drafts for use during Responding and Revising on Day 3, page 95A.

BELOW-LEVEL

Some children may have difficulty expressing their ideas in writing. If necessary, allow children to dictate their poetry lines for you to record. Ask children to read back the words you write.

ENGLISH-LANGUAGE LEARNERS

Children who have lived in warm climates near the Equator may not be familiar with winter. Provide books and pictures to help them understand the season. You may also provide shaved ice or ice cubes to further their understanding.

Grammar

Verbs That Tell About Now

5-DAY GRAMMAR

DAY 1	Introduce Verbs That Tell About Now
DAY 2	**Verbs That Tell About Now**
DAY 3	Words That Tell About Now
DAY 4	Action Game
DAY 5	Identify Verbs That Tell About Now

REVIEW

Review Verbs That Tell About Now Write the following sentences on the board. During Modeling, write the correct verb in each sentence.

> The bears _____ some fish.
> The bear _____ some fish.

MODEL If I want the first sentence to tell something that is happening now, I need to add a verb that tells about now. *Eat* would make sense: *The bears eat some fish.* The naming part, *bears,* tells about more than one bear. Now I'll try *eat* in the second sentence: *The bear eat some fish?* No, that isn't quite right. When the naming part of a sentence tells about only one, such as *bear*, we usually need to add *s* to the verb. The correct sentence is *The bear eats some fish.*

Use Verbs to Complete Sentences Have children copy and complete each of these sentences with a verb that tells about now.

> The bear _____ to the river.
> The cubs _____.

WRAP UP Read a Fish Story

Compare and Contrast Tell children that you will read a story about eating trout, a kind of fish. Then read aloud "The Rule." Discuss with children similarities and differences between "Fishing Bears" and "The Rule." (Both are about family groups, but one family is human and the other is animal. Characters in both stories eat fish—the bears like salmon, but Huey doesn't want to eat his trout.)

▲ "The Rule," pp. 55–64

S.S.R. Have children read silently from a book of their choice. See page 97J for tips on helping children choose books.

SKILL TRACE

VERBS THAT TELL ABOUT NOW

Introduce	68N
Reteach	T7
REVIEW	**93C, 95B, 97B, 97L**
T Test	Bk 1-5

ADVANCED

Help children find a story that is written in the past tense. Have them practice reading it aloud in a small group, changing it to the present tense. Though past-tense verbs have not yet been formally taught, an advanced reader can benefit from informally experimenting with verb tenses.

Grammar Resources

Grammar Jingles™ CD, **Primary, Track 8,** "Likes and Wishes"

Name _____

Verbs That Tell About Now

A **verb** can tell about now.

An **s** is added to some verbs that tell about now. The **s** is added when the verb tells what one person, place, or thing does.

Many girls run now.   One girl runs now.

▶ Write the correct verb under each picture. Use the words in the boxes.

| waves | runs | sit | kicks |

1. _____ sit
2. _____ runs
3. _____ waves
4. _____ kicks

122

SCHOOL-HOME CONNECTION

▲ Language Handbook, p. 122

Fishing Bears **93C**

Sharing Literature
Poem: "In the Summer We Eat"

Phonemic Awareness
Phoneme Isolation; Focus on /ī/

Phonics
REVIEW: Long Vowel /ī/*i*

Spelling
State the Generalization

Vocabulary
REVIEW: *during, ready*

High-Frequency Word
REVIEW: *both*

Reading

Rereading for Fluency
Pupil Edition
    "Fishing Bears," pp. 70–91

Making Connections, pp. 94–95

Independent Writing ✏️
Writing Process: Responding and Revising

Grammar
REVIEW: Verbs That Tell About Now

WARM UP

MORNING MESSAGE

Good Morning!

Today is _____.
During the summer, I like to _____.
When it's warm I can _____.
Both _____ and _____ grow best during the summer.

Introduce the Day

Remind children that the bears in "Fishing Bears" use the summer to fish and prepare for winter. Help children generate a message about summer by asking:

• **What do you like to do in the summer?**

• **What can you do in the summer that you can't do when it is cold?**

• **What kinds of plants do you think grow best in the summer?**

As you write the message, invite volunteers to write previously taught letters, words, and/or punctuation to reinforce skills. For instance, have volunteers write the words *during* and *Both*.

Read the Message

Read the message. Use the message to focus on selected skills that have been previously taught.

Apply Skills

Word Structure Have a volunteer frame the word *it's*. Elicit that it is a short way to say *it is*. Ask children which letter the apostrophe stands for. (the *i* in *is*)	**Phonics** Have a child point to and read a word with the long *i* sound. (like) Ask children to generate other words with the *i–e* pattern.

Sharing Literature

BUILD CONCEPT VOCABULARY

Connect to Prior Knowledge Explain to children that you are going to read a poem about some animals. Read the poem aloud. Then ask children what animals it is about and how they know. Remind them of the story "Fishing Bears" and what they know about bears and hibernation. Reread the poem and have children do the motions with you.

Multi-Meaning Words Discuss several meanings for the following words:
- play: We can *play* a game. What else can we *play*? (musical instruments, radio, cassette, CD, videotape, DVD, trick)
- fall: *Fall* is the name of a season. What might happen if you trip or stumble? (You might fall down.)

Phonemic Awareness

PHONEME ISOLATION

Words from "In the Summer We Eat" Read the word *sleep* slowly and ask children what vowel sound they hear in the middle. (/ē/) Continue with the following words.

peach (/ē/)   **den** (/e/)   **snow** (/ō/)   **play** (/ā/)
don't (/ō/)   **and** (/a/)   **flakes** (/ā/)   **seat** (/ē/)

FOCUS ON /ī/

Phoneme Substitution Tell children that you will say a word and they will change the middle sound to make a new word. Model by saying *found: If I change /ou/ to /ī/, I get* find. Continue with the following words:

Say:	Change:	Say:	Change:
chilled	/i/ to /ī/. (*child*)	pant	/a/ to /ī/. (*pint*)
mailed	/ā/ to /ī/. (*mild*)	blend	/e/ to /ī/. (*blind*)
grinned	/i/ to /ī/. (*grind*)	round	/ou/ to /ī/. (*rind*)

In the Summer We Eat

In the summer we eat,
(mime eating)
in the winter we don't;
(hold arms and shake head "no")
In the summer we'll play,
(wave hands like a playful cub)
in the winter we won't.
(hold arms and shake head "no")
All winter we sleep, each curled in a ball
(lean head on hands as if sleeping)
As soon as the snowflakes start to fall.
(wiggle fingers to show snowflakes)
But in spring we each come out of our den
(mime crawling out of a den)
And start to eat all over again.
(mime eating)

Zhenya Gai

ENGLISH-LANGUAGE LEARNERS

Visit *The Learning Site:* www.harcourtschool.com
See Language Support.

BELOW-LEVEL

If children have difficulty substituting medial vowel sounds, focus on initial sounds. Have them substitute /ī/ for the initial sound in these words: *ease* (eyes), *aim* (I'm), *ail* (I'll), *us* (ice), *eve* (I've).

OBJECTIVES

- *To generate the sound for long i, spelled i*
- *To blend sounds into words*
- *To read simple, regular words*

SKILL TRACE

/ī/i		
Introduce	68I–68L	
Reteach	S16-S17	
REVIEW	**68Q–68R, 93F–93G, 95E–95F**	

Phonics Resources

Phonics Express™ CD-ROM,
Level B Sparkle/Route 1/ Park

WORD WORK

Phonics
Long Vowel /ī/i *Review*

WORD BUILDING

b k l d m f n g r h i w a

Guided Practice Place the *Letter Cards m, i, l,* and *d* in a pocket chart. Have children use their *Word Builders* and *Word Builder Cards.* Model how to blend the word *mild.* Slide your hand under the letters as you slowly elongate the sounds—/mmmīīlld/. Then read the word naturally—*mild.* Have children do the same.

m	i	l	d

Have children build and read new words:

■ Change the *l* to *n.* What word did you make?

m	i	n	d

■ Change the *m* to *r.* What word did you make?

r	i	n	d

■ Add a *g* at the beginning. What word did you make?

g	r	i	n	d

■ Change *gr* to *h.* What word did you make?

h	i	n	d

■ Add *be* to the beginning. What word did you make?

b	e	h	i	n	d

■ Change *beh* to *w.* What word did you make?

w	i	n	d

Homograph Point out that the word *wind* can be pronounced two ways. Have children complete these sentences as you point to wind: To make some toys work, you have to _____ them. During a storm the _____ blows.

Apply Phonics

READ WORDS IN CONTEXT

Display *Teaching Transparency 87* or write the following sentences on the board or on chart paper. Have volunteers read the story one sentence at a time. Call on volunteers to underline or frame words with long *i*, spelled *i*.

▼ **Teaching Transparency 87**

LONG VOWEL /ī/*i*

What can we find to eat?
We can grind corn with the stone.
We could eat a pint of beans.
The beans are very mild.
I would not mind adding some spice.
What kind of spice shall we add?

"Fishing Bears"
Gather Around, Volume 1-5   87   Phonics: Long Vowel /ī/*i*
                                                                      Harcourt

Write Words Tell children to choose two long vowel *i* words and write them in their journal.

5-DAY PHONICS

DAY 1	Introduce /ī/*i*
DAY 2	Word Building with /ī/*i*
DAY 3	**Word Building with /ī/*i***
DAY 4	Word Building with /ī/*i* and /ī/*i-e*
DAY 5	Inflections *-ed, -ing*

REACHING ALL LEARNERS

Diagnostic Check: Phonics

If... children have difficulty decoding /ī/*i* words...

Then... read "Wild, Wild Things" with them and guide them in decoding the words with /ī/*i*.

◀ **Decodable Book 29**
"Wild, Wild Things"

ADDITIONAL SUPPORT ACTIVITIES

BELOW-LEVEL	Reteach, p. S16
ADVANCED	Extend, p. S17
ENGLISH-LANGUAGE LEARNERS	Reteach, p. S17

School-Home Connection

Take-Home Book Version

◀ Decodable Books
Take-Home Version

Spelling Words

1. find
2. kind
3. mind
4. mild
5. child
6. wild
7. day
8. play
9. sure
10. son

journal writing

Have children copy the Spelling Words into their journal.

Name _____

Spelling Lesson 3

▶ Unscramble the letters to write a Spelling Word.

1. licdh	2. yapl
child	play
3. usre	4. fdni
sure	find
5. dilm	6. nso
mild	son
7. yda	8. nidm
day	mind
9. inkd	10. idwl
kind	wild

Spelling Words

find
kind
mind
mild
child
wild
day
play
sure
son

SCHOOL-HOME CONNECTION: Have your child read each Spelling Word to you. Tell him or her to make a check mark next to all the words that have /ī/ as in *find.*

SPELLING PRACTICE BOOK
GATHER AROUND • LESSON 3 **71**

▲ Spelling Practice Book, p. 71

Spelling

5-DAY SPELLING	
DAY 1	Pretest; Word Sort
DAY 2	Word Building
DAY 3	**State the Generalization**
DAY 4	Review
DAY 5	Posttest; Writing Application

TEACH/MODEL

State the Generalization for /ī/i Write the Spelling Words on the board and have children read them aloud. Discuss what is the same about words 1–6. (They all have the sound /ī/; they all have *i*.) Have volunteers circle the letter that stands for /ī/ in each word. Emphasize that the letter *i* is used to spell the long *i* sound in these words.

Review the Generalization for /ā/ay Follow a similar procedure for words 7 and 8. Remind children that the letters *ay* are used to spell the long *a* sound, /ā/.

Review the High-Frequency Word and the Vocabulary Words Point out that the words *sure* and *son* do not follow the same patterns as the other words; they have neither the long *i* nor the long *a* sound.

BELOW-LEVEL

To help children spell these words, segment the phonemes as you slowly pronounce each word. Guide them in distinguishing the individual sounds and writing a letter that stands for each sound.

ADVANCED

Have children discover new words by changing the beginning letter in the *-ind* Spelling Words. Encourage them to see how many new words they can make. (bind, hind, rind, wind, blind, grind, behind)

Vocabulary

REVIEW WORDS IN CONTEXT

Use Words in Context Duplicate and distribute *Individual Word Cards* for *during* and *ready* (page T35). Have each child show one card to the group, say the word on the card, and use the word in a sentence.

> **REVIEW**
> **Vocabulary**
> **during   ready**

USE WORDS IN SENTENCES

Sentence Tag Game Write the following sentence frame on the board for children to use as reference: _____ **and I are ready to** _____ **during** _____. Have children play the following game. One child creates a sentence using the frame and the name of another child in the group. (Example: *Shanti* and I are ready to *dance* during *music class*.) The named child joins the first in acting out the sentence. Then the second child creates a new sentence, adding the name of a different child. Continue until every child has had a chance to create a sentence.

BELOW-LEVEL

Write *both, during,* and *ready* on sticky notes. As children reread the story "Fishing Bears," have them stick the note to the page on which the corresponding word occurs.

High-Frequency Words

REVIEW WORDS IN CONTEXT

Have children use the *Individual Word Card* for *both*. Ask them to use the word to describe two similar classroom objects—for example: *Both books have red covers.*

> **REVIEW**
> **High-Frequency Word**
> **both**

Words to Remember
WORD WALL

Match Words Have volunteers find, frame, and read the word *both*. Then have the group spell the word, clapping for each letter they say. Review other words in the same manner.

Read

FISHING BEARS

▲ *Pupil Edition*, pp. 70–91

FLUENCY ROUTINES For support, see Fluency Routine Cards in Theme Resources, pp. T83–T84.

READING

Rereading for Fluency

PARTNERS

Partner Reading

ON-LEVEL/ADVANCED Have each partner read two pages at a time. Point out that "Fishing Bears" is nonfiction and they should read as if they are telling someone information about bears. Remind partners that listening is just as important as reading; the listener should give feedback about how the reader sounds. INDEPENDENT

GROUPS

Choral Reading

BELOW-LEVEL/ENGLISH LANGUAGE LEARNERS Write selected sentences from the story on sentence strips and distribute them to each child. Before reading a page, discuss picture details that support the text. Then lead children in choral reading the page. Pause occasionally to model intonation and have children echo read sentences. TEACHER-DIRECTED

Brown bears look for fish in rivers.

They have small ears, small eyes, and a big long nose.

Managing Small Groups

Reread for fluency with children working individually, with partners, or in small groups. While you work with small groups, have other children do the following:

- **Self-Selected Reading**
- **Cross-Curricular Centers**
- **Practice Pages**
- **Journal Writing**

Use the suggested Classroom Management outline on page 7C for the whole-group/small-group schedule.

▲ Fishing Bears

Teacher Read-Aloud

Making Connections

Life in Alaska

Alaskan bears sleep during the long, cold winter. What do people who live in Alaska do to keep safe and warm in winter? Use the Internet to find out. Share one thing you learn.

Social Studies/ Technology CONNECTION

94

How Many Babies?

Most Alaskan mother bears have twins or triplets. If the mother bear has triplets, how many babies does she have? Make a chart of words like **twins** and **triplets**. Draw to show how many baby animals each word means.

Math CONNECTION

twins=   2

triplets=

quadruplets=

quintuplets =

Bear Captions

Choose a picture that you like from the story. Write a sentence or two to go with it. Say something different than what the author said. Write something silly if you like!

Writing CONNECTION

Wake up, little bear! It's time to go fishing.

95

Making Connections

SOCIAL STUDIES

Life in Alaska Locate Alaska on a globe or map. Encourage children to speculate on ways Alaskans might cope with their long winters. Then have children look up information to support or modify their thinking.

MATH

How Many Babies? Draw a chart with the headings *twins* and *triplets*. Call on children to draw animals of their choice to illustrate the words. Children may enjoy extending the activity by adding *quadruplets* and *quintuplets* to the chart. Explain that many animals, even cats and dogs, can have four or five babies at a time.

twins | triplets

WRITING

Bear Captions Have children page through the story, looking for a photograph that they especially like. After they have chosen a photograph, have them write a caption for it. If necessary, tell children to focus on actions because this strategy will help them think of a caption. Provide time for children to share their favorite photographs and their captions.

Wake up, little bear! It's time to go fishing.

5-DAY WRITING	
DAY 1	Prewriting
DAY 2	Drafting
DAY 3	**Responding and Revising**
DAY 4	Proofreading
DAY 5	Publishing

Writing Process

Poem

DAILY LANGUAGE PRACTICE

I like to pla the in snow.

I like to <u>play</u> <u>in the</u> snow.

RESPONDING AND REVISING

Read Drafted Poems Work with small groups. Have each child read aloud the poem he or she wrote during Drafting, page 93B.

> The grass dies.
> Leaves fall from trees.
> The wind blows
> And touches my nose.

Add Interesting Words Ask children to think of words that might make their poems a little more interesting. Suggest that they add some describing words or change a verb, for example.

> The grass <u>turns brown.</u>
> Red leaves <u>glide</u> from trees <u>and cover the ground.</u>
> The <u>chilly</u> wind blows
> And <u>stings</u> my nose.

Make Revisions Have children take turns reading their poem with a partner. As they read, ask children to add words that will help the reader or listener better picture what the poem tells about. Have partners also suggest words.

journal writing

Writing Prompt Have children choose a phrase from their revised poem, add words to make a complete thought, and write the new sentence in their journal.

BELOW-LEVEL

If children cannot think of ways to add vivid words to their poem, ask them questions such as *What does the grass look like when it dies? How do the leaves look when they fall?*

ADVANCED

Have children add additional lines to their poem, such as descriptions of snow.

Grammar

Verbs That Tell About Now

5-DAY GRAMMAR

DAY 1	Introduce Verbs That Tell about Now
DAY 2	Verbs That Tell About Now
DAY 3	**Verbs That Tell About Now**
DAY 4	Action Game
DAY 5	Identify Verbs That Tell About Now

REVIEW

Action Game Write *hop, walk, slide, smile,* and *wave* on index cards, and put the cards in a small bag or box. Have one child pick a card and pantomime the action. Choose a second child to create an oral sentence about what the first child is doing now. Remind children that in a sentence that tells about one person, they usually need to add *s* to the verb.

> **Latisha hops.**

Next, have both children pantomime the action. Ask a third child to create a sentence that describes what both of the other children are doing now:

> **Latisha and Malik hop.**

Continue in the same manner with the additional cards and new players. Pause occasionally to ask children when the action is happening. (now)

WRAP UP Read a Rhyme

Connect Ideas Across Text Have children recall what bears do during the winter. (hibernate) Then read aloud "Grandpa Bear's Lullaby." Ask children what time of year the poem tells about (the beginning of winter) and how they know. (The poem mentions winter several times.) Have children look back through "Fishing Bears" to find the page that tells about what bears do in the winter. (page 88) Discuss how the rhyme and the selection are alike. Remind children to listen to each other attentively and to ask questions if they don't understand what another child says.

▲ **Big Book of Rhymes, pp. 38–39**

 S.S.R. Have children read silently from a book of their choice. See page 97J for tips on helping children choose books.

SKILL TRACE

VERBS THAT TELL ABOUT NOW	
Introduce	68N
Reteach	T7
REVIEW	**93C, 95B, 97B, 97L**
T Test	Bk 1-5

BELOW-LEVEL

Allow children who have difficulty forming oral sentences to whisper the sentence to you first. Children's confidence will increase when they are sure they are saying a sentence correctly.

Name _____

Verbs That Tell About Now

▶ Underline the naming part of each sentence. Then write the verbs that tell about now.

1. The ducks fly by.
   _____ fly

2. Children slide on the slope.
   _____ slide

3. Marta makes a silly face.
   _____ makes

4. Carlos claps his hands.
   _____ claps

5. Mom and Dad sit on the bench.
   _____ sit

▲ **Language Handbook, p. 123**

Sharing Literature
Poem: "Jump or Jiggle"

Phonemic Awareness
Phoneme Blending; Focus on /i/

Phonics
Build Words

Spelling
Review

Vocabulary
REVIEW: *during, ready*

High-Frequency Word
REVIEW: *both*

Reading

Comprehension

(Focus Skill) Main Idea, pp. 96–97

Independent Writing ✎
Writing Process: Proofreading

Grammar
REVIEW: Verbs That Tell About Now

(WARM UP) MORNING MESSAGE

Good Morning!

Today is _____.

Sometimes I _____ fast.

Can you _____ up and down?

When I'm _____, I feel _____.

Introduce the Day

Tell children that they will listen to a poem that explores different ways creatures move. Guide children in generating a message about the ways animals and people move. Ask:

- **How do you move when you want to go fast?**
- **If you pretended to be a bunny, how would you move?**
- **Think about your favorite way to move. How does doing that make you feel?**

As you write the message, invite volunteers to write previously taught letters, words, and/or punctuation to reinforce skills. For instance, ask a volunteer to write the contraction *I'm.* Have another add the question mark at the end of the third sentence.

Read the Message

Read the message. Use the message to focus on selected skills that have been previously taught.

Apply Skills

Phonics Ask children to point out a word in the message that contains the vowel sound /ou/. (down) Have them generate more words that belong to the *-own* word family. (town, gown, frown, crown, drown)	**Vocabulary** Ask a child to point to the word *up* in the message. Then have someone identify the word in the same sentence that has the opposite meaning. (*down*) Have children think of other words that are opposites.

Sharing Literature

BUILD CONCEPT VOCABULARY

Connect to Prior Knowledge Invite volunteers to demonstrate the way that different animals move. Ask children to imagine the actions as you read aloud "Jump or Jiggle."

Respond to Literature Ask: *What does the poet say people do? Can people do the other actions too? Do you think the poet is trying to make us think and laugh?*

Create a Word Web Begin the web by writing *Actions* in the center oval. Ask children to name action words that tell how animals and people move. Review the completed web and have volunteers act out the actions.

Phonemic Awareness

PHONEME BLENDING

Words from "Jump or Jiggle" Segment the sounds in *hop:* (/h/ /o/ /p/). Ask children what word you are trying to say. (hop) Continue with the following words from the poem.

/l/ /ē/ /p/ (leap)   /j/ /u/ /m/ /p/ (jump) /g/ /l/ /ī/ /d/ (glide)
/b/ /u/ /g/ /z/ (bugs) /s/ /l/ /ī/ /d/ (slide)   /s/ /n/ /ā/ /k/ /s/ (snakes)
/k/ /r/ /ē/ /p/ (creep) /f/ /ī/ /n/ /d/ (find)   /p/ /ou/ /n/ /d/ (pound)

FOCUS ON /ī/

Phoneme Substitution Have children say *fin* and identify the vowel sound in the middle. (/i/) Model how to create a new word by substituting /ī/ for the medial vowel. Say *fine*. Ask children to create a new word for each of the words below by substituting /ī/ for the vowel sound in the middle.

pin (pine)   **band** (bind)   **pill** (pile)   **lit** (light)
man (mine)   **sled** (slide) **glade** (glide) **dim** (dime)

Jump or Jiggle

Frogs jump
Caterpillars hump

Worms wiggle
Bugs jiggle

Rabbits hop
Horses clop

Snakes slide
Sea gulls glide

Mice creep
Deer leap

Puppies bounce
Kittens pounce

Lions stalk—
But—
I walk!

Evelyn Beyer

ADVANCED

Have children think of other pairs of words that can be created by substituting the sound /ī/ for the medial vowel.

Phonics
Build Words *Review*

WORD BUILDING

OBJECTIVES

- *To recognize the sound-letter relationships /ī/i and /ī/i-e*

- *To read and write words with /ī/i and /ī/i-e*

Review Spelling for /ī/ List these words on the board: *find, fine, fly, flies.* Remind children that they have learned many spellings for the long *i* sound. As children read each word, underline *i* in *find, i* and *e* in *fine, y* in *fly,* and *ie* in *flies.*

Build and Read Words Display the *Letter Cards w, i, l,* and *d* in the pocket chart as children spell the word. Slide your hand slowly under the letters as you blend the sounds— /wwīīlld/. Then read the word naturally—*wild.* Have children repeat after you.

SKILL TRACE

	/ī/i	/ī/i-e
Introduce	68I–68L	Bk 1-4, 98I–98L
Reteach	S16-S17	Bk 1-4, S22-S23, T7
REVIEW	**68Q–68R,** **93F–93G,** **95E–95F**	
Review		Bk 1-4, 98Q–98R 119F–119G, 121E–121F, 151F
T Test		Bk 1-4
Maintain		**Bk 1-5, 95E–95F**

Ask volunteers to build new words:

- Take away the *l.* Add *e* after the *d.* Read the word.

- Change the *w* to *r.* Read the word.

- Change the *de* to *nd.* Read the word.

- Change the *r* to *m.* Read the word.

- Change the *n* to *l.* Read the word.

- Change the *d* to *e.* Read the word.

Phonics Resources

Phonics Express™ **CD-ROM, Level B** Roamer/Route 1/ Market; Sparkle/Route 6/Park

Phonics Practice Book, pp. 234–235

Homophones List these words on the board and have children read them aloud: *mind, mine, mined.* Ask which two words sound exactly the same. Point to the appropriate word and have children complete these sentences: *You think with your _____. The workers dug in the cave and _____ the coal.*

Apply Phonics

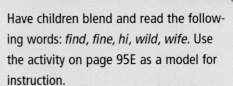

5-DAY PHONICS

DAY 1	Introduce /ī/i
DAY 2	Word Building with /ī/i
DAY 3	Word Building with /ī/i
DAY 4	**Word Building with /ī/i and /ī/i-e**
DAY 5	Inflections -ed, -ing

APPLY PHONICS SKILLS

Dictate Sentences Dictate the following sentences. Remind children to think about whether the long *i* words should be spelled with *i* alone or with a final *e* added.

> Mike has five fine mice.
> I am a kind child.

Have children write the sentences on a dry-erase board or in their journal.

Mike has five fine mice.

BELOW-LEVEL

Have children blend and read the following words: *find, fine, hi, wild, wife.* Use the activity on page 95E as a model for instruction.

ENGLISH-LANGUAGE LEARNERS

Some children may find the /ī/i spelling difficult. Give children cards for the words *find, fill, hi, hit, milk, mild, pine, pint, wild,* and *will.* Have children work in pairs or small groups to read the words aloud and sort them into piles according to short and long vowel sounds.

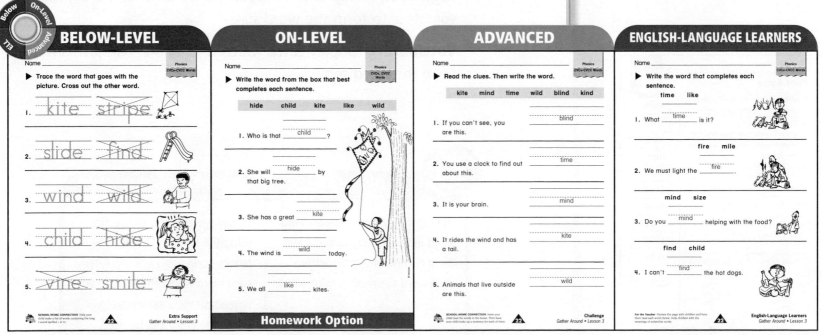

▲ Extra Support, p. 22	▲ Practice, p. 22	▲ Challenge, p. 22	▲ ELL, p. 22

Spelling Words

1. find
2. kind
3. mind
4. mild
5. child
6. wild
7. day
8. play
9. sure
10. son

Spelling

REVIEW

5-DAY SPELLING	
DAY 1	Pretest; Word Sort
DAY 2	Word Building
DAY 3	State the Generalization
DAY 4	**Review**
DAY 5	Posttest; Writing Application

Spelling Words Use a pocket chart and *Letter Cards* to form words. Have children listen to your directions and change one letter in each word to spell a Spelling Word. Have them write the Spelling Word on a sheet of paper or in their journal. Then have a volunteer change the *Letter Card* in the pocket chart so that children can self-check the word.

■ Form *king* in the pocket chart and have children read it aloud. **Which Spelling Word is made with one letter changed?** (*kind*)

■ Form *mile* in the pocket chart and have children read it aloud. **Which Spelling Word is made with one letter changed?** (*mild*)

■ Form *chill* in the pocket chart and have children read it aloud. **Which Spelling Word is made with one letter changed?** (*child*)

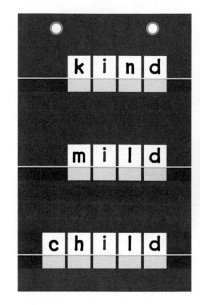

Follow a similar procedure with the following words: *fine (find)*, *plan (play)*, *mint (mind)*, *will (wild)*, *dad (day)*.

High-Frequency Word Display *Letter Cards* e, r, s, u. Ask a volunteer to form the word *sure*.

Vocabulary Display *Letter Cards* n, o, and s. Ask a volunteer to form the word *son*.

▲ Spelling Practice Book, p. 72

ADVANCED

After children form each Spelling Word in the activity above, have them change one more letter in each word to create a third word.

ENGLISH-LANGUAGE LEARNERS

Encourage children to practice using the Spelling Words in sentences during this activity. After each word is identified, have volunteers suggest sentences in which the word can be used.

Vocabulary

REVIEW WORDS

Generate Sentences Display *Word Cards* for *during* and *ready*. Have children read each word aloud. Ask volunteers to use the words in sentences.

> REVIEW
> ## Vocabulary
> **during   ready**

High-Frequency Words

REVIEW WORDS

Generate Sentences Display the *Word Card* for *both*. Have children read the word aloud. Ask volunteers to use the word in a sentence.

> REVIEW
> ## High-Frequency Word
> **both**

WRITE WORDS IN STORY CONTEXT

Reinforce Word Recognition Duplicate and distribute the Story Strips for "Fishing Bears" (page T67). Have children refer to the displayed *Word Cards* to complete the Story Strips. Partners can work together to read aloud the sentences and arrange them in story order.

> Brown bears eat ___ plants and animals.

> ___ the spring, bears fish in the river.

> The bear is ___ to catch a fish.

> During the winter, bears sleep in dens.

> Bears eat a lot to get ready to sleep.

BELOW-LEVEL

If children have difficulty identifying the missing words, then provide clues by telling them the first letter in the target word. After children write the word, ask them to read it aloud.

▲ *Pupil Edition*, pp. 70–91

OBJECTIVE

To identify the main idea of a selection

SKILL TRACE	
MAIN IDEA	
INTRODUCE	95I, 96–97
Reteach	S18–S19, T12
Review	99A, 119A 121I–123, 187A, 211A, 215I–217
T Test	Bk 1-5
Maintain	Bk 2-1

REACHING ALL LEARNERS

Diagnostic Check: Comprehension and Skills

If… children cannot understand the concept of main idea …

Then… read a set of simple directions and have children identify what the directions are telling them to do or make.

ADDITIONAL SUPPORT ACTIVITIES

BELOW-LEVEL	Reteach, p. S18
ADVANCED	Extend, p. S19
ENGLISH LANGUAGE LEARNERS	Reteach, p. S19

(**Focus Skill**) # Comprehension

Main Idea

TEACH/MODEL

Develop Concepts Remind children that the main idea is what a piece of writing is mainly about. Point out to children that understanding the main idea will help make clear what they read.

MODEL As I read this paragraph, I'll try to understand what it is mostly about: *Reading is fun. You can read funny books. You can read to learn lots of interesting things. You can share books with friends. You can read books everywhere you go.* The first sentence tells me that reading is fun. The other sentences give reasons why. So, I would say that the main idea is that reading is fun.

PRACTICE/APPLY

Recognize Main Idea Ask children to recall "Fishing Bears" and to think of the most important things in that selection. Read aloud *Pupil Edition* page 96 as children follow along. After reading the three sentence choices, ask children which one best tells the main idea of "Fishing Bears." Point out that, although many facts about Alaskan brown bears are given in the selection, most of the selection is about the way the bears hunt for food that they need to get them through the winter hibernation. Elicit that the third sentence tells the main idea. Then ask children why sentences 1 and 2 are not the main idea. (Each tells just one thing mentioned in the article, not what the whole article is about.)

Reread the Selection Have children reread "Fishing Bears" to confirm the main idea and to note details that help make the main idea clear and interesting.

TEST PREP

Model the Test Item Remind children that when they are taking a test, they should be sure to read everything carefully. Read aloud the paragraph about fish, the question, and the answer choices as children track the print. Guide children in choosing the correct answer.

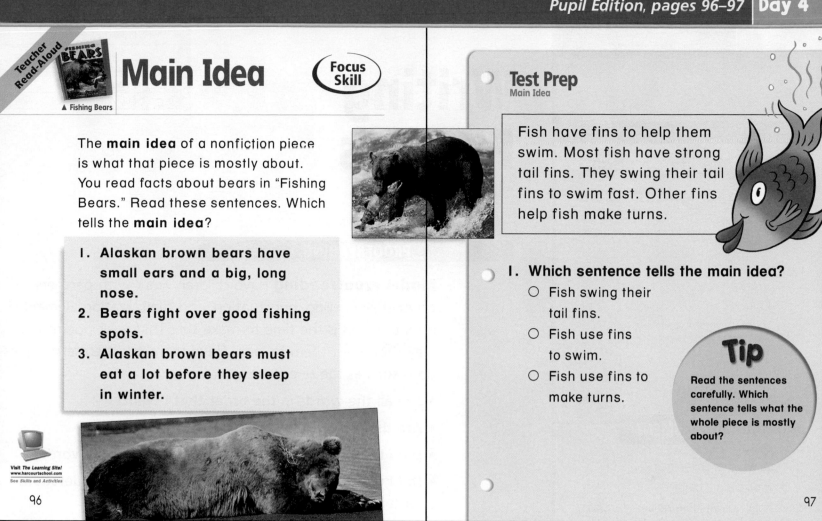

Focus Skill

Teacher Read-Aloud

▲ Fishing Bears

Main Idea

Focus Skill

The **main idea** of a nonfiction piece is what that piece is mostly about. You read facts about bears in "Fishing Bears." Read these sentences. Which tells the **main idea**?

1. Alaskan brown bears have small ears and a big, long nose.
2. Bears fight over good fishing spots.
3. Alaskan brown bears must eat a lot before they sleep in winter.

Visit *The Learning Site!*
www.harcourtschool.com
See *Skills and Activities*

96

Test Prep
Main Idea

Fish have fins to help them swim. Most fish have strong tail fins. They swing their tail fins to swim fast. Other fins help fish make turns.

1. **Which sentence tells the main idea?**
   ○ Fish swing their tail fins.
   ○ Fish use fins to swim.
   ○ Fish use fins to make turns.

Tip

Read the sentences carefully. Which sentence tells what the whole piece is mostly about?

97

Focus Skill

Visit *The Learning Site:*
www.harcourtschool.com

See Skill Activities and Test Tutors: Main Idea.

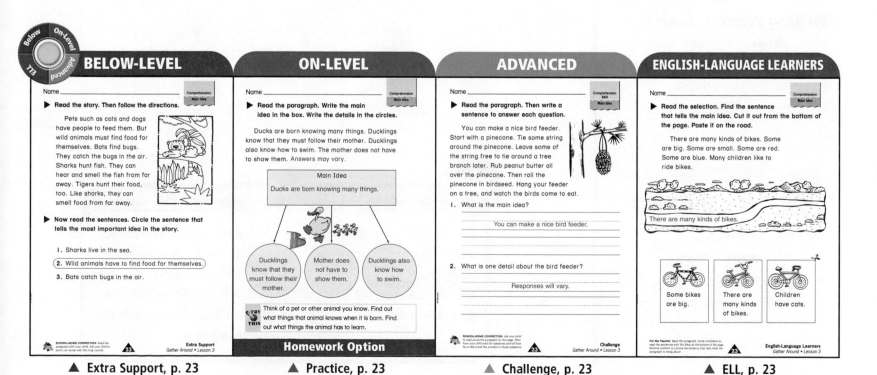

▲ Extra Support, p. 23   ▲ Practice, p. 23   ▲ Challenge, p. 23   ▲ ELL, p. 23

5-DAY WRITING	
DAY 1	Prewriting
DAY 2	Drafting
DAY 3	Responding and Revising
DAY 4	**Proofreading**
DAY 5	Publishing

DAILY LANGUAGE PRACTICE

Turn the lite on again?

Turn the <u>light</u> on again<u>.</u>

ONGOING ASSESSMENT

Note whether children are able to
- work with a partner.
- spell known high-frequency words correctly.
- listen attentively.

journal writing

Writing Prompt Have children draw a picture of an animal in a winter setting. Have them write one or two sentences about their picture.

technology

Visit *The Learning Site*:
www.harcourtschool.com
See Proofreading Makes Perfect.

LANGUAGE ARTS

Writing Process

Poem

PROOFREADING

Model Proofreading Have children work with partners to check their spelling, punctuation, and capitalization. Remind children that this is the time to make sure that their poems look the way they want them to look. Have them ask themselves questions such as the ones below:

- **Are all the words in the order that I want?**
- **Are they all spelled correctly?**
- **Did I leave enough space between letters and words?**
- **Did I use punctuation marks to help readers understand each line?**

Guide Editing As children proofread and make corrections, monitor their progress. Ask children how they feel about their writing now.

BELOW-LEVEL

Have children underline the describing words or other interesting words that they used to help the reader picture what the poem tells about.

ENGLISH-LANGUAGE LEARNERS

Have children work with partners to add color words or more precise nouns or verbs. Children may pantomime actions so that you can help them choose words that reflect their ideas.

Grammar

Verbs That Tell About Now

5-DAY GRAMMAR

DAY 1	Introduce Verbs That Tell About Now
DAY 2	Verbs That Tell About Now
DAY 3	Verbs That Tell About Now
DAY 4	**Action Game**
DAY 5	Identify Verbs That Tell About Now

REVIEW

Action Game: Thumbs Up, Thumbs Down Remind children that they have been learning about verbs that tell about now. Then play a game to give children practice identifying correct verbs. Tell children that you will say some sentences. If the sentence has the correct verb that tells about something that is happening now, children hold thumbs up. If the verb is not correct, children show thumbs down. Use sentences such as the following: *Matthew jumps.* (thumbs up) *Sara run.* (thumbs down) *Lilani and Roberto swim.* (thumbs up) *All the boys and girls plays.* (thumbs down) Once children get into the game, encourage them to suggest "thumbs up" or "thumbs down" sentences as well.

WRAP UP Revisit Literature

(Focus Strategy) Identify the Main Idea Reread the poem "Jump or Jiggle," page 95D. Then tell children to try to picture what is happening as you reread the poem. Ask children to finish this sentence: *This poem is mostly about _____.* (Possible response: the different ways animals and people move)

Next, reread the poem "In the Summer We Eat" (page 93E) as children act it out with you. Then ask children to finish this sentence: *"In the Summer We Eat" is mostly about _____.* (Possible response: the difference between what bears do in summer and winter)

S.S.R. Have children read silently from a book of their choice. See page 97J for tips on helping children choose books.

SKILL TRACE

VERBS THAT TELL ABOUT NOW

Introduce	68N
Reteach	T7
REVIEW	**93C, 95B, 97B, 97L**
T Test	Bk 1-5

ENGLISH-LANGUAGE LEARNERS

Some children may find it difficult to remember when a verb requires an *-s* at the end, since much of that knowledge is gained simply by listening to English correctly spoken. Help children identify verbs that agree with their subjects.

Name _____

Verbs That Tell About Now

► Add s to each verb. Write the word in the sentence.

stand

1. A man _____ stands _____.

run

2. A horse _____ runs _____.

dance

3. A dog _____ dances _____.

clap

4. A little girl _____ claps _____.

124

▲ Language Handbook, p. 124

Day at a Glance
Day 5

Sharing Literature
Big Book: *To Market, To Market*

Phonemic Awareness
Phoneme Isolation; Focus on Inflections *-ed, -ing*

Phonics
Inflections *-ed, -ing* (double final consonant)

Spelling
Posttest; Writing Application

Vocabulary
REVIEW: *during, ready*

High-Frequency Word
REVIEW: *both*

Reading
Rereading for Fluency
Pupil Edition
   "Fishing Bears," pp. 70–91
Self-Selected Reading

Independent Writing ✎
Writing Process: Publishing

Grammar
REVIEW: Verbs That Tell About Now

97C   Gather Around

WARM UP

MORNING MESSAGE
Good Morning!

Today is _____.

During the winter I like to _____.

When it is cold, I wear both _____ and _____.

When it snows, I am ready to _____.

Introduce the Day
Remind children that the bears in "Fishing Bears" slept during the winter. Guide children in generating a message about their winter activities. Ask:

• **What do you like to do in winter?**

• **What do you wear when it is cold?**

• **What can you do when it snows?**

As you write the message, invite volunteers to write previously taught letters, words, and/or punctuation to reinforce skills. For instance, have children join you in writing *During, ready,* and *both.* Have others add a capital letter at the beginning of each sentence and a period at the end.

Read the Message
Read the message. Use the message to focus on selected skills that have been previously taught.

Apply Skills

Phonics Point to the word *snows.* Have children read the word and identify the vowel sound. (/ō/) Elicit that the letters *ow* stand for the long o sound in *snows.*

Grammar Encourage children to note the action words in the message that tell about what is happening now.

Sharing Literature

LISTEN AND RESPOND

Reread Track the print as you reread the story. Encourage children to join in to read words they know.

Extend the Pattern Explain to children that a describing word is used to tell about each animal the lady brings home. Point out the describing word *fat*, which is used to tell about the pig. Have volunteers find the words *red, plump, live, spring, milking, white,* and *stubborn.* Write these words on the board. Have children think of other describing words that could be used for each animal in the story. Write these words on the board. Reread the story using the describing words that children suggested.

Phonemic Awareness

PHONEME ISOLATION

Words from the Big Book Remind children of the vegetables and animals in the story *To Market, To Market.* Ask children to identify the initial consonant sound as you say each word.

goose (/g/)	**duck** (/d/)	**cow** (/k/)	**horse** (/h/)
hen (/h/)	**pig** (/p/)	**lamb** (/l/)	**goat** (/g/)

FOCUS ON INFLECTIONS

Identify Base Words Remind children that they have learned the word endings *-ed* and *-ing.* Tell them that you will say several words with these endings. They will tell whether they hear *-ed* or *-ing.* Model by saying *walking. I hear the ending -ing in the word walk-ing.* Continue with these words:

running (-ing) **wanted** (-ed) **sipping** (-ing) **clapping** (-ing)
waited (-ed) **sailing** (-ing) **painted** (-ed) **driving** (-ing)

Have children say these words: *drumming-drummed.* Ask: *What is the base word—the shorter word you hear in* drumming *and* drummed? (drum) Continue with these word pairs:

runs-running (run)   **slipped-slipping** (slip)
waiting-waited (wait)   **sailing-sailed** (sail)

▲ **Big Book**

ENGLISH-LANGUAGE LEARNERS

Children might find the differing pronunciations of the *-ed* ending confusing. Have children practice the three ways *-ed* can be pronounced by saying the following words and having children repeat them after you: *wait-waited, jump-jumped, save-saved.*

OBJECTIVE

To recognize and read words with the inflections -ed, -ing

SKILL TRACE

INFLECTIONS *-ed, -ing* (double final consonant)	
INTRODUCE	97E–97F
Reteach	T6
Review	185H, 217F
Maintain	Bk 2-1

WORD WORK

Phonics
Inflections *-ed, -ing*

INTRODUCE SKILL

Understanding Inflections *-ed, -ing* (double final consonant) Have children turn to page 76 of "Fishing Bears" and read the last sentence. (This cub is napping on Mom!) Ask which word has an ending. (napping) Write the word *napping* on the board and ask children to name the base word. (nap) Write *nap* beneath *napping.* Then ask how the base word changed before the ending *-ing* was added. (The *p* was doubled.) Tell children that in some base words—ones with a short vowel followed by one consonant—the final consonant is doubled before the ending is added.

Base Words and Endings Write these words on the board:

tap	tapped	tapping
jog	jogged	jogging
bat	batted	batting

Read the words aloud, and ask children what endings were added to the base words. Have volunteers circle *-ed* and *-ing* in each word. Have another underline the base words. Ask how the spelling of the base words changed when the ending was added. (The last consonant was doubled.) Review the sounds for -ed in *tapped* (/t/), *jogged* (/d/), and *batted* (/ed/).

Compare Base Words Write the words *tape, taped, taping* above *tap, tapped, tapping.* Discuss the differences in vowel sounds and spelling patterns.

WORKING WITH PATTERNS

Analyze Inflections *-ed, -ing* (double final consonant) Display a chart like the following. Write the words *pat, flip, grin* in the left-hand blanks of the chart columns. Ask volunteers to fill in the spaces with the consonant that is doubled and the base word with the ending.

-ed ending	*-ing* ending
____ + __ + ed = ____	____ + __ + ing = ____
____ + __ + ed = ____	____ + __ + ing = ____
____ + __ + ed = ____	____ + __ + ing = ____

Apply Phonics

APPLY -ed, -ing ENDINGS

Write Words with -ed and -ing Write the following words and sentences on the board. Have children complete the sentences by filling in the blanks with the listed base words and adding the doubled consonant and the correct -ed or -ing ending for each.

snap   drag   chug   pop   bat

The branch ____ off the tree last night. (snapped)
We are ____ the branch out of the yard. (dragging)
Can you hear the train ____ down the track?
  (chugging)
The corn ____ when the pot was hot. (popped)
Today I ____ for the team. (batted)

5-DAY PHONICS	
DAY 1	Introduce /i/i
DAY 2	Word Building /i/i
DAY 3	Word Building with /i/i
DAY 4	Word Building with /i/i and /i/i-e
DAY 5	**Inflections -ed, and -ing**

BELOW-LEVEL

Some children may require extra practice in reading and writing words with a doubled final consonant before an ending. Have children build words using their *Word Builders* and *Word Builder Cards.* First, have children build the base word; then have them add the extra consonant and the ending. Give them these words to build: *nap, beg, rip, pop.*

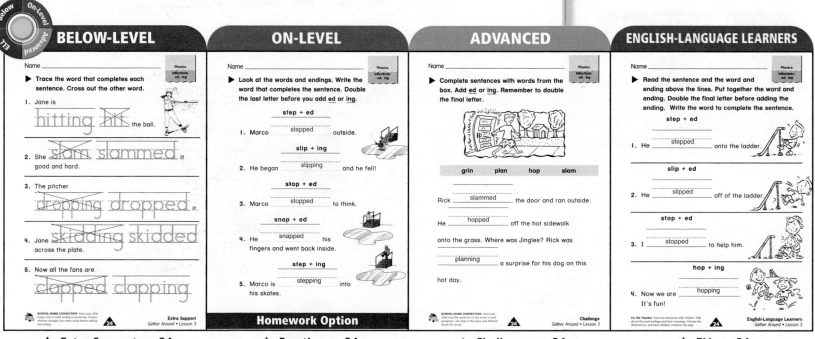

BELOW-LEVEL
▲ Extra Support, p. 24

ON-LEVEL
Homework Option
▲ Practice, p. 24

ADVANCED
▲ Challenge, p. 24

ENGLISH-LANGUAGE LEARNERS
▲ ELL, p. 24

5-DAY SPELLING	
DAY 1	Pretest; Word Sort
DAY 2	Word Building
DAY 3	State the Generalization
DAY 4	Review
DAY 5	**Posttest; Writing Application**

Spelling Words

1. find
2. kind
3. mind
4. mild
5. child
6. wild
7. day
8. play
9. sure
10. son

BELOW-LEVEL

Some children might need additional practice in using Spelling Words. Have children work in pairs. Have one child read a word from the spelling list and have the other child write the word and use it orally in a sentence.

ADVANCED

Have children create word chains using words from the spelling list and other words. Have them write their word chains in their journals.

Spelling

ASSESS/APPLY

Posttest Assess children's progress using the words and the Dictation Sentences from Day 1.

1. **find**   Did you **find** your boots?
2. **kind**   It was **kind** of you to share your toys.
3. **mind**   My **mind** grows as I learn new things.
4. **mild**   I like **mild** spring weather.
5. **child**   Did you see the **child** with his mother?
6. **wild**   Bears live in the **wild.**

Review

7. **day**   How many hours are there in one **day?**
8. **play**   It's fun to **play** in the park.

High-Frequency

9. **sure**   I am **sure** that I had my coat.

Vocabulary

10. **son**   Mr. Lopez's **son** looks just like him.

Writing Application Have children complete and illustrate the following sentence frames:

The **kind** of **wild** animal I like best is a _____.

It is fun to be a **child** because I can _____.

I use my **mind** to think about _____.

The kind of wild animal I like best is a tiger.

Vocabulary

USE WORDS IN SENTENCES

Display the following sentences and have volunteers complete them by filling in each sentence with the correct word. Then have another child frame the word as classmates reread each sentence aloud.

> **REVIEW**
> **Vocabulary**
> **during   ready**

> **You have learned a lot ____ this year.** (during)
> **Are you ____ to learn more?** (ready)

High-Frequency Words

Words to Remember

WORD WALL

Reinforce Words Hold up the *Word Card both.* Have children say the word and spell it. Have them say and spell the word again. Then put down the *Word Card* but keep your hand in the air. Ask children to say and spell the word one more time. Then have volunteers suggest sentences that include the word *both.* Finally, have children match the *Word Card* both with the same word in the display.

> **REVIEW**
> **High-Frequency Word**
> **both**

BELOW-LEVEL

Some children may need extra practice in spelling vocabulary or high-frequency words. Have children work in pairs at the display. First have one child spell a word, and have the other child say the word out loud and check the spelling. Then switch the activity by having the other child spell the word first.

▲ *Pupil Edition,* pp. 70–91

FLUENCY ROUTINES For support, see Fluency Routine Cards in Theme Resources, pp. T83–T84.

Rereading for Fluency

GROUPS

Echo Reading

🔵 **ENGLISH-LANGUAGE LEARNERS** Tell children that you will read the story one sentence at a time and that they should then read the same sentence, echoing what you read. Model expressive reading and encourage children to use expression. TEACHER-DIRECTED

This cub is napping on Mom!   This cub is napping on Mom!
These cubs are playing.   These cubs are playing.

PARTNERS

Partner Reading

🔵 **ON-LEVEL/BELOW-LEVEL** Have children work with partners to read the selection aloud. Remind them to read smoothly as if they are telling the information to someone. Suggest that each partner read one page at a time and reread if they think they can read more smoothly. INDEPENDENT

Managing Small Groups

Reread for fluency with children working individually, with partners, or in small groups. While you work with small groups, have other children do the following:

- **Self-Selected Reading**
- **Cross-Curricular Centers**
- **Practice Pages**
- **Journal Writing**

Use the suggested Classroom Management outline on page 7C for the whole-group/small-group schedule.

Self-Selected Reading

INDEPENDENT READING

Have children choose a book from the **Browsing Boxes** or the **Reading Center** to read independently during a sustained silent reading time. Children may also want to reread a story from their Pupil Edition. These are some books you may want to gather that relate to "Fishing Bears."

Decodable Books

Decodable Book 29
"Hi, Green Beans!" by Mary Hogan
"Wild, Wild Things" by Timothy Thomas

Cut-Out/Fold-Up Book

Find Something to Do
Practice Book, pp. 69–70

Books for All Learners

 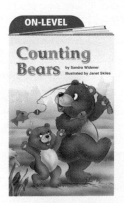  

Young Animals
by Lynn Trepicchio

Counting Bears
by Sandra Widener

The Wild Giant Panda
by Sandra Widener

Every Animal Has a Home
by Mindy Menschell

choosing books

To guide children in selecting books at their independent reading level, suggest that they read one or two pages of the book. If there are at least five words that the child can't read, he or she should try an easier book.

related books

- **Grizzly and the Bumble Bee**
  by Joy Cowley.
  The Wright Group, 1989.

  Grizzly Bear is stung by a bumble-bee and has a hard time telling people what happens. BELOW-LEVEL

- **A Friend for Growl Bear**
  by Margot Austin.
  Harper Collins, 1999.

  Growl Bear is just learning to talk, but he can only growl so he frightens all the other animals. ON-LEVEL

- **Three Pandas** by Jan Wahl.
  Boyd Mills Press, 2001.

  Three pandas leave the forest for the city and have crazy encounters with people. ADVANCED

- **Copy Me, Copycub** by Susan Winter.
  Harper Collins, 1999.

  Follow a mother bear and her cub through the seasons. ADVANCED

journal writing

Self-Selected Writing Have children write in their journal about a topic of their choice. They may want to illustrate their writing.

BELOW-LEVEL

If children have trouble forming their letters correctly (for example, if they frequently reverse letters), remind children to refer to the displayed alphabet.

ADVANCED

Have children write another poem based on a different season. Remind them of the writing process and encourage them to follow it as they create the new poem.

LANGUAGE ARTS

	5-DAY WRITING
DAY 1	Prewriting
DAY 2	Drafting
DAY 3	Responding and Revising
DAY 4	Proofreading
DAY 5	**Publishing**

Writing Process *Poem*

PUBLISHING

Copy and Illustrate Poems Provide children with construction or drawing paper. Have them write a clean copy of their poem. Encourage them to illustrate their poem. Remind them to sign their name on their poem.

Handwriting Remind children that poems are easier to read when their lines are separated. Tell children to make sure it is easy to see where one line ends and one begins by copying each line of poetry on its own separate line.

Display the Poems After poems have been read aloud, post them on a board or in the hallway for others to enjoy.

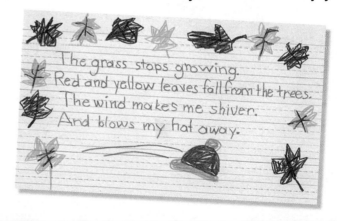

SCORING RUBRIC	4	3	2	1
FOCUS/IDEAS	Completely focused, purposeful.	Generally focused on task and purpose.	Somewhat focused on task and purpose.	Lacks focus and purpose.
ORGANIZATION	Presents material logically, adheres to topic.	Organization mostly clear, with few lapses; adheres to topic.	Some sense of organization but inconsistent or unclear in places.	Little or no sense of organization.
WORD CHOICE	Descriptive, imaginative, clear, and exact language.	Appropriate varied language; limited repetition.	Simplistic language; word choice unclear or inappropriate in places.	Simplistic language; word choice often unclear or inappropriate.
SENTENCES	Complete sentences with correct word order.	Most sentences are complete and have correct word order.	Frequent use of incomplete sentences and/or incorrect word order.	Demonstrates no understanding of complete sentences and correct word order.
DEVELOPMENT	Strong, specific supporting details.	Adequate support, mostly relevant details.	Limited supporting details.	Little or no development.
CONVENTIONS	Few, if any, errors in punctuation, capitalization, grammar, and spelling.	Some errors in punctuation, capitalization, grammar, and spelling.	Many errors in punctuation, capitalization, grammar, and spelling.	No meaningful use of punctuation, capitalization or grammar; frequent spelling errors.

5-DAY GRAMMAR	
DAY 1	Introduce Verbs That Tell About Now
DAY 2	Verbs That Tell About Now
DAY 3	Verbs That Tell About Now
DAY 4	Action Game
DAY 5	**Identify Verbs That Tell About Now**

Day 5

Grammar

Verbs That Tell About Now

REVIEW

Identify Verbs that Tell About Now Write the following verbs and sentences on the board. Have children choose one of the verbs to complete each sentence so that it tells about something that is happening now. Remind children that they might have to add *-s* to some words.

play   dig   nap

Anna ____ clams. Some bears ____ clams, too. (digs, dig)
Jeff ____ with his friends. Bear cubs ____, too. (plays, play)
The tired girl ____. Tired bear cubs ____, too. (naps, nap)

WRAP UP Author's Chair

Poetry Reading Invite children to take turns in the Author's Chair and share their poems. Encourage the authors to read their poems with expression and energy. You may want to make an audiotape of the performance so children can listen to it during free time.

Encourage children to speak in a voice loud enough for others to hear them and to hold their paper so the group can see the illustrations. Remind the audience to listen attentively and to applaud at the end of each poem.

S.S.R. Sustained Silent Reading

Have children read silently from a book of their choice. See page 97J for tips on helping children choose books.

SKILL TRACE

VERBS THAT TELL ABOUT NOW	
Introduce	68N
Reteach	T7
REVIEW	**93C, 95B, 97B, 97L**
T Test	Bk 1-5

ADVANCED

Have children look in books and magazines for sentences that contain verbs that tell about now.

technology

Visit *The Learning Site:*
www.harcourtschool.com
See Go for Grammar Gold, Multimedia Glossary.

Name _____

Verbs That Tell About Now

▶ Circle and write the correct verb.

(meet) meets

1. The children ____meet____ at Mike's house.

bring (brings)

2. Jane ____brings____ a snack.

(walk) walks

3. They ____walk____ to the park.

(sees) see

4. Joey ____sees____ a friend.

makes (make)

5. The children ____make____ a kite.

SCHOOL-HOME CONNECTION

125

▲ Language Handbook, p. 125

Fishing Bears **97L**

Guided Reading OPTIONS

Books for
All Learners
Reinforcing Skills and Strategies

■ BELOW-LEVEL

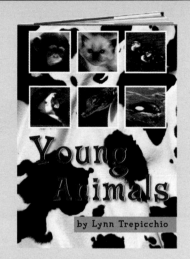

Young Animals

✓ **Phonics:** Long Vowel /ī/*i*

✓ **Vocabulary:** *during, ready*

✓ **High-Frequency Word:** *both*

✓ **Focus Skill:** Main Idea

SUMMARY Readers learn how animals care for their young.

 Visit *The Learning Site:*
www.harcourtschool.com
See Resources for Parents and
Teachers: Books for All Learners.

BEFORE READING

Build Background Ask children to share what they know about the birth of baby animals and how the babies are cared for by their parents.

Preview/Set Purpose Have children identify the title and help them read it. Point out the author and illustrator. Then have children look at the first few pages of the nonfiction book and predict what it is about. Have children set a purpose for reading, such as *I want to find out what mother animals do to take care of their babies*.

READING THE BOOK

Pages 2–5 Which young animal stays with its mother for awhile? (a young kangaroo) Which baby leaves right away? (a baby sea turtle) NOTE DETAILS

Pages 6–9 How is the birth of a baby killer whale different from the birth of an alligator? (A baby whale is born alive, and a baby alligator hatches from an egg.) MAKE COMPARISONS

Pages 10–12 When do young animals leave their parents? (when they are ready to take care of themselves) Is this the same with humans most of the time? Why do you think so? (Yes, because when children grow up they can live on their own and take care of themselves. Accept reasonable responses. Have children give reasons for their answers.) What is this story mostly about? (baby animals and how they are cared for) NOTE DETAILS, EXPRESS PERSONAL OPINIONS, MAIN IDEA

RESPONDING

Play a Fact Game Print these phrases on cards: *born in spring* and *carries her baby on her back*. Model how to play the game by reading each card and having children name the animal it describes. Have partners make several fact cards and play the game on their own.

Use Books for All Learners to promote oral reading fluency.

See **Fluency Routine Cards**, pp. T83–T84.

BELOW-LEVEL

Young Animals
by Lynn Trepicchio

ON-LEVEL

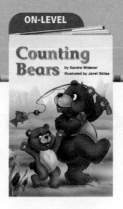

Counting Bears
by Sandra Widener
illustrated by Janet Skiles

ADVANCED

THE WILD GIANT PANDA
by Sandra Widener

▲ p. 97O

ELL

Every Animal Has a Home
by Mindy Menschell
illustrated by Tim Raouf

▲ p. 97P

■ ON-LEVEL

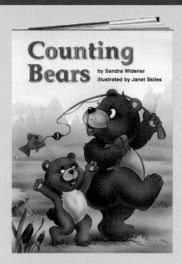

Counting Bears
by Sandra Widener
illustrated by Janet Skiles

Counting Bears

 Phonics: Long Vowel /ī/i

 Vocabulary: *during, ready*

 High-Frequency Word: *both*

✓ **Focus Skill: Main Idea**

SUMMARY Tiny bears and big, wild bears learn how to share fish in this rhymed story.

 Visit *The Learning Site*: www.harcourtschool.com
See Resources for Parents and Teachers: Books for All Learners.

BEFORE READING

Build Background Play simple counting, matching, and adding games with children. For example, lay out twenty game chips. Have children count them, and then divide them into two, four, five, and ten equal groups.

Preview/Set Purpose Have children identify the title and help them read it. Point out the author and illustrator. Then have children look at the first few pages of the book and predict what the story is about. Have children set a purpose for reading, such as *I want to find out if the bears can count and add.*

READING THE BOOK

Pages 2–5 How many bears are there all together? (ten) Why do the tiny bears go out in the boat? (They want to catch fish.) What do you notice about the words in this story? (They rhyme.) NOTE DETAILS; TEXT STRUCTURE

Pages 6–10 What is the problem in this story? (The tiny bears don't want to share the fish.) What happens to solve the problem? (A big bear suggests that they all share the tiny fish, and then the big bears will catch some big fish to share.) PLOT

Pages 11–16 How many fish does each bear get to eat? (two) What is this story mostly about? (bears who learn to share) NOTE DETAILS; MAIN IDEA

RESPONDING

Model the Story Provide groups of children with teddy bear graham crackers and goldfish crackers. Ask groups to use the "props" to act out the story. Invite children to equally divide and eat the "props" when they are done.

Books for All Learners

Reinforcing Skills and Strategies

■ ADVANCED

THE WILD GIANT PANDA
by Sandra Widener

The Wild Giant Panda

✓ **Phonics: Long Vowel /ī/i**

✓ **Vocabulary: *during, ready***

✓ **High-Frequency Word: *both***

✓ **Focus Skill: Main Idea**

SUMMARY   Readers learn about the giant panda, including where it lives, what it eats, and how it cares for its young.

Visit *The Learning Site:* www.harcourtschool.com
See Resources for Parents and Teachers: Books for All Learners.

BEFORE READING

Build Background Have children tell what they know about the giant panda. Show children a map of China and explain that this is where the giant panda lives in the wild.

Preview/Set Purpose Have children identify the title and help them read it. Point out the author and illustrator. Then have children look at the first few pages of the book and predict what it is about. Have children set a purpose for reading, such as *I want to find out if pandas eat honey.*

READING THE BOOK

Pages 2–5 What is one way that a giant panda is different from a black bear? (Possible response: The giant panda eats bamboo, and black bears don't.) COMPARE/CONTRAST

Pages 6–8 Why does the panda spend so much time looking for food? (It eats fifty pounds of bamboo a day.) How does it eat the tough leaves and stems? (It grinds them with big teeth.) DRAW CONCLUSIONS, NOTE DETAILS

Pages 9–13 Why did the Chinese love pandas long ago? (They believed pandas brought good luck.) NOTE DETAILS

Pages 14–16 What is this story mostly about? (the giant panda) MAIN IDEA

RESPONDING

Make Panda Posters Have pairs of children locate facts about giant pandas. Ask pairs to create posters that share facts from the book as well as those that they found. Children pair up and take turns telling each other facts about giant pandas.

▲ p. 97M   ▲ p. 97N

Managing Small Groups

While you work with small groups, have other children do the following:

- Self-Selected Reading
- Practice Pages
- Cross-Curricular Centers
- Journal Writing

■ ENGLISH-LANGUAGE LEARNERS

Every Animal Has a Home

✓ **Strong Picture Support**

✓ **Concept Vocabulary**

✓ **Theme Related**

SUMMARY Readers learn about the homes of common insects and larger animals.

 Visit *The Learning Site:* www.harcourtschool.com
See Resources for Parents and Teachers: Books for All Learners.

BEFORE READING

Build Background Work with children to make a list of the animals commonly seen in your area, including pets, farm animals, and wild animals. Guide children to name each animal's home.

Preview/Set Purpose Have children identify the title and help them read it. Point out the author and illustrator. Then have children look at the first few pages of the nonfiction book and predict what it is about. Have children set a purpose for reading, such as *I want to find out where bears live.*

READING THE BOOK

Pages 2–5 Where do spiders live? (on a web) How is a web a useful home for a spider? (They use their web to catch food.) SUMMARIZE, SPECULATE

Pages 6–9 Where do cows live? (in barns) What are two other animals that live in a barn? (Possible response: sheep and pigs) SUMMARIZE, MAKE COMPARISONS

Pages 10–12 What is this story mostly about? (the different homes of animals) MAIN IDEA

RESPONDING

Draw Animal Homes Ask children to choose one or more of the animals presented in the book and draw pictures of them in their homes. Discuss the names of the homes and guide children in adding labels to their pictures. For example, *A bear is in its den.*

Teacher Notes

Teacher Notes

Reading Selections

BIG BOOK

DECODABLE BOOK

Applies Long Vowel *o*

▲ Decodable Book 30
"Let's Go!"
"Flo Hippo"

PUPIL EDITION

Genre

Nonfiction

There are many ways an author can give information in nonfiction.

Look for:

• Ways the author lets you figure out answers to questions.

• Ideas the author gives about ways to learn from nature.

100

How to Be a Nature Detective

by Millicent E. Selsam
illustrated by Marlene Hill Donnelly

101

SUMMARY: *Nature detectives use clues about animals to answer questions.*

"How to Be a Nature Detective" is available on *Audiotext 5*.

Books for All Learners

Lesson Plans on pages 123M–123P

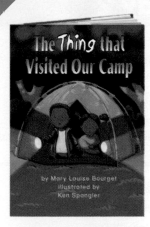

BELOW-LEVEL
- **Phonics:** Long Vowel /ō/o
- **Vocabulary:** *clues, detective, floor, nature, piece, pulls*

ON-LEVEL
- **Phonics:** Long Vowel /ō/o
- **Vocabulary:** *clues, detective, floor, nature, piece, pulls*

ADVANCED
- **Phonics:** Long Vowel /ō/o
- **Vocabulary:** *clues, detective, floor, nature, piece, pulls*

ELL
- *Strong Picture Support*
- *Concept Vocabulary*

MULTI-LEVELED PRACTICE

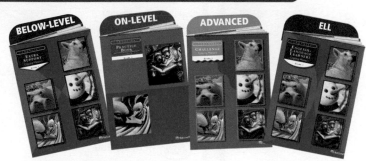

Practice Book, pp. 25–32

Extra Support, pp. 25–32

Challenge, pp. 25–32

English-Language Learners, pp. 25–32

 Technology

- *Phonics Express™ CD-ROM, Level B*
- *Writing Express™ CD-ROM*
- *Grammar Jingles™ CD, Primary*
- *Reading and Language Skills Assessment CD-ROM*
- *The Learning Site:* www.harcourtschool.com

ADDITIONAL RESOURCES

Phonics Practice Book, pp. 236–237, 286–287

Spelling Practice Book, pp. 73–74

Language Handbook, pp. 126–129

Read-Aloud Literature
- Big Book of Rhymes, p. 45

Teaching Transparencies 88–90, 108

Word Builders/Word Builder Cards

Letter Cards

Intervention Resource Resource Kit, Lesson 30

English-Language Learners Resource Kit, Lesson 30

 30 Minutes

ORAL LANGUAGE

- **Sharing Literature**

- **Phonemic Awareness**

 30 Minutes

WORD WORK

- **Phonics**

- **Spelling**

- **High-Frequency Words**

- **Vocabulary**

 45 Minutes

READING

- **Comprehension**
- **Fluency**

Daily Routines
- Morning Message
- Daily Language Practice
- Writing Prompt

- **Independent Reading**

 45 Minutes

LANGUAGE ARTS

- **Writing**

- **Grammar**

Daily Language Practice
Spiral Review

Day I

Sharing Literature, 98H
Big Book: Listen and Respond

Phonemic Awareness, 98H
Phoneme Isolation; Focus on /ō/

Phonics, 98I
Introduce: Long Vowel /ō/o

Spelling, 98K
Pretest; Word Sort **T**

High-Frequency Words, 98K
Review: *both* **T**

Vocabulary, 98K
Review: *during* **T**

Read
Apply Phonics, 98L

DECODABLE BOOK 30
"Let's Go!"

 Independent Reading
Books for All Learners

 **Writing Across the Curriculum,** 98M
Animal Features Chart

Writing Prompt
Have children describe the special feature of an animal and how this feature helps the animal survive.

Grammar, 98N
Introduce: Using *Am, Is,* and *Are*

Daily Language Practice
Can your go with me. (you, me?)

Day 2

Sharing Literature, 98P
Haiku: Listen and Respond

Phonemic Awareness, 98P
Phoneme Isolation; Focus on /ō/

Phonics, 98Q
Review: Long Vowel /ō/o

Spelling, 98Q
Word Building **T**

Vocabulary, 98S
Introduce: *clues, detective, floor, nature, piece, pulls* **T**

Word Power, pp. 98–99

Read
Read the Selection, 99A

PUPIL EDITION
"How to Be a Nature Detective,"
pp. 98–119

Comprehension

(Focus Skill) Main Idea **T**

(Focus Strategy) Read Ahead

 Independent Reading
Books for All Learners

 Shared Writing, 119B
Picture Caption

Writing Prompt
Have children draw a picture of an animal, then write a caption for their picture.

Grammar, 119C
Review: Using *Am, Is,* and *Are*

Daily Language Practice
I are going to school today (am, today.)

Focus Skill
Main Idea

Phonics
Long Vowel /ō/o

Focus of the Week:
• **VOCABULARY:** *clues, detective, floor, nature, piece, pulls*
• **COMPREHENSION:** Main Idea
• **GRAMMAR:** Using *am, is,* and *are*

Day 3

Sharing Literature, 119E
Poem: Build Concept Vocabulary

Phonemic Awareness, 119E
Matching and Isolating Phonemes;
Focus on /ō/

, 119F
Review: Long Vowel /ō/o

Spelling, 119H
State the Generalization **T**

Vocabulary, 119I
Review: *clues, detective, floor,
nature, piece, pulls* **T**

Read
Rereading for Fluency, 119J

**Making
Connections,**
120–121

Apply Phonics, 119G
DECODABLE BOOK 30
"Flo Hippo"

⦿ **Independent Reading**
Books for All Learners

✏ **Interactive Writing,** 121A
Newspaper Article

Writing Prompt
*Ask children to select a favorite sentence
from their article and copy it into their
journal.*

Grammar, 121B
Review: Using *Am, Is,* and *Are*

Daily Language Practice
Dont go oat in the cold. (Don't, out)

Day 4

Sharing Literature, 121D
Poem: Build Concept Vocabulary

Phonemic Awareness, 121D
Phoneme Isolation; Focus on /ō/o

, 121E
Build Words

Spelling, 121G
Review **T**

Vocabulary, 121H
Review: *clues, detective, floor,
nature, piece, pulls* **T**

Read
Comprehension, 121I

Focus Skill Main Idea,
pp. 122–123 **T**

⦿ **Independent Reading**
Books for All Learners

✏ **Independent Writing,** 123A
Riddle

Self-Selected Writing
*Have children write in their journal
about a topic of their choice.*

Grammar, 123B
Review: Using, *Am, Is,* and *Are*

Daily Language Practice
did you find any cluse? (Did, clues)

Day 5

Sharing Literature, 123D
Big Book: Develop Listening
Comprehension

Phonemic Awareness, 123D
Distinguish Phonemes; Focus on '*ve,
'd, 're*

, 123E
Introduce: Contractions '*ve, 'd, 're*

Spelling, 123G
Posttest; Writing Application **T**

Vocabulary, 123H
Review: *clues, detective, floor,
nature, piece, pulls* **T**

Read
Rereading for Fluency, 123I

**Self-Selected
Reading,** 123J

⦿ **Independent Reading**
Books for All Learners

✏ **Independent Writing,** 123K
Description of a Setting

Writing Prompt
*Have children write a description of their
favorite place in nature.*

Grammar, 123L
Review: Using *Am, Is,* and *Are*

Daily Language Practice
I dont know where they our. (don't, are)

How to Be a Nature Detective **98D**

Cross-Curricular Centers

MATH CENTER

Measure Footprints

Tell children that both animals and people can leave tracks or footprints. Set out a shoe box filled with sand or salt. Have children take turns stepping in the box and making a footprint. They can then measure the length of the footprint and record the results on a chart or graph.

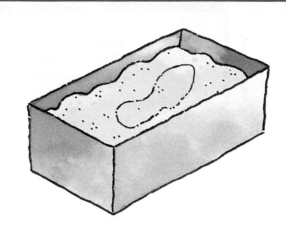

30 Minutes

Materials

- shoe box
- sand or salt
- rulers

COMPUTER CENTER

Animal Clues

Have children imagine that they are detectives tracking an animal. Tell them that they will create a "detective report." They can list the clues that they found at the scene. Children can tell how the clues describe the animal. Have them type their report using a word-processing program. They can draw pictures or use clip art to illustrate the report.

The prints might belong to a horse. It looks like the horse had on horseshoes.

30 Minutes

Materials

- computer
- word-processing program

ART CENTER

Vegetable and Fruit Prints

Tell children that they can use pieces of cut vegetables to make prints like the animal tracks in "How to Be a Nature Detective." Provide children with a variety of cut-up vegetable and fruit pieces that can be used to make prints. Show children how to dip the vegetable in paint and press it onto paper to make a print. Children can make a picture using the "vegetable tracks."

20 Minutes

Materials

- cut-up vegetables or fruits (potatoes, apples, carrots)
- finger paint
- construction paper
- paper towels

98E   Gather Around

MATH TECHNOLOGY ART LETTER AND WORD ABC SCIENCE

LETTER AND WORD CENTER

Words with Long Vowel *o*

Make several sets of word cards using story words from stories children have previously read. Divide the cards into piles. Have children read through a pile of cards and find words with the long vowel sound of o. They can then make a list of /ō/ words they find. When each child is done with a set of cards, he or she can exchange with another child and continue.

meadow   cozy   clothes   rope

15 Minutes

Materials
■ word cards with story words from previous lessons

SCIENCE CENTER

Animal Food

Display the *Big Book I Swam with a Seal*. Tell children to look at the pictures of the different animals. Have them choose several animals and find out what they eat. Provide resources for children to look through, such as magazines and nonfiction books. Ask them to make a two-column chart that tells the name of the animals and the food they eat.

Animal	Food
horse	hay
falcon	mice
cat	milk

30 Minutes

Materials
■ *Big Book I Swam with a Seal*
■ reference materials about animals
■ chart paper
■ markers

HOMEWORK FOR THE WEEK

The Homework Copying Master provides activities to complete for each day of the week.

 Visit *The Learning Site:* www.harcourtschool.com

See Resources for Parents and Teachers: Homework Helper.

Homework, p. T42 ▶

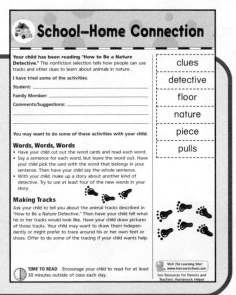

🚌 **School–Home Connection**

Your child has been reading "How to Be a Nature Detective." This nonfiction selection tells how people can use tracks and other clues to learn about animals in nature.

I have tried some of the activities.

Student: _____

Family Member: _____

Comments/Suggestions: _____

You may want to do some of these activities with your child.

Words, Words, Words
• Have your child cut out the word cards and read each word.
• Say a sentence for each word, but leave the word out. Have your child pick the card with the word that belongs in your sentence. Then have your child say the whole sentence.
• With your child, make up a story about another kind of detective. Try to use at least four of the new words in your story.

Making Tracks
Ask your child to tell you about the animal tracks described in "How to Be a Nature Detective." Then have your child tell what his or her tracks would look like. Have your child draw pictures of those tracks. Your child may want to draw them independently or might prefer to trace around his or her own feet or shoes. Offer to do some of the tracing if your child wants help.

⏱ **TIME TO READ** Encourage your child to read for at least 30 minutes outside of class each day.

clues
detective
floor
nature
piece
pulls

Visit *The Learning Site!* www.harcourtschool.com See Resources for Parents and Teachers: Homework Helper

How to Be a Nature Detective **98F**

Day at a Glance
Day 1

Sharing Literature
Big Book: *I Swam with a Seal*

Phonemic Awareness
Phoneme Isolation; Focus on /ō/

Phonics
INTRODUCE: Long Vowel /ō/o

Spelling
Pretest; Word Sort

High-Frequency Word
REVIEW: *both*

Vocabulary
REVIEW: *during*

Reading
Decodable Book 30
"Let's Go!"

Read

Writing Across the Curriculum ✏️
Animal Features Chart

Grammar
INTRODUCE: Using *Am, Is,* and *Are*

WARM UP · MORNING MESSAGE

Good Morning!

Today is _____.
Animals live in different places.
Some animals are wild.
Some animals live _____.
A _____ lives in the _____.

Introduce the Day

Tell children that they will revisit the *Big Book I Swam with a Seal*. Guide them in generating a message about where different animals live. Ask:

• **Where do seals and dolphins live?**

• **Where do moose and deer live?**

• **Some animals are not wild. Where might these animals live?**

As you write the message, ask volunteers to write known words. Have volunteers find and read the words they know in the message.

Read the Message

Read the message. Use the message to focus on selected skills that have been previously taught.

Apply Skills

High-Frequency Words This message contains several previously taught high-frequency words. Say these words: *a, the, some, animals, live, in,* and *different*. Ask volunteers to find and read these words in the message.	**Grammar** Point out the words *animals live* in the message. Remind children that the *s* at the end of *animals* means more than one. Point out the verb form that is used with telling about two or more (live).

Sharing Literature

LISTEN AND RESPOND

Read the Big Book Remind children that many animals have special features that help them survive in their environments. For example, a seal's flippers help it move quickly through the water. Read the *Big Book I Swam with a Seal* to children. Pause after reading about each animal and have volunteers tell something about what the animal is like or where it lives.

Respond to Literature Have children imitate the animals in the story. Tell them to move the way the story says the animals move. Children can also make the noises these animals might make.

▲ **Big Book**

Phonemic Awareness

PHONEME ISOLATION

Words from the Big Book Read aloud to children the title of the big book. Repeat the words *swam* and *seal*. Explain that both *swam* and *seal* begin with *s*, but *swam* includes the blend *sw*. Say the following words from the story and ask children to identify the words that begin with blends.

flipper	**funny**	**falcon**	skinny	**slithered**
snake	pranced	**pony**	flew	**sound**
turtle	trailed	**porcupine**	grass	**gull**

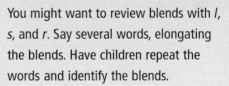

BELOW-LEVEL

You might want to review blends with *l*, *s*, and *r*. Say several words, elongating the blends. Have children repeat the words and identify the blends.

FOCUS ON /ō/

Identify Initial Phonemes Say the word *old* very slowly, and have children repeat the word. Say *I hear the sound /ō/ at the beginning of* old. Have children repeat the following words and tell the initial vowel sound of each:

oval (/ō/)	**open** (/ō/)	**ocean** (/ō/)	**only** (/ō/)
oboe (/ō/)	**older** (/ō/)	**odor** (/ō/)	**over** (/ō/)

OBJECTIVES

- *To generate the long vowel sound of o*
- *To build words using known letters and sounds*
- *To read simple, regular words*

SKILL TRACE

/ō/o	
INTRODUCE	**98I–98L**
Reteach	S22–S23
Review	98Q–98R; 119F–119G, 121E–121F

teaching tip

Build Vocabulary As you model blending the word *roll*, explain to children that *roll* has different meanings, such as a roll that you eat, to roll a ball, and a roll of tape.

30 Minutes

Materials

- mural paper
- pencils
- markers
- crayons

Phonics and Spelling
Long Vowel /ō/o *Introduce*

TEACH/MODEL

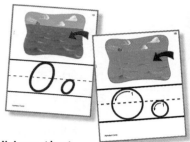

Introduce /ō/o Display *Alphabet Card Oo* and say the letter name. Tell children that the letter *o* can stand for the sound /ō/, the long vowel sound of *o* in words such as *old, over,* and *open.*

Hold up *Letter Card o* and say /ō/. Tell children that the /ō/ sound appears in the middle of the words *hold, sold,* and *toll.* Have children repeat the sound several times as you touch the card.

WORD BLENDING

c d f l l m o r s t

Words with /ō/o Blend and read the words *old, fold,* and *told.* As you demonstrate each step, using a pocket chart and *Letter Cards.* Have children repeat after you, using *Word Builders* and *Word Builder Cards.*

Follow the same procedure as children build and blend the words *cold, roll,* and *most.*

Phonics CENTER

O Around Our World

Have children travel around the classroom, looking for objects with names that contain the long vowel sound of *o*. Children can then return to the center and write a group list of /ō/ words on a sheet of mural paper. Each child can create an illustration to go with a word.

WORD BUILDING

c d f l l m o r s t

Build Spelling Words Place the letter *o* in a pocket chart. Have children do the same with their *Word Builders* and *Word Builder Cards*. Repeat with the letters *l* and *d*. Model how to blend the word *old*. Slide your hand under the letters as you slowly elongate the sounds—/ōōlldd/. Then read the word naturally—*old*. Have children do the same.

o l d

Have children build and read new words by telling them:

- Add an *f* to the beginning of *old*. What word did you make?

f o l d

- Change the *f* to *t*. What word did you make?

t o l d

- Change the *t* to *c*. What word did you make?

c o l d

- Change the *c* to *r*. Then change the *d* to *l*. What word did you make?

r o l l

- Change the *r* to *m*. Change the first *l* to *s*. Then change the second *l* to *t*. What word did you make?

m o s t

 Dictate Long /ō/*o* Words Dictate the words *cold* and *roll* and have children write them in their journal. Suggest that they either draw a picture or write about each word.

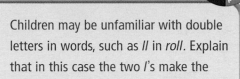

5-DAY PHONICS/SPELLING

DAY 1	Introduce /ō/*o*
DAY 2	Word Building with /ō/*o*
DAY 3	Word Building with /ō/*o*
DAY 4	Word Building with /ō/*o* and /ō/*o-e*
DAY 5	Contractions *'ve*, *'d*, *'re*

ENGLISH-LANGUAGE LEARNERS

Below · On-Level · Advanced · ELL

Children may be unfamiliar with double letters in words, such as *ll* in *roll*. Explain that in this case the two *l*'s make the same sound as one *l*.

Phonics Resources

Phonics Express™ CD-ROM, **Level B** Sparkle/Route 1/Harbor

Phonics Practice Book, pp. 236–237

Spelling Words

1. **old**
2. **fold**
3. **told**
4. **cold**
5. **roll**
6. **most**
7. **find**
8. **child**
9. **both**
10. **during**

Phonics and Spelling

	5-DAY SPELLING
DAY 1	Pretest; Word Sort
DAY 2	Word Building
DAY 3	State the Generalization
DAY 4	Review
DAY 5	Posttest; Writing Application

INTRODUCE THE WORDS

Pretest Read aloud the first word and the Dictation Sentence. Repeat the word as children write it. Write the correct spelling on the board and have children circle the word if they spelled it correctly and write it correctly if they did not. Repeat for words 2–10.

1. **old**   There is a hole in my **old** sneakers.
2. **fold**   Please **fold** the paper in half.
3. **told**   I **told** a story to the class.
4. **cold**   It gets very **cold** here in the winter.
5. **roll**   The gym teacher asked us to **roll** the ball.
6. **most**   The winner is the team with the **most** points.

Review

7. **find**   I can't **find** my glasses.
8. **child**   Things were different when I was a **child**.

High-Frequency

9. **both**   He asked **both** boys to play the game.

Vocabulary

10. **during**   We must be quiet **during** classes at school.

Word Sort Place cards with the labels *Long vowel o, Long vowel i,* and *-ing* at the top of a pocket chart. Write each Spelling Word on an index card. Display the cards and ask "Which words have the long vowel sound of *o*? Which words have the long vowel sound of *i*? What word is left over? Where does it go?" Place the words in the correct columns as children direct. Then have children read the words aloud.

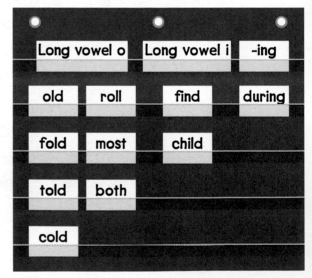

Long vowel o	Long vowel i	-ing
old roll	find	during
fold most	child	
told both		
cold		

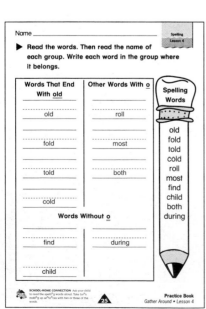

▲ Practice Book, p. 25

Apply Phonics

APPLY /ō/o

Write the following sentences on the board or chart paper. Have children read the first sentence as you track the print. Frame the words *hold* and *gold* and have children read them. Continue with the other sentences.

> I will **hold** on to the **gold** ring.
> Will you **go** to **both** shops?
> He **sold** his **old** car.

Have children read "Let's Go!" in *Decodable Book 30*.

Read

▲ **Decodable Book 30**
"Let's Go!"

School-Home Connection

Take-Home Book Version

◄ Decodable Books
Take-Home Version

ONGOING ASSESSMENT

Note how well children
- read sentences without modeling.
- decode words in "Let's Go!"
- complete long vowel /ō/o practice pages.

Managing Small Groups

Read the *Decodable Book* with small groups of children. While you work with small groups, have other children do the following:

- **Self-Selected Reading**
- **Practice Pages**
- **Cross-Curricular Centers**
- **Journal Writing**

Use the suggested Classroom Management outline on page 7C for the whole-group/small-group schedule.

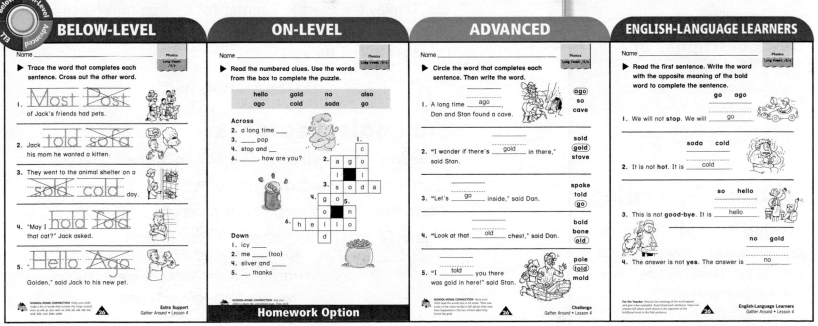

▲ Extra Support, p. 26   ▲ Practice, p. 26   ▲ Challenge, p. 26   ▲ ELL, p. 26

Writing Every Day

Day 1: Animal Features Chart
Have children create a chart telling about features of animals.

Day 2: Picture Caption
Have children look at a picture and write a caption to go with it.

Day 3: Newspaper Article
Have children work together to write a news story about an animal that escaped from the zoo.

Day 4: Riddle
Have children write an animal riddle that includes clues about the animal's identity.

Day 5: Description of a Setting
Have children write a description of a story setting.

journal writing

Writing Prompt Have children describe a special feature of an animal and how this feature helps the animal survive in its environment.

LANGUAGE ARTS

Writing Across the Curriculum

Animal Features Chart

BRAINSTORM

Discuss Animal Traits Remind children that many animals have special features that help them survive in nature. Many times these features allow the animal to eat the food it likes best. Provide an example, such as:

MODEL Seals have many special features that help them survive. They have flippers. Flippers help seals swim fast. They also have a thick layer of fat that helps keep them warm in cold water. Both of these features help seals catch the fish they like to eat.

Brainstorm Ideas Ask children to name other animals they know and to describe any special features these animals possess. Talk about how the animals use their special features. Include some of the animals from the story and challenge children to describe other animals they know about. Write their ideas on chart paper.

Display the Chart Read aloud the animal names and features, having children read decodable and previously taught words with you. Display the chart in a center for children to refer to as they write throughout the week. Allow children to suggest additions to the chart during the week.

Animals	Features
beaver	strong, flat tail to warn of danger
squirrel	sharp teeth to crack nutshells
giraffe	long neck to reach high leaves in trees

5-DAY GRAMMAR	
DAY I	Introduce Using *Am, Is,* and *Are*
DAY 2	Match Sentence Parts
DAY 3	*Am, Is, Are* Game
DAY 4	Sentences with *Am, Is,* and *Are*
DAY 5	Choose *Am, Is,* or *Are*

rammar

g Am, Is, *and* Are

TEACH/MODEL

Introduce Using *Am, Is,* and *Are*
Make word cards for *I, He, They, You, am, is, are* (two), and *six* (four) and a period (four). Form four sentences in a pocket chart, leaving out the verb.

Explain that the words *am, is,* and *are* tell about now. The word *am* is used to tell about yourself. *Is* tells about one person, place, animal, or thing. *Are* tells about more than one person, place, animal, or thing. Point out that *you* always takes the *are* form, whether it tells about one person or many. Add the *am, is, are,* and *are* cards. Have children read the sentences.

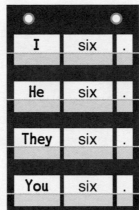

I	six	.
He	six	.
They	six	.
You	six	.

PRACTICE/APPLY

Display *Teaching Transparency 88* Model completing the first sentence with the correct form of the verb. Then have children identify which form of the verb correctly completes each sentence.

Revisit the Big Book

Pantomime Animals Reread the *Big Book I Swam with a Seal.* Have volunteers pantomime the actions of the different animals. The rest of the group can guess which animal is being pantomimed. Have children refer back to the big book if they need help.

Have children read silently from a book of their choice. See page 123J for tips on helping children choose books.

▲ **Big Book**

OBJECTIVE
To use am, is, *and* are
correctly in sentences

SKILL TRACE

USING *AM, IS,* AND *ARE*	
INTRODUCE	**98N**
Reteach	T7
Review	119C, 121B, 123B, 123L

▼ **Teaching Transparency 88**

USING *AM, IS,* AND *ARE*

1. I _____ a cat.
2. My nose _____ black.
3. My eyes _____ blue.
4. My tail _____ little.
5. My ears _____ big.
6. I _____ a happy cat.

"How to Be a Nature Detective"
Gather Around, Volume 1-5   88   Grammar: Using *Am, Is,* and *Are*
                                                                                   Harcourt

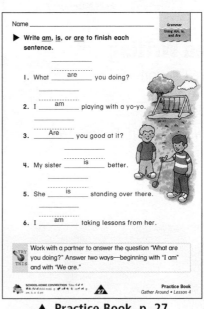

Name _____

Grammar
Using Am, Is,
and Are

► Write **am, is,** or **are** to finish each sentence.

1. What __are__ you doing?
2. I __am__ playing with a yo-yo.
3. __Are__ you good at it?
4. My sister __is__ better.
5. She __is__ standing over there.
6. I __am__ taking lessons from her.

TRY THIS Work with a partner to answer the question "What are you doing?" Answer two ways—beginning with "I am" and with "We are."

SCHOOL-HOME CONNECTION   27   **Practice Book**
                                                        Gather Around • Lesson 4

▲ **Practice Book, p. 27**

How to Be a Nature Detective   **98N**

Day at a Glance
Day 2

Sharing Literature
Haiku

Phonemic Awareness
Phoneme Isolation; Focus on /ō/

Phonics

REVIEW: Long Vowel /ō/o

Spelling
Word Building

Vocabulary
INTRODUCE: *clues, detective, floor, nature, piece, pulls*

Reading
Pupil Edition
   "How to Be a Nature Detective,"
   pp. 98–116

Shared Writing ✎
Picture Caption

Grammar
REVIEW: Using *Am, Is,* and *Are*

980   Gather Around

WARM UP
MORNING MESSAGE
Good Morning!

Today is _____.
We can use clues to answer a riddle.
A paw print shows us _____.
Clues can help answer questions like these:
_____? _____?

Introduce the Day

Tell children that they will read a selection about using clues in nature to figure out which animals have walked through a particular place. Help them create a message about different types of clues. Ask:

- **What happens when you walk in the house with mud on your shoes?**

- **What happens when an animal walks through the snow? What do you see?**

As you write the message, allow children to write words that they know. You may want to spell unfamiliar words and have children write the letters. Use this opportunity to develop new vocabulary.

Read the Message

Read the message. Use the message to focus on skills that have been previously taught.

Apply Skills

Phonics Focus on the word *shows* in the message. Remind children they have learned that one way to make the sound /ō/ is with *ow*. Have children name as many long vowel *o* words as they can that are spelled with *ow*.	**Grammar/Mechanics** Point out the colon after the word *these* in the message. Explain that this punctuation mark is used here to show that a list or a group of items will follow.

Sharing Literature

LISTEN AND RESPOND

Connect to Prior Knowledge Tell children that a discovery is something that we find out when we explore or study something. When we discover something, we learn something that we didn't know before. Ask children to describe discoveries that they or other people have made.

Respond to Literature Read the haiku. Help children understand that the button mentioned in the haiku is a belly button. The author looked closely at a frog and discovered that it doesn't have a belly button. Ask children to tell how they think the poet felt about making this discovery and why they think that.

Haiku

A discovery!
On my frog's smooth green belly
there sits no button.

Haiku, Yaku

Phonemic Awareness

PHONEME ISOLATION

Words from the Haiku Remind children that they heard the word *frog* in the haiku. Repeat the word and tell children that it begins with the blend /fr/. Say the following words from the haiku and ask children to identify the words that begin with blends and say the blends.

button	**my**	**smooth** /sm/
belly	**sits**	**green** /gr/

FOCUS ON /ō/

Phoneme Blending Tell children that you are going to say some words very slowly. Model by segmenting the word *hold* into phonemes—/h/ /ō/ /l/ /d/. Then say the word naturally—*hold*. Segment the following words, having children blend the sounds to say each word:

/r/ /ō/ /d/   (rode)   /m/ /ō/ /l/ /d/ (mold)   /n/ /ō/   (no)
/g/ /l/ /ō/ /b/ (globe)   /r/ /ō/ /b/   (robe)   /h/ /i/ /p/ /ō/ (hippo)

REACHING ALL LEARNERS

Diagnostic Check: Phonemic Awareness

If... children cannot identify words with medial /ō/ . . .

Then... have them practice identifying words with final /ō/, such as *grow, go, slow, bow, toe, Joe,* and *no.*

ADDITIONAL SUPPORT ACTIVITIES

BELOW-LEVEL   Reteach, p. S20

ADVANCED   Extend, p. S21

ENGLISH-LANGUAGE LEARNERS   Reteach, p. S21

How to Be a Nature Detective   **98P**

5-DAY SPELLING	
DAY 1	Pretest; Word Sort
DAY 2	**Word Building**
DAY 3	State the Generalization
DAY 4	Review
DAY 5	Posttest; Writing Application

OBJECTIVES

• *To blend sounds into words*

• *To read and write Spelling Words*

SKILL TRACE

/ō/o	
Introduce	98I–98L
Reteach	S22–S23
REVIEW	**98Q–98R, 119F–119G**
	121E–121F

Spelling Words

1. **old**
2. **fold**
3. **told**
4. **cold**
5. **roll**
6. **most**
7. **find**
8. **child**
9. **both**
10. **during**

Phonics and Spelling
Long Vowel /ō/o *Review*

WORD BUILDING

Blend and Read a Spelling Word Place *Letter Cards o, l, d* in a pocket chart. Ask children to name each letter as you place it in the chart. Slide your hand under the letters as you blend the sounds—/ōōlldd/. Have children repeat after you. Then read the word naturally—*old*, and have children do the same.

Build Spelling Words Ask children which letter you should add to make *old* become *fold*. *(f)* Continue building the Spelling Words shown in this manner and having children read them.

o	l	d
f	o	l	d
t	o	l	d
c	o	l	d
r	o	l	l
m	o	s	t

ADVANCED

Have children make lists of rhyming words with long *o*, using different spellings of the sound, such as *o-e, -ow*, and *-old*. Suggest that children keep the list for future writing assignments.

ENGLISH-LANGUAGE LEARNERS

To reinforce word meanings, use each Spelling Word in a sentence. If possible, use sentences that children can act out or draw.

Apply Phonics

READ WORDS IN CONTEXT

Write the following sentences on the board or on chart paper and have children read them aloud.

> The **child** can't **find** her dog.
> I **told** the class to **fold** the paper.
> We get **both** snow and rain **during** **cold** winters.
> I will **roll** that **old** ball.
> That bowl holds the **most** food.

Dictate Words Dictate to children several words from the pocket chart, and have them write the words on a dry-erase board or in their journal.

old
fold
told
cold
roll
most

5-DAY PHONICS/SPELLING

DAY 1	Introduce /ō/o
DAY 2	**Word Building with /ō/o**
DAY 3	Word Building with /ō/o
DAY 4	Word Building with /ō/o and /ō/o-e
DAY 5	Contractions 've, 'd, 're

Phonics Resources

Phonics Express™ CD-ROM, **Level B** Sparkle/Route 1/ Building Site, Train Station

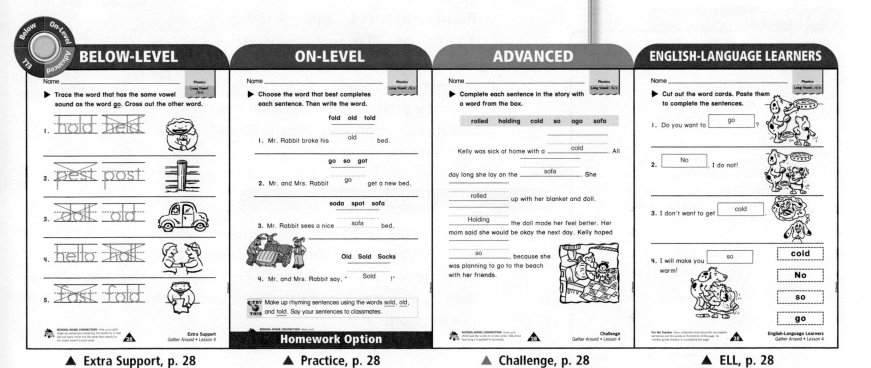

▲ Extra Support, p. 28   ▲ Practice, p. 28   ▲ Challenge, p. 28   ▲ ELL, p. 28

How to Be a Nature Detective   **98R**

Vocabulary

clues	things that help solve a problem or mystery
detective	a person who tries to solve crimes or mysteries
floor	the inside bottom surface of a room, where you walk
nature	all plant and animal life
piece	a part of something that is separated from the whole
pulls	to move something toward yourself

▼ **Teaching Transparency 89**

VOCABULARY

clues	detective	floor
nature	piece	pulls

The nature detective looks for clues. He sees tracks! The detective follows the tracks. The tracks go into the house and onto the floor.

The detective finds a torn piece of paper. He pulls out another piece of torn paper. The detective finds the dog with paper in its mouth. The problem is solved!

"How to Be a Nature Detective"
Gather Around, Volume 1-5

89

Vocabulary
Harcourt

Building Background

TALK ABOUT NATURE CLUES

Make a Nature Chart Tell children they are going to read a selection about being a nature detective. Ask children how they might guess that different animals have been or still are in a particular place. Tell children to think about clues they can see, hear, or smell. Guide children in completing a chart.

Animals	Clues
dog	paw prints, hairs, barking
bird	tracks, feathers, chirping
squirrel	nutshells, nest

Discuss Story Words Write the following words on the board: *claws, paws, toes, footprints, exactly, questions,* and *tires.* Point to each word and read it aloud. Ask volunteers to tell what each word means.

Vocabulary

INTRODUCE WORDS IN CONTEXT

Read Sentences Display *Teaching Transparency 89* or write the words and sentences on the board. Point to the words and read them to children. Track the print as you read aloud the sentences. Call on volunteers to reread each sentence.

> INTRODUCE
>
> **Vocabulary**
>
> | | |
> |---|---|
> | clues | nature |
> | detective | piece |
> | floor | pulls |

CHECK UNDERSTANDING

Every-Pupil Response Duplicate and distribute a set of the following Individual Word Cards for each child: *clues, detective, floor, nature, piece, pulls* (page T36). Say the words and have children hold up the appropriate Word Cards. Then ask volunteers to use the words in sentences.

Word Power

Words to Remember

clues

detective

floor

nature

piece

pulls

A **detective** looks for **clues**.
A **nature detective** looks for **clues**, too. They may be tracks in mud, in sand, or even on a **floor**. A **nature detective** sometimes **pulls** a stick or a **piece** of string out of a nest. Find out how to be a **nature detective**!

▲ How to Be a
Nature Detective

98

99

Word Power

Pages 98–99 Have children read aloud the Words to Remember. Then have children read aloud the sentences. Have children point to the Words to Remember in the sentences.

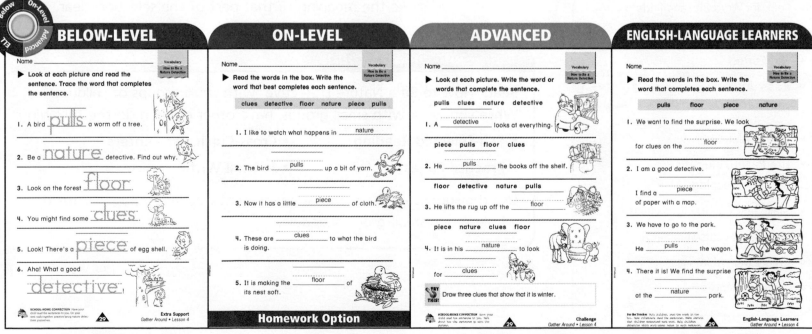

BELOW-LEVEL	**ON-LEVEL**	**ADVANCED**	**ENGLISH-LANGUAGE LEARNERS**
▲ Extra Support, p. 29	▲ Practice, p. 29	▲ Challenge, p. 29	▲ ELL, p. 29

How to Be a Nature Detective **98–99**

Phonics

Long Vowel /ō/o

Vocabulary

clues, detective, floor, nature, piece, pulls

Decodable Words

See the list on pp. T50–T51.

Comprehension

 Main Idea

 Read Ahead

Strategies
Good Readers Use

To Recognize Words

- Use Decoding/Phonics
- Look for Word Bits and Parts

To Gain Meaning

- Self-Correct
- **Read Ahead**
- Reread
- Reread Aloud
- Use Picture Clues to Confirm Meaning
- Make and Confirm Predictions
- Sequence Events/Summarize
- Create Mental Images
- Make Inferences

Prereading Strategies

PREPARING TO READ

Preview/Predict Have children read with you the title and author's name on page 101. Ask a volunteer to tell what a detective is. Then instruct children to look through the pictures in the selection. Have children predict what a nature detective might be.

Set Purpose Help children set a purpose for reading. If necessary, suggest that they read to find out what questions a nature detective tries to answer.

COMPREHENSION SKILL

Main Idea Tell children that the main idea of a story is the most important idea. Explain that many of the other ideas in the story, called details, tell more about the main idea. Ask volunteers to tell the main idea of other stories they have read. Suggest that children think about the main idea as they read the selection "How to Be a Nature Detective."

COMPREHENSION STRATEGY

Read Ahead Remind students that when they have difficulty understanding a word or a sentence, reading ahead might help them to figure out the meaning. Remind them that when they read ahead, they will discover more details that will make the meaning of that part of the selection clear.

Managing Small Groups

Read "How to Be a Nature Detective" with small groups of children. While you work with small groups, have other children do the following:

- **Self-Selected Reading**
- **Cross-Curricular Centers**
- **Practice Pages**
- **Journal Writing**

Use the suggested Classroom Management outline on page 7C for the whole-group/small-group schedule.

How to Be a Nature Detective

by Millicent E. Selsam
illustrated by Marlene Hill Donnelly

101

Guided Comprehension

Pages 100–101 Have children reread the title and review their predictions about what questions a nature detective might answer.

GENRE: Nonfiction

Read aloud the information about nonfiction on page 100. Tell children that nonfiction includes

• information about something real.

• settings that are real.

• topics that can be related to science and nature.

BELOW-LEVEL	ON-LEVEL	ADVANCED	ENGLISH-LANGUAGE LEARNERS
Before reading each spread in the selection, have children look at the illustrations and describe what is going on. If they mention any words that appear on the page, then point out these words. SMALL GROUP	As children read the selection, use the Guided Comprehension questions to direct their reading. WHOLE GROUP/SMALL GROUP	Have children share their predictions about the selection and then read the selection silently. After they read the selection, have children talk about whether or not their predictions were correct. SMALL GROUP/INDEPENDENT	Show children examples of animal tracks shown in nature books and magazines. After they read the selection, have children compare the tracks in the selection with the examples. SMALL GROUP
ADDITIONAL SUPPORT See Intervention Resource Kit, Lesson 30. *Intervention Teacher's Guide pp. 292–301*			**ADDITIONAL SUPPORT** See English Language Learners Resource Kit, Lesson 30. *English-Language Learners Teacher's Guide pp. 176–177*

"What happened?" a detective says.
"Who was here?
"Where did he go?"
A detective has many ways to find out.

One way is to look for the marks someone or something has made—fingerprints, footprints, the tracks made by bike tires.

Sometimes a detective finds a hair, a button, a piece of torn clothing. All these things are clues. They help a detective answer these questions: What happened? Who was here? Where did he go?

102

103

Guided Comprehension

Pages 102–103 Have children look at the illustration and describe what they see on the ground. Then have them read to find out what clues detectives use.

1 **NOTE DETAILS** What clues do detectives use? (fingerprints, footprints, tire tracks, hair, buttons, torn clothing)

2 **DRAW CONCLUSIONS** Who or what do you think made the tracks? Why do you think that? (Possible response: A person and an animal, such as a dog. One track looks like a shoe print. The other track looks like a paw print.)

3 **SPECULATE** Why do you think a detective looks for clues? (Possible response: The clues can help solve a problem or give an answer to a question.)

REACHING ALL LEARNERS

Diagnostic Check: Comprehension and Skills

If... children have difficulty identifying main ideas ...

Then... help them state a main idea for pages 102–103. Ask: Who are these pages about? (detectives) What do they do? (look for clues) Why do they do that? (to answer questions)

ADDITIONAL SUPPORT ACTIVITIES

BELOW-LEVEL	Reteach, p. S24
ADVANCED	Extend, p. S25
ENGLISH-LANGUAGE LEARNERS	Reteach, p. S25

102–103 Gather Around

You can be a detective too, a special kind of detective—a nature detective.

Nature detectives find tracks and clues that answer these questions: What animal walked here? Where did it go? What did it do? What did it eat?

104

Where does a nature detective look for clues? Almost anywhere—in a backyard, in the woods, in a city park.

You can find tracks in many places—in mud, in snow, in sand, in dust, even on the sidewalk or on the floor. Wet feet or wet muddy paws can make tracks anywhere.

105

Guided Comprehension

Pages 104–105 Have children look at the illustration and describe the setting. Then have them read to find out what the children are doing.

1 **NOTE DETAILS** How do nature detectives answer questions about what happened? (They find tracks and clues.)

2 **RELATE PICTURES TO TEXT** What are the children doing? (They are looking at tracks.)

3 **SPECULATE** Besides tracks, what might be a clue that an animal walked through this place? (Possible response: The animal might break tree branches or lose some fur.)

ENGLISH-LANGUAGE LEARNERS

Some English-language learners may have difficulties with homonyms. Take the opportunity to point out the three different spellings and meanings of the words *to, too,* and *two.*

BELOW-LEVEL

Suggest that children look for the smaller words in compound words, such as *backyard.* Have them write each word separately (*back, yard*), find the meanings of the words, and then "add" the words together like a "word addition problem" to find the meaning of the whole word (*back + yard = backyard, a yard in the back of a house*).

Here is a problem for a nature detective:

Here is a cat.

Here is a dog.

106

Here is a dish for the cat.

Here is a dish for the dog.

The cat's dish had milk in it. The dog's dish had meat in it. Who drank the milk? Who ate the meat?
Look at the tracks and see.

107

Guided Comprehension

Pages 106–107 Ask children to look at the illustrations and describe what they see. Then have children read to find out what the problem is.

1 **NOTE DETAILS** **What is the problem?** (We want to find out who drank the milk and who ate the meat.)

2 **MAKE PREDICTIONS** **How do you think a nature detective might solve this problem?** (Possible response: A nature detective might look for clues near the bowls, such as tracks or fur.)

SCIENCE

Animal Diets Tell children that both cats and dogs eat meat. Explain that we can guess that these animals eat meat since they both have sharp teeth. You may want to point out other members of the canine and feline families, such as wolves, foxes, lions, and tigers.

106–107 Gather Around

No claw marks!

Look at the tracks that go to the cat's dish. They were made by an animal that walks on four feet. And you can see claw marks in front of the toe marks.

A cat has four feet and sharp claws. But so does a dog.

Who went to the cat's dish? We still don't know.

Let's look for more clues.

Now look at the other tracks—the tracks that go to the dog's dish.

Did you ever watch a cat walk?

A cat walks on four feet. But the tracks of his hind feet fall exactly on the tracks of his front feet. So his footprints are one behind the other, in one line. They look like the footprints of an animal with only two feet. A cat pulls his claws in when he walks. So he does not leave claw marks.

108

109

Guided Comprehension

Pages 108–109 Have children look at the illustration and tell what is happening. Then ask children to read to find out how to tell the difference between a dog's and a cat's footprints.

1 MAKE COMPARISONS How are a cat's and a dog's feet alike? Find the words that tell you how. (*A cat has four feet and sharp claws. But so does a dog.*) **How are they different?** (A cat can pull his claws in, but a dog cannot.)

2 RELATE PICTURES TO TEXT You read that a cat pulls its claws in when it walks. Which picture shows this? (the picture on page 109)

3 (Focus Strategy) READ AHEAD Which animal do you think ate the meat? Why do you think so? (Possible response: The cat ate the meat; there are no claw marks near the dog's bowl.)

How to Be a Nature Detective **108–109**

Now do you know who drank the milk? (THE DOG!)
Now do you know who ate the dog food? (THE CAT!)

110

A nature detective can find many clues on a sandy beach.

When you walk on the beach in the morning, look for sea gull tracks. They can tell you which way the wind was blowing when the gulls were there.

111

Guided Comprehension

Pages 110–111 Have children read to find out which animal ate the meat and which drank the milk.

1 **NOTE DETAILS** Who ate the meat? (the cat) **Who drank the milk?** (the dog)

2 **EXPRESS PERSONAL OPINIONS** Were you surprised? (Possible response: Yes, because I know that cats usually drink milk. Accept all reasonable responses. Ask children to explain their answers.)

3 **DRAW CONCLUSIONS** Who or what do you think made the tracks on the beach? What makes you think that? (Possible response: A sea gull; the story tells us to look for sea gull tracks on a beach.)

110–111 Gather Around

MATH

Symmetry Have children look at the gull prints in the illustration. Ask them to imagine that they have a piece of paper shaped like the gull print. Ask: *If you folded the print down the middle, what would you notice about both sides of the print?* (They are the same size and shape.) Point out other natural objects that show symmetry, such as butterfly wings, leaves, and snowflakes. Use simple symmetrical paper shapes (square, heart, circle, flower) to demonstrate the concept of symmetry. Allow children to manipulate and fold the figures.

Like airplanes, sea gulls take off facing into the wind. First the gulls must run along the sand to get up speed for takeoff. As they run, their toes dig deeper into the sand.

Here all the gull toe tracks are in a line facing east. So you know that the wind came from the east.

112

113

Guided Comprehension

Pages 112–113 Ask children to look at the sea gull prints to see which way the sea gull was going. Have children read to find out which way the wind was coming from.

1 SUMMARIZE Describe how a sea gull takes off from the beach and flies. (Possible response: The sea gull faces into the wind. Then it runs on the sand to get up speed so it can take off.)

2 DRAW CONCLUSIONS How is a sea gull like a plane? (Possible responses: They both fly. They both take off facing into the wind.)

3 (Focus Skill) MAIN IDEA What is the main idea of these two pages? (Possible response: You can tell which way the wind was blowing by looking at the way the sea gull's tracks are facing.)

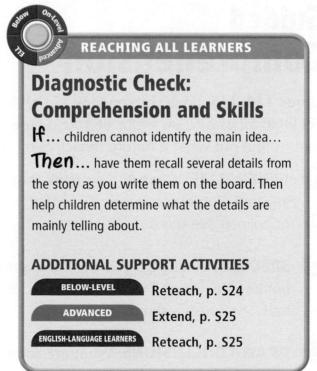

REACHING ALL LEARNERS

Diagnostic Check: Comprehension and Skills

If... children cannot identify the main idea...

Then... have them recall several details from the story as you write them on the board. Then help children determine what the details are mainly telling about.

ADDITIONAL SUPPORT ACTIVITIES

BELOW-LEVEL Reteach, p. S24

ADVANCED Extend, p. S25

ENGLISH-LANGUAGE LEARNERS Reteach, p. S25

How to Be a Nature Detective 112–113

Tracks are good clues for a nature detective. But there are other clues, too.

Who lives here?

Who ate here?

114

A nature detective learns to look and listen—and smell. She can find clues in a backyard, in the woods, or in a city park.

Who made that smell?

115

Guided Comprehension

Pages 114–115 Have children look at the illustrations and predict what kinds of clues might be found here. Then have children read to find out what a nature detective must do to find clues.

1 GENERALIZE What do you think these children are looking for? (Possible response: Clues that tell about what kinds of animals live there.)

2 SPECULATE Why do you think the girl on page 115 is holding her nose? (Possible responses: She smells something bad. She smells a skunk.)

3 DRAW CONCLUSIONS What are some clues these children might hear or smell? (Possible response: They might hear a bird singing or smell the scent of a skunk.)

Think and Respond

❶ How is a nature detective like other detectives?

❷ Which animal tracks do the detectives in the story look at?

❸ What surprise does the author give the reader about the dog and the cat?

❹ What are some good places to find nature clues?

❺ Which animals would you like to find out more about?

116   117

Think and Respond

❶ Possible response: He or she looks for clues that will answer questions. **MAKING COMPARISONS**

❷ dog, cat, and sea gull **RECALL DETAILS**

❸ The tracks show that the cat ate the dog food and the dog drank the milk, just the opposite of what might be expected. **AUTHOR'S CRAFT**

❹ in a backyard, in the woods, in a city park **RECALL DETAILS**

❺ Possible response: I'd like to find out more about sea gulls. I want to know what they eat and how they fly. (Accept all reasonable responses. Have children give reasons for their answer.) **EXPRESS PERSONAL OPINIONS**

About the Author

Millicent E. Selsam

Millicent Selsam always liked science and nature. She said, "I love to investigate everything." Before writing each book, she would read about the subject she wanted to share with children. Millicent Selsam wrote more than 130 books! She won many, many awards for her work. Her books have helped children learn to look at their world in a new way.

Meet the Illustrator

Marlene Hill Donnelly

Marlene Hill Donnelly draws things found in nature. Her work has been shown in zoos and aquariums across the United States. How did her pictures help you see nature in a new way?

Teacher Read-Aloud

Meet the Author and Illustrator

Pages 118–119 Explain that these pages tell about the people who wrote and illustrated "How to Be a Nature Detective." Identify Millicent E. Selsam in the photograph on page 118. Remind children that an **author** writes a selection, and an **illustrator** creates pictures to go with the writing. Read aloud pages 118–119.

Visit *The Learning Site:* **www.harcourtschool.com**

See Resources for Parents and Teachers: Author/Illustrator Features.

Retelling

COMPREHENSION FOCUS

Main Idea Remind children that the main idea is what a selection is mostly about. It is the most important idea. Explain that children should try to state the main idea in one sentence. Point out that there are many other sentences or ideas in the selection that give supporting details that tell about the main idea. Display *Teaching Transparency 108* or draw a similar chart on the board.

Work with children to complete the main idea box on the chart. (*We can use clues everywhere in nature to answer many questions and solve problems.*)

Remind children that details in the selection tell about this main idea. Ask questions and record children's responses in the detail boxes.

- **What are some of the questions that the clues answer?** (What animal walked here? Where did it go? What did it do? What did it eat?)

- **What are some of the clues that help answer the questions?** (Clues may be tracks made by the animals or things the animals left behind.)

- **Where can you look for clues?** (You can find clues in many places, such as your backyard, a park, the woods, in the snow, in the mud, or on a sidewalk.)

Help children use the chart to summarize the selection.

COMPREHENSION CHECK

▲ *End-of-Selection Test,* **Practice Book**, pp. **A45–A47**

▼ **Teaching Transparency 108**

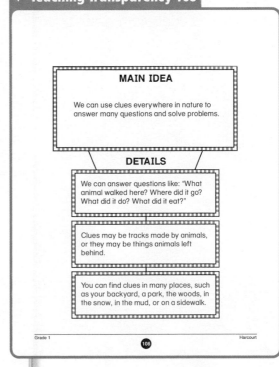

MAIN IDEA

We can use clues everywhere in nature to answer many questions and solve problems.

DETAILS

We can answer questions like: "What animal walked here? Where did it go? What did it do? What did it eat?"

Clues may be tracks made by animals, or they may be things animals left behind.

You can find clues in many places, such as your backyard, a park, the woods, in the snow, in the mud, or on a sidewalk.

Grade 1   108   Harcourt

How to Be a Nature Detective **119A**

DAILY LANGUAGE PRACTICE

I are going to school today

I <u>am</u> going to school today<u>.</u>

journal writing

Writing Prompt Have children draw a picture of an animal they know about. Then have them write a caption for their picture.

Shared Writing

Picture Caption

DRAW AND WRITE

Describe a Picture Show children a detailed picture of an animal. You may have an appropriate picture in a nature book, or you may choose an illustration from "How to Be a Nature Detective" or from other animal stories children have read. Ask them to name the animal and describe what it looks like. Record their ideas on chart paper.

Beaver
wide, flat tail
sharp teeth
webbed back feet

Write a Caption Read the notes aloud. Use them to write a caption for the picture. Ask children questions such as the following to elicit detailed ideas for the caption:

- **How does the beaver use its tail? For what does it use its teeth?**

- **Why do you think the beaver has claws on its front feet? Why would a beaver have webbed feet in the back?**

The beaver has a wide, flat tail. Its tail and webbed back feet help the beaver swim. Beavers use their sharp teeth to chew on trees and logs.

Use children's responses in forming a caption.

5-DAY GRAMMAR	
DAY 1	Introduce Using *Am*, *Is*, and *Are*
DAY 2	**Match Sentence Parts**
DAY 3	*Am*, *Is*, *Are* Game
DAY 4	Sentences with *Am*, *Is*, and *Are*
DAY 5	Choose *Am*, *Is*, or *Are*

Grammar

Using Am, Is, *and* Are

REVIEW

Review Using *Am, Is,* and *Are* Remind children that they can decide whether to use *am, is,* or *are* in a sentence by looking at who or what the sentence is about. Model using the word *is* in a sentence.

MODEL *Ruff is a dog.* I look at the sentence and it is about one person, place, animal, or thing, so it is correct to use the word *is.*

Continue modeling with the words *am* and *are.*

I am a detective. Cats and dogs are animals.

Match Sentence Parts Write several sentences with *am, is,* and *are* on sentence strips. Then cut the strips so that the naming part is separated from the telling part. Have children work in pairs to match the sentence parts.

That boy	is my brother.
The children	are at home.
I	am a good reader.

WRAP UP ## Recite a Rhyme

Read the Rhyme Read aloud "Oh Where, Has My Little Dog Gone?" on page 45 of the *Big Book of Rhymes.* Read the rhyme several times and have children chime in. Tell children to imagine that they are detectives looking for the lost dog. Ask what clues they are given that could help them find the dog.

S.S.R.
Sustained Silent Reading

Have children read silently from a book of their choice. See page 123J for tips on helping children choose books.

Oh Where Has My
Little Dog Gone?

Oh where, oh where has
my little dog gone?
Oh where,
oh where can he be?

With his ears cut short
and his tail cut long,
Oh where,
oh where can he be?

45

▲ Big Book of Rhymes, p. 45

SKILL TRACE

USING *AM, IS,* AND *ARE*	
Introduce	98N
Reteach	T7
REVIEW	119C, 121B, 123B, 123L

ENGLISH-LANGUAGE LEARNERS

Below · On-Level · Advanced · ELL

Use people in the room to reinforce subject-verb agreement. Point to the appropriate person or people as you make statements such as: *I am a teacher. Dan is a boy. She is a girl. They are children. We are friends.* Have children repeat after you and then make their own statements.

ADVANCED

Have children write their own sentences using *am, is,* and *are* to share with classmates.

Name _____

Using Am, Is, and Are

The words **am, is,** and **are** tell about now.
Use **am** to tell about yourself.
Use **is** to tell about one person, place, or thing.
Use **are** to tell about more than one person, place, or thing.

I am happy.	Mom is busy.	Pets are fun.

▶ Write am, is, or are to complete each sentence.

1. I _____ am _____ a girl named Molly.

2. My mother _____ is _____ a vet.

3. Five animals _____ are _____ in our home now.

126

SCHOOL-HOME CONNECTION

▲ Language Handbook, p. 126

How to Be a Nature Detective **119C**

Day at a Glance
Day 3

Sharing Literature
Poem: "Footprints in the Snow"

Phonemic Awareness
Matching and Isolating Phonemes; Focus on /ō/

Phonics
REVIEW: Long Vowel /ō/o

Spelling
State the Generalization

Vocabulary
REVIEW: *clues, detective, floor, nature, piece, pulls*

Reading
Rereading for Fluency
Pupil Edition
"How to Be a Nature Detective," pp. 100–116

Making Connections, pp. 120–121

Interactive Writing ✏
Newspaper Article

Grammar
REVIEW: Using *Am, Is,* and *Are*

WARM UP — MORNING MESSAGE

Good Morning!

Today is _____.

Have you ever seen footprints in the snow?

A person's footprint _____.

The tracks in the snow show _____.

Introduce the Day

Remind children that they read about animal tracks. Tell them that today they will read a poem about a cat's tracks in the snow. Guide them in generating a message about footprints in the snow. Ask:

- **What do people wear in the snow?**
- **What would a person's footprint look like?**
- **What can we find out if we follow tracks in the snow?**

Ask children to write words that they have already learned. For instance, they know the high-frequency words *have, you, in,* and *the*. As you say other words, such as *snow, show,* and *seen,* elongate the sounds and ask children to name the letters for the sounds they hear.

Read the Message

Read the message. Use the message to focus on skills that have been previously taught.

Apply Skills

Phonics Review the long vowel sound /ō/*ow.* Tell children that the word *snow* includes this sound and spelling. Ask children to find the other word in the message that has the long vowel sound /ō/*ow.* (show)

Word Structure Point out the word *footprints* in the message. Ask children to identify the two smaller words they see in this word. (*foot* and *prints*) Have children use these two smaller words to explain what a footprint is.

Sharing Literature

BUILD CONCEPT VOCABULARY

Connect to Prior Knowledge Ask children what they learned about the cat's tracks in "How to Be a Nature Detective." Help them recall that the cat's back feet fall exactly on the tracks of its front feet. Then read the poem "Footprints in the Snow."

Word-Learning Strategy Remind children that a detective is someone who tries to figure things out. Ask children to be "word detectives." Have them listen to some sentences and use words they know to determine the meanings of the underlined words: *I'll show you I can dance. That will <u>prove</u> I can do it. (show) We should stop talking. We <u>ought</u> to be quiet. (should)* Reread the poem and have children listen for the words *proves* and *ought*.

Phonemic Awareness

MATCHING AND ISOLATING PHONEMES

Words from "Footprints in the Snow" Tell children that you are going to say some words from the poem. Have them listen for words that end with the long vowel /ō/, as in *row*. Ask children to raise their hands each time they hear a word that ends with the long vowel sound of *o*.

one	window	**proves**
snow	**you**	know

FOCUS ON /ō/

Phoneme Substitution Tell children that you will say some words and they will change the vowel sound in the word to /ō/. Model by saying *mild, mold*. Continue with these words:

tilled (told)	**see** (so)	**guild** (gold)	**filled** (fold)
mist (most)	**held** (hold)	**past** (post)	**build** (bold)

Footprints in the Snow

When the cats make tracks,
there's just one set of tracks...

When they jump from the window
they put their feet in the same places.

This proves, as you ought to know,
that cats don't like snow.

Gavin Ewart

◀ "His Four Fur Feet," *Oo-pples and Boo-noo-noos: Songs and Activities for Phonemic Awareness,* pp. 83–84

ADVANCED

Have children segment the sounds they hear in the words in the Matching activity.

How to Be a Nature Detective **119E**

OBJECTIVES

- *To generate the long vowel sound of o*
- *To blend sounds into words*
- *To read simple, regular words*

SKILL TRACE

/ō/o	
Introduce	98I–98L
Reteach	S22–S23
REVIEW	98Q–98R; 119F–119G, 121E–121F

Phonics Resources

Phonics Express™ CD-ROM, **Level B** Sparkle/Route 4/Train Station

Phonics
Long Vowel /ō/o *Review*

WORD BUILDING

Guided Practice Place the letters *o, l, d* in a pocket chart. Have children do the same with their *Word Builders* and *Word Builder Cards.* Model how to blend the word *old.* Slide your hand under the letters as you slowly elongate the sounds—/ōōlldd/. Then read the word naturally—*old.* Have children do the same.

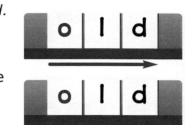

Have children build and read new words by telling them:

- Add *h* in front of *old.* What word did you make?

- Change the *h* to *s.* What word did you make?

- Change the *s* to *m.* What word did you make?

- Change the *l* to *s.* Change the *d* to *t.* What word did you make?

- Change the *o* to *i.* What word did you make?

- Change the *m* to *f.* What word did you make?

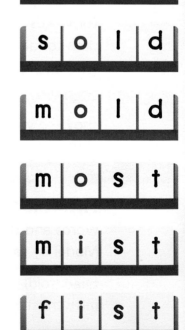

Continue word building with this word sequence: *fold, gold, bold, told, toll, tall, call, cold.*

Apply Phonics

READ WORDS IN CONTEXT

5-DAY PHONICS

DAY 1	Introduce /ō/o
DAY 2	Word Building with /ō/o
DAY 3	**Word Building with /ō/o**
DAY 4	Word Building with /ō/o and /ō/o-e
DAY 5	Contractions 've, 'd, 're

Display *Teaching Transparency 90* or write the following sentences on the board or on chart paper. Have volunteers read the story one sentence at a time. Call on volunteers to underline or frame words with the long vowel sound of *o*.

▼ Teaching Transparency 90

LONG VOWEL /ō/o

Long ago there was a hippo. He liked to go to the water hole. The old hippo played in the cold water. He also opened his mouth to drink. Now I have told you all I know about the hippo.

"How to Be a Nature Detective"
Gather Around, Volume 1-5

90

Phonics: Long Vowel /ō/o
Harcourt

Write Words Tell children to choose two words with the long vowel sound of *o* and write them in their journal.

REACHING ALL LEARNERS

Diagnostic Check: Phonics

If... children cannot decode words with long vowel /ō/o . . .

Then... have them read "Flo Hippo" in *Decodable Book 30* to reinforce the long vowel sound /ō/o.

◀ **Decodable Book 30** "Flo Hippo"

ADDITIONAL SUPPORT ACTIVITIES

BELOW-LEVEL	Reteach, p. S22
ADVANCED	Extend, p. S23
ENGLISH-LANGUAGE LEARNERS	Reteach, p. S23

School-Home Connection

Take-Home Book Version

◀ **Decodable Books** Take-Home Version,

5-DAY SPELLING

DAY 1	Pretest; Word Sort
DAY 2	Word Building
DAY 3	**State the Generalization**
DAY 4	Review
DAY 5	Posttest; Writing Application

Spelling Words

1. old
2. fold
3. told
4. cold
5. roll
6. most
7. find
8. child
9. both
10. during

journal  writing

Have children copy the Spelling Words into their journal.

WORD WORK

Spelling

TEACH/MODEL

State the Generalization for /ō/o Write the Spelling Words on the board and have children read them aloud. Discuss what is the same about words 1–6. (They all have the /ō/ sound; they all have o.) Have volunteers circle the letter that stands for /ō/ in each word. Tell children that the letter o is used to spell the /ō/ sound.

Review the Generalization for /ī/i Follow a similar procedure for words 7 and 8. Remind children that the letter i is used to spell the long i sound, /ī/.

Review the High-Frequency Word Point out that the o in *both* stands for the long vowel sound of o.

Review the Vocabulary Word Point out that the word *during* does not follow the same pattern as the other words.

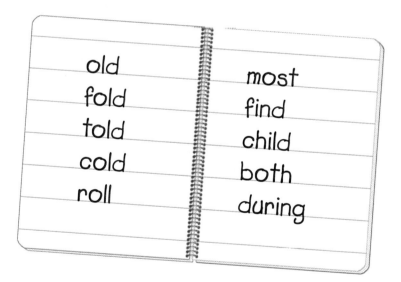

old
fold
told
cold
roll

most
find
child
both
during

ADVANCED	ENGLISH-LANGUAGE LEARNERS
Have children write Spelling Words 1–6 in their journal. Ask them to list as many other word forms as they can for each word; for example, *older, oldest; folded, folding.*	To check understanding of word meaning, ask children to spell each Spelling Word and then use it in a sentence. If necessary, clarify meanings of Spelling Words.

Word Sorts

Name _____

▶ Make cards for the Spelling Words. Lay them down and read them.

Spelling Words

1. Put the words with long o in one group and those without long o in another. Write the words on the chart.

2. Put the words with long i in one group and those without long i in another. Write the words on the chart.

Words With Long o		Words Without Long o	
old	roll	find	
fold	most	child	
told	both	during	
cold			

Words With Long i		Words Without Long i	
find		old	roll
child		fold	most
		told	both
		cold	during

Spelling Words
old
fold
told
cold
roll
most
find
child
both
during
My Own Word

SCHOOL-HOME CONNECTION Point to and read the Spelling Words aloud with your child. Talk about how the words are alike and how they are different.

SPELLING PRACTICE BOOK
GATHER AROUND • LESSON 4 **73**

▲ Spelling Practice Book, p. 73

119H Gather Around

Vocabulary

REVIEW WORDS IN CONTEXT

Read Words in Context Write the vocabulary words on the board. Write sentences from the story that include these words. Have children read the sentences aloud. Then ask children to help you create sentences using the vocabulary words.

Record the sentences on the board. Then read the sentences, tracking the print as you read.

> The detective found many clues.
>
> There is a piece of paper on the floor.

REVIEW

Vocabulary

clues　　　nature
detective　piece
floor　　　pulls

Words to Remember
WORD WALL

Complete Sentences Have children complete the following sentences with posted words. Point to the column in which the target word appears. Volunteers can frame the words as classmates read them aloud. Use a similar procedure to review other displayed words.

- The _____ helped us figure out what animal had been there. (clues)
- I love to read _____ books about plants and animals. (nature)
- I have the torn _____ of my shirt. (piece)
- A cat _____ in its claws when it walks. (pulls)
- She uses clues to solve crimes. She is a _____. (detective)
- Don't let the food fall on the _____. (floor)

BELOW-LEVEL

Instead of having children create their own sentences, provide these sentence frames. Have children complete them using the vocabulary words.

What _____ helped you get the answer? (clues)

A _____ uses clues to answer questions. (detective)

The dog left tracks on the _____. (floor)

We saw many animals along the _____ path. (nature)

I found a _____ of eggshell on the path. (piece)

The horse _____ the wagon. (pulls)

ADVANCED

Ask children to write more detailed sentences by adding descriptive words to the sentences created by the group.

teaching tip

Learned Words Examine the posted words and remove those that children understand, can spell, and can use with mastery.

Rereading for Fluency

PARTNERS

Partner Reading

⬤ **ON-LEVEL** Have children work in pairs to reread the selection two pages at a time. Remind them that readers should read smoothly as if they are telling the information to someone; listeners should follow along and give feedback. Suggest that they reread sections if they think they can read more smoothly. INDEPENDENT

Managing Small Groups

Reread for fluency with children working individually, with partners, or in small groups. While you work with small groups, have other children do the following:

- **Self-Selected Reading**
- **Cross-Curricular Centers**
- **Practice Pages**
- **Journal Writing**

Use the suggested Classroom Management outline on page 7C for the whole-group/small-group schedule.

Read

How to Be a Nature Detective

by Millicent E. Selsam
Illustrated by Marlene Hill Donnelly

▲ *Pupil Edition,* pp. 100–116

FLUENCY ROUTINES For support, see Fluency Routine Cards in Theme Resources, pp. T83–T84.

Making Connections

Nature Detective Walk

With your teacher, walk around your school or in a park. Look for clues that tell you which animals live there. Make a class list of your findings.

Science CONNECTION

Clues in Nature

animal tracks
empty nests
shells

Just In!

Write a TV news story for NDN, the Nature Detective Network. Tell about a nature clue you have found–or one you wish you had found!

Writing CONNECTION

Elephant tracks were seen in the schoolyard today!

Poster Paws

Find out how other animal tracks look. Draw a set of tracks and write the animal's name under them. Add your work to a class poster.

Art CONNECTION

120

121

Making Connections

SCIENCE

Nature Detective Walk If your school is in an urban area, you may want to conduct the nature walk at a local park. Suggest that children look for anthills, dog tracks, bird nests, molehills, spider webs, or any other signs that animals have been in the area. After the nature walk, ask children to report their findings. Have volunteers make a list of all the things the group saw. They can also make a list of animals that most likely live in the area. Post the list in the room.

WRITING

Just In! Tell children that their TV news stories can be real or make-believe. Prompt them with questions, such as:

- **What kinds of clues would you like to find?**
- **What do the clues mean?**
- **Where did you find the clues?**

When children have finished writing, ask them to present their news stories as a TV reporter would.

ART

Poster Paws Provide a variety of nature books for children to use as references. Children can use crayons or markers or make the prints using finger paint. They can cut shapes from a sponge and then dip them in paint to make their animal tracks. Display children's work on a bulletin board titled *Animal Tracks*.

LANGUAGE ARTS

Interactive Writing
Newspaper Article

DAILY LANGUAGE PRACTICE

Dont go oat in the cold.

<u>Don't</u> go <u>out</u> in the cold.

Writing Prompt Ask children to select a favorite sentence from the article and copy it into their journal.

SHARE THE PEN

Plan the Article Tell children that they are going to write a newspaper article about an animal that escaped from the zoo. Ask children questions to elicit ideas for the article. Write the questions on the board:

> What animal escaped from the zoo?
> How did the animal get out?
> Where did it go?
> What clues did it leave behind?
> Where did the detectives find the animal?

As children answer these questions, guide them to agree on the details of the article. Then have volunteers come to the board and help write notes that answer the questions.

Write the Article Use the notes and the sequence outlined in the questions to write the news article on chart paper. Ask children to "share the pen" by suggesting sentences that answer the questions. Have individuals contribute to the writing of the article by writing known words, sounds, and punctuation marks. Ask questions such as:

- **What is the first word of the sentence? How do you spell that word?**
- **Who can write the next word or words in the sentence?**
- **What punctuation mark goes at the end of the sentence?**

Read the Article Read the completed newspaper article. You may want to use a student word-processing program to publish the article. If possible, include clip art to illustrate it. Display the published work.

5-DAY GRAMMAR	
DAY 1	Introduce Using *Am, Is,* and *Are*
DAY 2	Match Sentence Parts
DAY 3	***Am, Is, Are* Game**
DAY 4	Sentences with *Am, Is,* and *Are*
DAY 5	Choose *Am, Is,* or *Are*

Day 3

Grammar

Using Am, Is, *and* Are

REVIEW

Review Using *Am, Is,* and *Are* Point out that *am* is used when the sentence starts with *I*. Explain that *is* is used when the sentence is about one person, place, animal, or thing, and *are* is used when the sentence is about more than one. Remind children that *are* is used when the sentence is about *you*, whether *you* means one person or more than one person.

Play a Game Write the following pronouns on index cards: *I, you, he, she, we, it, they.* Then make another set of index cards with words such as the following: *hungry, beautiful, funny, healthy, kind, nice, pretty, silly, young.*

Place the cards in two separate piles. Have children take turns picking one card from each pile. Have them look at the cards and make a sentence using the words *am, is,* or *are.*

SKILL TRACE

USING *AM, IS,* AND *ARE*	
Introduce	98N
Reteach	T7
REVIEW	119C, 121B, 123B, 123L

ADVANCED

Have children play the same game described in the activity. Tell children that they must add other words and details to their sentences.

WRAP UP

Revisit the Poem

Walk Like an Animal Reread the poem "Footprints in the Snow" on page 119E. Ask children to describe how a cat walks and what its tracks look like. Recall the other kinds of animal tracks children read about in "How to Be a Nature Detective." Have children describe how other animals walk and what their tracks might look like. Then ask volunteers to act out a walk or draw track pictures and have others guess the animal.

S.S.R.
Sustained Silent Reading

Have children read silently from a book of their choice. See page 123J for tips on helping children choose books.

Name _____

Using Am, Is, and Are

▶ Circle the words that complete the sentence. Color the picture the sentence tells about.

1. The pigs (are pink.) / is pink.

2. The dog (is hungry.) / are hungry.

3. The elephants is big. / (are big.)

4. I (am happy.) / is happy.

▶ Use <u>is</u> or <u>are</u> to complete the sentence.

5. The chick _____is_____ small.

SCHOOL-HOME CONNECTION
Ask your child to use *am, is,* and *are* at the beginning of questions. Answer the questions.

127

▲ Language Handbook, p. 127

How to Be a Nature Detective **121B**

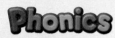

WARM UP — MORNING MESSAGE

Good Morning!

Today is _____.
You can see many things in nature.
On the ground you might see _____.
Up in a tree you might see _____.
Under the water you might see _____.

Introduce the Day

Tell children that today they are going to hear a riddle that gives clues about something they might see in nature. Guide them in writing a message about things they might see, hear, or smell while exploring nature. Ask:

- **What kinds of plants and animals live on the ground or underground?**
- **What kinds of animals climb trees?**
- **What plants and animals live underwater?**

As you write the message, ask volunteers to write known words and letters. Ask children to identify which words should be capitalized and where punctuation is needed.

Read the Message

Read the message. Use the message to focus on skills that have been previously taught.

Apply Skills

Phonics Remind children of two sounds they've learned: /ou/*ow* and /ī/*igh*. Say the sounds slowly and have children repeat after you. Ask children to find words in the message with these sounds. (*ground, might*)	**Concept Vocabulary** On the board, write these words from the message: *under, up, in.* Ask children to name the opposite of each word. (over, down, out)

Sharing Literature

BUILD CONCEPT VOCABULARY

Listen to a Poem Tell children you are going to read a poem that is a riddle. Remind them that they have to listen for clues. Read the poem, pausing for children to say the last line.

Explore a Word Remind children that they heard the word *chatter* in the poem. Say: *The word* chatter *describes the quick, clicking sounds that squirrels and other animals make.* Have children repeat the word. Then say: *Sometimes we say that people chatter. That means that they talk quickly because they're excited about something—and they keep talking about it.* Ask children if they ever chatter. Have volunteers use the word to tell about things they might chatter about—for example, a favorite television show or a new toy. Close by asking: *What word have we been talking about? When you chatter, do you speak slowly or quickly?*

> Chestnut-
> brown
> is the color
> for me,
> For I'm a nut
> about nuts, you see.
> From branch to
> branch
> I leap and whirl,
> Chitter and chatter,
> 'cause I'm . . .
>
> **a squirrel.**
>
> *Carol Diggory Shields*

Phonemic Awareness

PHONEME ISOLATION

Words from the Poem Remind children of the word *chestnut* from the poem. Tell children that you are going to say some words with the sound /ch/ and they will tell you whether the sound comes at the beginning or the end of the word. Model by saying *chestnut, beginning.* Continue with these words:

chitter (beginning)	**branch** (end)	**chatter** (beginning)
birch (end)	**pinch** (end)	**chirp** (beginning)

FOCUS ON /ō/

Distinguish Phonemes Tell children that you are going to say several words with the long vowel sound of *o*, and children will tell whether the /ō/ sound is at the beginning, middle, or end of the word. Say *open. Where do you hear the sound /ō/?* (beginning) Continue with these words:

over (beginning)	**hello** (end)	**rode** (middle)
note (middle)	**oval** (beginning)	**code** (middle)
old (beginning)	**go** (end)	**ago** (end)

ENGLISH-LANGUAGE LEARNERS

Children may have difficulty distinguishing the digraphs. Give several examples of words with the different sounds, pointing out the digraphs as you say the words. Have children repeat the words after you. Use words such as *with/wish, chip/ship, much/mush, patch/path.*

Phonics
Build Words Review

WORD BUILDING

OBJECTIVES

- *To discriminate between the sound-letter relationships /ō/o and /ō/o-e*

- *To read and write words with /ō/o and /ō/o-e*

SKILL TRACE

	/ō/o	/ō/o-e
Introduce	98I–98L	Bk 1-4, 216I–216L
Reteach	S22–S23	Bk 1-4, S46–S47, T12
REVIEW	98Q–98R, 119F–119G, 121E–121F	Bk 1-4, 216Q–216R, 245F–245G, 247E–249
T Test		Bk 1-4
MAINTAIN		Bk 1-5, 121E–121F

teaching tip

Build Vocabulary As you build the words *roll* and *role*, explain to children the difference in meaning between the two words.

Phonics Resources

Phonics Express™ CD-ROM, Level B Sparkle/Route 6/Market

Phonics Practice Book, pp. 216–221

Build and Read Words Use a pocket chart and *Letter Cards c, o, l, d, h, e, m, g, t, l, r,* and *s.* Display the letters *c, o, l,* and *d* in the pocket chart and ask children if each letter is a consonant or a vowel.

Place the letters close together. Slide your hand slowly under the letters as you blend the sounds—/kkōōlldd/. Then read the word naturally—*cold.* Have children repeat after you. Point out that the letters in *cold* follow the pattern *consonant, vowel, consonant, consonant.*

Ask volunteers to build new words in the pocket chart.

■ Change the *c* to *h.* Read the word.

■ Change the *d* to *e.* Read the word.

■ Change the *h* to *m.* Read the word.

■ Change the *e* to *d.* Read the word.

■ Change the *m* to *g.* Read the word.

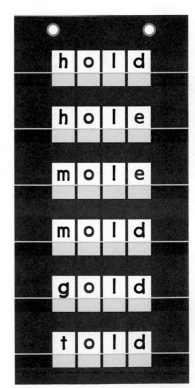

Continue word building with this word sequence: *told, toll, roll, role, sole, sold.*

Read Words—Write the words *hold, mole,* and *roll* on the board and have children read the words aloud.

5-DAY PHONICS	
DAY 1	Introduce /ō/o
DAY 2	Word Building with /ō/o
DAY 3	Word Building with /ō/o
DAY 4	**Word Building with /ō/o and /ō/o-e**
DAY 5	Contractions 've, 'd, 're

Day 4

Apply Phonics

APPLY PHONICS SKILLS

Dictate Sentences with /ō/o and /ō/o-e Dictate the following sentences:

> Her nose is cold.
> We both rode our bikes.

Have children write the sentences on a dry-erase board or in their journal.

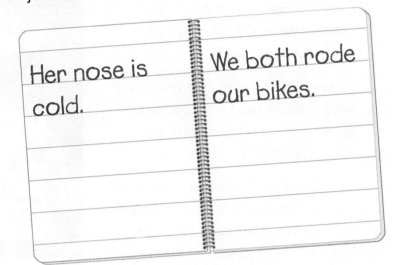

Her nose is cold.

We both rode our bikes.

BELOW-LEVEL

Children may need additional work with blending long vowel /ō/o and /ō/o-e words. Have children blend and read words such as *rope, nose, pole, bold, told, gold, hold, hole, hello,* and *robot.*

ADVANCED

Have children write other words with the long *o* spelled in different ways. Children may want to note rhyming words for use in today's writing activity.

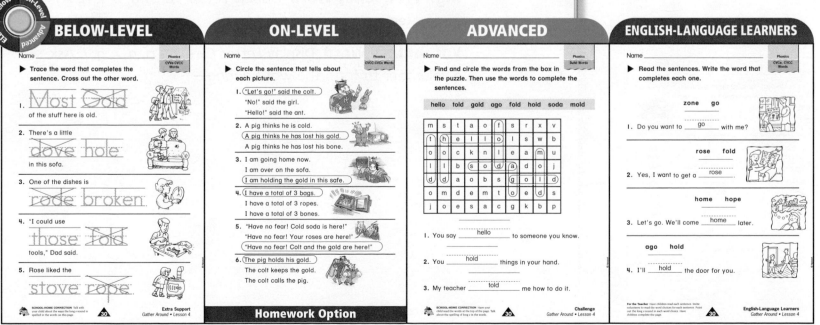

BELOW-LEVEL

Name _____

Phonics CVVe-CVCC Words

▶ Trace the word that completes the sentence. Cross out the other word.

1. Most ~~Gold~~
   of the stuff here is old.

2. There's a little ~~dove~~ hole
   in this sofa.

3. One of the dishes is ~~rode~~ broken

4. "I could use those ~~fold~~
   tools," Dad said.

5. Rose liked the stove ~~rope~~

SCHOOL-HOME CONNECTION Talk with your child about the ways the long *o* sound is spelled in the words on this page.

Extra Support *Gather Around • Lesson 4* 30

▲ Extra Support, p. 30

ON-LEVEL

Name _____

Phonics CVCC-CVCe Words

▶ Circle the sentence that tells about each picture.

1. ("Let's go!" said the colt.)
   "No!" said the girl.
   "Hello!" said the ant.

2. A pig thinks he is cold.
   (A pig thinks he has lost his gold.)
   A pig thinks he has lost his bone.

3. I am going home now.
   I am over on the sofa.
   (I am holding the gold in this safe.)

4. (I have a total of 3 bags.)
   I have a total of 3 ropes.
   I have a total of 3 bones.

5. "Have no fear! Cold soda is here!"
   "Have no fear! Your roses are here!"
   ("Have no fear! Colt and the gold are here!")

6. (The pig holds his gold.)
   The colt keeps the gold.
   The colt calls the pig.

Homework Option

▲ Practice, p. 30

ADVANCED

Name _____

Phonics Build Words

▶ Find and circle the words from the box in the puzzle. Then use the words to complete the sentences.

hello   told   gold   ago   fold   hold   soda   mold

m	s	t	a	o	f	s	r	x	v
t	h	e	l	l	o	l	s	w	b
o	o	c	k	n	l	e	a	m	u
l	l	b	s	o	d	a	d	o	j
d	d	a	o	b	s	g	o	l	d
o	m	d	e	m	t	o	e	d	s
j	o	e	s	a	c	g	k	b	p

1. You say ___hello___ to someone you know.

2. You ___hold___ things in your hand.

3. My teacher ___told___ me how to do it.

SCHOOL-HOME CONNECTION Have your child read the words at the top of the page. Talk about the spelling of long *o* in the words.

Challenge *Gather Around • Lesson 4* 30

▲ Challenge, p. 30

ENGLISH-LANGUAGE LEARNERS

Name _____

Phonics CVVe, CVCE Words

▶ Read the sentences. Write the word that completes each one.

zone   go

1. Do you want to ___go___ with me?

rose   fold

2. Yes, I want to get a ___rose___

home   hope

3. Let's go. We'll come ___home___ later.

ago   hold

4. I'll ___hold___ the door for you.

For the Teacher Have children read each sentence. Write solutions to read the word choices for each sentence. Point out the long *o* sound in each word choice. Have children complete the page.

English-Language Learners *Gather Around • Lesson 4* 30

▲ ELL, 30

Spelling Words

1. old
2. fold
3. told
4. cold
5. roll
6. most
7. find
8. child
9. both
10. during

Spelling

5-DAY SPELLING	
DAY 1	Pretest; Word Sort
DAY 2	Word Building
DAY 3	State the Generalization
DAY 4	**Review**
DAY 5	Posttest; Writing Application

REVIEW

Spelling Words Use a pocket chart and *Letter Cards* to form words. Have children listen to your directions and change one letter in each word to spell a Spelling Word. Have them write the Spelling Word on a sheet of paper or in their journal. Then have a volunteer change the *Letter Card* in the pocket chart so that children can self-check the word.

- Form *odd* in the pocket chart and have children read it aloud. **Which Spelling Word is made with one letter changed?** *(old)*

- Form *food* in the pocket chart and have children read it aloud. **Which Spelling Word is made with one letter changed?** *(fold)*

- Form *load* in the pocket chart and have children read it aloud. **Which Spelling Word is made with one letter changed?** *(told)*

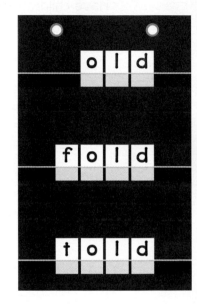

Follow a similar procedure with *colt (cold), toll (roll), moat (most), fond (find), mild (child)*.

High-Frequency Word Display *Letter Cards o, b, t, h*. Ask a volunteer to form the word *both*.

Vocabulary Word Display *Letter Cards u, d, n, r, g, i*. Ask a volunteer to form the word *during*.

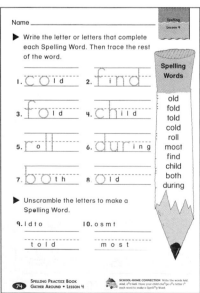

▲ Spelling Practice Book, p. 74

121G Gather Around

Vocabulary

WRITE WORDS IN STORY CONTEXT

Reinforce Word Recognition
Duplicate and distribute the Story Strips for "How to Be a Nature Detective" (page T68). Display *Word Cards* or write the vocabulary words on the board: *clues, detective, floor, nature, piece, pulls.* After children complete the Story Strip sentences, they can work with partners to check their work. The two partners can match their sentences and arrange the Story Strips to put story events in order.

REVIEW
Vocabulary

clues	nature
detective	piece
floor	pulls

ADVANCED

Have children write a paragraph or story that includes all the vocabulary words.

ENGLISH-LANGUAGE LEARNERS

Before completing the Story Strip activity, find a sentence from the story for each vocabulary word. Read each sentence, leaving the vocabulary word out. Ask children to complete each sentence using the correct word.

A _____ has many ways to get answers.

She may find a _____ of cloth.

She might find tracks on the _____.

All these things are _____.

A _____ detective can tell cat footprints.

A cat _____ its claws in when it walks.

Nature detectives look for clues everywhere!

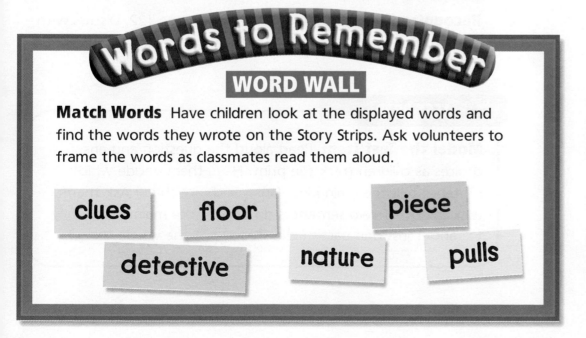

Words to Remember

WORD WALL

Match Words Have children look at the displayed words and find the words they wrote on the Story Strips. Ask volunteers to frame the words as classmates read them aloud.

clues   floor   piece

detective   nature   pulls

▲ **Pupil Edition, pp. 100–116**

OBJECTIVE

To identify the main idea of a story

SKILL TRACE

MAIN IDEA	
Introduce	69A, 93A, 95I–97
Reteach	S18–S19, S24–S25, S42–S43
REVIEW	**99A, 119A, 121I–123,**
	187A, 211A, 215I–217
T Test	Bk 1-5

REACHING ALL LEARNERS

Diagnostic Check: Comprehension

If... children cannot identify the main idea ...

Then... have them practice identifying the main idea of familiar books they have recently read.

ADDITIONAL SUPPORT ACTIVITIES

BELOW-LEVEL	Reteach, p. S24
ADVANCED	Extend, p. S25
ENGLISH-LANGUAGE LEARNERS	Reteach, p. S25

Focus Skill # Comprehension
Main Idea

TEACH/MODEL

Develop Concepts Remind children that the main idea of a story or article is what the story is mostly about. The main idea is the most important idea, and details give more exact information about the main idea.

> **MODEL** I read the story *I Swam with a Seal*, and I want to figure out what the main idea is. I read that the child swims with a seal, and that the seal wonders why the child doesn't have flippers. This same thing happens with other animals in the story. This story shows that all animals are different in the way they look, the things they do, and the places they live. This must be the main idea of the story.

PRACTICE/APPLY

Reread the Selection Have children reread "How to Be a Nature Detective," looking closely for the main idea. As children read, stop occasionally to ask them if a particular idea is a detail or the main idea. Explain how each fact and detail helps the reader to better understand the main idea—what the selection is mostly about. Then ask children to say a sentence that tells the main idea. Record their responses on the board or on chart paper and read the sentences aloud.

Recognize the Main Idea Read aloud page 122. Discuss with children the main idea of "How to Be a Nature Detective."

TEST PREP

Model the Test Item Read aloud the question and answer choices as children track the print. Have them decide which sentence tells the main idea. (answer choice three) Ask them why the other two sentences do not tell the main idea. (They tell about just one part of the story—not the whole thing.)

Teacher Read-Aloud

▲ How to Be a Nature Detective

Main Idea

 Focus Skill

You have learned that the **main idea** of a nonfiction piece is what that piece is mostly about. Think about "How to Be a Nature Detective." Which sentence tells the main idea?

1. A nature detective can find many clues on a sandy beach.
2. A nature detective uses sight, smell, and hearing to find clues about things in nature.
3. A cat does not leave claw marks in its tracks.

Visit *The Learning Site!*
www.harcourtschool.com
See Skills and Activities

122

Test Prep
Main Idea

Fox tracks are like dog tracks in some ways and cat tracks in other ways. Fox tracks are in one line like cat tracks. They show claw marks like dog tracks.

1. Which sentence tells the main idea?
   ○ Fox tracks show claw marks.
   ○ Fox tracks are in one line.
   ○ Fox tracks are like both dog tracks and cat tracks.

 Tip

Read the sentences carefully. Which sentence tells what the whole story is about?

123

Focus Skill

Visit *The Learning Site:*
www.harcourtschool.com

See Skill Activities and Test Tutors: Main Idea.

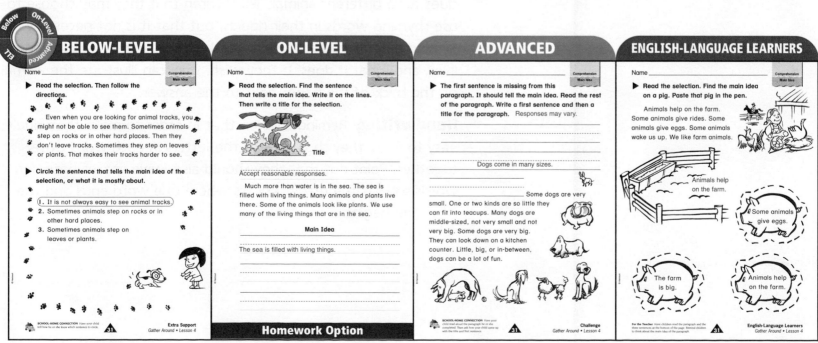

▲ Extra Support, p. 31   ▲ Practice, p. 31   ▲ Challenge, p. 31   ▲ ELL, p. 31

How to Be a Nature Detective **122–123**

Writing

Riddle

DAILY LANGUAGE PRACTICE

did you find any cluse?

<u>D</u>id you find any <u>clues</u>?

journal  writing

Self-Selected Writing Have children write in their journal about a topic of their choice. They may want to illustrate their writing.

teaching tip

Management Suggest that children proofread one another's work after they have proofread their own.

GENERATE IDEAS

Generate Clues Remind children that throughout this lesson they have worked with clues about animals. Display the Animal Features Chart they helped create (page 98M). Explain that these features can be used as clues. Tell children that they are going to write a riddle about an animal. Recall the squirrel poem, and explain that this is a kind of riddle. Show children how to use facts about animals to create clues for a riddle.

> I can use my sharp teeth to chop down a tree.
>
> I have a flat tail that is very strong, you'll see.
>
> My teeth and tail help me build my home.
>
> Can you guess who I am? (beaver)

Write a Riddle Have children write their own animal riddle. They may choose to use ideas from the chart or create their own clues for a different animal. Tell children that they may choose to use rhyming words in their riddles, but that it is not necessary. Remind children to use clues about how the animal looks, where it lives, and what it does. If they wish, they can illustrate the animal on the back of the paper next to the answer.

Handwriting Remind children that in order to make their riddles easy to read, they should place the letters in each word close together. Point out that they should also leave spaces between words so that the reader knows where one word ends and the next one begins.

5-DAY GRAMMAR

DAY 1	Introduce Using *Am, Is,* and *Are*
DAY 2	Match Sentence Parts
DAY 3	*Am, Is, Are* Game
DAY 4	**Sentences with *Am, Is,* and *Are***
DAY 5	Choose *Am, Is,* or *Are*

Grammar

Using Am, Is, *and* Are

REVIEW

Sentences with *Am, Is,* and *Are* Have children make word cards for *am*, *is*, and *are*. Write the following sentences on the board. Ask children to read them aloud, holding up the word that correctly completes each sentence:

Sal _____ a kitten. (is)

Kittens _____ little. (are)

I _____ happy to have a kitten. (am)

Chuckle _____ a cat. (is)

Cats _____ larger than kittens. (are)

I _____ larger than a cat. (am)

You _____ also larger than a cat. (are)

WRAP UP Share Ideas

Use the Author's Chair Ask children to share their riddles. Have their classmates guess which animal they are describing. Ask children to share their illustrations once their animals have been guessed. Suggest that children speak in a clear voice, loud enough for the audience to hear. Tell listeners to be polite and attentive. Remind children to use expression as they read their riddles.

S.S.R.
Sustained Silent Reading

Have children read silently from a book of their choice. See page 123J for tips on helping children choose books.

SKILL TRACE

USING *AM, IS,* AND *ARE*

Introduce	98N
Reteach	T7
REVIEW	119C, 121B, 123B, 123L

Grammar Resources

Grammar Jingles™ **CD, Primary,** Track 10, "All About Being"

Name _____

Using Am, Is, and Are

▶ Circle **am**, **is**, or **are** to complete each sentence correctly. Then write the word.

(is) are

1. Today _____is_____ the bike race.

is (am)

2. I _____am_____ ready.

am (are)

3. All my friends _____are_____ in the race, too.

(is) are

4. The race _____is_____ fun.

is (are)

5. My mom and dad _____are_____ here.

128

▲ Language Handbook, p. 128

How to Be a Nature Detective   **123B**

Day at a Glance
Day 5

Sharing Literature
Big Book: *I Swam with a Seal*

Phonemic Awareness
Distinguish Phonemes; Focus on
've, 'd, 're

Phonics
Contractions *'ve, 'd, 're*

Spelling
Posttest; Writing Application

Vocabulary
REVIEW: *clues, detective, floor,
nature, piece, pulls*

Reading

Rereading for Fluency
Pupil Edition
"How to Be a Nature Detective,"
pp. 100–116

Self-Selected Reading
Read

Writing ✏
Description of a Setting

Grammar
REVIEW: Using *Am, Is,* and *Are*

WARM UP MORNING MESSAGE

Good Morning!

Today is _____.

I would like to swim with a seal.

It would be fun to _____ with a rabbit.

Would you like to _____ with a _____?

Introduce the Day
Tell children that today they will revisit the story *I Swam with a Seal.*
Remind children that in this story, the children see different animals
doing what they like to do. Guide them in generating a morning
message about things animals do. Ask:

• **What do rabbits like to do?**

• **What is your favorite animal?**

• **What does that animal like to do?**

As you write the message, ask volunteers to write words, letters, or
sounds that they know. Remind children to begin each sentence
with a capital letter and end it with an end mark.

Read the Message
Read the message. Use the message to focus on skills that have
been previously taught.

Apply Skills

Concept Vocabulary Point
out the action words in the message. Tell children that seals swim
and rabbits hop. Have children
say other action words that tell
what animals do. (*run, gallop,
jump, trot, fly*)

Grammar/Mechanics Use the
message to review basic sentence punctuation and capitalization. Point out the differences
between statements and questions. Guide children to see that
a period ends a statement and a
question mark ends a question.

Sharing Literature

DEVELOP LISTENING COMPREHENSION

Connecting Texts Tell children that they are going to listen to *I Swam with a Seal*. Tell them to think about clues a nature detective might find that show that each of the animals in the story has passed by. For example, a nature detective might see ripples in the water that show where a seal has swum. Read the text. Pause to allow children to suggest clues for each animal.

Appreciating Language Focus children's attention on the author's use of action words in the story. Read the following line: *The hare glanced at me.* Talk about why the author chose the word *glanced* instead of just *looked*. Point to other action words in the story and have children act out and discuss their meanings: *sailed, slithered, pranced, whinnied, bothered, giggled.*

Phonemic Awareness

DISTINGUISH PHONEMES

Words from the Big Book Recall the animals named in the story. Say the word *seal* twice, the first time elongating the initial sound and the second time elongating the final sound. Ask children to identify the initial and final sounds they hear. (/s/ and /l/) Continue with the following words:

Word	falcon	snake	beaver	gull	porcupine
Initial Sound	/f/	/s/	/b/	/g/	/p/
Final Sound	/n/	/k/	/r/	/l/	/n/

FOCUS ON 've, 'd, 're

Count Syllables Tell children you are going to say some words or groups of words. Children will repeat after you, clapping out the word parts. Model by saying *they have* (clap twice) and *they've* (clap once). Continue with these words:

I've (once)	**I have** (twice)	**they'd** (once)	**they would** (twice)
we're (once)	**we are** (twice)	**he'd** (once)	**he had** (twice)

▲ **Big Book**

How to Be a Nature Detective **123D**

Phonics
Contractions 've, 'd, 're

✔ *Introduce*

OBJECTIVE

To recognize and read contrac-tions with 've, 'd, and 're

SKILL TRACE

CONTRACTIONS 've, 'd, 're	
INTRODUCE	Bk I-3, IIIE; Bk I-5, 123E–123F
Reteach	T8
Review	I55F, I85G
T Test	Bk I-5

ADVANCED

Suggest that children write sentences with contractions. Use the sentences to provide other children with practice identifying the two words that the con-tractions stand for.

Phonics Resources

Phonics Practice Book, pp. 286–287

WORKING WITH PATTERNS

Understand Contractions with *'ve, 'd,* and *'re* Write the following sentences on the board:

> I have seen that show.
> I've seen that show.

Underline *I have* and *I've*. Point out that *I've* is a contraction—a shorter way of saying *I have*. Ask children to name the letters that were dropped from *I have* to form the contraction *I've. (ha)*

Continue with the following sentences:

> We are going to school.   I would like to go home now.
> We're going to school.   I'd like to go home now.

Help children understand that *we're* is formed by dropping the *a* in *are* and adding an apostrophe, and *I'd* is formed by dropping the *woul* and adding an apostrophe. Tell children that *'d* can stand for *would*, *should*, or *had*.

Analyze Contractions Display a chart like the following:

Contractions with *'ve*	Contractions with *'d*	Contractions with *'re*
___ + ___ = ___	___ + ___ = ___	___ + ___ = ___
___ + ___ = ___	___ + ___ = ___	___ + ___ = ___

Write the following sentences on the board. Have children read each sentence. Ask a volunteer to underline each contraction and name the two words it stands for. Have the child then enter the information in the appropriate column in the chart. Continue with other sentences.

> We've been here.   (we + have = we've)
> I'd like to come here again.   (I + would = I'd)
> They're always here.   (they + are = they're)

Apply Phonics

APPLY PHONICS SKILLS

Write Contractions with 've, 'd, and 're Use the contractions chart to help children summarize what they have learned. Emphasize that in a contraction, an apostrophe takes the place of the missing letter or letters. Have children write three sentences in their journal, one with a 've word, one with a 'd word, and one with an 're word.

We're going to see our friends.
They'd like us to stay for a while.
I've never been to their new house.

5-DAY PHONICS

DAY 1	Introduce /ō/o
DAY 2	Word Building with /ō/o
DAY 3	Word Building with /ō/o
DAY 4	Word Building with /ō/o and /ō/o-e
DAY 5	**Contractions 've, 'd, 're**

ENGLISH-LANGUAGE LEARNERS

Use contractions in sentences about children. *You are a boy. You're a boy. They are girls. They're girls. We had better do our work. We'd better do our work.* Suggest that children practice pronouncing the contractions several times.

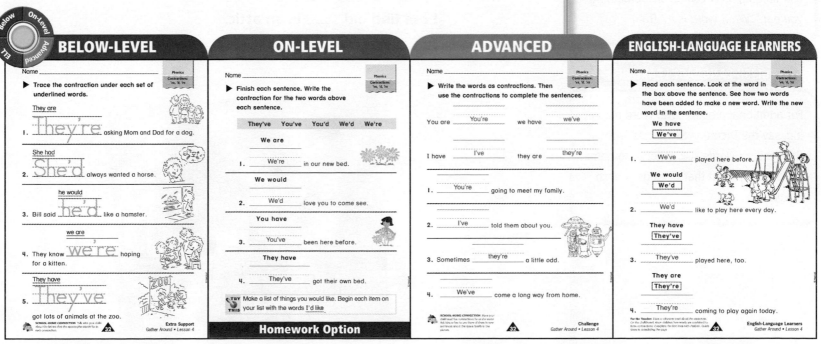

▲ Extra Support, p. 32   ▲ Practice, p. 32   ▲ Challenge, p. 32   ▲ ELL, p. 32

How to Be a Nature Detective **123F**

Spelling Words

1. old
2. fold
3. told
4. cold
5. roll
6. most
7. find
8. child
9. both
10. during

BELOW-LEVEL

Give children more practice in writing the Spelling Words. Give several clues for each word and have children write the Spelling Word that goes with each clue. For example, say *This word rhymes with* poll *and can mean "to go around and around," or it can mean "something you eat." What word is it?* (roll)

ENGLISH-LANGUAGE LEARNERS

For additional practice with word meaning, say the Dictation Sentences without the Spelling Words. Ask children to name the Spelling Word that belongs in each blank.

WORD WORK

Spelling

5-DAY SPELLING	
DAY 1	Pretest; Word Sort
DAY 2	Word Building
DAY 3	State the Generalization
DAY 4	Review
DAY 5	**Posttest; Writing Application**

ASSESS/APPLY

Posttest Assess children's progress using the words and the Dictation Sentences from Day 1.

1. **old**   There is a hole in my **old** sneakers.
2. **fold**   Please **fold** the paper in half.
3. **told**   I **told** a story to the class.
4. **cold**   It gets very **cold** here in the winter.
5. **roll**   The gym teacher asked us to **roll** the ball.
6. **most**   The winner is the team with the **most** points.

Review

7. **find**   I can't **find** my glasses.
8. **child**   Things were different when I was a **child**.

High-Frequency

9. **both**   He asked **both** boys to play the game.

Vocabulary

10. **during**   We must be quiet **during** classes at school.

Writing Application Have children complete and illustrate the following sentence frames:

Both my friend and I went _____.

I can find old _____ in an attic.

Max told a _____ story.

Vocabulary

USE WORDS IN SENTENCES

Reinforce Words Use the *Word Cards* for *clues, detective, floor, nature, piece,* and *pulls.* Hold up one of the cards and ask children to say the word and then spell it. Have children say the word and spell it again. Then put down the card but leave your hand up. Ask children to say and spell the word one more time. Continue this procedure with all the vocabulary words. When you complete this activity, ask volunteers to use the vocabulary words in sentences. Record the sentences on chart paper. Track the print as you read aloud each sentence.

> We can look for nature clues outside.
> I am a nature detective.
> May I have a piece of pizza?

REVIEW

Vocabulary

clues	nature
detective	piece
floor	pulls

Use these sentences to see if children have learned the meanings of the vocabulary words:

I spilled my milk on the _____.
I would like a _____ of cake.
The horse _____ the wagon.
I read about animals in a _____ book.
The _____ found many _____ on the path.

Words to Remember

WORD WALL

Match Words Have children write the vocabulary words on individual self-stick notes. Then have children take turns finding the displayed vocabulary words and sticking the notes to them.

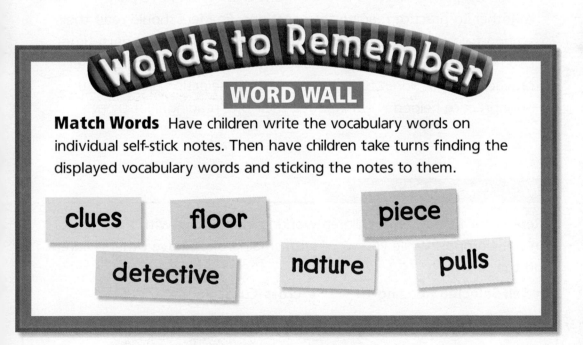

clues   floor   piece
detective   nature   pulls

Read

▲ *Pupil Edition*, pp. 100–116

FLUENCY ROUTINES For support, see Fluency Routine Cards in Theme Resources, pp. T83–T84.

Rereading for Fluency

GROUPS

Echo Reading

BELOW-LEVEL/ENGLISH-LANGUAGE LEARNERS Remind children that when they read aloud, they should read smoothly and with expression as if they were talking to someone. Have children track the print as you read aloud sentences or paragraphs and model proper intonation, phrasing, and expression. Then have children echo read. Reread as necessary to provide additional modeling. TEACHER-DIRECTED

PARTNERS

Repeated Reading

ON-LEVEL/ADVANCED Divide the selection into six to eight sections. Assign each section to a different child. Then have partners work together to practice reading their sections. Readers should read their section two or three times, trying to read more smoothly each time. Listeners should give feedback about how the readers sound. After practice, bring children together to read the selection aloud. Discuss how practice helped them improve their oral reading. INDEPENDENT

Managing Small Groups

Reread for fluency with children working individually, with partners, or in small groups. While you work with small groups, have other children do the following:

- **Self-Selected Reading**
- **Cross-Curricular Centers**
- **Practice Pages**
- **Journal Writing**

Use the suggested Classroom Management outline on page 7C for the whole-group/small-group schedule.

Self-Selected Reading

INDEPENDENT READING

Have children choose a book from the **Browsing Boxes** or the **Reading Center** to read independently during a sustained silent reading time. Children may also want to reread a story from their *Pupil Edition*. These are some books you may want to gather that relate to "How to Be a Nature Detective."

Decodable Books

Decodable Book 30
"Let's Go!" by Ann Miranda

"Flo Hippo" by Nancy Furstinger

Cut-Out/Fold-Up Book

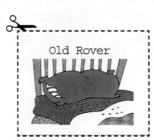

Old Rover

Old Rover
Practice Book, pp. 71–72

Books for All Learners

   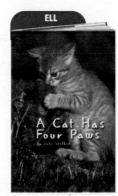

The Thing That Visited Our Camp
by Mary Louise Bourget

Girl Detectives
by Judith Brand

Looking for Clues
by Judith Brand

A Cat Has Four Paws
by Jake Walker

choosing books

Remind children to read one or two pages of a book to decide whether they need to select an easier book. If there are at least five words that the child can't read, he or she should try an easier book.

related books

- *The Monarch Butterfly* by Sarah Gaitanos. The Wright Group, 1996.

  Beautiful photographs help explain the process of a caterpillar turning into a butterfly. ON-LEVEL

- *If You Find A Rock* by Peggy Christian. Harcourt, 2000.

  Rocks and stones are for skipping, hiding things, climbing, and many other things. ADVANCED

- *Hide and Snake* by Keith Baker. Voyager, 1995.

  A snake plays hide-and-seek with the reader. BELOW-LEVEL

- *Animals in Camouflage* by Phyllis Limbacher Tildes. Charlesbridge, 2000. Riddles about animals that use camouflage to protect themselves. ON-LEVEL

How to Be a Nature Detective **123J**

Writing

Description of a Setting

5-DAY WRITING	
DAY 1	CROSS-CURRICULAR: Animal Features Chart
DAY 2	SHARED: Picture Caption
DAY 3	INTERACTIVE: Newspaper Article
DAY 4	INDEPENDENT: Riddle
DAY 5	INDEPENDENT: **Description of a Setting**

DISCUSS STORY SETTING

Make a Word List Remind children that the setting of a story tells where it takes place. Explain that they can use descriptive words to tell about a story setting. Have children look back at "How to Be a Nature Detective." Tell children that this story has different settings. Pick one of the settings and ask for words and phrases that can be used to describe this place, such as *outdoors, playground, trees,* and *rocks.*

Write a Description Tell children that they are going to write their own description of a story setting. They can use "How to Be a Nature Detective," or they may choose to describe the setting of a favorite story. Write the following questions on the board, and tell children that their descriptions should answer these kinds of questions:

- **Where is this place?**
- **What does it look like?**
- **What kinds of things can you see, hear, and smell here?**
- **What time of year is it?**

Suggest that children write three or four sentences to describe the setting. Ask children to share their descriptions with the class. If possible, children can display a picture from the story to accompany their presentation.

Handwriting Remind children to use their best handwriting when writing the sentences. Ask them to go back and check that there is proper spacing between letters and words. Have children look at their work and identify the word that they think shows their best handwriting.

DAILY LANGUAGE PRACTICE

I dont know where
they our.

I <u>don't</u> know where
they <u>are</u>.

ONGOING ASSESSMENT

Note whether children are able to
- spell known vocabulary words.
- say and write complete sentences.
- use knowledge of the basic rules of punctuation and capitalization.

ADVANCED

Have children choose another setting from "How to Be a Nature Detective" and write a description of it. Children can then illustrate the two settings they have described.

Writing Prompt Have children write a description of their favorite place in nature.

5-DAY GRAMMAR	
DAY 1	Introduce Using *Am, Is,* and *Are*
DAY 2	Match Sentence Parts
DAY 3	*Am, Is, Are* Game
DAY 4	Sentences with *Am, Is,* and *Are*
DAY 5	**Choose *Am, Is,* or *Are***

Day 5

Grammar

Using Am, Is, *and* Are

REVIEW

Choose *Am, Is,* or *Are* From the settings descriptions that children wrote in the Writing activity, page 123K, select sentences that contain forms of the verb *to be*, or use the sentences shown below. Tell children that you are going to read aloud some sentences and they will tell you whether to use *am, is,* or *are* to complete the sentence. Read the sentences aloud.

The trees _____ very tall. (are)
A girl _____ playing with a little dog. (is)
The beach _____ warm and sandy. (is)
I _____ walking through a green meadow. (am)

WRAP UP Revisit the Poem

Poem Innovation Reread the squirrel poem from Sharing Literature, page 121D. Ask children to use the pattern of the squirrel poem to innovate a poem about themselves. For example: *Dark brown hair is the color for me, / For I'm a nut about soccer you see. / I kick and kick to make the goal. / I also love airplanes, 'cause I'm . . . .* Tell children to be creative and not to worry about rhymes, but more about how they can describe themselves in a riddle.

S.S.R. Have children read silently from a book of their choice. See page 123J for tips on helping children choose books.

SKILL TRACE

USING *AM, IS,* AND *ARE*	
Introduce	98N
Reteach	T7
REVIEW	119C, 121B, 123B, 123L

technology

Visit *The Learning Site:*
www.harcourtschool.com
See Go for Grammar Gold, Multimedia Grammar Glossary.

BELOW-LEVEL

If children are unable to choose the correct verb form *am, is,* or *are*, provide sentence frames with a complete predicate such as, _____ *is shiny.* or _____ *am going to a party.* and have them supply the subject. Then have children read the sentences aloud.

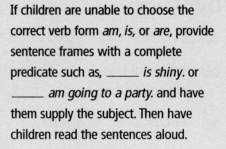

▲ Language Handbook, p. 129

How to Be a Nature Detective **123L**

Guided Reading OPTIONS

Books for All Learners

Reinforcing Skills and Strategies

■ BELOW-LEVEL

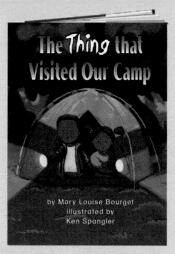

The *Thing* that Visited Our Camp

by Mary Louise Bourget
illustrated by Ken Spangler

The Thing That Visited Our Camp

 Phonics: Long Vowel /ō/o

 Vocabulary: *clues, detective, floor, nature, piece, pulls*

✓ **Focus Skill: Main Idea**

SUMMARY   A young boy becomes a detective after he finds his family's campsite in a mess.

 Visit *The Learning Site:*
www.harcourtschool.com
See Resources for Parents and
Teachers: Books for All Learners

BEFORE READING

Build Background Ask children to recall mystery stories they have read or viewed. Guide children to notice the following common elements of a mystery: a detective, a crime, the search for clues, and solving the crime by identifying the culprit.

Preview/Set Purpose Have children identify the title and help them read it. Point out the author and illustrator. Then have children look at the first few pages of the book and predict what it is about. Have children set a purpose for reading, such as *I want to find out what visited the camp.*

READING THE BOOK

Pages 2–6 Where does this story take place? (a family's campsite) What happens there? (Something made a mess of the family's camping supplies.) SETTING, SUMMARIZE

Pages 7–10 What clue does the boy find first? (claw marks on a roll of paper towels) What does he decide? (An animal made the mess.) What clues does the boy find next? (open food boxes and unopened boxes without food, all on the ground) What does he decide? (A hungry bear made the mess.) SUMMARIZE

Pages 11–12 What does the family do to protect its food from another bear visit? (put it into a special bear-proof locker) What is this story mostly about? (a campsite that is broken into by a bear) SUMMARIZE, MAIN IDEA

RESPONDING

Retell the Story Have volunteers retell the story. Encourage them to use the sequence words *first*, *next*, and *last*. Guide them in using proper phrasing, pitch, and modulation as they speak.

The Thing that Visited Our Camp

by Mary Louise Beurget
Illustrated by
Ken Spangler

Girl Detectives

by Judith Brand
illustrated by Jeff Seaver

LOOKING FOR CLUES

by Judith Brand
illustrated by Kevin Rechin

▲ p. 123O

A Cat Has Four Paws
by Jake Walker

▲ p. 123P

Oral Reading Fluency

Use Books for All Learners to promote oral reading fluency.

See **Fluency Routine Cards,** pp. T83–T84.

■ ON-LEVEL

Girl Detectives

 Phonics: Long Vowel /ō/*o*

 Vocabulary: *clues, detective, floor, nature, piece, pulls*

☑ **Focus Skill: Main Idea**

SUMMARY Two sisters use clues to find their friends in a detective game.

 Visit *The Learning Site:*
www.harcourtschool.com
See Resources for Parents and
Teachers: Books for All Learners.

BEFORE READING

Build Background Ask children to recall mystery stories they have read or viewed. Through discussion, help them to recognize that most mysteries have a detective that searches for clues to find an answer.

Preview/Set Purpose Have children identify the title and help them read it. Point out the author and illustrator. Then have children look at the first few pages of the book and predict what the story is about. Have children set a purpose for reading, such as *I want to find out what the girl detectives find.*

READING THE BOOK

Pages 2–6 What clues do Megan and Jo find first? (big and little tracks in the snow) Who do the girls think made the tracks? (A.J. and Jim) SEQUENCE, NOTE DETAILS

Pages 7–9 How does Megan know the muddy footprints on the porch weren't made by Evan? (They are much bigger than her foot, so they can't be a child's.) Would you say that Megan is a good detective? Why or why not? (Possible response: Yes, because she knows how to find clues.) SUMMARIZE; EXPRESS PERSONAL OPINIONS

Pages 10–13 What happens to make the girls think that Evan is behind the bush? (A branch has broken off and is lying on the snow.) CAUSE/EFFECT

Pages 14–16 What is this story mostly about? (two girls who play a detective game) MAIN IDEA

RESPONDING

Make a Comic Strip Have children draw comic strips to show the story. Encourage them to use speech bubbles to show what each character is saying.

Guided Reading OPTIONS

Books for All Learners

Reinforcing Skills and Strategies

■ ADVANCED

by Judith Brand
illustrated by Kevin Rechin

Looking for Clues

 Phonics: Long Vowel /ō/o

 Vocabulary: *clues, detective, floor, nature, piece, pulls*

✓ **Focus Skill: Main Idea**

SUMMARY A sister and brother become nature detectives and discover clues to animal life at a local park.

 Visit *The Learning Site:*
www.harcourtschool.com
See Resources for Parents and
Teachers: Books for All Learners.

BEFORE READING

Build Background Ask volunteers to share information about wild animals in your area, such as birds. Have children talk about what the animals eat, their homes, and where they've been seen.

Preview/Set Purpose Have children identify the title and help them read it. Point out the author and illustrator. Then have children look at the first few pages of the book and predict what it is about. Have children set a purpose for reading, such as *I want to find out what clues the children find.*

READING THE BOOK

Pages 2–5 What kind of animal has a big footprint with only two toes? (a deer) How do webbed feet help ducks swim fast? (The webbed feet can push a lot of water.) NOTE DETAILS, DRAW CONCLUSIONS

Pages 6–10 What clue did the snail leave behind? (a sticky trail) What do you think the trail is from? (Possible response: The snail's wet body dragging across the ground makes a trail. Accept reasonable responses. Encourage children to explain their responses.) NOTE DETAILS, SPECULATE

Pages 11–16 Think about everything you've read. What is this story mostly about? (Nolan and Roxann on a hunt for animals in their park) NOTE DETAILS, MAIN IDEA

RESPONDING

Play a Nature Detective Game Have partners print on cards the names of the animals in the book and lay the cards face-up on a table. To play the game, one partner gives a few clues about an animal, and the other must identify it.

BELOW-LEVEL

The Thing that Visited Our Camp

by Mary Louise Bourget
illustrated by Ken Spangler

▲ p. 123M

ON-LEVEL

Girl Detectives

by Judith Brand
illustrated by Jeff Seaver

▲ p. 123N

ADVANCED

LOOKING FOR CLUES

by Judith Brand
illustrated by Kevin Rechin

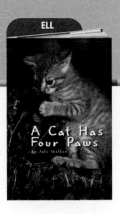

ELL

A Cat Has Four Paws

by Jake Walker

■ ENGLISH-LANGUAGE LEARNERS

A Cat Has Four Paws

 Strong Picture Support

 Concept Vocabulary

 Theme Related

SUMMARY This book of photographs introduces readers to the unique features of several animals.

 Visit *The Learning Site:*
www.harcourtschool.com
See Resources for Parents and Teachers: Books for All Learners.

BEFORE READING

Build Background Show a picture of a person and a cat. Guide children to name body parts both mammals have in common, such as eyes, legs, and ears.

Preview/Set Purpose Have children identify the title and help them read it. Point out the author and illustrator. Then have children look at the first few pages and predict what the nonfiction book is about. Have children set a purpose for reading, such as *I want to find out about animals' bodies.*

READING THE BOOK

Pages 2–5 How many paws does a cat have? (four) What is another animal with four paws? (Possible response: a bear) NOTE DETAILS, MAKE COMPARISONS

Pages 6–9 Think about the rabbit and the lion. What is one way they are alike? What is one way they are different? (Possible response: They are both covered with fur. The rabbit does not eat meat, and the lion does.) SPECULATE, COMPARE/CONTRAST

Pages 10–12 Which animal has a deep pouch? (a kangaroo) What is inside the pouch? (the kangaroo's baby) Would you like a pouch? Why or why not? (Possible response: Yes, because then I wouldn't need a backpack. Accept reasonable responses. Encourage children to explain their answers.) SUMMARIZE, EXPRESS PERSONAL OPINIONS

RESPONDING

Draw Animal Pictures Have children draw pictures of animals from the book. Discuss the animals' special features and help children to label their pictures with sentences like those in the book, such as *A lobster has two claws.*

Reading Selections

Applies Consonant /j/g, dge

▲ Decodable Book 31
"Roger's Gerbil"
"The Fudge Judge"
"Ginger"
"The Badgers Have a Picnic"

PUPIL EDITION

Genre

Fiction

In fiction, there can be a mix of realistic and make-believe parts.

Look for:

• Ways the story is like real life.

• Things that could not happen in real life.

The Puddle
by David McPhail

Award-Winning Author/ Illustrator

126

127

▼ **READING ACROSS TEXTS:**
"Time to Play"
GENRE: Poetry

SUMMARY: A boy plays at a puddle with several imaginary friends.

Comparing Fiction and Poetry

"The Puddle" is available on *Audiotext 5.*

124A   Gather Around

Books for All Learners

Lesson Plans on pages 155M–155P

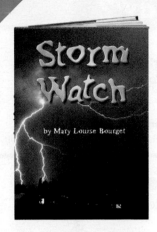

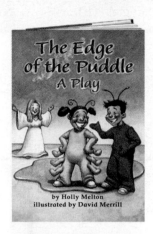

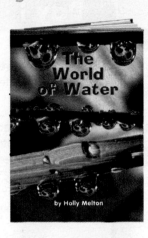

BELOW-LEVEL

- **Phonics: Consonants /j/ g, dge; Contraction 'd**
- **Vocabulary:** *angry, okay, nearly, sorry*

ON-LEVEL

- **Phonics: Consonants /j/ g, dge**
- **Vocabulary:** *angry, okay, nearly, sorry*

ADVANCED

- **Phonics: Consonants /j/ g, dge**
- **Vocabulary:** *angry, okay, nearly, sorry*

ELL

- **Strong Picture Support**
- **Concept Vocabulary**

MULTI-LEVEL PRACTICE

Practice Book, pp. 33–40

Extra Support, pp. 34–40

Challenge, pp. 34–40

English-Language Learners, pp. 34–40

 Technology

- *Phonics Express™ CD-ROM, Level B*
- *Writing Express™ CD-ROM*
- *Grammar Jingles™ CD, Primary*
- *Reading and Language Skills Assessment CD-ROM*
- *The Learning Site:* www.harcourtschool.com

ADDITIONAL RESOURCES

Phonics Practice Book, pp. 66–67, 68–69, 287, 308–311

Spelling Practice Book, pp. 75–76

Language Handbook, pp. 130–133

Read-Aloud Literature
- Big Book of Rhymes, p. 21
- Read-Aloud Anthology, p. 144

Teaching Transparencies 91–93, 110

Word Builders/Word Builder Cards

Letter Cards

Intervention Resource Kit, Lesson 31

English-Language Learners Resource Kit, Lesson 31

ORAL LANGUAGE

• **Sharing Literature**

• **Phonemic Awareness**

WORD WORK

• **Phonics**

• **Spelling**

• **Vocabulary**

READING

• **Comprehension**
• **Fluency**

Daily Routines
• **Morning Message**
• **Daily Language Practice**
• **Writing Prompt**

• **Independent Reading**

LANGUAGE ARTS

• **Writing**

• **Grammar**

Daily Language Practice
Spiral Review

Day 1

Sharing Literature, 124H
Big Book: Listen and Respond

Phonemic Awareness, 124H
Phoneme Matching; Focus on /j/

, 124I
Introduce: Consonants /j/g, dge

Spelling, 124K
Pretest; Word Sort **T**

Vocabulary, 124K
Review: *floor, piece* **T**

 Read
Apply Phonics, 124L

DECODABLE BOOK 31
"Roger's Gerbil"
"The Fudge Judge"

 Independent Reading
Books for All Learners

✏️ **Shared Writing,** 124M
Bingo Cards

Writing Prompt
Have children draw an animal they saw recently and write what it might have been thinking.

Grammar, 124N
Introduce: Verbs That Tell About the Past **T**

Daily Language Practice
I dansed with mi dog. (danced, my)

Day 2

Sharing Literature, 124P
Poem: Listen and Respond

Phonemic Awareness, 124P
Phoneme Addition; Focus on /j/

, 124Q
Review: Consonants /j/g, dge

Spelling, 124Q
Word Building **T**

Vocabulary, 124S
Introduce: *angry, nearly, okay, sorry* **T**

Word Power, pp. 124–125

 Read
Read the Selection, 125A

PUPIL EDITION
"The Puddle,"
pp. 124–149

Comprehension

(Focus Skill) Plot **T**

(Focus Strategy) Make Inferences

 Independent Reading
Books for All Learners

✏️ **Writing Across the Curriculum,** 149B
Class Book

Writing Prompt
Have children write about their favorite part of "The Puddle."

Grammar, 149C
Review: Verbs That Tell About the Past **T**

Daily Language Practice
the frog jumpd into the boat. (The, jumped)

Focus Skill

Plot

 Phonics

Consonant

/j/*g, dge*

Focus of the Week:
- VOCABULARY : *angry, nearly, okay, sorry*
- COMPREHENSION: Plot
- WRITING: Verbs That Tell About the Past

Day 3

Sharing Literature, 149E
   Poem: Build Concept Vocabulary

Phonemic Awareness, 149E
   Phoneme Addition; Focus on /j/

Phonics, 149F
   Review: Consonants /j/*g, dge*

Spelling, 149H
   State the Generalization **T**

Vocabulary, 149I
   Review: *angry, nearly, okay, sorry* **T**

Read

Rereading for Fluency, 149J

Reading Across Texts, 150–151
   "Time to Play"

Making Connections, 152–153

Apply Phonics, 149G
DECODABLE BOOK 31
   "Ginger"
   "The Badgers Have a Picnic"

⬤ **Independent Reading**
   Books for All Learners

✏ **Interactive Writing,** 153A
   Directions

Writing Prompt
   Have children write about and draw things they "see" on an imaginary trip.

Grammar, 153B
   Review: Verbs That Tell About the Past **T**

Daily Language Practice
   I'll pretend to fli to the stares. (fly, stars)

Day 4

Sharing Literature, 153D
   Poem: Listen and Respond

Phonemic Awareness, 153D
   Phoneme Substitution; Focus on /j/ and /s/

Phonics, 153E
   Build Words

Spelling, 153G
   Review **T**

Vocabulary, 153H
   Review: *angry, nearly, okay, sorry* **T**

Read

Comprehension, 153I

(Focus Skill) Plot,
   pp. 154–155 **T**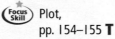

⬤ **Independent Reading**
   Books for All Learners

✏ **Independent Writing,** 155A
   Narrative Sentences

Self-Selected Writing
   Have children write about a topic of their choice.

Grammar, 155B
   Review: Verbs That Tell About the Past **T**

Daily Language Practice
   Do you want a peece of fudge. (piece, fudge?)

Day 5

Sharing Literature, 155D
   Big Book: Develop
   Listening Comprehension

Phonemic Awareness, 155D
   Phoneme Deletion; Focus on /d/, /t/, /ed/

Phonics, 155E
   Inflections *-ed, -ing*
   Contractions *'ve, 'd, 're* **T**

Spelling, 155G
   Posttest; Writing Application **T**

Vocabulary, 155H
   Review: *angry, nearly, okay, sorry* **T**

Read

Rereading for Fluency, 155I

Self-Selected Reading, 155J

⬤ **Independent Reading**
   Books for All Learners

✏ **Independent Writing,** 155K
   Letters

Writing Prompt
   Have children tell which character from "The Puddle" they would like to have as a friend and why.

Grammar, 155L
   Review: Verbs That Tell About the Past **T**

Daily Language Practice
   the frog and the pig hops into the puddle. (The, hop)

Cross-Curricular Centers

SOCIAL STUDIES CENTER

Puddle Rules

Remind children that the characters in the story "The Puddle" had a hard time playing together. Have children decide on at least three rules that the animals should follow the next time they play at the puddle. Have them make a poster of their rules. You may want to lightly draw write-on lines on the poster paper to help children write their letters and words neatly.

Puddle Rules
1. Don't splash.
2. Watch where you are going.
3. Don't drink all the water.
4. Be nice to the other animals.

30 Minutes

Materials

- poster paper
- crayons or markers

WRITING CENTER

Where Are They Now?

After children have read "The Puddle," place a copy of the story at the Writing Center with a sign that says, "Where are they now?" Have children choose an animal from the story and write about where it is and what it is doing, now that it is no longer at the puddle. Remind children to write complete sentences that begin with a capital letter and end with an end mark. Have children draw a picture to go with their writing.

He is swimming in a pond.

30 Minutes

Materials

- *Pupil Edition*
- small "Where are they now?" sign
- paper
- crayons or markers

SCIENCE CENTER

Evaporation Diagram

Have children draw a picture that shows how the sun's heat makes water dry up (evaporate). Suggest that children draw clothes drying on a clothesline, a wet dog lying in a sunny place, a puddle, or other subjects of their own choosing. Children may choose to add arrows or other symbols to show how the water turns into a gas and moves into the air.

20 Minutes

Materials

- drawing paper
- crayons or markers

HEALTH CENTER

All-Weather Wear

Make a set of weather cards: a sun labeled *hot*, rain-drops labeled *rainy*, and a snowman labeled *snowy*. Copy and distribute outlines of clothing, such as a base-ball cap, shorts, an umbrella, rain boots, mittens, and a woolen hat. Prepare a two-column floor chart with the headings *Weather* and *Clothes*. Have children cut out the clothing items. Then have them use the chart to match weather cards with appropriate clothing.

20 Minutes

Materials

■ set of weather cards (on index cards)
■ outlines of weather-related clothing
■ chart paper
■ scissors

COMPUTER CENTER

A Way to Play

Have children use a draw or paint program to create a picture that goes with one of the week's writing lessons. They could also cut and paste clip art to create a scene showing characters by a puddle. Have children type labels or sentences that tell about their pictures.

I'm flying to Zork.

40 Minutes

Materials

■ computer
■ software for creating pictures

HOMEWORK FOR THE WEEK

The Homework Copying Master provides activities to complete for each day of the week.

Visit *The Learning Site:* www.harcourtschool.com

See Resources for Parents and Teachers: Homework Helper.

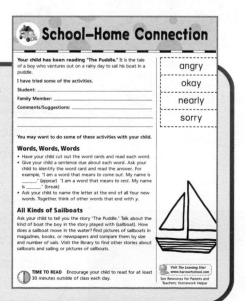

School–Home Connection

Your child has been reading "The Puddle." It is the tale of a boy who ventures out on a rainy day to sail his boat in a puddle.

I have tried some of the activities.

Student: _____

Family Member: _____

Comments/Suggestions: _____

| angry |
| okay |
| nearly |
| sorry |

You may want to do some of these activities with your child.

Words, Words, Words
• Have your child cut out the word cards and read each word.
• Give your child a sentence clue about each word. Ask your child to identify the word card and read the answer. For example, "I am a word that means to come out. My name is _____." (appear) "I am a word that means to rest. My name is _____." (break)
• Ask your child to name the letter at the end of all four new words. Together, think of other words that end with y.

All Kinds of Sailboats
Ask your child to tell you the story "The Puddle." Talk about the kind of boat the boy in the story played with (sailboat). How does a sailboat move in the water? Find pictures of sailboats in magazines, books, or newspapers and compare them by size and number of sails. Visit the library to find other stories about sailboats and sailing or pictures of sailboats.

TIME TO READ Encourage your child to read for at least 30 minutes outside of class each day.

Visit The Learning Site! www.harcourtschool.com See Resources for Parents and Teachers: Homework Helper

Homework, p. T43 ▶

Read

ORAL LANGUAGE

WARM UP

MORNING MESSAGE

Good Morning!

Today is _____.
We like to play with the animals.
_____ likes to hop with a _____.
_____ likes to crawl with a _____.
_____ likes to run with a _____.

Introduce the Day

Tell children that today they will revisit the book *I Swam with a Seal*. Guide them in generating a morning message about playing with animals. Ask:

• **Which animals hop in a pond? Which animals hop in the grass?**

• **Which bugs crawl across dirt? Which animals crawl near water?**

• **Which animals can run fast?**

As you write the message, ask volunteers to write previously taught letters, words, and/or punctuation to reinforce skills. For instance, have volunteers write *frog, toad,* or *bunny* in the third sentence and *spider, turtle,* or *crab* in the fourth sentence.

Read the Message

Read the message. Use the message to focus on selected skills that have been previously taught.

Apply Skills

Phonics Ask volunteers to point to words with *a. (today, play, a, crawl, animals)* Read aloud each word, emphasizing the different vowel sounds for *a*. Have children repeat after you. Then ask volunteers to tell which words have the same sound for *a*.

Grammar Ask a volunteer to find the words *like* and *likes* in the message. Have the volunteer tell how the two words are different. (*Likes* has an *-s* ending.) Point out that the verb *likes* tells about only one person, whereas *like* tells about more than one.

Sharing Literature

LISTEN AND RESPOND

Read *I Swam with a Seal* Tell children to close their eyes and listen as you read the story *I Swam with a Seal*. Suggest that they imagine themselves moving with each animal and responding to the animal's question. Pause after each page to allow children time to visualize themselves in the scene. Prompt them with questions such as *What are you doing? What do you see? What is the animal saying to you?*

Generate Animal Words and Action Words Ask children which animals were mentioned in the story. Write the names on the board. Then point to each name and ask children how that animal moved in the story. Write the action word next to the animal name. Then call on children to role-play each animal in action.

Phonemic Awareness

PHONEME MATCHING

Words from the Big Book Remind children of the seal in the story *I Swam with a Seal*. Say *seal* and *dream*, emphasizing the middle phoneme /ē/. Ask if both words have the same vowel sound in the middle (yes) and what that sound is. Continue with the following words from the Big Book.

snake, snail (yes; /ā/) **hill, build** (yes; /i/) **spied, by** (yes; /ī/)
moon, shone (no) **furry, purred** (yes; /ûr/) **look, stone** (no)

FOCUS ON /j/

Isolate Phonemes Have children say the word *giant* and tell what sound is heard at the beginning of the word. (/j/) Then tell them to clap when they hear you say a word that begins with /j/.

gym **gem** **pen** **germ** **good**

Remind children that a giant is huge. Tell them to listen for words that end with /j/. Model by saying, *When I say* huge, *I hear the /j/ sound at the end*. Have children clap for words with /j/:

cage **leg** **ledge** **lose** **budge**

▲ **Big Book**

◀ "Jennie Jenkins," *Oo-pples and Boo-noo-noos: Songs and Activities for Phonemic Awareness*, pp. 94–95

BELOW-LEVEL

Have children repeat one-syllable words that begin with the /j/ sound. Say the beginning sound two times before saying the word. For example: /j/, /j/, *gym*. Have children tap the beat as they repeat after you. Then have them practice saying words that end with /j/. Have them jump up when they say /j/.

ADVANCED

Have partners make up a silly alliteration for the /j/ sound. Share these examples: *Gigi the giraffe is at the gym; George the gerbil jumps on the gentle giant*. Children can draw pictures to go with their silly sayings.

Phonics and Spelling
Consonants /j/g, dge

Introduce

OBJECTIVES

- *To generate the sound for /j/g, dge*

- *To build words using those letters and sounds*

- *To read simple, regular words*

SKILL TRACE

	/j/g, dge
INTRODUCE	124I–124L
Reteach	S28–29
Review	124Q–124R, 149F–149G, 153E–153F

teaching tip

Point out the spelling patterns for soft *g*. Explain that the letter *g* often stands for the /j/ sound when it is followed by *e* or *i*.

BELOW-LEVEL

Help children understand that the letters *g* and *j* can stand for the same sound, /j/. Display *Picture Cards* for *jar* and *cage*, and have children name the pictured objects. Ask them where the sound /j/ is heard in each word. Then turn over the *Picture Cards* to reveal the names of the objects. Point out that the letter *j* stands for /j/ in *jar* and the letter *g* stands for /j/ in *cage*.

TEACH/MODEL

Introduce /j/g, dge Display *Alphabet Card Gg* and say the letter name. Remind children that they have learned the sound for *g* at the beginning of words like *goat*. Tell children that the letter *g* can also stand for the sound /j/, the soft sound of the letter *g* at the beginning of words such as *giraffe*, *gentle*, and *giant*.

Hold up the *Letter Card g* and say /j/. Tell children that the /j/ sound appears at the end of the words *cage*, *large*, and *page*. Have children repeat the sound several times as you touch the card.

Next, display *Letter Cards d, g,* and *e*. Explain that the letters *d, g,* and *e* together stand for the /j/ sound. Tell children that the *dge* spelling of the /j/ sound appears in the words *bridge*, *edge*, and *fudge*. Again have children repeat the sound. Explain that *dge* is usually at the end of a word.

WORD BLENDING

a   v   d   e   g   m   l   i

Words With /j/g, dge Blend and read the words *gem*, *edge*, and *village*. As you demonstrate each step, using a pocket chart and *Letter Cards*, have children repeat after you, using *Word Builders* and *Word Builder Cards*. After forming the word *village*, ask children to clap the word parts and tell how many they hear. (two)

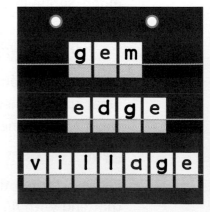

WORD BUILDING

Build Spelling Words Place the letter *a* in a pocket chart. Have children do the same with their *Word Builders* and *Word Builder Cards*. Repeat for the letters *g* and *e*. Model how to blend the word *age*. Slide your hand under the letters as you slowly elongate the sounds—/āājj/. Then read the word naturally—*age*. Have children do the same.

Have children build and read new words by telling them:

- Add a *p* in front of the *a*. What word did you make?

- Change the *p* to *c*. What word did you make?

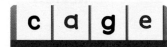

- Change the *c* to *b*. Add a *d* between the *a* and the *g*. What word did you make?

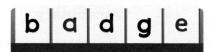

- Change the *a* to *u*. What word did you make?

- Change the *b* to *f*. What word did you make?

 Dictate Consonant /j/g, dge Words Dictate the words *cage* and *fudge* and have children write them in their journal. Suggest that they either draw a picture or write about each word.

5-DAY PHONICS/SPELLING

DAY 1	Introduce /j/g, dge
DAY 2	Word Building with /j/g, dge
DAY 3	Word Building with /j/g, dge
DAY 4	Word Building with /j/g, dge
DAY 5	Inflections -ed, -ing (drop e); Contractions 've, 'd, 're

teaching tip

Build Vocabulary As you model building the word *budge*, explain to children that the word means "to only move a little." Act out a sentence such as the following to clarify word meaning: *My heavy desk won't budge when I push it.* As you model building the word *fudge*, describe the soft candy.

BELOW-LEVEL

Some children may confuse long and short vowel sounds in words ending with *ge* and *dge*. Have them build and read the words *rid*, *ride*, and *ridge* for comparison. Point out that the vowel sound for a word ending with *dge* is always short.

Phonics Resources

 Phonics Express™ **CD-ROM, Level B** Sparkle/Route 1/ Fire Station

Phonics Practice Book, pp. 68–69

Spelling Words

1. age
2. page
3. cage
4. badge
5. budge
6. fudge
7. old
8. most
9. floor
10. piece

WORD WORK

5-DAY SPELLING

DAY 1	Pretest; Word Sort
DAY 2	Word Building
DAY 3	State the Generalization
DAY 4	Review
DAY 5	Posttest; Writing Application

Phonics and Spelling

INTRODUCE THE WORDS

Pretest Read aloud the first word and the Dictation Sentence. Repeat the word as children write it. Write the correct spelling on the board and have children circle the word if they spelled it correctly and write it correctly if they did not. Repeat for words 2–10.

1. **age**   I learned to ride a bike at the **age** of six.
2. **page**   What number is on the next **page** of your book?
3. **cage**   The tiger is asleep in his **cage**.
4. **badge**   A police officer wears a **badge**.
5. **budge**   The rock was so big we couldn't **budge** it.
6. **fudge**   Have you ever had **fudge** for dessert?

Review

7. **old**   How **old** are you?
8. **most**   **Most** children like pizza.

Vocabulary

9. **floor**   I cleaned the **floor** with a mop.
10. **piece**   I write with a **piece** of chalk.

Word Sort Place column heads *age*, *dge*, and *other* at the top of a pocket chart. Write each Spelling Word on an index card. Display the cards and ask "Which words have the letters *age*? Which words end with *dge*? Which words end with other letters?" Place the words in the correct column as children direct. Then have children

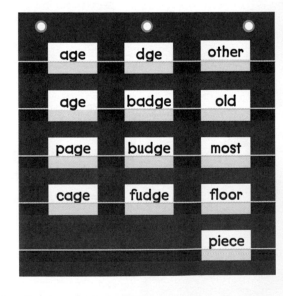

look at the words in the "other" column. Ask "Which two words are similar? How are they similar?" (Possible response: *old* and *most* both have the long *o* sound; *floor* and *piece* both have five letters.) After sorting, have children read the Spelling Words aloud.

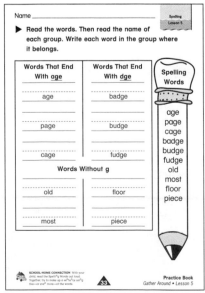

▲ Practice Book, p. 33

124K   **Gather Around**

Apply Phonics

Read

APPLY /j/ g, dge

Write the following sentences on the board or on chart paper. Have children read the first sentence as you track the print. Frame the words *Ginger* and *bridge* and have children read them. Continue with the other sentences.

> **Ginger** and I walked on the **bridge**.
> We looked over the **edge**.
> We saw a **large** fish in the water.

Have children read "Roger's Gerbil" and "The Fudge Judge" in *Decodable Book 31*.

▲ **Decodable Book 31**
"Roger's Gerbil"
"The Fudge Judge"

Managing Small Groups

Read the *Decodable Book* with small groups of children. While you work with small groups, have other children do the following:

- **Self-Selected Reading**
- **Cross-Curricular Centers**
- **Practice Pages**
- **Journal Writing**

Use the suggested Classroom Management outline on page 7C for the whole-group/small-group schedule.

School-Home Connection

Take-Home Book Version

◄ Decodable Books Take-Home Version

ONGOING ASSESSMENT

Note how well children
- read sentences without modeling.
- decode words in "Roger's Gerbil" and "The Fudge Judge."
- complete consonants /j/ g, dge practice pages.

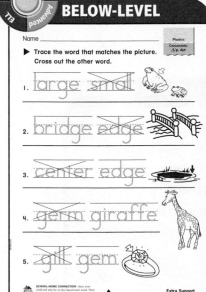

BELOW-LEVEL

▲ Extra Support, p. 34

ON-LEVEL

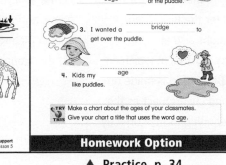

Homework Option

▲ Practice, p. 34

ADVANCED

▲ Challenge, p. 34

ENGLISH-LANGUAGE LEARNERS

▲ ELL, p. 34

Shared Writing *Bingo Cards*

DAILY LANGUAGE PRACTICE

I dansed with mi dog.

I danced with my dog.

Writing Every Day

Day 1: Bingo Cards
Have children make and use Animal Bingo Cards.

Day 2: Class Book
Have children make a group book about rainy weather.

Day 3: Directions
Have children write directions for making a toy boat or playing a game of hopscotch.

Day 4: Narrative Sentences
Have children write narrative sentences about a real or make-believe bug riding on a toy boat.

Day 5: Letters
Have children write a friendly letter from a character's point of view.

journal writing

Writing Prompt Have children recall an animal they saw recently. Have them draw the animal and write in a thought balloon what the animal might have been thinking.

BRAINSTORM

Brainstorm Animal Names Work with children to generate a list of at least twenty animal names on the board. Suggest that children start with animals mentioned in the big book *I Swam with a Seal*. Discuss some distinctive features of each animal, such as the slippery flippers of a seal or the floppy ears of a hare.

MAKE AND USE BINGO CARDS

Make Bingo Cards Distribute copies of the 16-Box Grid on page T25. Have children choose animal names from the board and write them in the boxes of their card in random order, one name per box.

Play Animal Bingo
Give each child a handful of markers, such as plastic counters or paper squares. Review how to play Bingo. Tell children that instead of

seal	hare	falcon	snake
pony	beaver	turtle	porcupine
dog	heron	moose	cat
frog	pig	alligator	elephant

calling out a number, you will describe one of the animals. After you describe an animal, call on a volunteer to say the animal's name. Check off the name on the board. Then have children find the name on their Bingo card and cover it with a marker. The game ends when a child has correctly covered four adjoining squares across, down, or diagonally.

BELOW-LEVEL	ENGLISH-LANGUAGE LEARNERS
Have children play partner Bingo or have them make and use a **3 x 3** grid for the Bingo card. Children might also enjoy a whole-body version, in which an oversized Bingo grid is made on the floor and children act as the markers, standing in the correctly labeled boxes.	Display the big book *I Swam with a Seal* during the Bingo game, and point to the correct animal picture before you check off the name on the board.

<table>
<tr><td colspan="2">5-DAY GRAMMAR</td></tr>
<tr><td>DAY 1</td><td>Introduce Verbs That Tell About the Past</td></tr>
<tr><td>DAY 2</td><td>Generate Sentences About the Past</td></tr>
<tr><td>DAY 3</td><td>Form Verbs and Sentences</td></tr>
<tr><td>DAY 4</td><td>Verb Game</td></tr>
<tr><td>DAY 5</td><td>Identify Verbs</td></tr>
</table>

Day 1

Grammar

Verbs That Tell About the Past

TEACH/MODEL

Introduce Verbs That Tell About the Past Remind children that a verb tells what someone or something does. Explain that verbs can be used to tell about the past. Write the following sentences on the board or on chart paper:

> I play today.
> I played last week.

Have children read the sentences aloud. Underline the words *play* and *played*, and ask children to tell the difference. Point out that adding the *-ed* ending to *play* changes the meaning of the action from "right now" to "a time in the past."

PRACTICE/APPLY

Display *Teaching Transparency 91* Have each child write *N* on one side of an index card and *P* on the other. Then read aloud each sentence on the transparency. Call on volunteers to point to each verb. Tell children to show *N* if the verb tells about now and *P* if the verb tells about the past. List the past-tense verbs on the board. Afterward, point out the *-ed* ending in each verb on the board.

WRAP UP Reread the Big Book

Relate Pictures to Text Invite children to join in as you reread *I Swam with a Seal*. Then read the story again, and ask questions like these about the illustrations: *How did the illustrator make the girl look like she is flying with her feet on the ground? How does the boy look like he is sliding along like a snake?*

S.S.R. *Sustained Silent Reading*

Have children read silently from a book of their choice. See page 155J for tips on helping children choose books.

▲ **Big Book**

OBJECTIVES

- *To identify and read verbs that tell about the past*

- *To distinguish between present-tense and past-tense verbs*

SKILL TRACE

VERBS THAT TELL ABOUT THE PAST

INTRODUCE	124N
Reteach	T9
Review	149C, 153B, 155B, 155L
T Test	Bk 1-5

▼ **Teaching Transparency 91**

VERBS THAT TELL ABOUT THE PAST

1. Ginny and Josh talk about their day.
2. Ginny crawled with a crab.
3. Josh marched with a monkey.
4. Ginny chirped with a bird.
5. Josh jumped with a rabbit.
6. Cory asks about the animals.
7. Ginny and Josh show pictures of the animals.

"The Puddle"
Gather Around, Volume 1-5
91
Grammar: Verbs That Tell About the Past
Harcourt

Name _____

► Write the word that best completes each sentence.

spilled	filled	needed	cleaned

1. Lenny ___needed___ to make some ice.

2. He ___filled___ the ice tray with water.

3. The water ___spilled___ all over.

4. Lenny ___cleaned___ up the mess.

TRY THIS Take turns with a partner reading the sentences and acting them out.

SCHOOL-HOME CONNECTION

35

Practice Book
Gather Around • Lesson 5

▲ **Practice Book, p. 35**

The Puddle **124N**

Sharing Literature
Poem: "It's Raining, It's Pouring"

Phonemic Awareness
Phoneme Addition; Focus on /j/

Phonics

REVIEW: Consonants /j/*g, dge*

Spelling
Building Words

Vocabulary
INTRODUCE: *angry, nearly, okay, sorry*

Reading
Pupil Edition
"The Puddle," pp. 124–149

Writing Across the Curriculum
Class Book

Grammar
REVIEW: Verbs That Tell About the Past

WARM UP

MORNING MESSAGE

Good Morning!

Today is _____.
What can we do on a rainy day?
We can _____ inside.
We can _____ outside.
We can look at _____ in the sky.

Introduce the Day

Tell children that today they will sing a song and read a story about a rainy day. Guide them in generating a morning message about rainy weather. Ask:

• **What do you like to do inside your home on a rainy day?**

• **What do you like to do outside on a rainy day?**

• **What might you see in the sky on a rainy day?**

As you write the message, invite volunteers to write previously taught letters, words, and/or punctuation to reinforce skills. For instance, have a volunteer write the words *dark clouds* or *a rainbow* in the last sentence.

Read the Message

Read the message. Use the message to focus on selected skills that have been previously taught.

Apply Skills

Word Structure Have children clap the syllables of these compound words as they read them aloud: *today, inside, outside.* Have children tell what two small words make up each one. Remind children that when they read new words they should look for word parts they know.

Concept Vocabulary Ask volunteers to demonstrate the meanings of the words *inside* and *outside.* Then review other positional words with children, such as *over, under, between,* and *around.* Have children demonstrate the meanings of those words.

Sharing Literature

LISTEN AND RESPOND

Connect to Prior Knowledge Ask children to share their thoughts and feelings about going outside on a rainy morning. As children speak, promote good oral communication by reminding them to stay on the topic.

Pantomime Actions Have children listen as you sing or recite "It's Raining, It's Pouring." Then have children join in with you. Teach the finger movements suggested in the poem and have children sing or say it again, adding the movements.

Phonemic Awareness

PHONEME ADDITION

Words from "It's Raining, It's Pouring" Tell children that you are going to ask them to make new words by adding sounds to the beginning of words. Model by saying *What word do I make if I say* old *with /k/ at the beginning? (cold)* Continue the procedure with the following words:

old: add /g/ (gold)   **add /h/** (hold)   **add /f/** (fold)
add /t/ (told)   **add /s/** (sold)   **add /b/** (bold)

or: add /p/ (pour)   **add /d/** (door)   **add /y/** (your)
add /s/ (sore)   **add /s//n/** (snore)   **add /m/** (more)

FOCUS ON /j/

Phoneme Blending Tell children that you are going to say some words very slowly and that they will blend the words together. Model by segmenting the word *page* into phonemes—/p//ā//j/. Then say it naturally—*page*. Segment the following words, having children blend the sounds to say the words:

/c//ā//j/ (cage)   /s//t//ā//j/ (stage)   /s//t//r//ā//n//j/ (strange)
/b/ /a/ /j/ (badge)   /b/ /u/ /j/ (budge)   /b/ /r/ /i/ /j/ (bridge)
/j/ /u/ /j/ (judge)   /ā/ /j/ (age)   /l/ /e/ /j/ (ledge)

Ask children how all the words are alike. (They all end with /j/.)

It's Raining, It's Pouring

It's raining, it's pouring, *(wiggle fingers down like rain)*
The old man is snoring. *(cover ears with hands and grimace)*
He went to bed *(hands together against cheek)*
And he bumped his head, *(tap top of head)*
And he wouldn't get up in the morning. *(shake head "no")*

REACHING ALL LEARNERS

Diagnostic Check: Phonemic Awareness

If... children cannot blend phonemes into words ...

Then... help children distinguish different letter sounds by stretching out each word as you show the motion of stretching out a piece of taffy. Then say the word naturally. Have children repeat the sounds, the actions, and the word.

ADDITIONAL SUPPORT ACTIVITIES

BELOW-LEVEL   Reteach, p. S26

ADVANCED   Extend, p. S27

ENGLISH-LANGUAGE LEARNERS   Reteach, p. S27

OBJECTIVES

- *To blend sounds into words*
- *To read and write Spelling Words*

5-DAY SPELLING

DAY 1	Pretest; Word Sort
DAY 2	**Word Building**
DAY 3	State the Generalization
DAY 4	Review
DAY 5	Posttest; Writing Application

SKILL TRACE

/j/g, dge	
Introduce	124I–124L
Reteach	S28–S29
REVIEW	**124Q–124R, 149F–149G, 153E–153F**

Spelling Words

1. age
2. page
3. cage
4. badge
5. budge
6. fudge
7. old
8. most
9. floor
10. piece

WORD WORK

Phonics and Spelling
Consonants /j/g, dge

Review

WORD BUILDING

Blend and Read a Spelling Word Place *Letter Cards a, g, e* in a pocket chart. Ask children to say the sound of each letter as you place it in the chart. Slide your hand under the letters as you blend the sounds—/āājj/. Have children repeat after you. Then read the word naturally—*age*, and have children do the same.

Build Spelling Words Ask children what letter you add to make *age* become *page*. (add a *p* in front of the *a*) Continue building the Spelling Words shown in this manner and having children read them.

BELOW-LEVEL

Have children work in pairs. One child says a Spelling Word and builds it using *Word Builder Cards*. The other child says a rhyming Spelling Word and builds it. Then children check the spelling of both words and continue.

ENGLISH-LANGUAGE LEARNERS

Have children act out dictated sentences that include the Spelling Words. For example: *I am a police officer. Here is my badge; Turn to page 10 in this book; I am trying to move this bookcase, but it won't budge.* This will help make word meanings more concrete.

Apply Phonics

READ WORDS IN CONTEXT

5-DAY PHONICS / SPELLING

DAY 1	Introduce /j/g, dge
DAY 2	**Word Building with /j/g, dge**
DAY 3	Word Building with /j/g, dge
DAY 4	Word Building with /j/g, dge
DAY 5	Inflections -ed, -ing (drop e) Contractions 've, 'd, 're

Write the following sentences on the board or on chart paper and have children read them aloud.

> Roger is writing a story about an **old** bird in a **cage**.
>
> He writes his name and **age** on the first **page**.
>
> He sits on the **floor** to write **most** of the story.
>
> He tells about Sweety the bird taking a **piece** of **fudge**.
>
> A man with a **badge** tells the bird to give the **fudge** back.
>
> Roger does not **budge** until the story ends.

 Dictate Words Dictate to children several words from the pocket chart, and have them write the words on a dry-erase board or in their journal.

age
page
cage
badge
budge
fudge

Phonics Resources

Phonics Express™ CD-ROM, **Level B** Sparkle/Route 2/Market

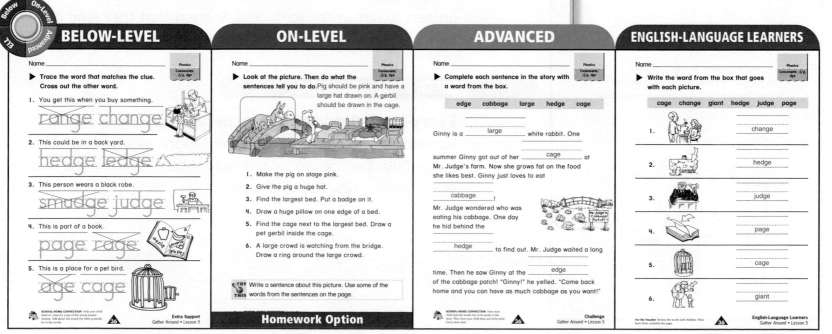

▲ Extra Support, p. 36   ▲ Practice, p. 36   ▲ Challenge, p. 36   ▲ ELL, p. 36

Vocabulary

angry   feeling or showing anger

nearly   almost

okay   all right

sorry   feeling sad about something

Building Background

TALK ABOUT PLAYING IN THE RAIN

Draw a Picture Tell children they are going to read a story about a boy who goes outside to play in the rain. Have children draw a picture of themselves playing in the rain or in puddles after a storm. Then have children tell about their pictures. Have volunteers describe puddles.

Discuss Story Words Write the words *alligator, elephant, gonna, steered,* and *worry* on the board, and discuss the meanings of the words. Elicit that *alligator* and *elephant* are names of animals. Explain that the word *gonna* is an informal way to say *going to*, as in *I'm gonna go outside now.*

Vocabulary

INTRODUCE WORDS IN CONTEXT

Read Sentences Display *Teaching Transparency 92* or write the words and sentences on the board. Point to the words and read them to children. Track the print as children read aloud the sentences. Call on pairs of volunteers to reread the sentences. Suggest that they read dramatically to show the meaning of the words *angry, sorry*, and *okay.*

> **INTRODUCE**
> ### Vocabulary
> angry   okay
> nearly   sorry

CHECK UNDERSTANDING

Every-Pupil Response Duplicate and distribute a set of Individual Word Cards for each child: *angry, nearly, okay, sorry* (page T36). Say the words and have children hold up the appropriate word cards. Ask volunteers to use the words in sentences.

▼ **Teaching Transparency 92**

VOCABULARY
angry   nearly   okay   sorry

"You <u>nearly</u> crashed into me," said Don.
"I'm <u>sorry</u>," said Pete. "Are you <u>angry</u> with me?"
"No," said Don. "I'm <u>okay</u>. You just surprised me."

"The Puddle"
Gather Around, Volume 1-5   92   Vocabulary
Harcourt

Word Power

Word Power

Pages 124–125 Have children read aloud the Words to Remember. Then have children read the sentences aloud. Have them point to the Words to Remember in the sentences.

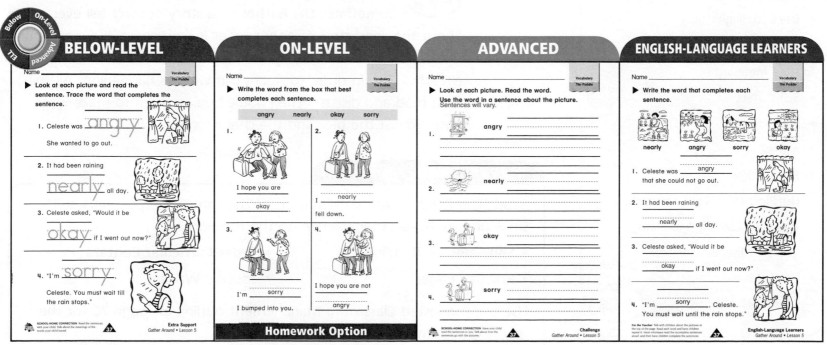

▲ Extra Support, p. 37

▲ Practice, p. 37

Homework Option

▲ Challenge, p. 37

▲ ELL, p. 37

The Puddle **124–125**

■ **Phonics**

Consonants /j/g, dge

■ **Vocabulary**

angry, nearly, okay, sorry

■ **Decodable Words**

See the list on pages T50–T51.

■ **Comprehension**

 Plot

 Make Inferences

Strategies Good Readers Use

To Recognize Words

• Use Decoding/Phonics

• Look for Word Bits and Parts

To Gain Meaning

• Self-Correct

• Read Ahead

• Reread

• Reread Aloud

• Use Picture Clues to Confirm Meaning

• Make and Confirm Predictions

• Sequence Events/Summarize

• Create Mental Images

• **Make Inferences**

READING

Prereading Strategies

PREPARING TO READ

Preview/Predict Discuss pages 126–127. Ask children to read the title and discuss puddles. Have children follow along as you read the name of the author/illustrator. Talk about the pictures on pages 128–131, what the boy is doing, and what might happen in the story.

Set Purpose Help children set a purpose for reading. If necessary, suggest that they read to find out what happens after the boy puts his boat in the puddle.

COMPREHENSION SKILL

Plot Explain to children that the *plot* of a story is what happens in that story. Usually the plot involves a character trying to solve a problem. Tell children that good readers think about the problem and make predictions about how it will be solved. Suggest that children predict how the boy will solve each problem as they read "The Puddle." Remind them to think about what has happened in the story before making their predictions. Then have them read to confirm their predictions.

COMPREHENSION STRATEGY

Make Inferences Help children understand that sometimes the author of a story doesn't tell everything about the characters or about what is happening in a story. Often readers must look for story clues and think about what they already know in order to figure out what is happening. As children read and discuss "The Puddle," guide them to make inferences about the plot and the characters.

Managing Small Groups

Read "The Puddle" with small groups of children. While you work with small groups, have other children do the following:

• **Self-Selected Reading**

• **Cross-Curricular Centers**

• **Practice Pages**

• **Journal Writing**

Use the suggested Classroom Management outline on page 7C for the whole group/small-group schedule.

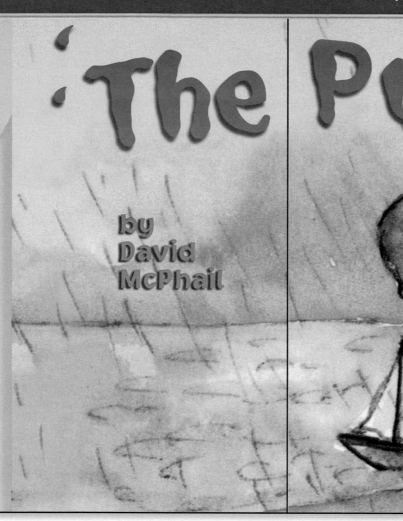

Genre

Fiction

In fiction, there can be a mix of realistic and make-believe parts.

Look for:

• Ways the story is like real life.

• Things that could not happen in real life.

126

127

Guided Comprehension

Pages 126–127 Have children reread the title and review their predictions about what the boy is doing and what might happen in the story.

GENRE: Fiction

Read aloud the information about fiction on page 126. Tell children that fiction includes

• characters that could be real.

• events that could happen.

• events that did not really happen.

BELOW-LEVEL	ON-LEVEL	ADVANCED	ENGLISH-LANGUAGE LEARNERS
Have children preview the pictures in the story and identify all the characters. As children read aloud, have them stop and talk about each new character that appears. SMALL GROUP	As children read the selection, use the Guided Comprehension questions to direct their reading. WHOLE GROUP/SMALL GROUP	Have children share their predictions about the story and then read the story silently. After reading, have children talk about whether or not their predictions were correct. Have them identify parts of the story that confirm their predictions. SMALL GROUP/ INDEPENDENT	Use realia such as a toy sailboat, a raincoat, and rain boots to preview the story concepts with children. Then have children read the story or follow along as they listen to a recording of it (Audiotext 5). SMALL GROUP
ADDITIONAL SUPPORT See Intervention Resource Kit, Lesson 31. *Intervention Teacher's Guide* pp. 302–311			**ADDITIONAL SUPPORT** See English-Language Learners Resource Kit, Lesson 31. *English-Language Learners Teacher's Guide* pp. 182–183

It was a rainy day.

128

I asked my mom if I could go out and sail my boat in the puddles. She said, "**Okay**, but *you* stay out of the puddles."

129

Guided Comprehension

Pages 128–129 Have children read the pages to find out what the boy and his mother are discussing.

1 SPECULATE **Why do you think the boy is staring out the window?** (Possible response: It is raining outside, and he is thinking about what he can do.)

2 NOTE DETAILS **What does the boy ask his mother?** (He asks if he can sail his boat in the puddles.)

3 (Focus Strategy) **MAKE INFERENCES** **Why do you think his mother tells him to stay out of the puddles?** (Possible response: She doesn't want him to get wet.)

Strategies Good Readers Use

(Focus Strategy) **Make Inferences**

Remind children that good readers use clues the author gives and what they know to figure out the story. Think aloud as you model how to make inferences:

MODEL The boy's mother tells him to stay out of the puddles. I know that when you go in puddles, you get wet. I think that she doesn't want him to get wet.

I got dressed in my rain boots and coat, and went to sail my boat in the largest puddle I could find.

130

A frog came along and sat down beside me. "Nice boat," he said.

131

Guided Comprehension

Pages 130–131 Have children read the pages to find out what the boy does.

1 **SEQUENCE What does the boy have to do before he goes outside?** (He has to put on his hat, rain boots, and coat.)

2 **DISTINGUISH BETWEEN FANTASY AND REALITY When the frog talks, what does that tell you about the kind of story this is? Why do you think so?** (Possible response: It's not about things that really happen; it's pretend. A real frog can't talk—it can only croak.)

3 **MAKE PREDICTIONS What do you think will happen next?** (Possible response: The boy will put the frog on the boat; the frog will jump on the boat.)

The Puddle 130–131

Then he jumped onto my boat and sailed away. "Come back!" I called, but he wouldn't listen.

132

A turtle floated by.
"Teatime," said the turtle. "Care to join me?"
"I can't," I said. "I need to get my boat back. Besides, I'm not allowed to go in puddles."

133

Guided Comprehension

Pages 132–133 Have children read to find out what happens to the boy's boat.

1 **CONFIRM PREDICTIONS** What does the frog do? Is that what you predicted would happen? (The frog takes the boy's boat; possible response: no, I thought the frog would play with the boy.)

2 **ILLUSTRATOR'S CRAFT** What makes the pictures funny? (the frog on the boat; the turtle on its back, drinking tea)

3 **NOTE DETAILS** Why can't the boy join the turtle for tea? (The boy has to get his boat back, and he isn't allowed to go in puddles.)

STUDENT SELF-ASSESSMENT

Have children ask themselves the following questions to assess how they are reading:

• How do I use letters and sounds I know to help me read the words?

• Do I go back and reread a word or a sentence when something doesn't seem right?

• Do I think about what has happened in the story and make predictions about what will happen next?

• Do I look for clues in the pictures to help me figure out how the characters feel and what they might be thinking?

But the frog steered my boat right into the turtle. CRASH!
The frog laughed. He thought it was funny.

The turtle didn't think it was funny at all.
She was angry.

134

Then an alligator offered to help.
"Want me to get your boat back
for you?" he asked.
"Really? That would be *great*!" I said.

135

Guided Comprehension

Pages 134–135 Have the children read to see if the boy finds any help to get his boat back.

1. **CAUSE/EFFECT** What makes the turtle angry? (The frog crashes the boat into the turtle.)

2. **RELATE PICTURES TO TEXT** How does the picture on page 134 help you understand the meaning of the word *steered*? (Possible response: The picture shows the frog steering the boat into the turtle.)

3. (Focus Strategy) **MAKE INFERENCES** Why do you think the alligator offers to help the boy? (Possible responses: He wants to do a good deed; he doesn't like what the frog did.)

BELOW-LEVEL

Ask children why they think the author wrote *CRASH* in all capital letters on page 134. Explain that the author wanted to let the reader know that the boat made a loud noise when it ran into the turtle. The capital letters show that the author was emphasizing the word. Have children reread the page with expression.

ADVANCED

Have children write the word *CRASH* vertically. Tell them to write words that begin with each letter of *CRASH*. The words must relate to the story so far. (**C**up, **R**ain, **A**ngry/**A**lligator, **S**ail/**S**hell/**S**aucer, **H**at)

So the alligator swam out to take my boat away from the frog. He did.

But the boat looked different than it did before.
"**Sorry**," he said.
"Don't worry about it," I told him.

136

137

Guided Comprehension

Pages 136–137 Have children read to find out what happens when the alligator goes to get the boat.

1 SPECULATE Do you think the alligator has a hard time getting the boat away from the frog? Why do you think so? (Possible response: Probably not, because the alligator is much bigger than the frog.)

2 DETERMINE CHARACTERS' EMOTIONS How do you think the boy feels when he gets his boat back? (Possible response: He may be happy that he gets it back but disappointed that it is broken.)

3 SUMMARIZE What has happened in the story so far? (A boy goes outside to sail his boat in a puddle. A frog takes the boat and crashes it into a turtle. An alligator gets the boat back, but the boat is broken.)

REACHING ALL LEARNERS

Diagnostic Check: Comprehension and Skills

If... children cannot retell the plot of the story ...

Then... have them look back at the pictures for clues about what happened first, next, and last.

ADDITIONAL SUPPORT ACTIVITIES

BELOW-LEVEL	Reteach, p. S30
ADVANCED	Extend, p. S31
ENGLISH-LANGUAGE LEARNERS	Reteach, p. S31

136–137 Gather Around

Next, a pig wanted to
swim in the puddle.

138

He took a running start,
jumped in, and splashed me.
"My mom's not gonna like this!"
I yelled to the pig.

139

Guided Comprehension

Pages 138–139 Have children read to find out what happens next at the puddle.

1 **SEQUENCE** **What animal comes next to visit the puddle, and what does he want to do?** (A pig comes to swim in the puddle.)

2 (Focus Strategy) **MAKE INFERENCES** **Why does the boy yell, "My mom's not gonna like this!"?** (Possible response: The pig splashes the boy, and the boy's mother told him to stay out of the puddles so he wouldn't get wet.)

3 **EXPRESS PERSONAL OPINIONS** **Do you think the pig tried to splash the boy on purpose? Why do you think so?** (Possible response: No; the pig was just trying to have some fun. Accept reasonable responses.)

ADVANCED

Point out to children that the story is told from the boy's point of view; the sentences tell what the boy sees, hears, thinks, and feels. Tell children to imagine what the other characters are thinking and feeling. Go back to some of the pages in the story and ask volunteers to tell how each character is feeling.

ENGLISH-LANGUAGE LEARNERS

Tell children that sometimes they may read words that are not formal English. Point out the word *gonna* on page 139. Explain that this is a word some people say that really stands for "going to." Have children reread the sentence, substituting "going to" for "gonna."

The Puddle **138–139**

Before long, a thirsty elephant showed up.

She drank . . .
and drank . . .

. . . until the puddle was **nearly** gone.

140

The other animals were upset with the elephant. "Put back the water!" they shouted.

141

Guided Comprehension

Pages 140–141 Ask children to identify the new animal on page 140 and to read to find out what happens.

1 **SEQUENCE** What words tell that a little bit of time passes before the elephant shows up? *(before long)*

2 **(Focus Strategy) MAKE INFERENCES** What is the problem? (Possible response: The elephant drank most of the puddle, and now the animals and the boy can't play in it.)

3 **CHARACTERS' EMOTIONS** Find the sentence that tells how the other animals feel, now that the puddle is almost gone. *(The other animals were upset with the elephant.)*

BELOW-LEVEL

Have children read aloud the sentence that begins with *She drank ...* on page 140. Direct their attention to the dots, or ellipsis points, after the word *drank*. Tell children that these dots mean there is a pause between the words, slightly longer than a comma. Have children practice reading the sentence with the ellipses.

140–141 Gather Around

So she did.

142

She left, and when the sun started to come out, the other animals left, too.

143

Guided Comprehension

Pages 142–143 Have children read to find out how the problem is solved.

1 **NOTE DETAILS** How is the problem solved? (The elephant puts the water back.)

2 **MAKE INFERENCES** Why do you think the animals leave? (Possible responses: They are tired of playing; the puddle is getting too small to play in; they don't like playing in the sun.)

3 **MAKE PREDICTIONS** What do you think will happen next? (Possible responses: The boy will continue playing; the boy will go home.)

ENGLISH-LANGUAGE LEARNERS

Review the names of the animals in the story as children point to pictures of them. Then call on volunteers to talk about large or unusual animals found in places they have lived before. Have them say the animal's name in their primary language and explain where the animal can be found. This will give children the opportunity to make a unique contribution to the group discussion.

Then the sun dried up
the rest of the puddle.
I took my boat home.

144

When I got there, my mom had a hot
bath waiting for me.
"Can I bring my boat?" I asked her.
"Of course," she said.

145

Guided Comprehension

Pages 144–146 Have children read to find out what the boy does next.

1 **INTERPRET CHARACTERS' MOTIVATIONS** **Why do you think the boy goes home?** (Possible response: He probably leaves because the puddle has dried up and he doesn't have enough water to play in.)

2 **SPECULATE** **Why do you think the boy wants to bring his boat when he takes his bath?** (Possible response: He wants to keep playing with it.)

3 **SEQUENCE** **Read page 146. What happens last?** (The boy takes a bath and plays with his boat.)

SCIENCE

Evaporation Reread the first sentence on page 144. Then ask children where the water goes after the puddle dries up. If necessary, introduce the word *evaporation*. Tell children that the water *evaporates*—changes from a liquid to a gas—and goes into the air. To demonstrate, have each child rub a little water on the back of his or her hand and blow on the water until it disappears.

And I did.

146

Think and Respond

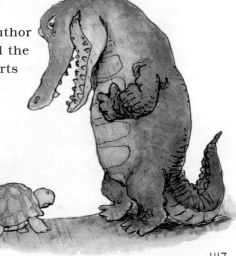

1. What is your favorite part of the story? Tell why.

2. What happens when the boy tries to sail his boat in the puddle?

3. How does the boy get his boat back?

4. What would you do if you could understand an animal talking to you?

5. How does the author mix the real and the make-believe parts of the story?

147

Think and Respond

1. Possible response: My favorite part of the story was when the pig jumped into the puddle. It made me think about the fun times I have had playing in puddles. **PERSONAL RESPONSE**

2. Animals come by and cause problems. A frog takes the boy's boat and crashes it into a turtle. An alligator gets the boat back, but the boat is broken. A pig splashes water on the boy. An elephant drinks all the water but then squirts it back into the puddle. **SUMMARIZE**

3. The alligator swims and gets the boat back from the frog and gives it to the boy. **IMPORTANT DETAILS**

4. Possible response: I would ask the animal to be my friend and to play with me. **GENERALIZE**

5. The beginning and the end are real. The middle is make-believe. **LITERARY ANALYSIS**

The Puddle **146–147**

Teacher Read-Aloud

Meet the Author/Illustrator

David McPhail

David McPhail grew up by the sea. He played in the woods and fields near his house. That is where he first got interested in animals. He likes to put animal characters in his stories.

He also likes to tell two stories in his books. He tells one in words and one in the illustrations. He believes that "each day is an adventure and each book is a new beginning."

David McPhail

 Visit *The Learning Site!* www.harcourtschool.com

148

149

Meet the Author/Illustrator

Pages 148–149 Explain that these pages tell about the person who wrote and illustrated "The Puddle." Identify David McPhail in the photograph on page 149. Remind children that an **author** sometimes both writes and illustrates a story. Read to children page 148.

Visit *The Learning Site:* **www.harcourtschool.com**
See Resources for Parents and Teachers:
Author/Illustrator Features.

Retelling

COMPREHENSION FOCUS

Focus Skill ★

Plot Remind children that the plot is what happens in a story. Usually the plot is about a character solving a problem. Have children recall the problems that arise when the boy tries to sail his boat in the puddle.

RETELL AND SUMMARIZE THE STORY

Complete a Problem-Solution Diagram Display *Teaching Transparency 110* or draw a similar chart on the board. Ask children these questions and record their responses on the chart:

- **Who is the story mostly about?**
- **What problem does he have during the story?**
- **How does he solve the problem?**

Review the information on the completed diagram. Help children use it to develop a one- or two-sentence summary of "The Puddle."

COMPREHENSION CHECK

▲ *End-of-Selection Test, Practice Book*, pp. A49–A51

▼ **Teaching Transparency 110**

Who?
boy

Problem?
The boy wants to play with his boat, but animals keep doing things to keep him from playing. Then the puddle dries up.

Solution?
The boy goes home to play with his boat while he takes a bath.

Grade 1   110   Harcourt

DAILY LANGUAGE PRACTICE

the frog jumpd into the boat.

The frog jumped into the boat.

journal writing

Writing Prompt Have children write about their favorite part of "The Puddle." Have them tell why they like that part. Suggest that they draw a picture to go with their writing.

Writing Across the Curriculum

Class Book

GENERATE IDEAS

Talk About Rainy Weather Have children share their ideas about rainy weather. Tell them to think of as many words and phrases as possible that tell about the things they see, do, and hear during a rainy day. Write their ideas in a word web on the board.

catch falling raindrops · drink hot cocoa · lightning · rainbows · **Rainy Weather** · thunder · dark clouds · howling wind · puddles

WRITE AND SHARE

Write Sentences Have each child write one or two sentences about rainy weather. Refer them to the word web for ideas. Review basic rules of grammar and punctuation, and remind children to include descriptive words in their sentences. Children may want to work with a partner to proofread their work. You might also consider having children type their sentences on the computer. After they finish writing, have children illustrate their sentences.

Share Sentences Have children read their sentences aloud. Encourage comments and discussion. Then help the group arrange their work into a book. Bind the pages together. Place the book in the Reading Center for children to read on their own.

Handwriting Review with children how to form capital *R* and lowercase *r* to write *rain*. Review other letters as needed.

Grammar

Verbs That Tell About the Past

5-DAY GRAMMAR

DAY 1	Introduce Verbs That Tell About the Past
DAY 2	**Generate Sentences About the Past**
DAY 3	Form Verbs and Sentences
DAY 4	Verb Game
DAY 5	Identify Verbs

REVIEW

Review Verbs That Tell About the Past Remind children that verbs can tell about the past. Write the following sentences on the board and have children read them aloud.

> A frog jumps on my boat.
> The frog steered my boat into a turtle.

Ask children to tell which sentence has a verb about the past. Then model changing a present-tense verb to a past-tense verb.

MODEL The word *jumps* tells about something that is happening now. If I change the ending *s* to *ed*, I will make the word *jumped*, which tells about the past.

Generate Sentences That Tell About the Past Help children recall the actions of the animals in the story "The Puddle." Ask questions such as these: *Who floated on his back? Who helped the boy? Who splashed the boy?* Have children say complete sentences, and write their responses on the board. Ask volunteers to circle the word that tells the action happened in the past.

WRAP UP
Listen to a Poem

Connect Ideas Across Texts Read "Where Go the Boats?" on page 144 of the *Read-Aloud Anthology*. Have children listen for where the boats are sailing. Then read the poem again, having children slowly move their hand as if it were a boat on the river. Have children tell how the poem is like "The Puddle."

▲ **"Where Go the Boats," p. 144**

S.S.R. *Sustained Silent Reading*

Have children read silently from a book of their choice. See page 155J for tips on helping children choose books.

SKILL TRACE

VERBS THAT TELL ABOUT THE PAST

Introduce	124N
Reteach	T9
REVIEW	149C, 153B, 155B, 155L
T Test	Bk 1-5

ENGLISH-LANGUAGE LEARNERS Below / On-Level / Advanced / ELL

Say the following word pairs aloud, emphasizing the three sounds *-ed* stands for, and have children repeat after you: *steer/steered, float/floated, laugh/laughed.* Remind children that they need to pronounce the endings so listeners know they are talking about the past.

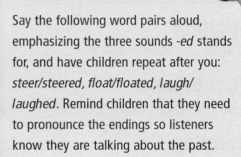

Name _____
Verbs That Tell About the Past

A verb can tell about the **past**. Some verbs that tell about the past end with **ed**.

Two goats played in their boat.
They jumped into the water.

▶ Write the verbs that tell about the past.

1. The goats painted their boat green. _____ painted
2. They shouted "Hello!" to all their friends. _____ shouted
3. They added a sail to their boat. _____ added
4. They sailed their boat on the lake. _____ sailed

130

▲ Language Handbook, p. 130

Sharing Literature
Poem: "To Walk in Warm Rain"

Phonemic Awareness
Phoneme Addition; Focus on /j/

Phonics
REVIEW: Consonants /j/*g*, *dge*

Spelling
State the Generalization

Vocabulary
REVIEW: *angry, nearly, okay, sorry*

Reading

Rereading for Fluency
Pupil Edition
  "The Puddle," pp. 126–146

Reading Across Texts
"Time to Play" pp. 150–151
Making Connections, pp. 152–153

Interactive Writing ✏
Directions

Grammar
REVIEW: Verbs That Tell About the Past

WARM UP MORNING MESSAGE

Good Morning!

Today is _____.
What clothes do you wear in the rain?
I wear a _____ on my body.
I wear _____ on my _____.
My _____ and _____ keep me dry.

Introduce the Day

Tell children that today they will reread a story and listen to a poem about playing in the rain. Guide them in generating a morning message about dressing for rainy weather. Ask:

• **What do you wear to keep dry in the rain?**

• **What might you wear on your head or feet to keep them dry?**

As you write the message, invite volunteers to write previously taught letters, words, and/or punctuation to reinforce skills. For instance, have a volunteer write the word *coat* or *raincoat* in the third sentence. Remind children that the first word of a sentence and the pronoun *I* are always capitalized.

Read the Message

Read the message. Use the message to focus on selected skills that have been previously taught.

Apply Skills

Phonics Ask volunteers to point to words that contain the long vowel sound /ē/. *(me, keep, body)* Point out the different spellings for the sound. Repeat the procedure for words with /ī/ (*I, my, dry*), /ā/ (*rain, today*), and /ō/ (*clothes, coat*).

High-Frequency Words Ask volunteers to point to and read known high-frequency words *what, do, you, in, the, I, a, on, my, and, keep,* and *me.* Remind children that the vowel sounds in these special words may not follow the regular spelling rules.

Sharing Literature

BUILD CONCEPT VOCABULARY

Connect to Prior Knowledge Tell children you are going to read a poem they have heard before entitled "To Walk in Warm Rain." As you read, have children imagine what the poem describes.

Explore a Word Remind children that they heard the phrase "drip like a drain" in the poem. Say: *When a drain keeps dripping, it can be very annoying. Something that is annoying bothers you.* Have children say *annoying*. Discuss annoying things—for example, an insect buzzing around your face or rain when you want to go out to play. Ask volunteers to use the word *annoying* to tell about other examples. Then ask: *What word have we been talking about? If something is annoying, does it bother you or do you like it?*

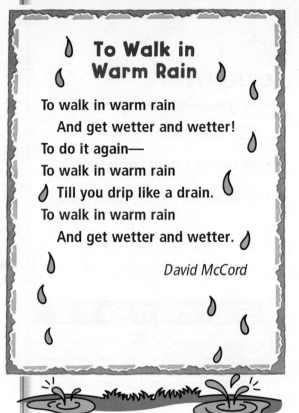

To Walk in Warm Rain

To walk in warm rain
   And get wetter and wetter!
To do it again—
To walk in warm rain
   Till you drip like a drain.
To walk in warm rain
   And get wetter and wetter.

David McCord

Phonemic Awareness

PHONEME ADDITION

Words from "To Walk in Warm Rain" Tell children that you are going to ask them what sound to add to change one word to another. Model by saying *and. If I want to change* and *to* hand, *what sound do I add at the beginning?* (/h/). Continue the procedure with the following words. For each word, specify whether the addition is at the beginning or at the end.

rain to *drain* (/d/)   *in* to *win* (/w/)   *till* to *still* (/s/)
to to *tooth* (/th/)   *rain* to *range* (/j/)   *and* to *sand* (/s/)

FOCUS ON /j/

Isolate Phonemes Tell children that you will say a pair of words, one of which has the /j/ sound. Tell them to listen to both words and then hold up one finger if the first word has the /j/ sound or two fingers if the second word has the /j/ sound. Model using the words *gas* and *gem*. Then say each of these pairs:

gas/<u>gem</u>   game/<u>germ</u>   <u>gym</u>/gift   <u>giraffe</u>/good
garden/<u>giant</u>   bu<u>dge</u>/bug   bag/ba<u>dge</u>   egg/e<u>dge</u>
le<u>dge</u>/leg   dog/do<u>dge</u>   <u>gentle</u>/great   hug/hu<u>ge</u>

BELOW-LEVEL

For the Isolate Phonemes activity, use only the first row of words, which have the /j/ or /g/ at the beginning of the word. Elongate each word as you say it, emphasizing the initial phoneme. Have children say each word as they decide whether the /j/ sound is in the first or second word.

OBJECTIVES

- *To generate the sounds for /j/g, dge*
- *To blend sounds into words*
- *To read simple, regular words*

SKILL TRACE

/j/g, dge	
Introduce	124I–124L
Reteach	S28–S29
REVIEW	124Q–124R, 149F–149G, 153E–153F

teaching tip

Build Vocabulary As children build and read new words, explain the meanings of unfamiliar words such as *wedge, wage,* and *lodge.* Use the words in sentences to clarify meaning. Whenever possible, tell children familiar synonyms for the words.

Phonics Resources

Phonics Express™ CD-ROM, **Level B** Sparkle/Route 6/ Building Site

---

Phonics
Consonants /j/g, dge

Review

WORD BUILDING

Guided Practice Place the letters *e, d, g, e* in a pocket chart. Have children do the same with their *Word Builders* and *Word Builder Cards.* Model how to blend the word *edge.* Slide your hand under the letters as you slowly elongate the sounds /eejj/. Then read the word naturally—*edge.* Have children do the same.

Have children build and read new words by telling them:

- Add *l* in front of *edge.* What word did you make?

- Change the *l* to *w.* What word did you make?

- Change the *e* to *a.* Take away the *d.* What word did you make?

- Change the *w* to *st.* What word did you make?

- Take away the *s.* Take away the *e.* What word did you make?

- Change the *t* to a *b.* What word did you make?

Continue word building with this word sequence: *badge, bridge, ridge, dodge, lodge, large.*

Apply Phonics

READ WORDS IN CONTEXT

Write the following sentences on the board or on chart paper or display *Teaching Transparency 93*. Have children read the story one sentence at a time. Call on volunteers to underline or frame words with /j/g, *dge*.

▼ **Teaching Transparency 93**

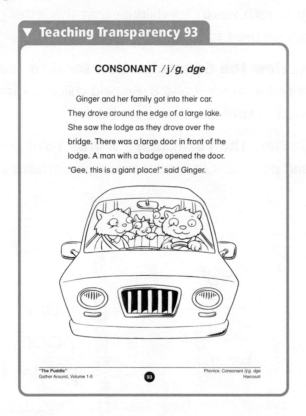

CONSONANT /j/g, *dge*

Ginger and her family got into their car. They drove around the edge of a large lake. She saw the lodge as they drove over the bridge. There was a large door in front of the lodge. A man with a badge opened the door. "Gee, this is a giant place!" said Ginger.

"The Puddle"
Gather Around, Volume 1-5   93   Phonics: Consonant /j/g, dge
                                                                            Harcourt

Write Words Tell children to choose two /j/g, *dge* words and write them in their journal.

5-DAY PHONICS	
DAY 1	Introduce /j/g, dge
DAY 2	Word Building with /j/g, dge
DAY 3	**Word Building with /j/g, dge**
DAY 4	Word Building with /j/g, dge
DAY 5	Inflections -ed, -ing (drop e) Contractions 've, 'd, 're

REACHING ALL LEARNERS

Diagnostic Check: Phonics

If... children cannot decode words with /j/g, *dge*...

Then... have them read decodable stories "Ginger" and "The Badgers Have a Picnic" in *Decodable Book 31* to reinforce /j/g, *dge*.

▲ **Decodable Book 31**
"Ginger," "The Badgers Have a Picnic"

ADDITIONAL SUPPORT ACTIVITIES

BELOW-LEVEL	Reteach, p. S28
ADVANCED	Extend, p. S29
ENGLISH-LANGUAGE LEARNERS	Reteach, p. S29

School–Home Connection

Take-Home Book Version

◄ Decodable Books Take Home Version pp. 17–32

Spelling Words

1. age
2. page
3. cage
4. badge
5. budge
6. fudge
7. old
8. most
9. floor
10. piece

journal writing

Have children copy the Spelling Words into their journal.

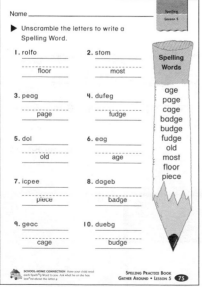

▲ Spelling Practice Book, p. 75

149H Gather Around

Spelling

5-DAY SPELLING	
DAY 1	Pretest; Word Sort
DAY 2	Word Building
DAY 3	State the Generalization
DAY 4	Review
DAY 5	Posttest; Writing Application

TEACH/MODEL

State the Generalization for /j/g, dge Write the Spelling Words on the board and have children read them aloud. Discuss what is the same about words 1–6. (They all have the /j/ sound; they all have g.) Have volunteers circle the letter(s) that stand for /j/ in each word. Tell children that the letter g and the letters dge can be used to spell the /j/ sound.

Review the Generalization for /ō/o Follow a similar procedure for words 7 and 8. Remind children that the letter o can be used to spell the long o sound, /ō/.

Review the Vocabulary Words Point out that the words floor and piece do not follow the same patterns as the other words.

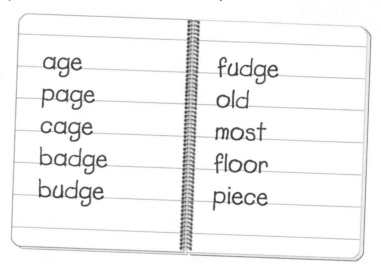

ENGLISH-LANGUAGE LEARNERS

While children are learning to spell a word, they are also learning the word's meaning and how to pronounce it. Suggest that children write each Spelling Word and, when appropriate, draw a picture to show its meaning. For example, have children draw pictures of a *cage*, a police *badge*, a pan of *fudge*, and an *old* car. Afterward, have children point to each picture, say the word, and then spell it aloud.

Vocabulary

Read Words in Context Copy the following sentences onto tagboard strips. Display the strips along with a picture of a tall cake. Track the print as children read the sentences aloud. Then ask half the group to read aloud the first sentence. Have the rest of the group read the second sentence. Continue alternating sentences several times.

> **REVIEW**
> **Vocabulary**
> angry   okay
> nearly   sorry

The cake nearly tipped over.

The baker was angry.

The little boy said he was sorry.

The baker smiled and said, "That's okay."

ADVANCED

Have children think of a character in a storybook who is angry about something or sorry about something. Have children draw a picture of the character and write a sentence that the character might say.

ENGLISH-LANGUAGE LEARNERS

Help children practice saying the words *angry, nearly, okay,* and *sorry* in sentences about their everyday life. Words that have abstract meaning can be clarified by using real-life examples.

Words to Remember

WORD WALL

Match Words Point to the following words on the sentence strips: *angry, nearly, okay, sorry*. Ask volunteers to find and point to the same words posted in the classroom. Have the group read the words aloud.

angry   nearly   okay   sorry

Read
The Puddle
by
David
McPhail

▲ *Pupil Edition*, pp. 126–146

FLUENCY ROUTINES For support, see Fluency Routine Cards in Theme Resources, pp. T83–T84.

Rereading for Fluency

GROUPS

Readers Theatre

⬤ **ON-LEVEL/ADVANCED** Have children work in small groups to dramatize the story. Have them create props as needed and devise sound effects if they wish. Have groups assign parts to individual children. Give groups time to practice before reading and acting out the story for classmates. INDEPENDENT

Managing Small Groups

Reread for fluency with children working individually, with partners, or in small groups. While you work with small groups, have other children do the following:

- **Self-Selected Reading**
- **Cross-Curricular Centers**
- **Practice Pages**
- **Journal Writing**

Use the suggested Classroom Management outline on page 7C for the whole-group/small-group schedule.

Tape-Assisted Reading

ENGLISH-LANGUAGE LEARNERS Conduct a picture walk to review the story events and to reinforce vocabulary such as the animal names, *teatime*, *steered*, *running start*, and *gonna*. Then have children track the print as they listen to *Audiotext 5*. Have them replay the tape and read along, trying to make their reading sound like the recording. INDEPENDENT

Partner Reading

BELOW-LEVEL Have partners take turns reading the story aloud. Point out that the story is written as if the boy is speaking, and they should read with expression to show how the boy and the other characters feel. Remind listeners to follow along and give feedback about how the readers sound. Monitor children and provide modeling as necessary. Later, suggest that children draw and write about their favorite part of the story. TEACHER-DIRECTED

The frog crashed the boat into the turtle.

4

Teacher Read-Aloud Poem

Time to Play

Mama says to play outside.
Wish I had a bike to ride.
I'll fly to the moon instead.
Steer the rocket in my head.
I'll pretend to find a star
no one else has seen so far.
Then I'll name it after me—
    Africa Lawanda Lee!
But for now I'll grab some chalk,
play hopscotch out on the walk.

by Nikki Grimes
illustrated by Floyd Cooper

150   151

Reading Across Texts

READ A POEM

Introduce the Poem Remind children that "The Puddle" was a story about a boy playing outside. Then have children describe the illustration of "Time to Play," and ask them what they think this poem will be about. (a girl playing outside) Remind children that a poem is a piece of writing in which the words are used in an imaginative way to tell about something special. Explain that often poems rhyme, as in this poem. Have children point to the title of the poem, and ask a volunteer to read it aloud.

Sharing a Poem Read the poem aloud as children track the print. Ask what pairs of words in the poem rhyme. *(outside, ride; instead, head; star, far; me, Lee; chalk, walk)* Reread the poem several times, and have children chime in for the rhyming words and other parts they know.

ABOUT THE POET

Nikki Grimes was born in Harlem, New York, in 1950. Although she loved to read, the books she read as a child did not seem to reflect who she was and her experiences. She remembers thinking as a child, "When I grow up, I'll write books about children who look and feel like me." So as an adult writer, Grimes creates African American characters like the children who will be reading her books. Grimes has won many awards, including the Coretta Scott King Award.

▲ The Puddle

Teacher Read-Aloud

Making Connections

An Alligator Friend

The alligator was a real friend to the boy. Think about something else the alligator and the boy could do together. Write about it.

Writing CONNECTION

152

Inside, Outside

The boy in *The Puddle* played outside. Playing inside can be fun, too. Draw and write about your favorite things to do both inside and outside.

Art CONNECTION

Sing a Puddle Song

Sing this song with classmates. Make up movements to go with it.

Music CONNECTION

They'll be coming 'round the puddle when they come . . .
They'll be coming 'round the puddle when they come . . .
They'll be coming 'round the puddle.
They'll be coming 'round the puddle.
They'll be coming 'round the puddle when they come.

153

Making Connections

WRITING

An Alligator Friend To get children started, prompt them with questions such as these: *Will they play together? Where will they go? What will they bring?* Suggest that partners discuss their ideas before writing them. If needed, show children pictures of water-related items, such as a beach ball, to generate ideas.

ART

Inside, Outside Have children brainstorm a list of activities to do indoors and outdoors. Have each child fold a sheet of paper in half, write INSIDE and OUTSIDE at the top of the two sections, draw a favorite activity in each category, and write a caption sentence under each picture.

INSIDE	OUTSIDE
play house	jump rope
read books	ride a bike
do puzzles	play soccer
play school	play tag
build with blocks	play hopscotch

MUSIC

Sing a Puddle Song Sing this song to the tune of "She'll Be Coming 'Round the Mountain." Other possible verses:
Mr. Froggie took my boat out for a sail…
Big Green 'Gator got my boat back from the frog…
You might consider putting a large paper "puddle" on the floor and having children circle around it as they sing the song.

LANGUAGE ARTS

5-DAY WRITING	
DAY 1	SHARED: Bingo Cards
DAY 2	CROSS-CURRICULAR: Class Book
DAY 3	**INTERACTIVE: Directions**
DAY 4	INDEPENDENT: Narrative Sentences
DAY 5	INDEPENDENT: Friendly Letter

DAILY LANGUAGE PRACTICE

I'll pretend to fli to the stares.

I'll pretend to <u>fly</u> to the <u>stars</u>.

journal writing

Writing Prompt Tell children to imagine riding on a boat or flying in a rocket. Have them list the things they "see" during their imaginary trip. Suggest that they draw pictures of the listed items. You may choose to have children use their ideas for a future story-writing assignment.

ADVANCED

Have children independently write directions for a favorite game or a craft project. Provide time for children to read aloud and demonstrate their directions for classmates.

Interactive Writing

Directions

SHARE THE PEN

Tap Prior Knowledge Have children recall the different games and activities that they read about in "The Puddle" and "Time to Play" and wrote about in the Making Connections activities, pages 152–153. Prompt them to mention the toy boat from "The Puddle" and the game of hopscotch from "Time to Play."

Write Directions Work with children to write directions for making a toy boat or playing a game of hopscotch. For the game of hopscotch, demonstrate the game as children help explain how to play it. For the toy boat, have children construct a simple toy boat as they explain how to make it step by step. You can use the following model as a guide for instruction. Call on volunteers to "share the pen," helping to write the directions by writing known words on chart paper.

How to Make a Toy Boat

What You Need: scissors, a sheet of paper, a straw, tape, clay, a foam tray

What You Do:

1. Cut the paper in two to make a triangle.
2. Tape the triangle to the straw to make a sail.
3. Use some clay to stick the straw onto the tray. Now you have a boat!
4. Make clay animals or people to put on the boat.

Grammar

Verbs That Tell About the Past

5-DAY GRAMMAR	
DAY 1	Introduce Verbs That Tell About the Past
DAY 2	Generate Sentences About the Past
DAY 3	**Form Verbs and Sentences**
DAY 4	Verb Game
DAY 5	Identify Verbs

REVIEW

Review Verbs That Tell About the Past Remind children that a verb tells what someone or something does. Have children brainstorm a list of verbs as you record them on the board. Then ask children how such a word can be changed to a word about the past, telling about something that has already happened.

Have volunteers take turns changing a word on the board to make it a verb that tells about the past. Help children remember that they must add *-ed* to most verbs to make them tell about the past. You may want to point out that the spellings of some verbs change to tell about the past. For example: *The turtle and the alligator* swim *in the water* would change to *The turtle and the alligator* swam *in the water*.

Form Sentences Have children make up a sentence using one of the verbs. Allow time for children to share their sentences with the group.

 shout   jump   float   look

 Revisit a Poem

Connecting Ideas Across Texts Recall with children the boy in "The Puddle." Ask: *Did he really meet all those animals at the puddle, or was he just pretending in that part of the story?* Help children understand that the boy had fun imagining the things that happened. Then reread aloud the poem "Time to Play" on *Pupil Edition* page 151. Ask children to name some things the girl is pretending while she plays, such as flying to the moon and finding a star. Ask children how the boy and girl are alike. (Both like to play outdoors; both have good imaginations.)

 S.S.R.
Have children read silently from a book of their choice. See page 155J for tips on helping children choose books.

SKILL TRACE

VERBS THAT TELL ABOUT THE PAST	
Introduce	124N
Reteach	T9
REVIEW	**149C, 153B, 155B, 155L**
T Test	Bk 1-5

BELOW-LEVEL

Call on a volunteer to act out an action word and then have the group tell what that child did. For example: *Latisha jumped.* Use verbs that do not need to have the spelling changed to add *-ed*. Write the sentence on the board and have the volunteer circle the verb. Repeat the procedure.

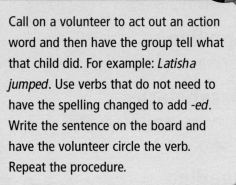

Name _____

Verbs That Tell About the Past

► Underline the verb that tells about the past.

1. fill	filled	2. picked	pick
3. shouted	shouts	4. want	wanted
5. jumped	jumping	6. roll	rolled
7. walk	walked	8. helped	help

► Change each verb to tell about the past.

9. look   looked

10. dance   danced

11. paint   painted

12. chirp   chirped

▲ Language Handbook, p. 131

The Puddle **153B**

Day at a Glance
Day 4

Sharing Literature
Poem: "Dangerous"

Phonemic Awareness
Phoneme Substitution; Focus on /j/ and /s/

Phonics
Build Words

Spelling
Review

Vocabulary
REVIEW: *angry, nearly, okay, sorry*

Reading

(Focus Skill) Comprehension
Plot, pp. 154–155

Independent Writing
Narrative Sentences

Grammar
REVIEW: Verbs That Tell About the Past

WARM UP — MORNING MESSAGE

Good Morning!

Today is _____.
I like to pretend when I play.
I can fly like a bird to _____.
I can move as fast as a _____.
I can jump over _____ in one hop!

Introduce the Day

Tell children that today they will listen to a poem about using imagination while playing indoors. Guide children in generating a morning message about pretending. Ask:

- **If you could fly like a bird, where would you go?**
- **What animal or thing do you wish you could beat in a race?**
- **What is the tallest thing you can imagine hopping over?**

Call on volunteers to help write the message. For instance, have them write the known high-frequency words *is, like, when, I, play, can, fly, move, one,* and *over*.

Read the Message

Read the message. Use the message to focus on selected skills that have been previously taught.

Apply Skills

Phonics Rewrite the fourth sentence, using *big giraffe*. Read the new sentence with children. Point out that *big* and *giraffe* both have the letter *g*. Have children say the sound of *g* in *big* (/g/) and then the sound of *g* in *giraffe* (/j/). Remind children that the letter *g* can sometimes stand for the sound /j/.

Grammar Circle the words *play* and *jump*. Ask children if these words tell about now or about the past. Then review the past-tense form of the verbs. Have volunteers say the verbs, write them on the board, and use them in sentences. (played, jumped)

Sharing Literature

LISTEN AND RESPOND

Connect to Prior Knowledge Ask volunteers to tell about the times they have used their imagination at home. Discuss the fun of acting like a make-believe character in a special place, like a princess in a castle or an explorer in the jungle.

Set a Purpose/Read Tell children the title of the poem, "Dangerous," and suggest that they listen to find out what the children in the poem are doing and where they are doing it. Then read the poem aloud.

Respond to the Poem Discuss the meaning of the word *dangerous*. Ask children whether they think exploring in the kitchen is really dangerous or whether the children in the poem are just pretending. Have children share their thoughts about the game that the poem's characters are playing in the kitchen. Then have children pantomime the actions as you reread the poem.

Dangerous

When we're
Hunting
We explore
Squares upon the
kitchen floor;
We must
Get from
Here to there
Without touching
Anywhere;
For this
Square is
Safe for us.
But that one is
Dangerous.

Dorothy Aldis

Phonemic Awareness

PHONEME SUBSTITUTION

Words from "Dangerous" Tell children that you will say a word and they will change the first or last sound to make a new word. Model by saying *get*. *If I change /g/ to /w/ at the beginning of* get, *I make a new word*, wet. Continue with these words:

here: change /h/ to /ch/ (cheer)   **safe:** change /f/ to /l/ (sail)
there: change /th/ to /hw/ (where) **floor:** change /ôr/ to /âr/ (flare)

FOCUS ON /j/ AND /s/

Phoneme Substitution Tell children that you will say a word and they will change the last sound to /j/ to make a new word. Model the first item by saying *ace*. *If I change /s/ to /j/, I get age.* Then have children say and change each of these words:

ace (age)   pace (page)   case (cage)
bus (budge)   less (ledge)   fuss (fudge)

ENGLISH-LANGUAGE LEARNERS

To help children focus on the final phoneme, segment each word into its onset and rime after you say it. For example, *pace, p-ace; case, c-ase*. Have children repeat after you before they change the final phoneme from /s/ to /j/. If needed, segment the answer and have children blend and say the new word.

OBJECTIVES

- *To discriminate between the sound-letter relationships /s/c and /j/g, dge*

- *To read and write words with /s/c and /j/g, dge*

SKILL TRACE

	/j/g, dge	/s/c
Introduce	124I–124L	Bk 1-4, 124I–124L
Reteach	S28	Bk 1-4, S28
REVIEW	124Q–124R, 149F–149G, 153E–153F	Bk 1-4, 124Q–124R 145F–145G, 151F; Bk 1-5, 153E–153F

Phonics Resources

Phonics Express™ CD-ROM, **Level B** Sparkle/Route 1/Fire Station (soft *g*); Roamer/Route 1/ Train Station (soft *c*)

Phonics Build Words *Review*

WORD BUILDING

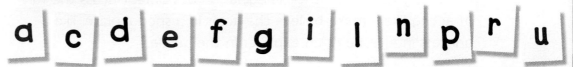

Build and Read Words Use a pocket chart and *Letter Cards a, c, d, e, f, g, i, l, n, p, r,* and *u.* Display the letters *p, a, g, e* in a pocket chart and ask children to spell the word.

Place the letters close together. Slide your hand slowly under the letters as you blend the sounds—/ppāājj/. Then read the word naturally—*page.* Have children repeat after you. Point out that the letters in *page* follow the pattern *consonant, vowel, consonant, e.*

Ask volunteers to build new words in the pocket chart.

- Change the *g* to *c.* Read the word.

- Change the *p* to *r.* Read the word.

- Change the *c* to *g.* Add an n between the *a* and *g.* Read the word.

- Change the *a* to *i.* Change the *n* to *d.* Read the word.

- Take away the *d.* Change the *g* to *c.* Read the word.

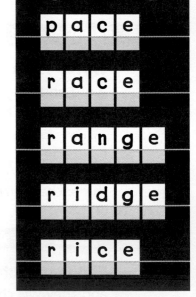

Continue word building with this word sequence: *nice, nudge, fudge, face, lace, ledge.*

Read Words Write the following words on the board. Point to each word and have children read it aloud.

page   **race**   **ridge**   **rice**

5-DAY PHONICS

DAY 1	Introduce /j/g, dge
DAY 2	Word Building with /j/g, dge
DAY 3	Word Building with /j/g, dge
DAY 4	**Word Building with /s/c and /j/g**
DAY 5	Inflections -ed, -ing (drop e) Contractions 've, 'd, 're

Apply Phonics

APPLY PHONICS SKILLS

Dictate Sentences Dictate the following sentences:

> Mom cooked rice on the range.
> My nice sister made fudge.

Have children write the sentences on a dry-erase board or in their journal.

> Mom cooked rice on the range.
>
> My nice sister made fudge.

BELOW-LEVEL

Have children blend and read the following words: *age, ace, nice, edge.* See page S28 for Word Blending instruction.

ENGLISH-LANGUAGE LEARNERS

Children may confuse the pronunciation of hard and soft sounds for *g* and *c.* Write the following words on the board, and read each one slowly: *game, gem, page, pig.* Have children repeat after you, feeling their throat, as they say each word. Point out that /g/ is formed in the back of the throat whereas /j/ is formed in the front of the mouth. Repeat the process for these hard and soft *c* words: *cat, cent, call, cell.*

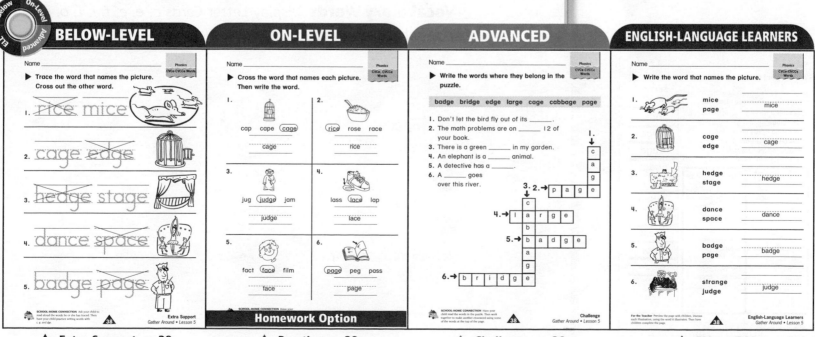

BELOW-LEVEL — ▲ Extra Support, p. 38

ON-LEVEL — ▲ Practice, p. 38

ADVANCED — ▲ Challenge, p. 38

ENGLISH-LANGUAGE LEARNERS — ▲ ELL, p. 38

Spelling Words

1. age
2. page
3. cage
4. badge
5. budge
6. fudge
7. old
8. most
9. floor
10. piece

BELOW-LEVEL

Make up riddles about Spelling Words based on rhyme and initial letter. For example: *It begins with* p *and rhymes with* wage. *(page)* Have children spell the correct answer.

Spelling

5-DAY SPELLING	
DAY 1	Pretest; Word Sort
DAY 2	Word Building
DAY 3	State the Generalization
DAY 4	Review
DAY 5	Posttest; Writing Application

REVIEW

Spelling Words Use a pocket chart and *Letter Cards* to form words. Have children listen to your directions and change one letter in each word to spell a Spelling Word. Have them write the Spelling Word on a sheet of paper or in their journal. Then have a volunteer change the *Letter Card* in the pocket chart so that children can self-check the word.

- Form *ate* in the pocket chart and read it with children. **Which Spelling Word is made with one letter changed?** *(age)*

- Form *pace* in the pocket chart and read it with children. **Which Spelling Word is made with one letter changed?** *(page)*

- Form *came* in the pocket chart and read it with children. **Which Spelling Word is made with one letter changed?** *(cage)*

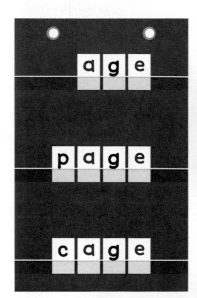

Follow a similar procedure with the following words: bulge *(budge)*, judge *(fudge, budge)*, must *(most)*, cold *(old)*, Madge *(badge)*.

Vocabulary Words Display Letter Cards *c, e, e, f, i, l, o, o, p, r.* Ask volunteers to form the words *floor* and *piece.*

Name _____

Word Sorts

▶ Make cards for the Spelling Words. Lay them down and read them.

1. Put the words with ge in one group and those without ge in another. Write the words on the chart.
2. Put the words with long a in one group and those without long a in another. Write the words on the chart.

Words With ge		Words Without ge	
age	badge	old	floor
page	budge	most	piece
cage	fudge		

Words With Long a	Words Without Long a	
age	badge	most
page	budge	floor
cage	fudge	piece
	old	

Spelling Words

age
page
cage
badge
budge
fudge
old
most
floor
piece
My Own Word

▲ Spelling Practice Book, p. 76

Vocabulary

WRITE WORDS IN STORY CONTEXT

REVIEW
Vocabulary
angry   okay
nearly   sorry

Reinforce Word Recognition
Duplicate and distribute the Story Strips for "The Puddle" (page T69). Display *Word Cards* or write the vocabulary words on the board: *angry, nearly, okay, sorry*. After children complete the Story Strip sentences, they can work with partners to check their work. The two partners can match their sentences and arrange the Story Strips to put story events in order.

> Mom said it was ___ to sail my boat in the puddles.

> The turtle was ___ when the frog crashed into her.

> The alligator said he was ___ about my boat.

> The elephant drank ___ all the water in the puddle.

To help children visualize and memorize vocabulary words, hold up a *Word Card*. Have children say and then spell the word. Have children say and spell the word again. Put down the *Word Card* but leave your hand up. Ask children to say and spell the word again.

Words to Remember

WORD WALL

Match Words Have children look at the displayed words and find the words they wrote on the Story Strips. Ask volunteers to frame the words as classmates read them aloud. Then have children read together all the words on display.

ADVANCED

Suggest that children find the words *angry, nearly, okay,* and *sorry* in the story "The Puddle." They can use self-stick notes to mark the pages that contain these words. Children can read the sentences containing those words in a small group.

Read

The Puddle
by David McPhail

▲ *Pupil Edition, pp. 126–146*

OBJECTIVE

To recognize and understand the plot of a story

SKILL TRACE	
PLOT	
Introduce	33A, 35I–37
Reteach	S6, S30, S48, T11
REVIEW	125A, 149A, 153I–155, 219A, 247A, 251I–253
T Test	Bk 1-5

REACHING ALL LEARNERS

Diagnostic Check: Comprehension and Skills

If... children cannot recognize the plot of a story ...

Then... have them tell something that happened to them. Prompt them to tell what happened first, next, after that, and last.

ADDITIONAL SUPPORT ACTIVITIES

BELOW-LEVEL Reteach, p. S30

ADVANCED Extend, p. S31

ENGLISH-LANGUAGE LEARNERS Reteach, p. S31

(Focus Skill) Comprehension

Plot

TEACH/MODEL

Develop Concepts Remind children that every story has a plot. The *plot* is the problem and how it is solved in the story. Point out that when we keep track of what happens in a story from beginning to end, we can better understand what the characters are doing and why they are doing these things.

> **MODEL** If I want to tell the plot of a story about me, I think about the most important events that happened. Then I tell them in order: I went to the pond. I put my fishing line in the water and waited a long time. Then I felt a strong tug. I caught a big fish! I reeled it in slowly so it wouldn't get away. I was proud, but then I felt sorry for the fish, so I threw it back into the water. I was happy to see the fish swim away.

PRACTICE/APPLY

Recognize the Plot of a Story Tell children to think about the plot of "The Puddle." Read aloud *Pupil Edition* page 154. Ask children which sentence best tells the plot. Then prompt them to tell about the most important parts. For example, say: *Tell me the most important thing that the alligator does.*

Reread the Selection Have children reread "The Puddle," paying close attention to the most important events and the order in which they happen. After reading, call on volunteers to summarize the story in a sentence or two.

TEST PREP

Model the Test Item Remind children that when they are taking a test, they should read carefully and try to remember who is in the story and what happens. Direct children to follow along as you read aloud the story on page 155. Read aloud the question and the answer choices as children follow along. Guide children in choosing the correct answer.

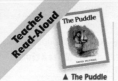

Teacher Read-Aloud

▲ The Puddle

Plot

Focus Skill

The **plot** of a story is what happens in that story. Think about the story "The Puddle." What happens in "The Puddle?" Choose the sentence that tells the **plot**.

1. **A frog takes a boy's boat and sails away.**
2. **A boy plays with an alligator.**
3. **A boy plays with animals in a puddle and goes home when the puddle dries up.**

Which sentence did you choose? Tell why.

Visit *The Learning Site!*
www.harcourtschool.com
See Skills and Activities

154

Test Prep
Plot

Sally had lost her Math book. At last she found it, but now she was late! She ran to the bus stop. Just then the bus came. The bus was late, too!

1. **Which sentence tells the plot of the story?**
   ○ Sally can't find a book at home.
   ○ Sally is late, but the school bus is late, too.
   ○ Sally runs to catch her bus.

Tip

Think of what the whole story is about. Then decide which sentence tells about the whole story.

155

Visit *The Learning Site:*
www.harcourtschool.com

See Skill Activities and Test Tutors: Plot.

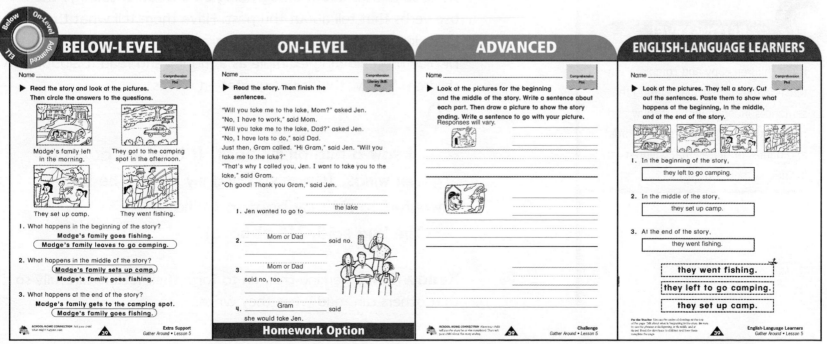

BELOW-LEVEL

Name _____ *Comprehension Plot*

▶ Read the story and look at the pictures. Then circle the answers to the questions.

Madge's family left in the morning. / They got to the camping spot in the afternoon.

They set up camp. / They went fishing.

1. What happens in the beginning of the story?
   Madge's family goes fishing.
   Madge's family leaves to go camping.

2. What happens in the middle of the story?
   Madge's family sets up camp.
   Madge's family goes fishing.

3. What happens at the end of the story?
   Madge's family gets to the camping spot.
   Madge's family goes fishing.

SCHOOL-HOME CONNECTION Ask your child what might happen next.

▲ *Extra Support Gather Around • Lesson 5*

ON-LEVEL

Name _____ *Comprehension Literary Skill Plot*

▶ Read the story. Then finish the sentences.

"Will you take me to the lake, Mom?" asked Jen.
"No, I have to work," said Mom.
"Will you take me to the lake, Dad?" asked Jen.
"No, I have lots to do," said Dad.
Just then, Gram called. "Hi Gram," said Jen. "Will you take me to the lake?"
"That's why I called you, Jen. I want to take you to the lake," said Gram.
"Oh good! Thank you Gram," said Jen.

1. Jen wanted to go to _____ the lake

2. _____ Mom or Dad _____ said no.

3. _____ Mom or Dad _____ said no, too.

4. _____ Gram _____ said she would take Jen.

Homework Option

ADVANCED

Name _____ *Comprehension Plot*

▶ Look at the pictures for the beginning and the middle of the story. Write a sentence about each part. Then draw a picture to show the story ending. Write a sentence to go with your picture.
Responses will vary.

SCHOOL-HOME CONNECTION Have your child tell you the story he or she numbered. Then ask your child about the story ending.

▲ *Challenge Gather Around • Lesson 5*

ENGLISH-LANGUAGE LEARNERS

Name _____ *Comprehension Plot*

▶ Look at the pictures. They tell a story. Cut out the sentences. Paste them to show what happens at the beginning, in the middle, and at the end of the story.

1. In the beginning of the story,
   they left to go camping.

2. In the middle of the story,
   they set up camp.

3. At the end of the story,
   they went fishing.

   they went fishing.
   they left to go camping.
   they set up camp.

For the Teacher: Focus on the order of drawings in the box at the page. Talk about what is happening in the story, the cues for each phrase at the beginning, in the middle, and at the end. Point the directions to children and have them complete the page.

▲ *English-Language Learners Gather Around • Lesson 5*

▲ Extra Support, p. 39   ▲ Practice, p. 39   ▲ Challenge, p. 39   ▲ ELL, p. 39

Writing
Narrative Sentences

5-DAY WRITING	
DAY 1	SHARED: Bingo Cards
DAY 2	CROSS-CURRICULAR: Class Book
DAY 3	INTERACTIVE: Directions
DAY 4	INDEPENDENT: **Narrative Sentences**
DAY 5	INDEPENDENT: Friendly Letter

DAILY LANGUAGE PRACTICE

Do you want a peece of fudge.

Do you want a <u>piece</u> of fudge<u>?</u>

journal writing

Self-Selected Writing Have children write in their journal about a topic of their choice. They may want to illustrate their writing.

ONGOING ASSESSMENT

Note whether children are able to
- make connections between sounds and letters in words.
- spell known high-frequency words.
- use knowledge of the basic rules of punctuation and capitalization.

BELOW-LEVEL

Have children copy and complete sentence frames rather than writing the sentences independently. Display and read aloud a list of descriptive words and names of places that children can include in their sentences.

GENERATE IDEAS

Visualize the Scene Remind children that the poem "Dangerous" and the story "The Puddle" are about children using their imagination. Tell children that they will be using their imagination to write about a bug on a toy boat. Have them close their eyes and imagine a real or make-believe bug on a boat. Prompt them with questions such as these:

- **What does the bug look like?**
- **What is the bug doing on the boat?**
- **Where does the bug want to go with the boat?**
- **What would the bug say if it could talk?**

DRAW AND WRITE

Make a Picture Have each child make a construction-paper picture of a bug on a boat. Have them use a paper triangle for the boat's sail and a half-circle for the boat's base. After gluing the boat onto construction paper, children can draw the bug on the boat and draw other details around the boat. Suggest that they show a puddle setting.

Write Narrative Sentences Have children use their ideas to write sentences about a bug riding on a boat. Encourage them to use verbs that tell about the past. Have them tell what the bug looks like, what the bug was doing, and where it was going. Display the following example as a model, and read it aloud with children. Review the use of quotation marks.

> I saw a bug on my boat. It had red dots and green wings. It was steering my boat. The bug wanted to ride my boat to China.
> The bug said, "All aboard!"

Handwriting Remind children to form their letters carefully so that others can read what they write.

Grammar

Verbs That Tell About the Past

5-DAY GRAMMAR	
DAY 1	Introduce: Verbs That Tell About the Past
DAY 2	Generate Sentences About the Past
DAY 3	Form Verbs and Sentences
DAY 4	**Verb Game**
DAY 5	Identify Verbs

REVIEW

Play a Verb Game Collect pictures of animals and glue them onto separate index cards to make picture cards. For each animal, make an "action card" that shows the present-tense verb on one side of the card and the past-tense form on the other. For example: *frog, jumps/jumped; dog, barks/barked; duck, quacks/ quacked; horse, trots/trotted; snake, slithers/slithered; turtle, crawls/crawled; ant, marches/marched.* Display the present-tense verbs in a pocket chart, and distribute the animal cards to children.

Call on a child to hold up his or her picture card. Have the group say the animal name. Then have the child point to the correct present-tense verb and say it. Lead the group in responding with a simple sentence that uses the verb, for example, *A frog jumps.* Then have the child act out the action. Have him or her turn over the action card and say the past-tense verb. Lead the group in responding with a sentence that tells about the action that was role-played: *The frog jumped.*

jumped

WRAP UP — Share Writing

Author's Chair Have children take turns sitting in the Author's Chair and reading aloud the sentences they wrote about a bug on a boat. Call on listeners to retell what the bug was doing and where it was going on the boat.

Encourage children to stay focused, asking them questions about where the bug went and what the bug did.

S.S.R. Sustained Silent Reading

Have children read silently from a book of their choice. See page 155J for tips on helping children choose books.

SKILL TRACE

VERBS THAT TELL ABOUT THE PAST	
Introduce	124N
Reteach	T9
REVIEW	**149C, 153B, 155B, 155L**
T Test	Bk 1-5

Grammar Resources

Grammar Jingles™ **CD, Primary, Track 9,** "What Happened?"

teaching tip

Show a video of animals in action. After each animal moves, pause the tape and ask children what the animal just did. List the past-tense verbs on the board. After the video, review the list of words with children.

Name _____

Verbs That Tell About the Past

▶ Add **ed** to the words in the boxes. Then write the correct word in each sentence.
Possible response.

fix	paint	move
	help	want

1. Last night I ___helped___ my mother.

2. We ___moved___ Max out of his doghouse.

3. We ___painted___ the walls.

4. We ___fixed___ the door.

5. Max ___wanted___ to get back in his home!

132

▲ Language Handbook, p. 132

ORAL LANGUAGE

WARM UP

MORNING MESSAGE

Good Morning!

Today is _____ .
What animals do you see on the land and in the sea? I see a _____ in the woods. Look at that large _____ over there! Do you see the _____ in the sea?

Introduce the Day

Tell children that today they will revisit the story *I Swam with a Seal*. Guide them in generating a message about animals. Ask:

- **What kinds of animals live in the woods?**
- **Which other animals live on land?**
- **Which animals live in the sea?**

As you write the message, invite volunteers to write previously taught letters, words, and/or punctuation to reinforce skills. For instance, have volunteers write the words *land* and *sea* and other words they know. Remind children that an exclamation mark is used to show strong feeling or surprise.

Read the Message

Read the message. Use the message to focus on selected skills that have been previously taught.

Apply Skills

High-Frequency Words Have volunteers point to and read known high-frequency words: *what, do, you, see, on, the, a, look, over,* and *there.*

Concept Vocabulary Write the words *big* and *giant* on the board, and have children read them aloud. Ask what word in the message has almost the same meaning as *big* and *giant.* (*large*) Point out that *giant* and *large* both have /j/ spelled *g*.

Sharing Literature

DEVELOP LISTENING COMPREHENSION

Focus Skill **Plot** Reread *Big Book I Swam with a Seal* to children, encouraging them to join in. As you read the story aloud, pause after every four or six pages and ask children to tell what has happened in the story so far.

Extend the Pattern Work with children to think of other animals that the children in the story could play with and how they would play with them. For example: *slide with a snail, run with a rhino,* and *paddle with a penguin.* Then recite the repeated pattern of the story, adding children's suggestions into the pattern.

Phonemic Awareness

PHONEME DELETION

Words from the Big Book Have children recall the hare from the story *I Swam with the Seal.* Tell children that you are going to ask them to make new words by taking away the beginning sound from words. Model with the word *hare: If I say* hare *without the /h/ sound at the beginning, I get* air. Continue the activity with these words from the story:

hill **without the /h/** (ill)   *flip* **without the /f/** (lip)
ground **without the /g/** (round)   *flick* **without the /f/** (lick)
trail **without the /t/** (rail)   *stalk* **without the /s/** (talk)
wall **without the /w/** (all)   *slap* **without the /s/** (lap)

FOCUS ON /d/, /t/, /ed/

Identify Final Sounds Tell children you will say some words with the ending *-ed* and they will tell what sound they hear at the end. Model by saying *When I say* showed, *I hear /d/ as the final sound. When I say* laughed, *I hear /t/ at the end. When I say* floated, *I hear /ed/.* Continue with the following words:

worked (/t/)	**cried** (/d/)	**played** (/d/)	**wanted** (/ed/)
waved (/d/)	**yelled** (/d/)	**splashed** (/t/)	**started** (/ed/)
rained (/d/)	**sailed** (/d/)	**dressed** (/t/)	**steered** (/d/)

▲ **Big Book**

BELOW-LEVEL

Have children look through "The Puddle" and point out words with the ending *-ed.* Read each word slowly, segmenting the phonemes. Have children repeat the word and identify the ending sound as /d/, /t/, or /ed/.

OBJECTIVE

To use common letter patterns to build and read words

SKILL TRACE

INFLECTIONS *-ed, -ing* (drop *e*)	
Introduce	37F
Reteach	T3
REVIEW	**67H, I55E**
T Test	Bk I-5

BELOW-LEVEL

Demonstrate action words to help children correctly use inflections *-ing* and *-ed*. For example, walk in front of the group and ask them to tell what you are doing. *(You are walking.)* Then stop the action and ask children what you just did. *(You walked.)* Write the two action words on the board and underline the *-ed* and *-ing*. Repeat with other action words, such as *dance* and *wave*.

Phonics
Inflections -ed,-ing

DEVELOP WORD MEANING

Review Words with Inflections *-ed* and *-ing* Remind children that in the story "The Puddle," the alligator chased the frog to get the boat back. Write the words *chase* and *chased* on the board, and have children read both words. Ask which word tells about something that happened in the past. *(chased)* Remind children that in a word like *chase*, which ends with an *e*, the final *e* is dropped when the ending *-ed* is added. Next, write *chasing*. Have children read the word and tell which letter was dropped from *chase* when the *-ing* was added. *(e)*

WORKING WITH PATTERNS

Read Words in Context On the board, write the following sentences and make a two-column chart that has the heading *Base Word* for the first column and the heading *Now or the Past?* for the second column. Have a volunteer read each sentence and identify the word that ends with *-ed* or *-ing*. Have children spell the base word and say whether the sentence tells about now or about the past. Record their responses in the chart.

> The girl is **dancing** on the stage.
> She **danced** for us last week.
> We **smiled** when we saw her.
> We are **writing** a thank-you note to her.

Build *-ed* and *-ing* Words Help children use plastic letters to build the words *dance, danced, dancing; smile, smiled*, and *smiling*. Model removing the *e* before adding *-ed* or *-ing*.

APPLY PHONICS SKILLS

 Write *-ed* and *-ing* Words Have children write two sentences in their journal, one with an *-ed* word and one with an *-ing* word. Have them choose one or two of these base words to use: *chase, bake, race, hike, smile, move, wave*.

Contractions 've, 'd, 're

5-DAY PHONICS

DAY 1	Introduce /j/g, dge
DAY 2	Word Building with /j/g, dge
DAY 3	Word Building with /j/g, dge
DAY 4	Word Building with /j/g, dge
DAY 5	**Inflections -ed, -ing (drop e)** **Contractions 've, 'd, 're**

DEVELOP WORD MEANING

Review Contractions Write the following on the board:

> I've played in the rain.
> I'd like to jump in the puddles, but I'd better not.
> You're going to get wet if you play in the rain.

Have children read aloud the first sentence. Ask what two words form the contraction *I've*. (I have) Write *I have* on the board. Ask a volunteer to show how the contraction is formed, by erasing *ha* and inserting an apostrophe. Continue in a similar manner with the other sentences.

SKILL TRACE

CONTRACTIONS 've, 'd, 're	
Introduce	123E–123F
Reteach	T8
REVIEW	**155F, 185G**
T Test	Bk 1-5

WORKING WITH PATTERNS

Form Contractions Write these word pairs on the board and have children form the contraction for each pair:

we have	she would	they are
you have	they would	we are

APPLY PHONICS SKILLS

Write Contractions Have children write three sentences in their journal, one with a 've word, one with a 'd word, and one with an 're word.

BELOW-LEVEL

Use stick-on labels and connecting cubes to make letter cubes for these word pairs: *I have, you have, we have, I would, she would, they would, they are, we are, you are.* Use the same color for all the letters and use a different color to make an apostrophe cube. Put together each pair of words to make a letter train. Have children form the contraction by removing the appropriate letter cubes and replacing them with the apostrophe cube.

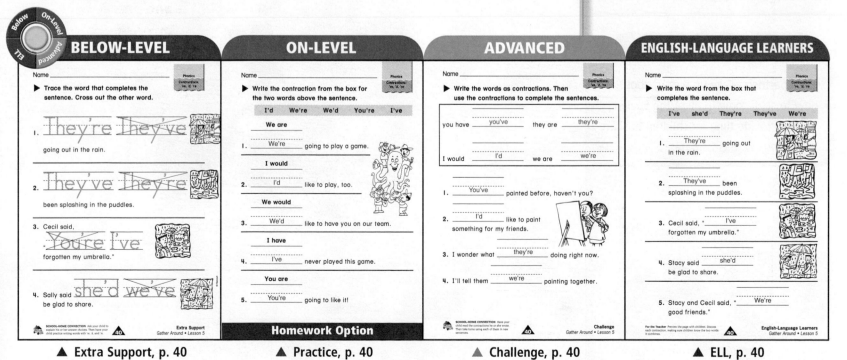

▲ Extra Support, p. 40	▲ Practice, p. 40	▲ Challenge, p. 40	▲ ELL, p. 40

5-DAY SPELLING	
DAY 1	Pretest; Word Sort
DAY 2	Word Building
DAY 3	State the Generalization
DAY 4	Review
DAY 5	**Posttest; Writing Application**

Spelling Words

1. **age**
2. **page**
3. **cage**
4. **badge**
5. **budge**
6. **fudge**
7. **old**
8. **most**
9. **floor**
10. **piece**

BELOW-LEVEL

Provide opportunities for children to use *Letter Cards*, letter stamps, sponge letters, and other manipulatives to form the Spelling Words. After children form each word, have them write it in their journal.

ADVANCED

Have partners make up a song about how to spell some or all of the Spelling Words. Provide time for children to share their songs with classmates.

Spelling

ASSESS/APPLY

Posttest Assess children's progress using the words and the Dictation Sentences from Day 1.

1. **age**   I learned to ride a bike at the **age** of six.
2. **page**   What number is on the next **page** of your book?
3. **cage**   The tiger is asleep in his **cage**.
4. **badge**   A police officer wears a **badge**.
5. **budge**   The rock was so big we couldn't **budge** it.
6. **fudge**   Have you ever had **fudge** for dessert?

Review

7. **old**   How **old** are you?
8. **most**   **Most** children like pizza.

Vocabulary

9. **floor**   I cleaned the **floor** with a mop.
10. **piece**   I write with a **piece** of chalk.

Writing Application Have children complete and illustrate the following sentence frames:

   The old floor _____ when I walked.

   I ate a _____ piece of fudge.

Vocabulary

USE WORDS IN SENTENCES

REVIEW
Vocabulary

angry	okay
nearly	sorry

Reinforce Usage List these words on the board and have children read them aloud: *angry, nearly, okay, sorry.* Then give each group of four children a set of Individual Word Cards (page T36) for the same set of words. Have children work together to think of four sentences that include the vocabulary words. When all the groups are ready, have them take turns saying their sentences, one sentence per child. Have speakers hold up their Word Card as they say the sentence. Record one sentence from each group on the board or on chart paper. Track the print as you reread the sentences with children.

Words to Remember

WORD WALL

Complete Sentences Have children complete the following sentences with words that have been displayed. Point to the column in which the target word appears. Volunteers can frame the words as classmates read them aloud.

- My mom said it was ＿＿ to play at your house. (okay)

- Oh no! It's ＿＿ time for dinner! (nearly)

- I hope my mom isn't ＿＿ with me for being late. (angry)

- I am ＿＿ for not getting home by 4:30. (sorry)

ENGLISH-LANGUAGE LEARNERS

Because some vocabulary words may be difficult to define, children need to work with them in context to understand their meaning. Have children complete these sentences orally:

The box of cereal was ＿＿ empty. (nearly)

My brother was ＿＿ when he looked inside the cereal box. (angry)

I told him I was ＿＿ for eating almost all of the cereal. (sorry)

He said, "That's ＿＿. I'll just eat a banana." (okay)

▲ *Pupil Edition*, pp. 126–146

FLUENCY ROUTINES For support, see Fluency Routine Cards in Theme Resources, pp. T83–T84.

teaching tip

Reading with "expression" refers to the ability to read with the rhythm and tone of spoken language—using appropriate phrasing and emphasis and pausing where appropriate. As you listen to children read, use these criteria to determine how much more fluency practice they need.

Rereading for Fluency

GROUPS

Readers Theatre

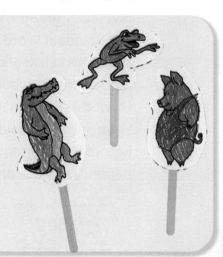

⬤ **BELOW-LEVEL/ENGLISH-LANGUAGE LEARNERS** Direct small groups of children to use the Character Cutouts (pages T19–T20) to make puppets. Tell them to color the cutouts and glue them onto craft sticks. Then have children take turns reading as others in the group use the puppets to act out the story. TEACHER-DIRECTED

PARTNERS

Partner Reading

⬤ **ON-LEVEL/ADVANCED** Have partners read two pages at a time. Encourage them to read with expression as if they are the boy telling the story. Suggest that they use different voices for the animal characters. Remind them that they can reread pages if they think they can improve their expression and read more smoothly. After reading, you might have partners meet in a group to share their ideas about how the animal characters sound. INDEPENDENT

Managing Small Groups

Reread for fluency with children working individually, with partners, or in small groups. While you work with small groups, have other children do the following:

- **Self-Selected Reading**
- **Cross-Curricular Centers**
- **Practice Pages**
- **Journal Writing**

Use the suggested Classroom Management outline on page 7C for the whole-group/small-group schedule.

Self-Selected Reading

INDEPENDENT READING

Have children choose a book from the **Browsing Boxes** or the **Reading Center** to read independently during a sustained silent reading time. Children may also want to reread a story from their *Pupil Edition*. These are some books you may want to gather that relate to "The Puddle."

Decodable Books

Decodable Book 31
"Roger's Gerbil" by Nancy Furstinger

"The Fudge Judge" by Nancy Furstinger

"Ginger" by Barbara Sobel

"The Badgers Have a Picnic" by Sheila Black

Cut-Out/Fold-Up Book

The Bridge

Practice Book, pp. 73–74

Books for All Learners

Storm Watch
by Mary Louise Bourget
BELOW-LEVEL

The Edge of the Puddle by Holly Melton
ON-LEVEL

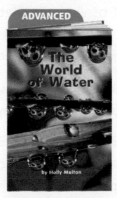

The World of Water by Holly Melton
ADVANCED

All Kinds of Weather by Irma Singer
ELL

related books

- **Water's Journey** by F. R. Robinson. Science Instant Reader, Harcourt, 1997. Rain falls from the sky and takes a long, long journey. BELOW-LEVEL
- **Pig Pig Grows Up** by David McPhail. Dutton Children's Books, 1980. Pig Pig refuses to grow up until a near disaster forces him to do it. BELOW-LEVEL
- **The Three Billy Goats Gruff** illustrated by Stephen Carpenter. HarperCollins, 1998. A classic tale of three goats who outsmart the troll that lives under the bridge. ON-LEVEL
- **Meet the Boxcar Children–The Adventures of Benny and Watch** by Gertrude Chandler. Albert Whitman & Company, 1998. Four orphaned siblings move into an abandoned boxcar until they are united with their grandmother. ADVANCED

Writing *Letters*

5-DAY WRITING	
DAY 1	SHARED: Bingo Cards
DAY 2	CROSS-CURRICULAR: Class Book
DAY 3	INTERACTIVE: Directions
DAY 4	INDEPENDENT: Narrative Sentences
DAY 5	**INDEPENDENT: Friendly Letter**

DAILY LANGUAGE PRACTICE

the frog and the pig hops into the puddle.

<u>T</u>he frog and the pig <u>hop</u> into the puddle.

journal  writing

Writing Prompt Have children tell which character from "The Puddle" they would like to have as a friend. Have them list reasons for their choice. They may want to draw a picture of the character.

BELOW-LEVEL

Work with children to write a group letter from one character's point of view. Have children "share the pen" as they contribute to the writing process.

GENERATE IDEAS

Tap Prior Knowledge Have children recall the different characters from "The Puddle," and ask them how the characters might feel about each other. Name pairs of characters, such as the boy and the frog, the frog and the turtle, the alligator and the boy, and the elephant and the pig. Ask children what each character might write in a letter to the other and how the receiver might respond. Then tell children that they will be writing letters as if they were one of the characters.

REVIEW AND WRITE

Review the Format of a Letter Display a sample letter and review the different parts. Remind children that a letter includes the date, the greeting, the body, the closing, and the signature. Tell children that their letter can include verbs that tell about the past, since the characters already visited the puddle.

> April 20, 200_
>
> Dear Mrs. Turtle,
>
> I am sorry that my boat crashed into you. I was having so much fun that I didn't see you floating by. I will buy you a new teapot and teacup. I hope we can still be friends.
>
> Sincerely,
> Mr. Frog

Write a Letter Have partners choose different characters from the story. Then have them each write a letter from that character's point of view. The letter should be written to the partner's character. Remind children to think about what happened at the puddle and how their character reacted.

Read and Respond Have partners exchange letters and respond to them as if they were the character from the story.

Handwriting Remind children to use the lines on their paper to help them write neatly. You might have children type their letters on a computer.

Grammar

Verbs That Tell About the Past

5-DAY GRAMMAR

DAY 1	INTRODUCE: Verbs That Tell About the Past
DAY 2	Generate Sentences About the Past
DAY 3	Form Verbs and Sentences
DAY 4	Verb Game
DAY 5	**Identify Verbs**

REVIEW

Identify Verbs That Tell About the Past Tell children that you will say some sentences and that they should repeat each one after you. After each sentence, ask whether the sentence contains a verb that tells about the past. Have children give a "thumbs-back" to show which verbs tell about something that already happened.

- Jill walked in the rain.
- Tom stays home in bed.
- Bert sailed his boat in the water.
- Rosa jumped in a puddle.
- Little bugs swim in the puddles.
- I looked at the dark clouds.
- Jenny sees a rainbow.

Write Sentences Have children write two sentences to add to the story, using verbs that end in *-ed* to tell about the past.

> We jumped for joy!
> Then we played a game of tag.

 WRAP UP ## Share Ideas

Author's Chair Have partners take turns sitting in the Author's Chair to read aloud the friendly letter they wrote in the Writing activity. Remind audience members to listen attentively and courteously to each author. When each child is finished reading, lead children in applause for the reader.

 S.S.R. *Sustained Silent Reading* Have children read silently from a book of their choice. See page 155J for tips on helping children choose books.

SKILL TRACE

VERBS THAT TELL ABOUT THE PAST

Introduce	124N
Reteach	T9
REVIEW	**149C, 153B, 155B, 155L**
T Test	Bk 1-5

ADVANCED

Have children conduct interviews with adults at school to learn about things they did as a young child. Have children write sentences about those activities and events. Tell them to underline the verbs that tell about the past. Provide time for children to share what they learned.

Grammar Resources

Visit *The Learning Source:*
www.harcourtschool.com

See Go for Grammar Gold, Multimedia Grammar Glossary.

Name _____

Verbs That Tell About the Past

► Write the verbs that tell about the past.

chirp   chirped

1. The birds _____ chirped _____ all night.

jumped   jump

2. The dog _____ jumped _____ on the bed.

splash   splashed

3. The fish _____ splashed _____ their water.

played   play

4. The cat _____ played _____ with her toys.

toss   tossed

5. Carmen _____ tossed _____ in her bed!

SCHOOL-HOME CONNECTION

133

▲ Language Handbook, p. 133

Books for All Learners

Reinforcing Skills and Strategies

■ BELOW-LEVEL

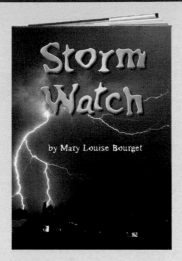

Storm Watch

☑ **Phonics: Consonant /j/g, dge;**
  Contraction 'd

☑ **Vocabulary: angry, nearly,**
  okay, sorry

☑ **Focus Skill: Plot**

SUMMARY Florida is home to many thunderstorms and hurricanes.

Visit *The Learning Site:*
www.harcourtschool.com
See Resources for Parents and
Teachers: Books for All Learners.

BEFORE READING

Build Background Invite children to share experiences they have had during a thunderstorm. Ask how they know a storm is coming.

Preview/Set Purpose Have children identify the title and help them read it. Point out the author and the illustrator. Then have children look at the first few pages of the book and predict what the story is about. Help children set a purpose for reading, such as *I want to find out more about storms.*

READING THE BOOK

Pages 2–3 How do maps help weather watchers? (Maps tell them about the wind, the clouds, and warm and cold air.) NOTE DETAILS, TEXT STRUCTURE

Pages 4–6 What do the labels on the diagram say? (*warm air, cold air, clouds, lightning*) How do they help you as you read? (The labels point out important information.) TEXT STRUCTURE, SPECULATE

Pages 7–9 How are lightning and thunder the same? (Both are part of a thunderstorm; they happen when warm air and cold air meet.) How are they different? (Lightning can harm you, but thunder cannot; you can see lightning but only hear thunder.) COMPARE/CONTRAST

Pages 10–12 What effects can be seen from a hurricane? (Housetops can be blown off and trees can be blown down.) CAUSE/EFFECT

RESPONDING

Write a Weather Story Invite each child to choose a weather phenomenon described in the book and write a story that includes it. Encourage them to incorporate information from the book into their story. Ask children to read their story aloud. Then challenge the rest of the group to briefly explain the plot of each story.

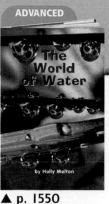

BELOW-LEVEL

Storm Watch

by Mary Louise Bourget

ON-LEVEL

The Edge of the Puddle
A Play

by Holly Melton
illustrated by David Merrill

ADVANCED

The World of Water

by Holly Melton

ELL

All Kinds of Weather

by Irma Singer
illustrated by Byron Gin

▲ p. 155O   ▲ p. 155P

Oral Reading Fluency

Use Books for All Learners to promote oral reading fluency.

See **Fluency Routine Cards**, pp. T83–T84.

■ ON-LEVEL

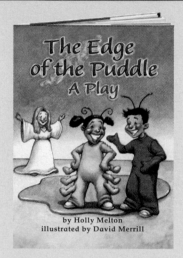

The Edge of the Puddle

 Phonics: Consonants /j/g, dge

 Vocabulary: angry, nearly, okay, sorry

 Focus Skill: Plot

SUMMARY   A caterpillar is unable to cross a large puddle until an ant comes up with a clever idea.

 Visit The Learning Site:
www.harcourtschool.com
See Resources for Parents and Teachers: Books for All Learners.

BEFORE READING

Build Background Have volunteers share experiences they may have had watching a caterpillar crawl. Ask children how a caterpillar moves and what a caterpillar might do if it encounters a large puddle.

Preview/Set Purpose. Have children identify the title and help them read it. Point out the author and the illustrator. Then have children look at the first few pages of the book and predict what the story is about. Help children set a purpose for reading, such as *I want to find out what happens to the caterpillar.*

READING THE BOOK

Pages 2–4 What must Caterpillar do to become a butterfly? (make a chrysalis) NOTE DETAILS

Pages 5–7 What problem does Caterpillar have? (Caterpillar is unable to cross the puddle and make a chrysalis.) How might Caterpillar solve the problem? (Possible response: He will ask a friend for help.) PLOT

Pages 8–12 What words would you use to describe Ant? (*helpful; kind; clever*) How do you know? (Ant says he will help Caterpillar and figures out how he can.) DETERMINE CHARACTERS' TRAITS

Pages 13–14 Why does Ant say there are alligators in the puddle? (He is being playful; he is joking with Caterpillar.) DRAW CONCLUSIONS, DETERMINE CHARACTERS' TRAITS

RESPONDING

Dramatic Reading Have children form groups of six and let them reread the story aloud. Assign each child one of the following parts: Storyteller, Caterpillar, Butterfly, Bee, Frog, or Ant. Allow children to reread the story several times to increase fluency. Encourage them to read with expression and use gestures to help convey the story. Then have each group perform its dramatic reading for the class.

Books for All Learners
Reinforcing Skills and Strategies

■ ADVANCED

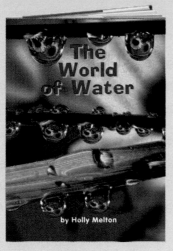

by Holly Melton

The World of Water

 Phonics: Consonants /j/ g, dge

 Vocabulary: *angry, nearly, okay, sorry*

 Focus Skill: Plot

SUMMARY The three forms of water are all around us.

 Visit *The Learning Site:*
www.harcourtschool.com
See Resources for Parents and
Teachers: Books for All Learners.

BEFORE READING

Build Background Have children tell where they see water all around them. Ask them what they would like to find out about water. Record their responses on a K-W-L chart.

Preview/Set Purpose. Have children identify the title and help them read it. Point out the author and the illustrator. Then have children look at the first few pages of the book and predict what the story is about. Help children set a purpose for reading, such as I want to find out why ice melts into water.

READING THE BOOK

Pages 2–5 How do the pictures help you learn about water? (They show the different forms and examples of water.) INTERPRET TEXT STRUCTURE

Pages 5–8 What causes ice and snow to melt? (heat from the sun) CAUSE/EFFECT

Pages 9–11 Why does the author say that water can seem angry? (It seems angry when it is raging, crashing against rocks, or moving very quickly.) AUTHOR'S CRAFT/DETERMINE IMAGERY

Pages 12–14 How does water vapor form? (It forms when water is heated.) NOTE DETAILS

Pages 15–16 How do you think the author feels about water? (She thinks that water is important because she says that we cannot live without it.) RECOGNIZE AUTHOR'S PURPOSE, THEME

RESPONDING

Make a Comic Strip Have each child create a comic strip showing how a drop of water goes through all three of its forms. Encourage children to use speech balloons and thought bubbles to show what the water droplet is saying and thinking.

Managing Small Groups

While you work with small groups, have other children do the following:
- Self-Selected Reading
- Practice Pages
- Cross-Curricular Centers
- Journal Writing

BELOW-LEVEL

Storm Watch
by Mary Louise Bourget

▲ p. 155M

ON-LEVEL

The Edge of the Puddle
A Play
by Holly Melton
illustrated by David Merrill

▲ p. 155N

ADVANCED
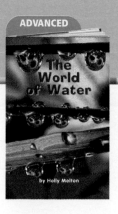
The World of Water
by Holly Melton

ELL

All Kinds of Weather
by Irma Singer
illustrated by Byron Gin

■ ENGLISH-LANGUAGE LEARNERS

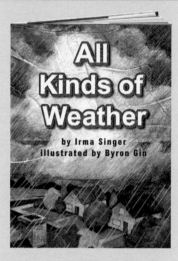

All Kinds of Weather

 Strong Picture Support

 Concept Vocabulary

 Theme Related

SUMMARY There are lots of things to do in every kind of weather.

 Visit *The Learning Site:*
www.harcourtschool.com
See Resources for Parents and
Teachers: Books for All Learners.

BEFORE READING

Build Background Have children discuss different types of weather. Ask them what kinds of things they can do when it is rainy, windy, snowy, or sunny.

Preview/Set Purpose Have children identify the title and help them read it. Point out the author and the illustrator. Then have children look at the first few pages of the book and predict what the story will be about. Have them set a purpose for reading, such as *I want to find out what the boy and girl do on a rainy day*.

READING THE BOOK

Pages 2–3 What do you think would be the best thing to do on a windy, rainy day? Why? (Possible response: The best thing to do would be to play a game inside, so we wouldn't get wet. Accept reasonable responses. Encourage children to explain their responses.) EXPRESS PERSONAL OPINIONS

Pages 4–6 What are the boy and girl doing outside in the rain? (splashing in puddles; tasting raindrops) NOTE DETAILS, RELATE PICTURES TO TEXT

Pages 7–9 What are the girls doing outside in the snow? (making a snowman; sledding down hills) NOTE DETAILS, RELATE PICTURES TO TEXT

Pages 10–12 What is this story mostly about? (There are lots of things to do in every kind of weather.) MAIN IDEA

RESPONDING

Pantomime Reread the story aloud to the class. As you read each page, have children pantomime the actions of the children in the story. After the rereading, review the different types of weather and have children recall the outdoor activities mentioned in the story for each type of weather.

Teacher Notes

Reading Selections

BIG BOOK

DECODABLE BOOK

Applies Long Vowel /(y)o͞o/u-e

▲ Decodable Book 32
"Queen June and the Rude Duke"
"Jules and Luke"

PUPIL EDITION

Genre

Fiction

Sometimes characters in fiction are funny.

Look for:

● things a character does or says that are funny.

● other funny parts of the story.

POPPLETON
Everyday

by Cynthia Rylant
illustrated by Mark Teague

158

159

SUMMARY: *Poppleton goes shopping for a bed and makes sure that he gets the perfect one.*

"Poppleton Everyday" is available on *Audiotext 5.*

156A   Gather Around

Books for All Learners

Lesson Plans on pages 185O–185R

Goldy and the Three Bears
by Lynn Trepicchio
illustrated by Lynn Titelman

All About Pigs
by Margaret Gallo

Little Pig at the State Fair
by Margaret Gallo
illustrated by Bob McMahon

The Furniture in My House
by Kathryn E. Lewis
illustrated by Jeff Shelly

BELOW-LEVEL
- Phonics: Long Vowel: /(y)ōō/u-e
- Vocabulary: *brought, few*
- High-Frequency Words: *boy, head, read*

ON-LEVEL
- Phonics: Long Vowel: /(y)ōō/u-e
- Vocabulary: *brought, few*
- High-Frequency Words: *head, read*

ADVANCED
- Phonics: Long Vowel: /(y)ōō/u-e
- Vocabulary: *brought, few*
- High-Frequency Words: *boy, head, read*

ELL
- *Strong Picture Support*
- *Concept Vocabulary*

MULTI-LEVELED PRACTICE

Practice Book, pp. 41–47

Extra Support, pp. 42–47

Challenge, pp. 42–47

English-Language Learners, pp. 42–47

Technology

- *Phonics Express™* CD-ROM, Level B
- *Writing Express™* CD-ROM
- *Grammar Jingles™* CD, Primary
- *Reading and Language Skills Assessment* CD-ROM
- *The Learning Site:* www.harcourtschool.com

ADDITIONAL RESOURCES

Phonics Practice Book, pp. 238–239, 297–300

Spelling Practice Book, pp. 77–78

Language Handbook, pp. 134–137

Read-Aloud Literature
- Big Book of Rhymes, p. 18
- Read-Aloud Anthology, pp. 32–36

Teaching Transparencies 94–96, 107

Word Builders/Word Builder Cards

Letter Cards

Intervention Resource Kit, Lesson 32

English-Language Learners Resource Kit, Lesson 32

Day 1

Day 2

ORAL LANGUAGE
30 Minutes

• **Sharing Literature**

• **Phonemic Awareness**

Sharing Literature, 156H
Big Book: Listen and Respond

Phonemic Awareness, 156H
Phoneme Isolation; Focus on /(y)ōō/

Sharing Literature, 156P
Poem: Listen and Respond

Phonemic Awareness, 156P
Phoneme Isolation; Focus on /(y)ōō/

WORD WORK
30 Minutes

• **Phonics**

• **Spelling**

• **Vocabulary**

• **High-Frequency Words**

**Phonics,** 156I
Introduce: Long Vowel /(y)ōō/u-e **T**

Spelling, 156K
Pretest; Word Sort **T**

Vocabulary, 156K
Review: *angry, sorry* **T**

Phonics, 156Q
Review: Long Vowel /(y)ōō/u-e **T**

Spelling, 156Q
Word Building **T**

Vocabulary, 156S
Introduce: *brought, few* **T**

High-Frequency Words, 156S
Introduce: *boy, head, read* **T**

Word Power, pp. 156–157

READING
45 Minutes

• **Comprehension**

• **Fluency**

Read
Apply Phonics, 156L

DECODABLE BOOK 32
"Queen June and the Rude Duke"

Read
Read the Selection, 157A

PUPIL EDITION:
"Poppleton Everyday,"
pp. 156–181

Comprehension

 Predict Outcomes

 Use Decoding/Phonics

Daily Routines
• **Morning Message**
• **Daily Language Practice**
• **Writing Prompt**

• **Independent Reading**

Independent Reading
Books for All Learners

Independent Reading
Books for All Learners

LANGUAGE ARTS
45 Minutes

• **Writing**

 Writing Process, 156M
Prewriting

Writing Prompt
Invite children to write the title of their favorite fantasy story and a sentence telling why they like it.

 Writing Process, 181B
Drafting

Writing Prompt
Have children draw and write about a place they have been, such as the park or the zoo.

• **Grammar**

Grammar, 156N
Introduce: Using *Was* and *Were* **T**

Grammar, 181C
Review: Using *Was* and *Were*

Daily Language Practice
Spiral Review

Daily Language Practice
where is your home (Where, home?)

Daily Language Practice
We was in the see. (were, sea)

156C Gather Around   **T=tested skill**

Focus Skill
Predict Outcomes

Phonics
Long Vowel
/(y)o͞o/u-e

Focus of the Week:
- VOCABULARY WORDS: *brought, few*
- HIGH-FREQUENCY WORDS:
  boy, head, read
- COMPREHENSION: Predict Outcomes
- WRITING PROCESS: A Fantasy Story

Day 3

Sharing Literature, 181E
Rhyme: Listen and Respond

Phonemic Awareness, 181E
Phoneme Blending; Focus on /(y)o͞o/

Phonics, 181F
Review: Long Vowel /(y)o͞o/u-e **T**

Spelling, 181H
State the Generalization **T**

Vocabulary, 181I
Review: *brought, few* **T**

High-Frequency Words, 181I
Review: *boy, head, read* **T**

Read
Rereading for Fluency, 181J

Making Connections,
182–183

Apply Phonics, 181G
DECODABLE BOOK 32
"Jules and Luke"

🔵 **Independent Reading**
Books for All Learners

✏️ **Writing Process,** 183A
Responding and Revising

Writing Prompt
Have children interview a friend about a place. Ask them to write questions and answers.

Grammar, 183B
Review: Using *Was* and *Were*

Daily Language Practice
Where was you and Bob (were, Bob?)

Day 4

Sharing Literature, 183D
Poem: Build Concept Vocabulary

Phonemic Awareness, 183D
Phoneme Addition; Focus on /(y)o͞o/
and /ā/

Phonics, 183E
Word Building **T**

Spelling, 185A
Review **T**

Vocabulary, 185B
Review: *brought, few* **T**

High-Frequency Words, 185B
Review: *boy, head, read* **T**

Read
Reread the Selection, 185B

🔵 **Independent Reading**
Books for All Learners

✏️ **Writing Process,** 185C
Proofreading

Writing Prompt
Have children write about a place they want to visit and explain why they want to go there.

Grammar, 185D
Review: Using *Was* and *Were*

Daily Language Practice
I were looking at a sel. (was, seal)

Day 5

Sharing Literature, 185F
Big Book: Develop Listening Comprehension

Phonemic Awareness, 185F
Phoneme Isolation; Focus on Contractions, Final /v/, /d/, /r/

Phonics, 185G
Contractions 've, 'd, 're **T**
Inflections -ed, -ing **T**

Spelling, 185I
Posttest; Writing Application **T**

Vocabulary, 185J
Review: *brought, few* **T**

High-Frequency Words, 185J
Review: *boy, head, read* **T**

Read
Rereading for Fluency, 185K

Self-Selected Reading, 185L

🔵 **Independent Reading**
Books for All Learners

✏️ **Writing Process,** 185M
Publishing

Self-Selected Writing
Have children write in their journal about a topic of their choice.

Grammar, 185N
Review: Using *Was* and *Were*

Daily Language Practice
Id like to visit Grandma, to. (I'd, too)

Cross-Curricular Centers

MATH CENTER

20 Minutes

How Many Pigs?

Show children the pig figures or blocks and a box top, identifying them as pigs and a bed. Tell children to guess how many pigs will fit in the bed, with none on top of any others. Have them discuss their ideas with a group; then have each child write an answer on a piece of paper. When all group members have guessed, have them put the pigs into the container, count to check their guesses, and write down the actual number. Children can repeat this activity with different sizes of box tops.

Materials

- several small plastic pig figures or rectangular blocks
- different sizes of box tops or other shallow rectangular containers
- paper and pencils

SCIENCE CENTER

30 Minutes

Home for Pig

Have pairs of children draw or make a model of a group of pigs in their home environment, such as a farm. Then have children make a list of the things pigs need to survive—water, food, and shelter.

Materials

- construction paper
- crayons or markers
- paper and pencils

SOCIAL STUDIES CENTER

40 Minutes

City Life or Farm Life

Have children work in pairs to create a poster that compares two different ways of life—life in the city and life on a farm. Tell children to think about the following things as they draw: where people live, what they do for work, how they get to work, and how they dress.

Materials

- poster board
- crayons or markers

LETTER AND WORD CENTER

Review Short *i*

Write the word *pig* on a transparency and place it on an overhead projector. Have children use *Word Builder Cards* to form the word and read it aloud. Have them work in pairs to change the letters to build and read other words, such as *big, wig, win, tin,* and other short *i* words.

20 Minutes

Materials
- overhead projector
- overhead transparency
- *Word Builder Cards*

COMPUTER CENTER

Write Fantasy Stories

Have children use a word processing program to write another fantasy story in addition to the one they create for this week's Writing Process activity. Children may want to write about another adventure with Poppleton the pig. Have children cut and paste clip art or use a draw or paint program to create the scenes.

30 Minutes

Materials
- computer
- word processing program
- clip art or software for creating pictures

HOMEWORK FOR THE WEEK

The Homework Copying Master provides activities to complete for each day of the week.

Visit *The Learning Site:* www.harcourtschool.com

See Resources for Parents and Teachers: Homework Helper.

Homework, page T44 ▶

School–Home Connection

Your child has been reading "At Home Around the World." This nonfiction selection tells about different kinds of houses in different parts of the world.
I have tried some of the activities.

Student: _____
Family Member: _____
Comments/Suggestions: _____

You may want to do some of these activities with your child.

Words, Words, Words
- Have your child cut out the word cards and read each word.
- Ask your child which two words rhyme. (*hold* and *old*) Together, think of other words that rhyme with *old*.
- Ask your child to find and read the cards with words that mean the opposite of *below, cool, same,* and *new.* (*above, warm, different,* and *old*)

Home Sweet Home
Ask your child to tell you about some of the houses in the story. Together, build a model of one kind of house. For example, you could use craft sticks (or sticks) and glue to make a log cabin, or toothpicks and scraps of cloth to make a tent.

 TIME TO READ Encourage your child to read for at least 30 minutes outside of class each day.

Visit *The Learning Site!* www.harcourtschool.com
See Resources for Parents and Teachers: Homework Helper

above
different
hold
old
warm
water
years

Day at a Glance
Day 1

Sharing Literature
Big Book: *To Market, To Market*

Phonemic Awareness
Phoneme Isolation; Focus on /(y)o͞o/

Phonics
INTRODUCE: Long Vowel /(y)o͞o/u-e

Spelling
Pretest; Word Sort

Vocabulary
REVIEW: *angry, sorry*

Reading
Decodable Book 32
"Queen June and the Rude Duke"

Read

Independent Writing 🖉
Writing Process: Prewriting

Grammar
INTRODUCE: Using *Was* and *Were*

WARM UP

MORNING MESSAGE

Good Morning!

Today is _____.

We like going to different places.

Places where I have gone are _____.

I saw _____ when I was at _____.

Introduce the Day

Tell children that today they will listen again to a story called *To Market, To Market*. Guide them in generating a message about different places. Ask:

- **Where are some places you have been?**
- **What did you do while you were there?**

As you write the message, have volunteers write previously taught letters, words, and/or punctuation to reinforce skills. For instance, ask a volunteer to write the letter *c* in *places*. Recall with children that the letter *c* sometimes stands for the /s/ sound.

Read the Message

Read the message. Use the message to focus on selected skills that have been previously taught.

Apply Skills

Phonics Ask a volunteer to point to two words that contain *wh. (where, when)* Review the /hw/ sound and have children point to other words displayed in the classroom with /hw/. Read these words with children while emphasizing the /hw/ sound.

High-Frequency Words Ask volunteers to point to and read known high-frequency words such as *are, different, gone, have, saw, to, when,* and *where*.

Sharing Literature

LISTEN AND RESPOND

Reread the Big Book Read aloud the *Big Book To Market, To Market* to children. Encourage children to join in.

Respond to Literature After reading, have children name the items purchased at the market. Make a list on the board or on chart paper. Then ask children to name items they usually get at the market and add them to the list.

▲ **Big Book**

Phonemic Awareness

PHONEME ISOLATION

Words from the Big Book Remind children of the goat in *To Market, To Market*. Say *goat*, emphasizing the final phoneme /t/. Ask what sound is at the end of the word. (/t/) Repeat the activity. Use animals from the big book and other animal names.

pig (/g/)   **hen** (/n/)   **trout** (/t/)   **dog** (/g/)
duck (/k/)   **cat** (/t/)   **goose** (/s/)   **sheep** (/p/)

FOCUS ON /(y)o͞o/

Identify Middle Phonemes Ask children to say the word *huge* slowly and tell what sound is heard in the middle. (/(y)o͞o/) Continue with the following words:

dune (/(y)o͞o/)   **prune** (/o͞o/)
mule (/(y)o͞o/)   **cute** (/(y)o͞o/)
rule (/o͞o/)   **tune** (/(y)o͞o/)

BELOW-LEVEL

Slowly elongate the vowel sound as you say each word to enable children to hear the vowel sound more easily. For example, say *huuuge.*

ADVANCED

Challenge children to segment /(y)o͞o/ words into all the component sounds. For example, have them say /h/ /(y)o͞o/ /j/.

OBJECTIVES

- *To generate the long vowel sound of u*
- *To build words using known letters and sounds*
- *To read simple, regular words*

SKILL TRACE

	/(y)o͞o/*u-e*
INTRODUCE	**156I–156L**
Reteach	S34–S35, T10
Review	156Q–156R, 181F–181G
Review	183E, 184–185
T Test	Bk 1-5
Maintain	Bk 2-1

teaching tip

Build Vocabulary As you model blending the word *cube*, explain to children that a cube is a three-dimensional square. Hold up an item that has a cube shape, such as a letter block.

15 Minutes

Materials

- overhead projector
- plastic letters

Phonics and Spelling
Long Vowel /(y)o͞o/*u-e*

✔ *Introduce*

TEACH/MODEL

Introduce /(y)o͞o/*u-e* Display *Alphabet Card Uu* and say the letter name. Tell children that the letter *u* can stand for the sound /(y)o͞o/, the long vowel sound of *u* in words such as *use* and *unicorn*.

Hold up *Letter Card u* and say /o͞o/. Tell children that the letter *u* can also stand for the sound /o͞o/, the long vowel sound of u in the middle of words such as *rude* and *tune*. Have children repeat the sound several times as you touch the card.

WORD BLENDING

b	c	e	g	h	l	r	s	t	u

Words with /(y)o͞o/*u-e* Blend and read the words *tube, cube, cute*. As you demonstrate each step using a pocket chart and *Letter Cards*, have children repeat after you using *Word Builders* and *Word Builder Cards*.

Follow the same procedure for: *use, rule, huge*.

Phonics CENTER

Word Building

Write the word *mule* on a transparency and place it on an overhead projector. Have children use plastic letters to form the word and read it aloud. Have them change letters to build and read other words, such as *flute, muse, use, rule,* and other long *u* words.

WORD BUILDING

Build Spelling Words Place the letter *t* in a pocket chart. Have children do the same with their *Word Builders* and *Word Builder Cards*. Repeat with the letters *u, b,* and *e*. Model how to blend the word *tube*. Slide your hand under the letters as you slowly elongate the sounds—/tt͞oobb/. Then read the word naturally—*tube*. Have children do the same.

| t | u | b | e |

Have children build and read new words by telling them:

■ Change the *t* to *c*. What word did you make?

| c | u | b | e |

■ Change the *b* to *t*. What word did you make?

| c | u | t | e |

■ Change the *t* to *s*. Take away the *c*. What word did you make?

| u | s | e |

■ Change the *s* to *l*. Add an *r* in front of the *u*. What word did you make?

| r | u | l | e |

■ Change the *r* to *h*. Change the *l* to *g*. What word did you make?

| h | u | g | e |

 Dictate Long Vowel /(y)͞oo/*u-e* Words Dictate the words *cube* and *huge* and have children write them in their journal. Suggest that they either draw a picture or write about each word.

5-DAY PHONICS/SPELLING

DAY 1	Introduce /(y)͞oo/*u-e*
DAY 2	Word Building with /(y)͞oo/*u-e*
DAY 3	Word Building with /(y)͞oo/*u-e*
DAY 4	Word Building with /(y)͞oo/*u-e*, /ā/*a-e*
DAY 5	Contractions *'ve, 'd, 're* Inflections *-ed, -ing*

BELOW-LEVEL

Help children by building words that rhyme so that only the first letter changes each time: *use, fuse; mule, rule.*

Phonics Resources

 ***Phonics Express™* CD-ROM, Level B** Sparkle/Route 2/Fire Station

Phonics Practice Book, pp. 238–239

Spelling Words

1. **tube**
2. **cube**
3. **cute**
4. **use**
5. **rule**
6. **huge**
7. **page**
8. **fudge**
9. **angry**
10. **sorry**

Phonics and Spelling

5-DAY SPELLING	
DAY 1	**Pretest; Word Sort**
DAY 2	Word Building
DAY 3	State the Generalization
DAY 4	Review
DAY 5	Posttest; Writing Application

INTRODUCE THE WORDS

Pretest Read aloud the first word and the Dictation Sentence. Repeat the word as children write it. Write the correct spelling on the board and have children circle the word if they spelled it correctly and write it correctly if they did not. Repeat for words 2–10.

1. **tube** We need a new **tube** of toothpaste.
2. **cube** She folded the paper into a **cube**.
3. **cute** That dog has a **cute** face.
4. **use** How do you **use** that tool?
5. **rule** The **rule** is "No talking."
6. **huge** That house is **huge**!

Review

7. **page** Emma turned the **page** of the book.
8. **fudge** Mom made **fudge** today.

Vocabulary

9. **angry** Tom was very **angry** with his friend Joe.
10. **sorry** Joe told Tom he was **sorry**.

Word Sort Place the numerals *3*, *4*, and *5* at the top of a pocket chart. Write each Spelling Word on an index card. Display the cards and ask "Which word is made of three letters? Which words are made of four letters? Which words are made of five letters?" Place the words in the correct columns as children direct. Have children read the words aloud.

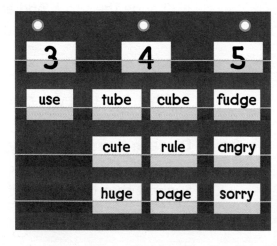

3	4	5
use	tube	cube	fudge
	cute	rule	angry
	huge	page	sorry

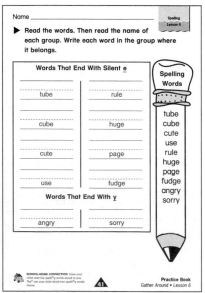

Name _____

▶ Read the words. Then read the name of each group. Write each word in the group where it belongs.

Words That End With Silent _e_

tube	rule
cube	huge
cute	page
use	fudge

Words That End With _y_

| angry | sorry |

Spelling Words
tube
cube
cute
use
rule
huge
page
fudge
angry
sorry

▲ Practice Book, p. 41

Apply Phonics

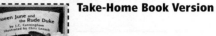

APPLY /(y)o͞o/u-e

Write the following sentences on the board or chart paper. Have children read the first sentence as you track the print. Frame the words *June* and *flute* and have children read them. Continue with the other sentences.

June learned to play the **flute**.
Duke Bruce had bad manners.
Use the paste in the **tube**.

Have children read "Queen June and the Rude Duke" in *Decodable Book 32.*

▲ **Decodable Book 32**
"Queen June and the Rude Duke"

School-Home Connection

Take-Home Book Version

◄ Decodable Books Take-Home Version

Managing Small Groups

Read the *Decodable Book* with small groups of children. While you work with small groups, have other children do the following:

- **Self-Selected Reading**
- **Practice Pages**
- **Cross-Curricular Centers**
- **Journal Writing**

Use the suggested Classroom Management outline on page 7C for the whole-group/small-group schedule.

ONGOING ASSESSMENT

Note how well children
- read sentences without modeling.
- decode words in "Queen June and the Rude Duke."
- complete long vowel /(y)o͞o/u-e practice pages.

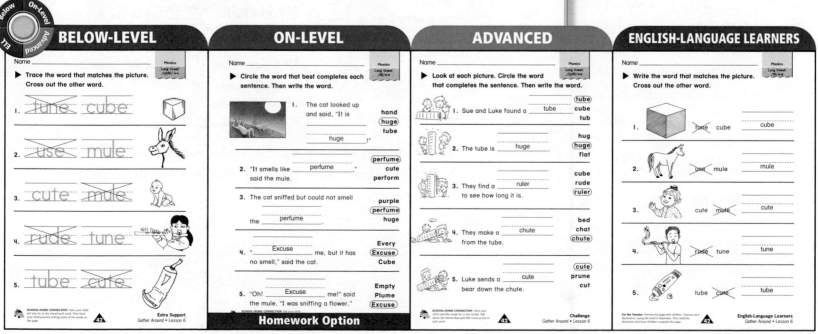

▲ Extra Support, p. 42   ▲ Practice, p. 42   ▲ Challenge, p. 42   ▲ ELL, p. 42

Writing Process
Fantasy Story

PREWRITING

Explore the Theme Tell children that they are going to write a fantasy story about themselves and a make-believe character as they explore a special place.

Discuss Elements of Fantasy Stories Ask children to think about a fantasy story they have read, such as "Frog and Toad All Year." Discuss how fantasy stories are different from stories about things that could really happen.

Fantasy Stories

• **have make-believe characters.**

• **have events that don't happen in real life.**

Create a Concept Map Tell children that they will write about an imaginary trip they take with a favorite toy or animal character. Have them begin by closing their eyes as you ask these questions:

• **Where do you go on your trip?**

• **Who is with you as you go exploring?**

• **What do you see there?**

• **What do you do?**

Record children's ideas on chart paper.

Tell children that they will use some ideas from the concept map to write a story. Save the map for Drafting on page 18 IB.

Day 1: Prewrite
Work together to create a concept map about a pretend trip.

Day 2: Draft
Have children complete sentence frames to write a fantasy story.

Day 3: Respond and Revise
Have children add a sentence to their story telling more details about their adventures.

Day 4: Proofread
Have children proofread their story.

Day 5: Publish
Have children make and illustrate a final copy of their fantasy story.

Writing Prompt Invite children to write the title of their favorite fantasy story and write a sentence telling why they like it.

5-DAY GRAMMAR	
DAY 1	Introduce Using *Was* and *Were*
DAY 2	Generate Sentences
DAY 3	Using *Was* and *Were*
DAY 4	Write Poem Frames
DAY 5	Identify *Was* and *Were*

Day 1

Grammar

Using Was *and* Were

TEACH/MODEL

Introduce Using *Was* and *Were* Write the following sentences on the board.

> Mom was upset.
>
> The animals were all over her house!

Ask a volunteer to read the first sentence. Ask children to tell the naming part of this sentence. (Mom) Ask how many people the sentence is about. (one) Frame the word *was*. Tell children that when a sentence tells about something that happened in the past and is about one person, the word *was* is used.

Ask a volunteer to read the second sentence. Ask children to tell the naming part of this sentence. (The animals) Ask how many animals the sentence is about. (more than one) Frame the word *were*. Tell children that when a sentence tells about more than one thing in the past, the word *were* is used.

PRACTICE/APPLY

Display *Teaching Transparency 94* Model using *was* and *were* to tell about the scene, such as *The dog and the cat were in the yard. The cat was in a tree.* Have children say sentences about the scene. List them on the board.

WRAP UP Tell a Story Game

Teach the Game Help children recall some of the fantasy stories they have read. Seat children in a circle and tell them that they will make up a story during the Tell a Story Game. Ask a volunteer to begin the story by completing the statement *Once upon a time there was a ____.* Moving around the circle, have children take turns adding to the story.

S.S.R. Have children read silently from a book of their choice. See page 185L for tips on helping children choose books.

OBJECTIVE

To understand the past-tense forms of be; to use correct subject-verb agreement

SKILL TRACE

USING *WAS* AND *WERE*	
INTRODUCE	156N
Review	181C, 183B, 185D, 185N

▼ **Teaching Transparency 94**

USING *WAS* AND *WERE*

"Poppleton Everyday"
Gather Around, Volume 1-5   94   Grammar: Using *Was* and *Were*
Harcourt

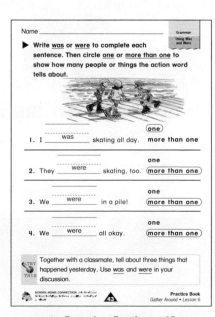

▲ **Practice Book, p. 43**

Sharing Literature
Poem: "This Little Pig Went to Market"

Phonemic Awareness
Phoneme Isolation; Focus on /(y)o͞o/

Phonics
REVIEW: Long Vowel /(y)o͞o/u-e

Spelling
Word Building

High-Frequency Words
INTRODUCE: *boy, head, read* (past tense)

Vocabulary
INTRODUCE: *brought, few*

Reading
Pupil Edition
"Poppleton Everyday,"
pp. 156–181

Independent Writing
Writing Process: Drafting

Grammar
REVIEW: Using *Was* and *Were*

WARM UP — MORNING MESSAGE

Good Morning!

Today is _____.

Another name for a market is a _____.

You can buy _____ at a market.

Shopping is fun because _____.

Introduce the Day
Tell children that today they will listen to a poem and read a story about pigs who go shopping. Guide children in writing a message about shopping at a market. Ask:

• **What is another name for a market?**

• **What can you buy at a market?**

As you write the message, have volunteers write previously taught letters, words, and/or punctuation to reinforce skills. For instance, begin the last sentence by writing *Shop*. Invite a volunteer to double the *p* and add *-ing* to form *Shopping*.

Read the Message
Read the message. Use the message to focus on selected skills that have been previously taught.

Apply Skills

Concept Vocabulary Ask a volunteer to point to the word that names a place. (market) Have volunteers name places where they like to go. (school, park, mall, restaurant) List the place names on the board and read the completed list. Ask children what is the same about all these words. (They all name places.)

Grammar/Mechanics Some of the places that children mention might be proper nouns. Ask a volunteer to point to the proper nouns and ask why those words are capitalized.

Sharing Literature

LISTEN AND RESPOND

Connect to Prior Knowledge Ask children to recall some nursery rhymes that they heard when they were younger. Ask if they recall the one about a pig that goes to the market. Invite children to chime in as you read the rhyme.

Choral Reading Write the following words each on a separate card: *market, home, roast beef, none, Wee-wee-wee.* Invite five volunteers to stand and hold the cards. Lead the group in saying *This little pig.* Then point to the first volunteer, who says *went to market.* Continue reading the rhyme in this manner.

Phonemic Awareness

PHONEME ISOLATION

Words from "This Little Pig Went to Market" Remind children that they heard the word *pig* in the rhyme. Repeat the word slowly and remind children that the first sound in *pig* is /p/. Say the following words and ask children to tell which sound they hear first in each word.

little (/l/)   **market** (/m/)   **roast** (/r/)
went (/w/)   **home** (/h/)   **beef** (/b/)

FOCUS ON /(y)o͞o/

Phoneme Blending Tell children that you are going to say some words very slowly and they will blend the words together. Model by segmenting the word *cute* into phonemes (/k/ /(y)o͞o/ /t/). Then say the word naturally—*cute.* Segment the following words, having children blend the sounds to say the words:

/f/ /(y)o͞o/ /z/ (fuse)   /d/ /(y)o͞o/ /k/ (duke)
/h/ /(y)o͞o/ /j/ (huge)   /(y)o͞o/ /z/ (use)
/d/ /(y)o͞o/ /n/ (dune)   /k/ /(y)o͞o/ /b/ (cube)

Ask children how all the words are alike. (They all have the /(y)o͞o/ sound.)

This Little Pig Went to Market

This little pig went to market,

This little pig stayed home,

This little pig had roast beef,

This little pig had none,

And this little pig cried:

"Wee-wee-wee-wee-wee-wee,"

All the way home!

Mother Goose

REACHING ALL LEARNERS

Diagnostic Check: Phonemic Awareness

If... children cannot correctly identify the sound /(y)o͞o/ in words ...

Then... point to a child and say *you.* Have children say the word *you* several times. Explain that the vowel sound in *fuse* and *cute* is exactly the same as in the word *you.*

ADDITIONAL SUPPORT ACTIVITIES

BELOW-LEVEL Reteach, p. S32

ADVANCED Extend, p. S33

ENGLISH-LANGUAGE LEARNERS Reteach, p. S33

OBJECTIVES

• To blend sounds into words

• To read and write Spelling Words

SKILL TRACE

/(y)o͞o/u-e	
Introduce	156I–156L
Reteach	S34–S35, T10
REVIEW	**156Q–156R, 181F–181G**
Review	183E, 184–185
T Test	Bk 1-5
Maintain	Bk 2-1

Spelling Words

1. **tube**
2. **cube**
3. **cute**
4. **use**
5. **rule**
6. **huge**
7. **page**
8. **fudge**
9. **angry**
10. **sorry**

5-DAY SPELLING	
DAY 1	Pretest; Word Sort
DAY 2	**Word Building**
DAY 3	State the Generalization
DAY 4	Review
DAY 5	Posttest; Writing Application

Phonics and Spelling
Long Vowel /(y)o͞o/u-e

✔ *Review*

WORD BUILDING

Blend and Read a Spelling Word
Place *Letter Cards t, u, b, e* in a pocket chart. Ask children to name the letters as you place them in the chart. Slide your hand under the letters as you blend the sounds /tto͞obb/. Have children repeat after you. Then read the word naturally—*tube*, and have children do the same.

Build Spelling Words Ask children which letter you should change to make *tube* become *cube*. (change *t* to *c*) After you make the change, have children read the new word. Continue building the Spelling Words shown in this manner and having children read them.

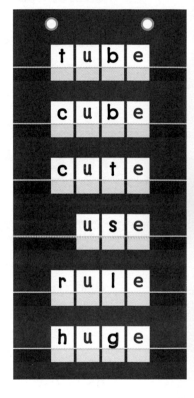

BELOW-LEVEL

Have children use *Word Builders* and *Word Builder Cards* to construct each Spelling Word as you do. After building each word, have children copy the word onto a piece of paper.

ENGLISH-LANGUAGE LEARNERS

After building each word, have children use it in a sentence. Record their sentences, underlining the Spelling Word in each. Have children pantomime any actions that are described.

Apply Phonics

READ WORDS IN CONTEXT

Write the following sentences on the board or on chart paper and have children read them aloud.

> The raft they **use** is **cute**.
>
> It is in the shape of a **cube**.
>
> We will follow the **rule** to be safe.
>
> I read each rule on the **page**.
>
> It's better to be safe than **sorry**.
>
> I will swim in the **huge tube**.
>
> Then I plan to eat some **fudge**.
>
> I will be **angry** if it's all gone.

Dictate Words Dictate several words from the pocket chart, and have children write the words on a dry-erase board or in their journal.

tube
cube
cute
use
rule
huge

5-DAY PHONICS/SPELLING

DAY 1	Introduce /(y)o͞o/u-e
DAY 2	**Word Building with /(y)o͞o/u-e**
DAY 3	Word Building with /(y)o͞o/u-e
DAY 4	Word Building with /(y)o͞o/u-e, /ā/a-e
DAY 5	Contractions 've, 'd, 're Inflections -ed, -ing

Phonics Resources

Phonics Express™ CD-ROM, **Level B** Sparkle/Route 2/ Harbor

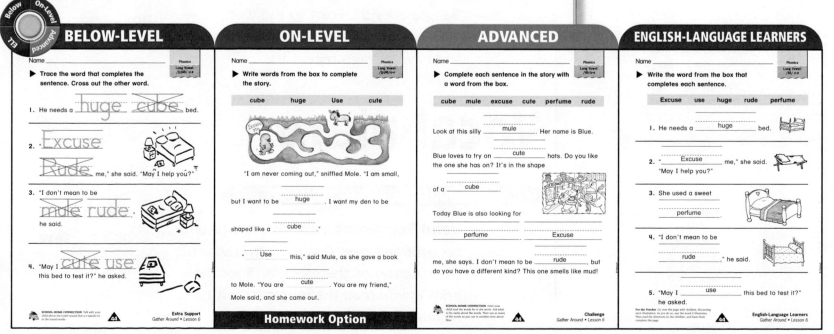

▲ Extra Support, p. 44   ▲ Practice, p. 44   ▲ Challenge, p. 44   ▲ ELL, p. 44

High-Frequency Words

boy	a young man
head	top part of body
read	understood words by looking

Vocabulary

brought	did bring
few	not many

Building Background

TALK ABOUT BEDS

Make a Bed Chart Ask children what kind of bed a baby sleeps in. (a crib) Then ask them why they don't sleep in cribs now. (Possible responses: I'm too big; I'm not a baby anymore.) Point out that in the story they will read, a pig that has gotten too big for his bed must buy a new one. Encourage children to talk about what kind of bed would be just right for them. Record children's responses on a chart under the heading *A Bed Just Right for Me.*

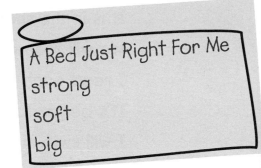

A Bed Just Right For Me
strong
soft
big

Discuss Story Words Write the words *crumbs, saleslady, enormous, decided,* and *certainly* on the board. Point to each word and read it aloud.

High-Frequency Words

IDENTIFY WORDS

Read Sentences Display *Teaching Transparency 95*. Point to the words *boy, head,* and *read*. Say each word and have children repeat it.

> **INTRODUCE**
>
> **High-Frequency Words**
> boy   read
> head

Vocabulary

INTRODUCE WORDS IN CONTEXT

Read Sentences Point to the words *brought* and *few*. Discuss with children the meaning of these words. Track the print as you read the sentences with children. Call on volunteers to reread each sentence.

> **INTRODUCE**
>
> **Vocabulary**
> brought   few

▼ **Teaching Transparency 95**

HIGH-FREQUENCY WORDS
boy   head   read

VOCABULARY WORDS
brought   few

The <u>boy</u> worked hard.
He <u>brought</u> a bag of apples.
A <u>few</u> had fallen on the ground.
A few had fallen on his <u>head</u>.
His head hurt a little bit.
At last the boy went home.
He <u>read</u> a book until Mom brought apple pie.

"Poppleton Everyday"
Gather Around, Volume 1-5   95   High-Frequency Words/Vocabulary
                                                 Harcourt

Word Power

Pages 156–157 Have children read aloud the Words to Remember. Then have children read the sentences aloud. Ask them to point to the Words to Remember in the sentences.

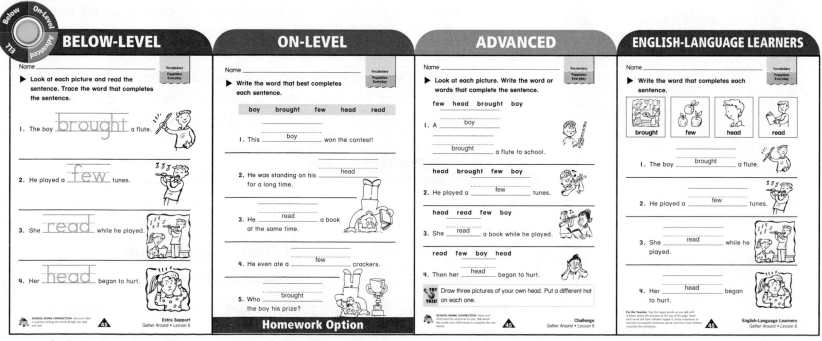

▲ Extra Support, p. 45　　▲ Practice, p. 45　　▲ Challenge, p. 45　　▲ ELL, p. 45

■ **Phonics**

Long Vowel /(y)o͞o/u-e

■ **High-Frequency Words**

INTRODUCE: *boy, head, read*
(past tense)

■ **Vocabulary**

INTRODUCE: *brought, few*

■ **Decodable Words**

See the list on pages T50–T51.

■ **Comprehension**

(Focus Skill) Predict Outcomes

(Focus Strategy) Use Decoding/Phonics

Strategies Good Readers Use

To Recognize Words

• **Use Decoding/Phonics** (Focus Strategy)

• Look for Word Bits and Parts

To Gain Meaning

• Self-Correct

• Read Ahead

• Reread

• Reread Aloud

• Use Picture Clues to Confirm Meaning

• Make and Confirm Predictions

• Sequence Events/Summarize

• Create Mental Images

• Make Inferences

READING

Prereading Strategies

PREPARING TO READ

Preview/Predict Discuss pages 158–159. Ask children to read aloud the title and discuss what they know about pigs. Have children follow along as you read the names of the author and the illustrator. Talk about the picture on pages 160–161 and what might happen in the story.

Set Purpose Help children set a purpose for reading. If necessary, suggest that they read to find out how Poppleton chooses his new bed.

COMPREHENSION SKILL

(Focus Skill) **Predict Outcomes** Explain to children that predicting outcomes means making a guess about how things might turn out or what things might happen next in a story. Have children discuss the outcomes of other stories they have read. Ask them to think about what might happen to Poppleton when he goes to buy a new bed.

COMPREHENSION STRATEGY

(Focus Strategy) **Use Decoding/Phonics** Explain to children that when they see a word they do not know, they can use what they know about letters and sounds to help them read the word. Write the word *show* on the board. Ask children what they could do if they did not know how to read this word. (Possible response: I could remember that *sh* stands for the /sh/ sound. The letters *ow* sometimes stand for the sound /ou/, but /shou/ doesn't make sense. *Ow* often stands for the long sound of *o*. I could then blend the sounds /sh/ and /ō/ together to read the word *show*.)

Managing Small Groups

Read "Poppleton Everyday" with small groups of children. While you work with small groups, have other children do the following:

• **Self-Selected Reading**

• **Cross-Curricular Centers**

• **Practice Pages**

• **Journal Writing**

Use the suggested Classroom Management outline on page 7C for the whole-group/small-group schedule.

CYNTHIA RYLANT
POPPLETON
Everyday
by MARK TEAGUE

Award-
Winning
Author and
Illustrator

Genre

Fiction

Sometimes characters in fiction are funny.

Look for:

• things a character does or says that are funny.

• other funny parts of the story.

POPPLETON
Everyday

by Cynthia Rylant
illustrated by Mark Teague

158

159

Guided Comprehension

Pages 158–159 Have children reread the title and review their predictions about how Poppleton chooses a bed or about what happens to him when he goes to buy the bed.

GENRE: Fiction

Read aloud the information about fiction on page 158. Tell children that fiction sometimes includes

• characters that do and say funny things.

• other funny things that happen.

BELOW-LEVEL	ON-LEVEL	ADVANCED	ENGLISH-LANGUAGE LEARNERS
After page 162, ask: *Where is Poppleton going?* Work with children to answer the question and to predict what might happen to Poppleton. Have children read pages 163–165. Then read the rest of the story aloud, tracking the print. SMALL GROUP	As children read the selection, use the Guided Comprehension questions to direct their reading. WHOLE GROUP/SMALL GROUP	Have children share their predictions about the story and then read the story silently. After reading, have children talk about whether or not their predictions were correct. SMALL GROUP/ INDEPENDENT	Use pictures of a pig, bed, salesperson, books, and bed store to preview the story concepts with children. Then have children read the story. Use the pictures to show the meaning of various sentences from the story. SMALL GROUP
ADDITIONAL SUPPORT See Intervention Resource Kit, Lesson 32. *Intervention Teacher's Guide pp. 312–321*			**ADDITIONAL SUPPORT** See English-Language Learners Resource Kit, Lesson 32. *English-Language Learners Teacher's Guide pp. 188–189*

THE NEW BED

One day Poppleton decided
to buy a new bed.
He liked his old bed.
But he'd had it since he was a boy.
Now he wanted a grown-up bed.

160

161

Guided Comprehension

Pages 160–161 Tell children that *Poppleton Everyday* is a chapter book. Ask children to explain what a chapter book is. Then have children locate the words *The New Bed* at the top of page 160, and ask what these words are. (the chapter title) Have children look at the illustrations and then read to find out about Poppleton.

① **USE PICTURE CLUES TO CONFIRM MEANING** **What can you tell about Poppleton by looking at his room?** (Possible response: Clothing and food are all over the room, which shows that Poppleton is not very neat.)

② (Focus Skill) **PREDICT OUTCOMES** **What will Poppleton do next? How do you know?** (Possible response: Since the last sentence says he wants a "grown-up bed," he will go out and look for a new bed.)

REACHING ALL LEARNERS

Diagnostic Check: High-Frequency Words

If... children cannot recognize and read the word *boy* and other high-frequency words ...

Then... write a sentence with the words in context, such as *Jen is a girl, and Luke is a boy*. Help children read the sentence and then find and read the story sentence with the same word.

ADDITIONAL SUPPORT ACTIVITIES

BELOW-LEVEL	Reteach, p. S36
ADVANCED	Extend, p. S37
ENGLISH-LANGUAGE LEARNERS	Reteach, p. S37

So Poppleton went to the bed store.

162

"Do you have a bed just right for a pig?"
he asked the saleslady.
"Hmmm," she said, looking Poppleton over.
"Right this way."

163

Guided Comprehension

Pages 162–163 Have children look at the illustrations and discuss what is happening. Then have them read to confirm their predictions and find out what happens to Poppleton at the bed store.

1 **DRAW CONCLUSIONS** What does *looking Poppleton over* mean? (Possible response: The saleslady is looking at Poppleton to figure out what kind and size of bed he will need.)

2 **MAKE JUDGMENTS** What kind of bed do you think Poppleton needs? Why do you think so? (Possible response: He probably needs a big bed because he is a big pig.)

Strategies
Good Readers Use

Focus Strategy **Use Decoding/Phonics**

Say the word *no*, and ask children to identify its vowel sound. (/ō/) Then have children look at pages 162–163 to locate other words in which *o* stands for the /ō/ sound. *(So, over)* Have children use what they know about letters and sounds to read these words.

Poppleton followed the saleslady to the biggest bed in the store.

It was vast! It was enormous!
"It's just my size!" said Poppleton.

164

165

Guided Comprehension

Pages 164–165 Have children look at the illustrations and read to find out about the bed that the saleslady shows Poppleton.

1 **ILLUSTRATOR'S CRAFT** Why do you think the artist made the bed the largest thing in these pictures? (Possible responses: to show how huge the bed is; to match the text "the biggest bed in the store")

2 **IDENTIFY WITH CHARACTERS** Do you think Poppleton likes this bed? How do you know? (Possible response: Yes, he says that the bed is just his size; he looks happy in the picture.)

ENGLISH-LANGUAGE LEARNERS

Point to the words *vast* and *enormous* on page 165. Explain that both of these words mean *very big*. Display pictures of enormous things, such as a mountain or an elephant. Have children name other things that are vast or enormous. Children can practice using the words in sentences.

164–165 Gather Around

He climbed on to test the bed.

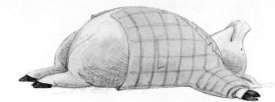

He lay on his back.

He lay on his side.

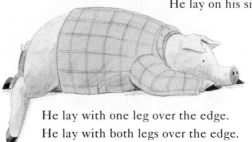

He lay with one leg over the edge.
He lay with both legs over the edge.

166

He lay on his head with his bottom in the air.

"How many different ways do you sleep?" asked the saleslady.
"About twenty," said Poppleton.

167

Guided Comprehension

Pages 166–167 Have children look at the illustrations and discuss what is happening. Then have them read to find out about the different ways Poppleton sleeps.

1 **NOTE DETAILS** In how many different ways does Poppleton sleep? (about 20)

2 **DRAW CONCLUSIONS** Why does Poppleton lie in so many different ways on the bed? (Possible response: He wants to see if the bed is comfortable in some of the different ways he sleeps.)

3 (Focus Strategy) **USE DECODING/PHONICS** How did using sounds for letters help you read the word *edge*? (Possible response: The letters *dge* can stand for the /j/ sound—the sound at the end of the word *edge*.)

MATH

Number Sense Have children write down how many different ways Poppleton lies on the bed in the bed store. (5) Then have them write down how many different ways he sleeps. (20) Tell children to write a number problem, such as:

If Poppleton sleeps in 20 different ways, but he only tests the bed in 5 ways, how many more ways can Poppleton lie on the bed to test it? (15)

20 – 5 = 15

"Do you have any books?" he asked.
The saleslady brought Poppleton a book.

168

Poppleton propped up some pillows
and read a few pages.
The saleslady looked at her watch.
"Do you want to buy the bed?"
she asked Poppleton.
"I don't know yet," said Poppleton.
"Do you have any crackers?"

169

Guided Comprehension

Pages 168–169 Have children read to find out another way in which Poppleton tests the bed.

1 **SPECULATE** **Why is Poppleton reading a book in bed?** (Possible response: He usually reads in bed, so he wants to see what it is like to read in the new bed.)

2 **INTERPRET CHARACTER'S MOTIVATIONS** **Why does Poppleton want crackers?** (Possible response: He often eats in bed and wants to try eating in the new bed.)

3 **(Focus Strategy)** **USE DECODING/PHONICS** **How did using what you know about letters and sounds help you read the words *asked* and *propped*?** (Possible responses: Both words have the ending -*ed*; I read the word without the ending and then tried the sound for that ending that sounded right – /t/.)

168–169 Gather Around

REACHING ALL LEARNERS

Diagnostic Check: Vocabulary

If... children cannot recognize and read the vocabulary words *brought* and *few* ...

Then... write each word on a separate sheet of construction paper. Write large so that the word fills the entire page. Have children trace the word with their index finger several times and say the word to themselves.

ADDITIONAL SUPPORT ACTIVITIES

BELOW-LEVEL Reteach, p. S36

ADVANCED Extend, p. S37

ENGLISH-LANGUAGE LEARNERS Reteach, p.S37

The saleslady brought Poppleton
some crackers.
He got crumbs everywhere.
"Do you want the bed?"
asked the saleslady.

170

"I don't know yet," said Poppleton.
"Do you have a TV?"
The saleslady brought Poppleton a TV.
He watched a game show.

171

Guided Comprehension

Pages 170–171 Have children read to find out how the saleslady helps Poppleton.

1 DETERMINE CHARACTER'S EMOTIONS How do you think the saleslady feels? How can you tell? (Possible response: impatient; she keeps asking "Do you want the bed?")

2 NOTE DETAILS Reread aloud the sentences that tell what the saleslady brought Poppleton. *(The saleslady brought Poppleton some crackers. The saleslady brought Poppleton a TV.)*

3 **(Focus Skill) PREDICT OUTCOMES** What do you predict Poppleton will do next? Explain. (Possible response: He may buy the bed because he feels comfortable in it and because the saleslady has been helpful.)

The saleslady checked her watch.
"Do you want the bed?"
she asked Poppleton.

"I don't know yet," said Poppleton.
"I have to check one more thing.
Do you have any bluebirds?"
"Pardon me?" said the saleslady.
"I always wake up to bluebirds,"
said Poppleton. "Do you have any?"

172

173

Guided Comprehension

Pages 172–173 Have children look at the illustrations. Then have them read to find out what Poppleton's last request is.

1 NOTE DETAILS What does Poppleton ask for this time? (bluebirds)

2 DRAW CONCLUSIONS What does Poppleton mean when he says he wakes up to bluebirds? (Possible response: He hears birds singing each morning when he wakes up.)

3 MAKE INFERENCES Why does the saleslady keep checking her watch? (Possible response: She is tired of waiting and wants Poppleton to hurry up and decide.)

Strategies Good Readers Use

Focus Strategy Use Decoding/Phonics

Ask children to identify a word that is a contraction. Have them name the two words that were joined to form *don't*. *(do not)* Remind them that the apostrophe takes the place of the letter or letters that are left out of the contraction.

172–173 Gather Around

The saleslady went outside
and got three bluebirds to come in
and sing to Poppleton.
Poppleton lay with his eyes closed
and a big smile on his face.

174

"*Now* do you want the bed?"
asked the saleslady.

175

Guided Comprehension

Pages 174–175 Have children look at the illustrations and discuss what is happening. Then have them read to find out how Poppleton feels now.

1 (*Focus Skill*) **PREDICT OUTCOMES** Do you think Poppleton will buy the bed? Explain. (Possible response: Yes, because he has a smile on his face.)

2 **PERSONAL RESPONSE** If you were the saleslady, would you have done all the things that Poppleton asked? Explain. (Possible response: Yes, because Poppleton seems willing to buy the bed if everything goes well. Accept reasonable responses. Have children give reasons for their answers.)

ADVANCED

Have children write a story about Poppleton going to buy some other item, such as a hammer or a jacket. Ask them what kind of store Poppleton would choose. Have them describe what Poppleton would check for and how he would test the item before buying it.

Poppleton tried on a new jacket in the department store.

"Certainly!" said Poppleton.

176

And he picked up the book, the crackers, the bluebirds, and the bed, and happily went home.

177

Guided Comprehension

Pages 176–177 Have children read to find out whether Poppleton finally buys a bed.

1 **(Focus Skill) PREDICT OUTCOMES Was your prediction about whether Poppleton would buy the bed correct? How do you know?** (Possible response: Yes; when asked if he will buy the bed, he says, "Certainly!" He also takes the bed with him when he leaves.)

2 **INTERPRET CHARACTER'S EMOTIONS How do you think Poppleton feels when he leaves the store?** (Possible response: He is happy because he has found the perfect new bed.)

BELOW-LEVEL

To help children decode compound words in the story, such as *saleslady* and *bluebirds*, cover one part of the word at a time and have children read the exposed word. Finally, uncover the whole compound word and have children read it.

176–177 Gather Around

178

Think and Respond

1 What does Poppleton do to test the bed before buying it?

2 Did you ever test something before making a decision? Tell what you did.

3 How does the saleslady feel about Poppleton? Give clues from the story that support your answer.

4 What did you learn about Poppleton's character from reading this story?

5 What did you like most about the story? What didn't you like? Tell why.

179

Think and Respond

1 He reads, eats crackers, watches TV, and listens to birds while lying on the bed. **SUMMARIZE**

2 Possible response: Yes, I tried on clothes before buying them. Accept reasonable responses. Have children give their own examples as they answer. **PERSONAL RESPONSE**

3 Possible response: She thinks he is hard to serve because he took so long to decide; she checked her watch and kept asking him if he wanted the bed. **INTERPRET CHARACTER'S EMOTIONS**

4 Possible responses: He is fussy; he is very careful before making a decision. **AUTHOR'S CRAFT**

5 Possible response: I liked the ways Poppleton tested the bed before he bought it. They were funny. Have children give reasons for their answers. **PERSONAL RESPONSE**

Meet the Author

CYNTHIA RYLANT

Cynthia Rylant grew up in the mountains of West Virginia. She spent a lot of time walking, playing, and thinking in the mountains. Now she likes to send copies of her books to her family. "They are all so proud and happy to receive them," she says. "It's nice to have a job people are so enthusiastic about!"

Cynthia Rylant

Meet the Illustrator

MARK TEAGUE

Mark Teague was working in a bookstore in New York City when he remembered how much he liked picture books as a child. He used to write and illustrate his own stories when he was a boy. He decided to try writing and illustrating children's books. He has illustrated more than fifteen of them.

Mark Teague

Visit *The Learning Site!*
www.harcourtschool.com

180

181

Meet the Author and the Illustrator

Pages 180–181 Explain that these pages tell about the people who wrote and illustrated the story "Poppleton Everyday." Identify Cynthia Rylant and Mark Teague in the photographs on pages 180–181. Remind children that an **author** writes a story, and an **illustrator** creates pictures to go with the writing. Read aloud pages 180–181.

Visit *The Learning Site:* www.harcourtschool.com
See Resources for Parents and Teachers:
Author/Illustrator Features.

Retelling

COMPREHENSION FOCUS

Focus Skill **Predict Outcomes** Remind children that to predict outcomes means to try to figure how things might turn out in a story or what might happen next in a story. Help children recall the predictions they made while reading "Poppleton Everyday."

RETELL AND SUMMARIZE THE STORY

Use a Story Web Ask children to think about the things Poppleton does in the story. Display *Teaching Transparency 107* or draw a similar chart on the board.

Write the title *The New Bed* in the center oval. Work with children to complete the first oval by having them tell the first thing Poppleton does in the story. Write a short sentence to tell what took place. (Poppleton decides to buy the bed.) Follow the same procedure to complete the web. Help children use the web to summarize the story.

COMPREHENSION CHECK

▲ *End-of-Selection Test*, Practice Book, pp. A53–A55

▼ **Teaching Transparency 107**

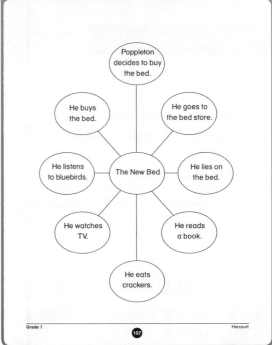

Poppleton decides to buy the bed.

He buys the bed.

He goes to the bed store.

He listens to bluebirds.

The New Bed

He lies on the bed.

He watches TV.

He reads a book.

He eats crackers.

Grade 1   107   Harcourt

5-DAY WRITING

DAY 1	Prewriting
DAY 2	**Drafting**
DAY 3	Responding and Revising
DAY 4	Proofreading
DAY 5	Publishing

LANGUAGE ARTS

Writing Process

Fantasy Story

DRAFTING

Review the Topic Tell children that they will write about an imaginary trip with an animal, a friend, or a favorite toy. Explain that they may use the details on the concept map they helped create in the Prewriting activity, page 156M.

Model Complete Sentences Select items from the concept map and model how to restate each idea in a complete sentence. Have children repeat the sentences.

Model Drafting Engage children in dictating sentences by completing the following sentence frames. Write their sentences on chart paper. Encourage children to suggest good action words and describing words.

_____ and I went to _____.
While we were there we _____.
When it was time to go home we _____.

Write Drafts Provide time for children to write a draft of their own story using the sentence frames. Suggest that children complete their own stories in ways that are different from what you have written on the chart.

Handwriting Remind children to form their letters carefully so that others can read what they write.

BELOW-LEVEL	**ADVANCED**
Encourage children to use what they know about letters and sounds to write words. Remind them to focus on getting their ideas down; they will have an opportunity to make corrections later on.	Have children create their own sentences without using the sentence frames. Tell children to use either *was* or *were* in their sentences.

journal writing

Writing Prompt Have children draw and write about a place that they have been, such as the park or the zoo.

ONGOING ASSESSMENT

As you observe children, note whether they
- accurately repeat a sentence.
- suggest describing words and action words.
- complete sentence frames.

Writing Resources

Writing Express ™ CD-ROM, Level B

5-DAY GRAMMAR

DAY 1	Using *Was* and *Were*
DAY 2	**Generate Sentences**
DAY 3	Using *Was* and *Were*
DAY 4	Write Poem Frames
DAY 5	Identify *Was* and *Were*

Grammar

Using Was *and* Were

REVIEW

Review Using *Was* and *Were* Remind children that *was* and *were* are used in sentences that tell about the past. *Was* is used when writing or speaking about one person, place, or thing. *Were* is used when writing or speaking about more than one person, place, or thing. Have children brainstorm places they were yesterday. Then model writing sentences using *was* and *were*.

MODEL If I want to write a sentence about where I was yesterday, I write *I was at school*. Since I am only talking about me, one person, and I want to tell about the past, I use *was*.

Generate Sentences Have children suggest sentences telling about the places they were yesterday. As you write the sentences, point out the words *was* and *were*.

WRAP UP **Listen to a Poem**

Talk About Places People Go

Remind children that in "Poppleton Everyday," Poppleton leaves his home to buy a bed. Ask children to discuss places people go every day when they leave their home, such as to work or to the park. Then ask children where they think animals go. Have children listen to a poem about some animals who go exploring. Read aloud "Night Runners."

▲ **Big Book of Rhymes, p. 18**

After reading, ask children if they predicted that the animals would go to sleep at sunrise. Discuss with children what they think it would be like to sleep during the day and go to school at night.

S.S.R. *Sustained Silent Reading*

Have children read silently from a book of their choice. See page 185L for tips on helping children choose books.

SKILL TRACE

USING *WAS* AND *WERE*

Introduce	156N
REVIEW	181C, 183B, 185D, 185N

ENGLISH-LANGUAGE LEARNERS

Children may benefit from a visual model. Draw on the board one stick figure of a person. Say *He was at home yesterday.* Draw several more stick figures and say *They were at home yesterday.* Emphasize the subject and verb of each sentence as you say it aloud. Repeat the activity with another drawing and ask children to create their own sentences using *was* or *were*.

Name _____

Using Was and Were

The words **was** and **were** tell about the past.
Use **was** to tell about one person, place, or thing.
Use **were** to tell about more than one person, place, or thing.

Our class play was funny.
The animals were silly.

▶ Write *was* or *were* to complete each sentence.

1. Dan _____ was _____ a caterpillar.

2. Some children _____ were _____ pigs.

3. Polly _____ was _____ a whale.

4. The songs _____ were _____ nice.

134

▲ **Language Handbook, p. 134**

Poppleton Everyday **181C**

Sharing Literature
Rhyme: "Roll Over"

Phonemic Awareness
Phoneme Blending; Focus on /(y)ōō/

Phonics
REVIEW: Long Vowel /(y)ōō/u-e

Spelling
State the Generalization

Vocabulary
REVIEW: brought, few

High-Frequency Words
REVIEW: boy, head, read (past tense)

Reading
Rereading for Fluency
Pupil Edition
"Poppleton Everyday,"
pp. 158–177

Read

Making Connections, pp. 182–183

Independent Writing ✎
Writing Process: Responding and Revising

Grammar
REVIEW: Using *Was* and *Were*

ORAL LANGUAGE

WARM UP

MORNING MESSAGE

Good Morning!

Today is _____.

Poppleton liked his new bed because _____.

I like to sleep in my bed because _____.

If I got a new bed it would be _____.

Introduce the Day
Recall with children that in the story "Poppleton Everyday," Poppleton went shopping for a new bed. Tell children that today they will hear a rhyme about a bed. Guide them in generating a message about beds. Ask:

• **What do you like about your bed?**

• **If you got a new bed, what would it be like?**

As you write the message, have volunteers write previously taught letters, words, and/or punctuation to reinforce skills. For instance, before writing *liked,* elongate the word—/lliīkktt/. Ask a volunteer to identify which letters stand for the /ī/ sound. Then call on a volunteer to write the word.

Read the Message
Read the message. Use the message to focus on selected skills that have been previously taught.

Apply Skills

Phonics Have a volunteer point to and read the word *sleep*. Ask which letters stand for the /ē/ sound. *(ee)* Have a volunteer point to another word with the long sound of e. *(be)*	**Grammar/Mechanics** Ask a volunteer to point to the word that describes Poppleton's bed. *(new)* Ask volunteers to suggest other words that could describe the bed.

Sharing Literature

LISTEN AND RESPOND

Connect to Prior Knowledge Ask children what they think might happen if ten pigs tried to sleep in one bed. Invite them to listen and join in as you recite "Roll Over."

Focus Skill **Predict Outcomes** Pause after the second or third verse and ask children to predict what will happen at the end of the rhyme. Read the remainder of the rhyme as children join in and ask them to confirm their predictions.

Phonemic Awareness

PHONEME BLENDING

Words from "Roll Over" Tell children that you are going to say some words very slowly. Model by segmenting the word *pig* into phonemes—(/p/ /i/ /g/). Then say the word *pig*. Segment the following words from the rhyme, having children blend the sounds to say the words.

/l/ /i/ /t/ /əl/ (little)   /b/ /e/ /d/ (bed)   /i/ /n/ (in)
/a/ /n/ /d/ (and)   /f/ /e/ /l/ (fell)   /n/ /ī/ /n/ (nine)
/s/ /i/ /ks/ (six)   /f/ /ī/ /v/ (five)   /f/ /ôr/ (for)

FOCUS ON /(y)o͞o/

Phoneme Substitution Tell children that you will say a word and they will change the middle vowel sound to make a new word. Model the first item by saying *mile*. *If I change /ī/ to /(y)o͞o/, I get* mule.

Say:	Phoneme Substitution	What is the word?
mile	change /ī/ to /(y)o͞o/	mule
coat	change /ō/ to /(y)o͞o/	cute
tone	change /ō/ to /(y)o͞o/	tune
cub	change /u/ to /(y)o͞o/	cube

Roll Over

*There were 10 in the bed
And the little pig said
"Roll over! Roll over!"
So they all rolled over
And one fell out.
*There were 9 in the bed
And the little pig said
"Roll over! Roll over!"
So they all rolled over
And one fell out.

Continue the verses in this manner, changing the number each time until you reach number one.

There was one in the bed
And the little pig said,
"Good night!"

◀ "Goin' to the Zoo," *Oo-pples and Boo-noo-noos: Songs and Activities for Phonemic Awareness*, p. 78

ENGLISH-LANGUAGE LEARNERS

Turn the Phoneme Blending activity into a name game by segmenting children's names into phonemes and having them identify whose name you are saying. Children may be more comfortable working with their names because they are confident about the pronunciation.

OBJECTIVES

- To generate the long vowel sound of u
- To blend sounds into words
- To read simple, regular words

SKILL TRACE

/(y)o͞o/u-e	
Introduce	156I–156L
Reteach	S34–S35, T10
REVIEW	**156Q–156R, 181F–181G**
Review	183E, 184–185
T Test	Bk 1-5
Maintain	Bk 2-1

Phonics Resources

Phonics Express™ CD-ROM,
Level B Sparkle/Route 4/Market

Phonics
Long Vowel /(y)o͞o/u-e

✔ *Review*

WORD BUILDING

c　d　e　J　k　l　L　n　p　r　u

Guided Practice Place the letters *p, r, u, n, e* in a pocket chart. Have children do the same with their *Word Builders* and *Word Builder Cards*. Model how to blend the word *prune*. Slide your hand under the letters as you slowly elongate the sound—/pprro͞onn/. Then read the word naturally— *prune*. Have children do the same.

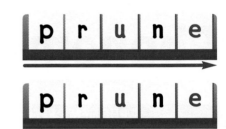

p	r	u	n	e

p	r	u	n	e

Have children build and read new words by telling them:

- Change the *p* and *r* to capital *J*. What word did you make?

J	u	n	e

- Change the capital *J* to small *d*. What word did you make?

d	u	n	e

- Change the *n* to *k*. What word did you make?

d	u	k	e

- Change the *d* to capital *L*. What name did you make?

L	u	k	e

- Change the capital *L* to small *l*. Add *c* after the *u*. Take away the *e*. What word did you make?

l	u	c	k

- Change the *l* to *d*. What word did you make?

d	u	c	k

Continue word building with this word sequence: *cute, cube, tube, tune, tub, rub.*

Apply Phonics

READ WORDS IN CONTEXT

Display *Teaching Transparency 96* or write the following sentences on the board or on chart paper. Have volunteers read the story one sentence at a time. Call on volunteers to underline or frame words with the long vowel sound of *u*.

▼ **Teaching Transparency 96**

LONG VOWEL /(y)o͞o/*u-e*

The dune was huge. There was a rule. Luke was sure of the rule: No tubes on the dune.

Luke used a box in the shape of a cube. He slid all the way down.

"Poppleton Everyday"
Gather Around, Volume 1-5

96

Phonics: Long Vowel /(y)o͞o/*u-e*
Harcourt

Write Words Tell children to choose two words with the long vowel sound of *u* and write them in their journal.

5-DAY PHONICS	
DAY 1	Introduce /(y)o͞o/*u-e*
DAY 2	Word Building with /(y)o͞o/*u-e*
DAY 3	**Word Building with /(y)o͞o/*u-e***
DAY 4	Word Building with /(y)o͞o/*u-e*, /ā/*a-e*
DAY 5	Contractions 've, 'd, 're Inflections -ed, -ing

REACHING ALL LEARNERS

Diagnostic Check: Phonics

If... children cannot read words with long vowel /(y)o͞o/*u-e* ...

Then... have them read "Jules and Luke" in *Decodable Book 32* to reinforce long vowel /(y)o͞o/*u-e*.

◀ **Decodable Book 32**
"Jules and Luke"

ADDITIONAL SUPPORT ACTIVITIES

BELOW-LEVEL	Reteach, p. S34
ADVANCED	Extend, p. S35
ENGLISH-LANGUAGE LEARNERS	Reteach, p. S35

School–Home Connection

Take-Home Book Version

◀ **Decodable Books Take-Home Version**

Spelling Words

1. tube
2. cube
3. cute
4. use
5. rule
6. huge
7. page
8. fudge
9. angry
10. sorry

journal writing

Have children copy the Spelling Words into their journal.

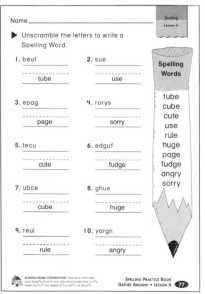

▲ Spelling Practice Book, p. 77

Spelling

5-DAY SPELLING
DAY 1	Pretest; Word Sort
DAY 2	Word Building
DAY 3	**State the Generalization**
DAY 4	Review
DAY 5	Posttest; Writing Application

TEACH/MODEL

State the Generalization for /(y)ōō/u-e Write the Spelling Words on the board and have children read them aloud. Discuss what is the same about words 1–6. (They all have the /(y)ōō/ or the /ōō/ sound; they all have *u* and a final *e*.) Have volunteers circle the letters that stand for /(y)ōō/ or /ōō/ in each word *(u-e)*. Tell children that the *u*-consonant-final *e* pattern shows that the *u* has the long sound in these words.

Review the Generalization for /j/g, dge Follow a similar procedure for words 7 and 8. Remind children that the letters *g* or *dge* can stand for the /j/ sound.

Review the Vocabulary Words Point out that the words *angry* and *sorry* do not follow the same patterns as the other words.

tube	huge
cube	page
cute	fudge
use	angry
rule	sorry

ADVANCED

Have children write a story in which they use one Spelling Word per story page in a complete sentence. Ask children to draw pictures to illustrate their sentences.

ENGLISH-LANGUAGE LEARNERS

While children are learning to spell a word, they are also learning the word's meaning and how to pronounce it. Provide children with a list of the Spelling Words and simple definitions. Have children read aloud each word and its meaning, while you listen for correct pronunciation.

Vocabulary

REVIEW WORDS IN CONTEXT

Read Words in Context Copy the following sentences onto tagboard strips. Use different colors either for the print or for the paper. Display the strips. Have children read the sentences aloud. Then have volunteers point to the words *brought* and *few*.

> REVIEW
> **Vocabulary**
> **brought   few**

Luke brought a friend home.

The friends played a few games.

High-Frequency Words

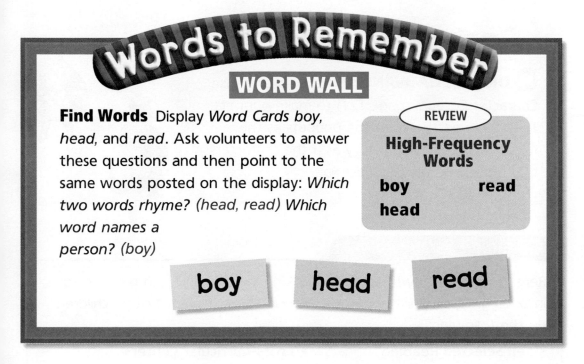

Words to Remember
WORD WALL

Find Words Display *Word Cards boy, head,* and *read.* Ask volunteers to answer these questions and then point to the same words posted on the display: *Which two words rhyme?* (head, read) *Which word names a person?* (boy)

> REVIEW
> **High-Frequency Words**
> **boy   read**
> **head**

boy   head   read

POPPLETON
Everyday

by Cynthia Rylant
illustrated by Mark Teague

▲ *Pupil Edition, pp. 158–177*

FLUENCY ROUTINES For support, see Fluency Routine Cards in Theme Resources, pp. T83–T84.

Rereading for Fluency

GROUPS

Echo Reading

🔵 **BELOW-LEVEL/ENGLISH-LANGUAGE LEARNERS** Tell children that you will read the first sentence of the story and that they will then read the same sentence, echoing what you read. Model expressive reading as you read the remaining sentences on the first page, and encourage children to use the same expression. Have children listen to how you change your voice for each sentence and how you use it to show a pause or stop. As you continue through the story, have children echo read longer passages and then full pages. TEACHER DIRECTED

PARTNERS

Partner Reading

🔵 **ON-LEVEL/ADVANCED** Have children use Character Cutouts (page T21) to make puppets. Then have partners use the puppets as they take turns reading the story as if the characters themselves are talking. INDEPENDENT

Managing Small Groups

Reread for fluency with children working individually, with partners, or in small groups. While you work with small groups, have other children do the following:

- **Self-Selected Reading**
- **Practice Pages**
- **Cross-Curricular Centers**
- **Journal Writing**

Use the suggested Classroom Management outline on page 7C for the whole-group/small-group schedule.

Making Connections

▲ Poppleton Everyday

It's Bedtime

Make a list of things you do to get ready for bed. Make a card to show each thing. Draw and write about it. Tape the cards together and share your list.

Writing CONNECTION

Where to Buy It

When Poppleton wanted a bed, he went to a bed store. Name other kinds of stores you go to for things you need. Make a list of different kinds of stores.

Social Studies CONNECTION

Grocery Store
Sports Store
Book Store

The New Bed

Cut out a bed shape. Find or draw pictures of things Poppleton might have on his new bed. Glue your pictures to the bed and share your work.

Art CONNECTION

The New Bed

182   183

Making Connections

WRITING

It's Bedtime Provide children with blank cards, tape, crayons, and markers. Remind them to write complete sentences. When children have finished their cards, help them tape the cards together.

SOCIAL STUDIES

Where to Buy It Organize children into small groups and have them list different kinds of stores. Then have them choose three or four stores to illustrate on a group poster. Have children write each store name and draw pictures of items that can be purchased there.

ART

The New Bed Tell children that a picture like this is called a collage. Have children work individually or in small groups. Provide them with construction paper and magazines to make their collage.

Day 3

LANGUAGE ARTS

5-DAY WRITING
DAY 1	Prewriting
DAY 2	Drafting
DAY 3	**Responding and Revising**
DAY 4	Proofreading
DAY 5	Publishing

Writing Resources

***Writing Express*™ CD-ROM, Post Office, Writing Workshop**

journal writing

Writing Prompt Have children interview a friend about a place. Ask them to write one question and answer.

Writing Process

Fantasy Story

RESPONDING AND REVISING

Reread the Stories Ask children to work with partners as they read aloud the drafts of their fantasy stories. Have partners think about questions they have as they listen. They can use these questions to prompt the writers to add details or make revisions.

Add a Sentence Children can add a sentence to their stories giving more details about their adventures. Remind them to insert describing words and action words as needed. For example, if a child has written about an adventure with a frog, he or she might add a sentence that tells something the frog said.

> Frog said, "Let's go."
> So we went to the pond. We saw turtles having a party.
> I'll always remember just Frog and me and the time that we danced on the lily pads in the pond. I'll never forget that night.

Make Revisions Ask volunteers to read their stories aloud to the group. Then ask all writers to examine their drafts. Ask:

- **Have you left out anything important?**
- **Do you want to change any words or add any words to make the sentences clearer?**

Provide time for children to make additional revisions if they wish.

Grammar

Using Was *and* Were

5-DAY GRAMMAR

DAY 1	Introduce Using *Was* and *Were*
DAY 2	Generate Sentences
DAY 3	**Using *Was* and *Were***
DAY 4	Write Poem Frames
DAY 5	Identify *Was* and *Were*

REVIEW

Review Using *Was* and *Were* Use *Word Cards was* and *were*, and the period *Punctuation Card*. Make word cards for *that, pig,* and *dirty*. Form the following sentence in a pocket chart, and have children read it: *that pig was dirty.*

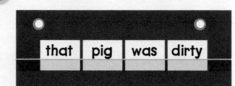

Ask why the word *was* is used instead of the word *were*. (because *pig* is one thing) Have volunteers correct the sentence by using self-stick notes to capitalize the first letter and adding a period at the end. Have children read it.

Form Sentences Use additional *Word Cards* and cards that you make to form the sentences shown in a pocket chart. Have children read each sentence. Ask volunteers to choose *was* or *were* to complete each sentence. Have them correct the sentences by capitalizing the first letters and adding end punctuation.

SKILL TRACE

USING *WAS* AND *WERE*

Introduce	156N
REVIEW	**181C, 183B, 185D, 185N**

ADVANCED

Write these forms of the word *be* on the board and have children read them: *am, is, are, was, were*. Remind children that *am, is,* and *are* are words people use to talk about something that happens in the present and that *was* and *were* are used for the past. Then have children work in pairs to interview one another. Have each child ask questions about what the partner is doing or feeling today and what the partner did or felt in the past (yesterday, last week).

WRAP UP Author's Chair

Share Writing Ask children to gather around the classroom Author's Chair. Have volunteers take turns reading their sentences from the Writing activity on page 183A and showing their pictures. Remind them to read and speak slowly and clearly so others can hear and understand. Lead children in showing a "thumbs-up" following each reader.

Have children read silently from a book of their choice. See page 185L for tips on helping children choose books.

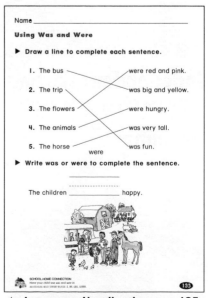

▲ Language Handbook, page 135

Poppleton Everyday **183B**

Day at a Glance
Day 4

WARM UP — MORNING MESSAGE

Good Morning!

Today is _____.

Do you think pigs are cute?

I like pigs because _____.

Pigs are _____, _____, and _____.

Introduce the Day

Tell children that today they will listen to a poem about a pig. Guide them in generating a message about pigs. Ask:

- **What do you like about pigs?**

- **How would you describe pigs?**

As you write the message, have volunteers write previously taught letters, words, and/or punctuation to reinforce skills. For instance, ask a volunteer to write *I* in the third sentence. Ask if the volunteer should write a capital *I* or a lowercase *i*. Remind children that the word *I* is always capitalized.

Read the Message

Read the message. Use the message to focus on selected skills that have been previously taught.

Apply Skills

Phonics Ask a volunteer to find a word that has long vowel /(y)o͞o/u-e. *(cute)* Read the word aloud with children, emphasizing the /(y)o͞o/ sound. Have children name other words having long vowel /(y)o͞o/u-e.

Grammar/Mechanics Have volunteers find the commas in the message. Remind them that commas tell them to pause slightly as they read. Explain that commas also separate items in a list. Have children practice reading the last line of the message, pausing at each comma.

Sharing Literature

BUILD CONCEPT VOCABULARY

Connect to Prior Knowledge Tell children you are going to read a poem about a pig who does not want his ears washed. Read the limerick with appropriate expression and rhythm. Invite responses.

Explore a Word Remind children that the pig "wept tears." Say: *We can tell from the word* tears *that the pig was crying. He was weeping. The word* weep *means "cry."* Have children say *weep.* Demonstrate the dramatic connotation of *weep* with the following sentence: *The sad story made me weep.* Have children use the word *weep* to dramatize situations that might make them cry. Close by asking children to repeat the word they have been talking about.

Phonemic Awareness

PHONEME ADDITION

Words from the Limerick Tell children you are going to ask them to make new words by adding sounds to the beginnings of words. Model by saying *What word do I make if I say* other *with /m/ at the beginning?* (mother) Continue the procedure with the following words:

ears
add /t/ to the beginning (tears)
add /f/ to the beginning (fears)
add /g/ to the beginning (gears)
add /h/ to the beginning (hears)

all
add /m/ to the beginning (mall)
add /t/ to the beginning (tall)
add /b/ to the beginning (ball)
add /f/ to the beginning (fall)

FOCUS ON /(y)o͞o/ AND /ā/

Distinguish Phonemes Have children say *sale.* Ask what sound is heard in the middle. (/ā/) Have children say *mule.* Ask what sound is heard in the middle. (/(y)o͞o/) Continue with the following words:

race (/ā/) **dune** (/(y)o͞o/) **rake** (/ā/) **rule** (/o͞o/)
pace (/ā/) **prune** (/o͞o/) **fake** (/ā/) **Luke** (/o͞o/)
flute (/o͞o/) **plate** (/ā/) **made** (/ā/) **rude** (/o͞o/)

Limerick from
A Book of Pigericks

There was a small pig who
    wept tears
When his mother said, "I'll
    wash your ears."
As she poured on the soap,
He cried, "Oh, how I hope
This won't happen again for
    ten years!"

Arnold Lobel

Phonics Build Words

5-DAY PHONICS	
DAY 1	Introduce /(y)ōō/u-e
DAY 2	Word Building with /(y)ōō/u-e
DAY 3	Word Building with /(y)ōō/u-e
DAY 4	**Word Building with /(y)ōō/u-e, /ā/a-e**
DAY 5	Contractions 've, 'd, 're Inflections -ed, -ing

OBJECTIVES

- *To discriminate between the sound-letter relationships /(y)ōō/u-e and /ā/a-e*

- *To read and write words with /(y)ōō/u-e and /ā/a-e*

SKILL TRACE

	/(y)ōō/u-e	/ā/a-e
Introduce	156I–156L	Bk 1-4, 36I–36L
Reteach	S34–S35, T10	
REVIEW	156Q–156R, 181F–181G, 183E, 184–85	Bk 1-4, 36Q–36R, 61F–61G, 63E–63F, 151F
T Test	Bk 1-5	Bk 1-4
MAINTAIN	Bk 2-1	65F, 183E–185

teaching tip

Build Vocabulary Explain that a *mane* is the hair on a horse's neck and a *pane* is a piece of glass that is part of a window.

Phonics Resources

Phonics Express™ CD-ROM, **Level B** Sparkle/Route 6/ Fire Station

Phonics Practice Book, pp. 200–205, 238–239

WORD BUILDING

Build and Read Words Use a pocket chart and *Letter Cards a, d, e, k, I, m, n, p, r, s, t,* and *u*. Display the letters *r, u, I,* and *e* in a pocket chart and ask children to spell the word.

Place the letters close together. Slide your hand slowly under the letters as you blend the sounds—/rrōōll/. Then read the word naturally—*rule*. Have children repeat after you. Discuss what a rule is. Point out that the letters in *rule* follow the pattern *consonant, vowel, consonant, e*.

Ask volunteers to build new words in the pocket chart.

- Change the *r* to *m*. Read the word.

- Change the *u* to *a*. Read the word.

- Change the *I* to *n*. Read the word.

- Change the *m* to *t*, and change the *a* to *u*. Read the word.

- Change the *t* to *d*. Read the word.

- Change the *d* to *p*, and change the *u* to *a*. Read the word.

Continue word building with this word sequence: *pale, tale, take, cake, cube, cute*.

Review the Skill Have children turn to pages 184–185 in their *Pupil Edition*. Read to them the information about long vowel /(y)ōō/u-e and discuss the questions on the page. Then model the test items by reading aloud the questions and discussing the answer choices. Use the tip on the page to help children select the correct answer.

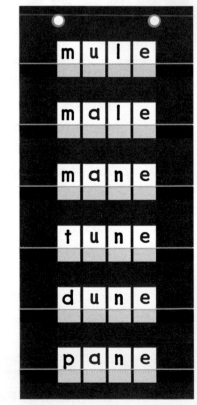

▲ *Poppleton Everyday*

Words with u-e

Teacher Read-Aloud

Phonics Skill

When the letter **u** is followed by a consonant and **e**, it can stand for the long sound of **u** as in <u>cute</u> and <u>June</u>. Read these sentences.

> Poppleton got a **huge** bed.
> He will **use** it right away.
> Did you think that was a **cute** story?

Now read the words in the box. Each one has the long sound of **u**.

tune	flute	cube

184

Test Prep
Words with u-e

1. **Choose a word that names the picture.**

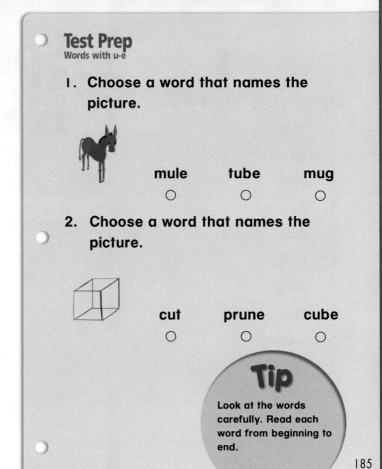

mule	tube	mug
○	○	○

2. **Choose a word that names the picture.**

cut	prune	cube
○	○	○

Tip

Look at the words carefully. Read each word from beginning to end.

185

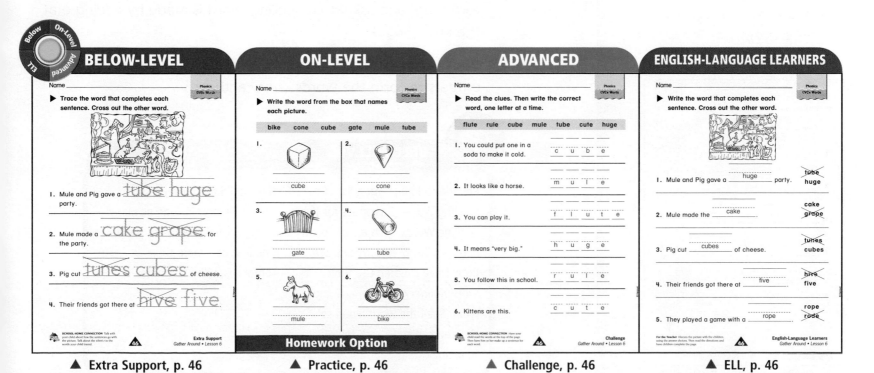

BELOW-LEVEL

Name _____

▶ Trace the word that completes each sentence. Cross out the other word.

1. Mule and Pig gave a ~~tube~~ huge party.

2. Mule made a cake ~~grape~~ for the party.

3. Pig cut ~~tunes~~ cubes of cheese.

4. Their friends got there at ~~hive~~ five.

▲ Extra Support, p. 46

ON-LEVEL

Name _____

▶ Write the word from the box that names each picture.

| bike | cone | cube | gate | mule | tube |

1. cube
2. cone
3. gate
4. tube
5. mule
6. bike

Homework Option

▲ Practice, p. 46

ADVANCED

Name _____

▶ Read the clues. Then write the correct word, one letter at a time.

| flute | rule | cube | mule | tube | cute | huge |

1. You could put one in a soda to make it cold.   c u b e

2. It looks like a horse.   m u l e

3. You can play it.   f l u t e

4. It means "very big."   h u g e

5. You follow this in school.   r u l e

6. Kittens are this.   c u t e

▲ Challenge, p. 46

ENGLISH-LANGUAGE LEARNERS

Name _____

▶ Write the word that completes each sentence. Cross out the other word.

1. Mule and Pig gave a huge party.   ~~tube~~ huge

2. Mule made the cake.   cake ~~grape~~

3. Pig cut cubes of cheese.   ~~tunes~~ cubes

4. Their friends got there at five.   ~~hive~~ five

5. They played a game with a rope.   rope ~~rode~~

▲ ELL, p. 46

Spelling Words

1. tube
2. cube
3. cute
4. use
5. rule
6. huge
7. page
8. fudge
9. angry
10. sorry

Spelling

5-DAY SPELLING	
DAY 1	Pretest; Word Sort
DAY 2	Word Building
DAY 3	State the Generalization
DAY 4	**Review**
DAY 5	Posttest; Writing Application

REVIEW

Spelling Words Use a pocket chart and *Letter Cards* to form words. Have children listen to your directions and change one letter in each word to spell a Spelling Word. Have them write the Spelling Word on a sheet of paper or in their journal. Then have a volunteer change the *Letter Card* in the pocket chart so that children can self-check the word.

- Form *tube* in the pocket chart and have children read it aloud. **Which Spelling Word is made with one letter changed?** *(cube)*

- Form *mule* in the pocket chart and have children read it aloud. **Which Spelling Word is made with one letter changed?** *(rule)*

- Form *cage* in the pocket chart and have children read it aloud. **Which Spelling Word is made with one letter changed?** *(page)*

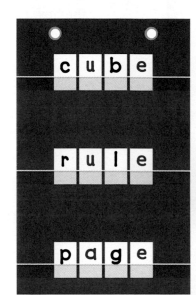

Follow a similar procedure with the following words: *mute* (cute), *fuse* (use) (one letter dropped), *budge* (fudge), *tune* (tube). Then form *hug*, and ask which Spelling Word is made by adding *e* at the end. *(huge)*

Vocabulary Display *Letter Cards a, r, r, r, g, o, s, n, y, y.* Ask volunteers to form the words *angry* and *sorry*.

BELOW-LEVEL	ADVANCED
Provide children with a list of the Spelling Words. Give clues for the Spelling Words, such as *This word begins with /k/ and rhymes with flute.* Have children use their *Word Builder Cards* to form the word. Spell the word aloud so children can self-check their spelling.	Have children make up silly sentences that include as many of the Spelling Words as possible. Children can share their sentences with classmates.

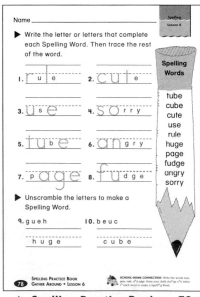

▲ Spelling Practice Book, p. 78

Vocabulary

REVIEW WORDS IN STORY CONTEXT

Reinforce Understanding
Duplicate and distribute
these Story Strips for "Poppleton
Everyday." (page T70) Display *Word Cards* or write these words on
the board: *brought, few*. Have children complete each sentence
with one of these words.

> **REVIEW**
> **Vocabulary**
> **brought   few**

The saleslady ____ Poppleton some crackers.

He tested the bed in a ____ different ways.

High-Frequency Words

REVIEW WORDS IN STORY CONTEXT

Reinforce Word Recognition
Duplicate and distribute these Story
Strips for "Poppleton Everyday."
(page T70) Display *Word Cards* or
write the high-frequency words on the board: *boy, head, read*.
Have children complete each sentence with one of these words.

> **REVIEW**
> **High-Frequency Words**
> **boy   read**
> **head**

Poppleton had his bed since he was a ____.

He lay with his ____ on the bed.

While on the bed, he ____ a book.

Then have them put all the Story Strips in order.

Reread the Selection Have children reread "Poppleton
Everyday" to see if they ordered the Story Strips correctly.

Read

▲ *Pupil Edition*, pp. 158–177

REACHING ALL LEARNERS

Diagnostic Check: Vocabulary and High-Frequency Words

If... children cannot recognize and read the words ...

Then... have them work in pairs practicing using the *Word Cards* from page T37 as flash cards.

ADDITIONAL SUPPORT ACTIVITIES

BELOW-LEVEL	Reteach, p. S36
ADVANCED	Extend, p. S37
ENGLISH-LANGUAGE LEARNERS	Reteach, p. S37

5-DAY WRITING

DAY 1	Prewriting
DAY 2	Drafting
DAY 3	Responding and Revising
DAY 4	**Proofreading**
DAY 5	Publishing

DAILY LANGUAGE PRACTICE

I were looking at a sel.

I <u>was</u> looking at a <u>seal</u>.

ONGOING ASSESSMENT

Note whether children are able to
- work with a partner.
- keep their writing on topic.
- spell known vocabulary and high-frequency words correctly.

journal writing

Writing Prompt Have children write about a place they want to visit and explain why they want to go there.

LANGUAGE ARTS

Writing Process

Fantasy Story

PROOFREADING

Model Proofreading Model how to proofread stories by asking questions such as:

- **Did you start each sentence with a capital letter?**
- **Did you use a capital letter for each character's name?**
- **Do all of your sentences end with ending punctuation marks?**
- **Can another person read your handwriting?**

Guide Editing If children answered no to any of these questions, guide them as they revise their work. Have them think of sound-letter relationships and words they know as they check the spelling of words. Suggest that children exchange their edited work with partners and proofread each other's stories.

Visit *The Learning Site:* **www.harcourtschool.com** See Proofreading Makes Perfect.

ADVANCED

Children may check their own spelling with an automatic spell checker if they are working on a computer, or use a dictionary if they are writing by hand.

Grammar

Using Was *and* Were

5-DAY GRAMMAR

DAY 1	Introduce Using *Was* and *Were*
DAY 2	Generate Sentences
DAY 3	Using *Was* and *Were*
DAY 4	**Write Poem Frames**
DAY 5	Identify *Was* and *Were*

REVIEW

Write Poem Frames Remind children that they use *was* and *were* when something happens in the past. Ask them when they use *was* (when writing about one person, place, or thing) and *were* (when writing about more than one person, place, or thing).

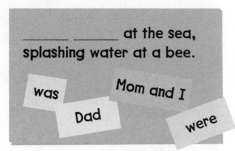

_____ _____ at the sea,
splashing water at a bee.

was   Mom and I   Dad   were

Write the following words on index cards with two-sided tape on the back: *Tom, We, Mom and I, You, Anna and Sean, Dad, was, were*. Also write the poem above on tagboard. Have volunteers use the cards to fill in the two blanks in the poem. As children read aloud various versions of the poem, have them tell why *was* or *were* is correct. Point out that *were* is always used with the word *you*.

SKILL TRACE

USING *WAS* AND *WERE*

| Introduce | 156N |
| **REVIEW** | **181C, 183B, 185D, 185N** |

Grammar Resources

Grammar Jingles™ **CD, Primary, Track 9,** "What Happened?"; **Track 10,** "All About Being"

WRAP UP Share Ideas

Connect Ideas Across Texts Ask children to describe the setting of "Poppleton Everyday." Tell children that the bed store was a new place for Poppleton to visit. Explain that you are going to revisit a story about people who move from place to place. Reread aloud "We Were Tired of Living in a House." Ask: *How do you think Poppleton would like to move around like the people in the story? Explain.* (Possible response: He probably wouldn't. He seemed to like being in his own home.)

▲ **"We Were Tired of Living in a House,"** pp. 32–36

S.S.R. Sustained Silent Reading

Have children read silently from a book of their choice. See page 185L for tips on helping children choose books.

Name _____

Using Was and Were

► Circle **was** or **were** to complete each sentence. Write the sentence.

1. The party ___ fun.   (was)   were

   The party was fun.

2. The hats ___ silly.   was   (were)

   The hats were silly.

3. Dad ___ busy.   (was)   were

   Dad was busy.

4. The cake ___ yummy.   (was)   were

   The cake was yummy.

► Draw a picture about a party you went to.

136   SCHOOL-HOME CONNECTION Ask your child to use *was* and *were* to tell about his or her picture.

▲ Language Handbook, p. 136

Poppleton Everyday **185D**

WARM UP — MORNING MESSAGE

Good Morning!

Today is _____.

Something silly that happened in To Market, To Market was _____.

Something silly that happened in school was _____.

Introduce the Day

Tell children that today they will revisit the story *To Market, To Market*. Recall some of the silly things that happen in the story. Guide them in generating a morning message about silly things that happen. Ask:

• **What is something silly that happened in the story?**

• **What is something silly that has happened to us here in school?**

As you write the message, have volunteers write previously taught letters, words, and/or punctuation to reinforce skills. For instance, before writing the word *was* in the last sentence, ask children which word belongs there—*was* or *were*. Invite a volunteer to write *was.*

Read the Message

Read the message. Use the message to focus on selected skills that have been previously taught.

Apply Skills

Phonics Ask a volunteer to point to the letter in the word *silly* that stands for the long e sound. *(y)* Ask children to name more words that end with y standing for the long e sound. (Possible responses: *funny, happy*)

High-Frequency Words Ask volunteers to dictate sentences that relate to the message and contain the words *boy, head,* and *read.* Add their sentences to the message.

Sharing Literature

DEVELOP LISTENING COMPREHENSION

Retell Story Events After reading the story, instruct partners to imagine that they are describing the book to someone who has not read it before. Have them take turns retelling the story events. Help children with their retellings by suggesting that they use the illustrations.

Extend the Pattern Ask children to suggest other animals for the story and where they go, or other items the woman might buy at the market to make something else for lunch. Recite the repeated pattern of the book, adding children's suggestions.

Phonemic Awareness

PHONEME ISOLATION

Words from the Big Book Help children recall the food words from *To Market, To Market.* *(potatoes, celery, beets, tomatoes, pea pods, peppers, cabbage, brown rice, okra, onions, carrot)* Say the word *carrot,* elongating the sounds, and have children do the same. Ask: *What is the first sound in* carrot? (/k/) Say the word *beets,* elongating the sounds, and have children do the same. Ask: *What is the last sound in* beets? (/s/) Continue with these words:

Initial Sound

celery (/s/)
tomatoes (/t/)
peppers (/p/)

Final Sound

onions (/z/)
brown (/n/)
rice (/s/)

FOCUS ON CONTRACTIONS, FINAL /v/, /d/, /r/

Identify Final Phonemes Say the word *they've,* elongating the sounds, and have children do the same. Model by saying, *If I listen for the last sound in* they've, *I hear* /v/. They've—/v/. Continue with the following words:

I'd (/d/)   **we're** (/r/)   **you've** (/v/)
you're (/r/)   **I've** (/v/)   **she'd** (/d/)

▲ **Big Book**

ADVANCED

Have children identify the initial sounds in all the food words from the big book. Note whether they name only the initial sounds or name the consonant blends as the initial sounds.

ENGLISH-LANGUAGE LEARNERS

Page through an illustrated cookbook. Point out different foods or dishes, name them, and ask children to repeat each word after you. Pictures will provide context for children to understand unfamiliar words.

Phonics
Contractions 've, 'd, 're

OBJECTIVE

To read contractions with 've, 'd, and 're

SKILL TRACE

CONTRACTIONS 've, 'd, 're	
Introduce	123E–123F
Reteach	T8
REVIEW	**I55E–I55F, I85G**
T Test	Bk I-5
Maintain	Bk 2-I

BELOW-LEVEL

Use *Word Builder Cards* and an apostrophe card for the words *they have.* Guide children as they remove the letters *h* and *a,* and insert an apostrophe to form the contraction *they've.* Follow a similar procedure with the words *you are, she would, you have,* and *we had.*

ENGLISH-LANGUAGE LEARNERS

Use contractions in sentences about children: *You are Brianna. You're Brianna. You have been to gym. You've been to gym. You would like to go to lunch. You'd like to go to lunch.*

DEVELOP WORD MEANING

Understand Contractions with 've, 'd, 're Write the following sentence pairs on the board:

I have seen that movie.
I've seen that movie.

She had gone to sleep.
She'd gone to sleep.

He would like to sleep.
He'd like to sleep.

We are tired.
We're tired.

Read the sentences to children and ask what makes the second sentence in each pair different from the first. (The second sentences all have contractions.)

Point out that the contraction *I've* stands for the words *I have, She'd* in this sentence stands for *She had, He'd* in this sentence stands for *He would,* and *We're* stands for *We are.* Remind children that a contraction is a short way of saying or writing two words. Point to the apostrophe in each contraction and ask which letters the apostrophe replaces. *(ha, ha, woul, a)*

WORKING WITH PATTERNS

Sort the Contractions Write *have, would,* and *are* on index cards. Arrange them side by side on a table. Then write these contractions on index cards: *you'd, we've, we're, they're, she'd, I've, you've, you're, I'd.* Have volunteers select a contraction index card, place it above the word that was shortened to form the contraction, and say the words that the contraction stands for.

she'd

would

APPLY PHONICS SKILLS

Write Contractions Have children write three sentences in their journal, one with a *'ve* word, one with a *'d* word, and one with a *'re* word.

Inflections -ed, -ing

5-DAY PHONICS

DAY 1	Introduce /(y)o͞o/u-e
DAY 2	Word Building with /(y)o͞o/u-e
DAY 3	Word Building with /(y)o͞o/u-e
DAY 4	Word Building with /(y)o͞o/u-e, /ā/a-e
DAY 5	**Contractions 've, 'd, 're Inflections -ed, -ing**

WORKING WITH PATTERNS

Identify Base Words and Endings Write the following words on the board:

| shop | shopping | shopped |
| trip | tripping | tripped |

Have children read the words aloud. Ask children what endings were added to the base words *shop* and *trip*. Have volunteers circle -*ed* and -*ing* in each word and underline the base words. Ask if the spelling of the base words changed when the ending was added. (Yes, the last consonant was doubled.)

Build and Blend Words Write the following words on chart paper: *stop, beg, walk, hop, jog, help,* and *tap.* Then write the endings -*ed* and -*ing*. Have children make words by adding an ending to each word. Have volunteers explain why they did or did not double the final consonant before adding each ending.

OBJECTIVES

• *To read inflectional endings* -ed *and* -ing

• *To understand that in some words, the final consonant is doubled before adding* -ed *or* -ing

SKILL TRACE

INFLECTIONS -ed, -ing (DOUBLED CONSONANT)

Introduce	97E–97F
Reteach	T6
REVIEW	**185H, 215I, 216–217**
Maintain	Bk 2-1

APPLY PHONICS SKILLS

Write Words Say the following words and have children write them in their journal: *rub, rubbing, rubbed, drop, dropping, dropped.* Post the words to help children check their work.

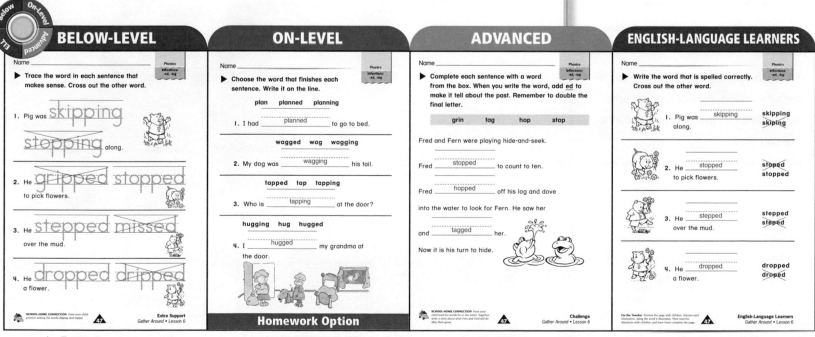

▲ Extra Support, p. 47   ▲ Practice, p. 47   ▲ Challenge, p. 47   ▲ ELL, p. 47

Spelling Words

1. tube
2. cube
3. cute
4. use
5. rule
6. huge
7. page
8. fudge
9. angry
10. sorry

ADVANCED

Have children make up and share songs about how to spell some or all of the Spelling Words and share the songs with classmates. A rhyming song might be particularly helpful in remembering the *u-consonant-e* words.

ENGLISH-LANGUAGE LEARNERS

Say each Spelling Word and ask volunteers to spell it. Provide extra practice with words children misspell or cannot use correctly.

Spelling

5-DAY SPELLING	
DAY 1	Pretest; Word Sort
DAY 2	Word Building
DAY 3	State the Generalization
DAY 4	Review
DAY 5	Posttest; Writing Application

ASSESS/APPLY

Posttest Assess children's progress using the words and the Dictation Sentences from Day 1.

1. tube — We need a new **tube** of toothpaste.
2. cube — She folded the paper into a **cube**.
3. cute — That dog has a **cute** face.
4. use — How do you **use** that tool?
5. rule — The **rule** is "No talking."
6. huge — That house is **huge**!

Review

7. page — Emma turned the **page** of the book.
8. fudge — Mom made **fudge** today.

Vocabulary

9. angry — Tom was very **angry** with his friend Joe.
10. sorry — Joe told Tom he was **sorry**.

Writing Application Have children complete and illustrate the following sentence frames:

Use the tube for ____.

That is a huge ____.

That is a huge dog.

Vocabulary

REVIEW

REVIEW

Complete Sentences Write the words *brought* and *few* on the board. Have children complete the following sentences.

Vocabulary
brought **few**

Jill ____ the ball to me. *(brought)*

Mom said, "We will be home in a ____ days." *(few)*

Have children make up new sentences using these words.

High-Frequency Words

Words to Remember
WORD WALL

Reinforce Words Write the words *boy, head,* and *read* on large self-stick notes. Hold up the note for *read*. Ask children to say and spell *read* (past tense). Next, have children say and spell the word again. Then put the note down, but keep your hand up. As children continue to look at your hand, have them say and spell *read* one more time. Finally, have a volunteer attach the self-stick note to the same word in the display. Use a similar procedure with the words *boy* and *head*.

REVIEW

High-Frequency Words

boy   read
head

ENGLISH-LANGUAGE LEARNERS

Below • On-Level • Advanced • ELL

Because high-frequency words may be difficult to define as well as pronounce, children need to work with them in context to understand their meaning and to practice their correct pronunciations. Have children complete these sentences orally.

The ____ and girl were brother and sister. (boy)

My hair grows on top of my ____. (head)

We ____ that story in class last week. (read)

▲ *Pupil Edition*, pp. 158–177

FLUENCY ROUTINES For support, see Fluency Routine Cards in Theme Resources, pp. T83–T84.

ENGLISH-LANGUAGE LEARNERS

Have children read along with *Audiotext 5*. Then have partners work together as described in the Repeated Reading activity.

Rereading for Fluency

GROUPS

Readers Theatre

ON-LEVEL/ADVANCED Have children take turns reading aloud, each child reading two pages at a time. Tell them to pretend they are reading the story to a very young child. Encourage them to read with expression, using different voices for the characters' dialogue and reading the other sentences in a dramatic way. Read aloud pages 160–163 to model. Monitor groups to provide support and encouragement. INDEPENDENT

> Do you want the bed?

PARTNERS

Repeated Reading

BELOW-LEVEL Have each partner choose a favorite part of the story to practice reading aloud. Tell them to choose at least two consecutive pages. Explain that readers should read their pages three times, trying to read more smoothly and with more expression each time; listeners should follow along and give feedback about how the readers sound. Monitor children closely, providing modeling and support. After practice, bring children together and invite volunteers to read aloud for the group. TEACHER DIRECTED

"It's just my size!" said Poppleton.

Managing Small Groups

Reread for fluency with children working individually, with partners, or in small groups. While you work with small groups, have other children do the following:

- **Self-Selected Reading**
- **Practice Pages**
- **Cross-Curricular Centers**
- **Journal Writing**

Use the suggested Classroom Management outline on page 7C for the whole-group/small-group schedule.

Self-Selected Reading

INDEPENDENT READING

Have children choose a book from the **Browsing Boxes** or the **Reading Center** to read independently during a sustained silent reading time. Children may also want to reread a story from their *Pupil Edition.* These are some books you may want to gather that relate to "Poppleton Everyday."

Decodable Books

Decodable Book 32
"Queen June and the Rude Duke" by J. C. Cunningham

"Jules and Luke" by Sunita Apte

Cut-Out/Fold-Up Book

Three Moles and a Mule *Practice Book*, pp. 75–76

Books for All Learners

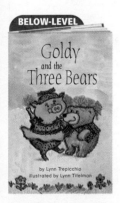

Goldy and the Three Bears by Lynn Trepicchio

All About Pigs by Margaret Gallo

Little Pig at the State Fair by Margaret Gallo

The Furniture in My House by Kathryn E. Lewis

choosing 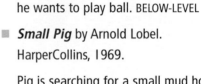 books

To guide children in selecting books at their independent level, suggest that they read one or two pages of the book. If there are at least five words that the child can't read, he or she should try an easier book.

related books

- **Boring Old Bed** by Joy Cowley. The Wright Group, 1996.

  Jim thinks his bed is boring, so he tries to sleep in other places around the house, but finds that his bed is the best place of all. BELOW-LEVEL

- **The Rainy Day Grump** by Deborah Eaton. Millbrook Press, 1998.

  Clay is grumpy because it's rainy and he wants to play ball. BELOW-LEVEL

- **Small Pig** by Arnold Lobel. HarperCollins, 1969.

  Pig is searching for a small mud hole. ADVANCED

- **Henry and Mudge and the Best Day** by Cynthia Rylant. Macmillan, 1995.

  The first day of May is a good day for Henry and his dog Mudge because it is Henry's birthday! ADVANCED

	5-DAY WRITING
DAY 1	Prewriting
DAY 2	Drafting
DAY 3	Responding and Revising
DAY 4	Proofreading
DAY 5	**Publishing**

DAILY LANGUAGE PRACTICE

Id like to visit Grandma, to.

I'd like to visit Grandma, too.

journal writing

Self-Selected Writing Have children write in their journal about a topic of their choice. They may want to illustrate their writing.

Writing Process

Fantasy Story

PUBLISHING

Copy and Illustrate Stories Have children copy their stories onto a clean sheet of paper. Remind them to include any corrections they made on the draft. Children should allow for correct letter formation and word spacing to make stories readable. Have children add illustrations to the final copies of their stories.

Share Stories Invite children to take turns sitting in the Author's Chair as they read their fantasy stories to an audience. Remind children to choose a voice that others will hear and to read clearly so that others will understand. You may also want to bind the stories into a booklet or display the finished work in the classroom.

SCORING RUBRIC				
	4	**3**	**2**	**1**
FOCUS/IDEAS	Completely focused, purposeful.	Generally focused on task and purpose.	Somewhat focused on task and purpose.	Lacks focus and purpose.
ORGANIZATION	Presents material logically, adheres to topic.	Organization mostly clear, with few lapses; adheres to topic.	Some sense of organization but inconsistent or unclear in places.	Little or no sense of organization.
WORD CHOICE	Descriptive, imaginative, clear, and exact language.	Appropriate varied language; limited repetition.	Simplistic language; word choice unclear or inappropriate in places.	Simplistic language; word choice often unclear or inappropriate.
SENTENCES	Complete sentences with correct word order.	Most sentences are complete and have correct word order.	Frequent use of incomplete sentences and/or incorrect word order.	Demonstrates no understanding of complete sentences and correct word order.
DEVELOPMENT	Strong, specific supporting details.	Adequate support, mostly relevant details.	Limited supporting details.	Little or no development.
CONVENTIONS	Few, if any, errors in punctuation, capitalization, grammar, and spelling.	Some errors in punctuation, capitalization, grammar, and spelling.	Many errors in punctuation, capitalization, grammar, and spelling.	No meaningful use of punctuation, capitalization or grammar; frequent spelling errors.

5-DAY GRAMMAR

DAY 1	Introduce Using *Was* and *Were*
DAY 2	Generate Sentences
DAY 3	Using *Was* and *Were*
DAY 4	Write Poem Frames
DAY 5	**Identify *Was* and *Were***

Grammar

Using Was *and* Were

REVIEW

Identify *Was* and *Were* Tell children that you will say some sentences and they will repeat each one after you. After each sentence, ask whether that sentence uses *was* or *were*.

• **Jack and Jill were up on the hill.**

• **The sink was full of dishes.**

• **Were the hot dogs good?**

Use *Was* and *Were* Write these sentences on the board without *was* and *were*, and have children read them.

———— **you and Lee at the party**

Lee ———— **at the party, but I stayed home**

Have volunteers add *was* or *were* and the correct ending punctuation marks.

SKILL TRACE

USING *WAS* AND *WERE*	
Introduce	156N
REVIEW	181C, 183B, 185D, 185N

 **technology**

Visit *The Learning Site:* www.harcourtschool.com See Go for Grammar Gold, Multimedia Grammar Glossary.

WRAP UP

Use the Alphabet

Play an Alphabet Game Ask children to name the things Poppleton tried out with the bed in the store. (book, crackers, TV, birds) Tell children they are going to play the "On Poppleton's Bed from A to Z" game. The game is played by naming things that begin with each letter of the alphabet that might be found on Poppleton's bed. Remind children that Poppleton's bed is enormous and can hold many things. The first volunteer might say *On Poppleton's bed there was an apple.* The next child could say *On Poppleton's bed there were balloons and a bicycle.* Continue until children have gone all the way through the alphabet.

S.S.R. *Sustained Silent Reading*

Have children read silently from a book of their choice. See page 185L for tips on helping children choose books.

Name _____

Using Was and Were

▶ Write was or were to complete the sentences.

Dear Gram,
  Last night we went to a play.

The story ___was___ wonderful.

The people ___were___ funny.

It ___was___ a very long play.

We ___were___ all tired!
          Love,
          Lilly

137

▲ Language Handbook, p. 137

Poppleton Everyday **185N**

Books for
All Learners
Reinforcing Skills and Strategies

■ BELOW-LEVEL

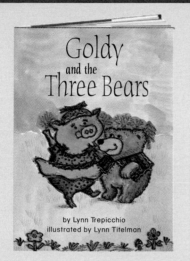

Goldy
and the
Three Bears

by Lynn Trepicchio
illustrated by Lynn Titelman

Goldy and the Three Bears

✓ **Phonics: Long Vowel /yōō, ōō/u-e**

✓ **High-Frequency Words:** *boy, read*

✓ **Vocabulary:** *brought, few*

✓ **Focus Skill: Predict Outcomes**

SUMMARY When Little Bear and his parents go in search of a new bed, they come home and find a surprise.

Visit *The Learning Site:*
www.harcourtschool.com
See Resources for Parents and
Teachers: Books for All Learners.

BEFORE READING

Build Background Have a volunteer summarize the story "Goldilocks and the Three Bears." Ask children if they have ever heard a different version of this story. Have volunteers describe some of the differences in detail or story line.

Preview/Set Purpose Have children identify the title and help them read it. Point out the author and the illustrator. Then have children look at the first few pages of the book and predict what the story is about. Help children set a purpose for reading, such as *I want to find out what happens to Goldy.*

READING THE BOOK

Page 2 How is this story different from the original story? (Little Bear is no longer a baby and he needs a new bed.) COMPARE/CONTRAST

Pages 5–6 How does Little Bear feel about the bed? (He dislikes it.) DETERMINE CHARACTERS' EMOTIONS

Pages 7–8 Why do you think Little Bear does not like either bed? (He is used to his old bed and neither of these beds seems as comfortable.) DRAW CONCLUSIONS

Pages 9–10 Who do you think is sleeping in the bed? (Goldy) What do you think will happen next? (Possible response: Father Bear will roar and wake her up.) PREDICT OUTCOMES

Pages 11–12 What happens after Goldy and the three bears go home? (They find a little boy sleeping in Little Bear's old bed.) SEQUENCE

RESPONDING

Put on a Puppet Show Have partners make finger puppets for Little Bear, Mama Bear, Papa Bear, Goldy, and the little boy. Direct partners to use their puppets to retell the story.

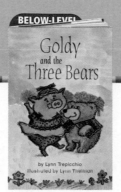

Goldy
and the
Three Bears

by Lynn Trepicchio
Illustrated by Lynn Trieman

All About Pigs

by Margaret Gallo

Little Pig at the State Fair

by Margaret Gallo
Illustrated by Bob McMahon

▲ p. 185Q

The Furniture in My House

by Kathryn E. Lewis
Illustrated by Jeff Shelly

▲ p. 185R

■ ON-LEVEL

All About Pigs

- ✔ **Phonics:** Long Vowel /yōō, ōō/u-e
- ✔ **High-Frequency Words:** *head, read, boy*
- ✔ **Vocabulary:** *brought, few*
- ✔ **Focus Skill:** Predict Outcomes

SUMMARY Duke, the pig, shares facts about pigs that many people may not know.

Visit *The Learning Site:*
www.harcourtschool.com
See Resources for Parents and Teachers: Books for All Learners.

BEFORE READING

Build Background Have children tell what they know about pigs. Ask them what they would like to find out about pigs. Record their responses on a K-W-L chart.

Preview/Set Purpose Have children identify the title and help them read it. Point out the author and the illustrator. Then have children look at the first few pages of the book and predict what the story is about. Help children set a purpose for reading, such as *I want to find out something I don't know about pigs.*

READING THE BOOK

Pages 2–4 How do pigs use their snouts? (They use their snouts to find food in the ground.) NOTE DETAILS

Pages 5–8 How does a mama pig care for her young? (She feeds them milk.) NOTE DETAILS

Pages 9–11 How do you know that pigs are smart? (They are able to do tricks.) DRAW CONCLUSIONS

Pages 12–13 Why do you think the boy sings a tune to his pet pig? (He is happy; he wants to make his pig feel loved.) SPECULATE

Pages 14–16 Why do you think the author wrote this story? (to tell facts about pigs that many people may not know) AUTHOR'S PURPOSE

RESPONDING

Pig Postcards Tell children to pretend they have gone on a field trip with Duke to learn about pigs. Have each child write on an index card a few facts he or she learned from *All About Pigs*. Encourage them to illustrate one of the facts on the other side. When all children have finished, have them switch postcards with a partner and read them aloud.

Books for All Learners

Reinforcing Skills and Strategies

■ ADVANCED

Little Pig at the State Fair

by Margaret Gallo
illustrated by Bob McMahon

Little Pig at the State Fair

✓ **Phonics:** Long Vowel /yo͞o, o͞o/*u-e*

✓ **High-Frequency Words:** *boy, head, read*

✓ **Vocabulary:** *brought, few*

✓ **Focus Skill: Predict Outcomes**

SUMMARY Although Little Pig does not win first prize at the State Fair, he does something far more important.

Visit *The Learning Site:*
www.harcourtschool.com
See Resources for Parents and
Teachers: Books for All Learners.

BEFORE READING

Build Background Have volunteers share experiences they have had participating in a contest. Encourage them to tell how they felt before, during, and after the contest.

Preview/Set Purpose Have children identify the title and help them read it. Point out the author and the illustrator. Then have children look at the first few pages of the book and predict what the story will be about. Have children set a purpose for reading, such as *I want to find out what happens to Little Pig.*

READING THE BOOK

Pages 2–3 What does June do after she brushes Little Pig? (She ties a bow on his head.) SEQUENCE

Pages 4–5 How does June feel about Little Pig's chances of winning the contest? (confident; hopeful) DETERMINE CHARACTERS' EMOTIONS

Pages 6–9 Do you think Little Pig will win the contest? Why? (Possible response: No, because he is too small.) PREDICT OUTCOMES

Pages 10–13 Why does Little Pig ring the fire alarm? (because he smells smoke) CAUSE/EFFECT

Pages 14–16 Why do you think the author decided to have Big Pig give Little Pig his prize? (Possible responses: She wanted to show that Big Pig was grateful; she wanted to show that being little is not a bad thing.) AUTHOR'S PURPOSE, THEME

RESPONDING

Retell the Story Have each child pick a partner and retell the story from Big Pig's point of view. Encourage children to use the sequence words *first*, *next*, and *last*. Guide children in staying on topic while speaking and listening attentively while others are speaking.

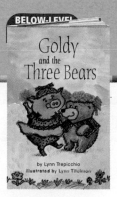

▲ p. 185O   ▲ p. 185P

Managing Small Groups

While you work with small groups, have other children do the following:

- Self-Selected Reading
- Practice Pages
- Cross-Curricular Centers
- Journal Writing

■ ENGLISH-LANGUAGE LEARNERS

The Furniture in My House

 Strong Picture Support

 Concept Vocabulary

 Theme Related

SUMMARY A boy tells about the different kinds of furniture in his house and what each is used for.

 Visit *The Learning Site:*
www.harcourtschool.com
See Resources for Parents and
Teachers: Books for All Learners.

BEFORE READING

Build Background Have children name the different types of furniture in their house. Write their responses on chart paper and have children repeat each word

Preview/Set Purpose Have children identify the title and help them read it. Point out the author and the illustrator. Then have children look at the first few pages of the book and predict what the story will be about. Help them set a purpose for reading, such as *I want to find out what kinds of furniture the boy talks about.*

READING THE BOOK

Pages 2–3 Where does Papa put the food? (on the table) NOTE DETAILS, RELATE PICTURES TO TEXT

Pages 4-–6 What does Mama do in the armchair? (She sits and reads.) NOTE DETAILS, RELATE PICTURES TO TEXT

Pages 7–9 How is a rocking chair different from an armchair? (A rocking chair rocks back and forth, but an armchair does not.) COMPARE/CONTRAST, RELATE PICTURES TO TEXT

Pages 10–12 How is your room the same as the boy's room? How is it different? (Possible response: Both rooms have a bed in them. My room does not have a desk.) COMPARE/CONTRAST

RESPONDING

Use a Model Display a toy dollhouse with all the people, rooms, and furniture described in the story. Invite children to manipulate the people and furniture to retell the story.

Teacher Notes

Teacher Notes

Reading Selections

BIG BOOK

DECODABLE BOOK

Applies Short Vowel /e/ea

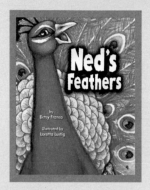

▲ Decodable Book 33
"All Kinds of Weather"
"Ned's Feathers"

PUPIL EDITION

Genre

Nonfiction

In nonfiction pieces, an author gives information about a topic.

Look for:

• Information about why sleep is important.

• Details and facts about sleep.

by Paul Showers
illustrated by Wendy Watson

▼ **READING ACROSS TEXTS:**
"Pretending"
GENRE: Poetry

SUMMARY: *This informational article explains how all animals and people need a certain amount of sleep each day.*

"Sleep Is for Everyone" is available on *Audiotext 5.*

Comparing Nonfiction and Poetry

Books for All Learners

Lesson Plans on pages 217M–217P

BELOW-LEVEL
- **Phonics: Short Vowel /e/ea**
- **Vocabulary: *afternoon, bicycle, carry, hours, parents***

ON-LEVEL
- **Phonics: Short Vowel /e/ea**
- **Vocabulary: *afternoon, bicycle, carry, hours, parents***

ADVANCED
- **Phonics: Short Vowel /e/ea**
- **Vocabulary: *afternoon, bicycle, carry, hours, parents***

ELL
- **Strong Picture Support**
- **Concept Vocabulary**

MULTI-LEVELED PRACTICE

Practice Book, pp. 48–55

Extra Support, pp. 49–55

Challenge, pp. 49–55

English-Language Learners, pp. 49–55

 Technology

- *Phonics Express™ CD-ROM, Level B*
- *Writing Express™ CD-ROM*
- *Grammar Jingles™ CD, Primary*
- *Reading and Language Skills Assessment CD-ROM*
- *The Learning Site: www.harcourtschool.com*

ADDITIONAL RESOURCES

Phonics Practice Book, pp. 182–183

Spelling Practice Book, pp. 79–80

Language Handbook, pp. 138–141

Read-Aloud Literature
- Big Book of Rhymes, p. 18

Teaching Transparencies 97–99, 108

Word Builders/Word Builder Cards

Letter Cards

Intervention Resource Kit, Lesson 33

English-Language Learners Resource Kit, Lesson 33

Sleep Is for Everyone,
pp. 188–209

Day 1

Day 2

30 Minutes

ORAL LANGUAGE

- **Sharing Literature**

Sharing Literature, 186H
Big Book: Build Concept Vocabulary

Sharing Literature, 186P
Poem: Build Concept Vocabulary

- **Phonemic Awareness**

Phonemic Awareness, 186H
Phoneme Isolation; Focus on /e/

Phonemic Awareness, 186P
Phoneme Isolation; Focus on /e/

30 Minutes

WORD WORK

- **Phonics**

Phonics, 186I
Introduce: Short Vowel /e/ea

Phonics, 186Q
Review: Short Vowel /e/ea

- **Spelling**

Spelling, 186K
Pretest; Word Sort **T**

Spelling, 186Q
Word Building **T**

- **Vocabulary**

Vocabulary, 186K
Review: *few* **T**

Vocabulary, 186S
Introduce: *afternoon, bicycle, carry, hours, parents* **T**

- **High-Frequency Words**

High-Frequency Words, 186K
Review: *boy* **T**

Word Power, pp. 186–187

45 Minutes

READING

- **Comprehension**
- **Fluency**

Read
Apply Phonics, 186L

DECODABLE BOOK 33
"All Kinds of Weather"

Read
Read the Selection, 187A

PUPIL EDITION
"Sleep Is for Everyone,"
pp. 186–211

Comprehension

 Focus Skill Main Idea **T**

 Focus Strategy Make Inferences

Daily Routines
- **Morning Message**
- **Daily Language Practice**
- **Writing Prompt**

- **Independent Reading**

 Independent Reading
Books for All Learners

 Independent Reading
Books for All Learners

45 Minutes

LANGUAGE ARTS

- **Writing**

 Shared Writing, 186M
Animal Chart

Writing Prompt
Have children draw an animal in its habitat and write about it.

Independent Writing, 211B
Story Response

Writing Prompt
Have children write a question about "Sleep Is for Everyone."

- **Grammar**

Grammar, 186N
Introduce: Using *Go* and *Went*

Grammar, 211C
Review: Using *Go* and *Went*

Daily Language Practice
Spiral Review

Daily Language Practice
i red a book about flowers. (I, read)

Daily Language Practice
the dogs can went home right now.
(The, go)

Focus Skill
Main Idea

Phonics
Short Vowel /e/ea

Focus of the Week:
- **VOCABULARY:** *afternoon, bicycle, carry, hours, parents*
- **COMPREHENSION:** Main Idea
- **WRITING:** Using *Go* and *Went*

Day 3

Sharing Literature, 211E
Poem: Listen and Respond

Phonemic Awareness, 211E
Phoneme Segmentation; Focus on /ē/ and /e/

Phonics, 211F
Review: Short Vowel /e/ea
Spelling, 211H
State the Generalization **T**
Vocabulary, 211I
Review: *afternoon, bicycle, carry, hours, parents* **T**

Read
Rereading for Fluency, 211J

Reading Across Texts, 212–213
"Pretending"

Making Connections, 214–215

Apply Phonics, 211G
DECODABLE BOOK 33
"Ned's Feathers"

 Independent Reading
Books for All Learners

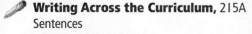 **Writing Across the Curriculum,** 215A
Sentences

Writing Prompt
Have children write about how they feel when they are asleep and awake.

Grammar, 215B
Review: Using *Go* and *Went*

Daily Language Practice
I go to Jim's house last week? (went, week.)

Day 4

Sharing Literature, 215D
Poem: Listen and Respond

Phonemic Awareness, 215D
Phoneme Isolation; Focus on /e/ and /a/

Phonics, 215E
Build Words
Spelling, 215G
Review **T**
Vocabulary, 215H
Review: *afternoon, bicycle, carry, hours, parents* **T**

Read
Comprehension, 215I

 Main Idea, pp. 216–217 **T**

 Independent Reading
Books for All Learners

 Independent Writing, 217A
Captions

Writing Prompt
Have children write two facts about an animal that lives in the forest.

Grammar, 217B
Review: Using *Go* and *Went*

Daily Language Practice
Steve and randy goed home. (Randy, went)

Day 5

Sharing Literature, 217D
Big Book: Develop Listening Comprehension

Phonemic Awareness, 217D
Phoneme Isolation: Focus on -er, -est

Phonics, 217E
Review: Inflections -er,-est; Inflections -ed, -ing **T**
Spelling, 217G
Posttest; Writing Application **T**
Vocabulary, 217H
Review: *afternoon, bicycle, carry, hours, parents* **T**

Read
Rereading for Fluency, 217I

Self-Selected Reading, 217J

 Independent Reading
Books for All Learners

 Interactive Writing, 217K
Facts List

Self-Selected Writing
Have children write about a topic of their choice.

Grammar, 217L
Review: Using *Go* and *Went*

Daily Language Practice
Is there a fether in my bed. (feather, bed?)

Sleep Is For Everyone   **186D**

Cross-Curricular Centers

SCIENCE CENTER

Observing Animals

Have children observe a classroom pet or a pet at home to see how long the animal sleeps. Prepare forms like the one pictured and have children fill them out. Children should record the dates and times the pet sleeps. After a week of observing, have children look at the forms together and tell if they see any patterns.

> Name of Animal: _____
>
> Date: _____
>
> Times seen sleeping:
>
> _____
>
> _____
>
> _____

Materials

- pet or animal to observe
- clock or timer
- observation forms

LETTER AND WORD CENTER

15 Minutes

/ē/ ea and /e/ ea Words

Have partners use *Letter Cards* or *Word Builder Cards* to make words that contain the letters *ea*. Then have children sort the words into two lists: those words that have the long vowel sound of e and those that have the short vowel sound of e. Have partners list their words. You may want to duplicate and distribute a two-column chart for partners to use to record their words.

Materials

- *Letter Cards* or *Word Builder Cards*
- copies of two-column chart

MATH CENTER

20 Minutes

Add Them Up!

Have partners work together to create math story problems from information in the selection. Post these sentences and the example in the center for children to refer to as they work. Have them share their finished problems with one another.

> Babies need 12 hours of sleep each night.
>
> Seven-year-olds need 10 hours of sleep each night.
>
> Grown-ups need 8 hours of sleep each night.
>
> Example: How much sleep do you and three friends need each night?
> 10 + 10 + 10 + 10 = 40 hours

Materials

- *Pupil Edition*, "Sleep Is for Everyone"

SCIENCE

LETTER AND WORD
ABC

MATH
+2

TECHNOLOGY

SOCIAL STUDIES

COMPUTER CENTER

Animal Dreams

Have children think of a pet they know. Then have them imagine a wonderful dream that the pet might have. Direct children in using artist's tools on the computer to draw a picture that shows what happens in the pet's dream. Then have them write sentences that tell about the dream.

Spike dreams about our cat Feathers.

45 Minutes

Materials
- word processing software and computer
- software for drawing

SOCIAL STUDIES CENTER

Night Jobs

Have children work together to brainstorm different jobs people do at night. Help children record their ideas on chart paper. Have groups illustrate a mural showing people who work at night. Each child can either draw pictures or cut pictures from old magazines. Have children label each person with the name of his or her job. At the end of the week, have groups share their murals. Ask contributors to tell what they added to the mural and explain the jobs.

Firefighter   cashier

45 Minutes

Materials
- butcher paper
- old magazines
- scissors
- glue
- crayons or markers

HOMEWORK FOR THE WEEK

The Homework Copying Master provides activities to complete for each day of the week.

   Visit *The Learning Site:* www.harcourtschool.com

See Resources for Parents and Teachers: Homework Helper.

School–Home Connection

Your child has been reading "Sleep Is for Everyone." This nonfiction story tells why and how people sleep.

I have tried some of the activities.

Student: _____
Family Member: _____
Comments/Suggestions: _____

You may want to do some of these activities with your child.

Words, Words, Words
- Have your child cut out the word cards and read each word.
- Have your child pick three new words to act out for you. Try to guess the words your child acts out.
- Say a sentence with each new word, but leave the word out. Have your child show the card with the missing word and then say the whole sentence.

Sleep Well!
Ask your child to describe how some animals sleep. If you have pets at home, take time to watch them sleep. Then remind your child that brown bears sleep all winter long; this is called hibernating. Have your child draw a picture to show what he or she would do if people slept during the whole winter.

| afternoon |
| bicycle |
| carry |
| hours |
| parents |

TIME TO READ Encourage your child to read for at least 30 minutes outside of class each day.

Visit The Learning Site!
www.harcourtschool.com
See Resources for Parents and Teachers: Homework Helper

Homework, p. T45 ▶

Day at a Glance
Day 1

Sharing Literature
Big Book: *To Market, To Market*

Phonemic Awareness
Phoneme Isolation; Focus on /e/

Phonics
INTRODUCE: Short Vowel /e/*ea*

Spelling
Pretest; Word Sort

Vocabulary
REVIEW: *few*

High-Frequency Word
REVIEW: *boy*

Reading
Decodable Book 33
"All Kinds of Weather"

Read

Shared Writing ✏
Animal Chart

Grammar
INTRODUCE: Using *Go* and *Went*

WARM UP

MORNING MESSAGE

Good Morning!

Today is _____.
We went to the grocery store.
_____ bought _____.
_____ bought _____.
_____ helped by _____.

Introduce the Day

Tell children they will reread the *Big Book To Market, To Market*, a story about a woman who buys food at a market. Ask children to tell what they bought at the grocery store the last time they went and how they helped at the store.

- **What did your family buy at the grocery store the last time you went?**
- **Did you help find things on the shelves or pick out fresh fruit or vegetables? How else did you help?**

As you write, ask volunteers to write previously taught letters, words, and/or punctuation. For instance, a volunteer can write the decodable and high-frequency words *morning, We, went, store, helped, by.* Remind children to capitalize the names of people.

Read the Message

Read the message. Use the message to focus on selected skills that have been previously taught.

Apply Skills

Grammar/Mechanics Ask children to identify nouns, such as *store*, people's names, and grocery items. Elicit from children that nouns begin with a capital letter if they name a particular person, place, or thing.	**Phonics** Ask a volunteer to point to a word that begins with the consonant blend *gr.* (grocery) Then have children name other words that begin with the same blend.

Sharing Literature

BUILD CONCEPT VOCABULARY

Vegetables

potatoes

celery

beets

tomatoes

peppers

(Focus Skill) **Main Idea** Reread *To Market, To Market*. Pause after reading pages 4–11, and ask children what the pages are mostly about. After you finish reading the story, have children fill in this sentence frame to state the main idea:

The lady finally bought ____ at the market because ____.

Generate Names of Vegetables
Ask children what the lady bought at the end of the story. (vegetables) Have children name the vegetables she bought. List them on chart paper. Then have children name other vegetables. Add them to the list. Read the list aloud. Ask volunteers to add pictures beside the names of the vegetables.

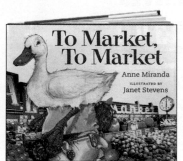

▲ **Big Book**

Phonemic Awareness

PHONEME ISOLATION

Words from the Big Book Say *head* slowly, elongating the sound /e/. Ask children what vowel sound they hear in the middle of the word. (/e/) Then say these words and have children touch their heads each time they hear a word with the sound /e/.

hen	trout	**pen**	cow	soup	**vegetables**
let	lamb	pig	**pepper**	**celery**	**everything**

FOCUS ON /e/

Isolate Phonemes Say the word *head* slowly, elongating the sound /e/. Ask children what vowel sound they hear in the middle of the word. (/e/) Then continue, using these words with *ea*:

read (/e/)   **bread** (/e/)   **lead** (/e/)   **dread** (/e/)

deaf (/e/)   **breath** (/e/)   **spread** (/e/)   **thread** (/e/)

Phonics and Spelling
Short Vowel /e/ea *Introduce*

OBJECTIVES

- *To generate the short vowel sound of /e/ea*

- *To build words using known letters and sounds*

- *To read simple, regular words*

SKILL TRACE

/e/ea	
INTRODUCE	186I–186L
Reteach	S40–S41
Review	186Q–186R, 211F–211G
Review	215E–215F

teaching tip

Build Vocabulary Tell children that they have learned how to read the words *read* and *lead* with the long vowel sound of *e*, but that they will now learn a different pronunciation for *ea*. Tell them that *read* (long *e*) and *read* (short *e*) have different meanings, as do *lead* (long *e*) and *lead* (short *e*). Talk about the meanings of the words.

TEACH/MODEL

Introduce /e/ea Display *Alphabet Cards Ee* and *Aa* together and say the letter names. Tell children that the letters *ea* can stand for the sound /e/, the short vowel sound of *e* in words such as *head* and *bread*.

Hold up *Letter Cards e* and *a* together and say /e/. Tell children that the sound /e/ appears in the middle of the words *head*, *bread*, and *lead*. Have children repeat the sound several times as you touch the cards.

WORD BLENDING

Words with /e/ea Blend and read the words *head*, *read*, and *instead*. As you demonstrate each step, using a pocket chart and *Letter Cards*, have children repeat after you, using *Word Builders* and *Word Builder Cards*.

Phonics CENTER

Post these words with the short vowel sound of *a*: *had*, *lad*, *Brad*. Have children use plastic letters to make words with the short vowel sound of *e* by adding an *e* in front of the *a* in each of the words (*head*, *lead*, *bread*). Then have children form other words with /e/ea.

head
lead
bread
read
thread

20 Minutes

Materials
■ plastic letters

WORD BUILDING

a b d e h l r v y

Build Spelling Words Place the letter *l* in a pocket chart. Have children do the same with their *Word Builders* and *Word Builder Cards*. Repeat for the letters *ea* together and then *d*. Model how to blend the word *lead*. Slide your hand under the letters as you slowly elongate the sounds—/lleedd/. Then read the word naturally—*lead*. Have children do the same.

Have children build and read new words by telling them:

- Change the *l* to *h*. What word did you make?

- Take away the *h*. Add a *b* and an *r* in front of *ead*. What word did you make?

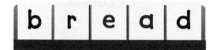

- Take away the *b*. What word did you make?

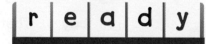

- Add a *y* after the *d*. What word did you make?

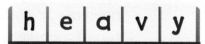

- Change the *r* to *h*. Change the *d* to *v*. What word did you make?

 Dictate Short /e/ea Words Dictate the words *bread*, *heavy*, and *head.* Have children write them in their journal. Suggest that they either draw a picture or write about each word.

Phonics Resources

Phonics Express™ CD-ROM, **Level B** Sparkle/Route 3/Train Station

Phonics Practice Book, pp. 182–183

Spelling Words

1. lead
2. head
3. bread
4. read
5. ready
6. heavy
7. rule
8. use
9. few
10. boy

Phonics and Spelling

5-DAY SPELLING	
DAY 1	Pretest; Word Sort
DAY 2	Word Building
DAY 3	State the Generalization
DAY 4	Review
DAY 5	Posttest; Writing Application

INTRODUCE THE WORDS

Pretest Read aloud the first word and the Dictation Sentence. Repeat the word as children write it. Write the correct spelling on the board and have children circle the word if they spelled it correctly and write it correctly if they did not. Repeat for words 2-10.

1. **lead**   I broke my pencil **lead.**
2. **head**   I have brown hair on my **head.**
3. **bread** You can make a sandwich with **bread.**
4. **read**   I **read** two books last week.
5. **ready** The soccer team is **ready** to play.
6. **heavy** Ten books are too **heavy** to carry.

Review

7. **rule**   Do you know the playground **rule?**
8. **use**   My sister let me **use** her bike.

Vocabulary

9. **few**   Only a **few** children are absent today.

High-Frequency

10. **boy**   That **boy** is my brother.

Word Sort Place the numerals *3*, *4*, and *5* at the top of a pocket chart. Write each Spelling Word on an index card. Display the cards and ask, "Which words are made of three letters? Which words are made of four letters? Which words are made of five letters?" Place the words in the correct columns as children direct. Then have children read the words aloud.

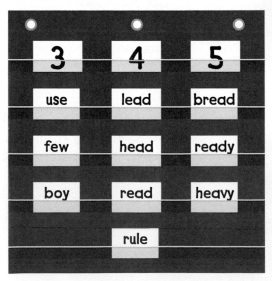

▲ Practice Book, p. 48

Apply Phonics

Read
All Kinds of Weather
by Sunita Apte
illustrated by John Wallace

▲ **Decodable Book 33**
"All Kinds of Weather"

APPLY /e/ea

Write the following sentences on the board or on chart paper. Have children read the first sentence as you track the print. Frame the word *heavy* and have children read it. Continue with the other sentences.

> That stack of books is **heavy**.
> I have **read** all of them.
> I have **read** about **bread** and **lead**.
> I'm **ready** for a new book.

Have children read "All Kinds of Weather" in *Decodable Book 33.*

Managing Small Groups

Read the *Decodable Book* with small groups of children. While you work with small groups, have other children do the following:

- **Self-Selected Reading**
- **Practice Pages**
- **Cross-Curricular Centers**
- **Journal Writing**

Use the suggested Classroom Management outline on page 7C for the whole-group/small-group schedule.

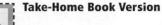

School-Home Connection

Take-Home Book Version

◀ Decodable Books
Take-Home Version

All Kinds of Weather
by Sunita Apte
illustrated by John Wallace

ONGOING ASSESSMENT

Note how well children
- decode words in "All Kinds of Weather."
- read sentences independently.
- complete short vowel /e/ea practice pages.

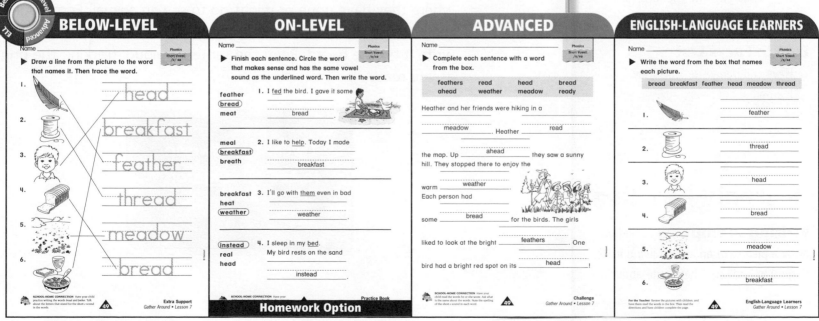

▲ Extra Support, p. 49   ▲ Practice, p. 49   ▲ Challenge, p. 49   ▲ ELL, p. 49

i red a book about flowers.

I <u>read</u> a book about flowers.

Writing Every Day

Day 1: Animal Chart
Work with children to fill in a chart about animals and where they live, and then create sentences about the animals.

Day 2: Story Response
Have children write interesting facts they learned from the story.

Day 3: Sentences
Have children write sentences that tell how many hours they spend sleeping or doing some other activity.

Day 4: Captions
Have children write captions for a mural they draw.

Day 5: Facts List
Have children write facts they learned about sleep.

Writing Prompt Have children draw a picture of an animal living in its natural habitat and then write about it.

Shared Writing
Animal Chart

BRAINSTORM

Discuss Animal Habitats Tell children that soon they will be reading about ways different animals sleep. Discuss with children the places where animals live. Ask children to name some of these places (habitats) and the kinds of animals that they might find there. Record their responses on a chart. You may want to have children add to the chart throughout the week. Keep this chart for use during the Writing Activity on Day 4, page 217A.

Place	Animals That Might Live There
farm	cows, chickens, sheep, horses
swamp	alligators, fish, snakes
forest	bears, squirrels, birds, deer
home	cats, dogs, gerbils, fish
zoo	monkeys, elephants, lions

CREATE SENTENCES

Dictate Sentences Read aloud children's responses on the chart. Then have children take turns dictating a sentence that tells where they have gone or might go to see an animal. Encourage them to use the ideas from the chart. Model a sentence and write it on the board. Read the sentence aloud, tracking the print as you read.

I went to a swamp to see an alligator.

Grammar

Using Go *and* Went

5-DAY GRAMMAR

DAY 1	**Introduce Using *Go* and *Went***
DAY 2	Generate Sentences
DAY 3	Sentence Frames
DAY 4	Play a Game
DAY 5	Write Sentences

TEACH/MODEL

Introduce Using *Go* and *Went* Have children walk to the window or to your desk saying, "I go to the _____." Have children walk back to their seat and say "I go back to my seat." Record the sentences on the board and read them aloud.

> **I go to the window.**
> **I go back to my seat.**

Explain that the sentences tell what is happening now. Have a volunteer underline *go.* Tell children that *go* is a verb that can be used to tell about now. Then replace the word *go* in both sentences with the word *went* and read the sentences aloud. Explain that *went* tells about something that has already happened.

PRACTICE/APPLY

Display *Teaching Transparency 97* Talk about the picture. Have children read each sentence and explain why the underlined word is correct by telling when the action takes place.

WRAP UP Reread the Big Book

Retell the Story Reread *To Market, To Market,* asking children to join in. Pause before the last word of each sentence so that children can supply the rhyming word. Then page through the book and have volunteers retell the story.

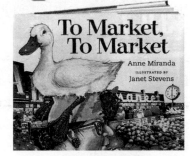

▲ Big Book

S.S.R.
Sustained Silent Reading

Have children read silently from a book of their choice. See page 217J for tips on helping children choose books.

OBJECTIVE

To use go *and* went *correctly in sentences to describe actions in time*

SKILL TRACE

USING *Go* AND *Went*	
INTRODUCE	**186N**
Review	211C, 215B, 217B, 217L
T Test	Bk 1-5

▼ **Teaching Transparency 97**

USING *GO* AND *WENT*

1. We <u>went</u> to the park.
2. Now we <u>go</u> home.
3. We <u>go</u> home on a bus.
4. Yesterday we <u>went</u> home in a car.

CITY PARK

"Sleep Is for Everyone"
Gather Around, Volume 1-5 ● 97
Grammar: Using Go and Went
Harcourt

Name _____

Grammar
Using Go and Went

▶ Write **go** or **went** to complete each sentence. Then circle **now** or **in the past** to show when each action took place.

1. You and I can __go__ to the zoo. — (now) / in the past

2. We __went__ last month. — now / (in the past)

3. We can __go__ again. — (now) / in the past

4. The goats __went__ from rock to rock last time. — now / (in the past)

Work with a partner to change the sentences. If it is in the past, make it tell about now. If it is about now, make it tell about something in the past. Use the words **go** and **went**.

SCHOOL-HOME CONNECTION
● 50
Practice Book
Gather Around ● Lesson 7

▲ Practice Book, p. 50

Sleep Is for Everyone **186N**

Sharing Literature
Poem: "Night Bear"

Phonemic Awareness
Phoneme Isolation; Focus on /e/

Phonics
REVIEW: Short Vowel /e/*ea*

Spelling
Word Building

Vocabulary
INTRODUCE: *afternoon, bicycle, carry, hours, parents*

Reading
Pupil Edition
"Sleep Is for Everyone," pp. 186–211

Interactive Writing ✏
Story Response

Grammar
REVIEW: Using *Go* and *Went*

ORAL LANGUAGE

WARM UP

MORNING MESSAGE
Good Morning!

Today is _____.
What do we do to get ready for sleep?
First we _____.
Next we _____.
Then we _____.

Introduce the Day

Tell children that they will listen to a poem about the way one child likes to sleep. Ask children what they do as they are getting ready to go to sleep.

- **How do you get ready for bed?**

- **What helps you go to sleep?**

As you write the message, invite volunteers to add letters, known words, and punctuation marks. Point out that the words *first, next,* and *then* tell readers that they are reading about steps that happen in a certain order.

Read the Message

Read the message. Use the message to focus on selected skills that have been previously taught.

Apply Skills

Phonics As you write the words in the message, have children sound out and spell decodable words such as *first, next, then, get, ready, sleep, for,* and *we.* Ask children what letters in *ready* stand for the sound /e/. *(ea)*

Grammar Read aloud the completed message. Have volunteers frame and read action verbs. Then have children pantomime the actions.

Sharing Literature

BUILD CONCEPT VOCABULARY

Connect to Prior Knowledge Ask volunteers to tell what a Teddy bear is. Then read "Night Bear." Discuss why the speaker is glad to have the Teddy bear.

Explore Synonyms Talk about the meaning of *snuggling.* Say: *When you snuggle something, you hug it and hold it close to you. The speaker is hugging and holding the bear close. The bear is snuggling close to the speaker's head.* Write *snuggle* on the board. Under it, list *hug* and *hold close.* Say these sentences and ask children to tell which words mean the same as snuggle: *The baby birds nestle together in their nest. I like to cuddle my kitten in my arms.* Add *nestle* and *cuddle* to the list. Read the completed list and emphasize that many different words have the same or almost the same meaning. Ask volunteers to choose words from the list to tell about things they like to snuggle.

Night Bear

In the dark of night
when all is still
And I'm half-sleeping in my bed;
It's good to know
my Teddy-bear
is snuggling at my head.

Lee Bennett Hopkins

Phonemic Awareness

PHONEME ISOLATION

Words from "Night Bear" Reread the poem "Night Bear" and have children listen for two words that rhyme. *(bed, head)* Ask children what vowel sound they hear in the middle of *bed* and *head.* *(/e/)* Then say these words, and have children tell which vowel sound they hear in the middle.

lead (/e/) **dark** (/är/) **read** (/e/) **sleep** (/ē/) **bread** (/e/)
Teddy (/e/) **good** (/ŏŏ/) **spread** (/e/) **dread** (/e/) **night** (/ī/)

FOCUS ON /e/

Blending Phonemes Tell children that you are going to say some words very slowly and they will blend the sounds together to make a word. Model by saying /h/ /e/ /d/, *head.* Continue with these words:

/b/ /r/ /e/ /d/ (bread)   /l/ /e/ /d/ (lead)   /d/ /e/ /f/ (deaf)
/s/ /p/ /r/ /e/ /d/ (spread)   /r/ /e/ /d/ (read)   /r/ /e/ /d/ /ē/ (ready)

Diagnostic Check: Phonemic Awareness

If... children have difficulty blending phonemes into words...

Then... repeat the phonemes of each word several times, blending the sounds more closely with each repetition until children are able to distinguish the word.

ADDITIONAL SUPPORT ACTIVITIES

BELOW-LEVEL	Reteach, p. S38
ADVANCED	Extend, p. S39
ENGLISH-LANGUAGE LEARNERS	Reteach, p. S39

OBJECTIVES

• *To blend sounds into words*

• *To read and write Spelling Words*

SKILL TRACE

lelea	
Introduce	186I–186L
Reteach	S40–S41
REVIEW	**186Q–186R, 211F–211G**
Review	215E–215F

Spelling Words

1. **lead**
2. **head**
3. **bread**
4. **read**
5. **ready**
6. **heavy**
7. **rule**
8. **use**
9. **few**
10. **boy**

Phonics and Spelling
Short Vowel /e/ea *Review*

WORD BUILDING

Blend and Read a Spelling Word
Have children recall that the letters *ea* together can stand for the sound /e/. Place *Letter Cards l, e, a, d* in a pocket chart, placing the *e* and *a* in at the same time. Ask children to name each letter as you place it in the chart. Slide your hand under the letters as you blend the sounds—/lleedd/. Have children repeat after you. Then read the word naturally—*lead,* and have children do the same.

Build Spelling Words Ask children which letter you should change to make *lead* become *head.* (change *l* to *h*) Continue building the Spelling Words shown in this manner and having children read them.

5-DAY SPELLING

DAY 1	Pretest; Word Sort
DAY 2	Word Building
DAY 3	State the Generalization
DAY 4	Review
DAY 5	Posttest; Writing Application

l	e	a	d

h	e	a	d

b	r	e	a	d

r	e	a	d

r	e	a	d	y

h	e	a	v	y

ADVANCED

Children can build words with the long vowel and short vowel sounds of *e.* As they build words, have them write them in two lists: one labeled *bead* and the other labeled *bread.*

ENGLISH-LANGUAGE LEARNERS

Reinforce the meaning of the Spelling Words for children who may be unfamiliar with them. Throughout the day, use the words in sentences, emphasizing the Spelling Word. Then point children to the spelling list and have them find the appropriate word. For example, say: *Are you ready for lunch? Who can find the word* ready *in the spelling list?*

Apply Phonics

READ WORDS IN CONTEXT

Write the following sentences on the board or on chart paper and have children read them aloud.

Mick **read** about making **bread**.
He used a **lead** pencil to make a list.
At the store, a **boy** put a **few heavy** sacks
in the car.
Mick wore a cook's hat on his **head**.
"I'll **use** a bowl to mix the batter," he said.
Now the **bread** is hot and **ready**.

 Dictate Words Dictate several words from the pocket chart, and have children write the words on a dry-erase board or in their journal.

lead
head
bread
read
ready
heavy

5-DAY PHONICS/SPELLING

DAY 1	Introduce /e/ea
DAY 2	**Word Building with /e/ea**
DAY 3	Word Building with /e/ea
DAY 4	Word Building with /e/ea and /a/a
DAY 5	Inflections -er, -est; Inflections -ed, -ing (double final consonant)

Phonics Resources

Phonics Express™ CD-ROM,
Level B Sparkle/Route 3/Park

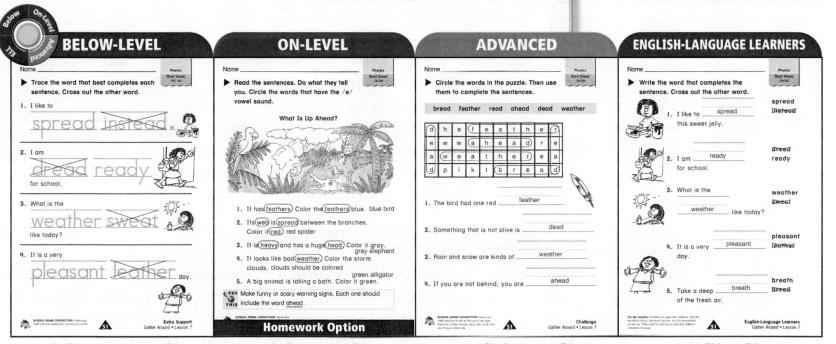

▲ Extra Support, p. 51   ▲ Practice, p. 51   ▲ Challenge, p. 51   ▲ ELL, p. 51

Vocabulary

afternoon the time after noon and before evening

bicycle a two-wheeled vehicle; a bike

carry take from one place to another

hours units of time that are sixty minutes long

parents fathers and mothers

Building Background

TALK ABOUT SLEEP

Make a K-W-L Chart Tell children they will read a selection about sleeping. Ask children what they already know about sleeping and write their responses in the first column of a K-W-L chart, such as *Teaching Transparency 104*. Then have children suggest questions for which they would like to find answers.

SLEEPING		
K—What We KNOW	**W—What We WANT to Know**	**L—What We LEARNED**
Animals sleep. We need sleep.	How much sleep do cats need? How much sleep do I need each night? Where do alligators sleep?	

Discuss Story Words List *attention, balloon, diaper, perfectly, pigeon, wander,* and *yawn* on the board. Point to each word and read it aloud. Talk about the meanings of the words and have volunteers use them in sentences.

Vocabulary

INTRODUCE WORDS IN CONTEXT

Read Sentences Display *Teaching Transparency 98* or write the words and sentences on the board. Point to each word and read it aloud. Track the print as you read aloud the sentences. Call on volunteers to reread each sentence.

INTRODUCE

Vocabulary

afternoon

bicycle   hours

carry   parents

CHECK UNDERSTANDING

Every-Pupil Response Duplicate and distribute a set of Individual Word Cards for each child: *afternoon, bicycle, carry, hours, parents* (page T37). As you give the meaning of each word, have children read aloud the correct Word Card and hold it up.

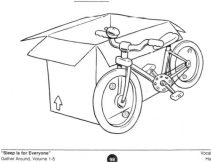

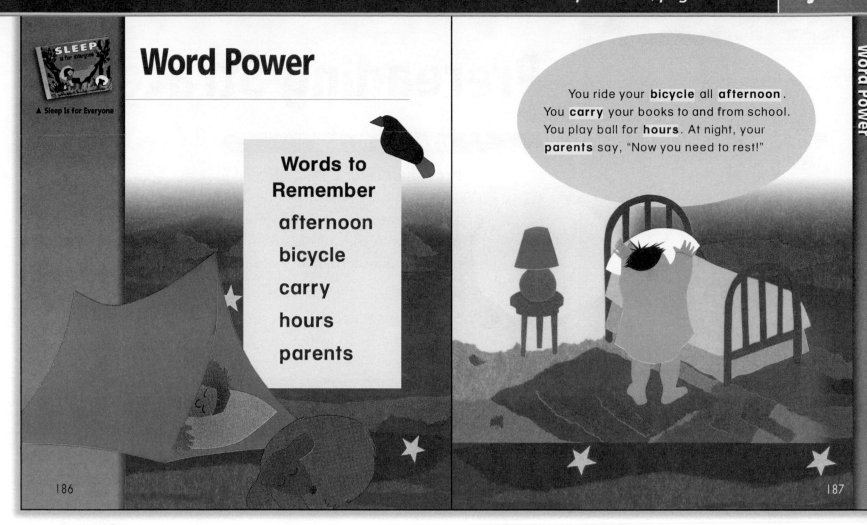

Word Power

Pages 186–187 Have children read aloud the Words to Remember. Then have children read the sentences aloud. Have children point to the Words to Remember in the sentences.

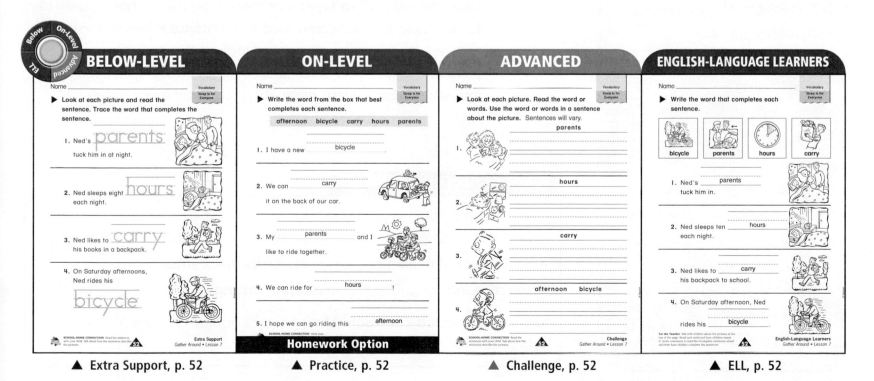

▲ Extra Support, p. 52   ▲ Practice, p. 52   ▲ Challenge, p. 52   ▲ ELL, p. 52

■ **Phonics**

Short Vowel /e/ea

■ **Vocabulary**

afternoon, bicycle, carry, hours, parents

■ **Decodable Words**

See the list on pages T50–T51.

■ **Comprehension**

 Main Idea

 Make Inferences

Strategies Good Readers Use

To Recognize Words

• Use Decoding/Phonics

• Look for Word Bits and Parts

To Gain Meaning

• Self-Correct

• Read Ahead

• Reread

• Reread Aloud

• Use Picture Clues to Confirm Meaning

• Make and Confirm Predictions

• Sequence Events/Summarize

• Create Mental Images

• **Make Inferences**

READING

Prereading Strategies

PREPARING TO READ

Preview/Predict Have children look at pages 188–189 and read aloud the title. Have them follow along as you read the author's and illustrator's names. Preview pages 190–193 and have children predict what they will learn as they read the selection. If they have any questions, add them to the second column of the K-W-L chart.

Set Purpose Help children set a purpose for reading. If necessary, suggest they read to find out how different animals sleep.

COMPREHENSION SKILL

 Main Idea Tell children that each selection they read has a main idea. The main idea is what the selection is mostly about. Sometimes one sentence on each page tells the page's main idea. Ask children to try to figure out the main idea as they read.

COMPREHENSION STRATEGY

Make Inferences Explain to children that sometimes we can learn more from a selection than the author tells us. Sometimes we can find clues in the pictures and use what we have already read to figure out more than the author actually says. For example, when children read the sentence *When a horse goes to sleep, its eyelids go down,* and look at the sleeping horse in the picture, they can infer that horses sleep standing up. By making an inference, children learn more about the way a horse sleeps.

Managing Small Groups

Read "Sleep Is for Everyone" with small groups of children. While you work with small groups, have other children do the following:

• **Self-Selected Reading**   • **Cross-Curricular Centers**

• **Practice Pages**   • **Journal Writing**

Use the suggested Classroom Management outline on page 7C for the whole-group/small-group schedule.

Genre

Nonfiction

In nonfiction pieces, an author gives information about a topic.

Look for:

• Information about why sleep is important.

• Details and facts about sleep.

188

SLEEP
Is for Everyone

by Paul Showers
illustrated by Wendy Watson

189

Guided Comprehension

Pages 188–189 Have children reread the title and review their predictions about what they will learn from "Sleep Is for Everyone."

GENRE: Nonfiction

Read aloud the information about nonfiction on page 188. Tell children that nonfiction includes

• facts about real people or animals.

• events that really happen.

BELOW-LEVEL	ON-LEVEL	ADVANCED	ENGLISH-LANGUAGE LEARNERS
Read aloud the first six pages of the story as children follow along. Have children list what they learned on the K-W-L chart. Read the pages and have them check off questions they can answer. SMALL GROUP	As children read the selection, use the Guided Comprehension questions to direct their reading. WHOLE CLASS/SMALL GROUP	Have children share their predictions about the selection and then read silently. Afterward, have children discuss whether their predictions were correct. INDIVIDUAL/SMALL GROUP	Before reading, point to key words in the story, such as *eyelids, standing up,* and so on. Ask children questions such as "Who is standing up? Whose eyelids are down?" Then have them read the text. SMALL GROUP
ADDITIONAL SUPPORT See Intervention Resource Kit, Lesson 33. *Intervention Teacher's Guide pp. 322–331*			**ADDITIONAL SUPPORT** See English-Language Learners Resource Kit, Lesson 33. *English-Language Learners Teacher's Guide pp. 194–195*

When a horse goes to sleep, its eyelids go down.

When a chicken goes to sleep, its eyelids go up. When a snake sleeps, its eyes stay open. Snakes have no eyelids.

When you go to sleep, which way do your eyelids go?

190

191

Guided Comprehension

Pages 190–191 Have children look at the illustrations and predict what they will learn about sleeping. Ask them why they think so. Then have them read to find out.

1 **NOTE DETAILS** What happens when a horse goes to sleep? (Its eyelids go down.)

2 **MAKE INFERENCES** Do you think a horse sleeps standing up or lying down? Why do you think so? (Possible response: Standing up, because the horses are standing up and the one with its eyelids down must be sleeping.)

3 **COMPARE AND CONTRAST** How are snakes different from chickens and horses? (Possible response: Snakes have no eyelids, so they sleep with their eyes open. Chickens and horses have eyelids. Accept reasonable responses.)

BELOW-LEVEL

Children can listen to "Sleep Is for Everyone" on cassette (*Audiotext 5,* or teacher-recorded). Have children look at the pictures and read along as they listen. The cassette provides a model of accurate decoding and fluent reading.

ENGLISH-LANGUAGE LEARNERS

Have children point to their eyelids and then find eyelids in the pictures. Ask volunteers to demonstrate actions such as *eyelids go up* and *eyelids go down.*

An elephant can sleep standing up.

192

A pigeon sits down when it sleeps. Pigs lie down to sleep. So do dogs. So do you. Sometimes dogs curl up. So do cats. Cows don't.
Do you?

193

Guided Comprehension

Pages 192–193 Have children look at the illustrations and tell what they notice about each of the sleeping animals. Then have them read to find more information.

1 (Focus Skill) **MAIN IDEA** How do animals sleep? (Possible response: They sleep in different ways: Some animals sleep standing up, others sit down, and others lie down.)

2 **COMPARE AND CONTRAST** Which animal so far sleeps most like an elephant? (the horse) How are they alike? (They both sleep standing up.)

3 **CLASSIFY** Which animal reminds you of the way you sleep? Why? (Possible responses: dogs and cats because they curl up; cows and pigs because they lie down.)

SOCIAL STUDIES

Elephants Around the World

Have children look at the picture on page 192. Explain that even though we see elephants in zoos, they are not native to the United States. Instead, they live in grassy areas in Africa and India. Show pictures of elephants in their natural habitat and have children describe what they notice about the elephants' surroundings. Help children find Africa and India on a globe.

194

Like birds and animals, people have to sleep. Some people sleep more than others. Jonathan is only six weeks old. He sleeps most of the time. He only wakes up when he wants to eat—or have his diaper changed.

195

Guided Comprehension

Pages 194–195 Have children look at the illustration on page 194 and tell what they think they will learn when they read the next page. Then have them read to find out.

1 (Focus Skill) **MAIN IDEA** What is the most important thing we find out about the baby's sleep? (He sleeps most of the time.)

2 **NOTE DETAILS** Why does Jonathan wake up? (He wakes up when he is hungry or needs his diaper changed.)

3 (Focus Strategy) **MAKE INFERENCES** Do you think you ever slept as much as Jonathan? Why or why not? (Possible response: Yes, when I was a baby I probably slept that much because babies need lots of sleep. Accept reasonable responses.)

REACHING ALL LEARNERS

Diagnostic Check: Comprehension and Skills

If... children cannot identify the main idea about Jonathan's sleep...

Then... have children recall that Jonathan wakes up only when he wants to eat or have his diaper changed. Explain that these are details, but they tell about a bigger idea—that Jonathan sleeps most of the time.

ADDITIONAL SUPPORT ACTIVITIES

BELOW-LEVEL Reteach, p. S42

ADVANCED Extend, p. S43

ENGLISH-LANGUAGE LEARNERS Reteach, p. S43

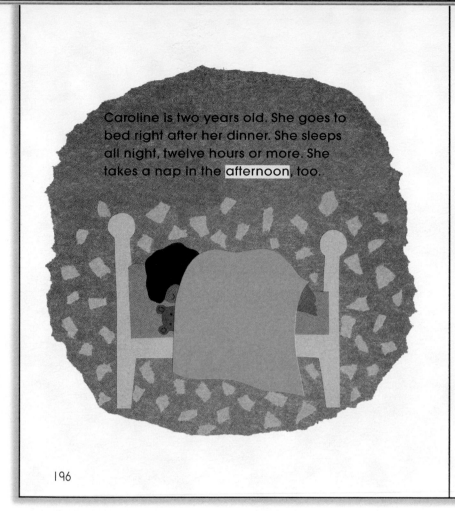

Caroline is two years old. She goes to bed right after her dinner. She sleeps all night, twelve hours or more. She takes a nap in the afternoon, too.

196

When Caroline doesn't get her nap, she is cranky. She cries. She throws things. But the next morning she feels fine—after she's had a good night's sleep.

197

Guided Comprehension

Pages 196–197 Have children look at the illustrations and predict what they will learn about the child. Then have them read to find out.

1 (Focus Skill) **MAIN IDEA** How much sleep do two-year-olds need? (They need an afternoon nap and at least twelve hours of sleep at night.)

2 **CAUSE/EFFECT** What happens if Caroline doesn't get enough sleep? Find the words that tell you this. *(When Caroline doesn't get her nap, she is cranky. She cries. She throws things.)*

3 **COMPARE AND CONTRAST** How are the needs of a baby and a two-year-old alike? How are they different? (Both need a lot of sleep, but a baby sleeps most of the time and a two-year-old is awake more.)

Strategies Good Readers Use

(Focus Strategy) **Make Inferences**

Remind children that readers sometimes must use clues from the selection and what they already know to figure out things the author doesn't explain. Model your thinking to help children with this strategy.

MODEL The selection doesn't tell me that Caroline needs a nap, but I can figure that out. I read that when Caroline doesn't get her nap, she is cranky, cries, and throws things. That must mean that she needs a nap to help her feel good.

Sleep Is for Everyone **196–197**

When people are little, they are growing, and they need a lot of sleep. As they grow bigger and older, they need less sleep. Schoolchildren need to sleep about ten to twelve **hours** a night.

Most grown-ups need only seven or eight hours. But babies, children, and grown-ups—all of them need to have their sleep.

198

199

Guided Comprehension

Pages 198–199 Remind children that they learned how much sleep a baby and small child need. Now have them predict what they will learn about sleep next. Then have them read to find out.

1 CONFIRM PREDICTIONS **Was your prediction correct?** (Possible response: Yes, I thought I would learn about how much sleep people need at different ages.)

2 (Focus Skill) MAIN IDEA **What is the most important thing you learned about sleep on these pages?** (Possible response: All people need to sleep, no matter how old they are.)

3 NOTE DETAILS **How much sleep do schoolchildren need each night?** (They need about ten to twelve hours.)

4 DRAW CONCLUSIONS **Why do small children need a lot of sleep?** (They are growing.)

MATH

Using the Clock
Remind children that the selection says that schoolchildren need to sleep about ten to twelve hours a night. Display a clock with movable hands. Explain that an hour

passes each time the little hand moves from one number to the next. Then use the clock to show what time children would wake up if they slept ten hours and went to bed at 7:00 PM (5:00 AM), 8:00 PM (6:00 AM), and 9:00 PM (7:00 AM) the night before.

Every part of your body has to rest after it does its work. Your arms need to rest after they **carry** heavy bundles. When you run fast, your legs work hard. They get tired, and you have to rest them.

200

201

Guided Comprehension

Pages 200–201 Direct children's attention to the illustration. Have children tell what they think the person in the picture is doing. Then have them read to find out.

1 (Focus Strategy) **MAKE INFERENCES Why do you think the child is resting?** (Possible response: The child has probably just done something tiring, such as hiking.)

2 (Focus Skill) **MAIN IDEA When does your body need to rest?** (after it does work) **Find the words that tell you this.** (*Every part of your body has to rest after it does its work.*)

3 **CAUSE/EFFECT What can make your legs get tired?** (Possible responses: running, hiking, playing tag, or swimming.)

REACHING ALL LEARNERS

Diagnostic Check: Comprehension and Skills

If... children cannot identify the main idea of the text on page 200...

Then... point out how the first sentence tells the main idea and the other sentences tell more about that idea. Have volunteers reread the main-idea sentence (the first sentence) and the two detail sentences. Then have children state the main idea in their own words.

ADDITIONAL SUPPORT ACTIVITIES

BELOW-LEVEL	Reteach, p. S42
ADVANCED	Extend, p. S43
ENGLISH-LANGUAGE LEARNERS	Reteach, p. S43

Your brain works hard, too. It never stops working. When you are awake, it helps you pay attention to the world around you—to the sights you see and the sounds you hear, and to the things you taste and smell and feel.

You can sit perfectly still and rest your arms and legs, but your brain isn't resting. It goes right on thinking as long as you are awake.

202

203

Guided Comprehension

Pages 202–203 Ask children to describe the child in the illustration and tell what they think the child is doing. Then have them read to find out.

❶ (Focus Strategy) **MAKE INFERENCES** **What is the child doing?** (The child is looking and listening; the child is eating.) **What parts of the child's body are working?** (Possible responses: The child's brain is working; the child's mouth, eyes, and ears are working.)

❷ **DRAW CONCLUSIONS** **Why doesn't your brain rest when you sit down after you exercise?** (Because you can still be busy thinking, even when your body is not moving.)

STUDENT SELF-ASSESSMENT

Have children ask themselves the following questions to assess how they are reading:

• **How do I use letters and sounds I know to help me read the words?**

• **Do I use the pictures and what I know so far about the selection to figure out things the author doesn't tell me?**

• **Can I read words that I have learned in other stories?**

At night your brain needs a rest from thinking. It needs to turn off the world—the way you turn off the light when you go to bed. Sleep is the time when part of your brain takes a rest.

204

Sometimes it is hard to go to bed. Perhaps I want to watch something on TV. But my mother makes me go to bed. Sometimes she is cross with me. That's because she is tired. Sometimes I'm cross. That's because I'm tired.

205

Guided Comprehension

Pages 204–205 Have children look at the illustrations and ask what the mother might be saying to the child. Then have them read to find out.

1 **DRAW CONCLUSIONS** Why is sleep important for your brain? (Possible response: Sleep is the time when your brain takes a rest.)

2 **SPECULATE** What do you think the mother is saying to the child? (Possible response: She is telling the child that it's time to go to bed. Accept reasonable responses.)

3 (Focus Strategy) **MAKE INFERENCES** How are the mother and child feeling when they are cross? (Possible response: They are upset and grumpy.)

ENGLISH-LANGUAGE LEARNERS

Point out words on page 205 that describe how people feel—*cross* and *tired*. Have children demonstrate facial expressions that convey the meanings of *cross* and *tired*.

Most of the time I go to bed when my parents tell me. It is warm under the covers. Sometimes I curl up. Or I stretch out and twist around. I yawn. I shut my eyes. I feel as if I am floating.

206

207

Guided Comprehension

Pages 206–207 Have children look at the illustration. Ask them to tell what the child is doing and explain how they know. Then have them read to find out how the child feels about doing this.

1 DETERMINE CHARACTERS' EMOTIONS How does the child feel about going to bed? (Possible responses: The child probably doesn't mind; the child likes feeling warm and cozy in bed. Accept reasonable responses. Encourage children to explain their responses.)

2 (Focus Strategy) **MAKE INFERENCES Does the child feel tired? How can you tell?** (Possible response: Yes, because the child yawns. Accept reasonable responses. Encourage children to explain their responses.)

BELOW-LEVEL

Before children read the page, have volunteers act out what they do just before they fall asleep. As needed, prompt them to stretch out, curl up, yawn, and close their eyes. Then have them read the text to find out what bedtime is like for the child in the selection.

206–207 Gather Around

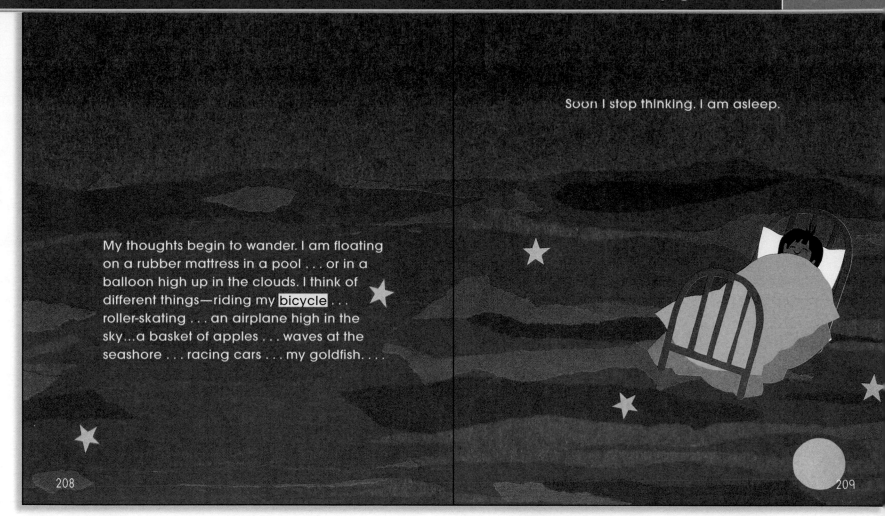

Soon I stop thinking. I am asleep.

My thoughts begin to wander. I am floating on a rubber mattress in a pool . . . or in a balloon high up in the clouds. I think of different things—riding my bicycle . . . roller-skating . . . an airplane high in the sky...a basket of apples . . . waves at the seashore . . . racing cars . . . my goldfish. . . .

208

209

Guided Comprehension

Pages 208–209 Have children look at the illustrations and tell what they think the child is thinking about. Then have them read to find out.

1 **UNDERSTAND FIGURATIVE LANGUAGE** What does the sentence "My thoughts begin to wander" mean? (Possible response: It means that the child's thoughts go from one idea to another.)

2 **SEQUENCE** When does the child stop thinking? (The child stops thinking when he (or she) falls asleep.)

ENGLISH-LANGUAGE LEARNERS

Explain that when someone wanders, he or she walks or moves without going anyplace in particular. Have children briefly act out *wandering*. Help children understand that when one's thoughts wander, they do not physically move, but they go from one idea to another. For example, the child thinks of an airplane, then a basket of apples, then waves at the seashore—with no real connection between the different thoughts.

Sleep Is for Everyone **208–209**

Think and Respond

1 Is "Sleep Is for Everyone" a good title for this selection? Why?

2 Why is sleep important?

3 When does your brain get a rest from thinking?

4 Do you like to go to bed on time or stay up late? Tell why.

5 What can happen to children when they don't get enough sleep?

About the Author
Paul Showers

Paul Showers was a writer and editor at newspapers. Then he started writing science books for children. He liked to listen to children play. This gave him ideas for his books. Paul Showers knew how to make science fun for children.

Meet the Illustrator
Wendy Watson

Wendy Watson grew up in a large family. She is the oldest of eight children. As a child, she loved to draw. She made pictures, books, and cards and gave them to people as presents. The pictures for *Sleep Is for Everyone* are made from cut paper. Wendy Watson is also a musician. She plays the piano and the cello.

Teacher Read-Aloud

210

211

Think and Respond

1 Possible response: Yes, because all people and animals need sleep. **MAKE JUDGMENTS**

2 Possible responses: It gives our bodies and minds a rest; it keeps us happy and healthy. **SUMMARIZE**

3 when you sleep **IMPORTANT DETAILS**

4 Responses will vary. Some children may say they like to go to bed on time because they like to feel good when they wake up; others may say they enjoy staying up late and are not sleepy when it is time to go to bed. Accept reasonable responses. Encourage children to explain their answers. **EXPRESS PERSONAL OPINIONS**

5 Possible response: They can get cranky. **CAUSE/EFFECT**

Meet the Author and Illustrator

Page 211 Explain that this page tells about the person who wrote and the person who illustrated the selection "Sleep Is for Everyone." Identify the author, Paul Showers, and the illustrator, Wendy Watson. Remind children that an author writes a story and an illustrator creates pictures to go with the writing. Read the page aloud.

 Visit *The Learning Site:* **www.harcourtschool.com**

See Resources for Parents and Teachers: Author/Illustrator Features.

Retelling

COMPREHENSION FOCUS

Complete the K-W-L Chart Revisit the K-W-L Chart from the Building Background activity, page 186S. Discuss the selection and record children's ideas in the third column of the chart—*What I Learned*. Talk about which questions were answered by the selection and which ones children may still want to investigate.

(Focus Skill) **Main Idea** Remind children that details in a selection tell about a main idea. Have children recall some of the facts they learned about sleep. Then have volunteers tell in their own words what the selection is mostly about. For example, all the information in "Sleep Is for Everyone" shows that sleep is important for all people and animals.

RETELL AND SUMMARIZE THE STORY

Use a Main Idea and Details Diagram Display *Teaching Transparency 108,* or draw a similar chart on the board. Work with children to state the main idea of the selection, and write it in the top box. (Possible response: All people and animals need to sleep.) Then ask volunteers to think of details from the selection that tell more about the main idea. You may want to have children page through the selection to help them recall details. As children respond, add their details to the diagram.

Help children use the Main Idea and Details diagram to summarize the story.

COMPREHENSION CHECK

▲ *End-of-Selection Test,*
Practice Book, pp. A57–A60

▼ **Teaching Transparency 108**

> **MAIN IDEA**
>
> All people and animals need to sleep.
>
> **DETAILS**
>
> Animals sleep in all kinds of ways. Horses and elephants stand up. Dogs and cats curl up.
>
> Small children need to sleep a lot because they are growing. Grown-ups don't need as much sleep, but they still need to sleep.
>
> Your brain keeps thinking as long as you are awake. Sleep is important because that's when your brain rests.

Grade 1   108   Harcourt

	5-DAY WRITING
DAY 1	SHARED: Animal Chart
DAY 2	**INDEPENDENT: Story Response**
DAY 3	CROSS-CURRICULAR: Sentences
DAY 4	INDEPENDENT: Captions
DAY 5	INTERACTIVE: Facts List

DAILY LANGUAGE PRACTICE

the dogs can went
home right now.

<u>T</u>he dogs can <u>go</u>
home right now.

journal writing

Writing Prompt Have children write a question they still have that they did not find an answer to as they read "Sleep Is for Everyone."

LANGUAGE ARTS

Writing
Story Response

DRAW AND WRITE

Revisit the K-W-L Chart Display the completed K-W-L Chart that was begun in Building Background on page 186S and read it aloud to children.

Create a Page Tell children to choose the most interesting fact they learned about sleeping from "Sleep Is for Everyone." Have them write the fact on paper and draw a picture to illustrate it. Then gather children's papers and bind

A snake can't shut its eyes. It sleeps with its eyes open.

them in a class book about sleep. Read it aloud to children, and place it in the Reading Center for children to enjoy.

Handwriting Point out how capital letters touch the top and bottom line of the paper. If children write two sentences, remind them that there should be a space between the period in the first sentence and the capital letter at the beginning of the second sentence.

BELOW-LEVEL

If children have difficulty putting their thoughts in writing, they can dictate a fact they learned from the selection and draw a picture to illustrate their idea.

ENGLISH-LANGUAGE LEARNERS

Have each child draw a picture to show the interesting fact and then dictate a caption for it. Record the sentence on a separate sheet of paper, and have the child copy it onto his or her paper.

Grammar

Using Go *and* Went

5-DAY GRAMMAR

DAY 1	Introduce Using *Go* and *Went*
DAY 2	**Generate Sentences**
DAY 3	Write Sentence Frames
DAY 4	Play a Game
DAY 5	Write Sentences

REVIEW

Review Using ***Go*** **and** ***Went*** Write these sentences on the board and have children read them.

> **In the afternoon the cows go to the barn.**
> **Last night the cows went to the barn.**

Ask children to underline the verb in each sentence. *(go, went)* Then model the correct use of *go* and *went*.

MODEL In the first sentence, the word *now* is a clue that the action is happening at this time. I use the word *go* to tell about an action that is happening now. The words *Last night* in the next sentence tell me that the action in the sentence has already happened. The word *went* tells about action in the past.

Generate Sentences Have volunteers dictate sentences using *go* and *went*. Write them on the board, and read them aloud with children. Have volunteers underline *go* and *went* and tell whether the action is happening now or in the past.

 WRAP UP

Read a Poem

Innovate on a Poem Reread the poem "Night Bear" from page 186P. Ask volunteers to share what stuffed animal or other object snuggles with them at night. Write their responses on large self-stick notes and post them on the board. Reread the poem several times, substituting children's responses for the word *Teddy-bear*. Point to the appropriate self-stick note as you read. Have children join in as they are able.

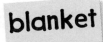 blanket

 pillow

 bunny

S.S.R. *Sustained Silent Reading*

Have children read silently from a book of their choice. See page 217J for tips on helping children choose books.

SKILL TRACE

USING *Go* **AND** *Went*

Introduce	186N
REVIEW	**211C, 215B, 217B, 217L**
T Test	Bk 1-5

BELOW-LEVEL
Below • On-Level • Advanced • ELL

If children still have difficulty using *go* and *went* correctly, write on the board several sentence frames like the following: *Yesterday I _____. Now I _____. Last Saturday I _____. Last week I _____. Right now I _____ again.* Have the children complete the sentences with *go* or *went*.

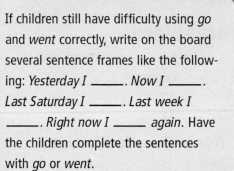

Name _____

Using Go and Went

> The word **go** tells about now.
> The word **went** tells about the past.

We go to the country.
They went to the country the other day.

▶ **Write go or went to complete the story.**

1. Last week we _____went_____ to a farm.

2. The ducks _____went_____ into the water.

3. The sheep _____went_____ into the barn.

4. Today I _____go_____ to the mountains.

138

SCHOOL-HOME CONNECTION

▲ **Language Handbook, p. 138**

Sleep Is for Everyone **211C**

Sharing Literature
Poem: "In the Night"

Phonemic Awareness
Phoneme Segmentation; Focus on /ē/ and /e/

Phonics
REVIEW: Short Vowel /e/ea

Spelling
State the Generalization

Vocabulary
REVIEW: *afternoon, bicycle, carry, hours, parents*

Reading

Rereading for Fluency
Pupil Edition
"Sleep Is for Everyone," pp. 188–209

Reading Across Texts
"Pretending," pp. 212–213
Making Connections, pp. 214–215

Writing Across the Curriculum ✎
Sentences

Grammar
REVIEW: Using *Go* and *Went*

ORAL LANGUAGE

WARM UP

MORNING MESSAGE

Good Morning!

Today is _____.

We think about different things at night.

_____ likes to think about _____.

_____ likes to pretend _____.

If you can't sleep, you can try _____.

Introduce the Day

Tell children they will listen to a poem about being awake in bed at night. Guide them in generating a message about going to sleep. Ask:

• **What kinds of things do you think about in bed at night?**

• **Do you have any tricks that you use when you want to fall asleep? What are they?**

As you write, ask volunteers to help by writing known letters, words, and/or punctuation. As you get to the end of each sentence, ask children to tell what kind of end mark you should use.

Read the Message

Read the message. Use the message to focus on selected skills that have been previously taught.

Apply Skills

Grammar Have children circle action verbs in the message. For example, children might have said that they pretend they are sailing on the ocean or that they try singing to themselves.

Phonics Have children help you spell the words *sleep* and *we* by telling you the vowels to use for the long vowel sound of *e* in those words. Ask children to name other words that have the sound /ē/ spelled *e* or *ee*.

Sharing Literature

LISTEN AND RESPOND

Connect to Personal Experiences Have children recall a time they woke up in the middle of the night. Ask them how it felt and how they passed the time before they fell back asleep. Then read "In the Night" and ask children to listen to find out what the person in the poem does when that happens.

Discuss the Poem Ask children what the person in the poem does when she wakes up before it's time to get up. (She hums a tune until she falls back asleep.) Ask children whether they think humming would work and why they think as they do. Then ask them for other suggestions they might like to add to the poem. Then reread the poem and encourage children to join in, especially on the rhyming words.

In the Night

When I wake up and it is dark
　And very far from day
I sing a humming sort of tune
　To pass the time away.

I hum it loud, I hum it soft,
　I hum it low and deep,
And by the time I'm out of breath
　I've hummed myself to sleep.

Marchette Chute

Phonemic Awareness

PHONEME SEGMENTATION

Words from "In the Night" Say the word *hum*, and have children segment the phonemes. (/h//u//m/) Continue with the following words from the poem:

day /d/ /ā/	**wake** /w/ /ā/ /k/	**pass** /p/ /a/ /s/
low /l/ /ō/	**deep** /d/ /ē/ /p/	**breath** /b/ /r/ /e/ /th/
time /t/ /ī/ /m/	**and** /a/ /n/ /d/	**night** /n/ /ī/ /t/

◀ "The Old Gray Horse," *Oo-pples and Boo-noo-noos: Songs and Activities for Phonemic Awareness*, p. 112

FOCUS ON /e/

Phoneme Isolation Tell children that they are going to play a game called "Head and Feet." You are going to slowly say some words, and they will tell what vowel sound they hear in the middle. They will point to their head if they hear the sound /e/ and to their feet if they hear the sound /ē/. Slowly say *breath. I hear the sound /e/ in breath, so I will point to my head.* Continue with these words:

deed /ē/	**thread** /e/	**red** /e/	**read** /ē/
sweet /ē/	**sweat** /e/	**head** /e/	**feed** /ē/
bead /ē/	**bread** /e/	**deaf** /e/	**leaf** /ē/

ENGLISH-LANGUAGE LEARNERS

Below　On-Level　Advanced　ELL

If children have difficulty distinguishing the long and short vowel sounds of *e*, say each sound slowly and have children watch your mouth. Then have them practice going back and forth several times between /ē/ and /e/.

OBJECTIVES

- *To generate the short and long vowel sounds of e*

- *To blend sounds into words*

- *To read simple, regular words*

SKILL TRACE

	/e/ea	/ē/ee,ea
Introduce	186I–186L	Bk 1-4, 8I–8L
Reteach	S40–S41	Bk 1-4, S4–S5, T2
REVIEW	**186Q–186R, 211F–211G 215E–215F**	**Bk 1-4, 8Q–8R, 29F–29G, 33E–33F**
T Test		Bk 1-4
MAINTAIN		Bk 1-5, 35E–35F, 211F–211G

Phonics Resources

Phonics Express™ CD-ROM, **Level B,** Sparkle/Route 3/Park

teaching tip

Point out that *beet* and *beat* sound the same but are spelled differently and have different meanings. Illustrate with these sentences: *A* beet *is a vegetable. Listen to the fast* beat *of the music.*

Phonics
Short Vowel /e/ea *Review*

WORD BUILDING

Guided Practice Place the letters *h, e, a, d* in a pocket chart, and have children do the same with their *Word Builders* and *Word Builder Cards.* Remind children that the letters *ea* together can stand for the sound /e/ or /ē/. Model how to blend the word *head.* Slide your hand under the letters as you slowly elongate the sounds /hheedd/. Then read the word naturally—*head.* Have children do the same.

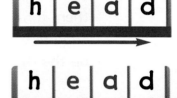

Have children build and read new words by telling them:

- Change the *a* to *e.* What word did you make?

- Change the *h* to *r.* What word did you make?

- Change the second *e* to *a.* What are two ways to say the word you made?

- Add a *b* in front of *r.* What word did you make?

- Take away the *r.* What word did you make?

- Change the *d* to *t.* What word did you make?

Continue word building with this word sequence: *beet, sweet, sweat, heat, heal, deal, deaf, leaf.*

Apply Phonics

READ WORDS IN CONTEXT

Display *Teaching Transparency 99* or write the following sentences on the board or on chart paper. Have volunteers read the story one sentence at a time. Call on volunteers to underline or frame words with /e/ spelled ea.

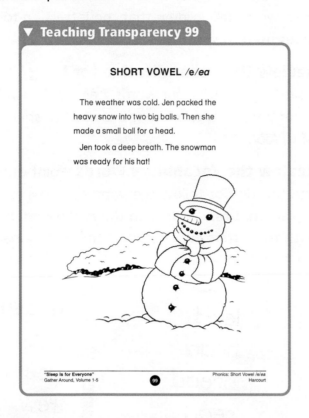

▼ **Teaching Transparency 99**

SHORT VOWEL /e/ea

The weather was cold. Jen packed the heavy snow into two big balls. Then she made a small ball for a head.

Jen took a deep breath. The snowman was ready for his hat!

"Sleep Is for Everyone"   Gather Around, Volume 1-5   **99**   Phonics: Short Vowel /e/ea   Harcourt

 Write Words Tell children to choose two words with /e/ spelled ea and write them in their journal.

5-DAY PHONICS	
DAY 1	Introduce /e/ea
DAY 2	Word Building with /e/ea
DAY 3	**Word Building with /e/ea**
DAY 4	Word Building with /e/ea and /a/a
DAY 5	Inflections -er, -est; Inflections -ed, -ing (double final consonant)

REACHING ALL LEARNERS

Below / On-Level / Advanced / ELL

Diagnostic Check: Phonics

If... students cannot decode words with short vowel /e/ea...

Then... have them read "Ned's Feathers" in *Decodable Book 33* to reinforce short vowel /e/ea.

◀ **Decodable Book 33**
"Ned's Feathers"

ADDITIONAL SUPPORT ACTIVITIES

BELOW-LEVEL	Reteach, p. S40
ADVANCED	Extend, p. S41
ENGLISH-LANGUAGE LEARNERS	Reteach, p. S41

School-Home Connection

Take-Home Book Version

◀ **Decodable Books
Take-Home Book Version**

Spelling Words

1. lead
2. head
3. bread
4. read
5. ready
6. heavy
7. rule
8. use
9. few
10. boy

journal writing

Have children copy the Spelling Words into their journal.

Spelling

5-DAY SPELLING	
DAY 1	Pretest; Word Sort
DAY 2	Word Building
DAY 3	State the Generalization
DAY 4	Review
DAY 5	Posttest; Writing Application

TEACH/MODEL

State the Generalization for /e/ea Write the Spelling Words on the board and have children read them aloud. Discuss what is the same about words 1–6. (They all have the sound /e/; they all have ea.) Have volunteers circle the letters that stand for /e/ in each word. Tell children that the letters *ea* together are some-times used to spell the sound /e/.

Review the Generalization for Long Vowel /o͞o/u-e Follow a similar procedure for words 7 and 8. Remind children that the letter pattern *u-consonant-e* is used to spell the long vowel sound of *u*, /o͞o/.

Review the Vocabulary Words Point out that the words *few* and *boy* do not follow the same patterns as the other words. Explain that *few* ends with the /o͞o/ sound, but that it is spelled with the letters *ew* instead of the *u-consonant-e* pattern.

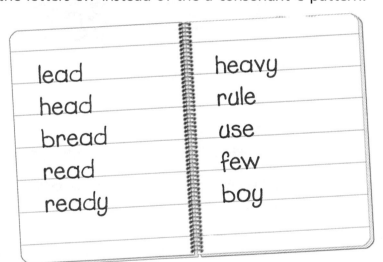

lead   heavy
head   rule
bread   use
read   few
ready   boy

ADVANCED

Have partners dictate the Spelling Words to one another, using each word in a sentence. Give them time to check their own work.

ENGLISH-LANGUAGE LEARNERS

As you teach children how to spell these words, help them learn each word's meaning. Say a sentence that can be pan-tomimed. As you say the sen-tence, emphasize the Spelling Word and have children pan-tomime the action with you. Then have them say and spell the word you used in the sentence.

Name _____

Word Sorts

▶ Make cards for the Spelling Words. Lay them down and read them.

1. Put the words with ea in one group and those without ea in another. Write the words on the chart.

2. Put the words with long u in one group and those without long u in another. Write the words on the chart.

Words With ea		Words Without ea	
lead	read	rule	few
head	ready	use	boy
bread	heavy		

Words With Long u	Words Without Long u	
rule	lead	ready
use	head	heavy
	bread	few
	read	boy

Spelling Words

lead
head
bread
read
ready
heavy
rule
use
few
boy
My Own Word

SCHOOL-HOME CONNECTION *Ask your child why he or she wrote the Spelling Words in each part of the chart.*

SPELLING PRACTICE BOOK
GATHER AROUND • LESSON 7 **79**

▲ Spelling Practice Book, p. 79

Vocabulary

REVIEW WORDS IN CONTEXT

Read Words in Context Display *Word Cards* for *afternoon, bicycle, carry, hours, parents*. Write the following sentences on tagboard strips. Track the print as you read the sentences aloud. Then have children read all the sentences together. Have volunteers choose a *Word Card*, read it aloud, and match it with the vocabulary word in the sentence.

My parents asked Uncle Rick to help me.

I see Uncle Rick each afternoon.

I ride my bicycle to his house.

I carry my homework with me.

We work on math and spelling for two hours.

Reinforce Words One by one, hold up a *Word Card* for each vocabulary word. Direct children to read the word, spell it, read it again, and spell it again. Put down the *Word Card*, but leave your hand up. Ask children to say and spell the word.

Words to Remember

WORD WALL

Match Words Point to the following words in the sentence-strip sentences: *afternoon, bicycle, carry, hours, parents.* Ask volunteers to find and point to the same words posted on the display. Have the group read the words aloud. Then have them read aloud all the words in the display.

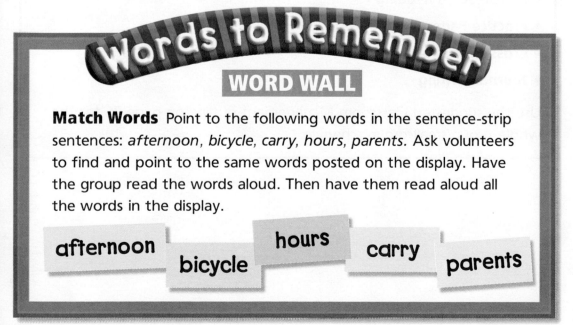

afternoon   hours   bicycle   carry   parents

BELOW-LEVEL

Display the *Word Cards* from the activity. Have children match each *Word Card* to a word in the selection "Sleep Is for Everyone." When children locate a word, have them read aloud the sentence in which the word is found.

ADVANCED

Children can write a few sentences about what they usually do after school. Tell them to use all the vocabulary words in their writing.

teaching tip

Learned Words Examine the posted words and remove those that children understand, can spell, and can use with mastery.

▲ *Pupil Edition, pp. 188–209*

FLUENCY ROUTINES For support, see Fluency Routine Cards in Theme Resources, pp. T83–T84.

Rereading for Fluency

GROUPS

Readers Theatre

● **ON-LEVEL/ADVANCED** Have children practice for a dramatic reading of the selection. Encourage them to bring in stuffed animals to use as props and to create visual effects to accompany their reading. Remind children to read smoothly as if they are telling the information to someone. You might want to videotape children's dramatic readings to share with classmates. INDEPENDENT

Managing Small Groups

Reread for fluency with children working individually, with partners, or in small groups. While you work with small groups, have other children do the following:

• **Self-Selected Reading**

• **Practice Pages**

• **Cross-Curricular Centers**

• **Journal Writing**

Use the suggested Classroom Management outline on page 7C for the whole-group/small-group schedule.

PARTNERS

Repeated Reading

⬤ **BELOW-LEVEL** Ask children to choose two consecutive pages they think give interesting information. Have partners work together to practice reading their pages. Each partner should read the pages aloud three times, trying to read more smoothly with each reading. The partner who listens should follow along, help with word identification, and give feedback about how the reader sounds. Suggest that children draw a picture to illustrate their pages and display it as they read the pages aloud to classmates. INDEPENDENT

GROUPS

Shared Reading

⬤ **ENGLISH-LANGUAGE LEARNERS** Read aloud pages 190–191 as children track the print. Point out that the commas, periods, and question mark helped you know how to read the sentences aloud. Reread the statement on page 190 and the question on page 191 and have children echo read each. Point out the difference in intonation. Reread the pages and invite children to join in. Continue through the rest of the selection. As children join in, note whether they use the appropriate intonation. Pause occasionally to reread sentences and model intonation and have them echo read. TEACHER-DIRECTED

Teacher Read-Aloud Poem

Pretending

When you are in bed and it's cold outside,
do you ever pretend that you have to hide?
Do you curl up your toes?
Do you wrinkle your nose?
Do you make yourself little so none of you shows?

Do you pull the sheet over the whole of your face
and pretend you are in some faraway place?
Mother thinks you are sleeping,
but she does not know
that all tucked in the bed, you have places to go.

by Bobbi Katz
illustrated by Melissa Iwai

212

213

Reading Across Texts

READ A POEM

Introduce the Poem Ask children what they usually think about before they fall asleep. Discuss the illustration and ask what they think the poem might be about. Remind children that a poem is a piece of writing in which the words are used in an imaginative way. Explain that often poems rhyme.

Sharing the Poem Read "Pretending" aloud. Ask children which words in the poem rhyme. *(outside, hide; toes, nose, shows; face, place; know, go)*

Rereading for a Purpose Ask children why they think the poem is called "Pretending." Ask them to tell what the poet was pretending to do in the poem. Then reread the poem, pausing at the end of each line so that children can say the rhyming words. Ask volunteers to share something they like to pretend at bedtime.

ABOUT THE POET

BOBBI KATZ has been writing children's books for over thirty years. Included in her long list of titles are many books of poetry. Some of her most popular titles include *Could We Be Friends?: Poems for Pals, 25 Great Grammar Poems with Activities*, and *Truck Talk: Rhymes on Wheels*.

Making Connections

▲ Sleep Is for Everyone

Making Connections

Your Favorite Dream

We all dream while we sleep. Draw and write about a funny or interesting dream you have had. If you can't remember any dreams, make one up!

Writing CONNECTION

I dreamed that I could fly.

214

Beds Around the World

Not everyone sleeps in a bed like Caroline's in the story. Have you ever slept in a hammock, or a bunk bed, or a mat on the floor? Find out about different ways to sleep. Share something you learn.

Social Studies CONNECTION

A Lullaby

Sing a lullaby for baby Jonathan in the story.

Music CONNECTION

Rock-a-bye, Jonathan, in mother's lap,
Babies like you need a long nap.
Rock-a-bye, Jonathan, in the car seat.
Sleep till it's time to wake up and eat!

215

Making Connections

WRITING

Your Favorite Dream Have children think of a dream that seems especially clear to them. Tell them to draw a picture that illustrates it and write sentences to describe what happened. If children cannot recall a dream they have had, tell them to make one up. Encourage them to be as imaginative as they can.

I dreamed
that I could
fly. I flew over
my house. Then
I landed in my
backyard!

SOCIAL STUDIES

Beds Around the World Help children use encyclopedias and books about life in other countries to learn more about how people sleep. Record their findings on a web, along with observations from their personal experience. Point out that the way people sleep often depends on the climate in which they live.

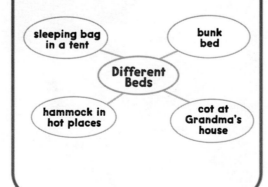

sleeping bag in a tent — bunk bed — Different Beds — hammock in hot places — cot at Grandma's house

MUSIC

A Lullaby Ask children what a lullaby is. Then have volunteers name different lullabies they know, for example, "Hush Little Baby," "Lullaby and Goodnight," or "Twinkle, Twinkle Little Star." Have volunteers take turns singing the lullabies they know for the baby Jonathan in the selection. Model by singing "Rock-a-Bye Jonathan" to the tune of "Rock-a-Bye Baby." Ask all children to join in.

5-DAY WRITING	
DAY 1	SHARED: Animal Chart
DAY 2	INDEPENDENT: Story Response
DAY 3	**CROSS-CURRICULAR: Sentences**
DAY 4	INDEPENDENT: Captions
DAY 5	INTERACTIVE: Facts List

Writing Across the Curriculum

Sentences

DAILY LANGUAGE PRACTICE

I go to Jim's house last week?

I <u>went</u> to Jim's house last week<u>.</u>

Writing Resources

Writing Express™ CD-ROM, Post Office, Gizmos and Gadgets

journal writing

Writing Prompt Have children write two sentences: one about how they feel when they are asleep and one about how they feel when they wake up. Children can illustrate their writing.

ENGLISH-LANGUAGE LEARNERS

Review with children the numbers from one to twelve in English.

GENERATE IDEAS

Talk About Time Remind children that young children should usually get from ten to twelve hours of sleep each night. Then have children tell when they went to sleep last night and what time they got up. Then guide them in figuring out how many hours of sleep they got.

DRAFT

Write Sentences Write these sentence frames on the board. Have children complete them or create sentences of their own.

I went to bed at _____ o'clock.
I got up at _____ o'clock.
I got _____ hours of sleep.

To vary the activity, have children write about the number of hours they go to school or spend on a long-term activity.

I went to bed at eight o'clock.
I got up at seven o'clock.
I got eleven hours of sleep.
I feel great!

Grammar

Using Go *and* Went

5-DAY GRAMMAR

DAY 1	Introduce Using *Go* and *Went*
DAY 2	Generate Sentences
DAY 3	**Sentence Frames**
DAY 4	Play a Game
DAY 5	Write Sentences

Day 3

REVIEW

Review Using *Go* **and** *Went* Choose samples of children's sentences from the Writing activity on page 215A and write them on the board.

I went to bed at eight o'clock.

Have the child who wrote the sentence underline the word *went*. Remind children that when they talk about something that happened in the past, they use the word *went*.

Ask a volunteer to change the word *went* to *go*. Explain that *go* is used to show action that is happening now.

Complete Sentence Frames Have children think of a place they went yesterday and a place they are going today. Then have them complete both of these sentences and read them to a partner.

I went ___ yesterday.
I can go ___ today.

SKILL TRACE

USING *Go* **AND** *Went*

Introduce	186N
REVIEW	211C, 215B, 217B, 217L
T Test	Bk 1-5

ADVANCED

Have children add times to their sentences using *o'clock*. Then have them add sentences to elaborate on the activities they did and are going to do.

WRAP UP Share a Poem

Express Opinions Tell children that all animals and people need to sleep, but they don't all sleep at the same time. Read the poem "Night Runners" on page 18 of the *Big Book of Rhymes*. Ask volunteers to tell whether or not they would like to stay awake all night and sleep all day like Raccoon and Rabbit. Ask them to explain why they feel as they do.

▲ Big Book of Rhymes p. 18

S.S.R. Reading

Have children read silently from a book of their choice. See page 217J for tips on helping children choose books.

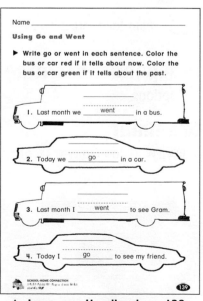

Name _____

Using Go and Went

▶ Write go or went in each sentence. Color the bus or car red if it tells about now. Color the bus or car green if it tells about the past.

1. Last month we ___went___ in a bus.

2. Today we ___go___ in a car.

3. Last month I ___went___ to see Gram.

4. Today I ___go___ to see my friend.

139

▲ Language Handbook, p. 139

Sleep Is for Everyone **215B**

Sharing Literature
Poem: "Keep a Poem in Your Pocket"

Phonemic Awareness
Phoneme Isolation; Focus on /e/ and /a/

Phonics
Build Words

Spelling
Review

Vocabulary
REVIEW: *afternoon, bicycle, carry, hours, parents*

Reading

Comprehension
(Focus Skill) Main Idea, pp. 216–217

Independent Writing
Captions

Grammar
REVIEW: Using *Go* and *Went*

ORAL LANGUAGE

WARM UP

MORNING MESSAGE

Good Morning!

Today is _____.

Bedtime is a special time of day.

"When I'm in bed, I feel _____," said _____.

"When I don't get enough sleep, I feel _____," said _____.

Introduce the Day

Tell children that they will listen to a poem that tells ways to keep from feeling lonely at night. Ask:

• **How do you feel when the lights are off and you are tucked in bed?**

• **How do you feel if you don't get enough sleep?**

As you write the message, have children write previously taught letters, words, and/or punctuation to reinforce skills. For example, as you write, have children help you with the spelling of the high-frequency words *when, said, day, don't,* and *is.* Have children help you add quotation marks to the dialogue.

Read the Message

Read the message. Use the message to focus on selected skills that have been previously taught.

Apply Skills

Phonics As you point to each of the following words, have children read the word aloud and tell what sound the *e* stands for in each: *bedtime* (the first *e*) /e/, *when* /e/, *bed* /e/, *feel* /ē/, *get* /e/, and *sleep* /ē/.

Grammar Have children point to and read describing words that tell about feelings in the message. Have volunteers explain what those words mean.

Sharing Literature

LISTEN AND RESPOND

Connect to Prior Knowledge Ask children if they have ever felt lonely when they were in bed at night. Then ask them if there was anything they did or thought about that made them feel better.

Read the Poem Read "Keep a Poem in Your Pocket" and have children listen to see what the poem in the pocket is for.

Discuss Poetic Language Reread the second verse and have children listen for words that show action. (*sing, bring, dance*) Point out that the poet wants us to think of a poem and a picture as more than just words or images on paper. Discuss with children what the words might mean. Then reread the poem and encourage children to pay close attention to the rhythm of the words.

Phonemic Awareness

PHONEME ISOLATION

Words from "Keep a Poem in Your Pocket" Say *poem* and ask children what sound they hear at the end of the word. (/m/) Continue with these words:

in (/n/)	**pocket** (/t/)	**head** (/d/)	**feel** (/l/)
dozen (/n/)	**dreams** (/z/)	**night** (/t/)	**bed** (/d/)
keep (/p/)	**your** (/r/)	**lonely** (/ē/)	**picture** (/r/)

FOCUS ON /e/ AND /a/

Phoneme Matching Tell children that you will say words in groups of three and they will tell which one has the sound /e/ in the middle and which word has the middle sound /a/. Model by saying *house, had, head. I hear /e/ in the middle of* head *and* had *has the middle sound /a/.* Continue with these sets of words:

weather, white, wag (weather, /e/; wag, /a/)
brag, bread, bring (bread, /e/; brag, /a/)
dad, dear, dread (dread, /e/; dad, /a/)
hilly, hat, heavy (heavy, /e/; hat, /a/)

Keep a Poem in Your Pocket

Keep a poem in your pocket
and a picture in your head
and you'll never feel lonely
at night when you're in bed.

The little poem will sing to you
the little picture bring to you
a dozen dreams to dance to you
at night when you're in bed.

So—
Keep a picture in your pocket
and a poem in your head
and you'll never feel lonely
at night when you're in bed.

Beatrice Schenk de Regniers

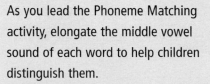

BELOW-LEVEL

As you lead the Phoneme Matching activity, elongate the middle vowel sound of each word to help children distinguish them.

ENGLISH-LANGUAGE LEARNERS

Some children may have difficulty distinguishing between the short vowel sounds of *a* and *e*. Repeat the sounds /e/ and /a/ a few times until children can say them. Then ask which vowel sound they hear in the middle of these words: cat (/a/), head (/e/), hat (/a/), bread (/e/).

Sleep Is for Everyone **215D**

WORD WORK

Phonics

Build Words *Review*

OBJECTIVES

- *To discriminate between sound-letter relationships /e/ea and /a/a*

- *To read and write words with /e/ea and /a/a*

SKILL TRACE

	/e/ea	/a/a
Introduce	186I–186L	Bk 1-1, 10I–10L
Reteach	S40–S41	Bk 1-1, S4–S5, T2
Review	186Q–186R, 211F–211G	Bk 1-1, 10Q–10R, 23F–23G, 25E–25F, 28I–28L, 28Q–28R, 41F–41G, 45E, 139E–139F
REVIEW	215E–215F	
T Test		Bk 1-1
MAINTAIN		Bk 1-2, 105E–105F
		Bk 1-4, 63E–63F
		Bk 1-5, 215E–215F

Phonics Resources

Phonics Express™ CD-ROM, **Level B**, Sparkle/Route 3/Park

WORD BUILDING

Build and Read Words Use a pocket chart and *Letter Cards a, b, d, d, e, h, l, r, t.* Display the letters *h, e, a,* and *d* in the pocket chart and ask children to spell the word.

Place the letters close together. Slide your hand slowly under the letters as you blend the sounds—/hheedd/. Then read the word naturally—*head.* Have children repeat after you. Point out that the letters in *head* follow the pattern *consonant, vowel, vowel, consonant.*

Ask volunteers to build new words in the pocket chart.

- Take away the *e.* Read the word.

- Change the *h* to *l.* Read the word.

- Add an *e* in front of the *a.* Read the word.

- Take away the *l.* Add an *r* in front of the *ead* and a *b* in front of the *r.* Read the word.

- Take away the *e.* Read the word.

- Take away the *r.* Read the word.

Continue word building with this word sequence: *dad, dread, thread, read.*

Read Words Write the words *head, had,* and *bread* on the board and have children read the words aloud.

Apply Phonics

5-DAY PHONICS	
DAY 1	Introduce /e/ea
DAY 2	Word Building with /e/ea
DAY 3	Word Building with /e/ea
DAY 4	**Word Building with /e/ea and /a/a**
DAY 5	Inflections -er, -est; Inflections -ed, -ing (double final consonant)

APPLY PHONICS SKILLS

Dictate Sentences with /e/ea, /a/a Dictate the following sentences:

Dad had the bread.
Brad's heavy coat made him sweat.

Have children write the sentences on a dry-erase board or in their journal.

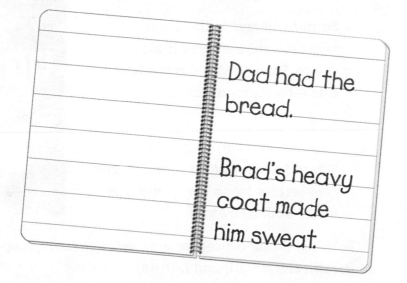

> Dad had the bread.
>
> Brad's heavy coat made him sweat.

BELOW-LEVEL

Give children additional practice spelling words with the short vowel sound of *a* and with the short vowel sound of *e* spelled *ea*. Have children blend and read the following words: *pad, sad, had, head, health, wealth.*

ENGLISH-LANGUAGE LEARNERS

Be sure that English-language learners understand the sentences that you dictate. Ask a volunteer to explain the meaning of unfamiliar words. Have children act out the meaning of unfamiliar words.

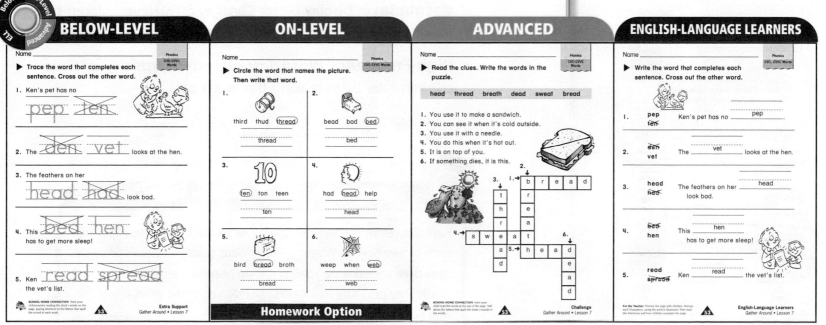

BELOW-LEVEL

Name _____

▶ Trace the word that completes each sentence. Cross out the other word.

1. Ken's pet has no ~~pep~~ ~~ten~~

2. The ~~den~~ ~~vet~~ looks at the hen.

3. The feathers on her ~~head~~ ~~had~~ look bad.

4. This ~~bed~~ ~~hen~~ has to get more sleep!

5. Ken ~~read~~ ~~spread~~ the vet's list.

▲ Extra Support, p. 53

ON-LEVEL

Name _____

▶ Circle the word that names the picture. Then write that word.

1. third thud (thread)
___thread___

2. bead bad (bed)
___bed___

3. (ten) ton teen
___ten___

4. had (head) help
___head___

5. bird (bread) broth
___bread___

6. weep when (web)
___web___

Homework Option

▲ Practice, p. 53

ADVANCED

Name _____

▶ Read the clues. Write the words in the puzzle.

head thread breath dead sweat bread

1. You use it to make a sandwich.
2. You can see it when it's cold outside.
3. You use it with a needle.
4. You do this when it's hot out.
5. It is on top of you.
6. If something dies, it is this.

▲ Challenge, p. 53

ENGLISH-LANGUAGE LEARNERS

Name _____

▶ Write the word that completes each sentence. Cross out the other word.

1. pep ~~ten~~ Ken's pet has no ___pep___

2. ~~den~~ vet The ___vet___ looks at the hen.

3. head ~~had~~ The feathers on her ___head___ look bad.

4. ~~bed~~ hen This ___hen___ has to get more sleep!

5. read ~~spread~~ Ken ___read___ the vet's list.

▲ ELL, p. 53

Spelling Words

1. lead
2. head
3. bread
4. read
5. ready
6. heavy
7. rule
8. use
9. few
10. boy

Spelling

5-DAY SPELLING	
DAY 1	Pretest; Word Sort
DAY 2	Word Building
DAY 3	State the Generalization
DAY 4	**Review**
DAY 5	Posttest; Writing Application

REVIEW

Spelling Words Use a pocket chart and *Letter Cards* to form words. Have children listen to your directions and change one or two letters in each word to spell a Spelling Word. Have them write the Spelling Word on a sheet of paper or in their journal. Then have a volunteer change the *Letter Card(s)* in the pocket chart so that children can self-check the word.

■ Form *load* in the pocket chart and have children read it aloud. **Which Spelling Word is made with one letter changed?** *(lead)*

■ Form *bead* and in the pocket chart and have children read it aloud. **Which Spelling Word is made with one letter added?** *(bread)*

■ Form *steady* in the pocket chart and have children read it aloud. **Which Spelling Word is made with two letters taken away and one letter added?** *(ready)*

Follow a similar procedure with *wavy (heavy), mule (rule), heat (head), red (read),* and *us (use).*

Vocabulary Display *Letter Cards e, f, w.* Have children take turns making the word *few.*

High-Frequency Word Display *Letter Cards o, y, b.* Have children take turns making the word *boy.*

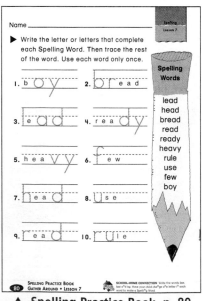

ADVANCED	ENGLISH-LANGUAGE LEARNERS
Have children write a story using some of their Spelling Words. Have them underline the Spelling Words. They can share their stories with classmates.	As you make each new Spelling Word, point to pictures or objects to help children understand the meaning of the word.

Vocabulary

Reinforce Word Recognition
Duplicate and distribute the Story Strips
for "Sleep Is for Everyone" (page T71).
Display *Word Cards* or write the
vocabulary words on the board:
afternoon, bicycle, carry, hours, parents.

REVIEW
Vocabulary
afternoon
bicycle   **hours**
carry   **parents**

Have children complete each sentence with a word from the list.
After children complete the Story Strip sentences, they can work
with partners to check their work. Then children can choose one
Story Strip that best tells what the selection is mainly about. Have
them glue it onto a sheet of paper and illustrate it.

All people need many ___ of sleep each night.

Little children nap in the ___.

Your arms need rest after you ___ heavy bundles.

Your legs need rest after you ride a ___.

___ need sleep, too.

BELOW-LEVEL

Give children Individual Word Cards
(page T37) for the vocabulary words. Say
each word and have children repeat it.
Then read the Story Strips again, helping
children fill in the vocabulary words. Have
them hold up and read aloud the Word
Card for the vocabulary word in each
sentence.

Words to Remember
WORD WALL

Match Words Have children look at the displayed words and
find the words they wrote on Story Strips. Ask volunteers to frame
the words as classmates read them aloud.

Read

▲ *Pupil Edition, pp. 188–209*

OBJECTIVE

To determine the main idea in a paragraph

SKILL TRACE

Main Idea	
Introduce	69A, 93A, 95I, 96–97
Reteach	S18–S19, S24–S25, S42–S43, T12
Review	99A, 119A, 121I, 122–123
REVIEW	**187A, 211A, 215I, 216–217**
T Test	Bk 1-5
MAINTAIN	Bk 2-1

REACHING ALL LEARNERS

Diagnostic Check: Comprehension and Skills

If... children have difficulty determining the main idea of a paragraph...

Then... have them reread pages of "Sleep Is for Everyone" and pause every few pages to tell the most important idea of the section they have just finished reading.

ADDITIONAL SUPPORT ACTIVITIES

BELOW-LEVEL	Reteach, p. S42
ADVANCED	Extend, p. S43
ENGLISH-LANGUAGE LEARNERS	Reteach, p. S43

⭐ Focus Skill Comprehension

Main Idea

TEACH/MODEL

Develop Concepts Remind children that the *main idea* is the most important idea in a story or a section of a story. The main idea is what that part of the selection is mostly about. Explain to children that knowing the main idea can help them understand what they are reading. Have children turn to page 200 in their *Pupil Edition*. Model how to determine the main idea.

MODEL   As I read a page or a section of the story, I try to figure out what it is mostly about. The sentences on page 200 tell about resting different parts of the body. Each one tells more about the first sentence *Every part of your body has to rest after it does its work.* The first sentence tells what this part of the story is mostly about. It tells the main idea.

PRACTICE/APPLY

Recognize Main Idea Now tell children they will think about the selection "Sleep Is for Everyone" and decide what it is mostly about. Read aloud *Pupil Edition* page 216 as children follow along. Emphasize that "Sleep Is for Everyone" includes many details that tell more about the author's most important idea. Discuss which sentence tells what the whole story is about and which sentence just tells more about the main idea.

Reread the Selection Have children reread "Sleep Is for Everyone." Pause from time to time and have children state what page or a section of the selection is mostly about. Help them to distinguish between main ideas and the interesting facts and details that tell more about those ideas. Then have children tell what the whole selection is mostly about.

TEST PREP

Model the Test Item Tell children that when they are reading a paragraph for a test, they should focus on what it is mainly about. Direct children to follow along as you read aloud the paragraph. Then read aloud the question and the answer choices. Guide children in choosing the correct answer.

Main Idea

Focus Skill

▲ Sleep Is for Everyone

The **main idea** of a selection is what that selection is mostly about. Think about "Sleep Is for Everyone" as you read these sentences.

All people and animals need sleep. People need less sleep as they grow older.

Which sentence tells the **main idea**? Why do you think so?

Visit *The Learning Site!*
www.harcourtschool.com
See Skills and Activities

216

Test Prep
Main Idea

Different animals sleep in different ways. Elephants and horses sleep standing up. Some birds sit down to sleep. Dogs lie down to sleep.

1. Which sentence best tells the main idea?
○ Some birds sit down to sleep.
○ Dogs lie down to sleep.
○ Different animals sleep in different ways.

Tip

Read the paragraph carefully. Which sentence tells what the whole paragraph is about?

217

Visit *The Learning Site:*
www.harcourtschool.com

See Skill Activities and Test Tutors: Main Idea.

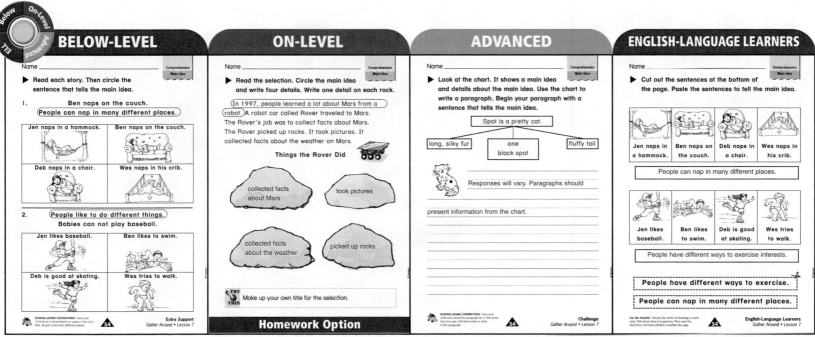

▲ Extra Support, p. 54   ▲ Practice, p. 54   ▲ Challenge, p. 54   ▲ ELL, p. 54

5-DAY WRITING	
DAY 1	SHARED: Animal Chart
DAY 2	INDEPENDENT: Story Response
DAY 3	CROSS-CURRICULAR: Sentences
DAY 4	INDEPENDENT: **Captions**
DAY 5	INTERACTIVE: Facts

LANGUAGE ARTS

Writing
Captions

DAILY LANGUAGE PRACTICE

Steve and randy goed home.

Steve and <u>R</u>andy <u>went</u> home.

ONGOING ASSESSMENT

Note whether children are able to
- correctly space letters and words in a sentence.
- write in complete sentences.
- use capitalization when needed.

journal writing

Writing Prompt Have children choose an animal that lives in the forest and write two facts about it.

ILLUSTRATE AND WRITE

Review Places Animals Live Display the chart created during Shared Writing on Day 1, page 186M. Review with children the different places where animals live. Then have children brainstorm other animals they know about and tell where they live. Add these to the chart.

Place	Animals That Might Live There
farm	cows, chickens, sheep, horses
swamp	alligators, fish, snakes
forest	bears, squirrels, birds, deer
home	cats, dogs, gerbils, fish
zoo	monkeys, elephants, lions

Write Captions Organize children into groups. Assign each group one place from the chart, such as farm or jungle. Give each group a large sheet of paper and have group members draw a picture of their place. Tell each group member to draw a picture of an animal sleeping (standing, lying down, curled up, and so on.) Then have each child write a caption to tell about the animal he or she drew.

Horses sleep standing up.

Handwriting Review with children how to form lowercase *a*, *e*, *o*, and *c*. Point out that if these letters are not formed clearly, readers may confuse them.

Grammar

Using Go *and* Went

5-DAY GRAMMAR

DAY 1	Introduce Using *Go* and *Went*
DAY 2	Generate Sentences
DAY 3	Write Sentences
DAY 4	**Play a Game**
DAY 5	Using *Go* and *Went*

Day 4

REVIEW

Play a Game Play "Where Did the Dog Go?" with children. Have one child be "it" and close his or her eyes. Then take a stuffed dog and have it "run" across the room and hide, such as behind a book, inside a desk, and so on. Then tell the child to open his or her eyes. The child who is "it" guesses where the dog has gone by asking questions that include the word *go*, such as "Did the dog go inside the closet?" You answer with a statement such as "No, the dog went toward the door." Guide children with statements using *toward* and *went* to direct them to the toy. After you model a few answers, have other children take over the role of "guide." When the child who is "it" asks, "Did the dog go to the fil-

ing cabinet?" the guide can say, "Yes, he went there. Go find him." Let children get the toy. Continue playing until all children get to play the game and practice using *go* and *went* correctly.

SKILL TRACE

USING *Go* **AND** *Went*

Introduce	186N
REVIEW	**211C, 215B, 217B, 217L**
T Test	Bk 1-5

ENGLISH-LANGUAGE LEARNERS

In the game, tell a child who is having difficulty asking a question to point to the place he or she guesses. Phrase a question such as *Did the dog go in the box?* and have the child repeat it.

WRAP UP Share Ideas

Use the Author's Chair Let groups share their murals and captions with classmates. Display each mural or have group members hold it up. Each child can sit in the Author's Chair to read the caption he or she wrote. Remind each speaker to read the caption clearly so that everyone can hear. Tell listeners to sit quietly, look at each speaker, and listen carefully. After each group is finished reading, have the listeners applaud.

S.S.R. Have children read silently from a book of their choice. See page 217J for tips on helping children choose books.

Name_____

Using Go and Went

▶ Write a sentence about somewhere you go now. Use go in your sentence. Draw a picture to show where you go.

_____
Responses will vary.

▶ Write a sentence about somewhere you went last year. Use went in your sentence. Draw a picture to show where you went.

_____
Responses will vary.

▲ Language Handbook, p. 140

Sleep Is for Everyone **217B**

Day at a Glance
Day 5

Sharing Literature
Big Book: *To Market, To Market*

Phonemic Awareness
Phoneme Isolation; Focus on Inflections -*er*, -*est*

Phonics
Inflections -*er*, -*est*; Inflections -*ed*, -*ing* (double final consonant)

Spelling
Posttest; Writing Application

Vocabulary
REVIEW: *afternoon, bicycle, carry, hours, parents*

Reading

Rereading for Fluency
Pupil Edition
"Sleep Is for Everyone," pp. 188–209

Self-Selected Reading

Interactive Writing
Facts List

Grammar
REVIEW: Using *Go* and *Went*

WARM UP MORNING MESSAGE

Good Morning!

Today is _____.
We like to go to special places.
One day _____ went _____.
One day _____ went _____.
_____ wants to go _____.

Introduce the Day

Tell children that today they will revisit the story *To Market, To Market*. Guide children in generating a message about going places. Ask:

- **What special place have you visited?**
- **What special place would you like to visit?**

As you write the message, invite children to write previously taught letters, words, and/or punctuation. For instance, pause while writing the last three sentences and ask children to write the appropriate word, *go* or *went*. Elicit from children which sentences talk about something that happened in the past.

Read the Message

Read the message. Use the message to focus on selected skills that have been previously taught.

Apply Skills

Grammar Ask children to point to words that are special names of places (proper nouns). Have them underline the capital letters.

Phonics Have children tell what letters stand for the sound of /ā/ as in *today*, *places*, and *day*.

Sharing Literature

DEVELOP LISTENING COMPREHENSION

(Focus Skill) Main Idea Remind children that they can better understand a story or selection when they think about what the story or a section of the story is mostly about. Reread *To Market, To Market*, and pause from time to time to ask *What are these pages mostly about?* Then have children identify the details in the pictures and the words that help tell about the main idea.

Extend the Pattern Have children suggest other animals that the woman might bring back home from the market. Write a frame to help children think of rhyming words.

> To market, to market,
> To buy a _____, (silly snake)
> Home again. . . .
> _____. (Uh-oh, did it swim into the lake?)

▲ **Big Book**

Phonemic Awareness

PHONEME ISOLATION

Words from the Big Book Repeat several times the names of the animals that appear in *To Market, To Market*. (pig, hen, goose, trout, lamb, cow, duck, goat) Have children tell which names

- **begin with the same sound.** (goose, goat)
- **end with the same sound.** (trout, goat)

FOCUS ON *-er, -est*

Distinguish Letter Patterns Tell children that when they hear a word that ends in *-er,* they will clap once. When they hear a word that ends in *-est,* they will clap twice. Model by saying *colder* and clapping once. *I hear -er at the end of* colder, *so I will clap once.* Continue with the following words:

thinner(1) **wisest**(2) **silliest**(2) **wilder**(1) **highest**(2)
slowest(2) **largest**(2) **smarter**(1) **lower**(1) **smaller**(1)

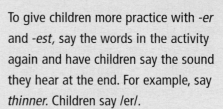

BELOW-LEVEL

To give children more practice with *-er* and *-est,* say the words in the activity again and have children say the sound they hear at the end. For example, say *thinner.* Children say /er/.

Phonics
Inflections -er, -est *Review*

OBJECTIVES

• *To identify and understand inflections -er, -est*

• *To use common letter patterns to read words*

SKILL TRACE

INFLECTIONS *-er, -est*	
Introduce	Bk 1-3, 143H
REVIEW	**217E**

ENGLISH-LANGUAGE LEARNERS

Have three children of different heights stand up in the front of the room. Write *tall*, *taller*, and *tallest* on large index cards. Guide children to order themselves in the positions of tall, taller, and tallest and have these children hold the cards in front of them. Then have them change positions and let volunteers rearrange them in the order of tall, taller, and tallest.

WORKING WITH PATTERNS

Review Words with *-er, -est* Draw three long lines on the board and label them long, longer, longest.

long _____

longer _____

longest _____

Have children read the words, and ask them how the words are alike. (They all have the word *long*.) Review with children that *-er* is added to words to compare two things and *-est* is added to compare more that two things. Use the lines on the board to illustrate this. Have a volunteer underline the *-er* and *-est*.

Listen for Meaning Use words such as *taller* and *tallest* in sentences. Have children tell whether you are comparing two or more than two and how they know. For example: *Juan is taller than Jimmy. George is the tallest boy in the class.*

Add Endings Make a chart like the one below. Write these base words: *cool*, *fast*, and *slow.* Work with children to fill in the rest of the chart. Then have volunteers use the words in sentences.

Base Word	-er	-est
cool	cooler	coolest
fast	faster	fastest
slow	slower	slowest

APPLY PHONICS SKILLS

 Write with Inflections Have children write in their journal sentences that have words with *-er* or *-est* endings.

The horse's tail is *longer* than the dog's tail.

Inflections -ed, -ing

 Review

5-DAY PHONICS	
DAY 1	Introduce /e/ea
DAY 2	Word Building with /e/ea
DAY 3	Word Building with /e/ea
DAY 4	Word Building with /e/ea and /a/a
DAY 5	**Inflections -er, -est; Inflections -ed, -ing (double final consonant)**

WORKING WITH PATTERNS

Analyze the Pattern Write these sentences on the board and have children read them aloud.

> The dogs wag their tails.
> The dogs wagged their tails.
> The dogs are wagging their tails.

Frame the words *wag* and *wagged*. Ask children how *wag* and *wagged* are different. (*Wagged* ends with *-ed* and has two *g*'s.) Follow the same procedure with *wag* and *wagging*. Then review with children that in a consonant-vowel-consonant word, the final consonant is doubled before *-ed* or *-ing* is added. Remind children of different pronunciations of *-ed* endings.

Build Words Make a chart like the one on page 217E, with columns headed *Base Word*, *-ed*, and *-ing*. Supply base words such as *tap*, *skip*, *hop* and *step*, and help children fill in the chart.

APPLY PHONICS SKILLS

 Write Sentences Ask children to choose one word from each column and write a sentence using that word.

OBJECTIVES

* To identify and understand inflections -ed, -ing

* To understand when to double the final consonant before adding -ed or -ing

* To use common letter patterns to read words

SKILL TRACE

Inflections -ed, -ing	
Introduce	97E–97F
Reteach	T6
REVIEW	**185H, 217F**
T Test	Bk 1-5

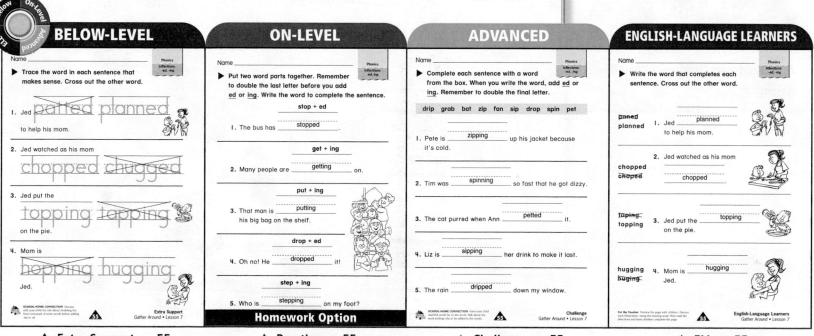

▲ Extra Support, p. 55   ▲ Practice, p. 55   ▲ Challenge, p. 55   ▲ ELL, p. 55

Spelling Words

1. lead
2. head
3. bread
4. read
5. ready
6. heavy
7. rule
8. use
9. few
10. boy

BELOW-LEVEL

Before giving the posttest, display the Spelling Words. Say each sentence in the posttest, and have children point to the Spelling Word they hear in the sentence. Then have them spell it.

ADVANCED

Children can create riddles for Spelling Words and share them with their classmates.

WORD WORK

Spelling

5-DAY SPELLING

DAY 1	Pretest; Word Sort
DAY 2	Word Building
DAY 3	State the Generalization
DAY 4	Review
DAY 5	**Posttest; Writing Application**

ASSESS/APPLY

Posttest Assess children's progress using the words and the Dictation Sentences from Day 1.

1. **lead**   I broke my pencil **lead.**
2. **head**   I have brown hair on my **head.**
3. **bread**   You can make a sandwich with **bread.**
4. **read**   I **read** two books last week.
5. **ready**   The soccer team is **ready** to play.
6. **heavy**   Ten books are too **heavy** to carry.

Review

7. **rule**   Do you know the playground **rule?**
8. **use**   My sister let me **use** her bike.

Vocabulary

9. **few**   Only a **few** children are absent today.

High-Frequency

10. **boy**   That **boy** is my brother.

Writing Application Have children complete and illustrate the following sentences:

I am ready for _____.

The _____ is heavy.

We use _____ to bake bread.

I am ready for soccer.

Vocabulary

USE WORDS IN SENTENCES

Reinforce Word Recognition and Meaning Display *Word Cards* or list these words on the board: *afternoon, bicycle, carry, hours, parents.* Have children read the words aloud. Then pantomime a scene to illustrate each word as children try to guess which word you are acting out. Have volunteers take turns helping you pantomime. Use actions such as carrying something from one place to another (carry), pointing to the three on the clock (afternoon), riding a bicycle (bicycle), holding a baby (parents), and looking at your watch (hours). Then have children suggest sentences for each pantomime. Write a sentence for each vocabulary word and read it aloud. Have children repeat it.

> **REVIEW**
>
> **Vocabulary**
> afternoon
> bicycle   hours
> carry   parents

afternoon   carry   parents

bicycle   hours

ADVANCED

Have children use the vocabulary words to write a set of rules about things they should do when they return home from school.

ENGLISH-LANGUAGE LEARNERS

Have children draw a picture of what they do in the afternoon. Then have them dictate sentences about the picture, using at least three vocabulary words. Have children circle the vocabulary words they used to tell about the picture.

Words to Remember

WORD WALL

Find and Read Words Have children look at the displayed words and find the words that were pantomimed. Ask volunteers to frame the words as children read them aloud. Then say the following clues. Have children look at the displayed words and read aloud words that fit each clue.

Find words that

- have the vowel sound /ī/ as in *bicycle*.
- end with *s* that sounds like /z/ as in *hours*.
- end with *s* that sounds like /s/ as in *parents*.

Read

▲ *Pupil Edition, pp. 188–209*

FLUENCY ROUTINES For support, see Fluency Routine Cards in Theme Resources, pp. T83–T84.

Rereading for Fluency

PARTNERS

Partner Reading

ADVANCED/ON-LEVEL Have partners take turns reading the selection aloud two pages at a time. Encourage children to read smoothly with expression as if they are talking. INDEPENDENT

GROUPS

Choral Reading

BELOW-LEVEL Tell children to look at pages 190–191 and tell in their own words what these pages are about. Then lead children in choral reading the pages. Reread sentences or sections to model fluency as necessary. Continue through the story in this way, discussing and choral reading two pages at a time. TEACHER-DIRECTED

> Horses close their eyelids when they sleep.

Managing Small Groups

Reread for fluency with children working individually, with partners, or in small groups. While you work with small groups, have other children do the following:

- **Self-Selected Reading**
- **Practice Pages**
- **Cross-Curricular Centers**
- **Journal Writing**

Use the suggested Classroom Management outline on page 7C for the whole-group/small-group schedule.

Self-Selected Reading

INDEPENDENT READING

Have children choose a book from the **Browsing Boxes** or the **Reading Center** to read independently during a sustained silent reading time. Children may also want to reread a story from their *Pupil Edition*. These are some books you may want to gather that relate to "Sleep Is for Everyone."

choosing books

Remind children to read one or two pages of a book to decide whether they need to select an easier book. If there are at least five words that the child can't read, he or she should try an easier book.

Decodable Books

Decodable Book 33
"All Kinds of Weather" by Sunita Apte

"Ned's Feathers" by Betsy Franco

Cut-Out/Fold-Up Book

Ready for Space
Practice Book, pp. 77–78

related books

- ***Goodnight Goodnight*** by Brenda Parkes. Rigby, 1898.

  A child dreams that storybook characters visit and play with her each night in her bed. BELOW-LEVEL

- ***The Sun Is My Favorite Star*** by Frank Asch. Gulliver Books, 2000.

  A little girl sings praises of the sun for all the things the sun does for us. ON-LEVEL

- ***Mabel Dancing*** by Amy Hest. Candlewick, 2000.

  A child dances her way through her dreams. ON-LEVEL

- ***What! Cried Granny: An Almost Bedtime Story*** by Kate Lum. Dial, 1999.

  Patrick has many excuses to delay his bedtime, but Granny springs into action. ADVANCED

Books for All Learners

| ***An Afternoon Nap*** by Beth Alley Wise | ***Ready, Set, Sleep!*** by Susan Blackaby | ***Jobs at All Hours*** by Susan Blackaby | ***Touch Your Nose, Wiggle Your Toes*** by Mindy Menschell |

5-DAY WRITING	
DAY 1	SHARED: Animal Chart
DAY 2	INTERACTIVE: Story Response
DAY 3	CROSS-CURRICULAR: Sentences
DAY 4	INDEPENDENT: Captions
DAY 5	**INTERACTIVE: Facts List**

DAILY LANGUAGE PRACTICE

Is there a fether in
my bed.

Is there a <u>feather</u> in
my bed<u>?</u>

journal writing

Self-Selected Writing Have
children write in their journal about a
topic of their choice. They may want to
illustrate their writing.

Interactive Writing

Facts List

SHARE THE PEN

Review the K-W-L Chart Display the K-W-L Chart children created during Building Background, page 186S, and Retelling, page 211A. Review with children the information on the chart. Work together to answer any unanswered questions from column 2. Add to the chart any other information that children have discovered about sleep.

Write About Sleep Tell children that they will work together to list some things they learned about sleep. Write a title at the top of a sheet of chart paper: *What We Learned.* Call on a volunteer to say one fact he or she learned about sleep. Have children help you write the fact on chart paper. Ask questions such as these.

• **What is the first word of the sentence?**

• **What is the first sound you hear in the word?**

• **What letter stands for that sound? Who would like to write it?**

What We Learned

All people and animals need
to sleep.

Babies need more sleep than
grown-ups do.

As you compose the sentences, continue to have children help by writing known consonants, vowels, words, and punctuation marks. Periodically, read what has been written while pointing to each word.

Read the Facts Read the sentences aloud. Pause occasionally to have children read aloud decodable and previously taught words.

5-DAY GRAMMAR

DAY 1	Introduce Using *Go* and *Went*
DAY 2	Generate Sentences
DAY 3	Sentence Frames
DAY 4	Play a Game
DAY 5	**Write Sentences**

Grammar

Using Go *and* Went

REVIEW

Complete Sentences Have children write *go* on the front of a sheet of paper and *went* on the back. Read the following sentences aloud, and have children hold up the word that correctly fills in each blank.

Now we ____ to school. (go)
Last night Dan ____ to the movies. (went)
We ____ to the park yesterday. (went)
Today we ____ to art class. (go)

Write Sentences Write these sentence frames on the board and have children complete them. Tell children that they can use clue words like *now, today, yesterday,* or *last week* to begin each sentence.

____ we go ____.
____ we went ____.

SKILL TRACE

USING *GO* AND *WENT*	
Introduce	186N
REVIEW	**211C, 215B, 217B, 217L**
T Test	Bk 1-5

technology

Visit *The Learning Site:*
www.harcourtschool.com
See Go for Grammar Gold, Multimedia Grammar Glossary

WRAP UP Revisit the Poems

Connect Ideas Across Texts Remind children that they read the poems "Pretending" (pages 212–213) and "Keep a Poem in Your Pocket" (page 215D). Reread both poems aloud and ask volunteers to tell how the two poems are alike. (Possible response: They both give ideas of things to do when you are trying to go to sleep.) Reread the poems for children to enjoy. Have them join in on the rhyming words and other parts they know.

S.S.R.

Have children read silently from a book of their choice. See page 217J for tips on helping children choose books.

Name ____

Using Go and Went

▶ Write **go** or **went** to complete the sentences. Make these sentences tell about now.

1. Today Dad and I ____ go ____ on a hike.

2. We ____ go ____ to the mountains.

▶ Make these sentences tell about the past.

3. Last month Mom and I ____ went ____ to the beach.

4. We ____ went ____ in the water.

141

▲ Language Handbook, p. 141

Sleep Is for Everyone　**217L**

Books for All Learners

Reinforcing Skills and Strategies

■ BELOW-LEVEL

by Beth Alley Wise
illustrated by Donna Perrone

An Afternoon Nap

✓ **Phonics:** Short Vowel /e/ *ea*

✓ **Vocabulary:** *afternoon, bicycle, carry, hours, parents*

✓ **Focus Skill:** Main Idea

SUMMARY A busy city in Spain comes to a quiet halt when everyone takes an afternoon siesta.

Visit *The Learning Site:*
www.harcourtschool.com
See Resources for Parents and
Teachers: Books for All Learners.

BEFORE READING

Build Background Invite children to share experiences they may have had while visiting a busy shop. Tell them that they are going to read a story about people who close their shops for an afternoon nap.

Preview/Set Purpose Have children identify the title and help them read it. Point out the author and the illustrator. Then have children look at the first few pages of the book and predict what the story is about. Help children set a purpose for reading, such as *I want to find out what happens to the people in the shops.*

READING THE BOOK

Pages 2–3 Why do workers bring food outside? (so people will buy the food) NOTE DETAILS

Pages 4–5 What do you think are in the boxes? (food and other things for the shops) What clues do you get from the story? (The shops sell food and other things and many people are buying these things.) DRAW CONCLUSIONS

Pages 6–7 For how long do the shops close? (two hours) NOTE DETAILS

Pages 8–10 Why do you think the owners pull down the blinds and close the doors? (so people will know that the shop is closed) DRAW CONCLUSIONS

Pages 11–12 What happens after the nap ends? (Everyone goes back to work in the shops.) SEQUENCE

RESPONDING

Retell the Story Have partners retell the story from the point of view of someone who works in a shop. Encourage children to use the sequence words *first, next,* and *last.* Bring the group together and have children tell the main idea of the story in one sentence.

An Afternoon Nap

by Beth Alley Wise
illustrated by Donna Perrone

READY, SET, SLEEP

by Susan Blackaby
illustrated by Mary Ann Lloyd

JOBS AT ALL HOURS

▲ p. 217O

Touch Your Nose, Wiggle Your Toes

by Mindy Menschell
illustrated by Jeff Mack

▲ p. 217P

■ ON-LEVEL

Ready, Set, Sleep!

 Phonics: Short Vowel /e/ea

 Vocabulary: afternoon, bicycle, carry, hours, parents

 Focus Skill: Main Idea

SUMMARY A boy is too excited to sleep on the night before a camping trip.

Visit The Learning Site:
www.harcourtschool.com
See Resources for Parents and Teachers: Books for All Learners.

BEFORE READING

Build Background Invite children to tell how they felt the night before going on a family vacation. Ask children what they do when they are unable to go to sleep.

Preview/Set Purpose Have children identify the title and help them read it. Point out the author and the illustrator. Then have children look at the first few pages of the book and predict what the story is about. Help children set a purpose for reading, such as *I want to find out what happens to the boy.*

READING THE BOOK

Pages 2–4 What did the boy help his dad do? (carry camping things to the van) NOTE DETAILS

Pages 5–7 What will the boy and his family do after they eat breakfast? (head out for the trip) SEQUENCE

Pages 8–10 What does the boy mean when he says "the bed felt like heaven"? (It was comfortable.) AUTHOR'S CRAFT, APPRECIATE LANGUAGE

Pages 11–13 Why do you think the boy cannot go to sleep? (He is excited about the camping trip.) Have you ever felt this way? When? (Possible response: Yes, before I went to see my cousins.) IDENTIFY WITH CHARACTERS

Pages 14–16 What is this story mostly about? (A boy is too excited to sleep on the night before a camping trip.) MAIN IDEA

RESPONDING

Pantomime the Story Form small groups. Have one child read the story aloud, while the other children act out what the boy, his mother, and his father do throughout the story. Let each group read and perform the story for the class.

Books for All Learners

Reinforcing Skills and Strategies

■ ADVANCED

Jobs at All Hours

 Phonics: Short Vowel /e/ea

 Vocabulary: *afternoon, bicycle, carry, hours, parents*

 Focus Skill: Main Idea

SUMMARY At almost any hour of the day, you can find people working on the job.

 Visit *The Learning Site:* www.harcourtschool.com

See Resources for Parents and Teachers: Books for All Learners.

BEFORE READING

Build Background Have children tell about the kinds of jobs held by their parents or others in the community. Encourage them to tell why each job is important.

Preview/Set Purpose Have children identify the title and help them read it. Point out the author and the illustrator. Then have children look at the first few pages of the book and predict what the story is about. Have children set a purpose for reading, such as *I want to find out if my favorite kind of job is in this book.*

READING THE BOOK

Pages 2–3 What kinds of jobs do you think might start at night? Why? (Possible responses: night watchman, police officer) SPECULATE

Pages 4–5 What does the author mean by "rush hour"? (Rush hour is a busy time of day when everyone is rushing to work and there are many cars on the road.) AUTHOR'S CRAFT, UNDERSTAND FIGURATIVE LANGUAGE

Pages 6–11 Why must firefighters be on the job at all times? (because fires could start at any time of the day or night) DRAW CONCLUSIONS

Pages 12–13 How do you think the author feels about jobs? (She thinks each job is necessary and important.) RECOGNIZE AUTHOR'S PURPOSE, THEME

Pages 14–16 What is this story mostly about? (People do all kinds of jobs at all hours.) MAIN IDEA

RESPONDING

Make a Map Have children draw a neighborhood map showing where each job would be performed. Invite children to use the map to tell a partner about a job and how the neighborhood benefits from that job.

BELOW-LEVEL

An Afternoon Nap
by Beth Alley Wise
illustrated by Donna Perrone

▲ p. 217M

ON-LEVEL

Ready, Set, Sleep
by Susan Blackaby
illustrated by Mary Ann Lloyd

▲ p. 217N

ADVANCED

JOBS AT ALL HOURS
BY SUSAN BLACKABY

ELL

Touch Your Nose, Wiggle Your Toes
by Mindy Menschell
illustrated by Jeff Mack

Managing Small Groups

While you work with small groups, have other children do the following:

- Self-Selected Reading
- Practice Pages
- Cross-Curricular Centers
- Journal Writing

■ ENGLISH-LANGUAGE LEARNERS

Touch Your Nose, Wiggle Your Toes

☑ **Strong Picture Support**

☑ **Concept Vocabulary**

☑ **Theme Related**

SUMMARY We have all sorts of body parts and each is used in a special way.

Visit *The Learning Site:*
www.harcourtschool.com
See Resources for Parents and
Teachers: Books for All Learners.

BEFORE READING

Build Background Play "Simon Says" with children, focusing on body parts described in the story. Then talk with children about different kinds of body parts and what they are used for.

Preview/Set Purpose Have children identify the title and help them read it. Point out the author and the illustrator. Then have children look at the first few pages of the book and predict what the story will be about. Help children set a purpose for reading, such as *I want to find out which body parts will be shown in the story.*

READING THE BOOK

Pages 2–4 What do you need to smell a rose? (your nose) NOTE DETAILS, RELATE PICTURES TO TEXT

Pages 5–7 What is the boy doing with his feet? (walking down the street) NOTE DETAILS, RELATE PICTURES TO TEXT

Pages 8–10 Why do you need your lips to eat chips? (So you can open your mouth and eat the chips.) DRAW CONCLUSIONS

Pages 11–12 What is this story mostly about? (We have all sorts of body parts.) How do you know? (Each page shows a different body part.) MAIN IDEA

RESPONDING

Draw and Label Body Parts Ask children to draw a picture of themselves and include the body parts mentioned in the story. Guide children in labeling the body parts in their pictures. Then write the following sentence frame on the board: *Look at my _____.* Read the frame with children, substituting different body part names in the blank, such as *Look at my ears.* Have children use their pictures, labels, and the sentence frame to identify each body part.

Teacher Notes

Reading Selections

BIG BOOK

DECODABLE BOOK

Applies Vowel Digraph /ōō/ oo

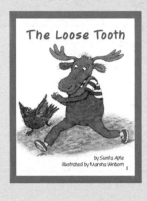

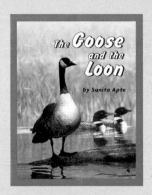

▲ Decodable Book 34
"The Loose Tooth"
"The Goose and the Loon"

PUPIL EDITION

Genre

Informational Fiction

Some fiction stories give information about things in the real world.

Look for:

• Parts of the story that are made-up.

• Information about different African animals.

220

Baboon

by Kate Banks

illustrated by Georg Hallensleben

221

▼ **READING ACROSS TEXTS:**
"Piggyback Ride"
GENRE: Nonfiction

SUMMARY: *A baby baboon learns about the world as his mother takes him on a walk.*

Comparing Informational Fiction and Nonfiction

 "Baboon" is available on *Audiotext 5.*

218A   Gather Around

Books for All Learners

Lesson Plans on pages 253M–253P

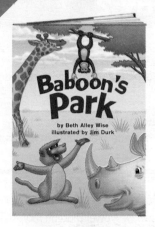

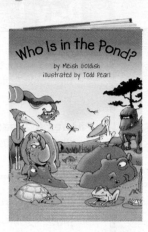

BELOW-LEVEL
- Phonics: Vowel Digraph /o͞o/ *oo*
- Vocabulary: *against, careful, fire, quietly, shook*

ON-LEVEL
- Phonics: Vowel Digraph /o͞o/ *oo*
- Vocabulary: *against, careful, fire, quietly, shook*

ADVANCED
- Phonics: Vowel Digraph /o͞o/ *oo*
- Vocabulary: *against, careful, fire, quietly, shook*

ELL
- Strong Picture Support
- Concept Vocabulary

MULTI-LEVELED PRACTICE

Practice Book, pp. 56–63

Extra Support, pp. 57–63

Challenge, pp. 57–63

English-Language Learners, pp. 57–63

Technology

- *Writing Express™* CD-ROM
- *Grammar Jingles™* CD, Primary
- *Reading and Language Skills Assessment* CD-ROM
- *The Learning Site:* www.harcourtschool.com

ADDITIONAL RESOURCES

Spelling Practice Book, pp. 81–82

Language Handbook, pp. 142–145

Read-Aloud Literature
- Read-Aloud Anthology, pp. 48–50

Teaching Transparencies 100–102, 109

Cross-Curricular Activity Cards, T14

Word Builders/Word Builder Cards

Letter Cards

Intervention Resource Kit, Lesson 34

English-Language Learners Resource Kit, Lesson 34

Day 1

ORAL LANGUAGE
 30 Minutes

- **Sharing Literature**

Sharing Literature, 218H
Big Book: Build Concept Vocabulary

- **Phonemic Awareness**

Phonemic Awareness, 218H
Phoneme Substitution; Focus on /ōō/

WORD WORK
 30 Minutes

- **Phonics**

, 218I
Introduce: Vowel Digraph /ōō/oo

- **Spelling**

Spelling, 218K
Pretest; Word Sort **T**

- **Vocabulary**

Vocabulary, 218K
Review: *carry, hours* **T**

READING
 45 Minutes

- **Comprehension**
- **Fluency**

Read
Apply Phonics, 218L

DECODABLE BOOK 34
"The Loose Tooth"

Daily Routines
- Morning Message
- Daily Language Practice
- Writing Prompt

- **Independent Reading**

 Independent Reading
Books for All Learners

LANGUAGE ARTS
 45 Minutes

- **Writing**

 Independent Writing, 218M
Talking Mural

Writing Prompt
Have children write sentences about "I Swam with a Seal."

- **Grammar**

Grammar, 218N
Introduce: Contractions with *not* **T**

Daily Language Practice
Spiral Review

Daily Language Practice
Last nite I go to a show. (night, went)

Day 2

Sharing Literature, 218P
Poem: Build Concept Vocabulary

Phonemic Awareness, 218P
Phoneme Manipulation; Focus on /ōō/

, 218Q
Review: Vowel Digraph /ōō/oo **T**

Spelling, 218Q
Word Building **T**

Vocabulary, 218S
Introduce: *against, careful, fire, quietly, shook* **T**

Word Power, pp. 218–219

Read
Read the Selection, 219A

PUPIL EDITION
"Baboon,"
pp. 218–247

Comprehension

(Focus Skill) Plot **T**

(Focus Strategy) Sequence Events/Summarize

 Independent Reading
Books for All Learners

 Independent Writing, 247B
Story Response

Writing Prompt
Have children write about what they would show Baboon in their neighborhood.

Grammar, 247C
Review: Contractions with *not* **T**

Daily Language Practice
I did'nt get to play the gam. (didn't, game)

Focus Skill ★

Plot

Phonics

Vowel Variant
/ōō/oo

Focus of the Week:
- VOCABULARY:
  against, careful, fire, quietly, shook
- COMPREHENSION: Plot
- WRITING: Contractions with *not*

Day 3

Sharing Literature, 247E
Song: Listen and Respond

Phonemic Awareness, 247E
Syllable Counting; Focus on /ōō/

Phonics, 247F
Review: Vowel Digraph /ōō/oo

Spelling, 247H
State the Generalization **T**

Vocabulary, 247I
Review: *against, careful, fire, quietly, shook* **T**

Read
Rereading for Fluency, 247J

Reading Across Texts, 248–249
"Piggy Back Ride"

Making Connections, 250–251

Apply Phonics, 247G
DECODABLE BOOK 34
"The Goose and The Loon"

⬤ **Independent Reading**
Books for All Learners

✎ **Writing Across the Curriculum,** 251A
Sentence Frames

Writing Prompt
Have children write about a baby animal they would like to be and explain why.

Grammar, 251B
Review: Contractions with *not* **T**

Daily Language Practice
Alex isnt redy for bed. (isn't, ready)

Day 4

Sharing Literature, 251D
Poem: Listen and Respond

Phonemic Awareness, 251D
Phoneme Blending; Focus on /ō/, /ōō/

Phonics, 251E
Build Words

Spelling, 251G
Review **T**

Vocabulary, 251H
Review: *against, careful, fire quietly, shook* **T**

Read
Comprehension, 251I

Focus Skill Plot,
pp. 252–253 **T**

⬤ **Independent Reading**
Books for All Learners

✎ **Interactive Writing,** 253A
Description

Writing Prompt
Have children write about what an animal might say if it could talk.

Grammar, 253B
Review: Contractions with *not* **T**

Daily Language Practice
Dad cant find his box of tules. (can't, tools)

Day 5

Sharing Literature, 253D
Big Book: Listen and Respond

Phonemic Awareness, 253D
Phoneme Manipulation: Focus on /ōō/, /m/, and /t/

Phonics, 253E
Phonograms -oom, -oot

Spelling, 253G
Posttest; Writing Application **T**

Vocabulary, 253H
Review: *against, careful, fire quietly, shook* **T**

Read
Rereading for Fluency, 253I

Self-Selected Reading, 253J

⬤ **Independent Reading**
Books for All Learners

✎ **Independent Writing,** 253K
Posters

Self Selected Writing
Have children write about a topic of their choice.

Grammar, 253L
Review: Contractions with *not* **T**

Daily Language Practice
Beth ha'snt ever lost a tuth. (hasn't, tooth)

Cross-Curricular Centers

SCIENCE CENTER

Baboon's Day

Have children pretend that a flashlight is the sun and a small toy animal is Baboon. Tell partners to experiment by moving the flashlight up and down slowly to see how Baboon's shadow changes as the sun rises, moves high in the sky, and then sets. Have children record what they see by drawing pictures showing Baboon, his shadow, and the position of the sun. Then provide a place in the room for children to post their work.

20 Minutes

Materials
- toy monkeys or other small plastic animals
- flashlights
- paper and crayons

LETTER AND WORD CENTER

/o͞o/oo Words

Create a bulletin board with areas marked for the endings *-ool, -oop, -oot, -oom, -oof, -oon, -oost, -ooth,* and *-oose.* Have children experiment with letter tiles to create /o͞o/oo words. Then have them use markers, crayons, or colored pencils to record on note cards each word they form. Children can then hang each word under the appropriate heading on the bulletin board. Pairs of children can then read all the words on the board that rhyme with their word.

tooth

moose

moon

20 Minutes

Materials
- letter tiles
- markers, crayons, and colored pencils
- colored note cards

MATH CENTER

Animal Groups

Have children write and illustrate math stories. Post the following frame for children to use: *Baboon saw _____, _____, and _____. How many animals did he see? He saw _____ animals.* Explain that children should fill in each blank with a number and the name of an animal. Tell children that they can write about more than two groups of animals. After writing their stories, children can draw pictures that show the same information and then count their animals to find the total. Display the stories for other children to solve.

turtle
crocodile
elephant
gazelle
rhinoceros
monkey

20 Minutes

Materials
- sentence frame
- list of animal names
- paper, pencils, crayons

ART CENTER

20-30 Minutes

Art Adventure

Provide books with pictures of wildlife and wild places in Africa. Have children look through the books, then draw or paint a picture of something Baboon might see on another day. Ask children to think about what Baboon would learn from the experience. Then have them write a caption using the sentence frame *The world is* _____. Bind children's pictures together to make a book. Have children decide as a group on a title for the book.

Materials

■ paint/crayons/markers
■ paintbrushes/water cups
■ books with pictures of African landscapes and animals

COMPUTER CENTER

20-30 Minutes

Publish a Story

Have partners work together to type sentences about things they could teach a pet living at home and how they might teach the pet. Then have children use the paint or draw program to illustrate the sentences. Print out the stories and display them for others to read.

I teach my pup how to sit and stay.

Materials

■ computer with a draw or paint program

HOMEWORK FOR THE WEEK

The Homework Copying Master provides activities to complete for each day of the week.

    Visit *The Learning Site:* www.harcourtschool.com

See Resources for Parents and Teachers: Homework Helper.

School–Home Connection

Your child has been reading "Baboon," a story about a baby baboon exploring the world with his mother.

I have tried some of the activities.

Student: _____
Family Member: _____
Comments/Suggestions: _____

_____

You may want to do some of these activities with your child.

Words, Words, Words
• Have your child cut out the word cards and read each word.
• Have your child act out the meaning of each word for you to guess the word.
• Have your child use the words in sentences and place the word cards in his or her word box.

Explore the World
Ask your child to tell you about the baby baboon's activities in "Baboon." Then talk about a human baby's activities. Together look at photographs that show your child learning to walk or crawl. Talk about how babies explore everything around them as part of learning and growing. Ask your child what kinds of things children of five or six years old do to learn.

| disappear |
| mouth |
| shook |
| ground |
| across |

TIME TO READ Encourage your child to read for at least 30 minutes outside of class each day.

Visit The Learning Site! www.harcourtschool.com
See Resources for Parents and Teachers: Homework Helper

Homework, p. T46 ▶

ORAL LANGUAGE

WARM UP MORNING MESSAGE
Good Morning!

Today is _____.
Do you have _____ like a whale or _____
like an ape?
I am like a _____ because _____.
I am different from a _____ because _____.

Introduce the Day

Tell children that they will be revisiting the book *I Swam with a Seal*. Guide the group in generating a message about similarities and differences.

• **Can you think of a way that you and a certain animal are alike? A way that you are different?**

• **Can you name animals that are similar to one another? In what ways are they alike?**

As you write the message, ask volunteers to write previously taught letters, words, and/or punctuation. For instance, have children write the high-frequency words *do, you, have,* and *like*.

Read the Message

Read the message. Use the message to focus on selected skills that have been previously taught.

Apply Skills

Phonics Remind children that words that end in *vowel-consonant*-e usually have a long vowel sound. Ask children to find words in the message that fit that pattern. (like, whale, ape) Ask children to read each word and then identify its vowel sound.	**Grammar/Mechanics** Ask children to name the punctuation marks they see in the message. Have them explain why the second sentence has a question mark at the end and the other sentences end with periods.

Sharing Literature

BUILD CONCEPT VOCABULARY

Revisit the Big Book As you read, track the print and invite children to join in. Discuss whether the story is "real" or "make-believe." Lead children to understand that some parts are realistic and others are make-believe.

Explore a Word Reread pages 26–27. Then say: *The speaker meandered with the moose. To meander means to "walk around slowly."* Have children say *meander*. Explain that when you meander, you take your time. Give examples such as: *People who like flowers might meander through a garden.* Ask volunteers to use the word *meander* to tell about places they like—for example, *I like to meander around the zoo so I can see every animal.* Then ask children to name the word they have been discussing. Ask: *If you meander, do you move slowly or quickly?*

▲ **Big Book**

Phonemic Awareness

PHONEME SUBSTITUTION

Words from the Big Book Tell children that you will say an animal name and they will change the first sound to make a new word. Model by saying *seal. If I change /s/ to /h/, I get* heal. Continue with these animal names:

Say:	Change:		Say:	Change:
hare	/h/ to /f/ (fare)		moose	/m/ to /g/ (goose)
dog	/d/ to /h/ (hog)		deer	/d/ to /ch/ (cheer)
horse	/h/ to /f/ (force)		mouse	/m/ to /h/ (house)

BELOW-LEVEL

If children are having difficulty substituting beginning sounds, have them say each original word as onset and rime (/s/, /ēl/). Then have them say the new beginning sound and the rime from the original word (/h/, /ēl/). Finally, model blending the new onset and the rime from the original word (/hēl/, *heal*). Have them repeat the word.

FOCUS ON /o͞o/

Phoneme Isolation Have children say *boot*. Ask: *Where do you hear the sound /o͞o/ in* boot—*at the beginning, in the middle, or at the end?* (middle) Continue with the following words:

ooze (beginning) **igloo** (end) **room** (middle)
loop (middle) **tooth** (middle) **loose** (middle)

OBJECTIVES

- *To generate the vowel sound /o͞o/, spelled oo*

- *To build words using known letters and sounds*

- *To read simple, regular words*

SKILL TRACE	
/o͞o/oo	
INTRODUCE	**218I–218L**
Reteach	S46–S47
Review	218Q–218R, 247F–247G
Review	251E–251F
T Test	Bk 2-1
Maintain	Bk 2-1

teaching tip

Pronunciation of some words with *oo* may vary by region. For example, the word *roof* may be pronounced /ro͞of/ or /ro͝of/. Adjust instruction as appropriate.

15 Minutes

Materials

- magnetic board with letters
- letter stamps, ink pads
- markers and crayons
- index cards
- alphabet blocks

Phonics and Spelling
Vowel Digraph /o͞o/oo

Introduce

TEACH/MODEL

Introduce /o͞o/oo Display the *Picture Card* moon. Point to the label and say *moon*. Tell children that two *o*'s together can stand for the sound /o͞o/, the vowel sound heard at the beginning of *ooze* and in the middle of *moon*.

Have children repeat the sound /o͞o/ several times as you tap the *oo* in the picture label *moon*.

moon

WORD BLENDING

Words with /o͞o/oo Blend and read the words *cool*, *boot*, and *tooth*. As you demonstrate each step, using a pocket chart and *Letter Cards*, have children repeat after you, using *Word Builders* and *Word Builder Cards*.

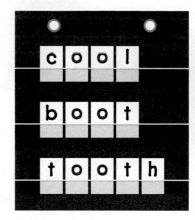

Phonics CENTER

Words with Vowel Digraph /o͞o/oo

Display the following words in the center: *boo, food, igloo, noon, room, hoop, smooth, tool, tooth, zoo*. Have children use a variety of materials to "print" the words. Then children can read the words to partners and spell the words aloud.

boo food igloo noon room hoop smooth tool tooth zoo

WORD BUILDING

Build Spelling Words Place the letter *c* in a pocket chart. Have children do the same with their *Word Builders* and *Word Builder Cards*. Repeat with the letters *o*, *o*, and *l*. Model how to blend the word *cool*. Slide your hand under the letters as you slowly elongate the sounds—/kko͞oll/. Then read the word naturally—*cool*. Have children do the same.

Have children build and read new words by telling them:

■ Change the *c* to *t*. What word did you make?

■ Change the *l* to *t*. What word did you make?

■ Add an *h* to the end of *toot*. What word did you make?

■ Change the first *t* in *tooth* to *b*. What word did you make?

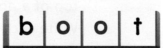

■ Take away the *h*. What word did you make?

 Dictate /o͞o/oo Words Dictate the words *tooth* and *cool* and have children write them in their journal. Suggest that they either draw a picture or write about each word.

ADVANCED

Have children use their *Word Builders* to experiment and build other /o͞o/oo words. Suggest that they work with blends as well as individual consonants.

Spelling Words

1. **cool**
2. **tool**
3. **toot**
4. **tooth**
5. **booth**
6. **boot**
7. **read**
8. **head**
9. **carry**
10. **hours**

Phonics and Spelling

5-DAY SPELLING	
DAY 1	Pretest; Word Sort
DAY 2	Word Building
DAY 3	State the Generalization
DAY 4	Review
DAY 5	Posttest; Writing Application

INTRODUCE THE WORDS

Pretest Read aloud the first word and the Dictation Sentence. Repeat the word as children write it. Write the correct spelling on the board and have children circle the word if they spelled it correctly and write it correctly if they did not. Repeat for words 2–10.

1. **cool** The fan kept me **cool**.
2. **tool** A hammer is a **tool**.
3. **toot** You can **toot** your horn while I play my drum.
4. **tooth** I have a loose **tooth**.
5. **booth** My father made a call from a phone **booth**.
6. **boot** I stepped in a puddle and got one **boot** wet.

Review

7. **read** Yesterday I **read** a book about monkeys.
8. **head** The king wore a crown on his **head**.

Vocabulary

9. **carry** A kangaroo can **carry** a baby in its pouch.
10. **hours** It takes two **hours** to get to my grandmother's house.

Word Sort Place the numerals *4* and *5* at the top of a pocket chart. Write each Spelling Word on an index card. Display the cards and ask "Which words have four letters? Which words have five letters?" Place the words in the correct columns as children direct. After words are sorted, have children read them aloud.

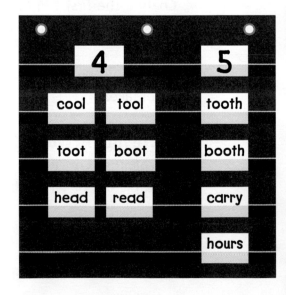

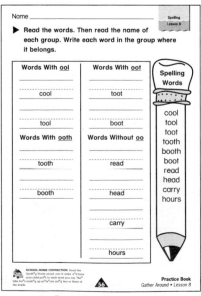

▲ Practice Book, p. 56

Apply Phonics

Read
The Loose Tooth

by Sunita Apte
Illustrated by Marsha Winborn

APPLY /o͞o/oo

Write the following sentences on the board or on chart paper. Have children read the first sentence. Frame the words *boot* and *too* and have children read them. Continue with the other sentences.

> One **boot** is **too** tight.
> The other **boot** is **too loose**.
> Next time I will **choose boots** that fit!

Have children read "The Loose Tooth" in *Decodable Book 34*.

▲ **Decodable Book 34**
"The Loose Tooth"

Managing Small Groups

Read the *Decodable Book* with small groups of children. While you work with small groups, have other children do the following:

- **Self-Selected Reading**
- **Practice Pages**
- **Cross-Curricular Centers**
- **Journal Writing**

Use the suggested Classroom Management outline on page 7C for the whole-group/small-group schedule.

School-Home Connection

Take-Home Book Version

The Loose Tooth

◄ **Decodable Books Take-Home Version**

ONGOING ASSESSMENT

Note how well children

- read sentences without modeling.
- decode words in "The Loose Tooth."
- complete /o͞o/oo practice pages.

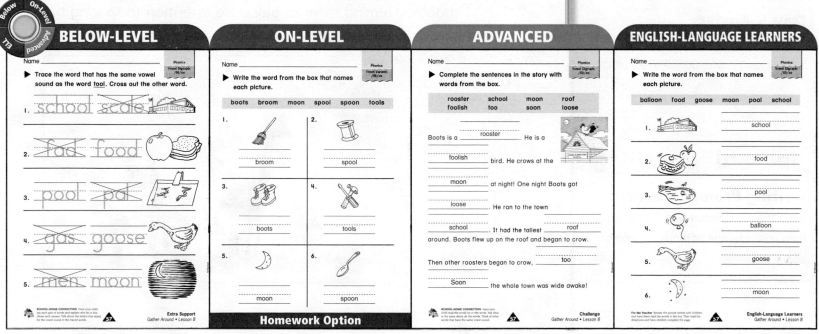

BELOW-LEVEL

Name _____
Phonics Vowel Digraph /o͞o/oo

▶ Trace the word that has the same vowel sound as the word <u>tool</u>. Cross out the other word.

1. school / ~~scale~~
2. ~~fad~~ / food
3. pool / ~~pal~~
4. ~~gas~~ / goose
5. ~~men~~ / moon

▲ Extra Support, p. 57

ON-LEVEL

Name _____
Phonics Vowel Variant /o͞o/oo

▶ Write the word from the box that names each picture.

| boots | broom | moon | spool | spoon | tools |

1. broom 2. spool
3. boots 4. tools
5. moon 6. spoon

▲ Practice, p. 57

Homework Option

ADVANCED

Name _____
Phonics Vowel Digraph /o͞o/oo

▶ Complete the sentences in the story with words from the box.

| rooster | school | moon | roof |
| foolish | too | soon | loose |

Boots is a ___ rooster ___. He is a ___ foolish ___ bird. He crows at the ___ moon ___ at night! One night Boots got ___ loose ___. He ran to the town ___ school ___. It had the tallest ___ roof ___ around. Boots flew up on the roof and began to crow.

Then other roosters began to crow, ___ too ___.

___ Soon ___ the whole town was wide awake!

▲ Challenge, p. 57

ENGLISH-LANGUAGE LEARNERS

Name _____
Phonics Vowel Digraph /o͞o/oo

▶ Write the word from the box that names each picture.

| balloon | food | goose | moon | pool | school |

1. school
2. food
3. pool
4. balloon
5. goose
6. moon

▲ ELL, p. 57

LANGUAGE ARTS

DAILY LANGUAGE PRACTICE

Last nite I go to a show.

Last <u>night</u> I <u>went</u> to a show.

Writing Every Day

Day 1: Talking Mural

Have children write their own speech bubble to add to a class mural.

Day 2: Story Response

Work together to teach Baboon about your school.

Day 3: Sentence Frames

Have children complete sentence frames to tell the names of baby animals.

Day 4: Description

Work together to describe the way different animals listen.

Day 5: Posters

Have children write and illustrate their own description of a lost animal.

journal writing

Writing Prompt Have children write the title *I Swam with a Seal* and then compose one or more sentences about the book.

LANGUAGE ARTS

Writing

Talking Mural

BRAINSTORM

Generate Dialogue Ideas Display and have children read aloud the *Animals* and *Special Parts* chart made during Sharing Literature, page 218H. Ask children to suggest other animals and parts of the animals' bodies to add to the chart.

Reread with children some of the questions from the big book *I Swam with a Seal*. Then have them make up questions that some of the animals on the chart might ask a child. Tell children they will write and illustrate similar questions to make a "talking" mural. Have children decide which idea from the chart they will write about.

MAKE THE MURAL

Write Questions Have children choose an animal from the chart and write a question that it might ask. For example, a child who chooses the giraffe might write *Where is your long neck, you funny giraffe?* Lay out a large sheet of butcher paper and have each child draw an illustration of their animal talking to a child. Then have them glue their question near the illustration. Help children make speech bubbles by drawing lines to connect their question to their animal.

Handwriting Because children will be writing within speech bubbles, remind them to pay close attention to spacing between words and letters within words.

Grammar

Contractions with Not

5-DAY GRAMMAR

DAY 1	Introduce Contractions with *Not*
DAY 2	Revise Sentences
DAY 3	Match Contractions with Meanings
DAY 4	Apostrophe Game
DAY 5	Write Contractions

TEACH/MODEL

Introduce Contractions with *Not* Write these sentences on the board and have children read them aloud:

> The seal did not look at me.
> The seal didn't look at me.

Point out that the word *didn't* is a shorter way of saying *did not*. Write *didn't* on the board. To demonstrate how the contraction is formed, write *didnot* beside *did not*. Then erase the *o* and insert an apostrophe to form *didn't*. Continue by forming contractions that stand for *is not, can not,* and *will not*. For *will not*, you will also need to point out that the *ill* is changed to an *o*.

PRACTICE/APPLY

Display *Teaching Transparency 100* Read each sentence aloud to children and have them repeat the two underlined words. Have children say the contraction that could replace the two words. Write the contraction above the words and help children reread the sentence with the contraction.

WRAP UP Share Ideas

Talk About the Mural Display the mural children made in their writing activity. Have volunteers read their question and tell about their illustration. Have others listen attentively and applaud when each speaker finishes.

Have children read silently from a book of their choice. See page 253J for tips on helping children choose books.

▲ Big Book

OBJECTIVE

To identify, read, and interpret contractions

SKILL TRACE

CONTRACTIONS WITH *NOT*	
INTRODUCE	218N
Review	247C, 251B, 253B, 253L
T Test	Bk 1-5

▼ **Teaching Transparency 100**

CONTRACTIONS WITH *NOT*

1. Baboon saw animals that <u>were not</u> like him.
2. Baboon <u>could not</u> tell why the turtle was so slow.
3. The crocodile <u>did not</u> see Baboon.
4. Mother <u>would not</u> let Baboon go near the fire.
5. Baboon <u>had not</u> seen a monkey before.
6. Baboon <u>will not</u> forget what he learned on his walk.

"Baboon"
Gather Around, Volume 1-5
100
Grammar: Contractions with *Not*
Harcourt

Name _____

Grammar Contractions With *Not*

▶ Write the word that best completes each sentence.

| isn't   don't   hasn't |

1. The spacecraft __hasn't__ landed yet.

| aren't   isn't   don't |

2. We __don't__ have long to wait until we reach Mars.

3. Mars has two moons, but they

| don't   isn't   aren't |

__aren't__ very big.

| don't   hasn't   doesn't |

4. Mars __doesn't__ have water.

TRY THIS Make two lists. Call one list "Things I Like" and the other list "Things I Don't Like." Which list is longer?

SCHOOL-HOME CONNECTION
58
Practice Book
Gather Around • Lesson 8

▲ Practice Book, p. 58

Sharing Literature
Poem: "The World"

Phonemic Awareness
Phoneme Manipulation; Focus on /o͞o/

REVIEW: Vowel Digraph /o͞o/oo

Spelling
Word Building

Vocabulary
INTRODUCE: *against, careful, fire, quietly, shook*

Reading
Pupil Edition
"Baboon," pp. 218–247

Interactive Writing ✏
Story Response

Grammar
REVIEW: Contractions with *Not*

WARM UP

MORNING MESSAGE

Good Morning!

Today is _____.
When I was little, I didn't know _____.
I hadn't yet learned to _____.
_____ showed me how to _____.
I learned to _____ by _____.

Introduce the Day

Tell children that today they will read a poem called "The World." Guide them in generating a message about how young children learn about the world. Ask:

• **What do you know now that you did not know when you were younger?**

• **Who taught you things you needed to know?**

• **How else did you learn when you were little?**

As you write the message, ask children to suggest words or phrases to complete the sentences. As you record children's responses, invite volunteers to write the day of the week and other familiar words.

Read the Message

Read the message. Use the message to focus on selected skills that have been previously taught.

Apply Skills

Grammar Have children find the contractions in the message. *(didn't, hadn't)* Ask children what two words each contraction stands for. Write the words in place of the contractions and have children read the message again.

Word Structure Ask children to identify the words in the message that have an *-ed* ending. *(learned, showed)* Have them name the base word for each word.

Sharing Literature

BUILD CONCEPT VOCABULARY

Connect to Prior Knowledge Tell children you are going to read a poem about growing up. Read "The World" and invite responses.

Explore a Word Remind children that the speaker thinks the world is very big. Say: *Many different words mean the same as* big, *such as* large, huge, *and* enormous. *Another word that means big is* gigantic. *Something gigantic is very big.* Have children repeat the word. Name some things that might be considered gigantic—for example, a mountain, the ocean, a skyscraper. Ask children to use the word *gigantic* to tell about things that seem very big to them. Then have children name the word they have been discussing. Ask: *What does gigantic mean?* (very big)

Phonemic Awareness

PHONEME MANIPULATION

Words from "The World" Tell children that you are going to ask them to make new words by adding sounds to the beginning of words from the poem. Model by saying *What word do I make if I say* all *with /t/ at the beginning? (tall)* Then say *What word do I make if I say* and *with /h/ at the beginning? (hand)* Continue with the following words:

all	and
add /s/ /m/ (small)	add /s/ (sand)
add /k/ (call)	add /b/ (band)
add /b/ (ball)	add /l/ (land)

FOCUS ON /ōō/

Phoneme Substitution Tell children that you are going to say some words and they will change the middle vowel sound to /ōō/. Model by elongating the vowel sound as you say *mice.* Then say *If I change /ī/ to /ōō/, I get* moose. Continue with the following words:

The World

The world is big,
And I am small.
The houses all
Are wide and tall.
I run and turn
And trip and fall!

I am so small!
I come and go.
I cannot see,
I cannot know.
I hope it won't
Be always so.

Barbara Young

REACHING ALL LEARNERS

Diagnostic Check: Phonemic Awareness

If... children cannot substitute medial phonemes to make new words . . .

Then... have them practice blending and segmenting the sounds in words you say. For example, Say /g/ /ōō/ /s/. *What's the word? (goose)* Then slowly say the sounds in *goose* again. Continue with the words *loose, cool, hoot, tool, loop.*

ADDITIONAL SUPPORT ACTIVITIES

BELOW-LEVEL	Reteach, p. S44
ADVANCED	Extend, p. S45
ENGLISH-LANGUAGE LEARNERS	Reteach, p. S45

Baboon **218P**

5-DAY SPELLING	
DAY 1	Pretest; Word Sort
DAY 2	**Word Building**
DAY 3	State the Generalization
DAY 4	Review
DAY 5	Posttest; Writing Application

Phonics
and Spelling
Vowel Digraph /o͞o/oo
Review

OBJECTIVES

• *To blend sounds into words*

• *To read and write Spelling Words*

SKILL TRACE

/o͞o/oo	
Introduce	218I–218L
Reteach	S46–S47
REVIEW	**218Q–218R, 247F–247G,**
Review	251E–251
T Test	Bk 2-1
Maintain	Bk 2-1

Spelling Words

1. **cool**
2. **tool**
3. **toot**
4. **tooth**
5. **booth**
6. **boot**
7. **read**
8. **head**
9. **carry**
10. **hours**

WORD BUILDING

Blend and Read a Spelling Word
Have children recall that the letters *oo* together can stand for the sound /o͞o/. Place *Letter Cards c, o, o, l* in a pocket chart, placing the *o*'s at the same time. Ask children to say the sound of each letter as you place it in the chart. Slide your hand under the letters as you blend the sounds—/kko͞oll/. Have children repeat after you. Then read the word naturally—*cool*, and have children do the same.

Build Spelling Words Ask children which letter you should change to make *cool* become *tool*. (change *c* to *t*) Continue building the Spelling Words shown in this manner and having children read them.

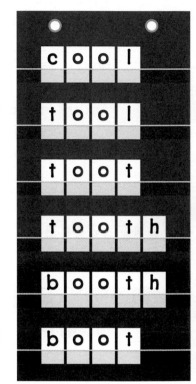

ADVANCED	ENGLISH-LANGUAGE LEARNERS
Provide opportunities for children to see Spelling Words as parts of longer words. Display the following words on a chart: *toolbox, toothpick, headband, tollbooth.* Ask children to identify the Spelling Word in each compound.	Children will benefit from additional context examples. On a cassette, record context sentences using the Spelling Words. Have children listen to and repeat the sentences.

Apply Phonics

READ WORDS IN CONTEXT

5-DAY PHONICS/SPELLING	
DAY 1	Introduce /o͞o/oo
DAY 2	**Word Building with /o͞o/oo**
DAY 3	Word Building with /o͝o/oo
DAY 4	Word Building with /ō/oa and /o͞o/oo
DAY 5	Phonograms -oom, -oot

Write the following sentences on the board or on chart paper and have children read them aloud.

> My big sister **read** for **hours**!
> In **cool** weather, my hat keeps my **head** warm.
> Sam's **boot** got stuck in the door of the **booth**.
> Is that **tool** too heavy for you to **carry**?
> My **tooth** is loose.
> The boat's horn gave a loud **toot**?

Dictate Words Dictate to children several words from the pocket chart, and have them write the words on a dry-erase board or in their journal.

cool
tool
toot
tooth
booth
boot

BELOW-LEVEL

Name _____

Phonics
Vowel Digraph /oo/oo

▶ Trace the word that answers the question or completes the sentence. Cross out the other word.

1. What helps you eat?
   ~~tooth~~ ~~balloon~~

2. When do you eat lunch?
   ~~mood~~ ~~noon~~

3. What cleans your hair?
   ~~shampoo~~ ~~bamboo~~

4. It's an ice house.
   ~~igloo~~ ~~school~~

5. This is a word to scare you.
   ~~soon~~ ~~boo~~

SCHOOL-HOME CONNECTION Have your child practice writing the words he or she traced on this page.

Extra Support
Gather Around • Lesson 8

59

▲ Extra Support, p. 59

ON-LEVEL

Name _____

Phonics
Vowel Variant /oo/oo

▶ Write the word from the box that best completes each sentence.

broom	food	noon	soon	spoon

1. It's almost ___noon___

2. Our friends will be here ___soon___

3. Bring the ___broom___ so I can sweep.

4. Is the ___food___ ready?

5. Use this big ___spoon___ to stir it.

Homework Option

▲ Practice, p. 59

ADVANCED

Name _____

Phonics
Vowel Digraph /oo/oo

▶ Complete the sentences in the story with words from the box.

shoot	cool	Balloons	school
foolish	noon	Roosters	mood

Mr. Pool is our coach. He teaches kids from our

___school___ to ___shoot___ and pass. Mr. Pool works hard to help us learn. On weekends, we meet at

twelve ___noon___

He's never in a bad ___mood___

Our team is called the Red ___Roosters___. We play

the Blue ___Balloons___ in our next game. Mr. Pool doesn't think "winning is everything." He thinks that's

___foolish___. He teaches us that it's better to just

have fun. We think he's very ___cool___

SCHOOL-HOME CONNECTION Have your child read the words he or she added to the story. Talk about the sound that oo stands for in the words.

59

Challenge
Gather Around • Lesson 8

▲ Challenge, p. 59

ENGLISH-LANGUAGE LEARNERS

Name _____

Phonics
Vowel Digraph /oo/oo

▶ Write the word that answers the question or completes the sentence. Cross out the other word.

1. What helps you eat?
   tooth
   ~~balloon~~   ___tooth___

2. When do you eat lunch?
   ~~mood~~
   noon   ___noon___

3. What cleans your hair?
   shampoo
   ~~bamboo~~   ___shampoo___

4. It's an ice house.
   igloo
   ~~boom~~   ___igloo___

5. This is a word to scare you.
   boo
   ~~soon~~   ___boo___

For the Teacher Preview the page with children. Discuss each illustration, using the word it illustrates. Then read the directions and have children complete the page.

59

English-Language Learners
Gather Around • Lesson 8

▲ ELL, p. 59

Vocabulary

against in contact with; upon

careful with care

fire what a match starts; hot, with red or yellow flames

quietly with little or no sound

shook made something shake

Building Background

TALK ABOUT LEARNING

Make a Web About Learning Tell children that they are going to read a story about a young baboon who explores the world around him. Explain that all youngsters have to learn about the world. Have children tell ways that young children learn. Record children's ideas in a concept web about learning.

Discuss Story Words Write *among*, *backward*, *disappear*, *gazelle*, *monkey*, and *rhinoceros* on the board. Point to each word and read it aloud. Elicit that *gazelle*, *monkey*, and *rhinoceros* are the names of animals. Discuss with children meanings for the remaining words.

Vocabulary

INTRODUCE WORDS IN CONTEXT

Read Sentences Display *Teaching Transparency 101*. Point to the words *against*, *careful*, *fire*, *quietly*, *shook*. Say each word and have children repeat it. Read the definitions of the words to children and discuss their meaning. Track the print as you read aloud the sentences. Call on volunteers to reread each sentence.

INTRODUCE

Vocabulary

against	quietly
careful	shook
fire	

▼ **Teaching Transparency 101**

VOCABULARY

against careful fire quietly shook

We shook hands with the man.
He told us to be careful with matches.
We had a fire drill.
We walked quietly out of the school.
We lined up against the fence.

"Baboon"
Gather Around, Volume 1-5   101   Vocabulary
Harcourt

218S Gather Around

▲ Baboon

Word Power

Words to Remember

against

careful

fire

quietly

shook

Baboon and his mother saw a **fire** in the forest. They watched it **quietly**.
Mother said, "We must be **careful**."
Then elephants walked by and **shook** the ground. Baboon leaned **against** his mother.

218

219

Word Power

Pages 218–219 Have children read aloud the Words to Remember. Then have children read the sentences aloud. Have children point to the Words to Remember in the sentences.

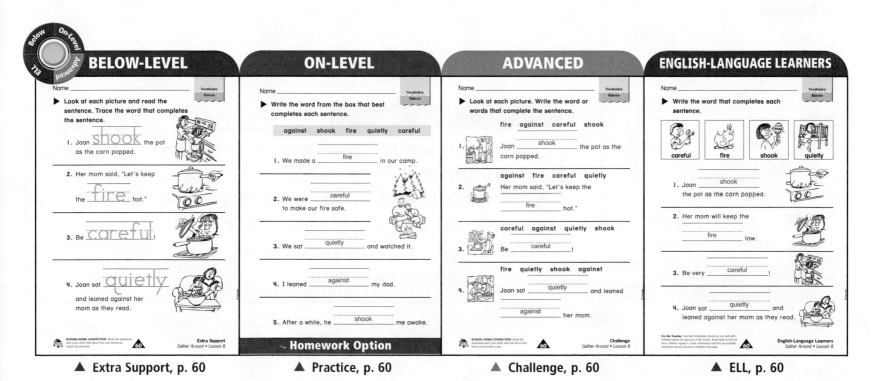

BELOW-LEVEL

Name _____

► Look at each picture and read the sentence. Trace the word that completes the sentence.

1. Joan __shook__ the pot as the corn popped.

2. Her mom said, "Let's keep the __fire__ hot."

3. Be __careful__!

4. Joan sat __quietly__ and leaned against her mom as they read.

▲ Extra Support, p. 60

ON-LEVEL

Name _____

► Write the word from the box that best completes each sentence.

| against | shook | fire | quietly | careful |

1. We made a ___fire___ in our camp.

2. We were ___careful___ to make our fire safe.

3. We sat ___quietly___ and watched it.

4. I leaned ___against___ my dad.

5. After a while, he ___shook___ me awake.

Homework Option

▲ Practice, p. 60

ADVANCED

Name _____

► Look at each picture. Write the word or words that complete the sentence.

fire against careful shook

1. Joan ___shook___ the pot as the corn popped.

against fire careful quietly

2. Her mom said, "Let's keep the ___fire___ hot."

careful against quietly shook

3. Be ___careful___!

fire quietly shook against

4. Joan sat ___quietly___ and leaned ___against___ her mom.

▲ Challenge, p. 60

ENGLISH-LANGUAGE LEARNERS

Name _____

► Write the word that completes each sentence.

| careful | fire | shook | quietly |

1. Joan ___shook___ the pot as the corn popped.

2. Her mom will keep the ___fire___ low.

3. Be very ___careful___!

4. Joan sat ___quietly___ and leaned against her mom as they read.

▲ ELL, p. 60

Baboon 218–219

Prereading Strategies

■ **Phonics**

Vowel Digraph /o͞o/ *oo*

■ **Vocabulary**

against, careful, fire, quietly, shook

■ **Decodable Words**

See the list on pp. T50–T51.

■ **Comprehension**

(Focus Skill) Plot

(Focus Strategy) Sequence Events/Summarize

PREPARING TO READ

Preview/Predict Discuss pages 220–221. Have children read aloud the title and the name of the author. Talk about the picture on pages 222–223 and what might happen to the baboons in the story.

Set Purpose Help children set a purpose for reading. If necessary, suggest that they read to find out how the mother baboon helps her baby.

COMPREHENSION SKILL

(Focus Skill) **Plot** Explain to children that "Baboon" is a fiction story so it has a beginning, a middle, and an end. Point out that there is also a problem to be solved. Tell children that as they begin to read they should decide what problem Baboon has.

COMPREHENSION STRATEGY

(Focus Strategy) **Sequence Events/Summarize** Explain to children that they can check their understanding of what they read by pausing from time to time to summarize what has happened so far. Retelling the events in order will help make the meaning clear.

Strategies Good Readers Use

To Recognize Words

• Use Decoding/Phonics

• Look for Word Bits and Parts

To Gain Meaning

• Self-Correct

• Read Ahead

• Reread

• Reread Aloud

• Use Picture Clues to Confirm Meaning

• Make and Confirm Predictions

• **Sequence Events/ Summarize** (Focus Strategy)

• Create Mental Images

• Make Inferences

Managing Small Groups

Read "Baboon" with small groups of children. While you work with small groups, have other children do the following:

• **Self-Selected Reading**

• **Cross-Curricular Centers**

• **Practice Pages**

• **Journal Writing**

Use the suggested Classroom Management outline on page 7C for the whole-group/small-group schedule.

Genre

Informational Fiction

Some fiction stories give information about things in the real world.

Look for:

- Parts of the story that are made-up.
- Information about different African animals.

220

Baboon

by Kate Banks

illustrated by
Georg Hallensleben

221

Guided Comprehension

Pages 220–221 Have children reread the title and review their predictions about what will happen to the baboons in the story.

GENRE: Informational Fiction

Read aloud the information about informational fiction on page 220. Tell children that informational fiction includes

- some parts that are made up.
- facts about real people, places, animals, or events.

BELOW-LEVEL	ON-LEVEL	ADVANCED	ENGLISH-LANGUAGE LEARNERS
Copy several times on chart paper the sentence frame *The world is _____*. Ask them to fill in the sentence frame each time Baboon learns something new about the world. Have them use their notes to summarize the story. SMALL GROUP	As children read the story, use the Guided Comprehension questions to direct their reading. WHOLE GROUP/SMALL GROUP	Have children share their predictions about the story and then read the story silently. After reading, have children talk about whether or not their predictions were correct. SMALL GROUP/INDE-PENDENT	Help children build meaning for action words they will encounter in the text. Explain and demon-strate phrases such as *opened his eyes, hid in the grass, lay down, leaped backward, stretched and blinked*. SMALL GROUP
ADDITIONAL SUPPORT See Intervention Resource Kit, Lesson 34. *Intervention Teacher's Guide pp. 332–341*			**ADDITIONAL SUPPORT** See English-Language Learners Resource Kit, Lesson 34. *English-Language Learners Teacher's Guide pp. 200–201*

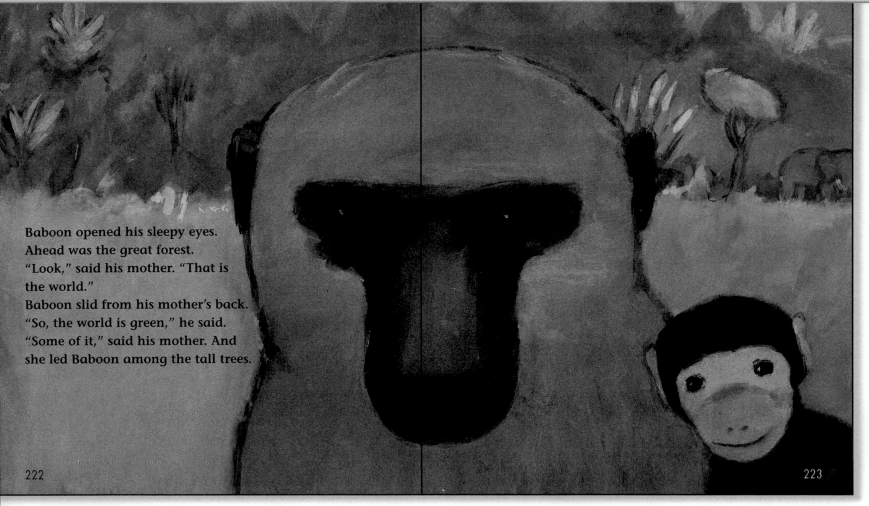

Baboon opened his sleepy eyes.
Ahead was the great forest.
"Look," said his mother. "That is
the world."
Baboon slid from his mother's back.
"So, the world is green," he said.
"Some of it," said his mother. And
she led Baboon among the tall trees.

222

223

Guided Comprehension

Pages 222–223 Ask children to describe the animals in the illustration. Have children read to find out more about Baboon.

1 **DRAW CONCLUSIONS** What is Baboon doing right before the story begins? (He is sleeping on his mother's back.)

2 **IMPORTANT DETAILS** What helped you know the answer to the first question? (The story said that Baboon opened his sleepy eyes and that he slid off his mother's back.)

3 **DRAW CONCLUSIONS** Why do you think Baboon says the world is green? (Possible response: He sees the green trees in the forest.)

BELOW-LEVEL

Have children listen to "Baboon" on cassette (*Audiotext 5* or child-recorded). You may want to have children follow along in their book or read along as they listen. The cassette provides children with a model for accurate decoding.

ENGLISH-LANGUAGE LEARNERS

Familiarize children with the animals and animal names in the story. Provide pictures of a baboon, an elephant, a gazelle, a rhinoceros, a crocodile, and a monkey. Have children suggest words and phrases that describe each animal.

A turtle sat in the middle of the road.
Its eyes were closed and it barely moved.
Baboon watched and waited for the turtle
to pass. He waited a long time.
"The world is slow," he said.
"It can be," said his mother.

224

225

Guided Comprehension

Pages 224–225 Briefly discuss the illustrations. Have children read to find out what Baboon says about the world and why.

1 **DRAW CONCLUSIONS** **Why does Baboon now think the world is slow?** (Possible response: He sees the turtle and it moves slowly.)

2 **INTERPRET CHARACTERS' MOTIVATION** **Why do you think Baboon's mother says, "It can be"?** (Possible response: She wants Baboon to know that only some things in the world are slow.)

3 **PLOT** **How does Baboon learn about the world?** (Each experience shows him something new about how the world might sometimes be.)

REACHING ALL LEARNERS

Diagnostic Check: Comprehension and Skills

If... children have difficulty identifying steps in the plot...

Then... help them focus on each of Baboon's experiences to determine what each one teaches him about the world.

ADDITIONAL SUPPORT ACTIVITIES

BELOW-LEVEL	Reteach, p. S48
ADVANCED	Extend, p. S49
ENGLISH-LANGUAGE LEARNERS	Reteach, p. S49

When the turtle had passed, Baboon followed his mother.
At the edge of the great forest, a fire burned in the bush.
Baboon moved close to the fire.
Soon he could feel its heat.
Baboon leaped backward.
"The world is hot!" he said.
"Not always," said his mother.

226

227

Guided Comprehension

Pages 226–227 Have children read to find out what Baboon and his mother are watching.

1 **NOTE DETAILS** What do Baboon and his mother see at the edge of the great forest? (a fire)

2 **DRAW CONCLUSIONS** Why does Baboon think that the world is hot? (He can feel the heat of the fire.)

3 **MAKE JUDGMENTS** Do you think Baboon's mother is right when she says, "Not always"? Why do you think so? (Possible response: Yes; the world isn't always hot. Accept reasonable responses. Encourage children to explain their responses.)

BELOW-LEVEL

Children may benefit from a review of strategies for decoding words with the ending -ed. Write the following words on word cards: *passed, followed, burned, leaped.* Ask volunteers to cover the final *ed* on each word and try to read the shorter word they see. Have the group read the word, first without and then with the ending. Ask children to find and read each -ed word on page 226.

She led Baboon to a small lake.
A crocodile lay on the sandy bank.
It opened its mouth wide.
"Careful," said Baboon's mother.
"The crocodile might eat you."
Baboon did not want to be eaten.
So he ran into the bush.
"The world is hungry," he said.
"Sometimes you are hungry, too,"
said his mother.

228

229

Guided
Comprehension

Pages 228–229 Ask children to look at the illustrations and describe the animal on page 229. Have them read to find out what warning Baboon's mother gives him.

1 **NOTE DETAILS** What warning does Baboon's mother give Baboon? (She tells him to be careful or the crocodile might eat him.)

2 **NOTE DETAILS** What does Baboon think about the world after learning about the crocodile? (The world is hungry.)

3 **SEQUENCE EVENTS/SUMMARIZE** What has happened in the story so far? (Baboon has seen the green forest, watched a slow turtle, felt the heat of a fire, and learned to be careful of crocodiles.)

Strategies
Good Readers Use

Focus Strategy
★ **Sequence Events/ Summarize**

Remind children that they can check their understanding of story events by stopping during their reading to tell what has happened so far. Recalling the events in order will make the meaning clear.

Soon the elephants came, four by four.
They thundered loud and shook the ground.
A gazelle passed. He was not slow like the
turtle, but quick and fast.

230   231

Guided Comprehension

Pages 230–231 Have children speculate about what Baboon is seeing and learning. Then have them read to find out.

1 NOTE DETAILS What animals does Baboon see in this part of the story? (elephants and a gazelle)

2 CAUSE/EFFECT What do you think Baboon thinks of the world now? Why do you think so? (Possible response: He probably thinks the world is loud, quick, and fast because of the way the elephants sound and the way the gazelle moves. Accept reasonable responses. Encourage children to explain their responses.)

STUDENT SELF-ASSESSMENT

Have children ask themselves the following questions to assess how they are reading:

- Do I notice patterns in the plot of the story? What is similar about all the events in the story so far?

- Do I pay attention to quotation marks and words that tell who is speaking so that I understand what is happening?

- Do I stop reading from time to time to recall the order of story events?

A rhinoceros darted out of the bushes.
He grunted at Baboon. Baboon was afraid.
"He will not hurt you," said his mother.

232

233

Guided Comprehension

Pages 232–233 Ask children to name the large animal in the picture. (rhinoceros) Have them read to find out what Baboon's mother tells him about the rhinoceros.

① INTERPRET STORY EVENTS How do you think Baboon's mother knows not to be afraid of the rhinoceros? (Possible response: She learned it from her mother; she knows from experience that rhinos don't bother baboons. Accept reasonable responses.)

② COMPARE AND CONTRAST How is Baboon different from the rhinoceros? How are they the same? (Possible response: The rhino is gray, large, and has horns; Baboon is brown, small, and without horns. They both have four legs, two ears, and a tail.)

ENGLISH-LANGUAGE LEARNERS

Help children understand the meaning of the word *darted*. Reread the first sentence on page 232 and explain that it means that the rhinoceros rushed or ran out of the bushes. Have children tell other words they know that describe the way an animal moves. (*run, crawl, hop, walk, gallop*) Record children's responses and discuss how the meanings of the words differ. Demonstrate the movements and have children say each word as they imitate the movement.

Baboon took his mother's hand, and they
started across a field.
Baboon hid in the tall grass.
His mother hid, too. When they found each
other, they lay down, side by side.
"The world is soft," said Baboon. And he
was happy.

234

235

Guided Comprehension

Pages 234–235 Have children predict something new that
Baboon will learn about the world. Have them read to find out.

1 **SPECULATE** **Why do you think Baboon and his mother
hide in the grass?** (Possible responses: They are hiding from
animals; they are playing a game.)

2 **CAUSE/EFFECT** **What makes Baboon think that the world
is soft?** (Possible response: The grass and his mother's fur
make the world seem soft.)

3 **DETERMINE CHARACTERS' EMOTIONS** **How do you
think Baboon and his mother feel about each other? Why do
you think so?** (Possible responses: They care about each
other; they hug, they are happy, and Baboon's mother
teaches him things. Accept reasonable responses.)

BELOW-LEVEL

Children may benefit from a review of how to read
sentences with commas. Remind children that
pausing each time they encounter a comma in the
text can help them better understand what they
read. Have children point out each sentence
containing a comma on page 234. Read each
sentence with appropriate pauses at commas.
Have children echo-read each sentence after you.

234–235 Gather Around

Baboon stretched and rolled over.
A bird flew by. A cloud passed
overhead. And Baboon fell asleep.
When he awoke, the sun was going down.
Baboon watched it disappear behind the trees.
"Come along," said his mother. And they
walked on.

236

237

Guided Comprehension

Pages 236–237 Have children look carefully at the details in the illustration. Then ask them to read to find out how the day is changing.

1 **NOTE DETAILS** When Baboon wakes up from his nap, what does he notice? (The sun is going down.) **Find the words that tell you this.** (*Baboon watched it disappear behind the trees.*)

2 **DRAW CONCLUSIONS** If the sun is going down, what time of day is it? (late afternoon or early evening)

3 **MAKE PREDICTIONS** Where do you think Baboon and his mother will go now? (Possible responses: to find food; to their home)

ENGLISH-LANGUAGE LEARNERS

Help children understand the sequence of events on page 236. Reread the page with children and ask volunteers to act out the following parts: bird, cloud, Baboon, sun, mother. Have the actors show the action as you read aloud the page. Then ask children to tell what happened first, second, third, and so on.

Baboon followed his mother up
a tree.
Across from him sat a monkey.
He was like Baboon.
"Is he the world, too?" asked Baboon.
"He is," said his mother. "Just as
you are."
Baboon watched quietly.
Then he followed his mother down
the tree.

238

239

Guided Comprehension

Pages 238–239 Have children examine the illustration and speculate about what Baboon might learn next.

1 **SPECULATE** **What do you think makes Baboon curious about the monkey?** (Possible response: The monkey looks like Baboon.)

2 **NOTE DETAILS** **How does Baboon's mother explain about the monkey?** (She says that the monkey is the world, just as Baboon is.)

3 **SPECULATE** **What do you suppose the monkey is thinking as he or she looks at Baboon?** (Possible response: Maybe the monkey is wondering if Baboon is the world or if Baboon would like to play. Accept reasonable responses. Encourage children to explain their responses.)

SCIENCE

Groups of Baboons Share the following information with children: Baboons travel together in large groups. The strongest male leads the group. The mothers and the babies stay in the middle of the group. Other adults watch for danger. Sometimes, the young baboons stop to play. Ask children what kinds of games they think the baboons might play.

Now the elephants were huddled together. The
gazelles were resting.
There was no more fire and the light was gone
from the sky.
Baboon climbed onto his mother's back.
"The world is dark," he said.
"Sometimes," whispered his mother, carrying
him home.

240

241

Guided Comprehension

Pages 240–241 Tell children to close their eyes and think about what Baboon's world is like at night. Then have them read to find out whether it is anything like what they imagined.

1 (Focus Strategy) **SEQUENCE EVENTS/SUMMARIZE** What happens when the sun goes down? (Elephants huddle together, gazelles rest, the world gets dark, and Baboon's mother carries him home.)

2 **NOTE DETAILS** What does Baboon think of the world now? (He thinks it is dark.)

3 **DRAW CONCLUSIONS** Why does Baboon's mother answer him and say, "Sometimes"? (because it isn't dark all the time)

ADVANCED

To develop children's use of descriptive language, have them reread the story description of nighttime on page 240. Have children imagine being at their own home as night comes. Ask them to think about what they might see or hear outside. Then tell children to write a sentence or two describing what night is like where they live.

Baboon looked around.
He blinked.
Everything was black as far as he could see.
He laid his head against his mother's soft neck.
"The world is big," he said.
"Yes," said his mother softly. "The world is big."

242   243

Guided Comprehension

Pages 242–243 Have children read to find out how the story ends.

1 **DRAW CONCLUSIONS** **What time of day is it at the end of the story? How do you know?** (It is nighttime; everything is black as far as Baboon can see.)

2 **PLOT** **How does the story end?** (Baboon learns that the world is big.)

Think and Respond

1. How did Baboon's mother help him learn about the world?

2. Tell about a time when you learned something new about a place you visited.

3. What clues let you know that the story happens all in one day?

4. What did you learn from reading this story?

5. What would you show Baboon if he came to visit your neighborhood?

244

245

Think and Respond

1. Possible responses: She showed him many different scenes and animals; she explained things to him and warned him about dangers. **SUMMARIZE**

2. Possible responses include descriptions of vacations, field trips, or family outings. Accept reasonable responses. **PERSONAL RESPONSE**

3. It goes from morning until dark. **SEQUENCE**

4. Possible response: A baby baboon rides on its mother's back; gazelles are fast animals; a crocodile will eat baboons, but a rhinoceros will not hurt them. **SUMMARIZE**

5. Possible responses: pets, plants, parks, and our school buildings, homes, and vehicles. Accept reasonable responses. Have children give reasons for their answers. **EXPRESS PERSONAL OPINIONS**

Teacher Read-Aloud

Meet the Author
Kate Banks

Kate Banks and her four-month-old son were looking at a picture of a mother baboon carrying her baby. That day, she began to think of the dialogue in "Baboon." Kate Banks likes watching, listening to, and being with children—she likes to write for them, too!

Kate Banks

Meet the Illustrator
Georg Hallensleben

Georg Hallensleben grew up in Germany. He loved riding his bike in the woods and drawing what he saw there. He used to bring his art supplies in a wooden case on his bike. He started drawing as a child and has never stopped!

G. Hallensleben

Visit *The Learning Site!*
www.harcourtschool.com

246

247

Meet the Author and Illustrator

Pages 246–247 Explain that these pages tell about the people who wrote and illustrated the story "Baboon." Identify Kate Banks in the photograph on page 246 and Georg Hallensleben in the photograph on page 247. Remind children that an **author** writes a story, and an **illustrator** creates pictures to go with the writing. Read aloud pages 246–247.

Visit *The Learning Site:* www.harcourtschool.com
See Resources for Parents and Teachers: Author/Illustrator Features.

Retelling

COMPREHENSION FOCUS

(Focus Skill) **Plot** Remind children that the plot of a story is what the story is about. Help them recall that a number of things happen to Baboon and these events help him to understand the world.

▲ *End-of-Selection Test*, Practice Book, pp. A61–A64

RETELL AND SUMMARIZE THE STORY

Use a Story Map Remind children that the events of a story are told in a special order and that the story makes sense because it has a beginning, a middle, and an end. Display *Teaching Transparency 109* or copy the story map onto the board.

Work with children to fill in the empty spaces in the story map. Begin by asking children to identify the first event. Record children's responses in the first section of the story map. Then have children name things that Baboon saw and learned on his walk. Record those responses in the middle part of the map. Finally, have children tell what Baboon did last and what he had learned. Help children use the story map to summarize the story.

▼ Teaching Transparency 109

Beginning
Baboon wakes up and goes for a walk with his mother.

Middle
Baboon sees a slow turtle. He sees a hot fire. He sees a hungry crocodile. He sees elephants, gazelles, and a rhinoceros. He naps in tall grass. He sees a monkey in a tree.

End
Baboon goes to sleep knowing the world is big.

Grade 1   109   Harcourt

DAILY LANGUAGE PRACTICE

I did'nt get to play the gam.

I <u>didn't</u> get to play the <u>game</u>.

Shared Writing *Story Response*

BRAINSTORM

Plan a Tour for Baboon Ask children to imagine that Baboon comes to visit your school. Write *Baboon's Tour* on chart paper. Ask children to suggest things in the school that they would show and explain to Baboon. Decide as a group the best order in which to show things to Baboon. Then record children's ideas on chart paper. Have children help you choose order words such as *first*, *second*, *next*, and *then* for the beginning of each sentence.

SHARE

Read and Display the Tour Plan Read the chart aloud to children. Display the chart in a center for children to refer to throughout the week.

Baboon's Tour
First, we will take him to the office.
Next, we will show him the lunchroom.
Then, we will let him play on the monkey bars.

journal writing

Writing Prompt Have children write about what they would like to show Baboon in their own neighborhood.

ADVANCED	ENGLISH-LANGUAGE LEARNERS
Have children make a poster that announces Baboon's visit to your school.	Have children draw on index cards pictures of the places and things that Baboon will be shown. Ask children to name these places and things in their first language. Then help them to write on the back of the cards the names in English.

5-DAY GRAMMAR

DAY 1	Introduce Contractions with *Not*
DAY 2	**Revise Sentences**
DAY 3	Match Contractions with Meanings
DAY 4	Apostrophe Game
DAY 5	Write Contractions

Grammar

Contractions with Not

REVIEW

Review Contractions with *Not* Write *was not* on the board and model forming a contraction.

MODEL I can write a shorter form of *was not* by putting the two words together and leaving out the *o* in *not*. I write an apostrophe to show where the *o* was left out. The new word, *wasn't*, is a contraction that stands for *was not*.

Revise Sentences Write the following sentences on the board:

> Baboon was <u>not</u> very big.
> The rhinoceros <u>did not</u> hurt him.
> Baboon learned he <u>should not</u> go near the crocodile.
> The gazelles <u>were not</u> slow like the turtle.

Have children read the sentences silently as you distribute five blank index cards to each child. As children read each sentence aloud, have them write on their cards the contraction for the underlined words. Direct a volunteer to reread the sentence, covering the underlined words with the contraction card.

WRAP UP Reenact the Story

Imagine a Jungle Have children imagine that the room is a jungle and they are young baboons. Tell them they will say what Baboon would say each time they see something new. Lead children to witness imaginary story events around the room. Point to a corner and say, "Look, I see a turtle!" Children should chant together, "The world is slow." Move around the room and repeat with other story events.

S.S.R. Sustained Silent Reading

Have children read silently from a book of their choice. See page 253J for tips on helping children choose books.

SKILL TRACE

CONTRACTIONS WITH *NOT*

Introduce	218N
REVIEW	247C, 251B, 253B, 253L
T Test	Bk 1-5

ENGLISH-LANGUAGE LEARNERS

Below On-Level Advanced ELL

Some children may have difficulty pronouncing the final sounds in contractions. Model pronunciation of the final cluster of consonant sounds and have children say it several times before adding the beginning syllable. For example, exaggerate the cluster /dnt/ and have children repeat it several times. When they are successful, have children add the beginning of the word to say *didn't*.

Name _____

Contractions with Not

There is a short way to write words with **not**. An apostrophe (') shows where letters are left out.

| is + not = isn't | do + not = don't |
| did + not = didn't | will + not = won't |

► Circle and write the word that completes the sentence.

wasn't (didn't)
1. Bill ___ know what the loud sound was.   _____ didn't

isn't (won't)
2. Now he ___ turn on the light.   _____ won't

(isn't) don't
3. Bill ___ afraid of the dark.   _____ isn't

(hasn't) don't
4. He ___ called his mom or dad.   _____ hasn't

142

SCHOOL-HOME CONNECTION

▲ Language Handbook, p. 142

Sharing Literature
Song: "The Bear Went Over the Mountain"

Phonemic Awareness
Syllable Counting; Focus on /oo/

Phonics
REVIEW: Vowel Digraph /oo/oo

Spelling
State the Generalization

Vocabulary
REVIEW: *against, careful, fire, quietly, shook*

Reading

Rereading for Fluency
Pupil Edition
"Baboon," pp. 220–243

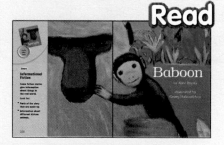

Read

Reading Across Texts
"Piggyback Ride," pp. 248–249
Making Connections, pp. 250–251

Writing Across the Curriculum
Sentence Frames

Grammar
REVIEW: Contractions with *Not*

WARM UP
MORNING MESSAGE
Good Morning!

Today is _____.
I like to explore _____.
It's fun to snoop around at _____, too.
One time _____ saw a _____!

Introduce the Day
Tell children that today they will sing a song about exploring called "The Bear Went Over the Mountain." Guide children in generating a message about exploring. Ask:

- **Where do you like to go exploring?**
- **What have you seen or discovered while exploring?**

As you write the message, ask children to suggest words or phrases to complete the sentences. Choose a child to write his or her name in the last sentence. Then help the child complete the sentence with the name of something interesting he or she once saw. As you record children's responses, invite volunteers to write the words they can sound out.

Read the Message
Read the message. Use the message to focus on selected skills that have been previously taught.

Apply Skills

Grammar Help children recall that a noun names a person, place, animal, or thing. Direct children to identify nouns in the message and then tell in which category the word fits.	**Phonics** Remind children that the letters *oo* can stand for the sound /oo/. Have children frame and read two words with the sound /oo/oo. (*snoop, too*)

Sharing Literature

LISTEN AND RESPOND

Connect to Prior Knowledge Ask children to tell about a time when they went for a walk in a new place. Have them tell where they went and what they saw and did there. Then teach them the song "The Bear Went Over the Mountain."

Respond to Literature Lead children in singing the song again while a volunteer acts out the words. Have children replace the words *the bear* with the volunteer's name. Pause after the first verse and have the child tell what he or she "saw." Use the child's idea to replace the words *The other side of the mountain*. Repeat to give several volunteers a turn.

Phonemic Awareness

SYLLABLE COUNTING

Words from "The Bear Went Over the Mountain" Tell children you will say a word from the song and they should repeat the word and clap the syllables. Model the process by saying *over*, and then clapping twice as you repeat the word. Say the following words and have children repeat and clap for them.

bear (I clap)	**do** (I clap)	**you** (I clap)
very (2 claps)	**side** (I clap)	**mountain** (2 claps)
went (I clap)	**other** (2 claps)	**happily** (3 claps)

Continue with these animal names: *baboon, turtle, crocodile, elephants, gazelle, rhinoceros, monkey.*

FOCUS ON /o͞o/

Identify Phonemes Tell children that you are going to say some words, and they will tell whether they hear /o͞o/ at the beginning, middle, or end of the word. Model by saying *moon. I hear /o͞o/ in the middle of* moon. Continue with these words:

booth (middle)	**oops** (beginning)	**too** (end)	**soon** (middle)
tool (middle)	**ooze** (beginning)	**coo** (end)	**spoon** (middle)

The Bear Went Over the Mountain

The bear went over the mountain,
The bear went over the mountain,
The bear went over the mountain,
To see what he could see.
And what do you think he saw?
And what do you think he saw?

The other side of the mountain,
The other side of the mountain,
The other side of the mountain,
Is all that he did see!

So the bear went down the mountain,
So the bear went down the mountain,
So the bear went down the mountain.
Very hap-pi-ly.

Traditional (to the tune of "For He's a Jolly Good Fellow")

◀ "Fooba-Wooba John," *Oo-pples and Boo-noo-noos: Songs and Activities for Phonemic Awareness*, pp. 72–73

ADVANCED

Say a series of /o͞o/ words to children. Have them experiment with substituting other vowel sounds in the words to make new words. Try these words: *mood, fool, pool, broom, hoop, droop, stoop, troop, root.* Have children tell what each new word means and then have them use it in a sentence.

OBJECTIVES

- *To generate the sound for vowel digraph /ōō/oo*

- *To blend sounds into words*

- *To read simple, regular words*

SKILL TRACE

	/ōō/oo
Introduce	218I–218L
Reteach	S46–S47
REVIEW	**218Q–218R, 247F–247G**
Review	251E–251F
T Test	Bk 2-1
Maintain	Bk 2-1

 Phonics Resources

Phonics Express™ **CD-ROM, Level C** Scooter/Route 6/Train Station, Harbor

Phonics
Vowel Digraph /ōō/oo

WORD BUILDING

Guided Practice Place the letters *s*, *c*, *o*, *o*, and *t* in a pocket chart. Have children do the same with their *Word Builders* and *Word Builder Cards.* Model how to blend the word *scoot*. Slide your hand under the letters as you slowly elongate the sounds—/sskkōōtt/. Then read the word naturally— *scoot*. Have children do the same.

Have children build and read new words by telling them:

■ Change the *t* to *p*. What word did you make?

■ Change the *s* to *d*. Change the *c* to *r*. What word did you make?

■ Take away one *o*. What word did you make?

■ Change the *d* to *s*. Change the *r* to *t*. What word did you make?

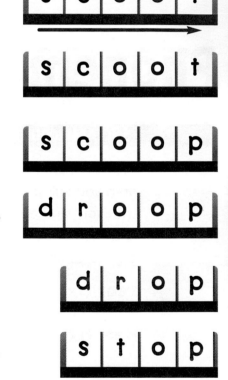

Continue word building with this word sequence: *stoop, stool, tool, fool, food, mood, moon, spoon.*

Apply Phonics

READ WORDS IN CONTEXT

Display *Teaching Transparency 102* or write the following sentences on the board or on chart paper. Have volunteers read the story one sentence at a time. Call on volunteers to underline or frame words with /oo/oo.

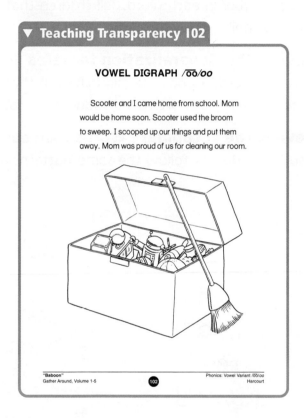

▼ **Teaching Transparency 102**

VOWEL DIGRAPH /oo/oo

Scooter and I came home from school. Mom would be home soon. Scooter used the broom to sweep. I scooped up our things and put them away. Mom was proud of us for cleaning our room.

"Baboon"
Gather Around, Volume 1-5

102

Phonics: Vowel Variant /oo/oo
Harcourt

 Write Words Tell children to choose two /oo/oo words and write them in their journal.

Day 3

5-DAY PHONICS	
DAY 1	Introduce /oo/oo
DAY 2	Word Building with /oo/oo
DAY 3	**Word Building with /oo/oo**
DAY 4	Word Building with /ō/oa and /oo/oo
DAY 5	Phonograms with -oom, -oot

REACHING ALL LEARNERS

Diagnostic Check: Phonics

If... children cannot decode words with /oo/oo ...

Then... have them read "The Goose and the Loon" in *Decodable Book 34.*

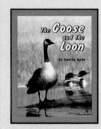

◀ **Decodable Book 34**
"The Goose and the Loon"

ADDITIONAL SUPPORT ACTIVITIES

BELOW-LEVEL	Reteach, p. S46
ADVANCED	Extend, p. S47
ENGLISH-LANGUAGE LEARNERS	Reteach, p. S47

 **School–Home Connection**

Take-Home Book Version

 ◀ **Decodable Books Take-Home Version**

Spelling Words

1. cool
2. tool
3. toot
4. tooth
5. booth
6. boot
7. read
8. head
9. carry
10. hours

journal writing

Writing Prompt Have children copy the Spelling Words into their journal. Encourage them to add illustrations to show the meanings of the words.

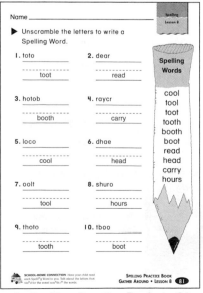

▲ Spelling Practice Book, p. 81

Spelling

5-DAY SPELLING	
DAY 1	Pretest; Word Sort
DAY 2	Word Building
DAY 3	**State the Generalization**
DAY 4	Review
DAY 5	Posttest; Writing Application

TEACH/MODEL

State the Generalization for /o͞o/oo Write the Spelling Words on the board and have children read them aloud. Discuss what is the same about words 1–6. (They all have the sound /o͞o/; they all have the letters *oo*.) Have volunteers circle the letters that stand for /o͞o/ in each word. Tell children that the letters *oo* are used to spell the sound /o͞o/.

Review the Generalization for /e/ea Follow a similar procedure for words 7 and 8. Remind children that the letters *ea* can be used to spell the short vowel sound of *e*, /e/.

Review the Vocabulary Words Point out that the words *carry* and *hours* do not follow the same patterns as the other words.

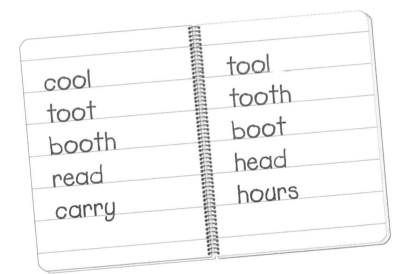

BELOW-LEVEL

To help children focus on the letters in the Spelling Words, give clues about the spelling of each word. For example, say "Find the word that has five letters, begins with *t* and ends with *th*." (tooth) Have children say, spell, and say the word again. Then have them write the word.

ADVANCED

Have children work in pairs and take turns writing questions and answers that include the Spelling Words. For example, the first child might write *Will you please carry this tool?* The second could answer *This tool is cool. I read about it.*

Vocabulary

REVIEW WORDS IN CONTEXT

Read Words in Context Copy the following poem onto chart paper and track the print as volunteers read each line aloud. Help children read the words *yawn* and *dawn* in lines 6 and 8. Have children think of actions to go with each line. Have children reread the poem and do the actions.

> REVIEW
>
> **Vocabulary**
> **against   quietly**
> **careful   shook**
> **fire**

Dragon Dream

A dragon came into my room.
Her footsteps shook the house!
When she said hello to me,
Fire came from her mouth.
I told her to be careful,
But she smiled and gave a yawn.
She snuggled up against me
And snored quietly 'til dawn.

Reinforce Words As you show each word card, have children say the word, spell it, say it again, and spell it again. Put down the word card, but continue to hold up your hand as if holding the card. Have children mentally picture the word as they say and spell the word two more times.

ADVANCED

Provide opportunities for higher-level thinking by having children draw pictures they can use to explain the meaning of each vocabulary word. Then have them explain their drawings to English-language learners.

ENGLISH-LANGUAGE LEARNERS

Reinforce children's understanding of the words by leading them in pantomiming the following sentences:

I leaned against the wall.
I put out the fire.
I was careful when I held the baby.
I shook the tree and an apple fell.
I tiptoed quietly across the room.

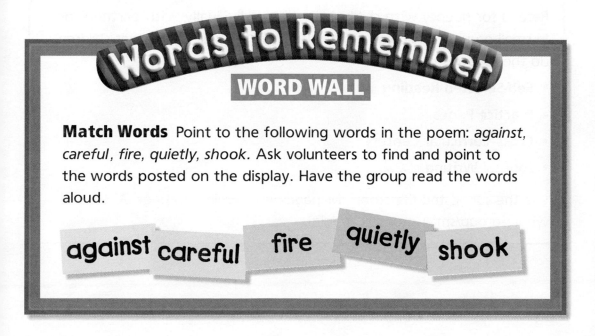

Words to Remember

WORD WALL

Match Words Point to the following words in the poem: *against, careful, fire, quietly, shook.* Ask volunteers to find and point to the words posted on the display. Have the group read the words aloud.

against careful fire quietly shook

▲ *Pupil Edition, pp. 220–243*

FLUENCY ROUTINES For support, see Fluency Routine Cards in Theme Resources, pp. T83–T84.

Rereading for Fluency

GROUPS

Choral Reading

⬤ **BELOW-LEVEL** Remind children that in "Baboon," some sentences tell what happens and others tell what the characters say. Read aloud page 222 as children track the print. Ask volunteers to read the words Baboon's mother and Baboon say. Point out that quotation marks appear at the beginning and end of the dialogue and they are a signal that the words should be read as if the characters are speaking to each other. Have children echo read the dialogue. Then lead children in choral reading the story. Pause occasionally to model reading dialogue with the appropriate expression and have children echo read. Encourage children to reread the story using the Character Cutouts (page T22) to role-play the dialogue. TEACHER-DIRECTED

Managing Small Groups

Reread for fluency with children working individually, with partners, or in small groups. While you work with small groups, have other children do the following:

• **Self-Selected Reading**

• **Practice Pages**

• **Cross-Curricular Centers**

• **Journal Writing**

Use the suggested Classroom Management outline on page 7C for the whole-group/small-group schedule.

PARTNERS

Partner Reading

● **ON-LEVEL/ADVANCED** Have partners take turns reading the story aloud one page at a time. Remind them to read smoothly and with expression as if they were telling the story to someone. Point out that they can use punctuation, such as quotation marks, as a guide to how the sentences should sound. Suggest that they reread sentences or pages if they think they can improve their reading. INDEPENDENT

INDIVIDUALS

Tape-Assisted Reading

● **ENGLISH-LANGUAGE LEARNERS** Conduct a brief picture walk to review story events and to reinforce vocabulary such as animal names and words that describe settings. Then have children track the print and read along with *Audiotext 5.* Tell them to try to make their voice sound like the recording. INDEPENDENT

Teacher
Read-Aloud
Magazine Article

Piggyback Ride

Mother bears give their cubs a ride when they get tired. Do your parents give you piggyback rides?

The water is not safe for baby grebes. Big fish eat little chicks. Mom and dad make great lifeboats.

This frog has two tadpoles on its back. They are on their way to a pool of water. The tadpoles will grow up there.

Young lemurs hold on tight when they go piggybacking. Lemur parents swing from trees with their babies on board!

248

249

Reading Across Texts

READ A SCIENCE ARTICLE

Build Background Ask children if they have ever seen a mother animal carry her baby. Have them tell how the mother held the baby. List children's responses on the board.

Set Purpose/Read Read aloud the title and have children preview the illustrations. Remind children that this piece is called an *article*. An article is shorter than a story and most often gives information about real things. Help children set a purpose for reading, such as to find out why animal mothers carry their babies. Then read aloud "Piggyback Ride" while children follow along.

SUMMARIZE/EXTEND

Check Understanding Ask how and why different mother animals carry their babies. Lead children to summarize the article. Then have them tell about other ways mother animals care for their babies.

SCIENCE

Animal Cards Organize children into groups and have them follow the directions on the card. Have children share their cards with the class and explain how the mother animal cares for her baby.

CROSS-CURRICULAR ACTIVITY CARD 7

Make Animal Cards

1. Find out about animal mothers that help their babies.
2. Fold a sheet of paper in half.
3. Draw an animal mother on the outside.
4. Write "Guess How I Help My Baby."
5. Draw how she helps on the inside.
6. Share your animal card with classmates.

▲ **Cross-Curricular Activity Card, p. T14**

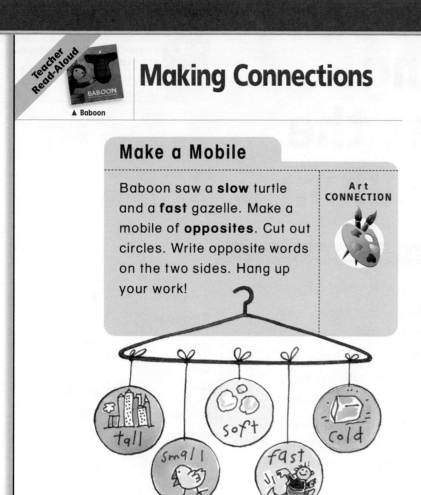

Making Connections

▲ Baboon

Make a Mobile

Baboon saw a **slow** turtle and a **fast** gazelle. Make a mobile of **opposites**. Cut out circles. Write opposite words on the two sides. Hang up your work!

Art
CONNECTION

Mobile Sentences

Write pairs of sentences using words from your mobile. Draw pictures to go with them. Share your work.

Writing
CONNECTION

Ice is cold.   This tea is hot.

Animals Baboon Saw

Baboon saw a monkey that looked a lot like him. Find out more about monkeys or another animal the Baboon saw. Use encyclopedia software or the Internet. Draw and write about the animal. Share your work.

Science/
Technology
CONNECTION

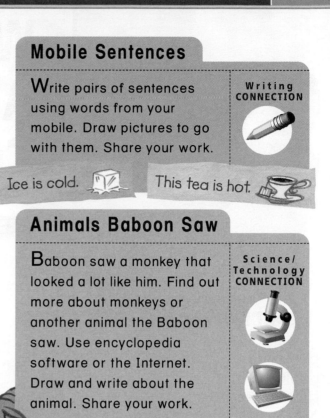

A rhinoceros has horns on its snout.

250

251

Making Connections

ART

Make a Mobile Help children brainstorm a list of opposites. Provide paper circles, a hole punch, string, a hanger, and crayons or markers for each child. Demonstrate how to write words with opposite meanings on either side of a circle and tell them to draw pictures to illustrate the words. Help children punch a hole at the top of their circles for attaching a length of string, and tie the string to attach the circles to the hanger.

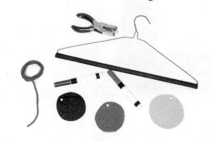

WRITING

Mobile Sentences Write *dark* and *light* on the board. Ask children to name something that is dark and something that is light. Use children's ideas to write sentences on the board such as *Nighttime is dark. Morning is light.* Then ask children to use the opposites on their mobile to write similar sentences. Remind children to illustrate their sentences. Display the sentence pairs in a center where children can read each other's work.

SCIENCE/TECHNOLOGY

Animals Baboon Saw Help children recall other animals that appear in the story "Baboon" and discuss what the story and illustrations tell about each animal. Then have children choose an animal they would like to learn more about. Help children use electronic or conventional encyclopedias to find out facts about their animal. Have children write and draw about something they learned. Provide time for children to share their work.

DAILY LANGUAGE PRACTICE

Alex isnt redy for bed.

Alex <u>isn't</u> <u>ready</u> for bed.

journal writing

Writing Prompt Have children write about a baby animal they would like to be and explain why.

ADVANCED

Tell children to write their own sentences about the names of baby animals without the sentence frame.

ENGLISH-LANGUAGE LEARNERS

To familiarize children with the terms for animal babies, compile children's captioned drawings into a class book. Arrange a time for classmates to read the book together.

Writing Across the Curriculum *Sentence Frames*

GENERATE IDEAS

Tap Prior Knowledge Point out that there are special names for some animal babies, such as cubs for baby bears. Ask children to think of special names for baby cats, dogs, and other animals. Write children's responses in two columns on chart paper.

Adult Animals	Animal Babies
bear	cub
cat	kitten
dog	puppy
chicken	chick
duck	duckling
pig	piglet
goose	gosling
frog	tadpole
cow	calf
horse	colt

DRAFT

Complete a Sentence Frame Have children copy the following sentence frame and complete it, using words from the chart. Suggest that if children wish, they may write additional sentences describing the baby animal. Tell children to illustrate their sentences.

A baby _____ is called a _____.

A baby pig is called a piglet.

Grammar
Contractions with Not

5-DAY GRAMMAR

DAY 1	Introduce Contractions with *Not*
DAY 2	Revise Sentences
DAY 3	**Match Contractions with Meanings**
DAY 4	Apostrophe Game
DAY 5	Write Contractions

REVIEW

Match Contractions with Meanings Make word cards for the following contractions and words. Display the cards in random order. Have children take turns matching the cards and using the contractions in sentences.

don't	do not	shouldn't	should not
hasn't	has not	wouldn't	would not
can't	can not	couldn't	could not
won't	will not	weren't	were not

won't   will not   shouldn't   should not

WRAP UP Read a Story

Connect Ideas Across Texts Remind children that the story they just read tells about a number of things that happen to Baboon on an ordinary day. Tell children that you are going to read another story, "Alexander and the Terrible, Horrible, No Good, Very Bad Day," about all the things that happen to a little boy on a not-so-ordinary day.

▲ **Read-Aloud Anthology, pp. 48–50**

(Focus Skill) **Plot** Help children recall some of the things that happen to Baboon. Discuss similarities and differences between Baboon's and Alexander's experiences. Ask children whether they feel more like Baboon or Alexander today, and have them tell why.

Have children read silently from a book of their choice. See page 253J for tips on helping children choose books.

SKILL TRACE

CONTRACTIONS WITH *NOT*	
Introduce	218N
REVIEW	247C, 251B, 253B, 253L
T Test	Bk 1-5

BELOW-LEVEL

Provide extra practice for children who have difficulty matching the contraction *won't* to the meaning *will not*. Write on the board *We won't forget.* Have children read the sentence. Then cover the word *won't* with a word card that says *will not* and have children read the sentence again. Repeat with additional sentences containing the contraction *won't*.

Name _____

Contractions with Not

▶ Read each sentence. Write the contraction for the underlined words.

isn't	wasn't	don't
aren't	weren't	didn't
hasn't	haven't	won't

1. This <u>is not</u> a flower. _____ isn't

2. These <u>are not</u> frogs. _____ aren't

3. This <u>was not</u> fixed. _____ wasn't

4. They <u>are not</u> sad. _____ aren't

5. They <u>do not</u> fly. _____ don't

SCHOOL-HOME CONNECTION

▲ **Language Handbook, p. 143**

Baboon **251B**

Day at a Glance
Day 4

Sharing Literature
Poem: "When You Talk to a Monkey"

Phonemic Awareness
Phoneme Blending; Focus on /ō/, /o͞o/

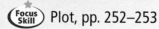

Phonics
Build Words

Spelling
Review

Vocabulary
REVIEW: *against, careful, fire, quietly, shook*

Reading

Read

Baboon

Comprehension
(Focus Skill) Plot, pp. 252–253

Interactive Writing ✏
Description

Grammar
REVIEW: Contractions with *Not*

WARM UP MORNING MESSAGE

Good Morning!

Today is _____.

_____, _____, and _____ make good pets.

Some _____ can learn to _____.

_____ and _____ don't make good pets.

I would like a _____ for a pet.

Introduce the Day
Tell children that they are going to read a poem about talking to a monkey. Explain that some people have monkeys as pets. They talk to the monkeys and train them. Ask:

- **What other animals make good pets?**
- **What are some things that pets can learn to do?**
- **What are some animals that would *not* make good pets?**

As you write the message, have children suggest ways to complete the sentences. Have them suggest correct capitalization and punctuation. Ask volunteers to write familiar words or letters.

Read the Message
Read the message. Use the message to focus on selected skills that have been previously taught.

Apply Skills

Concept Vocabulary Discuss with children some differences between wild animals and tame animals. Have children name animals that are often kept as pets. Then have them name animals that usually live in wild areas away from people.

Phonics Have volunteers point to words that include the letter *p*. Have children say each word aloud and tell what sound the *p* stands for. Then have them tell whether they hear the sound /p/ at the beginning, in the middle, or at the end of the word.

Sharing Literature

LISTEN AND RESPOND

Connect to Prior Knowledge Have children tell what they do to show they are listening to a teacher, parent, or friend. Explain that you are going to read a poem about how a monkey acts when he listens. Ask children to listen to find out whether or not the monkey does the same things they do.

Read and Dramatize the Poem Read the poem aloud. Have children discuss the monkey's actions. Help children create motions to express these actions and perform them as you reread the poem.

Phonemic Awareness

PHONEME BLENDING

Words from "When You Talk to a Monkey" Tell children that you are going to say some words very slowly. Model by segmenting the word *tail* into phonemes (/t/ /ā/ /l/). Then say the word *tail*. Segment the following words from the poem, having children blend the sounds to say the words.

/m/ /är/ /k/ (mark)   /s/ /ā/ (say)   /w/ /ī/ /z/ (wise)
/s/ /ē/ /m/ /z/ (seems) /o/ /n/ (on)   /a/ /n/ /d/ (and)
/j/ /u/ /s/ /t/ (just)   /b/ /i/ /g/ (big)   /h/ /e/ /d/ (head)

FOCUS ON /ō/, /o͞o/

Distinguish Phonemes Tell children that you are going to say some words and they will say the vowel sound they hear in the middle of each one. Model by saying *toot. I hear /o͞o/ in the middle of* toot. Continue with these words:

road (/ō/)   **noon** (/o͞o/)   **roam** (/ō/)
boat (/ō/)   **boot** (/o͞o/)   **proof** (/o͞o/)
hoop (/o͞o/)   **roast** (/ō/)   **roost** (/o͞o/)

When You Talk to a Monkey

When you talk to a monkey
   He seems very wise.
He scratches his head,
   And he blinks both his eyes;
But he won't say a word.
   He just swings on a rail
And makes a big question mark
   Out of his tail.

Rowena Bennett

ENGLISH-LANGUAGE LEARNERS

If children have difficulty hearing medial sounds, model how to segment the words into phonemes. Have children look in a mirror as they repeat the segmented sounds. Have children watch the movement of your mouth as you blend the sounds. Then have them look in the mirror and try to make the same movements as they blend the sounds themselves.

Phonics
Build Words *Review*

OBJECTIVES

- *To discriminate between the sound-letter relationships /ō/oa and /o͞o/oo*

- *To read and write words with /ō/oa and /o͞o/oo*

SKILL TRACE

	/o͞o/oo	/ō/oa
Introduce	218I–218L	Bk 1-3, 144I–144L
Reteach	S46–S47	Bk 1-3, S34–S35, T12
Review	218Q–218R, 247F–247G	Bk 1-3, 144Q–144R 165F–165G, 171F–171
REVIEW	**251E–251F**	
T Test	Bk 2-1	Bk 1-3
MAINTAIN		Bk 1-4, 33E–33F Bk 1-5, 251E–251F

Phonics Resources

Phonics Express™ **CD-ROM,**
Level B Bumper/Route 1/Market

WORD BUILDING

Build and Read Words Use a pocket chart and *Letter Cards a, b, e, f, g, m, o, o, p, r, s,* and *t.* Display the letters *b, o, o,* and *m* in the pocket chart. Remind children that the letters *oo* together can stand for the sound /o͞o/.

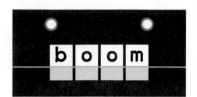

Place the letters close together. Slide your hand slowly under the letters as you blend the sounds—/bbo͞omm/. Then read the word naturally—*boom.* Have children repeat after you. Discuss the meaning of *boom.* Point out that the letters in *boom* follow the pattern *consonant, vowel, vowel, consonant.*

Ask volunteers to build new words in the pocket chart.

- Change the *m* to *st.* Read the word.

- Change the second *o* to *a.* Read the word.

- Change the *b* to *r.* Read the word.

- Change the *a* to *o.* Change the *st* to *m.* Read the word.

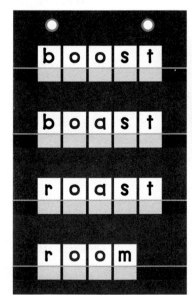

Continue word building with this word sequence: *roam, root, boot, boat, coast, coat, coal, cool.*

Write the words *boost, boast,* and *cool* on the board and have children read the words aloud.

5-DAY PHONICS	
DAY 1	Introduce /o͞o/oo
DAY 2	Word Building with /o͞o/oo
DAY 3	Word Building with /o͞o/oo
DAY 4	Word Building with /ō/oa and /o͞o/oo
DAY 5	Phonograms -oom, -oot

Day 4

Apply Phonics

APPLY PHONICS SKILLS

Dictate Sentences Dictate the following sentences:

> I have a filling in my tooth.
> Help me find my other boot.

Have children write the sentences on a dry-erase board or in their journal.

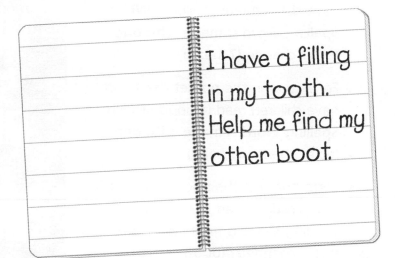

I have a filling
in my tooth.
Help me find my
other boot.

BELOW-LEVEL

If children have difficulty remembering longer sentences, dictate these shorter sentences using the same Spelling Words:
Look at my tooth.
This is my boot.

ENGLISH-LANGUAGE LEARNERS

Before giving dictation, make sure children are familiar with the meaning of all the words in the sentences. If necessary, explain what a dental filling is.

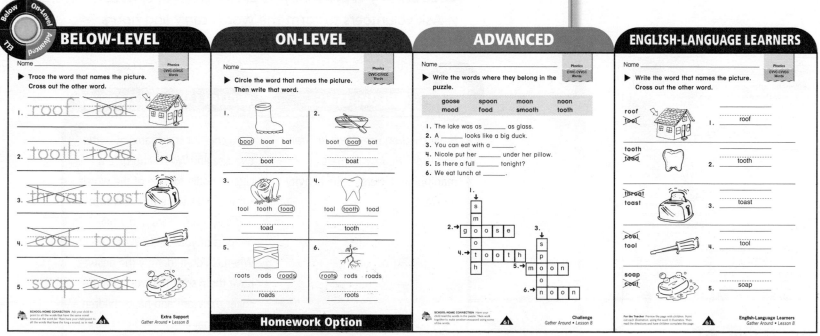

BELOW-LEVEL

Name _____
▶ Trace the word that names the picture. Cross out the other word.
1. roof ~~tool~~
2. tooth ~~toad~~
3. ~~throat~~ toast
4. ~~cool~~ tool
5. soap ~~coat~~

▲ Extra Support, p. 61

ON-LEVEL

Name _____
▶ Circle the word that names the picture. Then write that word.
1. (boot) boat bat — boot
2. boot (boat) bat — boat
3. tool tooth (toad) — toad
4. tool (tooth) toad — tooth
5. roots rods (roads) — roads
6. (roots) rods roads — roots

▲ Practice, p. 61

Homework Option

ADVANCED

Name _____
▶ Write the words where they belong in the puzzle.

goose	spoon	moon	noon
mood	food	smooth	tooth

1. The lake was as _____ as glass.
2. A _____ looks like a big duck.
3. You can eat with a _____.
4. Nicole put her _____ under her pillow.
5. Is there a full _____ tonight?
6. We eat lunch at _____.

▲ Challenge, p. 61

ENGLISH-LANGUAGE LEARNERS

Name _____
▶ Write the word that names the picture. Cross out the other word.
1. roof ~~tool~~ — roof
2. tooth ~~toad~~ — tooth
3. ~~throat~~ toast — toast
4. ~~cool~~ tool — tool
5. soap ~~coat~~ — soap

▲ ELL, p. 61

Spelling Words

1. cool
2. tool
3. toot
4. tooth
5. booth
6. boot
7. read
8. head
9. carry
10. hours

Spelling

5-DAY SPELLING	
DAY 1	Pretest; Word Sort
DAY 2	Word Building
DAY 3	State the Generalization
DAY 4	**Review**
DAY 5	Posttest; Writing Application

REVIEW

Spelling Words Use a pocket chart and *Letter Cards* to form words. Have children listen to your directions and change one letter in each word to spell a Spelling Word. Have them write the Spelling Word on a sheet of paper or in their journal. Then have a volunteer change the *Letter Card* in the pocket chart so that children can self-check the word.

■ Form *held* in the pocket chart and have children read it aloud. **Which Spelling Word is made with one letter changed?** (head)

■ Form *road* in the pocket chart and have children read it aloud. **Which Spelling Word is made with one letter changed?** (read)

■ Form *boom* in the pocket chart and have children read it aloud. **Which Spelling Word is made with one letter changed?** (boot)

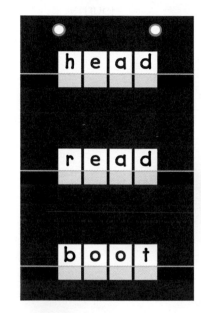

Follow a similar procedure with the following words: *teeth (tooth), tooth (booth), root (toot, boot), coop (cool), fool (cool, tool).*

Vocabulary Words Display *Letter Cards a, c, h, o, r, r, r, s, u,* and *y.* Ask volunteers to form the words *carry* and *hours.*

BELOW-LEVEL

Have children use *Word Builders* and *Word Builder Cards* as they manipulate letters in the activity above.

ENGLISH-LANGUAGE LEARNERS

On a chart or transparency, write two Spelling Words and give a clue or riddle for one of the words. For example, write *tool* and *tooth* and say, "I am sharp and white. I am part of your smile. What am I?" When children identify the answer, have them spell the word. Then cover the word and have children spell it again.

Name _____

▶ Write the letter or letters that complete each Spelling Word. Then trace the rest of the words.

1. c o o l   2. t o o th

3. h o u r s   4. t o o

5. t o o t   6. c a r r y

7. r e a d   8. b o o th

Spelling Words
cool
tool
toot
tooth
booth
boot
read
head
carry
hours

▶ Unscramble the letters to make a Spelling Word.

9. o t b o   b o o t

10. e h a d   h e a d

▲ Spelling Practice Book, p. 82

Vocabulary

WRITE WORDS IN STORY CONTEXT

Reinforce Word Recognition

Duplicate and distribute the Story Strips for "Baboon," page T72. Display *Word Cards* or write the vocabulary words on the board: *against, careful, fire, quietly, shook*. Have children complete each sentence with a word from the list. After children complete the Story Strip sentences, they can work with partners to check their work. Partners can then put the Story Strips in correct sequence.

REVIEW

Vocabulary

against   quietly

careful   shook

fire

BELOW-LEVEL

Help children focus on the features of each word, one word at a time. Ask them to look for familiar word endings, blends, and vowel pairs. After each discussion, have children think about the features as they try writing the word from memory. Revisit the word and have children evaluate and adjust their strategies until they are successful in writing the word from memory.

> Baboon learned to be _____ so he would not get hurt.

> He felt the heat of the forest _____.

> He hid _____ from the crocodile.

> The ground _____ when the elephants walked.

> Baboon put his head _____ his mother's neck and went to sleep.

Words to Remember

WORD WALL

Match Words Have children look at the displayed words and find the words they wrote on the Story Strips. Ask volunteers to frame the words as classmates read them aloud.

Read

▲ *Pupil Edition*, pp. 220–243

OBJECTIVE

To understand and summarize the plot of a story

SKILL TRACE

PLOT	
Introduce	Bk 1-5, 9A, 33A, 35I
Reteach	S48–S49, T1 1
REVIEW	**125A, 153I, 149A, 219A, 247A, 251I**
T TEST	Bk 1-5

REACHING ALL LEARNERS

Diagnostic Check: Comprehension

If... children cannot summarize the plot of the story . . .

Then... page through the story together, looking at the pictures and rereading selected text. Decide together how the events can be included in a summary.

ADDITIONAL SUPPORT ACTIVITIES

BELOW-LEVEL Reteach, p. S48

ADVANCED Extend, p. S49

ENGLISH-LANGUAGE LEARNERS Reteach, p. S49

READING

Focus Skill Comprehension

Plot

TEACH/MODEL

Develop Concepts Remind children that when we talk about the plot of the story, we mean the events that happen as characters figure things out or solve a problem. Point out that paying attention to what happens helps us to understand the plot, or what the whole story is about.

MODEL Tammy can't find her cat Puff. She looks in the places where Puff usually hides or naps, but the cat is not there. In the front yard, Tammy sees the neighbor's dog looking up in a tree, excited and barking. Tammy asks her dad to get the ladder. I can tell that Tammy found her cat in the tree. These events form the plot of the story.

PRACTICE/APPLY

Understand Plot Tell children that they will now summarize the plot of the story. Read aloud *Pupil Edition* page 252 as children follow along. Discuss the pictures and what happens in the story. Point out that Baboon sees a forest and meets a monkey, but these do not tell what the whole story is about.

Reread the Selection Have children reread "Baboon," paying close attention to the things that Baboon sees and does. Ask children to tell the main events in the plot of the story.

TEST PREP

Model the Test Item Remind children that when they are taking a test, they should read carefully and think about which are the important events in the story. Direct children to follow along as you read the story aloud. Read aloud the question and the answer choices, and guide children in choosing the correct answer.

Plot

▲ **Baboon**

Focus Skill

You have learned that the **plot** of a story is what that story is about. Read these three sentences about the story "Baboon."

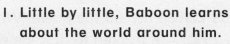
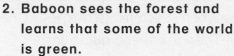

1. Little by little, Baboon learns about the world around him.
2. Baboon sees the forest and learns that some of the world is green.
3. Baboon meets a monkey that looks a lot like him.

Which sentence do you think best tells the plot of the whole story? Why?

Visit *The Learning Site!*
www.harcourtschool.com
See *Skills and Activities*

252

Test Prep
Plot

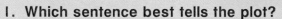

The animals felt heat and saw flames. It was a forest fire! The birds flew away. Raccoon and his friends ran to the pond. "We're safe here," said Raccoon.

1. **Which sentence best tells the plot?**
   ○ Raccoon and his friends run to a pond.
   ○ The animals escape from a forest fire.
   ○ Animals feel the heat from a forest fire.

Tip

Remember that the plot is what happens in a story. Read all the sentences carefully before you answer.

253

Visit *The Learning Site*

www.harcourtschool.com

See Skill Activities and Test Tutors: Plot.

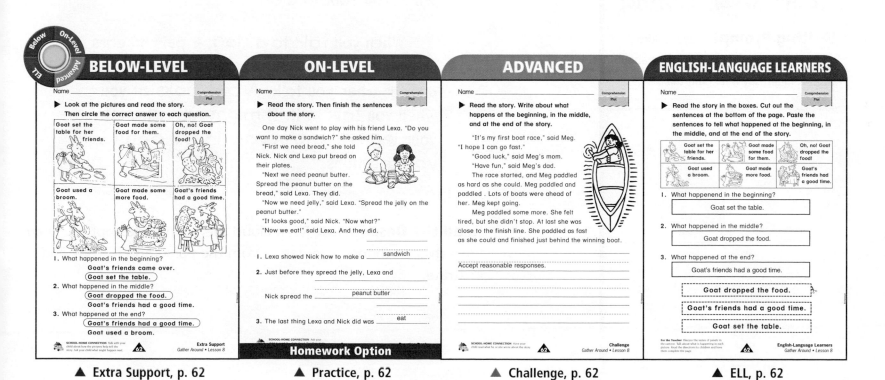

BELOW-LEVEL

Name _____ Comprehension Plot

▶ Look at the pictures and read the story. Then circle the correct answer to each question.

| Goat set the table for her friends. | Goat made some food for them. | Oh, no! Goat dropped the food! |
| Goat used a broom. | Goat made some more food. | Goat's friends had a good time. |

1. What happened in the beginning?
   Goat's friends came over.
   (Goat set the table.)
2. What happened in the middle?
   (Goat dropped the food.)
   Goat's friends had a good time.
3. What happened at the end?
   (Goat's friends had a good time.)
   Goat used a broom.

SCHOOL-HOME CONNECTION Talk with your child about how the pictures help tell the story. Ask your child what might happen next.

Extra Support
Gather Around • Lesson 8

▲ **Extra Support, p. 62**

ON-LEVEL

Name _____ Comprehension Plot

▶ Read the story. Then finish the sentences about the story.

One day Nick went to play with his friend Lexa. "Do you want to make a sandwich?" she asked him.
"First we need bread," she told Nick. Nick and Lexa put bread on their plates.
"Next we need peanut butter. Spread the peanut butter on the bread," said Lexa. They did.
"Now we need jelly," said Lexa. "Spread the jelly on the peanut butter."
"It looks good," said Nick. "Now what?"
"Now we eat!" said Lexa. And they did.

1. Lexa showed Nick how to make a _____ sandwich
2. Just before they spread the jelly, Lexa and Nick spread the _____ peanut butter
3. The last thing Lexa and Nick did was _____ eat

SCHOOL-HOME CONNECTION Ask your...

Homework Option

▲ **Practice, p. 62**

ADVANCED

Name _____ Comprehension Plot

▶ Read the story. Write about what happens at the beginning, in the middle, and at the end of the story.

"It's my first boat race," said Meg. "I hope I can go fast."
"Good luck," said Meg's mom.
"Have fun," said Meg's dad.
The race started, and Meg paddled as hard as she could. Meg paddled and paddled. Lots of boats were ahead of her. Meg kept going.
Meg paddled some more. She felt tired, but she didn't stop. At last she was close to the finish line. She paddled as fast as she could and finished just behind the winning boat.

Accept reasonable responses.

SCHOOL-HOME CONNECTION Have your child read what he or she wrote about the story.

Challenge
Gather Around • Lesson 8

▲ **Challenge, p. 62**

ENGLISH-LANGUAGE LEARNERS

Name _____ Comprehension Plot

▶ Read the story in the boxes. Cut out the sentences at the bottom of the page. Paste the sentences to tell what happened at the beginning, in the middle, and at the end of the story.

| Goat set the table for her friends. | Goat made some food for them. | Oh, no! Goat dropped the food! |
| Goat made a broom. | Goat made more food. | Goat's friends had a good time. |

1. What happened in the beginning?
   Goat set the table.
2. What happened in the middle?
   Goat dropped the food.
3. What happened at the end?
   Goat's friends had a good time.

   Goat dropped the food.
   Goat's friends had a good time.
   Goat set the table.

For the Teacher: Discuss the names of panels in the cartoon. Talk about what is happening in each picture. Read the directions to children and have them complete the page.

English-Language Learners
Gather Around • Lesson 8

▲ **ELL, p. 62**

5-DAY WRITING	
DAY 1	INDEPENDENT: Talking Mural
DAY 2	SHARED: Story Response
DAY 3	CROSS-CURRICULAR: Sentence Frames
DAY 4	**INTERACTIVE: Description**
DAY 5	INDEPENDENT: Posters

Interactive Writing *Write a Description*

SHARE THE PEN

Describe How Pets Listen Reread the poem "When You Talk to a Monkey" on page 25 ID. Ask children to describe what the poem says a monkey does when it listens. (scratches its head, blinks, swings, curls its tail) Then ask these questions:

- **Have you ever seen a pet do any of the things the poet describes?**

- **What does a dog do when you talk to it? a cat? other pets?**

- **What do people do when they listen that pets do not do?**

Tell children that you are going to record their ideas in a paragraph. Point out that the first sentence will be indented. Each time a volunteer offers an idea, have the group suggest ways to word a sentence telling that idea. As you record the responses, point out that you write the sentences one after another rather than starting each one on a new line. Choose volunteers to write parts of words, phrases, and familiar words such as contractions.

When You Talk to a Pet

When you talk to a dog, it puts its ears up and wags its tail. A dog doesn't answer when you talk. A cat looks at you when you talk to it. It might rub against your leg or jump in your lap. It can't ask you questions.

Read the Description Read aloud the finished description. Then have children choose a sentence from the paragraph to copy and illustrate.

DAILY LANGUAGE PRACTICE

Dad cant find his box of tules.

Dad <u>can't</u> find his box of <u>tools</u>.

ONGOING ASSESSMENT

Note whether children are able to
- make connections between sounds and letters in words.
- spell known high-frequency and vocabulary words.
- use knowledge of the basic rules of punctuation and capitalization.
- correctly write contractions with *not*.

journal writing

Writing Prompt Have children choose an animal or pet and write about what it might say if it could talk.

5-DAY GRAMMAR	
DAY 1	Introduce Contractions with *Not*
DAY 2	Revise Sentences
DAY 3	Match Contractions with Meanings
DAY 4	**Apostrophe Game**
DAY 5	Write Contractions

Day 4

Grammar

Contractions with Not

REVIEW

Play an Apostrophe Game Have children sit in a circle. Write the following sentences on the board or on chart paper:

> Soo's mother has not told her about the
>   surprise party.
> She said we should not tell Soo about the party.
> Kim does not know where the party will be.
> Jerry is not sure what he will give to Soo.
> Jason and Keesha have not made gifts yet.

Ask volunteers to read each sentence and underline the words that could be replaced by a contraction. Write the contraction without the apostrophe. Ask children to tell which letters were left out when forming the contraction. Point out that the apostrophe should be placed where letters have been left out. Have children pass the chalk around the circle while they recite the alphabet. When they reach the letter that begins the contraction, the child holding the chalk comes to the board to add the apostrophe. On the next round, that child begins passing the chalk.

WRAP UP Revisit a Song

Reading Across Texts Revisit the song "The Bear Went Over the Mountain," page 247E. Ask children to sing the song and think about how the song is similar to the story "Baboon." (Both are about animals who explore their world.) Then discuss ways that the story and song are different. (The bear only sees the other side of the mountain. Baboon discovers many new things about the world.) Then lead children in singing a new version of the song by changing *The bear* to *Baboon* in each line.

S.S.R. Sustained Silent Reading

Have children read silently from a book of their choice. See page 253J for tips on helping children choose books.

Name _____

Contractions with Not

▶ Read each sentence. Write the contraction for the underlined words.

isn't	wasn't	don't
aren't	weren't	didn't
hasn't	haven't	won't

1. Many people <u>are not</u> ready.   aren't

2. They <u>have not</u> put away
   their things.   haven't

3. The train <u>will not</u> go yet.   won't

4. The alarm <u>has not</u>
   buzzed yet.   hasn't

5. We <u>were not</u> late!   weren't

144

▲ Language Handbook, p.144

Baboon **253B**

Day at a Glance
Day 5

Sharing Literature
Big Book: *I Swam with a Seal*

Phonemic Awareness
Phoneme Manipulation;
Focus on /o͞o/, /m/, and /t/

Phonics
Phonograms -oom, -oot

Spelling
Posttest; Writing Application

Vocabulary
REVIEW: *against, careful, fire, quietly, shook*

Reading
Rereading for Fluency
Pupil Edition
"Baboon," pp. 220–243

Self-Selected Reading

Read

Independent Writing ✎
Posters

Grammar
REVIEW: Contractions with *Not*

WARM UP MORNING MESSAGE

Good Morning!

Today is _____.
A _____ uses its _____ when it _____.
A _____ doesn't need _____
because _____.
I don't have _____. I have _____ instead.

Introduce the Day

Tell children that today they will revisit the story *I Swam with a Seal*. Guide them in generating a morning message about animals and their bodies. Ask:

• **What animals use special body parts for the things they do? When do they use those parts?**

• **Why don't all animals have those parts?**

• **What is a part of an animal's body that you don't have? What do you have instead?**

As you write the message, ask volunteers to write word beginnings, endings, familiar words, and punctuation marks. Where appropriate, have children write whole phrases.

Read the Message

Read the message. Use the message to focus on selected skills that have been previously taught.

Apply Skills

Phonics Remind children that they have learned different ways to spell the short vowel sound of e, /e/. Point out the words *when* and *instead*. Ask children to name the letters that stand for that sound in each word. (e, ea)

Grammar Have children identify the contractions in the message. *(doesn't, don't)* Then have volunteers tell the two words that each contraction stands for.

Sharing Literature

LISTEN AND RESPOND

(Focus Skill) **Plot** As you reread the *Big Book I Swam with a Seal*, pause occasionally to have children summarize the story events to that point. Have them explain what happens to the children each time they meet one of the animals. (The animal thinks they are funny because they are different.) Lead a discussion about what the children in the story learn about themselves.

Speak for the Characters Display the first page of the story. Have a volunteer read the seal's question and tell how the child might answer it. (I use my arms and legs to help me swim.) Then ask volunteers to recall other animals from the story and tell how the children could answer their questions.

▲ **Big Book**

Phonemic Awareness

PHONEME MANIPULATION

Words from the Big Book Tell children that you will say a word, and they will change the last sound of the word to make a new word. Model by saying *seal. If I change /l/ to /t/, I get* seat. Continue the activity with these words:

snail; change /l/ to /k/ (snake)
gum; change /m/ to /l/ (gull)
dot; change /t/ to /g/ (dog)
moon; change /n/ to /s/ (moose)

cap; change /p/ to /t/ (cat)
hot; change /t/ to /p/ (hop)
peep; change /p/ to /k/ (peek)
sleeve; change /v/ to /p/ (sleep)

FOCUS ON /o͞o/, /m/, and /t/

Phoneme Addition Tell children they will make some words by adding beginning sounds to the endings /o͞om/ and /o͞ot/. Model by saying *If I add /b/ to /o͞om/, I get* boom. Have children blend together the following sounds to make words:

-oot
add /s/ /k/ (scoot)
add /r/ (root)
add /h/ (hoot)
add /b/ (boot)

-oom
add /r/ (room)
add /b/ /l/ (bloom)
add /d/ (doom)
add /z/ (zoom)

BELOW-LEVEL

Children who have difficulty changing the final sound of a word may benefit from more practice with identifying final sounds. First model by saying a series of words that end with the same sound, and then identifying the sound. Continue the activity with other series of words with the same end sounds and have children identify the sounds.

Baboon **253D**

OBJECTIVES

- To discriminate between words with different patterns

- To use common vowel spelling patterns to read words

SKILL TRACE

PHONOGRAMS -oom, -oot	
INTRODUCE	253E–253F

Phonics

Phonograms -oom, -oot

WORKING WITH PATTERNS

Listen for Rhyming Words Say the words *broom* and *zoom*. Ask children how the words are the same. (They both end with /o͞om/. They rhyme.) Using the words *bloom, mom, room, come, groom,* and *loom,* have children show "thumbs up" when they hear a word that rhymes with *broom*.

Then say *boot* and *toot*. Ask how these words are the same. (They both end with /o͞ot/. They rhyme.) Have children show "thumbs up" when they hear a word that rhymes with *boot*. Say *root, scoot, spot, hot, hoot,* and *shoot*.

Discriminate Sounds As you read the following words, have children say whether each one rhymes with *boom* or *boot*.

groom	scoot	root	room
bloom	zoom	shoot	hoot

Build Words Write the phonograms *-oom* and *-oot* to head two columns on a chart. Have children suggest words that end with either *-oot* or *-oom* and say what letter or letters are needed to start the words. Have children read each word as it is added to the chart. Then read both sets of words together. End the activity by pointing to words at random and having children read them.

-oot	-oom
boot	boom
toot	doom
root	room
scoot	broom
hoot	bloom
shoot	zoom

Apply Phonics

5-DAY PHONICS

DAY 1	Introduce /o͞o/oo
DAY 2	Word Building with /o͞o/oo
DAY 3	Word Building with /o͞o/oo
DAY 4	Word Building with /ō/oa and /o͞o/oo
DAY 5	**Phonograms -oom, -oot**

APPLY PHONICS SKILLS

Write Words with -oom and -oot Have children write in their journal at least one word for each phonogram. Then have them write sentences using their words.

I use a broom to sweep the room.

ADVANCED

Have children build rhyming words with other /o͞o/ phonograms. Write -oose, -oon, -ool, and -oop on a chart. Have children experiment with letter tiles to find pairs of rhyming words with each ending.

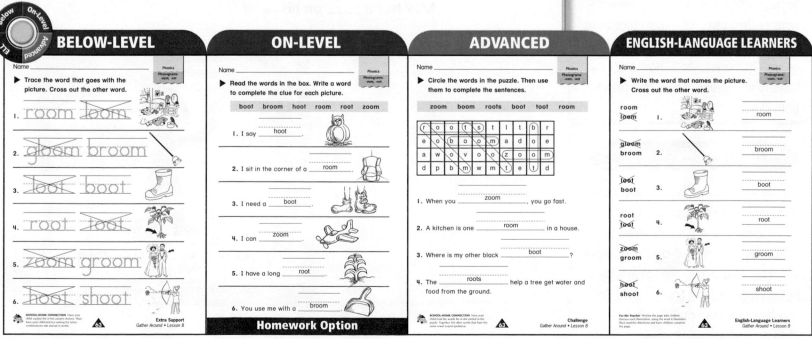

BELOW-LEVEL	ON-LEVEL	ADVANCED	ENGLISH-LANGUAGE LEARNERS

▲ Extra Support, p. 63   ▲ Practice, p. 63   ▲ Challenge, p. 63   ▲ ELL, p. 63

Spelling Words

1. cool
2. tool
3. toot
4. tooth
5. booth
6. boot
7. read
8. head
9. carry
10. hours

BELOW-LEVEL

To reinforce spelling patterns through kinesthetic activity, have children form the Spelling Words with plastic letters. Then have them record the words in their journal.

ADVANCED

To help children make spelling observations of their own, have them take turns making up two clues about the spelling of each of the list words. Have the group identify the Spelling Words that match both clues.

ENGLISH-LANGUAGE LEARNERS

Display the Spelling Words on word cards and make up sentences using each one. For example, say "Make a call from a phone booth." Have one child pantomime the action and identify the Spelling Word in the sentence. Have another child find and read that word card. Finally, have children read, spell, and reread the word.

WORD WORK

Spelling

5-DAY SPELLING	
DAY 1	Pretest; Word Sort
DAY 2	Word Building
DAY 3	State the Generalization
DAY 4	Review
DAY 5	**Posttest; Writing Application**

ASSESS/APPLY

Posttest Assess children's progress using the words and the Dictation Sentences from Day 1.

1. **cool** The fan kept me **cool**.
2. **tool** A hammer is a **tool**.
3. **toot** You can **toot** your horn while I play my drum.
4. **tooth** I have a loose **tooth**.
5. **booth** My father made a call from a phone **booth**.
6. **boot** I stepped in a puddle and got one **boot** wet.

Review

7. **read** Yesterday I **read** a book about monkeys.
8. **head** The king wore a crown on his **head**.

Vocabulary

9. **carry** A kangaroo can **carry** a baby in its pouch.
10. **hours** It takes two **hours** to get to my grandmother's house.

Writing Application Have children complete and illustrate the following sentence frames:

I can carry the tool to ____.

My boot is too ____.

Max has a ____ on his head.

Vocabulary

USE WORDS IN SENTENCES

Reinforce Usage and Meaning

Display *Word Cards* or list these words on the board: *against, careful, fire, quietly, shook.* Have children read the words. Ask volunteers to use the words in sentences that tell about interesting things they have seen or done. Write the sentences on chart paper, leaving a blank where each vocabulary word goes. Track the print as you read the sentences aloud. Then have other children pick the card with the word needed to complete each sentence.

> **REVIEW**
>
> **Vocabulary**
>
> against   quietly
>
> careful   shook
>
> fire

Words to Remember

WORD WALL

Complete Sentences Have children complete the following sentences with words that have been displayed. Point to the column in which the target word appears. Volunteers can frame the words as classmates read them aloud.

• **Be ____ not to leave trash on the path.** (careful)

• **Sandy moved ____ to get close to a bunny.** (quietly)

• **Dan leaned ____ a tree to rest.** (against)

• **John saw some trees that had been in a ____.** (fire)

• **When Kim ____ the tree, an apple fell.** (shook)

BELOW-LEVEL

For children who have difficulty generating sentences, suggest scenarios that will prompt ideas. For example, say *Imagine you are exploring. What would you need to be careful about?* or *How could you use* quietly *to tell what you would do if you wanted to see an animal in the wild?*

ENGLISH-LANGUAGE LEARNERS

To help children understand the meaning of vocabulary words, provide more practice using the words in context. Write these sentences on a chart. Read and discuss them.

> **The dog shook to get dry.**
>
> **I lean against the tree.**
>
> **I am careful with the baby.**
>
> **We tiptoed quietly.**
>
> **We sat by the fire.**

Children can then copy and illustrate the sentences to make a picture dictionary.

▲ *Pupil Edition, pp. 220–243*

FLUENCY ROUTINES For support, see Fluency Routine Cards in Theme Resources, pp. T83–T84.

Rereading for Fluency

GROUPS

Readers Theatre

⬤ **ON-LEVEL/ADVANCED** Assign small groups different parts of the story for a dramatic reading. Have children choose roles: Baboon, Baboon's mother, and narrator. Before practicing their parts, have group members take turns reading aloud as they think about how the baboons' voices might sound and how the narrator can read expressively to describe the events. Encourage groups to practice their readings several times, trying to read more smoothly and expressively with each reading. Then have the groups present their readings in turn. INDEPENDENT

PARTNERS

Repeated Reading

⬤ **BELOW-LEVEL/ENGLISH-LANGUAGE LEARNERS** Have partners choose their favorite parts of the story to practice reading aloud. Direct them to read the pages three times, trying to read more smoothly and expressively with each reading. Remind them that when they listen to each other, they should follow along and give feedback. Monitor children closely, providing modeling, support, and encouragement. After practice, gather children together and invite volunteers to read aloud for the group. TEACHER-DIRECTED

Managing Small Groups

Reread for fluency with children working individually, with partners, or in small groups. While you work with small groups, have other children do the following:

- **Self-Selected Reading**
- **Cross-Curricular Centers**
- **Practice Pages**
- **Journal Writing**

Use the suggested Classroom Management outline on page 7C for the whole-group/small-group schedule.

Self-Selected Reading

INDEPENDENT READING

Have children choose a book from the **Browsing Boxes** or the **Reading Center** to read independently during a sustained silent reading time. Children may also want to reread a story from their *Pupil Edition*. These are some books you may want to gather that relate to "Baboon."

choosing ★ books

To guide children in selecting books at their independent reading level, suggest that they read one or two pages of the book. If there are at least five words that the child can't read, he or she should try an easier book.

related books

- *How the Sky Got Its Stars* by Gail Tuchman. Instant Readers, Harcourt, 1997.

  This is a Hopi legend that tells how all the animals helped to make things on the earth, except for Coyote, until he decides to play with the stars. BELOW-LEVEL

- *Gift from the Sea* by Kate Banks. Farrar, Straus & Giroux, 2001.

  A rock holds many, many secrets from the past. ON-LEVEL

- *Up the Mountain* by Charlotte Agell. Dorling-Kindersley, 2000.

  A rainy day leads to adventures for four friends, Cat, Dragon, Chicken, and Rabbit. ON-LEVEL

- *Lionel at Large* by Stephen Krensky. Puffin, 1986.

  Lionel must endure many things, including eating green beans. ADVANCED

Decodable Books

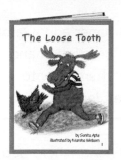 

Decodable Book 34
"The Loose Tooth" by Sunita Apte

"The Goose and the Loon" by Sunita Apte

Cut-Out/Fold-Up Book

The Zoo Race
Practice Book, pp. 79–80

Books For All Learners

Baboon's Park
by Beth Alley Wise

Around the Zoo with Baboon by Meish Goldish

Who Is in the Pond? by Meish Goldish

Let's Visit the Zoo by Kate Morgan

Writing
Posters

5-DAY WRITING	
DAY 1	INDEPENDENT: Talking Mural
DAY 2	SHARED: Story Response
DAY 3	CROSS-CURRICULAR: Sentence Frames
DAY 4	INTERACTIVE: Description
DAY 5	INDEPENDENT: **Posters**

DAILY LANGUAGE PRACTICE

Beth ha'snt ever lost
a tuth.

Beth <u>hasn't</u> ever lost
a <u>tooth</u>.

journal writing

Self-Selected Writing Have children write in their journal about a topic of their choice. They may want to illustrate their writing.

BELOW-LEVEL

If children have difficulty thinking of details to include in the description of the lost pet, have them make their illustration first and then describe the pet they have drawn.

GENERATE IDEAS

Elicit Describing Words Explain that when people lose a pet, they often put up posters around the neighborhood so that people will help find the pet. Ask children to tell what information would help neighbors who are looking for the lost pet. If necessary, point out that the poster should give a description of the animal that includes its size, color, and name. Discuss other details children might include, such as the phone number of the pet's owner. Record the poster ideas on chart paper.

DRAFT

Create Posters Give each child a sheet of lined paper and a large sheet of drawing paper. Have children write their description and other information on the lined paper. Then show them how to glue the written information onto the larger sheet, leaving room to draw a picture of the pet.

Handwriting Point out that posters are usually hung where people can read them from the street, so the letters need to be large, clear and carefully formed so they can be read from a distance.

5-DAY GRAMMAR

DAY 1	Introduce Contractions with *Not*
DAY 2	Revise Sentences
DAY 3	Match Contractions with Meanings
DAY 4	Apostrophe Game
DAY 5	**Write Contractions**

Grammar

Contractions with Not

REVIEW

Write Contractions Write the following sentences on the board:

> I do not have paper.
> We should not run in the halls.
> My friends have not called yet.
> Was not that fun?

Tell children to read the sentences aloud and identify the words that can be rewritten as contractions. Have children come to the board to demonstrate how to form contractions.

WRAP UP Share Ideas

Use the Author's Chair Have volunteers read aloud their lost animal posters. Suggest that children show their illustration first, then read the sentences they wrote. Ask children to explain how their description would help people to recognize the pet.

Remind listeners to sit quietly and be attentive. Tell them to ask the authors questions if they do not understand what they hear or if they want to know more. After each reading, lead children in applause for the author.

S.S.R. Have children read silently from a book of their choice. See page 253J for tips on helping children choose books.

SKILL TRACE

CONTRACTIONS WITH *NOT*

INTRODUCE	218N
REVIEW	247C, 251B, 253B, 253L
T TEST	Bk 1-5

BELOW-LEVEL

Some children may have difficulty understanding where to place the apostrophe. Have them use letter tiles to spell word pairs such as *did not* or *has not*. Then have children push the words together. Point to the *o* in *not* and explain that it will be dropped out to form a contraction. Tell children to remove the *o* and to put an apostrophe in its place. If there is no apostrophe tile, create one on an index card or blank tile.

ENGLISH-LANGUAGE LEARNERS

Visit The Learning Site:
www.harcourtschool.com
See Go for Grammar Gold, Multimedia Grammar Glossary.

Name _____

Contractions with Not

▶ Match each pair of words with its contraction.

isn't	wasn't	don't
aren't	wouldn't	can't
hasn't	haven't	won't

1. is not   aren't
2. have not   don't
3. will not   wasn't
4. was not   isn't
5. do not   haven't
6. are not   won't
7. can not   wouldn't
8. would not   can't

SCHOOL-HOME CONNECTION
Ask your child to read the contractions in the boxes and tell what two words form them.

145

▲ Language Handbook, p.145

***Baboon* 253L**

Books for All Learners

Reinforcing Skills and Strategies

■ BELOW-LEVEL

Baboon's Park

 Phonics: Vowel Digraph /oo/oo

 Vocabulary: *against, careful, fire, quietly, shook*

 Focus Skill: Plot

SUMMARY Baboon is unhappy because he doesn't have a park, so his friends come up with a creative solution.

 Visit *The Learning Site:* www.harcourtschool.com See Resources for Parents and Teachers: Books for All Learners.

BEFORE READING

Build Background Have children tell about the kinds of equipment they might see on a playground. Let volunteers tell about their favorite things to play with on a playground.

Preview/Set Purpose Have children identify the title and help them read it. Point out the author and the illustrator. Then have children look at the first few pages of the book and predict what the story is about. Have children set a purpose for reading, such as *I want to find out what Baboon's park looks like.*

READING THE BOOK

Pages 2–3 Who sent Baboon a letter? (his friend Tiger) NOTE DETAILS

Pages 4–5 How does Baboon feel when he is talking to Ape? (sad) What clues do you get from the story? (He is not in the mood to play and he begins to cry.) DETERMINE CHARACTERS' EMOTIONS

Pages 6–7 What problem does Baboon have? (He wants a park like Tiger's park.) PLOT

Pages 8–10 How is Baboon's problem solved? (Ape's dad and Baboon's dad use the other animals to make a park.) PLOT

Pages 11–12 Do you think you would like Baboon's park? Why or why not? (Possible response: Yes, because I would like to play with Baboon.) MAKE JUDGMENTS

RESPONDING

Draw a Park Invite each child to draw a park that contains some of the things shown and described in the story. Have children share their drawings and point out the elements from the story.

Oral Reading Fluency

Use Books for All Learners to promote oral reading fluency.

See **Fluency Routine Cards**, pp. T83–T84.

▲ p. 2530   ▲ p. 253P

■ ON-LEVEL

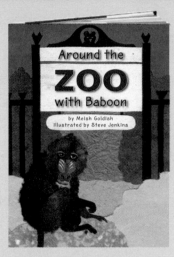

Around the Zoo with Baboon

 Phonics: Vowel Digraph /o͞o/oo

 Vocabulary: *against, careful, fire, quietly, shook*

 Focus Skill: Plot

SUMMARY Baboon learns about his animal neighbors when he is brought to the zoo.

 Visit *The Learning Site:*
www.harcourtschool.com
See Resources for Parents and
Teachers: Books for All Learners.

BEFORE READING

Build Background Invite children to share experiences they may have had making new friends. Have volunteers tell how they have felt when they met someone new.

Preview/Set Purpose Have children identify the title and help them read it. Point out the author and the illustrator. Then have children look at the first few pages of the book and predict what the story is about. Help children set a purpose for reading, such as *I want to find out what Baboon does at the zoo.*

READING THE BOOK

Pages 2–4 What words would you use to describe how Baboon feels? (*curious, friendly, happy, polite*) DETERMINE CHARACTERS' TRAITS

Pages 5–7 What does Baboon do after Goose invites her to come in the pool? (She climbs around the zoo and meets Peacock.) SEQUENCE

Pages 8–10 Why do you think Baboon does not sit on the roof with Rooster? (She wants to meet all of her new neighbors.) PLOT

Pages 11–13 What is this story mostly about? (Baboon learns about her animal neighbors when she is brought to the zoo.) MAIN IDEA

Pages 14–16 How does the story end? (Baboon is happy because she made many friends.) PLOT

RESPONDING

Act It Out Invite groups of children to act out *Around the Zoo with Baboon.* Encourage them to include Baboon saying *"good afternoon"* and other dialogue from the story.

Books for
All Learners
Reinforcing Skills and Strategies

■ ADVANCED

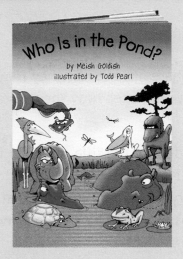

Who Is in the Pond?
by Meish Goldish
illustrated by Todd Pearl

Who Is in the Pond?

☑ **Phonics: Vowel Digraph /o͞o/oo**

☑ **Vocabulary:** *against, careful, fire, quietly, shook*

☑ **Focus Skill: Plot**

SUMMARY Animals use a pond of water in different ways.

**Visit *The Learning Site:*
www.harcourtschool.com**
See Resources for Parents and Teachers: Books for All Learners.

BEFORE READING

Build Background Have children tell about the kinds of animals that may live near a pond. Encourage them to tell in what ways the animals may need the pond.

Preview/Set Purpose Have children identify the title and help them read it. Point out the author and the illustrator. Then have children look at the first few pages of the book and predict what the story is about. Have children set a purpose for reading, such as *I want to find out which animals are in the pond.*

READING THE BOOK

Pages 2–4 Why do the fish swim away from the pelican? (They do not want to be eaten by the pelican.) PLOT

Pages 5–6 How are the pelican and the hippo alike? (They both find food in the pond.) MAKE COMPARISONS

Pages 7–10 What do the baboons do after they drink from the pond? (They groom each other.) SEQUENCE

Pages 11–12 How do you know that there are people near the pond? (There is a grass hut in the picture on page 11.) RELATE PICTURES TO TEXT

Pages 13–16 Why do you think the crocodile does not chase the turtle? (The turtle hides in the mud on the bottom of the pond; the turtle is difficult to see.) PLOT

RESPONDING

Retell the Story Have children retell the story from the point of view of one of the animals in the story. Encourage them to use the sequence words *first, next,* and *last.* Invite them to elaborate by telling how each animal feels about using the pond. Guide children in staying on topic while speaking.

Managing Small Groups

While you work with small groups, have other children do the following:
- Self-Selected Reading
- Practice Pages
- Cross-Curricular Centers
- Journal Writing

BELOW-LEVEL	ON-LEVEL	ADVANCED	ELL
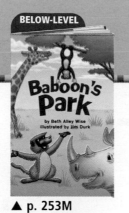	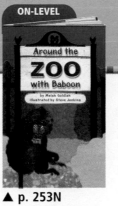		
▲ p. 253M	▲ p. 253N		

■ ENGLISH-LANGUAGE LEARNERS

Let's Visit the Zoo

 Strong Picture Support

 Concept Vocabulary

 Theme Related

SUMMARY Many kinds of animals live in the zoo, and each one is different.

 **Visit *The Learning Site:*
www.harcourtschool.com**
See Resources for Parents and Teachers: Books for All Learners.

BEFORE READING

Build Background Have volunteers talk about the kinds of animals that live in the zoo. Let children share experiences they may have had visiting a zoo.

Preview/Set Purpose Have children identify the title and help them read it. Point out the author and the illustrator. Then have children look at the first few pages of the book and predict what the story will be about. Help children set a purpose for reading, such as *I want to find out which animals are in this zoo.*

READING THE BOOK

Pages 2–4 What has black and white stripes? (a zebra) NOTE DETAILS, RELATE PICTURES TO TEXT

Pages 5–7 What has a very long neck? (a giraffe) NOTE DETAILS, RELATE PICTURES TO TEXT

Pages 8–11 How are camels and kangaroos different? (Camels have humps and kangaroos have pouches.) COMPARE/CONTRAST

Page 12 How do the pictures help you learn about the animals? (Possible responses: They help me remember what each animal looks like; the pictures help me see what is special about each animal.) DETERMINE TEXT STRUCTURE

RESPONDING

Sort the Animals Invite children to cut out magazine pictures of animals from the story, as well as other animals, including pets and farm animals. Help children sort the pictures into the following categories—pets, farm animals, zoo animals.

Theme Wrap-Up & Review

Making Connections

Pupil Edition
Page through the stories with children. Have volunteers identify particular characters and the type of environment they live in. Discuss: *Which environment do you like best? Why?* Have children draw and write about their choices. Ask children to share and compare their responses with others.

Big Books
Have volunteers summarize the stories using sequence words such as *first, next,* and *last.* Page through the books as they summarize the events. Discuss: *Who is your favorite character in each book? Why?* Encourage volunteers to turn to specific pages and explain the reasons for their choices. Ask other children to share their choices as well.

Theme Project

Dioramas
Revisit the dioramas with children. Have children assess their own work by describing what they learned from their research and by working on the diorama. Children might like to add drawings of the places they learned about in this theme to their portfolios. Discuss how investigating another environment relates to the theme "Going Places."

Cross-Curricular Centers

Visit the various centers and review activities in which children participated during this theme.

SCIENCE
Discuss what children learned about birds, bears, pigs, and animal eating and sleeping habits. Talk about the signs of spring. Have children explain how the sun's heat makes water dry up and how the sun creates shadows.

MATH
Discuss number sense, estimation, and measurement by reviewing children's work.

SOCIAL STUDIES
Ask children to share their bird's-eye view of their school, home, or neighborhood. Using a globe, review what children learned about seasons around the world. Have children talk about city life versus farm life and about jobs people do at night.

HEALTH
Review the chart showing clothing appropriate for different types of weather.

COMPUTER
Ask children to choose a piece of writing to read aloud to the group.

ARTS
Ask volunteers to share a favorite drawing or their bird collage. Have children sing their innovation on "The Bear Went Over the Mountain."

REVIEW

Phonics

Long Vowel Word Game Have groups use their *Word Builders* and *Word Builder Cards* to play a Long Vowel Game. Have them use *ai*, *ay*, and *igh* word patterns. One child should say a word, while the other children use their *Word Builder Cards* to spell it. Correct responses earn one point. Have children take turns calling out words. The player with the most points at the end of the game is the winner.

Comprehension

Main Idea Review the concept of main idea—what a story is mostly about. Have partners pick a favorite book from the Browsing Boxes and read it aloud together. Provide each pair with an index card and have them write a sentence on it that tells the main idea of the story.

Grammar

Verbs To review verbs, ask children to play a Silly Verb Game. Reproduce the text from a few pages in one of the theme's stories, but delete the action verbs. Do not show the page to children. Brainstorm a list of verbs with children and write them on the board. Have children take turns picking a verb from the list. Substitute each verb in place of the missing verb. When the story is complete, read the silly new version to children.

Vocabulary

Charades Provide small groups with copies of the word cards, pages T34–T38. Have children sit in a circle. Have one child pick a card and act out the word. The other players guess the word. The first player to respond correctly must use the word in a sentence.

High-Frequency Words

Play a Game Distribute to pairs of children copies of the word cards for high-frequency words, pages T34–T38. Have partners turn the cards face down. One player picks a card and writes a blank for each letter on a sheet of paper. The other player guesses letters and fills in the blanks. After each round, have children use the high-frequency word in a sentence.

Spelling

Word Building Have children use their *Word Builders* and *Word Builder Cards* to review Spelling Words. Start with the sequence *right, might, mind, find, fold, told, tube*, and *tooth*. Then have children build *those, rode, most, use, rule, child*.

Name _____

Practice Test

▶ Read each sentence. Look at how the two words are spelled. Fill in the oval next to the correct word.

SAMPLE: Most _____ birds are out in the daytime.
  ◯ wiled   ⬤ wild

1. Some birds only come out at _____.
  ⬤ night   ◯ nite

2. _____ night birds see in the dark.
  ◯ Must   ⬤ Most

3. Lots of birds can fly _____ in the sky.
  ◯ hie   ⬤ high

4. Do not try to put a wild bird in a _____.
  ⬤ cage   ◯ caje

5. That would make the bird _____.
  ◯ aingry   ⬤ angry

SPELLING PRACTICE BOOK
THEME 6 PRACTICE TEST 83

▲ Spelling Practice Book, pp. 83–84

▲ *Little Fox Goes to the End of the World*
by Ann Tompert, illustrated by John Wallner

THEME: Going Places

Little Fox fantasizes about going to the end of the world. She expresses to her mother the places, animals, and challenges she meets along the way. Even though her mother questions some of Little Fox's brave adventures, Little Fox always has solutions to convince her mother that everything will work out.

GENRE: Animal Fantasy

SUMMARY: Little Fox's fantastical journey through a deep forest, icy mountains, hot desert, crocodile filled river, and open sea lead her to the end of the world. At each place, brave Little Fox is faced with challenges that she conquers with ease. Throughout the trip, her mother is there for encouragement and reassurance.

Library Books

ACCESS PRIOR KNOWLEDGE

Talk about places around the world. Write *forest* on the board and elicit from children some animals that could been seen there. Then ask them to name other places around the world and describe the setting and common animals that exist at that place.

DEVELOP VOCABULARY AND CONCEPTS

Discuss problems and solutions. Encourage children to think of ways to solve the following problems:

- **What could you do if you get lost?**
- **What could you do if you feel very hot?**
- **What could you do if you are scared of an animal?**

After children suggest several solutions, ask these additional questions using these story words and talk about their meanings: *strayed, den, lend, lasso, capture.*

- **If a little fox *strayed* from its *den*, what could happen?**
- **How do you ask someone to *lend* you something?**
- **How do you *capture* something with a *lasso*?**

INTRODUCE THE BOOK

Discuss settings and characters. Display the book *Little Fox Goes to the End of the World*. Read aloud the title, and the author's and illustrator's names. Preview the illustrations that display the different settings in the story, and elicit from children where the settings take place. Then have a volunteer point out and name some of the characters in the story.

SET PURPOSE/PREDICT

Set purposes for reading. Have children set a purpose for reading the story. (Possible response: to find out how Little Fox gets to the end of the world) Have children predict from the illustrations what is going to happen to Little Fox on her journey.

Directed Reading Focus on making inferences by asking questions such as the following:

- **Why do you think Little Fox's mother is so scared and Little Fox is so brave throughout the story?**
- **What were some of the ways Little Fox solved her problems?**

Independent Reading After children have read the story on their own, have them think of some other ways Little Fox will solve her problems. Children can draw and write about their ideas.

Teacher Read-Aloud As you read the story, pause and have children predict how Little Fox will solve her problems. For example, when Little Fox encounters bears in the deep forest, have children predict how Little Fox will make friends with the bears.

PERSONAL RESPONSE:

- **How did the Little Fox finally get to the end of the world?**
- **What were some of the items Little Fox used to help her travels around the world and how did these items help her?**
- **If you were Little Fox, how would you get to the end of the world?**

SOCIAL STUDIES: Writing Postcards Explain to children that people like to travel many different places around the world. Remind children about postcards and have them tell about them. Then have them create a postcard from a place that Little Fox visited. Direct children to write a postcard to Little Fox's mother, pretending to be Little Fox. Display postcards on a bulletin board. INDIVIDUAL

ENGLISH-LANGUAGE LEARNERS

Point out to children the past-tense verbs in the story, such as *called, asked, cried, said, shouted, exclaimed,* and *laughed.* Use each word in a sentence; then encourage volunteers to use a word in a sentence.

Library Books

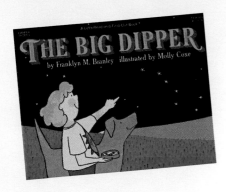

▲ *The Big Dipper*
**by Franklyn M. Branley,
illustrated by Molly Coxe**

THEME: Going Places
In this book, children will be introduced to simple astronomical facts and to the pleasures of stargazing.

GENRE: Nonfiction
SUMMARY: A little girl shares with the reader her knowledge of the stars, including information about the Big Dipper, the North Star, and the Little Dipper.

About the Author
The Big Dipper was written by **Franklyn M. Branley.** Mr. Branley, an astronomer, has written many books for children on scientific subjects. He is former chairman of the Hayden Planetarium of the American Museum of Natural History in New York City, and lives in Sag Harbor, New York.

ACCESS PRIOR KNOWLEDGE

Talk about stars. Tell children that people have been looking at the stars and studying them for a long, long time. Have children share facts they know about the stars. Ask whether children have ever seen the Big Dipper and what they know about it.

DEVELOP VOCABULARY AND CONCEPTS

Have children arrange stars in patterns. Draw and cut out six stars. Have six children arrange the stars in a design that they like. Then have six other children arrange the stars in a different design. Continue, perhaps varying the number of stars, until all of the children have participated. As children do this activity, use these story words and talk about their meanings: *touch, almost, direction, imagine, toward.*

INTRODUCE THE BOOK

Discuss this nonfiction book. Display the book *The Big Dipper*. Read aloud the title and share the information about the author. Tell children that this is not a make-believe story, but a book of real facts. Then preview the illustrations and have children tell what they think they might learn from reading this book. (Possible response: true information about stars)

SET PURPOSE/PREDICT

Children set purposes for reading. Ask children to predict the kinds of facts they might learn from this book. Have them set a purpose for reading. (Possible response: to find out why the author named the book *The Big Dipper*.)

Directed Reading Help children make connections between text and illustrations by asking questions such as the following:

Page 13: **What did the girl draw? What do the numbers mean?**
Page 17: **What are the stars you see in this picture?**

Partner Reading As children read the book, encourage them to pause frequently to discuss the information and the illustrations. Suggest that partners reread together any pages they may not understand.

Independent Reading After rereading the story on their own, children can draw and write in their journal about what they learned.

Teacher Read-Aloud As you read the book aloud to children, you may want to pause occasionally to have volunteers retell in their own words the information on the page.

OPTIONS FOR RESPONDING

PERSONAL RESPONSE:

- **Why is it important to look at the illustrations when you read about facts?**
- **Why do you think the author chose to write about the Big Dipper instead of another group of stars?**
- **What is the most interesting fact you learned from this book? Why does that interest you?**

SCIENCE: Use a Compass Provide an inexpensive compass for children to use. Explain how to use the compass, and have children experiment with it. Children can make signs for the classroom, showing the directions north, south, east, and west. They can then play games using the direction words to direct classmates to move around the room. SMALL GROUP

ENGLISH-LANGUAGE LEARNERS

Use the illustrations to help children understand the meanings of words such as *night, stars, dipper, handle,* and *bowl*. Have children point to the appropriate part of the illustration as they repeat the word.

▲ *Peeping and Sleeping*
**by Fran Manushkin,
illustrated by Jennifer Plecas**

THEME: Going Places

Children will see how a boy named
Barry learns something new by taking a
night walk to the pond with his father.

GENRE: Realistic Fiction

SUMMARY: When Barry hears a
peeping sound in the night, his father
takes him down to the pond to discover
the cause for himself. Barry is delighted
to see the tiny frogs called *spring peepers*. Barry and his father take off their
slippers and hop home, imitating the
peepers. At home, Barry finds one of the
peepers in his slipper. Soon the little
frog is on his way back to the pond, and
Barry is fast asleep.

About the Author

Fran Manushkin was born in Chicago,
Illinois. She is the youngest of five chil-
dren. She taught school, and at one
time, she was a tour guide at Lincoln
Center for the Performing Arts in New
York City.

Library Books

Talk about frogs. Ask children what they know about frogs, and where
they live, what they eat, the sounds they make, and so on. After children
have shared their information, you may want to tell them that there are
many different kinds of frogs, including large ones with deep voices and little
tiny ones with high voices that say, "Peep peep."

DEVELOP VOCABULARY AND CONCEPTS

Children play a game that previews the plot. Choose one child to be
"It." This child covers his or her eyes as you hide a toy frog or picture of a frog
in the classroom. The child then searches for the hidden frog, while the other
children call out *peep-peep*. Children should speak very softly when "It" is far
from the frog, and louder as "It" gets closer. After the frog is found, you can
play the game again with a new "It" and a new hiding place. As children do
this activity, use these story words and talk about their meanings: *promise,
surrounded, guessed, zillion.*

INTRODUCE THE BOOK

Discuss the setting. Display the book *Peeping and Sleeping*. Read aloud
the title and share the information about the author. Then preview the illustrations and have children tell what time of day this story takes place. Ask
children how a night-time setting might be important to the story.

SET PURPOSE/PREDICT

Have children set purposes for reading. Ask children to draw pictures
in their journal to predict who might be peeping and who might be sleeping in
the story. Then have them set a purpose for reading. (Possible response: to find
out what the people in the story are doing outside at night in their pajamas)

Directed Reading Focus on making predictions by asking questions such as the following:

Page 12: **What do you think Barry will see?**
Page 26: **Where do you think the sound is coming from?**

Partner Reading As children read the book, encourage them to pause after reading each page to talk about what is happening in the story and what might happen next.

Independent Reading After reading the story on their own, children can return to their journals and write or draw to confirm their predictions about who was peeping and who was sleeping.

Teacher Read-Aloud Help children identify with story characters by telling them to imagine how they would feel if they were doing what Barry does in the story.

OPTIONS FOR RESPONDING

PERSONAL RESPONSE:

- **Why did Barry's father take Barry to the pond at night in his pajamas?**
- **How did the frog that was in Barry's slipper know the way back to the pond?**
- **Why did Barry say that his father wouldn't hear another peep out of him?**

SCIENCE: All About Spring Have children recall that the little frogs are called spring peepers and that the story takes place on a warm spring night. Discuss what else children know about the weather during that season and events that take place in nature at that time. Then children can draw pictures that show plants and animals in springtime. Have them write captions for their pictures. INDIVIDUAL

ENGLISH-LANGUAGE LEARNERS

Below | On-Level | Advanced | ELL

Explain to children that *peep-peep* is the way we describe in English the sound the little frogs make. Help children appreciate the word play in the phrases *peep-leap* and *peep-sleep* by showing what *leap* and *sleep* mean and emphasizing the rhymes.

Assessing Student Progress
to Modify Instruction

- **End-of-Selection Tests** (in Practice Book)

- **Oral Reading and Fluency Assessment**

Monitoring of Progress

END-OF-SELECTION TESTS

IF you want to monitor children's progress in selection vocabulary and comprehension	**Then** administer the multiple-choice and short answer diagnostic **End-of-Selection Tests**.

Multiple Measures

Anecdotal Records To track the progress of individual children's literacy development, establish procedures for keeping anecdotal records. Consider setting aside several pages in a spiral notebook for each child in the class. Focus on one to three behaviors or understandings during each week.

Checklists Use the checklists on pages R20–R21 to track children's progress in Listening, Speaking, Viewing, Reading, and Writing.

Portfolios Have children keep copies of their works-in-progress and final drafts of writing assignments In a Working Portfolio. Encourage children to choose their best work and keep it in a Show Portfolio. Use teacher-student conferences to review children's progress in writing.

Reading Notebooks To learn about children's independent or self-selected reading, have children keep a log of their reading in a Reading Notebook. Encourage them to keep lists of titles, authors, and genres that they enjoy.

- **Reading and Language Skills Assessment: Book 1-5 Posttest**
- **Reading and Language Skills Assessment: End-of-Year Test**
- **Holistic Assessment Book 1-5**

Summative Assessment

READING AND LANGUAGE SKILLS ASSESSMENT: Posttest **IF** you want to evaluate a child's mastery of the skills in this theme,	**Then** administer the **Reading and Language Skills Assessment**.
END-OF-YEAR READING AND LANGUAGE SKILLS ASSESSMENT **IF** you want to evaluate a child's mastery of the skills in themes 1–6,	**Then** administer the **End-of-Year Reading and Language Skills Assessment**.
HOLISTIC ASSESSMENT **IF** you want to know more about a child's ability to read a passage and apply literal, inferential, and critical thinking skills in a global and holistic manner, revising and editing skills in writing, and how he or she responds to multiple-choice and short and extended open-ended questions,	**Then** administer the **Holistic Assessment**.

Additional Support Activities

Going Places
Additional Support Activities

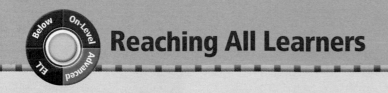

Additional Support Activities
Phonemic Awareness

**For More
Intensive Instruction**

**See Intervention
Resource Kit, Lesson 27** for additional **preteach** and **reteach** activities.

■ BELOW-LEVEL

Reteach: Distinguish Long Vowel /ī/

Tell children you will be saying pairs of words. Have them tell you which word in each pair has the sound /ī/ as in *tight*.

light, lit

bit, bite

sight, sit

flight, flit

fit, fight

kit, kite

high, hay

late, light

rate, right

might, mate

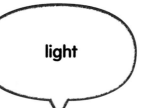

light

■ ADVANCED

Extend: Substitute Phonemes

Tell children you will be saying some words with the long *i* sound. Tell them to listen to the word to see where the /ī/ sound occurs, and then make a different word by changing the /ī/ sound to a different vowel sound.

light

sight

fight

flight

high

sigh

might

right

■ ENGLISH-LANGUAGE LEARNERS

Reteach: Listen for /ī/

Help children focus on the sound. Ask children to slowly segment the sounds in the following words:

high   **fight**   **might**   **sigh**   **right**

Ask children how all the words are the same, leading them to conclude that they all have the same vowel sound—/ī/.

For More Language Development

See English-Language Learners Resource Kit, Lesson 27 for additional **preteach** and **reteach** activities.

Additional Support Activities

■ BELOW-LEVEL

Reteach: Word Blending

Work with children to make and blend /ī/*igh* words. As you demonstrate each step, using a pocket chart and *Letter Cards,* have children repeat the steps after you, using their *Word Builders* and *Word Builder Cards (e, f, g, h, i, l, s, t)*. Use the following as a model for blending instruction for the word *sight.* Hold up the *s* card and say /ss/. Hold up the *i, g,* and *h* cards together and say /īī/. Hold up the *t* card and say /tt/. Have children blend the word *sight* along with you.

Have children blend and read new words by telling them:

For More Intensive Instruction

See Intervention Resource Kit, Lesson 27 for additional **preteach** and **reteach** activities.

- Add *l* after the *s.* What word did you make?

s	l	i	g	h	t

- Take away the *igh.* In their place add *ee.* What word did you make?

s	l	e	e	t

- Change the *s* to *f.* What word did you make?

f	l	e	e	t

- Take away the *ee.* In their place add *igh.* What word did you make?

f	l	i	g	h	t

- Take away the *l.* What word did you make?

f	i	g	h	t

■ ADVANCED

Extend: Write Rhymes

Suggest that children begin by listing all the -*ight* words they can think of. Then have them make up a poem of two to four lines that contains -*ight* rhymes. Children can then exchange poems with a partner and read their partner's poem aloud.

■ ENGLISH-LANGUAGE LEARNERS

Reteach: Reading *igh* Words

Have children work in small groups to reinforce the relationship between the spelling *igh* and the /ī/ sound. Make and distribute word cards with -*igh* and -*ight* words to each group. Each child can pick a card, read the word aloud, and then use the word in a sentence. Repeat until each child has picked and read at least one card.

**For More
Language Development**

See **English-Language
Learners Resource Kit,
Lesson 27** for additional
preteach and **reteach**
activities.

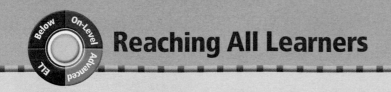

Reaching All Learners

Additional Support Activities
Comprehension and Skills

■ BELOW-LEVEL

Reteach: Identify Plot

Divide the class into groups. Assign each group a story the class has read recently. Have each group discuss the plot of the assigned story and decide what happens at the beginning, what happens in the middle, and what happens at the end. When all groups have finished, have each group tell their classmates what they have determined about the story's plot.

For More Intensive Instruction

See Intervention Resource Kit, Lesson 27 for additional **preteach** and **reteach** activities.

■ ADVANCED

Extend: Three-Person Stories

Arrange children in groups of three to practice applying plot elements. Tell each child to create a sentence that will serve as the beginning of a story. Then have children give their paper to the group member on their right. Each child reads the beginning and adds a sentence to make the middle of the story. Have children switch again and write a sentence to end the story.

> The boy ran up a hill.
> The wind blew his kite away.
> He went home and made a new kite.

■ ENGLISH-LANGUAGE LEARNERS

Reteach: Pantomime

Have groups of children pantomime the events of "The Story of a Blue Bird." Tell them to act out their pantomimes in sections, clearly showing the beginning, middle, and end of the story. After they have practiced, allow children to present their pantomimes to the group.

For More Language Development

See English-Language Learners Resource Kit, Lesson 27 for additional **preteach** and **reteach** activities.

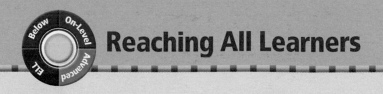
Additional Support Activities
Phonemic Awareness

■ **BELOW-LEVEL**

Reteach: Blend Words with /ā/

Tell children that together you will make words. First, you will say a consonant sound, then they will say the long vowel sound of *a*, and then together you will say the word you made. Model by saying, *If I say /r/, you will say /ā/, and then together we will say* ray. Continue with the following sounds and words:

/b/ *(bay)*	/s/ *(say)*	/w/ *(way)*
/j/ *(jay)*	/h/ *(hay)*	/p/ *(pay)*
/d/ *(day)*	/l/ *(lay)*	/m/ *(may)*

Then tell children that you will turn the activity around. They will say /ā/ first, and then you will say a consonant sound to add and make a word. Model by saying, *You will say /ā/, I will say /p/, and then together we will say* ape. Continue with these sounds and words.

/d/ *(aid)*	/j/ *(age)*	/m/ *(aim)*
/b/ *(Abe)*	/s/ *(ace)*	/t/ *(ate)*

For More Intensive Instruction

See Intervention Resource Kit, Lesson 28 for additional **preteach** and **reteach** activities.

■ ADVANCED

Extend: Phoneme Substitution

Tell children that you will say some words and they will change the vowel sound to the long vowel sound of *a* to make a new word. Model by saying *food*. *If I change the vowel sound to /ā/, the word is now* fade. Continue with the following words:

woo *(way)*	**all** *(ail)*	**stew** *(stay)*
odd *(aid)*	**bee** *(bay)*	**grow** *(gray)*
rise *(raise)*	**am** *(aim)*	**brown** *(brain)*

■ ENGLISH-LANGUAGE LEARNERS

Reteach: Identify and Segment Words with /ā/

To help children identify words with the long vowel sound of *a* and associate meanings with those words, provide pairs of pictures or objects, one with /ā/ and one without. Name the items for children and have them point to the picture whose name has the sound /ā/ and then repeat and segment the picture name. For example, you might show pictures representing *night* and *day*. Say the appropriate name as you show each picture and model: *Night/day.* Hold up the day picture and say: *This picture's name has the sound /ā/. I would point to it and say* day. /d/ /ā/.

Continue showing and naming the pictures, having children point to, name, and segment the name of the /ā/ object in each pair.

night	**day** *(day, /d/ /ā/)*
bay	**river** *(bay, /b/ /ā/)*
robin	**jay** *(jay, /j/ /ā/)*
brown	**gray** *(gray, /g/ /r/ /ā/)*
clay	**glue** *(clay, /k/ /l/ /ā/)*

For More Language Development

See English-Language Learners Resource Kit, Lesson 28 for additional **reteach** activities.

Additional Support Activities

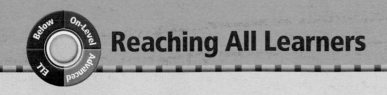

For More Intensive Instruction

See Intervention Resource Kit, Lesson 28 for additional **preteach** and **reteach** activities.

■ BELOW-LEVEL

Reteach: Word Blending

Demonstrate making and blending the words *say*, *sail*, *mail*, *play*, *rain*, and *brain*, using a pocket chart and *Letter Cards.* Have children repeat each step after you, using their *Word Builders* and *Word Builder Cards.*

■ Place the letters *s*, *a*, and *y* in the pocket chart with the *s* separated from the *a* and *y*, which are together. Have children do the same.

■ Point to *s*. Say /ss/. Point to the *a* and *y* and say /āā/.

■ Slide *ay* next to the *s*. Move your hand under the letters and blend the sounds, elongating them—/ssāā/. Have children repeat after you.

■ Then have children read the word *say* aloud.

FROG AND TOAD
ALL YEAR
by Arnold Lobel

■ ADVANCED

Extend: Create an /ā/ Rap

Have children work alone or with a partner to create their own rap presentation, using as many words with the long vowel sound of *a* as possible. Encourage children to tape-record their rap and play it back for classmates. If a number of different raps are recorded, more advanced children may listen to make a list of all the /ā/ words they hear.

> I'm Dee Jay
> And I'm here to say . . .

■ ENGLISH-LANGUAGE LEARNERS

Reteach: Read Words with /ā/

Work individually with children to read very simple text that has examples of words with long vowels /ā/*ai, ay*, such as the stories in *Decodable Book 28*. Read one page at a time aloud, pausing for the child to provide each word with /ā/*ai, ay*. Before going on to the next page, either point to something in the illustration that relates to an /ā/ word and have the child say the word and find it on the page, or point to an /ā/ word and ask a question about it. For example, point to the word *rain* and say *What is this word? Where do you see rain in the picture?* You may want to have the child retell what happens on that page before going on.

For More Language Development

See English-Language Learners Resource Kit, Lesson 28 for additional **reteach** activities.

Additional Support Activities
Vocabulary and High-Frequency Words

■ BELOW-LEVEL

Reteach: Review Vocabulary

Display *Word Cards caught, hurried, near,* and *son* or write the words on the board. Have children find each word in "Frog and Toad All Year" and read aloud the sentence that contains the word. You may wish to follow the same procedure to review the high-frequency words *cold* and *sure*.

For More Intensive Instruction

See Intervention Resource Kit, Lesson 28 for additional **preteach** and **reteach** activities.

Reteach: Talk About It

Display the *Word Cards* for the high-frequency words *cold* and *sure*. Point to the word *cold* and have children turn to *Pupil Edition*, page 45. Read this page aloud and have children look for and point to the word *cold*. Then call on a child to read aloud the sentence with the word *cold*. Use page 56 to review the word *sure*. Follow a similar procedure to reteach the vocabulary words *caught, hurried, near,* and *son*.

cold   sure

■ ADVANCED

Extend: Play a Matching Game

Distribute Individual Word Cards *caught, hurried, near*, and *son* to children. Have children make a second card for each word, giving the definition of the word. Have them play a matching game with a partner by mixing up a set of all eight cards and placing them facedown. Players take turns turning over two cards at a time. If the two cards have a matching word and definition, the player keeps both cards. If not, the cards are turned facedown again. Play continues until all the cards are matched. Follow a similar procedure to review the high-frequency words *cold* and *sure*.

hurried

moved fast

■ ENGLISH-LANGUAGE LEARNERS

Reteach: Identify Vocabulary

Display *Word Cards caught, hurried, near*, and *son*. Say each word aloud as you show it, and have children repeat after you. Then mix up the cards and place them faceup on a table in front of children. Call the words out at random and have children take turns picking up the card for the word you say and repeating it. When children seem fairly confident with identifying the words, review the meanings of the words, using a combination of definitions, drawings, pantomime, and example sentences as needed. Repeat the process of having children identify and name the *Word Cards*, but this time call out definitions. Follow a similar procedure to reteach the high-frequency words *cold* and *sure*.

For More Language Development

See English-Language Learners Resource Kit, Lesson 28 for additional **reteach** activities.

Additional Support Activities
Phonemic Awareness

■ BELOW-LEVEL

Reteach: Blend Onsets and Rimes

Model how to blend an onset and rime by saying /p/ /īn/, /pīn/.
What word did I say? (pine) Say the following words as onsets and
rimes and have children say the blended words.

/m/ /īn/ *(mine)*	/f/ /īn/ *(fine)*
/r/ /īs/ *(rice)*	/r/ /īnd/ *(rind)*
/l/ /īn/ *(line)*	/m/ /īld/ *(mild)*
/f/ /īnd/ *(find)*	/n/ /īt/ *(night)*
/p/ /īl/ *(pile)*	/p/ /īnt/ *(pint)*
/l/ /īt/ *(light)*	/w/ /īld/ *(wild)*

**For More
Intensive Instruction**

**See Intervention
Resource Kit, Lesson 29**
for additional **preteach**
and **reteach** activities.

■ ADVANCED

Extend: Distinguish /ī/ from Other Vowel Sounds

Read the following groups of words. Have children identify the words that contain the sound /ī/ by saying "first," "second," or "third."

bond	bind	**band** (second)
lit	let	**light** (third)
mill	mile	**milk** (second)
wild	will	**wilt** (first)

Extend the activity by saying the following and having children identify the two words that have the sound /ī/.

mine	mind	**mint** (first and second)
fin	fine	**find** (second and third)
hind	hid	**hide** (first and third)

■ ENGLISH-LANGUAGE LEARNERS

Reteach: Listen for /ī/

Have children repeat after you as you say the following, elongating the long vowel sound of *i*. As you say the last sentence, reach into the air and pretend to take the word.

> /ī/, /mīn/ *Mine* has the sound /ī/.
> /ī/, /chīld/ *Child* has the sound /ī/.
> *Child* has the sound /ī/. *Child* is mine.

Say the following words. When children hear *a* word with /ī/, they should say "*(Word)* is mine" as they pantomime taking it.

nine	time	cup
light	hot	hide
child	name	pie

You may also want children to tell the meaning of each /ī/ word.

For More Language Development

See English-Language Learners Resource Kit, Lesson 29 for additional reteach activities.

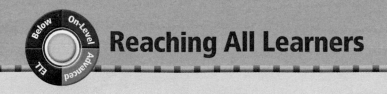

Additional Support Activities

For More Intensive Instruction

See Intervention Resource Kit, Lesson 29 for additional **preteach** and **reteach** activities.

■ **BELOW-LEVEL**

Reteach: Word Blending

Demonstrate making and blending *find*, *mind*, *kind*, *wild*, *mild*, and *child*, using a pocket chart and *Letter Cards*. Have children repeat the steps using their *Word Builders* and *Word Builder Cards*. Use the following to model blending for the word *find*. Hold up the *f* card and say /ff/. Hold up the *i* card and say /ī̆/. Hold up the *n* and card and say /nn/. Hold up the *d* card and say /dd/.

■ Place letters *f, i, n, d* in the pocket chart with the letters separated. Have children do the same.

■ Point to *f* Say /ff/. Point to *i*. Say /ī̆/.

■ Slide the *i* next to the *f*. Move your hand under the letters and blend the sounds, elongating them—/ffī̆/. Have children repeat after you.

■ Point to *n*. Say /nn/. Point to *d*. Say /dd/. Slide the letters together and say /nndd/, elongating the sounds. Have children do the same.

■ Slide the *nd* next to the *fi*. Slide your hand under *find* and blend by elongating the sounds—/ffī̆nndd/. Have children do the same.

■ Then, have children read the word *find* along with you.

FISHING BEARS

■ ADVANCED

Extend: What Will I Find?

Tell children you want to create a group story with long *i* words. Explain that each child will add a sentence or a phrase with at least one long *i* word. Start the story with:

What will I find when I turn on the light?
I will find a *white* rabbit.

Point out that the word *white* contains the long vowel sound of *i*. Have each child repeat the story to that point before extending it. For example, the first child might say:

What will I find when I turn on the light?
I will find a *white* rabbit and a *pile* of carrots.

After each turn, ask the group to identify the long *i* word that was just added. Continue playing until children can no longer remember the whole story.

■ ENGLISH-LANGUAGE LEARNERS

Make word cards for *child, mild, wild, nine, line, fine, dine, shine, spine,* and *pine.* Hold up and read aloud each card. Have children repeat the word. Call on children to choose a word card and act out the word or use it in a sentence.

child

shine

nine

**For More
Language Development**

**See English-Language
Learners Resource Kit,
Lesson 29** for additional
reteach activities.

Additional Support Activities
Comprehension and Skills

For More Intensive Instruction

See Intervention Resource Kit, Lesson 29 for additional **preteach** and **reteach** activities.

■ **BELOW-LEVEL**

Reteach: Practice Main Ideas

Write the following sentences on strips. Call on children to come to the front of the room and display each strip so the group can read it aloud.

Rover can pull a sled.
Lad helps Jane cross the street.
Bears fish in the river.
Lions lie in the sun and rest.
Shep herds the sheep.
Elephants like to squirt water.
Rex keeps the house safe.
Birds fly south in the fall.

On construction paper, write the main ideas, *Dogs do many jobs* and *Animals live in the wild,* one to a sheet, and place them in two different areas of the classroom.

Guide children in placing the sentences with the correct main idea. If necessary, tell children that *Rover, Lad, Shep,* and *Rex* are all names of dogs in these sentences.

(Dogs do many jobs: Rover can pull a sled. Lad helps Jane cross the street. Shep herds the sheep. Rex keeps the house safe. Animals live in the wild: Bears fish in the river. Lions lie in the sun and rest. Elephants like to squirt water. Birds fly south in the fall.)

■ ADVANCED

Extend: Main Idea Charts

Challenge children to find other articles and stories, and to create main idea charts for them. Have them copy a chart like the one shown here. Then have them fill in the chart with the main idea and a few important details from their article.

Encourage children to share their charts with the class by using them to summarize articles or stories they have read.

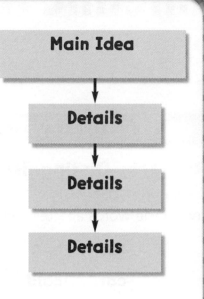

■ ENGLISH-LANGUAGE LEARNERS

Reteach: What's the Main Idea?

Call on one child to follow these directions as you say them one sentence at a time:

Stand up. Walk to my desk. Pick up my pencil. Walk over to (name of child). Give him/her the pencil. Walk back to your desk. Sit down.

Help children use one sentence to describe what happened: *(Name) brought a pencil to (Name).* Continue with other simple sets of directions and have children state the main idea in each set.

**For More
Language Development**

See English-Language Learners Resource Kit, Lesson 29 for additional **reteach** activities.

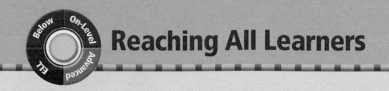

Additional Support Activities
Phonemic Awareness

**For More
Intensive Instruction**

See Intervention
Resource Kit, Lesson 30
for additional **preteach**
and **reteach** activities.

■ **BELOW-LEVEL**

Reteach: Distinguish Long *o* Words

Tell children that you are going to say pairs of words. Have them listen to the words and tell which word has the sound /ō/ as in *open*.

hope,	**hop**
cat,	**cold**
toll,	**ten**
under,	**over**
road,	**rod**
man,	**mold**
pole,	**pull**
sold,	**sell**
fist,	**fold**
hello,	**help**
poke,	**pick**

■ ADVANCED

Extend: Sort Long Vowel *o* Words

Put together a group of *Picture Cards*. Use all of the pictures for words that have the long vowel sound of *o*. Mix in some pictures for words with different vowel sounds. For long *o* words, use the following pictures: *boat, ghost, globe, goat, piano, pillow, robot, rose, tomato, yo-yo, zero*. Place them so that the word side is not showing.

Have children pick up a card and name the picture. If the name has the long vowel sound of *o*, children put the picture in one pile. They make a second pile for all words that do not have the long vowel sound of *o*.

■ ENGLISH-LANGUAGE LEARNERS

Reteach: Long Vowel Sound of *o*

Help children reinforce word meanings for words with the long vowel sound of *o*. Display the *Picture Cards* for the following words and say each word aloud: *boat, ghost, globe, goat, piano, robot, rose*. Have children repeat the words after you. Then ask them what sound they heard in each word. Help them say the sound /ō/ correctly.

For More Language Development

See English-Language Learners Resource Kit, Lesson 30 for additional **reteach** activities.

Additional Support Activities

■ BELOW-LEVEL

Reteach: Word Blending

Demonstrate making and blending *sold*, *roll*, *robot*, and *mold*, using a pocket chart and *Letter Cards.* Have children repeat the steps, using their *Word Builders* and *Word Builder Cards.*

- Place the letters *s, o, l, d* in the pocket chart with the letters separated. Have children do the same.

- Point to *s*. Say /ss/. Point to *o*. Say /ōō/. Point to *l*. Say /ll/. Point to *d*. Say /dd/.

- Slide the *s* next to the *o*. Move your hand under the letters and blend the sounds, elongating them—/ssōō/. Have children repeat after you.

- Slide *l* next to *so*. Slide your hand under *sol* and blend by elongating the sounds—/ssōōll/. Have children repeat.

- Slide *d* next to *sol*. Next, slide your hand under *sold* and blend by elongating the sounds—/ssōōlldd/. Have children repeat.

- Then have children read the word *sold* along with you.

Follow the same procedure to blend the other words.

For More Intensive Instruction

See Intervention Resource Kit, Lesson 30 for additional **preteach** and **reteach** activities.

■ ADVANCED

Extend: Rhyming Words in Sentences

Help children use rhyming words in sentences. First brainstorm a list of rhyming words with the long vowel sound of *o*.

so	old	bowl
go	cold	pole
row	fold	roll
bow	gold	toll
yo-yo	hold	stroll
tow	told	troll

Ask children to use these rhyming words in sentences or riddles.

> I wear my old gold coat when it is cold.

> I put the toll in the bowl for the troll.

■ ENGLISH-LANGUAGE LEARNERS

Reteach: Charades

Assign each child one word with the long vowel sound of *o* and whisper it in his or her ear. Use words such as *phone, robot, hello, no, gold,* and *hold*. Have the child pantomime the meaning of his or her word for the other children to guess. Help children write their words on the board. You may want to model for children by pretending to talk on a telephone for the word *phone.*

For More Language Development

See English-Language Learners Resource Kit, Lesson 30 for additional **reteach** activities.

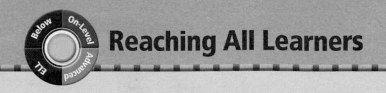

Additional Support Activities
Comprehension and Skills

■ BELOW-LEVEL

Reteach: Main Idea

Remind children that the main idea of a story tells what the story is mostly about. The main idea is the most important idea in the story. Write the following sentences on the board. Tell children that one of the sentences is a main idea and the others tell more about this main idea. Read the sentences and have children tell which is the main idea.

> Animals leave tracks when they walk.
> Each animal makes its own sound.
> A nature detective can look and
> listen for clues that will tell which
> animals are in the area.

Help children understand why the first and second sentences are not the main idea. Explain that both of these sentences tell about clues that nature detectives can use to figure out the kinds of animals that are in the area. These details tell more about the main idea, but they are not the main idea.

For More Intensive Instruction

See Intervention Resource Kit, Lesson 30 for additional **preteach** and **reteach** activities.

■ ADVANCED

Extend: Extend the Story

Ask children to tell the main idea of "How to Be a Nature Detective." (A nature detective can look, smell, and listen for clues about animals.) Have them recall some of the details in the story that support this idea.

Ask children to choose one or two more animals that a nature detective could look for, and tell about clues these animals would leave behind. Then ask children to write about their ideas. Ask volunteers to share their work with the class.

■ ENGLISH-LANGUAGE LEARNERS

Reteach: Main Idea vs. Details

Remind children that the main idea of a story or article is what it is mostly about. Tell children that the ideas that tell more about the main idea are called details. Write these sentences on the board. Read the sentences aloud to children. As children direct, label each sentence *main idea* or *detail*.

Like airplanes, seagulls take off facing into the wind. (detail)
You can find tracks in many places—in mud, in snow, in sand, in dust, even on the sidewalk or on the floor. (detail)
A cat has four feet and sharp claws. So does a dog. (detail)
Nature detectives find tracks and use clues to answer their questions. (main idea)

For More Language Development

See English-Language Learners Resource Kit, Lesson 30 for additional reteach activities.

Additional Support Activities
Phonemic Awareness

■ BELOW-LEVEL

Reteach: Step and Blend

Use masking tape to make three connecting squares on the floor. Make the squares large enough for a child to step from one square to the next. Have a child stand inside the first square as he or she says the word *gem*. Then have the child listen as you elongate the word, stretching out the sounds—*/jjeemm/*. Repeat, having the child say the elongated sounds with you. As the child blends one sound to the next, have him or her step from one square to the next. After the last square, have the child jump out. Say the word naturally and have the child say it after you. Repeat the procedure several times with other three-phoneme words such as *gym*, *page*, *ledge*, *wedge*, *badge*, *budge*, and *fudge*. This will help children listen for individual letter sounds while blending them into words.

**For More
Intensive Instruction**

**See Intervention
Resource Kit, Lesson 31**
for additional **preteach**
and **reteach** activities.

■ ADVANCED

Extend: Segment Recorded Words

Have children segment words by following instructions on audio-tape. Collect toys, pictures, and other visual representations for these words: *giraffe, cage, giant, bridge, cabbage, orange, pigeon, badger*. Then make a recording of instructions for children to listen to and follow at a Listening Center. Give step-by-step directions for each word. Use a format similar to this one: *Touch the spotted animal. Say* giraffe. (pause) *Now say the sounds you hear in the word* giraffe. (pause) *Good! Now say the sounds with me—/j/ /ûr/ /a/ /f/. What was the word?* (pause) *That's right,* giraffe!

■ ENGLISH-LANGUAGE LEARNERS

Reteach: Sing and Blend

Have children blend sounds into words as they sing modified versions of familiar songs. Have them first blend onsets and rimes. Then after some practice, switch to the more difficult skill of blending phonemes. For example: */k/-age* (onset and rime), */k/ /ā/ /j/* (phonemes). Whenever possible, show a picture card for the word being blended. Sing the following song to the tune of "Little Green Frog."

> */k/ /āj/ said the little green frog one day.*
> */k/ /āj/ said the little green frog.*
> */k/ /āj/ said the little green frog one day,*
> *Then he said, "Cage, cage, cage, cage."*

Repeat with these words: *page, badge, ledge, wedge, budge, fudge, nudge, gym, giraffe.*

For More Language Development

See English-Language Learners Resource Kit, Lesson 31 for additional **reteach** activities.

Additional Support Activities

Phonics

■ BELOW-LEVEL

Reteach: Word Blending

Demonstrate making and blending *age, cage, page, badge, budge,* and *fudge,* using a pocket chart and *Letter Cards,* and have children repeat the steps using their *Word Builders* and *Word Builder Cards.*

■ Place the letters *f, u, d, g,* and *e* in the pocket chart with the *f* and *u* separated, and the *dge* together. Have children do the same.

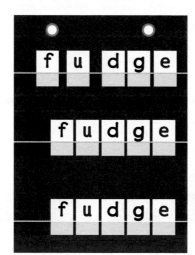

■ Point to *f* and say /ff/. Point to *u* and say /uu/.

■ Slide the *u* next to the *f*. Move your hand under the letters and blend the sounds, elongating them /ffuu/. Have children repeat after you.

■ Point to *dge.* Say /j/. Have children do the same.

■ Slide *dge* next to *fu.* Slide your hand under *fudge* and blend by elongating the sounds /ffuujj/. Have children do the same.

■ Then have children read the word *fudge* along with you.

**For More
Intensive Instruction**

**See Intervention
Resource Kit, Lesson 31**
for additional **preteach**
and **reteach** activities.

■ ADVANCED

Extend: The Little Engine That Could

Write and photocopy a list of words that includes a variety of previously taught letters and words, including /j/g, dge words. Draw and photocopy a boxcar train that has an empty boxcar for each /j/g, dge word on the word list. Then distribute the lists and the trains. Have children write on each boxcar a /j/g, dge word from the list. Model how to fill in the first boxcar. Point out to children that the word engine—which is the name of a machine that pulls a train—has the /j/ sound spelled with g. Write engine on the first boxcar. When children finish their word trains, have partners read them to each other. You may choose to read aloud the story The Little Engine That Could before children complete this activity.

■ ENGLISH-LANGUAGE LEARNERS

Reteach: Words with /j/g, dge

Children learning English may be more familiar with the hard sound of g /g/. Point out that g and dge can stand for the sound of soft g /j/. Write the following words on the board: age, cage, stage, page, vegetable, gem, fudge, judge, bridge, badge, edge. Track the print as you read the words aloud and have children read along with you. To reinforce vocabulary, ask volunteers to explain what each word means, assisting them as necessary.

For More Language Development

See English-Language Learners Resource Kit, Lesson 31 for additional reteach activities.

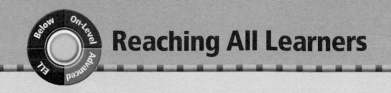
Additional Support Activities
Comprehension and Skills

**For More
Intensive Instruction**

**See Intervention
Resource Kit, Lesson 31**
for additional **preteach**
and **reteach** activities.

■ BELOW-LEVEL

Reteach: Reorder Story Events for Plot

Remind children that a story is made up of a series of events. A story has a problem and a solution. Write the following sentences on sentence strips and display them out of order.

Read aloud the sentences together. Work with children to rearrange the strips to show what happened in "The Puddle."

A boy put his toy boat in a puddle.

A frog jumped onto the boat and sailed away.

The frog steered the boat into a turtle.

An alligator helped.

A pig wanted to swim in the puddle.

A thirsty elephant drank...and drank.

The sun came out and dried up the puddle.

The boy went home.

■ ADVANCED

Extend: Continue the Story

Have children recall the characters and the plot of the story "The Puddle." Then ask children to think of another animal that could come to the puddle, and have them suggest what it might do. Have partners write sentences about such an animal to add to the story, and then draw a picture to go with their writing. Remind children to write complete sentences that begin with a capital letter and end with an end mark. Allow time for children to share their sentences and pictures.

■ ENGLISH-LANGUAGE LEARNERS

Reteach: Record and Compare Story Plots

Give each pair of children the following *Picture Cards: bird, boy, cage, sun, wolf, house.* Tell children to work together to think of a story that includes those characters and things. Have partners tape record their stories. Suggest that they practice before making the recording. Remind children to speak slowly and clearly when they make their recording. Children may want to draw a picture to go with their story. When all the partners finish, have the group listen to the stories. Point out that the stories include the same characters and things, but they have different plots—they do not tell about the exact same events.

Use the recordings to assess children's abilities to enunciate words, pronounce letter sounds, and express ideas. Help children with these skills as needed.

For More Language Development

See English-Language Learners Resource Kit, Lesson 31 for additional **reteach** activities.

Additional Support Activities
Phonemic Awareness

■ BELOW-LEVEL

Reteach: Listen for /(y)o͞o/

Tell children that you will be saying pairs of words. Slowly say the words below, emphasizing the vowel sound in each. Have volunteers tell you which word in each pair has the sound /(y)o͞o/ as in *cube* or the /o͞o/ sound as in *prune*.

cub	**cube**		**mule**	male
Jane	**June**		flake	**fluke**
rule	rub		tub	**tune**
cute	cut		**mute**	mate

For More Intensive Instruction

See Intervention Resource Kit, Lesson 32 for additional **preteach** and **reteach** activities.

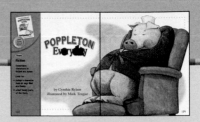

■ ADVANCED

Extend: Generate Sentences

Have children make up oral sentences, including as many words as they can with the sound /(y)o͞o/ or /o͞o/. For example:

June used her flute to play a tune.

■ ENGLISH-LANGUAGE LEARNERS

Reteach: Listen for /(y)o͞o/

Hum a simple tune and invite children to hum along. Say *tune* and have children repeat the word after you. Explain that what you are humming is called a tune and that *tune* contains the long vowel sound /o͞o/. Tell children that whenever they hear a word with the long vowel sound /o͞o/ as in *tune* or /(y)o͞o/ as in *cute*, they should hum a tune. Say each word and have children repeat it after you.

me	mule	such	mat	tube
say	mute	sack	mitt	rule
cat	cube	June	look	cute

**For More
Language Development**

**See English-Language
Learners Resource Kit,
Lesson 32** for additional
reteach activities.

Additional Support Activities

■ **BELOW-LEVEL**

Reteach: Decode Words with Long Vowel /(y)o͞o/u-e

Have children list the following words from *Teaching Transparency 96* (page 18IG) on paper:

dune	**tubes**
huge	**used**
Luke	**cube**
rule	

Tell children to write each letter of a word under that word and to say each letter as they write it. Remind children that the final e is silent. Have them underline the letter that has the sound /(y)o͞o/ or the sound /o͞o/.

dune

d   (children say /d/)

u   (children say /o͞o/ and
        underline the *u*)

n   (children say /n/)

e   (silent)

**For More
Intensive Instruction**

**See Intervention
Resource Kit, Lesson 32**
for additional **preteach**
and **reteach** activities.

■ ADVANCED

Extend: Write a Story

Have children write a short story about any topic they choose. Tell them to use the long vowel /(y)ōō/u-e words they wrote in their journal, as well as other long vowel /(y)ōō/u-e words. Allow children time to illustrate their story and to highlight the long vowel /(y)ōō/u-e words they used.

■ ENGLISH-LANGUAGE LEARNERS

Reteach: Build Words

Have children use their *Word Builder Cards* to build the word *rule*. Have them repeat the word after you several times, elongating the vowel sound. Next, have them change the *u* to *o*. Say *role* and have children repeat it after you several times. Ask children to touch their hand to their lips as they repeat the words *rule, role* several times. Have children tell if they can feel and hear the difference between the two vowel sounds. Remind children that *rule* contains the sound of long *u*. Follow the same procedure with the words *dune, dine* and *Luke, lake*.

For More Language Development

See English-Language Learners Resource Kit, Lesson 32 for additional **reteach** activities.

Additional Support Activities
Vocabulary and High-Frequency Words

■ BELOW-LEVEL

Reteach: Practice High-Frequency Words

Display *Word Cards* for *boy*, *head*, and *read* or write the words on the board. Have children find each word in "Poppleton Everyday" and read aloud the sentence that contains the word. Ask children to discuss each word's meaning as it is used in the story. Work with children to use each high-frequency word in a sentence of their own. Write the sentences on the board.

For More Intensive Instruction

See Intervention Resource Kit, Lesson 32 for additional **preteach** and **reteach** activities.

boy   head   read

Reteach: Practice New Vocabulary

Display *Word Cards* for *brought* and *few*. Have children identify the word that completes each of these sentences:

**Everyone at the party liked the cookies Manuel
_____.** *(brought)*

I don't have many pencils, but I do have a _____.
(few)

■ ADVANCED

Extend: Write a Short Story

Have children write the high-frequency words *boy, head,* and *read* on a sheet of paper or chart paper. Then tell children to write a short story in which they use each of these words in a sentence. Remind children to create a main character for their story who has to solve a problem. Allow children time to share their stories.

■ ENGLISH-LANGUAGE LEARNERS

Reteach: Act Out High-Frequency Words

Use a marker to write each of these words on a large index card: *boy, head, read.* Hold up the cards one at a time, reading each word and prompting children to echo you. Have children work with partners to point to an example or act out the meaning of each word.

For More Language Development

See English-Language Learners Resource Kit, Lesson 32 for additional **reteach** activities.

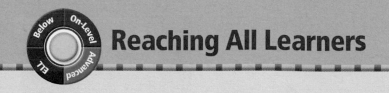
Additional Support Activities
Phonemic Awareness

**For More
Intensive Instruction**

**See Intervention
Resource Kit, Lesson 33**
for additional **preteach**
and **reteach** activities.

■ BELOW-LEVEL

Reteach: Blending Word Parts

If children have trouble blending several phonemes together to
make a word, give them fewer, bigger word parts to work with.
Segment the following words into two parts and have children
blend the parts and say the words naturally:

/l/ /ed/ (lead)   /br/ /ed/ (bread)

/h/ /ed/ (head)   /r/ /ed/ (read)

/thr/ /ed/ (thread)   /spr/ /ed/ (spread)

/red/ /ē/ (ready)   /hev/ /ē/ (heavy)

■ ADVANCED

Extend: Mystery Commands

Tell children you will give them some commands. Explain that they must listen carefully and blend one or more words in the command to know what to do. Use directions like these:

- **Raise your arm above your /h/ /e/ /d/** (head) **and keep it /s/ /t/ /e/ /d/ /ē/.** (steady)

- **Pretend to butter some /b/ /r/ /e/ /d/.** (bread)

- **Touch your /h/ /e/ /d/.** (head)

- **Wipe /s/ /w/ /e/ /t/** (sweat) **from your forehead.**

■ ENGLISH-LANGUAGE LEARNERS

Reteach: Phoneme Isolation

Display the *Picture Card* for *bread*. Have children identify the picture, say the word *bread*, and say the sound they hear in the middle of the word (/e/). Tell children that you will say some words and they will repeat each one, giving "thumbs up" for words with the sound /e/ in the middle. If children have difficulty distinguishing /e/, suggest that they say *bread* before they repeat each word, comparing the sounds of the middle vowels. Use the following words:

head	dead	deed	sweat	spread	sweet
leaf	deaf	cliff	breath	seed	head

For More Language Development

See English-Language Learners Resource Kit, Lesson 33 for additional **reteach** activities.

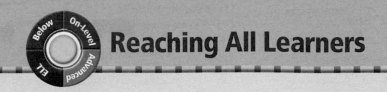
Additional Support Activities

■ **BELOW-LEVEL**

Reteach: Word Blending

Reinforce /e/ea and /ē/ee by using a pocket chart and *Letter Cards* to make and blend words. Have children repeat the steps using their *Word Builders* and *Word Builder Cards*.

■ Place the letters *h, e, a,* and *d* in the pocket chart with the *e* and *a* close together. Have children do the same.

■ Point to *h* and say /h/. Point to *e* and *a* and say /e/.

■ Slide the *ea* next to the *h*. Move your hand under the letters and blend the sounds, elongating them—/hhee/. Have children repeat after you.

■ Point to *d* and say /d/. Have children do the same.

■ Slide the *d* next to *hea*. Slide your hand under *head* and blend by elongating the sounds—/hheedd/. Have children repeat after you.

■ Then have children read the word *head*.

Repeat with the words *heed, bread, bead, sweat,* and *sweet*. Point out that the letters *e* and *a* together can have the sounds /e/ and /ē/; the letters *ee* spell /ē/.

For More Intensive Instruction

See Intervention Resource Kit, Lesson 33 for additional **preteach** and **reteach** activities.

SLEEP
Is for Everyone

■ ADVANCED

Extend: Rhyming Words

Have children substitute letters and make words that rhyme with *head, deed, sweat, sweet, leaf, deaf, heed* and other words with *ea* and *ee.* Remind them that they can also think of rhyming C-V-C words, such as *fed* and *bed.* Then have them use the words from their lists to write a poem.

The bread smelled sweet.
I gave it to Pete.

■ ENGLISH-LANGUAGE LEARNERS

Reteach: Rhyming Words

Help children generate pairs of rhyming words that they can refer to as they write a poem. As children suggest words, write them on the board or on chart paper. Explain what each word means or have volunteers do so. When appropriate, you may wish to draw simple pictures beside words to reinforce meaning. Then have children use the words to write, dictate, or say a two-line poem.

bread/head	health/wealth
read/thread	dread/lead

For More Language Development

See English-Language Learners Resource Kit, Lesson 33 for additional **reteach** activities.

English-Language Learners
Write-On Wipe-Off Board

Additional Support Activities
Comprehension and Skills

■ BELOW-LEVEL

Reteach: Identifying Main Idea

Remind children that the main idea of a selection tells what the selection is mostly about. It's the most important idea of the story. Write the following sentences on the board. Tell children that one of the sentences tells the main idea of the selection and that the others are details—they tell little things about the main idea, but they are not the main idea. Read the following sentences aloud and have children tell which one is the main idea.

> **An elephant can sleep standing up.**
>
> **Jonathan is only six weeks old, so he sleeps most of the time.**
>
> **Animals and people of all ages need to sleep.** (main idea)
>
> **Part of your brain rests while you sleep.**

Help children understand why the third sentence is the main idea and the other sentences are not. Although the other sentences are connected to the main idea, each tells only one detail about it. Together, however, they explain who sleeps and why they need to sleep.

For More Intensive Instruction

See Intervention Resource Kit, Lesson 33 for additional **preteach** and **reteach** activities.

■ ADVANCED

Extend: Extend the Selection

Have children discuss the main idea of the selection. Work with them to come up with one sentence that tells what the selection is mostly about. Then have them brainstorm ideas for new parts that could be added to "Sleep Is for Everyone."

Bats sleep during the day and fly around at night. They still need to sleep, just not at night.

Emphasize that the new parts must tell something about the main idea. For example, children might consider a part that tells which creatures need the most sleep and which need the least sleep, which animals sleep during the day and are awake at night, or tips for a good night's sleep. If they wish, they can look back at their K-W-L chart for ideas. Have each child write a new page for the selection.

■ ENGLISH-LANGUAGE LEARNERS

Reteach: Identify Main Ideas in Familiar Tales

To reinforce the concept of main idea, tell children a short fable, such as "The Tortoise and the Hare" or "King Midas and the Golden Touch." End the story with the moral. Then ask children to tell the main idea of the story. Ask volunteers to tell traditional tales they know. When speakers finish, help children identify the main idea of the story.

For More Language Development

See English-Language Learners Resource Kit, Lesson 33 for additional **reteach** activities.

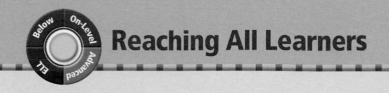
Additional Support Activities
Phonemic Awareness

**For More
Intensive Instruction**

**See Intervention
Resource Kit, Lesson 34**
for additional **preteach**
and **reteach** activities.

■ BELOW-LEVEL

Reteach: Blend Words with /oo/

Tell children that you are going to say some words very slowly. Tell
them to listen carefully and then blend the sounds to make a word.
Model by segmenting the word *noon* into phonemes. (/n/ /oo/ /n/)
Then say it naturally—*noon*. Segment the following words, having
children blend the sounds to say the words:

/g/ /oo/ /s/ (goose)

/l/ /oo/ /s/ (loose)

/h/ /oo/ /t/ (hoot)

/s/ /t/ /oo/ /l/ (stool)

/s/ /k/ /oo/ /p/ (scoop)

/k/ /oo/ /l/ (cool)

/l/ /oo/ /p/ (loop)

/d/ /r/ /oo/ /l/ (drool)

■ ADVANCED

Extend: Manipulate Phonemes

Have children form words by deleting phonemes. Ask them to say:

bloom without the /l/	(boom)
proof without the /r/	(poof)
booth without the /th/	(boo)
goose without the /s/	(goo)
zoom without the /m/	(zoo)
boost without the /s/	(boot)
balloon without the /b/ and /ə/	(loon)
roost without the /s/	(root)

■ ENGLISH-LANGUAGE LEARNERS

Reteach: Act Out /o͞o/ Words

Tell children that you will say a series of words. Explain that some words will have /o͞o/, while others will not. Direct children to stand up and listen carefully as you call out each word. Instruct them to stand still if the word they hear does not contain /o͞o/. Direct them to act out the word if they do hear /o͞o/. Use words such as these:

<u>bear</u>	<u>broom</u>	<u>moose</u>
<u>tooth</u>	worry	bunny
<u>groom</u>	<u>scoop</u>	<u>bloom</u>
<u>roof</u>	third	<u>goose</u>

For More Language Development

See English-Language Learners Resource Kit, Lesson 34 for additional **reteach** activities.

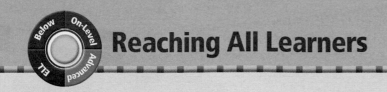

Additional Support Activities
Phonics

■ BELOW-LEVEL

Reteach: Word Blending

Demonstrate making and blending *too, tooth, moo, moon, goo,* and *goof* using a pocket chart and *Letter Cards*. Have children repeat the steps using their *Word Builders* and *Word Builder Cards*. After you blend and read *too*, have children listen as you say *tooth*.

Ask children what they notice about the first part of the word. Then ask them to watch for the letters of the short word *too* as you build and blend *tooth*. Do the same for *moo* before blending *moon* and for *goo* before blending *goof*.

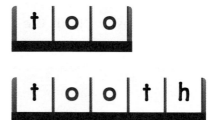

For More Intensive Instruction

See Intervention Resource Kit, Lesson 34 for additional **preteach** and **reteach** activities.

■ ADVANCED

Extend: Write Rhyming Riddles

Have children find as many pairs of rhyming words with /o͞o/ as they can. Have them record the pairs they find and try to find a pair that they can use in a rhyming riddle. Post this example:

> **I am bigger than a goose.**
> **I'm a big, furry _____.** (moose)

Have children post their rhyming riddles in a center for others to guess. Near the riddles, display a list of /o͞o/ words for answer choices.

■ ENGLISH-LANGUAGE LEARNERS

Reteach: Reading *oo* Words

Have children work in small groups to reinforce the relationship between the spelling *oo* and the sound /o͞o/. Make and distribute word cards with *oo* words to each group. Each child can pick a card, read the word aloud, and then use the word in a sentence. Repeat until each child has picked and read at least one card.

For More Language Development

See **English-Language Learners Resource Kit, Lesson 34** for additional **reteach** activities.

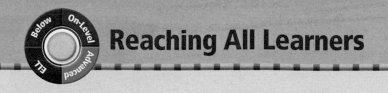
Additional Support Activities
Comprehension and Skills

**For More
Intensive Instruction**

**See Intervention
Resource Kit, Lesson 34**
for additional **preteach**
and **reteach** activities.

■ BELOW-LEVEL

Reteach: Plot

Remind children that *plot* means the important things that happen in a story. Tell children that some story events are important and others are not. Point out that in this story, the events that helped Baboon learn were important. Write the following events on sentence strips.

Baboon saw a turtle.

He saw a forest fire.

He saw a crocodile.

He saw elephants and a gazelle.

He saw a rhinoceros.

Baboon stretched.

He took a nap.

He saw a monkey.

He saw the day change to night.

Have children tell which strips name important events and which do not. Then lead children to summarize the plot in a statement, such as *Baboon saw many things and learned about the world.*

Extend: Write in Baboon's Journal

Ask children to think about which story events were most important to the plot. Then have them imagine that Baboon is keeping a journal about what he learns. Have them use the story events to write Baboon's journal entry for the day described in the story. Allow children to read their journal entries to a group of classmates.

■ **ENGLISH-LANGUAGE LEARNERS**

Reteach: Tell a Cloze Summary

Page through the story, helping children summarize the important events of the plot. Say *Baboon saw a _____. He said, "The world is _____."* Have children look at the illustration and supply the last word of each statement. If children need quite a bit of coaching, repeat the activity until they can supply the words independently.

For More Language Development

See English-Language Learners Resource Kit, Lesson 34 for additional **reteach** activities.

Teacher Notes

Theme Resources

Going Places
Theme Resources

Phonics
Long Vowel /ī/igh

OBJECTIVES

- *To generate the sound for long vowel /ī/igh*
- *To distinguish /ī/ in spoken words*
- *To blend and read words with long vowel /ī/igh*

Focus

Write the word *night* on the board and read it. Ask children what vowel sound they hear in the word. (/ī/) Underline the *igh* and remind children that these letters can represent /ī/. Change the beginning of *night* to make *might* and *sight*. Read each word, emphasizing /ī/. Have children repeat the words.

Reteach the Skill
Phonemic Awareness

Phoneme Isolation Tell children to listen as you say two words. Ask them to repeat only the word that has /ī/. Use these words:

right	*rate*
knit	*slight*
fight	*fit*
sigh	*sea*
bread	*bright*
light	*late*
high	*hoe*

Word Blending

Distribute Word Builder Cards *r, i, g, h,* and *t.* Blend and read the word *right* with children. As you model each step in your Word Builder, have children repeat after you.

- Place the letters *r, i, g, h,* and *t* in the Word Builder, separated from each other.
- Point to *r.* Say /r/.
- Slide *i, g,* and *h* together. Move your hand under the letters and say /ī/.
- Slide *igh* next to *r.* Move your hand under the letters and blend the sounds—/rrī/.
- Point to *t.* Say /t/.
- Slide *t* next to *righ.* Move your hand under *right* and blend by elongating the sounds—/rrītt/.
- Read the word *right* naturally.

Follow the same procedure for *light* and *fight.*

Summarize/Assess

Write the word *might* on the board and have children read it. Then dictate *bright, tight,* and *sigh.* Have children use their sound-letter knowledge to write the words.

Word Structure
Inflections: -ed, -ing

OBJECTIVES

- *To identify words with the inflections* -ed *and* -ing
- *To drop the final* e *before adding* -ed *or* -ing
- *To use inflectional endings to interpret meaning*

Focus

Write the words *liked* and *liking* on the board. Touch *liked* and say *Yesterday I liked my lunch.* Then touch *liking* and say *I am liking the weather today.* Remind children that the ending *-ed* shows that something happened in the past. The ending *-ing* shows that something is going on now. Write the word *like* on the board and point out the *e* on the end. Explain that when a word ends with *e*, the *e* is dropped before *-ed* or *-ing* is added.

Reteach the Skill

Kinesthetic Model   Write the following words on the board: *please*, *place*, *race*, and *share*. Then write the endings *ed* and *ing* on index cards that can be held up to the words on the board. Give each child a card with an ending. Name one of the words, and have a child add his or her ending to the word by holding the card up to the word, covering the final *e* with the card. Then ask the child to read the new word. Point out that to add the ending, they must drop the final *e*. Then follow the suggestions in **Summarize/Assess**.

Auditory Model   Read each sentence aloud. Have children identify the word with an *-ed* or *-ing* ending and tell whether the action is happening now or in the past.

Kevin shared some raisins.
Mary is sharing the book.
Bill traded with Sue.
Bill is trading pictures.
Carol whistled for the dog.
Carol is whistling a happy song.

Then follow the suggestions in **Summarize/ Assess**.

Visual Model   Write the following base words on the board:

care   joke   race

Have children fold sheets of paper in thirds to make three columns. Tell children to write each base word in the first column. In the second column, have them write each base word and add the ending *-ed*. In the third, have them add the ending *-ing*. Remind children to drop the final *e* before they add the endings. Have children read aloud each row of words. Then follow the suggestions in **Summarize/Assess**.

Summarize/Assess

Check children's understanding of the lesson by having them summarize what they learned. (The endings *-ed* and *-ing* can be added to words to tell when something happened. When a word ends with *e*, the *e* is dropped before the ending *-ed* or *-ing* is added.) To reinforce this lesson, help children look in stories they have read previously for words that end with *-ed* and *-ing*. Remind children to use what they know about adding the endings *-ed* and *-ing* to words that end in *e* to help them read unfamiliar words.

Phonics
Long Vowel /ā/ *ai, ay*

OBJECTIVES

- *To generate the sound for long vowel /ā/ai, ay*
- *To distinguish /ā/ in spoken words*
- *To blend and read words with long vowel /ā/ai, ay*

Focus

Write the words *say* and *rain* on the board and read them. Ask children what vowel sound they hear in the words. (/ā/) Underline the *ay* and *ai* and remind children that these letters can represent /ā/. Change *say* to make *way* and change *rain* to make *pain*. Read each word, emphasizing /ā/. Have children repeat the words.

Reteach the Skill
Phonemic Awareness

Phoneme Deletion   Tell children to listen as you say a word. Ask them to repeat the word without its final sound, changing the /ā/ word into a new one. Use these words:

train	(tray)
sail	(say)
grain	(gray)
raid	(ray)
stain	(stay)
hail	(hay)

Word Blending

Distribute Word Builder Cards *d*, *a*, and *y*. Blend and read the word *day* with children. As you model each step in your Word Builder, have children repeat after you.

- Place the letters *d*, *a*, and *y* in the Word Builder, separated from each other.

- Point to *d*. Say /d/.

- Slide *a* and *y* together. Move your hand under the letters and say /ā/.
- Slide *ay* next to *d*. Move your hand under the letters and blend the sounds—/ddāā/.

- Read the word *day* naturally.
- Distribute Word Builder cards *m*, *a*, *i*, and *n*.

Blend and read the word *main*. Have children repeat the steps after you.
- Place *m*, *a*, *i*, and *n* in the Word Builder. Slide *a* and *i* together.
- Point to *m*. Say /m/. Point to *ai*. Say /ā/.
- Slide *ai* next to *m*. Move your hand under *mai*

and blend the sounds, elongating them—/mmāā/.
- Point to *n*. Say /n/.

- Slide *n* next to *mai*. Move your hand under main and blend by elongating the sounds—/mmāānn/
- Read the word *main* naturally.

Follow the same procedure for *play* and *grain*.

Summarize/Assess

Write the word *way* on the board and have children read it. Dictate *stay* and *hay*. Write the word *pain* on the board and have children read it. Dictate *stain* and *gain*. Have children use their sound-letter knowledge to write the words.

Grammar
Verbs

OBJECTIVES
- *To identify verbs*
- *To use verbs in sentences*

Focus
Remind children that verbs tell what someone or something does.

Reteach the Skill
Visual Model   Write on the board and have children read:

> **The mouse ran into the barn.**

Ask children to tell which word tells what the mouse did. (ran) Point out that *ran* is an action word, or a verb. Call on volunteers to name other verbs that would make sense in the sentence. (possible responses: *looked, hopped, raced,* or *crept*) Have each child say a sentence about an animal doing something, and then tell what verb they used. Then follow the suggestions in **Summarize/Assess**.

Auditory Model   Ask children to name things they have done today. After each response, repeat the verb the child used and write it on the board. After several responses, help children read the list of verbs. Point out that verbs tell what someone or something does. Then say the following sentences and ask children to suggest a verb to fit in the blank.

> **We _____ on the bus.**
> **Tom _____ up the hill.**
> **Karen _____ at the circus.**
> **Three elephants _____ in the water.**
> **The boys and girls _____ at school.**

Point out that verbs tell what someone or something does. Finally, follow the suggestions in **Summarize/Assess**.

Kinesthetic Model   Write the following words on cards: *jump, cut, hop, fly, sing, swim, wiggle, sleep*. Have children select a card and pantomime the word. When the action is guessed, have volunteers use the word in sentences. Then follow the suggestions in **Summarize/Assess**.

Summarize/Assess
Check children's understanding of the lesson by asking them to summarize what they learned. (Verbs are the words that tell what someone or something does.) Have each child write a sentence and underline the verb. Remind children that knowing about verbs can help them make their writing clear and interesting.

Word Structure
Inflections: -ed, -ing

OBJECTIVE
- *To identify words with the inflections -ed and -ing*
- *To double the final consonant before adding -ed or -ing*
- *Use inflectional endings to interpret meaning.*

Focus
Write the words *stopped* and *stopping* on the board. Touch *stopped* and say *Yesterday the bus stopped*. Then touch *stopping* and say *The bus is stopping at the school*. Remind children that the ending *-ed* shows that something happened in the past. The ending *-ing* shows that something is going on now. Write the word *stop* on the board. Point out that the word ends with one *p*. Then point to *stopped* and *stopping* and ask how many *p*'s are in each word. Explain that when a word ends with a short vowel and a single consonant, the consonant is doubled before adding *-ed* or *-ing*.

Reteach the Skill
Kinesthetic Model   Write the following words on index cards: *drop, stop, hop, skip, clap*. Make a second set of cards with the endings *ed, ing, ped*, and *ping*. Have a child choose a word and read it. Pronounce the word with an *-ed* or *-ing* ending, and have the child choose the ending card that will correctly complete the word. Ask the child to use the new word in a sentence. Then follow the suggestions in **Summarize/Assess**.

Auditory Model   Read each sentence aloud. Have children identify the word with *-ed* or *-ing* ending and tell whether the action is happening now or in the past.

> **Pam gripped the bat.**
> **Pam is gripping the bat.**
> **Ray stopped the game.**
> **Ray is stopping the game.**

Then follow the suggestions in **Summarize/Assess**.

Visual Model   Write the following chart on the board:

	-ed	-ing
They grip the bat.	They _____ the bat.	They are _____ the bat.
They stop the game.	They _____ the game.	They are _____ the game.
They slip on the ice.	They _____ on the ice.	They are _____ on the ice.
They nap every day.	They _____ every day.	They are _____ every day.

Have volunteers complete the sentences in columns 2 and 3 by adding the ending to the base word. Remind children to double the final consonant before adding the endings. Then follow the suggestions in **Summarize/Assess**.

Summarize/Assess
Check children's understanding of the lesson by having them summarize what they learned. (The endings *-ed* and *-ing* can be added to words to tell about when something happened. When a word ends with a short vowel sound and one consonant, the consonant is usually doubled before the ending is added.) To reinforce this lesson, help children look in selections they have read for words that end with *-ed* and *-ing*. Ask them to tell the base word of each word they find that has a double consonant in front of the ending. Remind children to use the strategies from this lesson to help them read unfamiliar words.

Verbs That Tell About Now

OBJECTIVES
- *To identify verbs in present tense*
- *To use verbs in sentences*

Focus

Prepare word cards for *run* and *runs*. Read the words with children. Remind them that a verb can tell about something that happens now. An *s* is added to some verbs that tell about what one person, place, or thing does now. Write on the board and have children read:

> I _____ .
> She _____ .
> The dog _____ .
> We _____ .

Have children choose the word card that completes each sentence on the board, hold the word in the blank, and read the complete sentence.

Reteach the Skill

Visual Model   Make and randomly distribute word cards for *I*, *He*, *She*, *We*, *They*, *A frog*, and *Frogs*. Write on the board and have children read:

> _____ **hop.**   _____ **hops.**

Ask, "Who has a card for a word that fits in the first blank?" Have children with the cards for *I*, *They*, and *Frogs* come to the board, and one at a time, hold the word card in the blank as the rest of the group reads the sentence. Do the same for the second blank, having children with the cards for *He*, *She*, and *A frog* take turns holding their cards in the blank. Point out that *s* is added to some verbs when one person or thing is doing the action. Invite volunteers to share their sentences with the group. Then follow the suggestions in **Summarize/Assess.**

Auditory Model   Ask children to listen to these sentences: *We walk. Jeff walks.* Have children repeat the sentences. Then ask, "How did the word *walk* change when *Jeff* was the naming part of the sentence?" (The sound /s/ was added.) Point out that we add an *s* to some verbs when one person or thing is doing the action. Tell children you will say a verb and a sentence. They must use the correct form of the verb to complete the sentence.

> *play: My brother* ____(plays)____ .
> *sing: Mandy and Susan* ____(sing)____ .
> *jump: I* ____(jump)____ .
> *work: Dad* ____(works)____ .
> *squawk: Our pet bird* ____(squawks)____ .

Then follow the suggestions in **Summarize/Assess.**

Kinesthetic Model   Have children perform actions such as walking, jumping, hopping, reading, and writing individually and in small groups. During each performance, have other children tell what the performer does, using sentences such as *James writes* and *Randy, Marta, and Tamika read*. Record the sentences on the board, and call on volunteers to underline the verb in each one. Then follow the suggestions in **Summarize/Assess.**

Summarize/Assess

Check children's understanding of the lesson by asking them to summarize what they learned. (Some verbs can tell about things that happen now. An *s* is added to some verbs that tell what one person or thing does.) Write *ride* and *rides* on the board. Ask children to write a sentence using each word. Remind children that using the correct forms of verbs will help them write clear, correct sentences.

Word Structure
Contractions: 've, 'd, 're

OBJECTIVES
- *To identify contractions with 've, 'd, and 're*
- *To use contractions to interpret meaning*

Focus

Remind children that a contraction is a shorter way to express two words that are usually said together. The apostrophe in a contraction shows where a letter or letters have been left out. Write these words on the board and ask children which ones are contractions and how they can tell:

wed	Ivy	you're
we'd	I've	your

Erase the words that are not contractions and then say word sets, asking children to tell which contraction goes with each set of words: *I have* (I've), *you are* (you're), *we would* (we'd).

Reteach the Skill

Visual Model   Write on index cards these word sets: *I have, she would, we are, you are, you have, they have, you would, they are, he would*. On another set of index cards, write the corresponding contractions: *I've, she'd, we're, you're, you've, they've, you'd, they're, he'd*. Give each child a card. Have children walk around the room to find their partner, the person holding the corresponding contraction or word set. Ask the partners to read aloud the word set and the contraction. Have them tell what letters are replaced by the apostrophe. Encourage children to use the contraction in a sentence. Then follow the suggestions in **Summarize/Assess**.

Auditory Model   Read aloud one of the sentences below. Have a volunteer repeat the sentence, this time using a contraction for the underlined words. After saying the sentence, ask the child to repeat just the contraction and the words it stands for.

I <u>have</u> come to help. (I've)
<u>We have</u> played that game. (We've)
I <u>would</u> like a snack. (I'd)
<u>They are</u> coming home. (They're)
<u>We are</u> going to play. (We're)
<u>She should</u> play with you. (She'd)

Then write *are, have,* and *would* on the board. Say a contraction with one of the words and have children tell which word is in the contraction. Some words to use are: *you're, I've, he'd, they're, you'd, we've, they'd, we're*. Then follow the suggestions in **Summarize/Assess**.

Kinesthetic Model   Write on the board several word sets that can be made into contractions, such as *you have, we have, I would, he would, we are,* and *they are*. Have children choose one of the word pairs and write it on a sentence strip. Encourage children to name the contraction that can be made by combining the two words. Then ask children to cut out the letters that don't appear in the contraction. Have them glue the remaining letters together and add an apostrophe to make the contraction. Invite children to share their contractions and to use them in sentences. Then follow the suggestions in **Summarize/Assess**.

Summarize/Assess

Check children's understanding of the lesson by having them summarize what they learned. (Contractions are a short way of saying and writing two words as one. The contraction 've means *have*, 're means *are*, and 'd usually means *would*. Knowing contractions can help you decode.) Reinforce this lesson by helping children find contractions in stories they have read. Remind them to use what they know about contractions as they read.

Grammar
Verbs That Tell About the Past

OBJECTIVES
- *To identify verbs that tell about the past*
- *To use verbs that tell about the past in sentences*

Focus
Say *Today I work hard*. Ask when you are working. (today) Then say *Yesterday, I worked hard*. Ask when you worked. (yesterday) Remind children that verbs can tell about the past.

Reteach the Skill
Visual Model   Write on the board and have children read:

jump	*jumped*
hop	*hopped*
shout	*shouted*

Ask children which words tell about things that happened in the past and how they know. (*jumped, hopped, shouted*; because they end with *-ed*.) Have children complete these sentences three times, using words from the board:

Now I ____. (jump, hop, shout)

A long time ago I ____. (jumped, hopped, shouted)

Ask each child to say a sentence telling something he or she did yesterday. Ask other children to identify the verb in each sentence. Then follow the suggestions in **Summarize/Assess**.

Auditory Model   Tell children you will say a sentence. They should say *today* or *yesterday* to tell whether the sentence tells about now, or whether it tells about the past. Use these sentences:

I am reading.
Kevin played his guitar.
Marcie climbed a tree.
You are listening.
Ann jumped over a puddle.
Nayla lifted the big bag.
We pushed our bikes up the hill.

Lastly, follow the suggestions in **Summarize/Assess**.

Kinesthetic Model   Write the following words on cards: *hopped, skipped, played, lifted, run, fall, sing, marched, ride*. Then write the word *now* at one end of the board and *the past* at the other end. Have children choose a card, read the word, and place it under the word on the board that indicates whether the word tells about now or the past. Then follow the suggestions in **Summarize/Assess**.

Summarize/Assess
Check children's understanding of the lesson by asking them to summarize what they learned. (A verb can tell about the past. Most verbs that tell about the past end with *-ed*.) Have each child write a sentence about the past. Encourage them to illustrate their sentences. Remind them that knowing about verbs that tell about the past can help them write clear, interesting sentences.

Phonics
Long Vowel /(y)o͞o/u-e

OBJECTIVES

- *To generate the sound for long vowel /(y)o͞o/u-e*
- *To distinguish /(y)o͞o/ in spoken words*
- *To blend and read words with long vowel /(y)o͞o/u-e*

Focus

Write the word *tube* on the board and read it. Say /(y)o͞o/ and tell children that the letter *u* has its long sound in *tube*. Point to the *e* at the end of the word, and remind children that the letter *e* at the end of a word often signals that the vowel in the middle will make its long sound.

Reteach the Skill
Phonemic Awareness

Phoneme Isolation   Tell children to listen as you say two words. Ask them to repeat only the word that says /(y)o͞o/. Use these words:

tune	town
cube	code
hug	huge
tube	tub
mile	mule
road	rude
cut	cute

Word Blending

Distribute Word Builder Cards *c*, *u*, *t*, and *e*. Blend and read the words *cut* and *cute* with children. As you model each step in your Word Builder, have children repeat after you.

- Place the letters *c*, *u*, and *t* in the Word Builder,  separated from each other.
- Point to *c*. Say /k/. Point to *u*. Say /u/.
- Slide *u* next to *c*. Move your hand under the letters  and blend the sounds, elongating them—/kkuu/.
- Point to *t*. Say /t/.
- Slide *t* next to *cu*. Move your hand under *cut* and blend by elongating the sounds—/ccuutt/.
- Read the word *cut* naturally.
- Add *e* after *t*. Point to *e*. Remind children 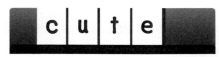 that the letter *e* often signals that the vowel in the middle makes its long sound.
- Blend the sounds again, this time using /(y)o͞o/ in place of /u/. Move your hand under the letters, elongating them—/kk(y)o͞ott/.
- Read the word *cute* naturally.

Follow the same procedure for *cub* and *cube*.

Summarize/Assess

Write the word *huge* on the board and have children read it. Then dictate *rude*, *mule*, and *tune*. Have children use their sound-letter knowledge to write the words.

 **Plot**

TESTED SKILL

ALTERNATIVE TEACHING STRATEGIES

OBJECTIVE
To recognize the elements of plot

Focus

Share the following information with children:

Every story has a beginning, a middle, and an ending. Events happen in each part of the story, and when you put them all together you have the whole *plot*. Knowing what happens and when it happens will help you to understand the plot of a story.

Reteach the Skill

Visual Model Write this simple story on sentence strips:

Pat went to the park.
Pat fed the ducks.
Pat went home.

Read the story aloud. Ask children to tell what happens in the beginning of the story. Remind them that the beginning comes before any other part of the story. Then ask them to tell you what happens in the middle of the story. Finally, have them tell you what happens at the end of the story, and remind them that the ending of the story is the last thing that happens. Then mix up the sentence strips and have children repeat the process. Have them discuss how the plot changed as the beginning, middle, and ending of the story changed. Then follow the suggestions in **Summarize/Assess**.

Kinesthetic Model Distribute art supplies for children to make simple puppets. Divide children into small groups. Have each group decide on a fable or tale they want to act out with their puppets. Help them first to write the beginning, middle, and ending of the story on paper. Then have them dramatize the plot of their story with their puppets. Ask the audience to identify the beginning, middle, and ending of each puppet show. Then follow the suggestions in **Summarize/Assess**.

Auditory Model Read aloud a short fable or tale. Have partners orally interview one another. Model questions such as, *What was the first thing that happened in the story? What happened in the middle of the story? What was the last thing that happened in the story? What was the whole story about?* Then have pairs work together to write the beginning, middle, and ending of the story. Then follow the suggestions in **Summarize/Assess**.

Summarize/Assess

Ask children to summarize what they have learned. (Every story has a beginning, a middle, and an ending. Events happen in each part of the story, and when you put them all together you have the whole *plot*.) To reinforce ideas, have children identify the beginning, middle, and ending of another story they have read.

Comprehension
Main Idea

OBJECTIVES
- *To read nonfiction for pleasure and/or information*
- *To determine important ideas in texts*

Focus

Ask children to listen as you name some objects: *soccer ball, football, rubber ball, playground ball*. Then ask what word tells what all the objects were. (balls) Explain that, since all the things you named were balls, you could say that the word *balls* tells the main idea of the list. Then tell children that information that you read also has a main idea. If you tell someone what a book or article is about, you are telling the main idea.

Reteach the Skill

Visual Model   Have children draw pictures of things they see on their way home from school. Display and discuss the pictures. Point out that these pictures show many things, but that there might be a way to tell what all the pictures are about. Through discussion, help children dictate a sentence about the pictures and write it on the board. For example, *We see a lot on our way home from school.* Then point out that this sentence tells the main idea of the pictures. Last, follow the suggestions in **Summarize/Assess**.

Kinesthetic Model   Put on display a group of items that can be used for writing, such as a pen, a pencil, a crayon, a piece of chalk, an eraser, paper. Tell children to think about a way to tell someone what kind of objects these are. Ask them to suggest what they would tell someone about all these objects. Explain that telling what all these objects are used for is telling the main idea. Point out that information that you read also has a main idea. The main idea is what the information is about. Then follow the suggestions in **Summarize/Assess**.

Auditory Model   Have children listen as you read the following paragraph. Ask them to think about what it is about.

> **Kevin likes many kinds of fruit in his lunches. Sometimes he has an apple. Other times he has a banana. Every now and then, he likes to have a peach. His favorite fruit of all is pears.**

Ask children to tell what the paragraph was about. Help them put their ideas into a complete sentence. Explain that a sentence that tells what a story or a paragraph is about tells the main idea of the paragraph. Then follow the suggestions in **Summarize/Assess**.

Summarize/Assess

Check children's understanding of the lesson by having them summarize what they learned. (The main idea is what a story or paragraph is about.) To reinforce this lesson, have children find pictures they like in books or magazines. Have them show the pictures to the class and give a sentence that tells what the picture is about. Point out that there are some objects in the picture that are not mentioned when you tell the main idea. Explain that the main idea is only the most important idea in a picture or in what you read. Remind children that paying attention to the main idea will help them understand and remember what they read.

Make Tree Frog Models

1. Make two tree frogs out of clay.
2. Make one little and one big.
3. Press the frogs against something smooth.
4. See which frog stays on longest.

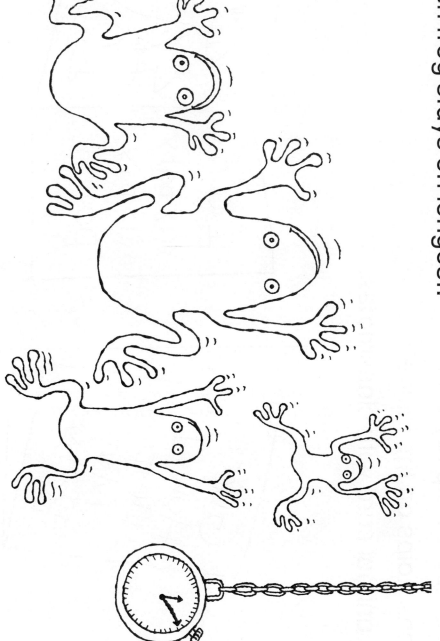

Harcourt

Make Animal Cards

1. Find out about animal mothers that help their babies.

2. Fold a sheet of paper in half.

3. Draw an animal mother on the outside.

4. Write "Guess How I Help My Baby."

5. Draw how she helps on the inside.

6. Share your animal card with classmates.

Guess
How I
Help
My
Baby

I carry
my baby
in my
pouch.

Description

Score of 4 ☆ ☆ ☆ ☆

🙂	My description has a title.
🙂	My description tells what something looks like.
🙂	My description is all about one thing.
🙂	My description has details to help my reader see what I am telling about.
🙂	My description has describing words.

Information Writing

Score of 4 ☆ ☆ ☆ ☆

☺	My information writing has a title.
☺	My information writing tells about something that is true.
☺	My information writing is all about one thing.
☺	My information writing has details to help my reader understand what I am writing about.

Harcourt

Harcourt

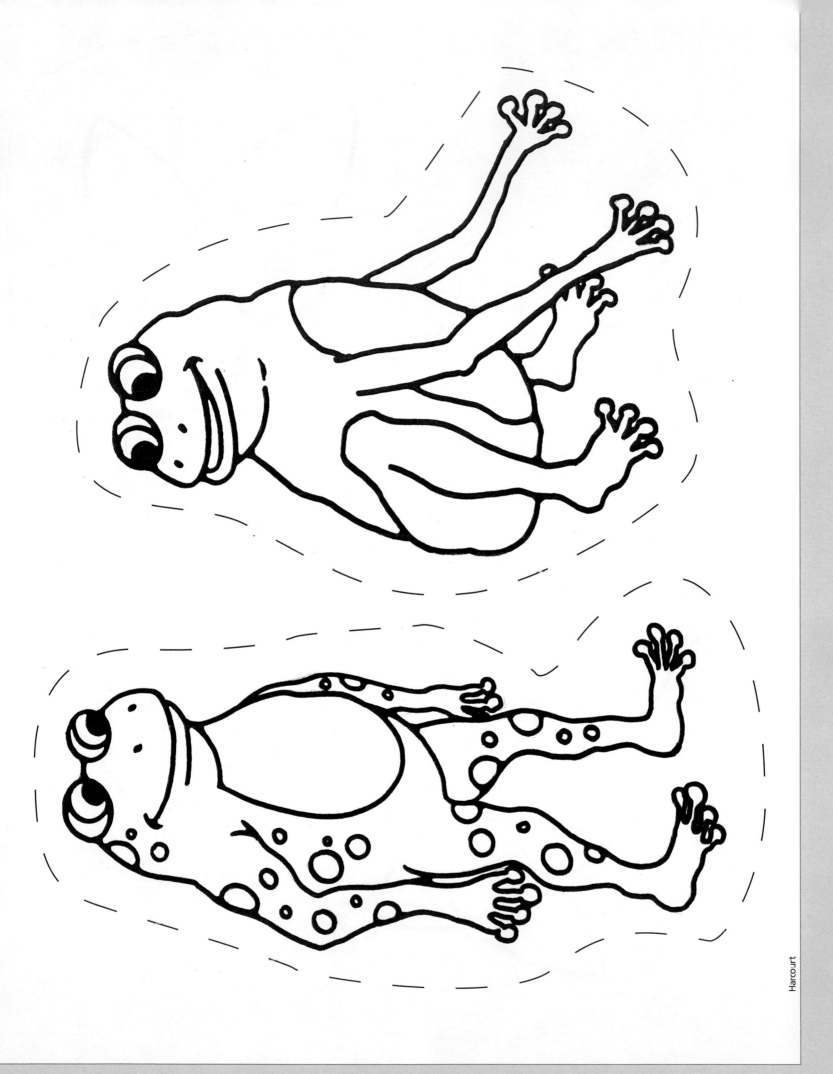

T18 **Gather Around**

CHARACTER CUTOUTS: Frog and Toad All Year

Harcourt

Harcourt

CHARACTER CUTOUTS: Poppleton Everyday

CHARACTER CUTOUTS: Baboon

Harcourt

Wordscope

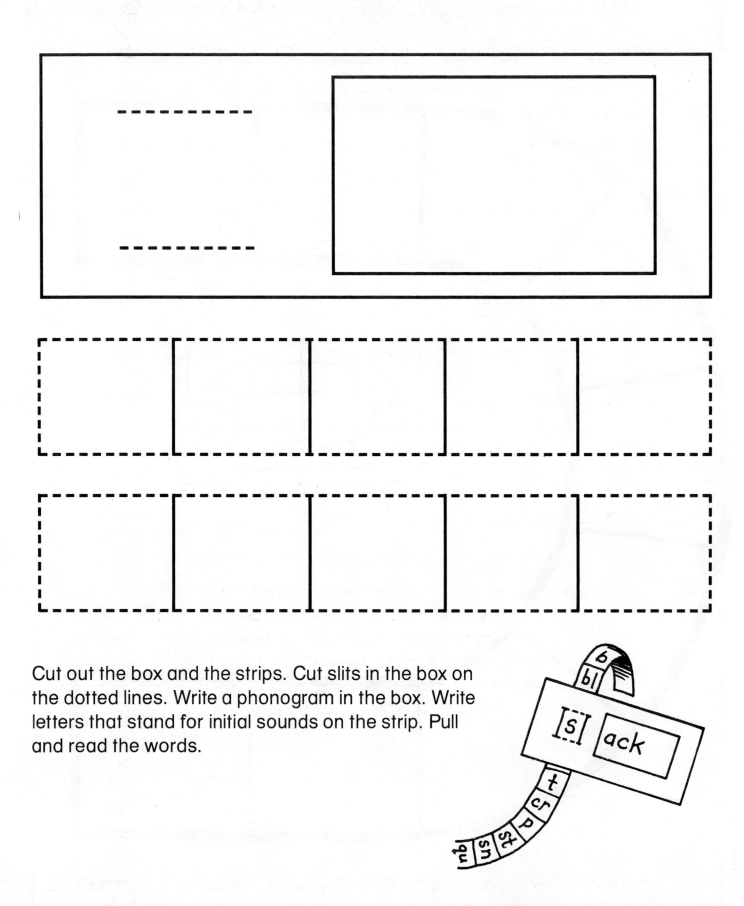

Cut out the box and the strips. Cut slits in the box on the dotted lines. Write a phonogram in the box. Write letters that stand for initial sounds on the strip. Pull and read the words.

Game Board

1. Make two copies.   **2.** Cut out.   **3.** Glue onto a file folder.

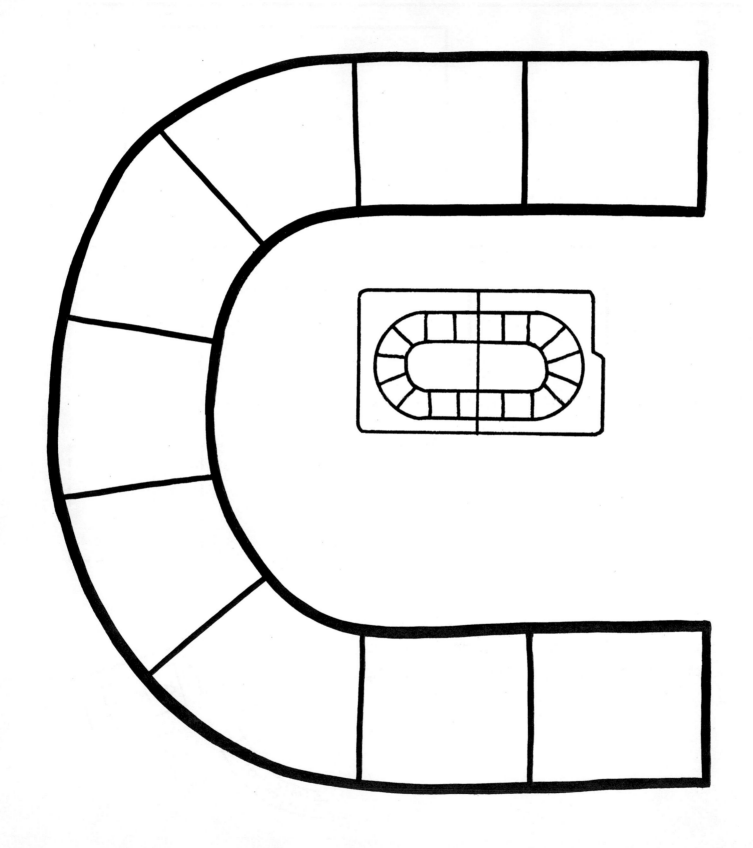

Harcourt

16-Box Grid

Use for word sorts and games.

Harcourt

Sum It Up

Write or draw.

Story Event	Story Event	Story Event

What happened in the whole story?

Harcourt

Making Predictions

What will happen in the story?

What really happened?

What was surprising?

 # News from

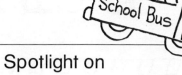

Dear Family,
    I'd like to take a
moment to talk about

Spotlight on

Something to Try at Home

From Your Child

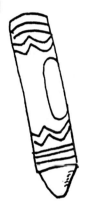

We have been very
busy lately!

BOOK CORNER

Harcourt

Reading Log

Keeping Track
of Reading

_____
(name)

Book Title _____

Author _____

What did you think of the book? _____

_____

_____

_____

Tape the cars together. Fold the book to store it.

Children can make an accordion book to keep a record of books they have read. Make several copies of the train cars to use.

Harcourt

Pop-Up Book

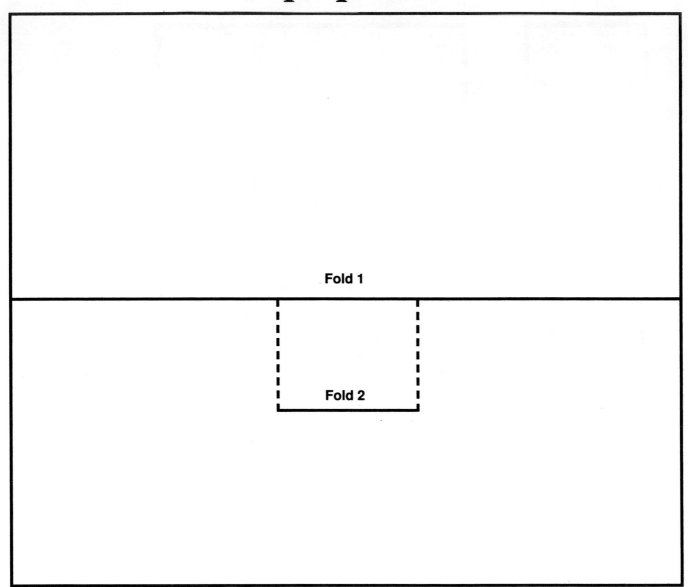

Fold 1

Fold 2

1. Cut out the book. Fold the book in half.
2. Cut on the dotted lines through both layers.
3. Fold on the solid lines. Open and refold so the box will pop out.
4. Glue it inside a cover.
5. Glue a picture on the pop-up.

My Writing Log

Name _____

My ideas for writing:	I wrote my first copy.	I made changes	I published my writing.

Make copies of the Writing Log for children to keep in their portfolios. Keep a log of progress by placing check marks, a rubber stamp, or a date for each writing idea that is developed.

Harcourt

K-W-L Chart

K	W	L
What I Know	What I Want to Know	What I Learned

Harcourt

Index of High-Frequency Words and Vocabulary

The Story of a Blue Bird

afraid
flew
join
learn
nothing
thought
wonder

How to Be a Nature Detective

clues
detective
floor
nature
piece
pulls

Sleep Is for Everyone

afternoon
bicycle
carry
hours
parents

Frog and Toad All Year

caught
cold
hurried
near
son
sure

The Puddle

angry
nearly
okay
sorry

Baboon

against
careful
fire
quietly
shook

Fishing Bears

both
during
ready

Poppleton Everyday

boy
brought
few
head
read

The Story of a Blue Bird	The Story of a Blue Bird
afraid	wonder
flew	
join	
learn	
nothing	
thought	

Frog and Toad All Year	Fishing Bears
caught	both
cold	during
hurried	ready
near	
son	
sure	

clues	angry
detective	nearly
floor	okay
nature	sorry
piece	
pulls	

Harcourt

Poppleton Everyday	Sleep Is for Everyone
boy	afternoon
brought	bicycle
few	carry
head	hours
read	parents

Harcourt

against

careful

fire

quietly

shook

Harcourt

 # School-Home Connection

Your child has been reading "The Story of a Blue Bird." It tells of a young bird who overcomes his fear of flying and goes exploring with other young birds.

I have tried some of the activities.

Student: _____

Family Member: _____

Comments/Suggestions: _____

_____

You may want to do some of these activities with your child.

Words, Words, Words

Label an empty tissue or shoe box for word cards. Print your child's name on the box, for example, **Molly's Words**. Your child will add word cards for each new story.

- Have your child cut out the word cards and read each word.
- Think of a sentence for each word but leave the word out. Ask your child to complete the sentence by choosing the word card and saying the word. Then your child can create a new sentence with the same word.
- Have your child identify and read the five words that show action. (*flew, join, learn, thought, wonder*)

What Makes a Nest?

Ask your child what birds use to make their nests. Different birds build different kinds of nests. Materials include grass, pine needles, straw, hair, feathers, pebbles, and dirt. Take your child on a walk to observe nests in your neighborhood. Find books at the library about birds and how they build nests, one tiny piece at a time.

Harcourt

🕐 **TIME TO READ** Encourage your child to read for at least 30 minutes outside of class each day.

| afraid |
| flew |
| join |
| learn |
| nothing |
| thought |
| wonder |

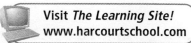 **Visit *The Learning Site!*** www.harcourtschool.com

See Resources for Parents and Teachers: Homework Helper

School–Home Connection

Your child has been reading "Frog and Toad All Year: The Corner," a story about Frog's search for spring which is "just around the corner."

I have tried some of the activities.

Student: _____

Family Member: _____

Comments/Suggestions: _____

_____

_____

You may want to do some of these activities with your child.

Words, Words, Words

- Have your child cut out the word cards and read each word.
- Ask your child to use each word in a sentence that shows the meaning of the word, for example, "People are *working* to repair the road."
- Have your child find and read the two words that begin with *c* and the two words that begin with *s*.

Figures of Speech

Explain that "just around the corner" is a figure of speech, or a way of saying one thing to mean something else. For example, just around the corner means "very soon" or "very near." Talk about other sayings such as "It's raining cats and dogs" and "I have a frog in my throat." Your child may like to draw pictures of the literal meanings of these expressions.

| caught |
| cold |
| hurried |
| near |
| son |
| sure |

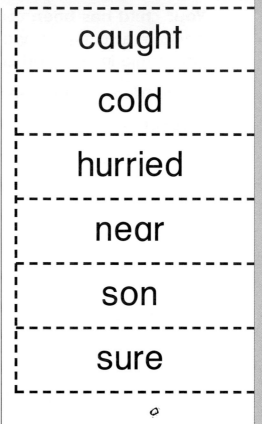

Harcourt

 TIME TO READ Encourage your child to read for at least 30 minutes outside of class each day.

Visit *The Learning Site!*
www.harcourtschool.com

See Resources for Parents and Teachers: Homework Helper

# School–Home Connection

Your child has been reading "Fishing Bears." This nonfiction story tells about the lives of Alaskan brown bears.

I have tried some of the activities.

Student: _____

Family Member: _____

Comments/Suggestions: _____

_____

_____

You may want to do some of these activities with your child.

Words, Words, Words
- Have your child cut out the word cards and read each word.
- Have your child make up questions using the words on the cards. Make up an answer to each question, and use the same new word your child used.
- Together, make up a sentence using all three new words. Write the sentence for your child, and have your child draw a picture to go with the sentence.

Let's Go Fishing
Ask your child to tell you how brown bears catch fish. Together, talk about how people catch fish. Look in magazines, catalogs, and books for pictures of people fishing. Then talk about where you would go and what you would do if you could go fishing together.

 TIME TO READ Encourage your child to read for at least 30 minutes outside of class each day.

 Visit *The Learning Site!* www.harcourtschool.com

See Resources for Parents and Teachers: Homework Helper

Harcourt

 # School-Home Connection

Your child has been reading "How to Be a Nature Detective." This nonfiction selection tells how people can use tracks and other clues to learn about animals in nature.

I have tried some of the activities.

Student: _____

Family Member: _____

Comments/Suggestions: _____

_____

_____

You may want to do some of these activities with your child.

Words, Words, Words
- Have your child cut out the word cards and read each word.
- Say a sentence for each word, but leave the word out. Have your child pick the card with the word that belongs in your sentence. Then have your child say the whole sentence.
- With your child, make up a story about another kind of detective. Try to use at least four of the new words in your story.

Making Tracks
Ask your child to tell you about the animal tracks described in "How to Be a Nature Detective." Then have your child tell what his or her tracks would look like. Have your child draw pictures of those tracks. Your child may want to draw them independently or might prefer to trace around his or her own feet or shoes. Offer to do some of the tracing if your child wants help.

clues
detective
floor
nature
piece
pulls

TIME TO READ Encourage your child to read for at least 30 minutes outside of class each day.

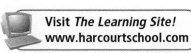 **Visit *The Learning Site!*** www.harcourtschool.com

See Resources for Parents and Teachers: Homework Helper

Harcourt

School–Home Connection

Your child has been reading "The Puddle." It is the tale of a boy who ventures out on a rainy day to sail his boat in a puddle.

I have tried some of the activities.

Student: _____

Family Member: _____

Comments/Suggestions: _____

_____

_____

angry
okay
nearly
sorry

You may want to do some of these activities with your child.

Words, Words, Words

- Have your child cut out the word cards and read each word.
- Give your child a sentence clue about each word. Ask your child to identify the word card and read the answer. For example, "I am a word that means *to come out*. My name is _____." (appear) "I am a word that means *to rest*. My name is _____." (break)
- Ask your child to name the letter at the end of all four new words. Together, think of other words that end with *y*.

All Kinds of Sailboats

Ask your child to tell you the story "The Puddle." Talk about the kind of boat the boy in the story played with (sailboat). How does a sailboat move in the water? Find pictures of sailboats in magazines, books, or newspapers and compare them by size and number of sails. Visit the library to find other stories about sailboats and sailing or pictures of sailboats.

Harcourt

TIME TO READ   Encourage your child to read for at least 30 minutes outside of class each day.

Visit *The Learning Site!* www.harcourtschool.com

See Resources for Parents and Teachers: Homework Helper

School–Home Connection

"Your child has been reading "Poppleton Everyday: The New Bed." It tells the story of a pig in search of the best grown-up bed he can find. Poppleton uses many tests to be sure that the bed he finds is perfect for him.

I have tried some of the activities.

Student: _____

Family Member: _____

Comments/Suggestions: _____

_____

_____

You may want to do some of these activities with your child.

| boy |
| brought |
| few |
| head |
| read |

Words, Words, Words

• Have your child cut out the word cards and read each card.
• Have your child lay the word cards on the table. Then think of a sentence and have your child supply the missing word by identifying the word card and saying the word. For example, "It is good to take a walk and breathe fresh _____." (*air*)
• Have your child use the words in sentences and place the word cards in his or her word box.

The Right Bed for Me

Ask your child how Poppleton tested a bed before he bought it. Then ask your child to describe the tests he or she would do before purchasing a bed. Suggest that your child draw pictures to show himself or herself conducting the tests (sleeping, jumping, standing, rolling on the bed, watching TV, and so on).

Harcourt

TIME TO READ Encourage your child to read for at least 30 minutes outside of class each day.

Visit *The Learning Site!* www.harcourtschool.com

See Resources for Parents and Teachers: Homework Helper

 # School–Home Connection

Your child has been reading "Sleep Is for Everyone."
This nonfiction story tells why and how people sleep.

I have tried some of the activities.

Student: _____

Family Member: _____

Comments/Suggestions: _____

_____

_____

You may want to do some of these activities with your child.

Words, Words, Words

- Have your child cut out the word cards and read each word.
- Have your child pick three new words to act out for you. Try to guess the words your child acts out.
- Say a sentence with each new word, but leave the word out. Have your child show the card with the missing word and then say the whole sentence.

Sleep Well!

Ask your child to describe how some animals sleep. If you have pets at home, take time to watch them sleep. Then remind your child that brown bears sleep all winter long; this is called hibernating. Have your child draw a picture to show what he or she would do if people slept during the whole winter.

afternoon

bicycle

carry

hours

parents

TIME TO READ Encourage your child to read for at least 30 minutes outside of class each day.

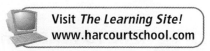
Visit *The Learning Site!*
www.harcourtschool.com

See Resources for Parents and Teachers: Homework Helper

Harcourt

 # School-Home Connection

Your child has been reading "Baboon," a story about a baby baboon exploring the world with his mother.

I have tried some of the activities.

Student: _____

Family Member: _____

Comments/Suggestions: _____

_____

_____

You may want to do some of these activities with your child.

Words, Words, Words

- Have your child cut out the word cards and read each word.
- Have your child act out the meaning of each word for you to guess the word.
- Have your child use the words in sentences and place the word cards in his or her word box.

Explore the World

Ask your child to tell you about the baby baboon's activities in "Baboon." Then talk about a human baby's activities. Together look at photographs that show your child learning to walk or crawl. Talk about how babies explore everything around them as part of learning and growing. Ask your child what kinds of things children of five or six years old do to learn.

TIME TO READ Encourage your child to read for at least 30 minutes outside of class each day.

disappear

against

careful

fire

quietly

shook

Harcourt

Visit *The Learning Site!*
www.harcourtschool.com

See Resources for Parents and
Teachers: Homework Helper

Additional Reading
Gather Around

This list is a compilation of the additional theme- and topic-related books cited in the lesson plans. You may wish to use this list to provide children with opportunities to read at least twenty minutes a day outside of class.

THEME 6: GOING PLACES

Agell, Charlotte. *Up the Mountain.* Dorling-Kindersley, 2000. A rainy day leads to adventures for Cat, Dragon, Chicken, and Rabbit. AVERAGE

Asch, Frank. *The Sun is My Favorite Star.* Gulliver Books, 2000. A little girl sings praises of the sun for all the things the sun does for us. AVERAGE

Austin, Margot. *Friend for Growl Bear.* HarperCollins, 1999. Growl Bear is just learning to talk, but he can only growl, so he frightens all the other animals. AVERAGE

Baker, Keith. *Hide and Snake.* Voyager, 1995. A snake plays hide-and-seek with the reader. EASY

Banks, Kate. *Gift from the Sea.* Farrar, Straus & Giroux, 2001. A rock holds many secrets from the past. AVERAGE

Burton, Virginia Lee. *The Little House.* Houghton Mifflin, 1969. A pretty little house in the country watches the city build up all around her until she is moved back to the country. ☙ *Caldecott Medal; ALA Notable Book.* CHALLENGING

Carpenter, Stephen. *The Three Billy Goats Gruff.* HarperCollins, 1998. Three goats outsmart a troll that lives under a bridge. AVERAGE

Chandler, Gertrude. *Meet the Boxcar Children: The Adventures of Benny and Watch.* Albert Whitman & Company, 1998. Four orphaned siblings move into an abandoned boxcar until they are united with their grandmother. CHALLENGING

Christian, Peggy. *If You Find a Rock.* Harcourt, 2000. Rocks and stones are for skipping, climbing, and hiding things. CHALLENGING

Cowley, Joy. *Boring Old Bed.* The Wright Group, 1996. Jim thinks his bed is boring, and tries to sleep in other places around the house. However, he realizes that his bed is the best place of all. EASY

Cowley, Joy. *Grizzly and the Bumble-Bee.* The Wright Group, 1989. Grizzly Bear is stung by a bumble-bee and has a hard time telling people what happened. EASY

Eastman, P.D. *Are You My Mother?* Random House, 1960. A newly hatched bird goes on an adventure in search of his mother. EASY

Eaton, Deborah. *Dream Around the World.* Instant Reader, Harcourt 1997. A boy falls asleep and dreams about traveling the world. EASY

Eaton, Deborah. *The Rainy Day Grump.* Millbrook Press, 1998. Clay is grumpy because it's rainy and he wants to play ball. EASY

Gaitanos, Sarah. *The Monarch Butterfly.* The Wright Group, 1996. Beautiful photographs help explain the process of a caterpillar turning into a butterfly. AVERAGE

Gibbons, Gail. *Frogs.* Holiday House, 1993. This informational book about frogs, explains their beginnings as tadpoles and how they differ from toads. CHALLENGING

Hest, Amy. *Mabel Dancing.* Candlewick, 2000. A child dances her way through her dreams. AVERAGE

Krensky, Stephen. *Lionel at Large.* Puffin, 1986. Lionel must endure many things, including eating green beans. CHALLENGING

Leaf, Munro. *The Story of Ferdinand.* Puffin Books, 1977. A little Spanish bull would rather sit and smell the flowers than fight. AVERAGE

Lobel, Arnold. *Frog and Toad Together.* HarperCollins, 1972. Classic companion stories in one compilation including "A List," "Cookies," and "The Dream." ☙ *Newbery Honor; ALA Notable Book.* AVERAGE

Lobel, Arnold. *Small Pig.* HarperCollins, 1969. Pig is searching for a small mud hole. CHALLENGING

Lum, Kate. *What! Cried Granny: An Almost Bedtime Story.* Dial 1999. Patrick's many excuses delay his bedtime, but Granny springs into action. ☙ *ALA Notable Book; SLJ Best Book; Children's Choice.* CHALLENGING

McPhail, David. *Pig Pig Grows Up.* Dutton Children's Books, 1980. Pig Pig refuses to grow up until a near disaster forces him to. ☙ *Children's Choice. EASY*

Moffatt, Judith. *Who Stole the Cookies?* Grossett & Dunlap, 1996. A series of animals bicker over stolen cookies until the thief appears in a cave. EASY

Parkes, Brenda. *Goodnight Goodnight.* Rigby, 1898. Each night, a child dreams that storybook characters visit her. EASY

Robinson, F.R. *Henry.* Instant Reader, Harcourt, 1997. Henry is a little different from the other members of his family. EASY

Robinson, F.R. *Water's Journey.* Instant Reader, Harcourt, 1997. Rain falls from the sky and travels a long way to the ground. EASY

Rylant, Cynthia. *Henry and Mudge and the Best Day.* Macmillan, 1995. The first day of May is a good day for Henry and his dog Mudge because it is Henry's birthday. CHALLENGING

Tildes, Phyllis. *Animals in Camouflage.* Limbacher. Charlesbridge, 2000. Riddles about animals that use camouflage to protect themselves. AVERAGE

Tuchman, Gail. *How the Sky Got Its Stars.* Instant Readers, Harcourt, 1997. A Hopi legend tells how all animals, except for Coyote, created things on Earth. Then Coyote plays with the stars and makes something, too. EASY

Wahl, Jan. *Three Pandas.* Boyd Mills Press, 2001. Three Pandas leave the forest and head for the city, where they encounter many people. CHALLENGING

Winter, Susan. *Copy Me, Copycub.* HarperCollins, 1999. Follow a mother bear and her cub through the four seasons. CHALLENGING

Pupil Edition Word Lists: Level 5

The following words appear in the *Pupil Edition* stories in Level 5.

Key	
*	High-Frequency Word in Level 5
italics	Story Word in Level 5
red	Word appears for the first time in Level 5
normal type	Decodable Word or Known Word*

* Known words were taught in Trophies Kindergarten Program, in the Inventory Unit, or in Levels 1, 2, 3, or 4.

The Story of a Blue Bird

a, about, afraid*, all, am, and, *answered*, are, as, ask, asked, at, away, back, be, been, before, beyond, big, bird, birds, bit, blue, born, brother, but, by, called, came, *colorful*, come, couldn't, didn't, does, don't, ever, everyone, everywhere, fast, flew*, flock, fluttering, fly, flying, for, forgot, from, go, going, gone, green, grew, had, happened, *happily*, have, he, here, high, him, his, home, how, I, if, *imagining*, in, is, it, join*, joined, kept, know, learn*, like, little, look, looked, looking, low, make, Mama, me, might, morning, mother, nest, next, night, no, nothing*, now, of, Oh, on, one, or, other, out, *pool*, said, sat, seen, she, sister, sleep, so, someone, spread, still, stop, story, *suddenly*, surprised, tell, tested, that, the, their, them, there, they, thinking, this, thought*, to, together, too, tree, trees, up, upon, us, walked, was, watching, water, well, what, when, where, while, why, wings, with, wonder*, wondered, wonderful, yes, you, your

Frog and Toad All Year

a, again, all, along, am, an, and, another, are, around, asked, asleep, back, be, been, bigger, birds, but, cake, came, caught*, chasing, *clothes*, cold*, come, coming, corner, cried, day, did, down, dry, father, find, flowers, for, found, frog, frog's, garden, go, good, got, grass, gray, had, happy, has, have, his, home, house, hurried*, I, if, in, is, it, just, lizard, look, make, me, *meadow*, mother, much, mud, must, my, near*, no, not, of, Oh, old, on, only, other, out, outside, path, pebbles, pine, *pollywog*, rain, ran, right, river, said, saw, see, side, singing, sitting, small, some, son*, soon, *spoiled*, spring, stand, started, stop, stopped, story, stove, stump, sun, sure*, tail, tea, tell, than, that, the, their, there, they, this, three, *tired*, to, toad, too, tree, until, very, waiting, walked, wanted, was, we, went, were, wet, what, when, while, who, will, *woods*, working, worm, year, yes, you, your

Fishing Bears

a, about, again, air, *Alaskan*, also, an, and, animals, are, at, baby, be, bear, bears, big, bigger, both*, brown, by, called, can, catch, clams, count, *cozy*, cub, cubs, deep, den, dens, dig, do, doing, during*, ears, eat, eating, ends, *enemies*, eyes, fat, feet, fighting, find, fish, fishing, flat, food, for, from, furry, get, good, ground, hard, have, healthy, her, *hibernate*, hibernating, hind, how, in, is, it, keeping, keeps, leave, legs, live, long, look, lot, makes, male, many, marks, Mom, most, mother, mothers, napping, near, need, next, nose, of, on, one, or, over, picture, plants, playing, pouncing, ready*, rest, river, rivers, safe, *salmon*, sleep, small, smell, sneak, some, spot, spring, stand, stands, stay, the, their, them, then, these, they, think, this, three, time, to, toe, toes, tracks, trail, triplets, trying, twins, under, up, *usually*, walk, walking, warm, water, what, when, why, will, wins, winter, with, work, years, you

How to Be a Nature Detective

a, across, again, ahead, all, almost, an, and, animal, another, answer, anywhere, apart, are, as, at, ate, away, baby, back, backyard, bank, be, began, behind, belly, big, bike, bullfrog, but, button, by, came, can, carefully, cat, cat's, catch, city, claw, *claws*, clothing, clues*, coming, could, course, crayfish, day, deer, detective*, detectives, did, dinner, dish, do, does, doesn't, dog, dog's, don't, down, drank, drink, dust, eat, empty, even, ever, *exactly*, fall, far, fat, fawn, feet, find, finds, fingerprints, floor*, food, *footprints*, for, found, four, fox, from, front, go, goes, going, had, hair, hands, happened, has, have, he, help, her, here, hind, his, hoof, how, hurry, if, in, into, is, it, jumps, kind, know, last, leave, leaves, left, let's, lickety, like, line, little, long, look, looks, made, make, many, mark, marks, means, meat, milk, more, mother, mud, muddy, nature*, near, night, not, now, of, on, once

one
only
or
other
out
page
park
paw
paws
picture
piece*
pile
places
prints
problem
pulls*
puts
questions
rabbit
raccoon
raccoons
rest
right
river
round
sand
sat
says
see
sharp
shells
sidewalk
single
slithered
snake
snow
snowy
so
somebody
someone
something
sometimes
special
split
still
take
that
the
them
then
there
these
they
things
this
those
tires
to
toe
toes
too
torn
toward
track
tracks
tree
two
walk
walked
walks
was
watch
water
way
ways
we
webbed
went
were
wet

what
when
where
which
who
why
will
with
woods
you

The Puddle
a
about
all
alligator
allowed
along
an
and
angry*
animals
asked
at
away
back
bath
be
before
beside
boat
boots
bring
but
by
called
came
can
can't
care
coat
come
could
course
crash
day
did
didn't
different
don't
down
drank
dressed
dried
elephant
find
floated
for
frog
from
funny
get
go
gone
gonna
got
great
had
he
help
her
him
home
hot
I
I'm
if
in
into

it
join
jumped
largest
laughed
left
like
listen
long
looked
me
mom
mom's
my
nearly*
need
next
nice
not
of
offered
okay*
onto
other
out
pig
puddle
puddles
put
rain
rainy
really
rest
right
running
said
sail
sailed
sat
she
shouted
showed
so
sorry*
splashed
start
started
stay
steered
sun
swam
swim
take
teatime
than
that
the
then
there
they
think
thirsty
this
thought
to
told
too
took
turtle
until
up
upset
waiting
want
wanted
was
water
went
were
when

with
worry
would
wouldn't
yelled
you
your

Poppleton Everyday
a
about
air
always
and
any
asked
at
back
bed
big
biggest
bluebirds
book
books
both
bottom
boy*
brought*
but
buy
certainly
check
checked
climbed
closed
come
crackers
crumbs
day
decided
different
do
don't
edge
enormous
everyday
everywhere
eyes
face
*few**
followed
for
game
got
grown-up
had
happily
have
he
he'd
head*
her
his
Hmmm
home
how
I
in
it
it's
just
know
lay
leg
legs
liked
looked
looking
many

me
more
my
new
now
old
on
one
outside
over
pages
pardon
picked
pig
pillows
Poppleton
propped
read*
right
said
saleslady
she
show
side
since
sing
size
sleep
smile
so
some
store
test
the
thing
this
three
to
TV
twenty
up
vast
wake
want
wanted
was
watch
watched
way
ways
went
with
yet
you

Sleep Is for Everyone
a
about
after
afternoon*
airplane
all
am
an
and
animals
apples
are
arms
around
as
asleep
at
attention
awake
babies
balloon
basket

because
bed
begin
bicycle*
bigger
birds
body
brain
bundles
but
can
Caroline
carry*
cars
cats
changed
chicken
children
clouds
covers
cows
cranky
cries
cross
curl
diaper
different
dinner
do
does
doesn't
dogs
don't
down
eat
eight
elephant
every
everyone
eyelids
eyes
fast
feel
feels
fine
floating
for
from
get
go
goes
goldfish
good
grow
growing
grown-ups
had
hard
has
have
he
hear
heavy
helps
her
high
his
horse
hours*
I
I'm
if
in
is
isn't
it
its
Jonathan
less
lie

light
like
little
long
lot
makes
mattress
me
more
morning
most
mother
my
nap
need
needs
never
next
night
night's
no
of
off
old
older
on
only
open
or
others
out
parents*
part
pay
people
perfectly
perhaps
pigeon
pigs
pool
racing
rest
resting
riding
right
roller-skating
rubber
run
schoolchildren
seashore
see
seven
she
she's
shut
sights
sit
sits
six
sky
sleep
sleeps
smell
snake
snakes
so
some
sometimes
soon
sounds
standing
stay
still
stop
stops
stretch
takes
taste
tell
ten

than
that's
the
their
them
they
things
think
thinking
thoughts
throws
time
tired
to
too
turn
TV
twelve
twist
two
under
up
wakes
wander
want
wants
warm
watch
waves
way
weeks
when
which
with
work
working
works
world
yawn
years
you
your

Baboon
a
across
afraid
against*
ahead
along
always
among
and
are
around
as
asked
asleep
at
awoke
baboon
baboon's
back
backward
bank
barely
be
behind
big
bird
black
blinked
burned
bush
bushes
but
by
came
can
careful*

carrying
climbed
close
closed
cloud
come
could
crocodile
dark
darted
did
disappear
down
each
eat
eaten
edge
elephants
everything
eyes
far
fast
feel
fell
field
fire*
flew
followed
for
forest
found
four
from
gazelle
gazelles
going
gone
grass
great
green
ground
grunted
had
hand
happy
he
head
heat
hid
him
his
home
hot
huddled
hungry
hurt
in
into
is
it
its
just
laid
lake
lay
leaped
led
light
like
long
look
looked
loud
middle
might
monkey
more
mother
mother's

mouth
moved
neck
no
not
now
of
on
onto
opened
other
out
over
overhead
pass
passed
quick
quietly*
ran
resting
rhinoceros
road
rolled
said
sandy
sat
see
she
shook*
side
sky
sleepy
slid
slow
small
so
soft
softly
some
sometimes
soon
started
stretched
sun
tall
that
the
then
there
they
thundered
time
to
together
too
took
tree
trees
turtle
up
waited
walked
want
was
watched
were
when
whispered
wide
will
world
yes
you

Decodable Book Word Lists Level 5

The following decodable words appear in the *Decodable Books* in Level 5.

Key	
red	Word appears for the first time in Level 5
normal type	Decodable Word

Seeing the Sights
a
all
and
as
back
be
best
bike
bright
bus
but
by
car
cross
eating
flight
fly
for
fun
get
getting
high
home
in
is
it's
jet
light
lights
lunch
might
nice
night
on
pack
seas
see
seeing
ship
sights
sky
snacks
spot
stopping
stuck
sunshine
take
the
tight
time

travel
traveling
while

The Light Fight
a
all
and
as
bad
bright
can't
Clark
dark
day
dreams
drive
fight
first
for
fright
fun
gives
good
got
had
he
his
I
I'm
in
is
it
leave
light
long
Mark
me
might
morning
much
mumbled
night
nightlight
off
on
right
see
shouted
sigh
sights
sleep
sleepy

started
stop
store
that
the
then
tight
turn
turned
went
with

Daisy
a
all
always
and
art
at
Blaine
but
called
Daisy
down
fails
flair
for
going
grins
hand
her
hogging
hogs
humming
in
it's
job
just
lots
making
milk
Miss
needs
never
nice
no
Oh
paint
play
plays
puddles
rain
raise
rest

rests
she
sit
speak
spilling
splashes
splashing
stains
the
things
time
trail
wailed
wait
whispered
whispering
white
wink
with

A Gray Day
a
are
asks
at
bay
bird
but
by
clay
clouds
cries
dark
day
digging
dock
end
get
glad
gray
he
hidden
his
I
I'm
in
is
it
it's
Jay
Kay
making
may

mumbles
near
not
OK
on
pail
rays
sand
she
stay
stayed
sun's
that
the
things
tray
way
well
will

One Rainy Day
a
and
be
Blaine
bright
cards
care
chair
cried
day
for
Gail
get-well
got
here
in
it
left
made
mail
milk
Mom
mop
more
my
no
on
pail
paint
painted

plain
rainy
rest
sailing
sat
set
sick
sit
stains
surprise
take
tape
that
the
this
toast
trail
train
tray
tripped
up
we'll
went
will
with

Rain, I Say
a
again
all
another
as
away
can
can't
care
clay
day
days
fun
garden
gets
go
gray
ground
grow
hard
hasn't
I
if
in
inside
is

it
just
let
like
maybe
much
my
no
plants
play
playing
quite
rain
rained
rays
say
sky
stay
sun
the
this
today
way
while
why
will
with

Hi, Green Beans!
a
and
at
beans
beetles
bigger
can
deep
dig
dirty
falls
find
garden
getting
green
grow
Hi
holes
I
I'll
inches
it
it's
kind

last
leaves
lots
lunch
make
makes
mild
mind
munching
my
nice
on
plant
plants
rain
rise
say
scat
see
seeds
small
spot
spring
stems
sunlight
sunny
sunshine
tall
the
time
wait
will
with

Wild, Wild Things
a
all
and
bit
blinding
boring
cats
child
day
days
Di
dogs
find
fish
flies
found
happy
has

ice
is
isn't
it
kind
likes
mice
mild
mind
named
now
off
OK
or
pets
place
quite
rain
rather
she
snow
still
storming
tame
that
that's
the
they're
things
thinks
turtles
when
where
wild
wildest

Let's Go!
again
and
bet
bundle
bundled
called
cold
cried
did
don't
fall
fell
fluffy
froze
fun
go
groaned

grumbled
hold
I
is
Jo
last
let's
like
make
moaned
Mom
my
no
nose
now
prints
sighed
skate
snow
so
that
the
this
time
told
up
we
we'll
went
will
wind

Flo Hippo
a
air
and
any
banjo
Bo
can
Chimp
class
cried
dance
don't
dressed
ever
fast
faster
Flo
floating
for
fro
fun

fun
go
gold
had
Hippo
his
how
I
I'll
I'm
in
is
it
just
keep
kept
let's
like
more
most
mumbled
no
off
Oh
on
over
play
played
please
see
she
show
slow
so
songs
spun
stop
the
this
time
to
told
twirled
up
way
well
what
when
won't
yo-yo

Roger's Gerbil

a
and
as
cage
can't
curled
ear
for
gentle
gerbil
gerbil's
giggled
Ginger
Ginger's
grinned
had
hand
he
he's

his
how
I
in
is
it
kept
large
let
like
little
look
looks
lots
me
name
nap
needs
new
pet
picked
playthings
Ranger
Roger
Roger's
rubbed
sat
she
shouted
sweet
tall
that
that's
the
think
thinking
twitched
up
what's
whiskers

The Fudge Judge

a
as
badge
be
big
bit
bridge
bright
budge
bulge
cannot
cried
crossed
day
dripped
each
edge
fudge
gold
grinned
had
hard
he
Hedgehog
help
his
hot
I

I'm
in
into
it
judge
judged
large
melting
more
mumbled
never
nibbled
no
nose
on
pick
quills
smudge
sparkled
Spike
stage
started
stuck
sun
the
then
town
tummy
walked
was
wedge
will
winner
with

Ginger

a
asked
at
back
be
but
called
cried
dad
danger
day
did
didn't
dog
find
for
found
frisky
full
gentle
get
Ginger
Ginny
Ginny's
got
hedge
help
her
hugged
is
just
last
leash
like
liked

name
next
park
plunged
she
so
spice
that
the
there
upset
was
we
when

The Badgers Have a Picnic

a
and
asked
at
Badgers
basket
big
bridge
by
can
cheese
chirped
cried
dodge
eat
forgot
fudge
get
giggled
ginger
Ginny
grumbled
help
here
I
I'll
if
is
it
it's
Jack
just
lake
large
let's
little
Madge
much
need
orange
pack
picnic
said
salad
sandwiches
see
she
sick
sit
smile
smiled
snaps

sniffed
something
that
the
this
we
we'll
wedge
yelled

Queen June and the Rude Duke

a
acted
again
all
always
and
bad
ball
band
best
big
Bruce
but
came
crown
cubes
cute
dance
day
Duke
ever
filled
flutes
gave
had
he
huge
ice
in
June
June's
liked
manners
named
never
night
once
one
or
played
playing
please
prunes
Queen
queen
quite
rude
say
seen
she
silly
so
stuffed
thanks
the
time
tricks

tunes
upon
visit
with

Jules and Luke

a
across
along
always
and
are
at
camp
chilly
cold
could
doesn't
don't
dunes
eat
flute
grapes
has
his
hot
huge
hum
I
if
in
is
it
Jules
June
likes
Luke
March
matter
mule
name
night
on
or
peaches
plays
prunes
rest
rule
sand
set
small
snack
stop
that's
the
then
travel
tunes
up
wish
with

All Kinds of Weather

across
all
and
best
bundle

can
changes
chilly
fall
flowers
for
fun
gardens
get
head
healthy
heavy
hot
ice
in
instead
is
it
it's
jackets
keep
kind
kinds
leaves
like
meadows
might
most
muggy
outside
picnics
places
planting
pleasant
pumpkins
raking
ready
same
shade
skating
sledding
snow
spread
spring
start
stays
summer
sweat
sweaters
swimming
the
time
up
weather
what
when
will
winter
year

Ned's Feathers

a
after
all
and
as
bad
be
bread
cried
down

feathers
fine
fluffed
for
fox
fox's
get
go
going
got
he
headed
his
home
I
I'll
instead
just
long
lunch
meadow
mumbled
my
Ned
Ned's
pleasant
ready
road
said
sandwich
screamed
she
shopped
shopping
shortcut
skipped
smiled
spotted
take
that
the
think
this
those
to
way
weather
will
yum

The Loose Tooth

a
as
bad
bit
by
chicken
choose
clucked
coop
cried
dentist
didn't
doctor
doomed
down
felt
fixed
food
gobbling
goose

had
he
hen
her
his
hooting
hurt
I'll
I'm
in
it
loose
mood
moose
moose's
napping
no
noon
not
on
pain
raccoon
right
room
roost
sat
scooted
she
silly
sit
snoop
soon
started
stool
such
taking
that
the
this
to
tool
tooth
who's
window

The Goose and the Loon

a
all
and
another
are
back
birds
by
can
cannot
catches
close
cold
don't
feathers
fish
flies
food
for
funny
gets
giggle

has
hear
in
into
is
it
it's
keep
kind
kinds
lake
lakes
land
light
like
look
loon
makes
might
mild
moon
nest
north
on
one
or
roost
shore
slide
so
sound
south
the
there
these
thick
to
too
trees
turns
warm
water
waterproof
weather
when

Cumulative Word List
Level 5

The following words appear in the *Pupil Edition* stories and the *Decodable Books* in Level 5.

Key	
*	High-Frequency Word in Level 5
italics	Story Word in Level 5
red	Word appears for the first time in Level 5
normal type	Decodable Word or Known Word*

* Known words were taught in Trophies Kindergarten Program, in the Inventory Unit, or in Levels 1, 2, 3, or 4.

a	apart	barely	blinked	bushes	chasing
about	apples	basket	blue	but	check
across	are	bath	bluebirds	button	checked
acted	arms	bay	Bo	buy	cheese
afraid*	around	be	boat	by	chicken
after	art	beans	body	cage	child
afternoon*	as	bear	book	cake	children
again	ask	bears	books	called	chilly
against*	asked	because	boots	came	Chimp
ahead	asks	bed	boring	camp	chirped
air	asleep	been	born	can	choose
airplane	at	beetles	both*	can't	city
Alaskan	ate	before	bottom	cannot	clams
all	*attention*	began	boy*	car	Clark
alligator	awake	begin	brain	cards	class
allowed	away	behind	bread	care	claw
almost	awoke	belly	bridge	careful*	*claws*
along	babies	beside	bright	carefully	clay
also	baboon	best	bring	Caroline	climbed
always	baboon's	bet	brother	carry*	close
am	baby	beyond	brought*	carrying	closed
among	back	bicycle*	brown	cars	*clothes*
an	*backward*	big	Bruce	cat	clothing
and	backyard	bigger	budge	cat's	cloud
angry*	bad	biggest	bulge	catch	clouds
animal	badge	bike	bullfrog	catches	clucked
animals	Badgers	bird	bundle	cats	clues*
another	ball	birds	bundled	caught*	coat
answer	*balloon*	bit	bundles	*certainly*	cold*
answered	band	black	burned	chair	*colorful*
any	banjo	Blaine	bus	changed	come
anywhere	bank	blinding	bush	changes	coming

coop	didn't	ends	flew*	gazelles	hair
corner	different	*enemies*	flies	gentle	hand
could	dig	*enormous*	flight	gerbil	hands
couldn't	digging	even	Flo	gerbil's	happened
count	dinner	ever	floated	get	*happily*
course	dirty	every	floating	get-well	happy
covers	*disappear*	everyday	flock	gets	hard
cows	dish	everyone	floor*	getting	has
cozy	do	everything	flowers	giggle	hasn't
crackers	dock	everywhere	fluffed	giggled	have
cranky	doctor	*exactly*	fluffy	Ginger	he
crash	dodge	eyelids	flute	ginger	he'd
crayfish	does	eyes	flutes	Ginger's	he's
cried	doesn't	face	fluttering	Ginny	head*
cries	dog	fails	fly	Ginny's	headed
crocodile	dog's	fall	flying	gives	healthy
cross	dogs	falls	followed	glad	hear
crossed	doing	far	food	go	heat
crown	don't	fast	*footprints*	gobbling	heavy
crumbs	doomed	faster	for	goes	hedge
cub	down	fat	forest	going	Hedgehog
cubes	drank	father	forgot	gold	help
cubs	dreams	fawn	found	goldfish	helps
curl	dressed	feathers	four	gone	hen
curled	dried	feel	fox	*gonna*	her
cute	drink	feels	fox's	good	here
dad	dripped	feet	fright	goose	Hi
Daisy	drive	fell	frisky	got	*hibernate*
dance	dry	felt	fro	grapes	hibernating
danger	Duke	few*	frog	grass	hid
dark	dunes	field	frog's	gray	hidden
darted	during*	fight	from	great	high
day	dust	fighting	front	green	him
days	each	filled	froze	grew	hind
decided	ear	find	fudge	grinned	Hippo
deep	ears	finds	full	grins	his
deer	eat	fine	fun	groaned	Hmmm
den	eaten	fingerprints	funny	ground	hogging
dens	eating	fire*	furry	grow	hogs
dentist	edge	first	Gail	growing	hold
detective*	eight	fish	game	grown-up	holes
detectives	*elephant*	fishing	garden	grown-ups	home
Di	elephants	fixed	gardens	grumbled	hoof
diaper	empty	flair	gave	grunted	hooting
did	end	flat	*gazelle*	had	horse

hot	just	looking	mood	north	peaches
hours*	Kay	looks	moose	nose	pebbles
house	keep	loon	moose's	not	people
how	keeping	loose	mop	nothing*	*perfectly*
huddled	keeps	lot	more	now	perhaps
huge	kept	lots	morning	of	pet
hugged	kind	loud	most	off	pets
hum	kinds	low	mother	offered	pick
humming	know	Luke	mother's	Oh	picked
hungry	laid	lunch	mothers	OK	picnic
hurried*	lake	made	mouth	okay*	picnics
hurry	lakes	Madge	moved	old	picture
hurt	land	mail	much	older	piece*
I	large	make	mud	on	pig
I'll	largest	makes	muddy	once	*pigeon*
I'm	last	making	muggy	one	pigs
ice	laughed	male	mule	only	pile
if	lay	Mama	mumbled	onto	pillows
imagining	leaped	manners	mumbles	open	pine
in	learn*	many	munching	opened	place
inches	leash	March	must	or	places
inside	leave	mark	my	orange	plain
instead	leaves	Mark	name	other	plant
into	led	marks	named	others	planting
is	left	matter	nap	out	plants
isn't	leg	mattress	napping	outside	play
it	legs	may	nature*	over	played
it's	less	maybe	near*	overhead	playing
its	let	me	nearly*	pack	plays
Jack	let's	*meadow*	neck	page	playthings
jackets	lickety	meadows	Ned	pages	pleasant
Jay	lie	means	Ned's	pail	please
jet	light	meat	need	pain	plunged
Jo	lights	melting	needs	paint	*pollywog*
job	like	mice	nest	painted	*pool*
join*	liked	middle	never	pardon	Poppleton
joined	likes	might	new	parents*	pouncing
Jonathan	line	mild	next	park	prints
judge	listen	milk	nibbled	part	problem
judged	little	mind	nice	pass	propped
Jules	live	Miss	night	passed	prunes
June	lizard	moaned	night's	path	puddle
jumped	long	mom	nightlight	paw	puddles
jumps	look	mom's	no	*paws*	pulls*
June's	looked	*monkey*	noon	pay	pumpkins

put	rule	showed	snow	stems	test
puts	run	shut	snowy	still	tested
Queen	running	sick	so	stool	than
queen	safe	side	soft	stop	thanks
questions	said	sidewalk	softly	stopped	that
quick	sail	sigh	some	stopping	that's
quietly*	sailed	sighed	somebody	stops	the
quills	sailing	sights	someone	store	their
quite	salad	silly	something	storming	them
rabbit	*saleslady*	since	sometimes	story	then
raccoon	*salmon*	sing	son*	stove	there
raccoons	same	singing	songs	stretch	these
racing	sand	single	soon	stretched	they
rain	sandwich	sister	sorry*	stuck	they're
rained	sandwiches	sit	sound	stuffed	thick
rainy	sandy	sits	sounds	stump	thing
raise	sat	sitting	south	such	things
raking	saw	six	sparkled	*suddenly*	think
ran	say	size	speak	summer	thinking
Ranger	says	skate	special	sun	thinks
rather	scat	skating	spice	sun's	thirsty
rays	schoolchildren	skipped	Spike	sunlight	this
read*	scooted	sky	spilling	sunny	those
ready*	screamed	sledding	splashed	sunshine	thought*
really	seas	sleep	splashes	sure*	thoughts
rest	seashore	sleeps	splashing	surprise	three
resting	see	sleepy	split	surprised	throws
rests	seeds	slid	*spoiled*	swam	thundered
rhinoceros	seeing	slide	spot	sweat	tight
riding	seen	slithered	spotted	sweaters	time
right	set	slow	spread	sweet	tired
rise	seven	small	spring	swim	*tired*
river	shade	smell	spun	swimming	*tires*
rivers	sharp	smile	stage	tail	to
road	she	smiled	stains	take	toad
Roger	she's	smudge	stand	takes	toast
Roger's	shells	snack	standing	taking	today
rolled	ship	snacks	stands	tall	toe
roller-skating	shook*	snake	start	tame	*toes*
room	shopped	snakes	started	tape	together
roost	shopping	snaps	started	taste	told
round	shore	sneak	stay	tea	too
rubbed	shortcut	sniffed	stayed	teatime	took
rubber	shouted	snoop	stays	tell	tool
rude	show		*steered*	ten	tooth

torn	turtles	waiting	we'll	wide	worm
toward	TV	wake	weather	wild	*worry*
town	twelve	wakes	webbed	wildest	would
track	twenty	walk	wedge	will	wouldn't
tracks	twins	walked	weeks	wind	*yawn*
trail	twirled	walking	well	window	year
train	twist	walks	went	wings	years
travel	twitched	*wander*	were	wink	yelled
traveling	two	want	wet	winner	yes
tray	under	wanted	what	wins	yet
tree	until	wants	what's	winter	yo-yo
trees	up	warm	when	wish	you
tricks	upon	was	where	with	your
triplets	upset	watch	which	won't	yum
tripped	us	watched	while	wonder*	
trying	*usually*	watching	whiskers	wondered	
tummy	vast	water	whispered	wonderful	
tunes	very	waterproof	whispering	*woods*	
turn	visit	waves	white	work	
turned	wailed	way	who	working	
turns	wait	ways	who's	works	
turtle	waited	we	why	world	

Cumulative Word List
Levels 1, 2, 3, 4 and 5

The following words appear in the *Pupil Edition* stories and the *Decodable Books* in Levels 1, 2, 3, 4 and 5.

Key	
*	High-Frequency Word in Level 5
italics	Story Word in Level 5
red	Word appears for the first time in Level 5
normal type	Decodable Word or Known Word*

* Known words were taught in Trophies Kindergarten Program, in the Inventory Unit, or in Levels 1, 2, 3, or 4.

a	*among*	attics	basket	Benny	blinding
about	an	awake	bat	Benny's	blinked
above	and	away	batch	beside	blocks
Abuela	angry*	awoke	bath	best	blowing
Abuela's	animal	babies	baths	bet	blows
Abuelita	animals	baboon	bats	Beth	blue
across	Ann	baboon's	batter	better	bluebirds
act	another	baby	bay	Betty	blur
acted	answer	back	be	beyond	Bo
ad	*answered*	*backward*	beach	bib	boast
add	ant	backyard	beans	bicycle*	boat
adopted	ants	bad	bear	big	boats
afraid*	any	badge	bear's	bigger	body
after	anything	Badgers	bears	biggest	bong
afternoon*	anywhere	bag	beat	bike	book
again	apart	bags	beautiful	bill	books
against*	apartment	bake	because	bin	boot
ago	apple	baked	bed	Bing	boots
agrees	apples	ball	bee	Bing's	boring
ahead	are	*balloon*	been	bins	Boris
air	arf	balls	bees	bird	born
airplane	arm	bam	beetle	birdbath	both*
Alaskan	arms	band	beetles	birds	bottle
Alex	around	banjo	before	birthday	bottom
all	art	bank	beg	bit	Bow-Wow
alligator	as	banner	began	bite	bowl
allowed	ask	barely	begin	bits	box
almost	asked	bark	behind	bitten	boxes
along	asks	barked	being	black	boxy
also	asleep	barking	Bell	Blaine	boy*
always	at	barks	belly	Blake	brain
am	ate	barn	Ben	Blanch	branch
America	*attention*	Bart	bench	Blanch's	branches

brave
bread
breeze
bricks
bridge
bright
bring
brings
brother
brought*
brown
Bruce
brush
brushes
bubbles
Buck
Bud
Bud's
budge
bug
bugs
bulge
bullfrog
bullfrogs
bump
bumps
bunch
bundle
bundled
bundles
bunny
Burk
Burk's
burned
burns
burnt
Burt
Burt's
bus
bush
bushes
busy
but
butterfly
button
buy
buy
buzz

buzzes
buzzing
Buzzy
by
cabin
cage
cake
cakes
call
called
calling
calls
came
Camila
camp
camping
can
can't
candle
cannot
cans
cap
caps
car
cards
care
careful*
carefully
Carmen
Caroline
carry*
carrying
cars
cart
cash
Cass
cat
cat's
catch
catches
caterpillar
Catnip
cats
caught*
cave
caves
Cecil
Cecil's

cells
center
certainly
Chad
Chad's
chair
champ
chance
change
changed
changes
chased
chasing
chat
check
checked
checks
cheer
cheered
cheers
cheese
chess
chest
Chet
Chet's
chick
chicken
chicks
child
children
chilly
Chimp
Chip
chips
chirped
chirps
chomp
choose
chop
chrysalis
Chuck
Chuck's
chuckle
chug
chums
churned
Cindy
Cindy's

circle
circles
circus
city
clams
clank
clapped
claps
Clark
Clark's
class
claw
claws
clay
clean
cleaned
cleaning
cleanup
clear
click
climb
climbed
close
closed
cloth
clothes
clothing
cloud
clouds
clown
clowns
cluck
clucked
clucks
clues*
clunk
clutched
coach
coached
coal
coat
cold*
collected
colorful
come
comes
coming
complain

cook
cookies
coop
corn
corner
Corwin
Corwin's
couch
could
couldn't
count
countries
country
course
cove
covers
cows
cozy
crack
crackers
cracks
cranky
crash
crate
crawl
crawls
crayfish
creak
cream
creek
creep
creeps
cried
cries
crisp
croak
croaked
croaking
croaks
crocodile
crops
cross
crossed
crouching
crow
crowd
crowded
crown

crows
crumbs
crunch
crush
cry
crying
cub
cubes
cubs
cuddle
cup
curl
curled
curls
Curtis
curve
cut
cute
Dad
Daisy
damp
Dan
Dan's
dance
dances
dancing
danger
dark
darted
darts
dashed
dashes
Dave
Dave's
days
deal
Dean
dear
decided
deep
deer
den
Dennis
dens
dentist
desert
detective*
detectives

Di	dripped	everybody	fills	flutes	fur
diaper	drips	everyday	find	fluttering	furry
did	drive	everyone	finds	fly	Gail
didn't	drone	everything	fine	flying	game
different	drones	everywhere	fingerprints	foam	garden
dig	drop	*exactly*	fingers	follow	gardens
digger	dropped	eyelids	fire	followed	gate
digging	drops	eyes	firm	food	gave
digs	drum	face	first	*footprints*	*gazelle*
dinner	dry	fails	fish	for	gazelles
dip	duck	fall	fished	forest	gear
dipped	ducklings	falls	fishes	forests	gentle
dirt	ducks	family	fishing	forever	gerbil
dirty	dug	fan	fit	forget	gerbil's
disappear	Duke	fans	Fitch	forgot	Gert
dish	dump	far	five	formed	get
dive	dumped	farm	fix	fort	get-well
diver	dunes	fast	fixed	forth	gets
do	during*	faster	fizz	found	getting
dock	dust	fat	flair	four	giant
doctor	each	father	flash	fox	gift
dodge	ear	fawn	flashes	fox's	giggle
does	ears	feast	flat	Freddy	giggled
doesn't	Earth	feathers	flea	Freddy's	ginger
dog	east	fed	fleas	free	Ginger's
dog's	easy	feed	Fletch	fresh	Ginny
dogs	eat	feeding	flew*	fried	Ginny's
doing	eaten	feeds	flies	friend	girl
doll	eating	feel	flight	friend's	give
dolls	eats	feelers	flip	friends	gives
don't	edge	feeling	flippers	fries	glad
doomed	Edith	feels	flips	fright	glances
door	egg	feet	Flo	frisky	glow
Doreen	eggs	Felix	float	fro	glowing
Doris	eight	fell	floated	frog	glows
Dot	*elephant*	fellow	floating	frog's	go
Dot's	elephants	felt	floats	frogs	gobble
down	Ellen	female	flock	from	gobbled
downtown	else	fence	floor*	front	gobbling
Dr.	Emily	Fern	flop	frosting	goes
drank	empty	fetch	flops	frosty	going
dream	end	few*	Flora	frown	gold
dreaming	ends	fiddle	flower	frowns	goldfish
dreams	*enemies*	field	flowers	froze	gone
dressed	*enormous*	fight	flowing	fudge	*gonna*
dried	even	fighting	fluffed	full	good
drink	ever	fill	fluffy	fun	good-by
drip	every	filled	flute	funny	goose

gosh	happen	hide-and-seek	hunters	Jo	lamps
got	happened	high	hunting	Joan	land
gowns	happens	hill	hurls	job	landed
grab	*happily*	hills	hurried*	jog	landing
grabs	happy	him	hurry	jogs	lands
grains	hard	himself	hurt	join*	Lang
Gram	harder	hind	hurts	joined	laps
Gram's	has	Hip	hush	Jonathan	Larch
Gramps	hasn't	hippo	I	Josh	large
grand	hat	Hippo	I'll	judge	largest
granddad	hatch	his	I'm	judged	last
Grandma	hatched	hisses	ice	Jules	latch
Grandpa	have	hit	if	jumble	late
grapes	he	hits	*imagining*	jump	laugh
grass	he'd	hive	important	jumped	laughed
grassy	he's	hogging	in	jumps	lay
gray	head*	hogs	inch	June	lays
great	headed	hold	inches	June's	leading
green	heal	holds	insect	junk	leads
greens	healthy	hole	inside	junks	leafy
grew	heap	holes	instead	just	leap
grin	heaped	home	into	Kate	leaped
grinned	hear	homes	is	Kate's	learn*
grins	heard	honey	island	Kathy	leash
groaned	heat	hoof	isn't	Kay	least
groans	heavy	hooting	it	keep	leave
grouchy	hedge	hop	it's	keeping	leaves
ground	Hedgehog	hops	itch	keeps	led
grove	held	horse	its	kept	Lee
grow	hello	hot	Jack	Kern	Lee's
growing	help	hound	jackets	kick	left
growls	helped	hours*	Jake	kicking	leg
grown-up	helper	house	Jake's	Kim	legs
grown-ups	helping	houses	Jan	kind	less
grows	helps	how	Jane	kinds	let
grubs	hen	how's	Jane's	king	let's
grumble	hens	howdy	jar	Kirk	lets
grumbled	her	howl	Jay	kite	library
grunted	Herb	huddled	Jean	kites	lick
gurgle	Herbert	huff	Jeff	kitten	lickety
Gus	here	hug	jelly	kittens	licks
had	here's	huge	Jen	kitty	lie
hair	Hi	hugged	jerk	know	lift
ham	*hibernate*	hugs	jet	knows	light
hand	hibernating	hum	jiggle	laid	lights
hands	hid	humming	Jill	lake	like
hang	hidden	hungry	Jill's	lakes	liked
Hap	hide	hunt	jingle	lamp	likes

lime	mark	mole's	naps	old	Patty's
line	market	Mom	narrow	older	paw
Ling	marks	mom's	Nate	on	*paws*
lips	Martha	Moms	nature*	once	pay
listen	mash	*monkey*	Neal	one	peach
lit	mask	mood	near*	only	peaches
little	mat	moose	nearly*	onto	peacock
live	mate	moose's	neat	open	pebbles
lived	math	mop	neck	opened	peck
lives	matter	more	nectar	or	peep
Liz	mattress	morning	Ned	orange	pen
lizard	Max	Morris	Ned's	other	pens
load	may	Mort	need	others	people
log	maybe	Mort's	needed	our	peppy
long	me	most	needs	out	perfect
look	*meadow*	mother	nest	outside	*perfectly*
looked	meadows	mother's	nests	over	perhaps
looking	meal	mothers	never	overhead	pet
looks	means	mound	new	own	pets
loon	meat	mouth	news	owner	pick
loose	meet	move	newspaper	pack	picked
lost	meets	moved	next	packed	picking
lot	Meg	moves	nibble	paddle	picks
lots	melting	mow	nibbled	page	picnic
loud	mess	Mr.	nice	pages	picnics
love	met	much	Nick	pail	picture
low	mice	mud	night	pain	pie
lucky	Mick	muddy	night's	paint	piece*
Lucy	middle	Muff	nightlight	painted	pig
Luke	might	Muff's	nine	pal	*pigeon*
lunch	Mike	muffin	no	pals	pigs
Mack	Mike's	muggy	nodded	Pam	Pike
mad	mild	mule	noon	pan	pile
made	milk	mumble	Norm	pants	pillow
Madge	mind	mumbled	north	Papa	pillows
mail	mine	mumbles	nose	pardon	pinch
make	miss	mums	not	parents*	pine
makes	Miss	munch	note	park	ping
making	missed	munching	nothing*	part	pink
male	misses	must	now	parts	Pinky
mall	Mitch	my	number	pass	pins
Mama	mitts	name	Oak	passed	Pip
man	mix	named	of	past	pitch
manners	mixed	Nan	off	Pat	pitcher
many	mixer	nap	offered	patch	place
map	moaned	napper	Oh	path	places
march	moans	napping	OK	pats	plain
marched	mole		okay*	Patty	plan

plane	pup	red	rubs	seashore	shouted
plant	pup's	Reed	rude	seat	shouts
planted	puppy	Reed's	ruff	see	show
planting	purple	rest	rule	seeds	showed
plants	purr	resting	rum-a-tum-tum	seeing	showers
plates	purrs	rests	rumble	seems	shows
play	put	reward	run	seen	shut
played	puts	Rex	running	sees	shy
playing	quack	rhinoceros	runs	sell	sick
plays	quacked	Rick	rush	sent	Sid
playthings	quacking	Ricky	rushes	served	side
pleasant	quacks	Ricky's	sack	set	sidewalk
please	Queen	rid	sad	Seth	sideways
plips	queen	riddle	safe	Seth's	sigh
plop	questions	ride	safety	sets	sighed
plops	quick	rides	said	seven	sights
plums	quietly*	riding	sail	shade	silk
plunged	quill	right	sailed	Shadow	silly
poked	quills	ring	sailing	Shadow's	since
pokes	quilt	rise	salad	shake	sing
pole	Quinn	river	saleslady	shall	singing
pollen	Quinn's	Rivera	salmon	shame	single
pollywog	Quint	Rivera's	Sam	share	sings
Pom-Pom	quit	rivers	same	sharp	sir
pond	quite	road	Sanchez	she	sister
pong	rabbit	roam	sand	she'll	sit
pool	rabbits	Rob	sandwich	she's	sits
pop	raccoon	robot	sandwiches	shed	sitting
Poppleton	raccoons	rock	sandy	sheep	six
pops	race	rocks	sang	sheet	size
pot	races	rode	sat	shell	skate
pouncing	racing	rods	saw	shells	skating
pounding	rain	Roger	say	shelter	skin
pout	rained	Roger's	says	shelters	skinny
prance	rainy	roll	scare	Sherm	skins
pretty	raise	rolled	scared	shines	skipped
prince	rake	roller-skating	scarf	ship	skipping
prints	raked	room	scat	Shirl	skips
problem	raking	rooms	scatter	shook*	sky
propped	ran	roost	school	shopped	slaps
prunes	Ranger	rope	schoolchildren	shopping	sled
puddle	rather	rose	scooted	shops	sledding
puddles	rattle	round	score	shore	sleep
puff	rays	rowed	scores	short	sleeping
puffed	reaches	rows	screamed	shortcut	sleeps
Puffy	read*	rub	sea	shots	sleepy
pulls*	ready*	rubbed	seals	should	slept
pumpkins	really	rubber	seas	shout	slid

slide	socks	spread	storming	tag	there
slip	sod	spreads	story	tail	these
slithered	soft	spring	stove	tails	they
Sloan	softly	sprinkle	stream	take	they're
Sloan's	some	spun	street	takes	thick
slouched	somebody	spy	streets	taking	thin
slow	someone	squirrels	stretch	tale	thing
slurped	something	squirt	stretched	tales	things
sly	sometimes	stage	stretches	talk	think
smack	son*	stains	stripes	talking	thinking
small	songs	stand	strong	tall	thinks
smart	soon	standing	stronger	tame	third
smash	sore	stands	stuck	tap	thirsty
smell	sores	star	stuff	tape	thirty
smile	sorry*	stars	stuffed	tapped	this
smiled	sort	start	stump	taps	thorns
smiles	sorted	started	such	taste	those
Smith	sorts	startle	sudden	tea	thought*
Smiths	sound	starts	*suddenly*	teach	thoughts
smoke	sounds	starving	suds	teacher	thousand
smudge	soup	state	summer	team	thousands
snack	south	states	sun	tears	three
snacks	sowbugs	stay	sun's	teased	throat
snake	space	stayed	sunburn	teatime	throws
snakes	spark	stays	sunk	Ted	thump
snaps	sparkle	*steered*	sunlight	teeth	thundered
snatched	sparkled	stems	sunny	tell	tickle
sneak	speak	steps	sunshine	telling	tickles
sneaked	special	stern	sure*	tells	tied
sniff	spelling	stick	surf	ten	tiger
sniffed	Spencer	sticks	surprise	tent	tight
sniffing	spend	still	surprised	tents	Tim
sniffs	spice	stilts	surprises	tepee	time
snoop	spied	stir	swam	tepees	times
snore	Spike	stirring	sweat	Tess	tip
snoring	spilling	stone	sweaters	test	Tip
snorted	spinning	stool	sweet	tested	tips
snow	spins	stop	swim	Texas	*tired*
Snowball	splash	stopped	swimmer	than	*tires*
snowing	splashed	stopping	swimming	thank	to
snowman	splashes	stops	swings	thanked	toad
snowy	splashing	store	swirl	thanks	toast
snug	split	stores	swirled	that	today
snuggle	*spoiled*	stories	swish	that's	Todd
so	sports	stork	switch	the	Todd's
soaked	spot	stork's	Tad	their	toe
sobs	spots	storm	tadpole	them	*toes*
sock	spotted	stormed	tadpoles	then	together

told	tub	vole's	whale	wish	zap
Tomás	tug	waggles	wham	wished	zing
tongue	tugs	wailed	what	with	zip
tongues	tumble	wait	what's	woke	
too	tumbles	waited	wheat	won't	
took	tummy	waiting	wheels	wonder*	
tool	tunes	wake	wheeze	wondered	
tooth	turf	wakes	when	wonderful	
top	turn	walk	where	*woods*	
tops	turned	walked	which	wore	
tore	turning	walking	whiff	work	
torn	turns	walks	while	worker	
toss	turtle	wall	whip	workers	
tossed	turtles	walls	whir	working	
touch	TV	*wander*	whirl	works	
toward	twelve	want	whish	world	
towers	twenty	wanted	whiskers	worm	
town	twice	wants	whisper	*worry*	
towns	twigs	warm	whispered	would	
tows	twinkle	was	whispering	wouldn't	
track	twins	wasn't	whispers	wow	
tracks	twirl	watch	whistle	write	
trail	twirled	watched	whistles	writing	
train	twist	watching	white	yak's	
trap	twitch	water	White's	yaks	
trash	twitched	waterproof	whiz	yams	
travel	two	waved	who	yard	
traveling	umbrella	waves	who's	yarn	
tray	Uncle	waxy	why	*yawn*	
treat	under	way	wide	year	
treats	United States	ways	wiggle	years	
tree	of America	we	wiggled	yell	
trees	unroll	we'll	wiggles	yelled	
treetop	until	we're	wild	yellow	
tricking	up	weather	wildest	yells	
tricks	upon	web	will	yes	
tried	upset	webbed	win	yet	
tries	upside	wedge	wind	yip-yip	
trip	us	weeds	window	yips	
triplets	use	weeks	windy	yo-yo	
tripped	used	welcome	wings	York	
trips	*usually*	well	wink	you	
Trish	van	went	winked	you're	
trots	vast	were	Winkle	young	
truck	very	weren't	Winky	your	
trucks	vet	west	winner	yowls	
try	visit	wet	wins	yuck	
trying	vole	whack	winter	yum	

The little blue bird was _____ to fly.

He left the nest to look for _____ .

"I _____ where nothing is," thought the little blue bird.

A green bird asked the blue bird to _____ him.

The blue bird and the green bird _____ with a flock of birds.

The little blue bird forgot he was afraid to _____ how to fly.

The little blue bird _____ hard.

Frog and Toad were _____ in the rain.

They got wet and _____.

Frog said, "Stand _____ the stove to get dry."

One day, Frog's dad said, "_____, spring is just around the corner."

At last, Frog and Toad _____ outside.

They wanted to make _____ spring had come again.

Harcourt

Brown bears eat _____ plants and animals.

_____ the spring, bears fish in the river.

The bear is _____ to catch a fish.

During the winter, bears sleep in dens.

Bears eat a lot to get ready to sleep.

Harcourt

A _____ has many ways to get answers.

She may find a _____ of cloth.

She might find tracks on the _____.

All these things are _____.

A _____ detective can tell cat footprints.

A cat _____ its claws in when it walks.

Nature detectives look for clues everywhere!

Mom said it was _____ to sail my boat in the puddles.

The turtle was _____ when the frog crashed into her.

The alligator said he was _____ about my boat.

The elephant drank _____ all the water in the puddle.

Harcourt

Poppleton had his bed since he was a _____.

The saleslady _____ Poppleton some crackers.

He tested the bed in a _____ different ways.

He lay with his _____ on the bed.

While on the bed, he _____ a book.

Harcourt

All people need many _____ of sleep each night.

Little children nap in the _____.

Your arms need rest after you _____ heavy bundles.

Your legs need rest after you ride a _____.

_____ need sleep, too.

Harcourt

Baboon learned to be _____ so he would not get hurt.

He felt the heat of the forest _____.

He hid _____ from the crocodile.

The ground _____ when the elephants walked.

Baboon put his head _____ his mother's neck and went to sleep.

The Writing Process

1. Prewrite

Draw or list some ideas. Choose one to write about.

2. Draft

Write about your idea. Don't worry about making mistakes.

> My dog is named ruff. He is brown and
> white he does tricks.

254

Writer's Handbook

3. Revise

Talk about your work. Make it better.

> My dog is named rutt. He is brown ~~and~~ with
> white, he does, tricks. I love my dog!
>   spots.   lots of

4. Proofread

Read your story and fix the mistakes.

> My dog is named Ruff. He is brown ~~and~~ with
> white, he does, tricks. I love my dog!
>   spots.   lots of

5. Publish

Create a finished copy of your story. Share your writing.

> My Dog
> by Daniel Ruiz
> My dog is named Ruff.
> He is brown with white
> spots. He does lots of
> tricks. I love my dog!

255

Introduce the Writer's Handbook

Tell children that the Writer's Handbook has three sections that will help them when they write—*The Writing Process, Models for Writing* and *Words For Writing.* Invite children to preview the handbook and tell how they think they might use each section.

The Writing Process

Teach

Tell children that they can use pages 254 and 255 when they need to remember the five steps of the Writing Process. Read these pages to children and discuss how these pages might be useful.

Practice/Apply

Have children work with a partner to use the five steps of the Writing Process to write one sentence. Invite children to read their completed sentences to the group. Have them tell what they did to the sentence during each step.

Models for Writing

You can look at these writing models when you need to
write something special.

Fantasy Story

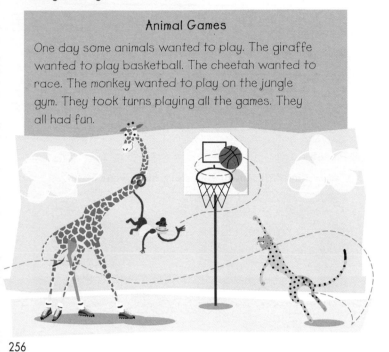

Animal Games

One day some animals wanted to play. The giraffe
wanted to play basketball. The cheetah wanted to
race. The monkey wanted to play on the jungle
gym. They took turns playing all the games. They
all had fun.

256

Poem

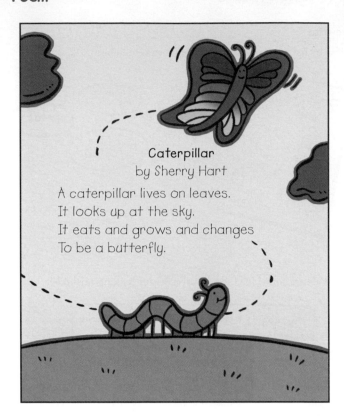

Caterpillar
by Sherry Hart
A caterpillar lives on leaves.
It looks up at the sky.
It eats and grows and changes
To be a butterfly.

257

Models for Writing

Teach

Tell children pages 256 and 257 are the second section of their handbook. Explain that these pages
show two models that they can use to help them
with two types of writing—A Fantasy Story and a
Poem. Read the pages to children and ask them
when they might be able to use these pages.
(when I am writing a fantasy story or a poem)

Practice and Apply

Write the following poem on the board and read
it to children.

**Roses are red. Violets are
blue. Sugar is sweet and so
are you.**

Tell children that there is something wrong with
the way this poem is written. Ask them to look at
the poem model on page 257 and try to figure out
what needs to be changed. (The poem needs to
be written like a verse and not just like a group of
sentences.) Have a volunteer tell where each line
needs to begin and end as you rewrite the poem
correctly. Ask children how the model helped them
to know this information. Ask how they can use
these models to improve their own writing.

Words for Writing

People Words

baby

boy

doctor

girl

mail carrier

man

police officer

teacher

woman

258

Verbs

draw

drive

eat

jump

play

read

run

skate

swing

walk

259

People Words and Verbs

Teach

Tell children that this is the third section of their Writer's Handbook. Explain that the next four pages contain lists of words that they can use when they write—words that name people, verbs or action words, feeling words, and food words. Read the people words and verbs to children. Discuss how these words might be useful.

Practice and Apply

Write the following sentence frame on the board and read it to children.

That _____ can _____ good pictures!

Have children use pages 258 and 259 to find the words that complete the sentence. Have them spell the words as you write them in the blanks. Ask children to suggest ways they might use the words in their own writing.

Words For Writing

Feeling Words

excited happy hungry

mad proud

sad scared shy

sick tired

260

Food Words

apple bread cake

carrots eggs

pancakes pizza sandwich

spaghetti taco

261

Feeling Words and Food Words

Teach

Call attention to the pictures that correspond to each feeling word. Have volunteers tell what feeling is depicted in each picture. Then read the words to children. Follow a similar procedure to introduce the food words.

Practice and Apply

Write the following sentence frame on the board and read it to children.

I am so _____ that I could eat a _____, a _____, and a _____.

Have children use pages 260 and 261 to find words to complete the sentence. Have them spell the words as you write them in the blanks. Ask children to suggest ways they might use the words in their own writing.

Introducing the Glossary

Explain to children that a glossary is often included in a book so that readers can look up words used in the book. Tell children that the words in a glossary are listed in alphabetical order. Have children say the alphabet aloud. Then ask them questions such as: Would the word *apple* be found near the beginning of the glossary or near the end? Would *monkey* be found at the beginning, in the middle, or at the end of the glossary?

■ Read aloud the introductory paragraph in the *Pupil Edition* to children. Have them page through the Glossary, and ask them what they notice about the entries. Then choose a word from the Glossary and model using guide words and alphabetical order to look it up. Have children read the sentence. Then have them tell how the sentence and the picture, if there is one, help them understand the meaning of the word.

■ Select several other words, with and without accompanying illustrations, and have children practice looking them up, using guide words and alphabetical order. Discuss the meanings of the words. Have children explain how using guide words and alphabetical order helped them locate the words.

■ Tell children to use the Glossary to check the meanings of vocabulary words as they read and to help them better understand the meanings of words they don't know. Then discuss the differences and similarities between this Glossary and a classroom dictionary, being sure that children recognize that words in a glossary and a dictionary are in alphabetical order. Conclude with the idea that lists in books that people use to look up information are usually arranged in alphabetical order.

Glossary

What is a Glossary?

A glossary can help you read a word. You can look up the word and read it in a sentence. Some words have a picture to help you.

car·ry   Albert can **carry** two bags.

(A)

a·fraid   The tiger is **afraid** of the bunny.

afraid

af·ter·noon   I have a snack in the **afternoon**.

a·gainst   Stand up **against** the wall.

ang·ry   A leaky pen makes me **angry**.

angry

(B)

bi·cy·cle   Lee rode her **bicycle** to the park.

---

both   Can we have **both** kinds of ice cream?

boy   The **boy** has brown hair.

brought   The waiter **brought** us our pizza.

careful

(C)

care·ful   Be **careful** with the flower vase!

car·ry   Albert can **carry** two bags.

caught   Lilly **caught** a butterfly in a net.

carry

---

cold   I put on a coat when I am **cold**.

(D)

de·tec·tive   A **detective** looks for clues.

detective

(F)

few   We only have a **few** more tickets to the fair.

fire   Dad lit a **fire** to help us stay warm.

fire

flew   The airplane **flew** over the city.

---

floor

floor   Clean the **floor** with a mop.

(H)

head

head   He has no hair on his **head**.

hur·ried   We **hurried** inside to get out of the rain.

(J)

join   Do you want to **join** our game?

(L)

learn   Let's **learn** a new song.

266

(N)

na·ture   Animals, plants, and the sky are parts of **nature**.

near   The park is **near** the school.

near·ly   The bucket is **nearly** full.

no·thing   I have **nothing** in my pocket.

nothing

(O)

o·kay   You fell down. Are you **okay**?

(P)

par·ents   I call my **parents** Mama and Papa.

parents

267

---

piece

piece   Do you want a **piece** of cake?

pulls   The boy **pulls** the string to ring the bell.

pulls

(Q)

qui·et·ly   Talk **quietly** in the library.

(R)

read   Tammy **read** two books last night.

read·y   Are you **ready** to go?

(S)

shook   The baby **shook** her rattle.

268

son   The boy is his dad's **son**.

sor·ry   Abby was **sorry** she spilled the milk.

sure   I am **sure** my answer is right.

son

(T)

thought   Fred **thought** of a new game to play.

sorry

(W)

won·der   I **wonder** how big that ship is.

269

GLOSSARY   **Gather Around**   **T79**

Oral Reading Fluency

What Is Oral Reading Fluency?

Research recognizes fluency as a strong indicator of efficient and proficient reading. A fluent reader reads orally with accuracy and expression, at a speech-like pace. Oral reading fluency is an assessment of accuracy and rate. It is expressed as the number of words read correctly per minute (WCPM).

Oral reading fluency is an important goal of reading instruction in the elementary grades. If a reader devotes most of his or her attention to pronouncing words, comprehension and meaning will suffer. Students who read fluently can devote more attention to meaning and thus increase comprehension.

The oral reading passage and recording form that follows provides a tool for gathering quantitative information about an individual's oral reading. Use the passages provided in each Teacher's Edition to collect a one-minute sample of a child's oral reading periodically throughout the school year. Track the child's progress and development on the Oral Reading Recording Forms completed and collected throughout the school year.

The passages provided were written with controlled vocabulary and progressive levels of difficulty. The originality of the passages ensures that children will not already be familiar with the content.

Administering the Oral Reading Passage

For administering the assessment you will need
- a stopwatch or a watch with a second hand
- a clean copy of the passage for the child to read
- a copy of the Recording Form version of the same passage to mark as the child reads

1. Explain the task. The child is to read the passage aloud, beginning and ending with your signals.
2. Use a stopwatch to time a one-minute interval inconspicuously. Tell the child when to begin and when to end reading. Put a slash mark on the Recording Form after the last word the child reads.
3. As the child reads, record reading errors unobtrusively on the Recording Form. Mark mispronunciations, substitutions, omissions of a sound or word, and other errors. Do not count repetitions or self-corrections as reading errors.

Scoring the Oral Reading Fluency Rate

Complete the Oral Reading Fluency Form and save it. Use the completed forms to track growth and progress throughout the school year and to share the results with parents or guardians.

To Compute the Fluency Rate

1. Total the number of words the child read in one minute.
2. Total the number of reading errors the child made.
3. Subtract the number of reading errors from the number of words read to get the total words read correctly per minute (WCPM).

Total Words Read Per Minute   _____

Number of Errors   _____

Number of Words Read Correctly (WCPM)   _____

Interpreting the Oral Reading Fluency Rate

See the tables of norms provided in the *Oral Reading Fluency Assessment* to make a normative interpretation of a student's oral reading fluency score. Children who read significantly below the oral reading fluency norms will need additional word recognition instruction, more frequent monitoring of performance, and building fluency strategies such as repeated reading, echo reading, tape assisted reading, and partner reading.

Oral Reading Passage

Passage 1C

There are many beautiful colors all around us. The sky is blue, and the grass is green. Flowers and birds are all colors. When you paint a picture, you may need many colors. You can start with only yellow, red, and blue paints. Did you know that you can make other colors by mixing these three colors? Mix a bit of blue paint with a bit of yellow paint. You will get the color green. If you put blue, red, and yellow paint together, you will get brown. White paint will make your colors look lighter. By mixing colors you will have new colors to use. With all these colors you can paint a pretty picture.

Oral Reading Fluency Recording Form

Child _____   Date _____

Passage IC   Word Count 116

There are many beautiful colors all	6
around us. The sky is blue, and the	14
grass is green. Flowers and birds are all	22
colors. When you paint a picture, you	29
may need many colors. You can start	36
with only yellow, red, and blue paints.	43
Did you know that you can make other	51
colors by mixing these three colors?	57
Mix a bit of blue paint with a bit of	67
yellow paint. You will get the color	74
green. If you put blue, red, and yellow	82
paint together, you will get brown.	88
White paint will make your colors look	95
lighter. By mixing colors you will have	102
new colors to use. With all these colors	110
you can paint a pretty picture.	116

Fluency Score

Total Words Read Per Minute _____

Number of Errors _____

Number of Words Read Correctly (WCPM) _____

Fluency Routine Card 1
Echo Reading

1. Have students turn to the first page and point to the beginning of the sentence.
2. Read the sentence aloud as students track the print.
3. Then have students track the print and read the sentence aloud by themselves, matching your intonation and expression.
4. Continue through the rest of the selection.

Harcourt

Fluency Routine Card 2
Choral Reading

1. Tell students to track the print of the selection and read with you.
2. Remind students to use the same expression and intonation as you do.
3. Organize students into groups and assign groups alternating pages, verses, or lines.
4. Read the selection aloud, having students read their assigned parts along with you. Be sure they track the print as they read.

Harcourt

Fluency Routine Card 3
Partner Reading

1. Have students work with a partner.
2. As the first student reads the selected text aloud, the partner should listen actively and follow along.
3. Partners should provide word-identification assistance as needed.
4. At the end of the reading, listening partners should provide feedback on fluency behaviors.
5. Have partners switch roles and repeat the procedure.

Harcourt

Fluency Routine Card 4
Tape-Assisted Reading

1. Set up a listening center with headphones and a cassette or CD player, so that students may work independently.
2. As students listen to an audio recording of the selected text, they should follow along as they track the print.
3. Have students replay the recording. This time the student should subvocalize, or read aloud quietly, imitating the expression and phrasing of the recording.

Once students are confident that they can read the text fluently, have them read it orally to you. Provide feedback as needed.

Harcourt

Fluency Routine Card 5
Repeated Reading

1. Have students choose a section of the text on which to practice the pace of their reading.
2. The student should read the passage aloud once.
3. Talk to the student about phrases and sentences that should be read more quickly.
4. Model reading at an appropriate speed.
5. The student then repeats the reading about three or four times until he or she reads at a speech-like pace.

Harcourt

Fluency Routine Card 6
Shared Reading

1. Conduct a picture walk to introduce the book and to tap students' prior knowledge of the topic.
2. Read aloud the text as students track the print.
3. Encourage students to join in as they are able.
4. Talk with students about the expression and intonation you used while reading.

Harcourt

Fluency Routine Card 7
Readers Theatre

Tell students that in Readers Theatre readers use only their voices to bring text to life, and no memorization is needed. Over the course of several days, they will practice reading their parts and finally perform for an audience.

Preparing to Read Provide each student with a copy of the script. Read the script aloud, modeling fluent and expressive reading as students follow along.

Discuss with students how a particular character might feel or act, and how the character might sound.

1. Organize students into groups and assign a role to each student in the group. You may choose to have students exchange roles for each rereading, so that they will have read the entire script by the end of the week.
2. Have students assume their roles and read the script.
3. Circulate among the groups, providing feedback and support.
4. On the assigned day, have each group perform their reading before an audience. You may choose to invite special guests, such as parents or the principal, to the reading.

Harcourt

Additional Resources

Going Places
Additional Resources

Setting the Stage

Designing a Space

One of the keys to productive learning is the physical arrangement of your classroom. Each classroom has unique characteristics, but the following areas should be considered in your floor plan.

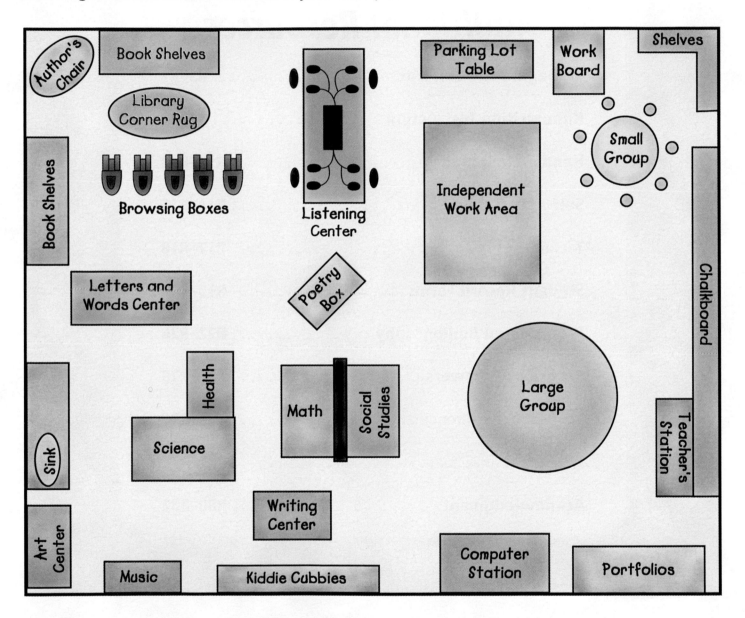

When arranging your classroom, consider traffic patterns and usage of areas. Place quiet centers near small group and independent work areas. Provide some private spaces for children to work.

Tip: A three-sided cardboard divider can instantly become a "private office" or a portable learning center.

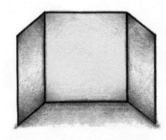

Organizing Materials

- Make certain each work area has the supplies needed to perform the required tasks. Add new supplies as activities change.

- Plan for the accommodation of complete and incomplete tasks and materials storage.

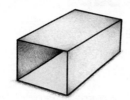

three-sided box for supplies or work　　**inside-a-box viewing center**

bins, tins, and plastic storage bags

Introducing the Centers

Before beginning a routine, acquaint children with procedures for and use of each area. All center activities should involve literacy with a balance of reading and writing tasks.

- Label each center with its name, its icon (which will also appear on the Work Board—see page R4), and a symbol to indicate the number of children who can use the center.

- Help children understand how much time they will spend in a center. For example, they can read several books from the Browsing Boxes, listen to one tape recording in the Listening Center, and play one phonics game in the Letter and Word Center.

- Show children how to use the tape recorder, computer, headphones, and overhead projector. Demonstrate proper usage of art supplies.

Tips

Keeping the Room Organized

- Clean and resupply each center as needed.

- Get children into the habit of returning materials to their proper places.

- Determine the placement of items and centers by usage. For example, you'll need a wastebasket in the Art Center. Science and Art Centers need to be located nearest the sink.

- Set aside time once a day for room cleaning. Assign specific tasks for each child.

- Have a "parking lot" table for children to store unfinished projects that require more than one day for completion.

Beginning a Routine

Establish Flexible Work Groups

In order for you to work with small guided reading groups without interruption, the other class members must clearly understand what they are to do. To plan a series of tasks that the other children can do independently, establish small work groups. These are heterogeneous groups of children who are scheduled for the same center activities on a daily basis. You can change these groups as often as you like.

Introduce a Work Board

One way to schedule classroom activity is with a Work Board. A typical Work Board includes the names of small group members and icons that represent independent tasks. A Work Board can be a pocket chart with cards, a cork board, a peg board with hooks, or a magnetic board. Its design should be flexible, enabling you to move cards on a daily basis.

Carrie Joshua Derek Suwanna Dillon	Mickey Dante Maritza Ty Karla
ABC **Letter and Word Center**	🔬 **Science Center**
🔬 **Science Center**	📝 **Math Center**
🎨 **Art Center**	ABC **Letter and Word Center**

Introduce the Icons Icons are simple shapes that children can easily recognize and connect with a center in the classroom. Make icons consistent throughout the year. Label each activity center with the icon. Sample reproducible icons are available in *Guess Who Teacher's Edition*, pages TI3–TI8.

Organize the Work Board One way to set up your Work Board is to place groups of names as shown in the sample above. Next to each group, place icons to represent activities for the day. Rotate group cards each day, giving each group a new set of activities. Further options are provided by using an icon that represents "free choice" of three or more additional activities. At the end of the week, change the icons to provide a new set of activities for the next week.

Using the Work Board

- If a child is working on a task in a center and is called to a small group session, he or she can return to that same center once instruction is finished.

- Children not engaged in a teacher-directed small group activity who have completed their other assignments should check the Work Board to follow the routine listed for them.

- If the maximum number of children is using a center, a child can move to the next task shown on the Work Board and return to the previous one at a later time.

- If a task requires more than one day for completion, children can store their projects in the classroom "parking lot" (a large table) and return to it on another day.

Tracking Progress

There are various ways to keep track of what children are doing during the course of a day.

Kid Watching   Observe children throughout the day. Determine which children are unable to finish all the activities for the day, but are working to capacity, and which children are not completing tasks because they are spending too much time in one center. Visit the centers. Note activities that work well and those that do not.

Portfolios   Have children store products they take from center activities in a portfolio created from a file folder, carton, or even a paper bag with handles. These products can be shared during conferences with children.

Conferencing   Set up a conference schedule to spend ten minutes each week looking through children's portfolios and talking with them about activities they have enjoyed, books they have read, games they have played, art they have created, and so on.

Managing the Classroom

Setting Up Centers

Planning Activities for Classroom Centers

Many of the materials for ongoing centers are at your fingertips. Base center activities on literacy skills children are learning throughout the year. The following are suggestions for particular centers.

Reading Center

This center is a large area in your classroom that can include the following:

Listening Station Include a tape recorder and headsets. Provide *Audiotext* and a variety of commercial tapes and tapes recorded by volunteers and children. If you are providing text with a tape, make multiple copies and store the tape and books in a plastic bag. Suggest an extension activity following listening.

Poetry Box Arrange a large box with copies of poems, rhymes, and finger plays that have been shared during reading time. The poems can be presented as large or small posters, in small books, as puzzles, or as copies for children to illustrate and take home.

Browsing Boxes Provide boxes of books for each small reading group. Use color-coded boxes or bins that hold fifteen or more books. Provide multiple copies if possible. Books can include those that have been shared during group sessions and books that are appropriate for independent reading. Children can choose books to read from their assigned box.

Classroom Library One corner of your room can house books children can freely choose and enjoy on their own. Include books of all kinds: Big Books, library books, and books children have made.

Letter and Word Center

Organize this center on a table in one corner of the classroom. Include activities for building and reading words. Children can use an overhead projector and plastic or cardboard letter shapes to form words to project on the wall. Provide small slates for writing words and word building pocket charts with letters and cards. Store sets of word cards from stories children are reading. Provide supplies for making rhyming words flip books, word slides, word wheels, and phonics game boards.

Computer Center

Children can write with the computer by using word processing software, such as *ClarisWorks for Kids* or interact with literature software, such as *Instant Readers* and *Living Books*™.

Writing Center

This should be a clearly defined space where writing materials are stored. Your display of learned words might also be nearby for handy reference. Organize all materials in labeled containers.

blank books	a variety of paper	stationery and envelopes
stickers	rubber stamps	poster board
pencils	markers	staplers and staple remover
glue	hole punch and yarn	date stamp

Other materials might include an alphabet chart and picture dictionaries.

Curriculum Centers

Provide reading and writing activities in curriculum centers. Ideas are suggested in each lesson's Cross-Curricular Center ideas. Provide materials as needed for children to:

■ create graphs in the Math Center.

■ perform an experiment and keep a log in the Science Center.

■ make a map in the Social Studies Center.

■ create new verses to perform a song in the Music Center.

■ create artwork in the Art Center in response to stories.

Handwriting

Individual children come to first grade with various levels of handwriting skills, but they all have the desire to communicate effectively. To learn correct letter formation, they must be familiar with concepts of

- position (top, middle, bottom; on, above, below).
- size (tall, short).
- direction (left, right; up, down; over, around, across).
- order (first, next, then, last).
- open and closed.
- spacing.

The lessons in *Trophies* build on these concepts in both formal and informal handwriting lessons so that children develop the skills they need to become independent writers. To assess children's handwriting skills, have them write each capital and lowercase letter of the alphabet. Note whether children use correct formation, appropriate size and spacing.

Stroke and Letter Formation

The shape and formation of letters taught in *Trophies* are based on the way experienced writers write their letters. Most are formed with a continuous stroke, so children do not often pick up their pencils when writing a single letter. Letter formation is simplified through the use of "letter talk"—an oral description of how the letter is formed. Models for manuscript and D'Nealian Handwriting are used in this program to support different writing systems.

Learning Modes

A visual, kinesthetic, tactile, and auditory approach to handwriting is used throughout *Trophies*. To help children internalize letter forms, each letter is taught in the context of how it looks, the sound it stands for, and how it is formed.

Position for Writing

Establishing the correct posture, pencil grip, and paper position for writing will help prevent handwriting problems later on.

Posture   Children should sit with both feet on the floor and with hips to the back of the chair. They can lean forward slightly but should not slouch. The writing surface should be smooth and flat and at a height that allows the upper arms to be perpendicular to the surface and the elbows to be under the shoulders.

Writing Instrument   An adult-sized number-two lead pencil is a satisfactory writing tool for most children. However, use your judgment in determining what type of instrument is most suitable for a child, given his or her level of development.

Hand Dominance   To determine each child's hand dominance, observe him or her at play and note which hand is the preferred hand. Watching the child turn a doorknob, roll a ball, build a block tower, or turn the pages in a book will help you note hand dominance.

Paper Position and Pencil Grip The paper is slanted along the line of the child's writing arm, and the child uses his or her nonwriting hand to hold the paper in place. The child holds the pencil slightly above the paint line—about I inch from the lead tip.

Reaching All Learners

The best instruction builds on what children already know and can do. Given the tremendous range in children's experience with writing materials prior to first grade, a variety of approaches will be needed. Throughout *Trophies*, viable alternatives are suggested for reaching all learners.

Extra Support For children with limited print concepts, one of the first and most important understandings is that print carries meaning and that writing has real purpose. Provide many opportunities for writing in natural settings. For example, children can

- make a class directory listing names and phone numbers of their classmates.
- record observations in science.
- write and illustrate labels for art materials.
- draw and label maps, pictures, graphs, and picture dictionaries.

ELL English language learners can also participate in meaningful print experiences. They can

- write signs, name tags, and messages.
- label pictures.
- join in shared writing experiences.

Challenge To ensure the continued rapid advancement of children who come to first grade already writing, provide

- exposure to a wide range of reading materials.
- opportunities for independent writing on self-selected and assigned topics.
- explicit instruction in print conventions (punctuation, use of capital letters).
- introduce simple editing marks and encourage children to proofread and edit their own work.

The handwriting strand in *Trophies* teaches correct letter formation and spacing and provides a variety of opportunities to help children become fluent, confident writers. Materials and activities include

- handwriting activities in the *Teacher's Edition.*
- *Alphabet Cards* showing correct strokes.
- handwriting practice and guidelines in the *Language Handbook.*
- reproducible models for manuscript and D'Nealian Handwriting.

Handwriting
Uppercase Manuscript Alphabet

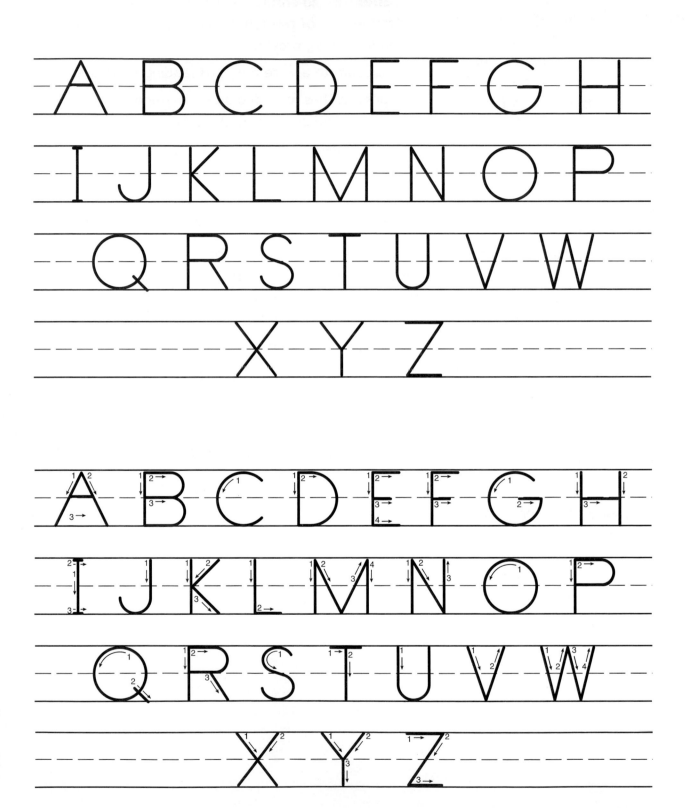

Handwriting
Lowercase Manuscript Alphabet

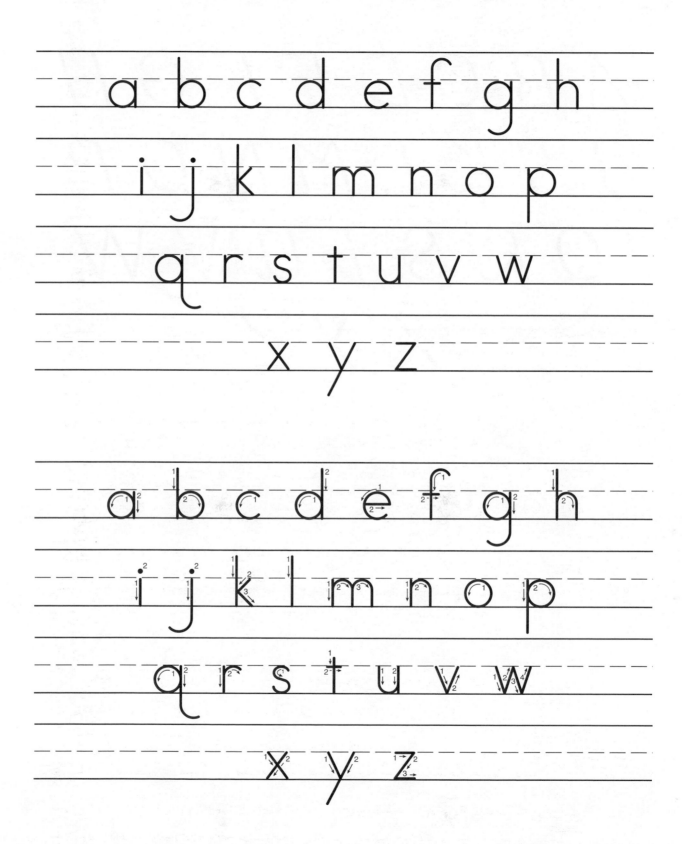

Handwriting
D'Nealian Capital Alphabet

Handwriting
D'Nealian Lowercase Alphabet

a b c d e f g h
i j k l m n o p
q r s t u v w
x y z

My Reading Log

Name _____

1. Title _____

2. Author _____

3. What is this book about?

_____

_____

_____

4. What is your favorite part?

_____

_____

_____

Harcourt

Thinking About My Reading and Writing

Name _____

When I read,

1. I think about what I already know.	🙂	😐	🙁
2. I picture in my mind what I am reading about.	🙂	😐	🙁
3. I think about what is going to happen next in a story.	🙂	😐	🙁
4. I ask myself if what I'm reading makes sense.	🙂	😐	🙁
5. When I read by myself, I feel like this.	🙂	😐	🙁

When I write,

1. I think about who will read my writing.	🙂	😐	🙁
2. I list or draw my ideas.	🙂	😐	🙁
3. I write in complete sentences.	🙂	😐	🙁
4. I begin my sentences with a capital letter.	🙂	😐	🙁
5. I put an end mark at the end of each sentence.	🙂	😐	🙁

Harcourt

Thinking About My Listening and Speaking

Name _____

When I speak,

1. I use words that my audience will understand.	😊	😐	☹
2. I speak clearly and look at my audience.	😊	😐	☹
3. I speak loudly and slowly before a group.	😊	😐	☹
4. I use objects and movements to help show what I mean.	😊	😐	☹
5. I answer questions that my audience asks.	😊	😐	☹
6. I use words that describe my ideas and feelings.	😊	😐	☹

When I listen,

1. I pay attention.	😊	😐	☹
2. I picture in my mind what the speaker is saying.	😊	😐	☹
3. I ask questions if I don't understand or want to know more.	😊	😐	☹
4. I take notes and follow directions.	😊	😐	☹

STUDENT SELF-ASSESSMENT FORMS

Harcourt

Traveling on the Internet

There are so many things to see and do on the Internet that new users may wish they had a "tour guide" to help them see the most interesting sites and make sure they don't miss anything. There are many ways to become a savvy Web traveler—one is by learning the language. Here are some common terms.

bookmark A function that lets you return to your favorite Web sites quickly.

browser Application software that allows you to navigate the Internet and view a Web site.

bulletin board/newsgroup Places to leave an electronic message or to share news that anyone can read and respond to.

chat room A place for people to converse online by typing messages to each other. Once you're in a chat room, others can contact you by e-mail. Some online services monitor their chat rooms and encourage participants to report offensive chatter. Some allow teachers and parents to deny children access to chat rooms altogether.

cookie When you visit a site, a notation known as a "cookie" may be fed to a file in your computer. If you revisit the site, the cookie file allows the Web site to identify you as a return guest—and offer you products tailored to your interests or tastes. You can set your online preferences to limit or let you know about cookies that a Web site places on your computer.

cyberspace Another name for the Internet.

download To move files or software from a remote computer to your computer.

e-mail Messages sent to one or more individuals via the Internet.

filter Software that lets you block access to Web sites and content that you may find unsuitable.

ISP (Internet Service Provider) A service that allows you to connect to the Internet.

junk e-mail Unsolicited commercial e-mail; also known as "spam."

keyword A word you enter into a search engine to begin the search for specific information or Web sites.

links Highlighted words on a Web site that allow you to connect to other parts of the same Web site or to other Web sites.

listserv An online mailing list that allows individuals or organizations to send e-mail to groups of people at one time.

modem An internal or external device that connects your computer to a phone line that can link you to the Internet.

password A personal code that you use to access your Internet account with your ISP.

privacy policy A statement on a Web site describing what information about you is collected by the site and how this information is used.

search engine A function that helps you find information and Web sites. Accessing a search engine is like using the catalog in a library.

URL (Uniform Resource Locator) The address that lets you locate a particular site. For example, **http://www.ed.gov** is the URL for the U.S. Department of Education. All government URLs end in **.gov**. Nonprofit organizations and trade associations end in **.org**. Commercial companies now end in **.com**, and non-commercial educational sites end in **.edu**. Countries other than the United States use different endings.

virus A file maliciously planted in your computer that can damage files and disrupt your system. Antivirus software is available.

Web site An Internet destination where you can look at and retrieve data. All the Web sites in the world, linked together, make up the World Wide Web or the "Web."

Visit *The Learning Site!*
www.harcourtschool.com

Harcourt

My Rules for Internet Safety

I agree that

- **I will never give out private information,** such as my last name, my address, my telephone number, or my parents' work addresses or telephone numbers on the Internet.

- **I will never give out the address or telephone number** of my school on the Internet without first asking an adult's permission.

- **I understand which sites I can visit** and which ones are off-limits.

- **I will tell an adult right away** if something comes up on the screen that makes me feel uncomfortable.

- **I will never agree to meet in person** with anyone I meet online.

- **I will never e-mail a person any pictures** of myself or my classmates without an adult's permission.

- **I will tell an adult** if I get an inappropriate e-mail message from anyone.

- **I will remember that going online** on the Internet is like going out in public, so all the safety rules I already know apply here as well.

- **I know the Internet is a useful tool,** and I will always use it responsibly.

- **I will follow these same rules when I am at home,** in school, at the library, or at a friend's.

X _____   _____
(Student signs here)   (Parent/Guardian signs here)

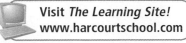
Visit *The Learning Site!*
www.harcourtschool.com

Harcourt

Using the Student Record Form

Using the Student Record Form

The record form on the following pages is a tool for tracking each student's progress toward grade-level standards. In addition to formal records on assessment results and instructional plans, you may also wish to complete this form several times yearly for each student. Make one copy of the form for each student. Record the date at the top of the column, and use the codes provided to record student progress. You may wish to add comments at the bottom or on the back of the form.

Sharing Student Progress with Family Members

The record form can be one vehicle for communicating with families about how students are making progress toward grade-level standards. Explain that students are expected to master the standards toward the end of the school year. Therefore, a code of B, or Beginning, at the start of the year is expected for most students. After that time, most students should be receiving a P for Making Progress, and by the end of the year they should meet or exceed each standard.

Students who are not making progress, of course, require intervention and frequent assessment to monitor progress and adapt instruction. Explain to family members the levels of support offered by *Trophies* and how you are using these tools to help their students succeed. On the other hand, some students may begin to meet or exceed the standards early in the year. For these families, you can explain how you are using *Trophies* to extend and accelerate progress. (For more information about levels of support in *Trophies*, see Theme Assessment to Plan Instruction at the beginning of each theme.)

Encouraging Family Involvement

Besides explaining student progress, there are several things you can do to encourage parents and guardians to support their students' achievement:

- Use the School-Home Connections pages in the Theme Resources section to suggest activities and reading materials on a weekly basis.
- Copy the Additional Homework Ideas pages at the beginning of each theme, and send them home with students. Encourage family members to use at least one activity per day.
- Have students use My Reading Log (provided in this tabbed section) daily, to record their reading outside of class. Stress repeatedly that sustained daily reading is essential to student growth. Request that parents or guardians sign off on the My Reading Log form, to encourage them to monitor students' reading.
- Above all, offer praise and recognition for all efforts that family members make to support students' literacy.

Student Record Form

Student _____ Teacher _____ Grade _____

	Date___	Date___	Date___	Date___	Date___	Date___
WORD ANALYSIS, FLUENCY, AND SYSTEMATIC VOCABULARY DEVELOPMENT						
Match oral words to printed words.						
Identify the title and author of a reading selection.						
Identify letters, words, and sentences.						
Distinguish initial, medial, and final sounds in single-syllable words.						
Distinguish long- and short-vowel sounds in orally stated single-syllable words.						
Create and state a series of rhyming words, including consonant blends.						
Add, delete, or change target sounds to change words.						
Blend two to four phonemes into recognizable words.						
Segment single syllable words into their components.						
Generate the sounds from all the letters and letter patterns, including consonant blends and long- and short-vowel patterns, and blend those sounds into recognizable words.						
Read common, irregular sight words.						
Use knowledge of vowel digraphs and r-controlled letter-sound associations to read words.						
Read compound words and contractions.						
Read inflectional forms and root words.						
Read common word families.						
Read aloud with fluency in a manner that sounds like natural speech.						
Classify grade-appropriate categories of words.						
READING COMPREHENSION						
Identify text that uses sequence or other logical order.						
Respond to *who, what, when, where,* and *how* questions.						
Follow one-step written instructions.						
Use context to resolve ambiguities about word and sentence meanings.						
Confirm predictions about what will happen next in a text by identifying key words.						
Relate prior knowledge to textual information.						
Retell the central ideas of simple expository or narrative passages.						
LITERARY RESPONSE AND ANALYSIS						
Identify and describe the elements of plot, setting, and character(s) in a story, as well as the story's beginning, middle, and ending.						
Describe the roles of authors and illustrators and their contributions to print materials.						
Recollect, talk, and write about books read during the school year.						

Harcourt

WRITING STRATEGIES

Select a focus when writing.					
Use descriptive words when writing.					
Print legibly and space letters, words, and sentences appropriately.					

WRITING APPLICATIONS
(Genres and Their Characteristics)

Write brief narratives describing an experience.					
Write brief expository descriptions of a real object, person, place, or event, using sensory details.					

WRITTEN AND ORAL ENGLISH LANGUAGE CONVENTIONS

Write and speak in complete, coherent sentences.					
Identify and correctly use singular and plural nouns.					
Identify and correctly use contractions and singular possessive pronouns in writing and speaking.					
Distinguish between declarative, exclamatory, and interrogative sentences.					
Use a period, exclamation point, or question mark at the end of sentences.					
Use knowledge of the basic rules of punctuation and capitalization when writing.					
Capitalize the first word of a sentence, names of people, and the pronoun *I*.					
Spell three- and four-letter short-vowel words and grade-level-appropriate sight words correctly.					

LISTENING AND SPEAKING STRATEGIES

Listen attentively.					
Ask questions for clarification and understanding.					
Give, restate, and follow simple two-step directions.					
Stay on the topic when speaking.					
Use descriptive words when speaking about people, places, things, and events.					

SPEAKING APPLICATIONS
(Genres and Their Characteristics)

Recite poems, rhymes, songs, and stories.					
Retell stories using basic story grammar and relating the sequence of story events by answering *who, what, when, where, why,* and *how* questions.					
Relate an important life event or personal experience in a simple sequence.					
Provide descriptions with careful attention to sensory detail.					

Comments:

Harcourt

Key:

B = Beginning

P = Making Progress

M = Meets Standard

E = Exceeds Standard

Professional Bibliography

Adams, M. J. 1990. *Beginning to Read: Thinking and Learning About Print.* Cambridge: Massachusetts Institute of Technology Press.

Adams, M. J., et al. 1998. "The Elusive Phoneme: Why Phonemic Awareness Is So Important and How to Help Children Develop It," *American Educator: The Unique Power of Reading and How to Unleash It,* Vol. 22, Nos. 1 and 2, 18–29.

Adams, M. J.; R. Treiman; and M. Pressley. 1998. "Reading, Writing, and Literacy," in *Handbook of Child Psychology: Child Psychology in Practice* (Fifth edition). Vol. 4. Edited by I. E. Sigel and K. A. Renninger. New York: Wiley.

Allen, L. 1998. "An Integrated Strategies Approach: Making Word Identification Instruction Work for Beginning Readers," *The Reading Teacher,* Vol. 52, No. 3, 254–68.

American Association of School Librarians and the Association of Educational Communications and Technology. 1998. *Information Power: Building Partnerships for Learning.* Chicago: American Library Association.

Anderson, R. C., et al. 1985. *Becoming a Nation of Readers: The Report of the Commission on Reading.* Washington, D.C.: National Academy of Education, Commission on Education and Public Policy.

Anderson, R. C.; P. T. Wilson; and L. G. Fielding. 1988. "Growth in Reading and How Children Spend Their Time Outside of School," *Reading Research Quarterly,* Vol. 23, No. 3, 285–303.

Anderson, R. C., and W. E. Nagy. 1991. "Word Meanings," in *Handbook of Reading Research.* Vol. 2. Edited by R. Barr, et al. New York: Longman.

Ball, E. W., and B. A. Blachman. 1991. "Does Phoneme Awareness Training in Kindergarten Make a Difference in Early Word Recognition and Developmental Spelling?" *Reading Research Quarterly,* Vol. 26, No. 1, 49–66.

Barinaga, M. 1996. "Giving Language Skills a Boost," *Science,* Vol. 271, 27–28.

Baumann, J. F., and E. J. Kame'enui. 1991. "Research on Vocabulary Instruction: Ode to Voltaire," in *Handbook of Research on Teaching the English Language Arts.* Edited by J. Flood, J. J. D. Lapp, and J. R. Squire. New York: Macmillan.

Beck, I., et al. 1996. "Questioning the Author: A Year-Long Classroom Implementation to Engage Students with Text," *The Elementary School Journal,* Vol. 96, 385–414.

Beck, I., et al. 1998. "Getting at the Meaning: How to Help Students Unpack Difficult Text," *American Educator: The Unique Power of Reading and How to Unleash It,* Vol. 22, Nos. 1 and 2, 66–71, 85.

Beck, I., et al. 1997. *Questioning the Author: An Approach for Enhancing Student Engagement with Text.* Newark, Del.: International Reading Association.

Berninger, V. W., et al. 1994. "Developmental Skills Related to Writing and Reading Acquisition in the Inter-mediate Grades," *Reading and Writing: An Interdisciplinary Journal,* Vol. 6, 161–96.

Berthoff, A. E. 1984. "Recognition, Representation, and Revision," in *Rhetoric and Composition: A Sourcebook for Teachers and Writers.* Edited by R. Graves. Portsmouth, N.H.: Boynton Cook.

Blachman, B. A., et al. 1994. "Kindergarten Teachers Develop Phoneme Awareness in Low-Income, Inner-City Classrooms," *Reading and Writing: An Interdisciplinary Journal,* Vol. 6, 1–18.

Blachowicz, C. L. Z., and P. Fisher. 1996. *Teaching Vocabulary in All Classrooms.* Englewood Cliffs, N.J.: Merrill/Prentice Hall.

Bloom, B. S., ed. 1985. *Developing Talent in Young People.* New York: Ballantine Books.

Bus, A. G.; M. H. vanIJzendoorn; and A. D. Pellegrini. 1995. "Joint Book Reading Makes for Success in Learning to Read: A Meta-Analysis on Inter-generational Transmission of Literacy," *Review of Educational Research,* Vol. 65, 1–21.

Byrne, B., and R. Fielding-Barnsley. 1995. "Evaluation of a Program to Teach Phonemic Awareness to Young Children: A One- and Three-Year Follow-Up and a New Preschool Trial," *Journal of Educational Psychology,* Vol. 87, No. 3, 488–503.

California Department of Education. 1996. *Connect, Compute, and Compete: The Report of the California Education Technology Task Force.* Sacramento: California Department of Education.

California Department of Education. 1994. *Differentiating the Core Curriculum and Instruction to Provide Advanced Learning Opportunities.* Sacramento: California Department of Education.

California Department of Education. 1998. *English-Language Arts Content Standards for California Public Schools, Kindergarten Through Grade Twelve.* Sacramento: California Department of Education.

California Department of Education. 1995. *Every Child a Reader: The Report of the California Reading Task Force.* Sacramento: California Department of Education.

California Department of Education. 1998. *Fostering the Development of a First and a Second Language in Early Childhood.* Sacramento: California Department of Education.

California Department of Education. 1999. *Reading/Language Arts Framework for California Public Schools: Kindergarten Through Grade Twelve.* Sacramento: California Department of Education.

California Department of Education. 1996. *Recommended Readings in Literature, Kindergarten Through Grade Eight* (Revised annotated edition). Sacramento: California Department of Education.

Calkins, L. 1996. "Motivating Readers," ERIC Clearinghouse on Assessment and Evaluation (No. SP525606), *Instructor,* Vol. 106, No. I, 32–33.

Campbell, F. A., and C. T. Ramsey. 1995. "Cognitive and Social Outcomes for High-Risk African American Students at Middle Adolescence: Positive Effects of Early Intervention," *American Educational Research Journal,* Vol. 32, 743–72.

Carlisle, J. F., and D. M. Nomanbhoy. 1993. "Phonological and Morphological Awareness in First-Graders," *Applied Psycholinguistics,* Vol. 14, 177–95.

Carnine, D.; J. Silbert; and E. J. Kame'enui. 1990. *Direct Instruction Reading.* Columbus, Ohio: Merrill Publishing Company.

Chall, J.; V. Jacobs; and L. Baldwin. 1990. *The Reading Crisis: Why Poor Children Fall Behind.* Cambridge: Harvard University Press.

Cornwall, A., and H. Bawden. 1992. "Reading Disabilities and Aggression: A Critical Review," *Journal of Learning Disabilities,* Vol. 25, 281–88.

Corson, D. 1995. *Using English Words.* Dordrecht, Netherlands: Kluwer.

Cunningham, A. E., and K. E. Stanovich. 1993. "Children's Literacy Environments and Early Word Recognition Subskills," *Reading and Writing: An Interdisciplinary Journal,* Vol. 5, 193–204.

Cunningham, A. E., and K. E. Stanovich. 1998. "What Reading Does for the Mind," *American Educator: The Unique Power of Reading and How to Unleash It,* Vol. 22, Nos. I and 2, 8–15.

Cunningham, P. M. 1998. "The Multisyllabic Word Dilemma: Helping Students Build Meaning, Spell, and Read 'Big' Words," *Reading and Writing Quarterly,* Vol. 14, 189–218.

Daneman, M. 1991. "Individual Differences in Reading Skills," in *Handbook of Reading Research* (Vol. 2). Edited by R. Barr, M. L. Kamil, P. B. Mosenthal, and P. D. Pearson. New York: Longman.

Defior, S., and P. Tudela. 1994. "Effect of Phonological Training on Reading and Writing Acquisition," *Reading and Writing,* Vol. 6, 299–320.

Delpit, L. D. 1986. "Skills and Other Dilemmas of a Progressive Black Educator," *Harvard Educational Review,* Vol. 56, 379–85.

Dickinson, D. K., and M. W. Smith. 1994. "Long-Term Effects of Preschool Teachers' Book Readings on Low-Income Children's Vocabulary and Story Comprehension," *Reading Research Quarterly,* Vol. 29, No. 2, 104–22.

Dillard, A. 1998. "What Reading Does for the Soul: A Girl and Her Books," *American Educator: The Unique Power of Reading and How to Unleash It,* Vol. 22, Nos. I and 2, 88–93.

Ediger, M. 1988. "Motivation in the Reading Curriculum," ERIC Clearinghouse on Assessment and Evaluation (No. CS009424).

Ehri, L. 1994. "Development of the Ability to Read Words: Update," in *Theoretical Models and Processes of Reading.* Edited by R. Ruddell, M. Ruddell, and H. Singer. Newark, Del.: International Reading Association.

Ehri, L. C., and S. McCormick. 1998. "Phases of Word Learning: Implications for Instruction with Delayed and Disabled Readers," *Reading and Writing Quarterly,* Vol. 14, 135–63.

Ehri, L. C. 1991. "Development of the Ability to Read Words," in *Handbook of Reading Research* (Vol. 2). Edited by R. Barr, et al. New York: Longman.

Ehrlich, M. F.; B. Kurtz-Costess; and C. Loridant. 1993. "Cognitive and Motivational Determinants of Reading Comprehension in Good and Poor Readers," *Journal of Reading Behavior,* Vol. 25, No. 4, 365–81.

Eisenberg, M., and R. Berkowitz. 1990. *Information Problem Solving: The Big Six Skills Approach to Library and Information Skills Instruction.* Norwood, N.J.: Ablex.

Englert, C. S., et al. 1995. "The Early Literacy Project: Connecting Across the Literacy Curriculum," *Learning Disability Quarterly,* Vol. 18, 253–75.

Epstein, J. L. 1995. "School-Family-Community Partnerships: Caring for Children We Share," *Phi Delta Kappan,* Vol. 76, No. 9, 701–2.

Felton, R. H., and P. P. Pepper. 1995. "Early Identification and Intervention of Phonological Deficits in Kindergarten and Early Elementary Children at Risk for Reading Disability," *School Psychology Review,* Vol. 24, 405–14.

Fielding, L. G., and Pearson, P. D. 1994. "Synthesis of Research—Reading Comprehension: What Works," *Educational Leadership,* Vol. 51, No. 5, 62–7.

Fielding-Barnsley, R. 1997. "Explicit Instruction in Decoding Benefits Children High in Phonemic Awareness and Alphabet Knowledge," *Scientific Studies of Reading,* Vol. I, No. I, 85–98.

Fitzgerald, J. 1995. "English-as-a-Second-Language Learners' Cognitive Reading Processes: A Review of Research in the U.S.," *Review of Educational Research,* Vol. 65, 145–90.

Flower, L. 1985. *Problem-Solving Strategies for Writing.* New York: Harcourt Brace Jovanovich.

Foorman, B., et al. 1998. "The Role of Instruction in Learning to Read: Preventing Reading Failure in At-Risk Children," *Journal of Educational Psychology,* Vol. 90, 37–55.

Foster, K. C., et al. 1994. "Computer-Assisted Instruction in Phonological Awareness: Evaluation of the DaisyQuest Program," *Journal of Research and Development in Education,* Vol. 27, 126–37.

Fuchs, L. S., et al. 1993. "Formative Evaluation of Academic Progress: How Much Growth Can We Expect?" *School Psychology Review,* Vol. 22, No. I, 27–48.

Gambrell, L. B., et al. 1996. *Elementary Students' Motivation to Read.* Reading Research Report No. 52. Athens, Ga.: National Reading Research Center.

Gardner, H. 1983. *Frames of Mind: The Theory of Multiple Intelligences.* New York: Basic Books.

Gersten, R., and J. Woodward. 1995. "A Longitudinal Study of Transitional and Immersion Bilingual Education Programs in One District," *Elementary School Journal,* Vol. 95, 223–39.

Giles, H. C. 1997. "Parent Engagement as a School Reform Strategy," ERIC Clearinghouse on Urban Education (Digest 135).

Goldenberg, C. N., and R. Gallimore. 1991. "Local Knowledge, Research Knowledge, and Educational Change: A Case Study of Early [First-Grade] Spanish Reading Improvement," *Educational Researcher,* Vol. 20, No. 8, 2–14.

Goldenberg, C. 1992–93. "Instructional Conversations: Promoting Comprehension Through Discussion," *The Reading Teacher,* Vol. 46, 316–26.

Good, R. III; D. C. Simmons; and S. Smith. 1998. "Effective Academic Interventions in the United States: Evaluating and Enhancing the Acquisition of Early Reading Skills," *School Psychology Review,* Vol. 27, No. 1, 45–56.

Greene, J. F. 1998. "Another Chance: Help for Older Students with Limited Literacy," *American Educator: The Unique Power of Reading and How to Unleash It,* Vol. 22, Nos. 1 and 2, 74–79.

Guthrie, J. T., et al. 1996. "Growth of Literacy Engagement: Changes in Motivations and Strategies During Concept-Oriented Reading Instruction," *Reading Research Quarterly,* Vol. 31, 306–25.

Hanson, R. A., and D. Farrell. 1995. "The Long-Term Effects on High School Seniors of Learning to Read in Kindergarten," *Reading Research Quarterly,* Vol. 30, No. 4, 908–33.

Hart, B., and T. R. Risley. 1995. *Meaningful Differences in the Everyday Experience of Young American Children.* Baltimore: Paul H. Brookes Publishing Co.

Hasbrouck, J. E., and G. Tindal. 1992. "Curriculum-Based Oral Reading Fluency Norms for Students in Grades 2 Through 5," *Teaching Exceptional Children,* Vol. 24, 41–44.

Hiebert, E. H., et al. 1992. "Reading and Writing of First-Grade Students in a Restructured Chapter I Program," *American Educational Research Journal,* Vol. 29, 545–72.

Hillocks, G., Jr. 1986. *Research on Written Composition: New Directions for Teaching.* Urbana, Ill.: National Council for Teachers of English.

Honig, B.; L. Diamond; and L. Gutlohn. 2000. *Teaching Reading Sourcebook for Kindergarten Through Eighth Grade.* Emeryville, CA: CORE, Consortium on Reading Excellence.

Honig, B.; L. Diamond; and R. Nathan. 1999. *Assessing Reading: Multiple Measures for Kindergarten Through Eighth Grade.* Emeryville, CA: CORE, Consortium on Reading Excellence.

Hoover-Dempsey, K. V., and H. M. Sandler. 1997. "Why Do Parents Become Involved in Their Children's Education?" *Review of Educational Research,* Vol. 67, No. 1, 3–42.

Hunter, M., and G. Barker. 1987. "If at First . . . : Attribution Theory in the Classroom," *Educational Leadership,* Vol. 45, No. 2, 50–53.

Jimenez, R. T.; G. E. Garcia; and P. D. Pearson. 1996. "The Reading Strategies of Latina/o Students Who Are Successful Readers: Opportunities and Obstacles," *Reading Research Quarterly,* Vol. 31, 90–112.

Juel, C. 1991. "Beginning Reading," in *Handbook of Reading Research* (Vol. 2). Edited by R. Barr, M. L. Kamil, P. B. Mosenthal, and P. D. Pearson. New York: Longman.

Juel, C. 1988. "Learning to Read and Write: A Longitudinal Study of 54 Children from First Through Fourth Grades," *Journal of Educational Psychology,* Vol. 80, 437–447.

Kame'enui, E. J. 1996. "Shakespeare and Beginning Reading: 'The Readiness Is All,'" *Teaching Exceptional Children,* Vol. 28, No. 2, 77–81.

Kuhn, M. R., and S. A. Stahl. 1998. "Teaching Children to Learn Word Meanings from Context: A Synthesis and Some Questions," *Journal of Literacy Research,* Vol. 30, No. 1, 119–38.

Lance, K. C.; L. Welborn; and C. Hamilton-Pennell. 1993. *The Impact of School Library Media Centers on Academic Achievement.* San Jose, Calif.: Hi Willow Research and Publishing.

Leather, C. V., and L. A. Henry. 1994. "Working Memory Span and Phonological Awareness Tasks as Predictors of Early Reading Ability," *Journal of Experimental Child Psychology,* Vol. 58, 88–111.

Levy, B. A.; A. Nicholls; and D. Kohen. 1993. "Repeated Readings: Process Benefits for Good and Poor Readers," *Journal of Experimental Child Psychology,* Vol. 56, 303–27.

Liberman, I. Y.; D. Shankweiler; and A. M. Liberman. 1991. "The Alphabetic Principle and Learning to Read," in *Phonology and Reading Disability: Solving the Reading Puzzle.* Edited by D. Shankweiler and I. Y. Liberman. Ann Arbor: University of Michigan Press.

Lie, A. 1991. "Effects of a Training Program for Stimulating Skills in Word Analysis in First-Grade Children," *Reading Research Quarterly,* Vol. 26, No. 3, 234–50.

Lipson, M. Y., and K. K. Wixson. 1986. "Reading Disability Research: An Interactionist Perspective," *Review of Educational Research,* Vol. 56, 111–36.

Louis, K. S.; H. M. Marks; and S. Kruse. 1996. "Teachers' Professional Community in Restructuring Schools," *American Educational Research Journal* (Vol. 33).

Lundberg, I.; J. Frost; and O. P. Petersen. 1988. "Effects of an Extensive Program for Stimulating Phonological Awareness in Preschool Children," *Reading Research Quarterly,* Vol. 23, 263–284.

Lyon, G. R. 1995. "Toward a Definition of Dyslexia," *Annals of Dyslexia,* Vol. 45, 3–27.

Lyon, G. R., and V. Chhabra. 1996. "The Current State of Science and the Future of Specific Reading Disability," *Mental Retardation and Developmental Disabilities Research Reviews,* Vol. 2, 2–9.

Markell, M. A., and S. L. Deno. 1997. "Effects of Increasing Oral Reading: Generalization Across Reading Tasks," *The Journal of Special Education,* Vol. 31, No. 2, 233–50.

McCollum, H., and A. Russo. 1993. *Model Strategies in Bilingual Education: Family Literacy and Parent Involvement.* Washington, D.C.: United States Department of Education.

McGuinness, D.; C. McGuinness; and J. Donahue. 1996. "Phonological Training and the Alphabetic Principle: Evidence for Reciprocal Causality," *Reading Research Quarterly*, Vol. 30, 830–52.

McWhorter, J. 1998. *The Word on the Street: Fact and Fable about American English.* New York: Plenum.

Moats, L. C. 1995. *Spelling: Development, Disability, and Instruction.* Baltimore: York Press.

Moats, L. C. 1998. "Teaching Decoding," *American Educator: The Unique Power of Reading and How to Unleash It*, Vol. 22, Nos. 1 and 2, 42–49, 95–96.

Moffett, J., and B. J. Wagner. 1991. *Student-Centered Language Arts, K-12.* Portsmouth, N.H.: Boynton Cook.

Morrow, L. M. 1992. "The Impact of a Literature-Based Program on Literacy, Achievement, Use of Literature, and Attitudes of Children from Minority Backgrounds," *Reading Research Quarterly*, Vol. 27, 250–75.

Mosenthal, P. 1984. "The Problem of Partial Specification in Translating Reading Research into Practice," *The Elementary School Journal*, Vol. 85, No. 2, 199–227.

Mosenthal, P. 1985. "Defining Progress in Educational Research," *Educational Researcher*, Vol. 14, No. 9, 3–9.

Mosteller, F.; R. Light; and J. Sachs. 1996. "Sustained Inquiry in Education: Lessons from Skill Grouping and Class Size," *Harvard Educational Review*, Vol. 66, No. 4, 797–842.

National Center to Improve the Tools of Educators. 1997. *Learning to Read, Reading to Learn—Helping Children to Succeed: A Resource Guide.* Washington, D.C.: American Federation of Teachers.

National Research Council. 1998. *Preventing Reading Difficulties in Young Children.* Edited by M. S. Burns, P. Griffin, and C. E. Snow. Washington, D.C.: National Academy Press.

National Research Council. 1999. *Starting Out Right: A Guide to Promoting Children's Reading Success.* Edited by M. S. Burns, P. Griffin, and C. E. Snow. Washington, D.C.: National Academy Press.

Neuman, S. B. 1996. "Children Engaging in Storybook Reading: The Influence of Access to Print Resources, Opportunity, and Parental Interaction," *Early Childhood Research Quarterly*, Vol. 11, 495–513.

O'Connor, R. E.; J. R. Jenkins; and T. A. Slocum. 1995. "Transfer Among Phonological Tasks in Kindergarten: Essential Instructional Content," *Journal of Educational Psychology*, Vol. 87, 202–17.

Pearson, P. D., et al. 1992. "Developing Expertise in Reading Comprehension," in *What Research Says to the Teacher.* Edited by S. J. Samuels and A. E. Farstrup. Newark, Del.: International Reading Association.

Pearson, P. D., and K. Camperell. 1985. "Comprehension in Text Structures," in *Theoretical Models and Processes of Reading.* Edited by H. Singer and R. B. Ruddell. Newark, Del.: International Reading Association.

Perfetti, C. A., and S. Zhang. 1995. "The Universal Word Identification Reflex," in *The Psychology of Learning and Motivation* (Vol. 33). Edited by D. L. Medlin. San Diego: Academic Press.

Phillips, L. M.; S. P. Norris; and J. M. Mason. 1996. "Longitudinal Effects of Early Literacy Concepts on Reading Achievement: A Kindergarten Intervention and Five-Year Follow-Up," *Journal of Literacy Research*, Vol. 28, 173–95.

Pinnell, G. S., and L C. Fountas. 1997. *Help America Read: A Handbook for Volunteers.* Portsmouth, N.H.: Heinemann.

Pressley, M.; J. Rankin; and L. Yokoi. 1996. "A Survey of Instructional Practices of Primary Teachers Nominated as Effective in Promoting Literacy," *The Elementary School Journal*, Vol. 96, 363–84.

Purcell-Gates, V.; E. McIntyre; and P. Freppon. 1995. "Learning Written Storybook Language in School: A Comparison of Low-SES Children in Skills-Based and Whole-Language Classrooms," *American Educational Research Journal*, Vol. 32, 659–85.

Robbins, C., and L. C. Ehri. 1994. "Reading Storybooks to Kindergartners Helps Them Learn New Vocabulary Words," *Journal of Educational Psychology*, Vol. 86, No. 1, 54–64.

Rosenshine, B., and C. Meister. 1994. "Reciprocal Teaching: A Review of the Research," *Review of Educational Research*, Vol. 64, No. 4, 479–530.

Ross, S. M., et al. 1995. "Increasing the Academic Success of Disadvantaged Children: An Examination of Alternative Early Intervention Programs," *American Educational Research Journal*, Vol. 32, 773–800.

Ruddell, R.; M. Rapp Ruddell; and H. Singer, eds. 1994. *Theoretical Models and Processes of Reading* (Fourth edition). Newark, Del.: International Reading Association.

Ryder, R. J., and M. F. Graves. 1994. "Vocabulary Instruction Presented Prior to Reading in Two Basal Readers," *Elementary School Journal*, Vol. 95, No. 2, 139–53.

Sacks, C. H., and J. R. Mergendoller. 1997. "The Relationship Between Teachers' Theoretical Orientation Toward Reading and Student Outcomes in Kindergarten Children with Different Initial Reading Abilities," *American Educational Research Journal*, Vol. 34, 721–39.

Samuels, S. J. 1979. "The Method of Repeated Reading," *The Reading Teacher*, Vol. 32, 403–08.

Sanacore, J. 1988. "Linking Vocabulary and Comprehension Through Independent Reading," ERIC Clearinghouse on Assessment and Evaluation (No. CS009409).

Shefelbine, J. 1991. *Encouraging Your Junior High Student to Read.* Bloomington, Ind.: ERIC Clearinghouse on Reading, English, and Communication.

Shefelbine, J. L. 1990. "Student Factors Related to Variability in Learning Word Meanings from Context," *Journal of Reading Behavior,* Vol. 22, No. 1, 71–97.

Shore, W. J., and F. T. Durso. 1990. "Partial Knowledge in Vocabulary Acquisition: General Constraints and Specific Detail," *Journal of Educational Psychology,* Vol. 82, 315–18.

Shore, B. M., et al. 1991. *Recommended Practices in Gifted Education: A Critical Analysis.* New York: Teachers College Press.

Simmons, D. C., and E. J. Kame'enui. 1996. "A Focus on Curriculum Design: When Children Fail," in *Strategies for Teaching Children in Inclusive Settings.* Edited by E. Meyen, G. Vergason, and R. Whelan. Denver: Love Publishing.

Simmons, D. C., and E. J. Kame'enui, eds. 1998. *What Reading Research Tells Us About Children with Diverse Learning Needs: Bases and Basics.* Mahwah, N.J.: Lawrence Erlbaum Associates.

Sindelar, P. T.; L. Monda; and L. O'Shea. 1990. "Effects of Repeated Readings on Instructional- and Mastery-Level Readers," *Journal of Educational Research,* Vol. 83, 220–26.

Slavin, R. E.; N. L. Karweit; and B. A. Wasik, eds. 1993. *Preventing Early School Failure: Research, Policy, and Practice.* 1993. Boston: Allyn and Bacon.

Snider, V. E. 1995. "A Primer on Phonological Awareness: What It Is, Why It's Important, and How to Teach It," *School Psychology Review,* Vol. 24, 443–55.

Spear-Swerling, L., and R. J. Sternberg. 1998. "Curing Our 'Epidemic' of Learning Disabilities," *Phi Delta Kappan,* Vol. 79, No. 5, 397–401.

Spear-Swerling, L., and R. J. Sternberg. 1996. *Off Track: When Poor Readers Become Learning Disabled.* Boulder, Colo.: Westview Press.

Stanovich, K. E. 1986. "Matthew Effects in Reading: Some Consequences of Individual Differences in the Acquisition of Literacy," *Reading Research Quarterly,* Vol. 21, 360–407.

Stanovich, K. E. 1994. "Constructivism in Reading Education," *The Journal of Special Education,* Vol. 28, 259–74.

Stanovich, K. E. 1993–94. "Romance and Reality," *The Reading Teacher,* Vol. 47, 280–90.

Sulzby, E., and W. Teale. 1991. "Emergent Literacy," in *Handbook of Reading Research* (Vol. 2). Edited by R. Barr, M. L. Kamil, P. B. Mosenthal, and P. D. Pearson. New York: Longman.

Topping, K. 1998. "Effective Tutoring in America Reads: A Reply to Wasik," *The Reading Teacher,* Vol. 52, No. 1, 42–50.

Torgesen, J. K. 1998. "Catch Them Before They Fall: Identification and Assessment to Prevent Reading Failure in Young Children," *American Educator: The Unique Power of Reading and How to Unleash It,* Vol. 22, Nos. 1 and 2, 32–39.

Treiman, R. 1985. "Onsets and Rimes as Units of Spoken Syllables: Evidence from Children," *Journal of Experimental Child Psychology,* Vol. 39, 161–81.

Treiman, R.; S. Weatherston; and D. Berch. 1994. "The Role of Letter Names In Children's Learning of Phoneme-Grapheme Relations," *Applied Psycholinguistics,* Vol. 15, 97–122.

Vandervelden, M. C., and L. S. Siegel. 1995. "Phonological Recoding and Phoneme Awareness in Early Literacy: A Developmental Approach," *Reading Research Quarterly,* Vol. 30, 854–73.

Vellutino, F. R., et al. 1996. "Cognitive Profiles of Difficult-to-Remediate and Readily Remediated Poor Readers: Early Intervention as a Vehicle for Distinguishing Between Cognitive and Experiential Deficits as Basic Causes of Specific Reading Disability," *Journal of Educational Psychology,* Vol. 88, 601–38.

Wagner, R. K., et al. 1993. "Development of Young Readers' Phonological Processing Abilities," *Journal of Educational Psychology,* Vol. 85, 83–103.

Walberg, H. J. 1984. "Families as Partners in Educational Productivity," *Phi Delta Kappan,* Vol. 65, No. 6, 397–400.

Wasik, B. A., and R. E. Slavin. 1993. "Preventing Early Reading Failure with One-to-One Tutoring: A Review of Five Programs," *Reading Research Quarterly,* Vol. 28, 178–200.

Wells, G. 1986. *The Meaning Makers: Children Learning Language and Using Language to Learn.* Portsmouth, N.H.: Heinemann.

White, T. G.; M. F. Graves; and W. H. Slater. 1990. "Growth of Reading Vocabulary in Diverse Elementary Schools: Decoding and Word Meaning," *Journal of Educational Psychology,* Vol. 82, 281–90.

Whitehurst, G. J., et al. 1994. "Outcomes of an Emergent Literacy Intervention in Head Start," *Journal of Educational Psychology,* Vol. 86, 542–55.

Yopp, H. K. 1988. "The Validity and Reliability of Phonemic Awareness Tests," *Reading Research Quarterly,* Vol. 23, No. 2, 159–77.

Program Reviewers

Dr. Judylynn Baily-Mitchell
Principal
West Salisbury
Elementary School
Salisbury, Maryland

Dr. Judith F. Barry
Coordinator of Reading/
Language Arts
Taunton Public Schools
Taunton, Massachusetts

Carol Berman
Lead Teacher
Crestview Elementary School
Miami, Florida

Angela Berner
Language Arts Staff Developer
Huntington Unified
School District
Administration Offices
Huntington Station, New York

Susan Birch
Teacher
Dunns Corners
Elementary School
Westerly, Rhode Island

Candace Bouchard
Teacher
Sandburg Elementary School
San Diego, California

Sandra Carron
Teacher
Moreno Valley Unified
School District
Moreno Valley, California

Loretta Cudney
Teacher
Riverside Unified School District
Riverside, California

Justyne Davis
Teacher
Wallbridge Community
Education Center
St. Louis, Missouri

Dr. Ann Dugger
Reading Teacher/Title I
Will Rogers Elementary School
Stillwater, Oklahoma

Rosemary Foresythe
Reading Specialist
West Pottsgrove
Elementary School
Pottstown, Pennsylvania

Stanley Foster
Teacher
Magnolia Avenue School
Los Angeles, California

Kimberly Griffeth
Teacher
Fulton Elementary
Aurora, Colorado

Jeffrey Guerra
Teacher
Westchase Elementary School
Tampa, Florida

Anne Henry
Teacher
Northern Hills
Elementary School
Edmond, Oklahoma

Carol Hookway
Teacher
Memorial Elementary School
Natick, Massachusetts

Arlene Horkey
Curriculum Technology Specialist
Belleair Elementary School
Clearwater, Florida

Carolyn M. Horton
District Reading Facilitator
Cedar Rapids Community
School District,
Educational Service Center
Cedar Rapids, Iowa

Patty Jacox
Teacher
Lansing Elementary School
Aurora, Colorado

Beverly Keeley
Teacher
Grant Foreman
Elementary School
Muskogee, Oklahoma

Rebecca L. Kelly
Teacher
Wekiva Elementary School
Longwood, Florida

Lisa Leslie
Teacher
Costello Elementary School,
Troy Public Schools
Troy, Michigan

Arlene D. Loughlin
Student Achievement Specialist
Curlew Creek
Elementary School
Palm Harbor, Florida

Christin Machado
Teacher
Jefferson Elementary School
Burbank, California

Alicia L. Marsh
Teacher
Pearl Sample
Elementary School
Culpeper, Virginia

K. Gale Martin
Teacher
JEB Stuart Elementary School
Richmond, Virginia

Anne M. Merritt
Teacher
Citrus Glen Elementary School
Ventura, California

Joan Miller
Teacher
Carlton Hills Elementary School
Santee, California

Bobbie A. Overbey
Teacher
Carillon Elementary School
Oviedo, Florida

Katherin Pagakis
English Teacher
Washington Elementary School
Waukegan, Illinois

Barbara Pitts
Administrator
Joy Middle School
Detroit, Michigan

Sundee Preedy
Teacher
Aloma Elementary School
Winter Park, Florida

Dr. Carolyn Reedom
Principal
Vanderberg Elementary School
Henderson, Nevada

Dorina Rocas
Teacher
Corono-Norco Unified
School District
Corona, California

Josephine Scott
Language Arts
Curriculum Director
Columbus City School District,
Columbus, Ohio

Renee Siefert
Teacher
Serrano Elementary School
Moreno Valley, California

Gayle E. Sitter
Mathematics Resource
Educational Leadership Center
Teacher ELC-7
Orlando, Florida

Linda Smolen
Director of Reading
Buffalo City School District,
Buffalo, New York

Gail Soft
Teacher
Vermillion Primary School
Maize, Kansas

Alejandro Soria
Teacher
Leo Politi Elementary
Los Angeles, California

Jan Strege
Vice-Principal
Schlegel Road
Elementary School
Webster, New York

Dahna Taylor
Teacher
Chavez Elementary School
San Diego, California

Dr. Sandra Telfort
Teacher
Palmetto Elementary School
Miami, Florida

Dana Thurm
Teacher
Olivenhain Pioneer
Elementary School
Carlsbad, California

Geralyn Wilson
Literacy Coordinator
James McCosh Intermediate
Chicago, Illinois

John L. York
Teacher
Cedar Heights
Elementary School
Cedar Falls, Iowa

Maureen A. Zoda
Reading Specialist Coordinator
Meadow Brook
Elementary School
East Longmeadow,
Massachusetts

KINDERGARTEN REVIEWERS

Janice Allocco
Teacher
Klem Road South
Elementary School
Webster, New York

Irma A. Barr
Teacher
Embassy Creek
Elementary School
Cooper City, Florida

Dikki Cie Chanski
Teacher
Martell Elementary School
Troy, Michigan

Rosemary Gaskin
Teacher
Broad Rock Elementary School
Richmond, Virginia

Carol Grenfell
District Language
Arts Specialist
Ventura Unified School District
Ventura, California

Cathleen Hunter
Teacher
Peterson Elementary
Huntington Beach, California

Karen A. Kuritar
Teacher
Allen Elementary School
Dayton, Ohio

Charlotte Otterbacher
Teacher
Hamilton Elementary
Troy, Michigan

Gwendolyn Perkins
Teacher
Ginter Park Elementary School
Richmond, Virginia

Kelly Schmidt
Teacher
Public School #225 Seaside
Rockaway Parkway, New York

Corene Selman
Teacher
Westwood Early
Childhood Center
Woodward, Oklahoma

Laureen B. Stephens
Teacher
Mountainview
Elementary School
Saycus, California

Pam Styles
Teacher
World of Wonder Community
School
Dayton, Ohio

Scope and Sequence

Reading

Concepts about Print	GR K	GR I	GR 2	GR 3	GR 4	GR 5	GR 6
Understand that print provides information	▨						
Understand how print is organized and read	▨						
Know left-to-right and top-to-bottom directionality	▨						
Distinguish letters from words	▨						
Recognize name	▨						
Name and match all uppercase and lowercase letter forms	▨						
Understand the concept of word and construct meaning from shared text, illustrations, graphics, and charts	▨						
Identify letters, words, and sentences	▨	▨					
Recognize that sentences in print are made up of words	▨	▨					
Identify the front cover, back cover, title page, title, and author of a book	▨	▨					
Match oral words to printed words	▨	▨					

Phonemic Awareness	GR K	GR I	GR 2	GR 3	GR 4	GR 5	GR 6
Understand that spoken words and syllables are made up of sequences of sounds	▨						
Count and track sounds in a syllable, syllables in words, and words in sentences	▨	▨		▨			
Know the sounds of letters	▨	▨					
Track and represent the number, sameness, difference, and order of two or more isolated phonemes	▨	▨					
Match, identify, distinguish, and segment sounds in initial, final, and medial position in single-syllable spoken words	▨	▨					
Blend sounds (phonemes) to make words or syllables	▨	▨	▨				
Track and represent changes in syllables and words as target sound is added, substituted, omitted, shifted, or repeated	▨	▨					
Distinguish long- and short-vowel sounds in orally stated words		▨					
Identify and produce rhyming words	▨	▨					

Decoding: Phonic Analysis	GR K	GR I	GR 2	GR 3	GR 4	GR 5	GR 6
Understand and apply the alphabetic principle	▨	▨					
Consonants: single, blends, digraphs in initial, final, medial positions	•	•	•	▨	▨	▨	▨
Vowels: short, long, digraphs, r-controlled, variant, schwa		•	•	▨	▨	▨	▨
Match all consonant and short-vowel sounds to appropriate letters	•	•					
Understand that as letters in words change, so do the sounds	•	•					
Blend vowel-consonant sounds orally to make words or syllables	•	•					
Blend sounds from letters and letter patterns into recognizable words	▨	▨					

Decoding: Structural Analysis	GR K	GR I	GR 2	GR 3	GR 4	GR 5	GR 6
Inflectional endings, with and without spelling changes: plurals, verb tenses, possessives, comparatives-superlatives		•	•	▨	▨	▨	▨
Contractions, abbreviations, and compound words		•	•				
Prefixes, suffixes, derivations, and root words			•	•	•	•	•
Greek and Latin roots					•	•	•
Letter, spelling, and syllable patterns		▨	▨	▨	▨	▨	▨
Phonograms/word families/onset-rimes	▨	▨					
Syllable rules and patterns				•			

Key

Shaded area   Explicit Instruction/Modeling/Practice and Application

•   Tested
    Assessment resources include: Kindergarten Assessment Handbook; Placement and Diagnostic Assessments, Grades 1, 2, and 3–6;
    Reading and Language Skills Assessments, Grades 1–6; Holistic Assessments, Grades 1–6; End-of-Selection Tests, Grades 1–6; and
    Oral Reading Fluency Assessment, Grades 1–6

	GR K	GR 1	GR 2	GR 3	GR 4	GR 5	GR 6
Decoding: Strategies							
Visual cues: sound/symbol relationships, letter patterns, and spelling patterns		▓	▓	▓	▓	▓	▓
Structural cues: compound words, contractions, inflectional endings, prefixes, suffixes, Greek and Latin roots, root words, spelling patterns, and word families		▓	▓	▓	▓	▓	▓
Cross check visual and structural cues to confirm meaning			▓	▓	▓	▓	▓
Syllabication rules and patterns			▓	▓	▓	▓	▓
Word Recognition							
One-syllable and high-frequency words	•	•	•				
Common, irregular sight words	•	•	•				
Common abbreviations			•				
Lesson vocabulary		•	•	•	•	•	•
Fluency							
Read aloud in a manner that sounds like natural speech		•	•				
Read aloud accurately and with appropriate intonation and expression			•	•			
Read aloud narrative and expository text with appropriate pacing, intonation, and expression				•	•	•	•
Read aloud prose and poetry with rhythm and pace, appropriate intonation, and vocal patterns							
Vocabulary and Concept Development							
Academic language	▓	▓	▓	▓	▓	▓	▓
Classify-categorize		•	▓	•	▓	•	▓
Antonyms		▓	•	•	•	▓	▓
Synonyms		▓	•	•	•	▓	▓
Homographs				•	•	▓	▓
Homophones			•	•	•	•	▓
Multiple-meaning words			•	•	▓	•	▓
Figurative and idiomatic language			▓	▓	▓	▓	•
Context/context clues			•	•	•	•	•
Content-area words			▓	▓	▓	▓	▓
Dictionary, glossary, thesaurus			▓	▓	•	•	▓
Foreign words			▓	▓	▓	▓	▓
Connotation-denotation					▓	•	•
Word origins (acronyms, clipped and coined words, regional variations, etymologies, jargon, slang)					▓	▓	▓
Analogies					▓	▓	▓
Word structure clues to determine meaning			•	•	•	•	•
Inflected nouns and verbs, comparatives-superlatives, possessives, compound words, prefixes, suffixes, root words			•	•	•	•	•
Greek and Latin roots, prefixes, suffixes, derivations, and root words					•	•	•
Develop vocabulary							
Listen to and discuss text read aloud	▓	▓	▓	▓	▓	▓	▓
Read independently	▓	▓	▓	▓	▓	▓	▓
Use reference books			▓	▓	▓	▓	▓
Comprehension and Analysis of Text							
Ask/answer questions	▓	▓	▓	▓	▓	▓	▓
Author's purpose				•	•	•	•
Author's perspective						•	•
Propaganda/bias							•

Key
Shaded area Explicit Instruction / Modeling / Practice and Application
• Tested
Assessment resources include: Kindergarten Assessment Handbook; Placement and Diagnostic Assessments, Grades 1, 2, and 3–6; Reading and Language Skills Assessments, Grades 1–6; Holistic Assessments, Grades 1–6; End-of-Selection Tests, Grades 1–6; and Oral Reading Fluency Assessment, Grades 1–6

	GR K	GR I	GR 2	GR 3	GR 4	GR 5	GR 6
Background knowledge: prior knowledge and experiences							
Cause-effect			•	•	•	•	•
Compare-contrast			•	•	•	•	•
Details		•	•	•	•	•	•
Directions: one-, two-, multi-step	•	•	•	•	•		
Draw conclusions				•	•	•	•
Fact-fiction							
Fact-opinion				•	•	•	•
Higher order thinking							
Analyze, critique and evaluate, synthesize, and visualize text and information							
Interpret information from graphic aids			•	•	•	•	•
Locate information		•	•	•	•	•	•
Book parts				•			•
Text features				•		•	
Alphabetical order		•					
Main idea: stated/unstated		•	•	•	•	•	•
Main idea and supporting details				•	•	•	•
Make generalizations							
Make inferences			•	•	•	•	•
Make judgments							
Make predictions/predict outcomes							
Monitor comprehension							
Adjust reading rate, create mental images, reread, read ahead, set/adjust purpose, self-question, summarize/paraphrase, use graphic aids, text features, and text adjuncts							
Paraphrase/restate facts and details			•	•	•	•	•
Preview							
Purpose for reading							
Organize information							
Alphabetical order							
Numerical systems/outlines							
Graphic organizers							
Referents							
Retell stories and ideas							
Sequence		•	•	•	•	•	•
Summarize			•	•	•	•	•
Text structure							
Narrative text			•	•	•	•	•
Informational text (compare and contrast, cause and effect, sequence/chronological order, proposition and support, problem and solution)					•	•	•
Study Skills							
Follow and give directions			•	•	•		
Apply plans and strategies: KWL, question-answer-relationships, skim and scan, note taking, outline, questioning the author, reciprocal teaching							
Practice test-taking strategies							

Key

Shaded area Explicit Instruction / Modeling / Practice and Application

•   Tested

Assessment resources include: Kindergarten Assessment Handbook; Placement and Diagnostic Assessments, Grades 1, 2, and 3–6; Reading and Language Skills Assessments, Grades 1–6; Holistic Assessments, Grades 1–6; End-of-Selection Tests, Grades 1–6; and Oral Reading Fluency Assessment, Grades 1–6

Research and Information

	GR K	GR 1	GR 2	GR 3	GR 4	GR 5	GR 6
Use resources and references		░	░	░	░	░	░
Understand the purpose, structure, and organization of various reference materials							
Title page, table of contents, chapter titles, chapter headings, index, glossary, guide words, citations, end notes, bibliography	░	░	░	•	░	░	•
Picture dictionary, software, dictionary, thesaurus, atlas, globe, encyclopedia, telephone directory, on-line information, card catalog, electronic search engines and data bases, almanac, newspaper, journals, periodicals	░	░	•	•	•	•	•
Charts, maps, diagrams, timelines, schedules, calendar, graphs, photos	░	░	•	•	░	░	•
Choose reference materials appropriate to research purpose							•

Viewing/Media

	GR K	GR 1	GR 2	GR 3	GR 4	GR 5	GR 6
Interpret information from visuals (graphics, media, including illustrations, tables, maps, charts, graphs, diagrams, timelines)	░	░	•	•	•	•	•
Analyze the ways visuals, graphics, and media represent, contribute to, and support meaning of text			░	░	░	░	░
Select, organize, and produce visuals to complement and extend meaning			░	░	░	░	░
Use technology or appropriate media to communicate information and ideas		░	░	░	░	░	░
Use technology or appropriate media to compare ideas, information, and viewpoints				░	░	░	░
Compare, contrast, and evaluate print and broadcast media					░	░	░
Distinguish between fact and opinion					░	░	░
Evaluate the role of media					░	░	░
Analyze media as sources for information, entertainment, persuasion, interpretation of events, and transmission of culture						░	░
Identify persuasive and propaganda techniques used in television and identify false and misleading information							░
Summarize main concept and list supporting details and identify biases, stereotypes, and persuasive techniques in a nonprint message							░
Support opinions with detailed evidence and with visual or media displays that use appropriate technology							░

Literary Response and Analysis

Genre Characteristics

	GR K	GR 1	GR 2	GR 3	GR 4	GR 5	GR 6
Know a variety of literary genres and their basic characteristics	░	░	•	•	•	•	•
Distinguish between fantasy and realistic text	░	░	░	░	░	░	░
Distinguish between informational and persuasive texts	░	░	░	░		░	░
Understand the distinguishing features of literary and nonfiction texts: everyday print materials, poetry, drama, fantasies, fables, myths, legends, and fairy tales	░	░	•	•	•	░	░
Explain the appropriateness of the literary forms chosen by an author for a specific purpose							

Literary Elements

Plot/Plot Development

	GR K	GR 1	GR 2	GR 3	GR 4	GR 5	GR 6
Important events	░	•	•	•	•	•	•
Beginning, middle, end of story	░	•	•				
Problem/solution		░	•				
Conflict				•			
Conflict and resolution/causes and effects					•	•	•
Compare and contrast		░	░	░	░	░	░

Character

	GR K	GR 1	GR 2	GR 3	GR 4	GR 5	GR 6
Identify	░	•	░	░	░	░	░
Identify, describe, compare and contrast			•	•	•	•	•
Relate characters and events					•	•	•

Key

Shaded area — Explicit Instruction/Modeling/Practice and Application

• — Tested

Assessment resources include: Kindergarten Assessment Handbook; Placement and Diagnostic Assessments, Grades 1, 2, and 3–6; Reading and Language Skills Assessments, Grades 1–6; Holistic Assessments, Grades 1–6; End-of-Selection Tests, Grades 1–6; and Oral Reading Fluency Assessment, Grades 1–6

	GR K	GR 1	GR 2	GR 3	GR 4	GR 5	GR 6
Traits, actions, motives				•	•	•	•
Cause for character's actions					•		
Character's qualities and effect on plot							•
Setting							
Identify and describe	▓	•	•	•	•	•	•
Compare and contrast			•	•	•	•	•
Relate to problem/resolution							
Theme							
Theme/essential message				•	•	•	•
Universal themes							
Mood/Tone							
Identify						▓	•
Compare and contrast							•

Literary Devices/Author's Craft

	GR K	GR 1	GR 2	GR 3	GR 4	GR 5	GR 6
Rhythm, rhyme, pattern, and repetition	▓	▓	▓	▓	▓	▓	▓
Alliteration, onomatopoeia, assonance, imagery		▓	▓	▓	▓	▓	▓
Figurative language (similes, metaphors, idioms, personification, hyperbole)		▓	▓	•	•	•	•
Characterization/character development		▓	▓	•	•		
Dialogue		▓	▓	•	•	•	•
Narrator/narration		▓	▓		•	•	•
Point of view (first-person, third-person, omniscient)		▓	▓		•	•	•
Informal language (idioms, slang, jargon, dialect)		▓	▓	▓	▓	▓	▓

Response to Text

	GR K	GR 1	GR 2	GR 3	GR 4	GR 5	GR 6
Relate characters and events to own life	▓	▓	▓	▓	▓	▓	▓
Read to perform a task or learn a new task	▓	▓	▓	▓	▓	▓	▓
Recollect, talk, and write about books read	▓	▓	▓	▓	▓	▓	▓
Describe the roles and contributions of authors and illustrators	▓	▓	▓	▓	▓	▓	▓
Generate alternative endings and identify the reason and impact of the alternatives			▓	▓	▓	▓	▓
Compare and contrast versions of the same stories that reflect different cultures			▓	▓	▓	▓	▓
Make connections between information in texts and stories and historical events				▓	▓	▓	▓
Form ideas about what had been read and use specific information from the text to support these ideas			▓	▓	▓	▓	▓
Know that the attitudes and values that exist in a time period or culture affect stories and informational articles written during that time period					▓	▓	▓
Explore origin and historical development of words and changes in sentence patterns over the years							▓

Self-Selected Reading

	GR K	GR 1	GR 2	GR 3	GR 4	GR 5	GR 6
Select material to read for pleasure	▓	▓	▓	▓	▓	▓	▓
Read a variety of self-selected and assigned literary and informational texts	▓	▓	▓	▓	▓	▓	▓
Use knowledge of authors' styles, themes, and genres to choose own reading			▓	▓	▓	▓	▓
Read literature by authors from various cultural and historical backgrounds	▓	▓	▓	▓	▓	▓	▓

Cultural Awareness

	GR K	GR 1	GR 2	GR 3	GR 4	GR 5	GR 6
Connect information and events in texts to life and life to text experiences	▓	▓	▓	▓	▓	▓	▓
Compare language, oral traditions, and literature that reflect customs, regions, and cultures	▓	▓	▓	▓	▓	▓	▓
Identify how language reflects regions and cultures				▓	▓	▓	▓
View concepts and issues from diverse perspectives				▓	▓	▓	▓
Recognize the universality of literary themes across cultures and language							▓

Key

Shaded area   Explicit Instruction / Modeling / Practice and Application

•   Tested

Assessment resources include: Kindergarten Assessment Handbook; Placement and Diagnostic Assessments, Grades 1, 2, and 3–6; Reading and Language Skills Assessments, Grades 1–6; Holistic Assessments, Grades 1–6; End-of-Selection Tests, Grades 1–6; and Oral Reading Fluency Assessment, Grades 1–6

	GR K	GR 1	GR 2	GR 3	GR 4	GR 5	GR 6
Writing							
Writing Strategies							
Writing process: prewriting, drafting, revising, proofreading, publishing							
Collaborative, shared, timed writing, writing to prompts		•	•	•	•	•	•
Evaluate own and others' writing							
Proofread writing to correct convention errors in mechanics, usage, punctuation, using handbooks and references as appropriate				•	•	•	•
Organization and Focus							
Use models and traditional structures for writing							
Select a focus, structure, and viewpoint							
Address purpose, audience, length, and format requirements							
Write single- and multiple-paragraph compositions			•	•	•	•	•
Revision Skills							
Correct sentence fragments and run-ons					•	•	•
Vary sentence structure, word order, and sentence length							
Combine sentences					•	•	•
Improve coherence, unity, consistency, and progression of ideas							
Add, delete, consolidate, clarify, rearrange text							
Choose appropriate and effective words: exact/precise words, vivid words, trite/overused words						•	•
Elaborate: details, examples, dialogue, quotations							
Revise using a rubric							
Penmanship/Handwriting							
Write uppercase and lowercase letters							
Write legibly, using appropriate word and letter spacing							
Write legibly, using spacing, margins, and indention							
Writing Applications							
Narrative writing (stories, paragraphs, personal narratives, journal, plays, poetry)		•	•	•	•	•	•
Descriptive writing (titles, captions, ads, posters, paragraphs, stories, poems)		•	•	•	•	•	•
Expository writing (comparison-contrast, explanation, directions, speech, how-to article, friendly/business letter, news story, essay, report, invitation)			•	•	•	•	•
Persuasive writing (paragraph, essay, letter, ad, poster)						•	•
Cross-curricular writing (paragraph, report, poster, list, chart)							
Everyday writing (journal, message, forms, notes, summary, label, caption)							
Written and Oral English Language Conventions							
Sentence Structure							
Types (declarative, interrogative, exclamatory, imperative, interjection)		•	•	•	•	•	•
Structure (simple, compound, complex, compound-complex)		•	•	•	•	•	•
Parts (subjects/predicates: complete, simple, compound; clauses: independent, dependent, subordinate; phrase)		•	•	•	•	•	•
Direct/indirect object							
Word order		•					
Grammar							
Nouns (singular, plural, common, proper, possessive, collective, abstract, concrete, abbreviations, appositives)		•	•	•	•	•	•
Verbs (action, helping, linking, transitive, intransitive, regular, irregular; subject-verb agreement)		•	•	•	•	•	•
Verb tenses (present, past, future; present, past, and future perfect)		•	•	•	•	•	•
Participles; infinitives							

Key

Shaded area Explicit Instruction / Modeling / Practice and Application

• Tested

Assessment resources include: Kindergarten Assessment Handbook; Placement and Diagnostic Assessments, Grades 1, 2, and 3–6; Reading and Language Skills Assessments, Grades 1–6; Holistic Assessments, Grades 1–6; End-of-Selection Tests, Grades 1–6; and Oral Reading Fluency Assessment, Grades 1–6

	GR K	GR 1	GR 2	GR 3	GR 4	GR 5	GR 6
Adjectives (common, proper; articles; comparative, superlative)		•	•	•	•	•	•
Adverbs (place, time, manner, degree)				•	•	•	•
Pronouns (subject, object, possessive, reflexive, demonstrative, antecedents)		•	•	•		•	•
Prepositions; prepositional phrases					•	•	•
Conjunctions							
Abbreviations, contractions				•	•	•	•

Punctuation

	GR K	GR 1	GR 2	GR 3	GR 4	GR 5	GR 6
Period, exclamation point, or question mark at end of sentences		•	•	•	•	•	•
Comma			•	•	•	•	•
Greeting and closure of a letter			•	•	•	•	•
Dates, locations, and addresses			•	•	•	•	•
For items in a series			•	•	•	•	•
Direct quotations							
Link two clauses with a conjunction in compound sentences					•	•	•
Quotation marks			•	•	•	•	•
Dialogue, exact words of a speaker				•	•	•	•
Titles of books, stories, poems, magazines						•	•
Parentheses/dash/hyphen					•	•	•
Apostrophes in possessive case of nouns and in contractions				•	•	•	•
Underlining or italics to identify title of documents					•	•	•
Colon					•	•	•
Separate hours and minutes					•	•	•
Introduce a list					•	•	•
After the salutation in business letters						•	•
Semicolons to connect independent clauses							

Capitalization

	GR K	GR 1	GR 2	GR 3	GR 4	GR 5	GR 6
First word of a sentence, names of people, and the pronoun *I*	•	•	•	•	•	•	•
Proper nouns, words at the beginning of sentences and greetings, months and days of the week, and titles and initials of people		•	•	•	•	•	
Geographical names, holidays, historical periods, and special events							•
Names of magazines, newspapers, works of art, musical compositions, organizations, and the first word in quotations when appropriate							•
Use conventions of punctuation and capitalization							

Spelling

	GR K	GR 1	GR 2	GR 3	GR 4	GR 5	GR 6
Spell independently by using pre-phonetic knowledge, sounds of the alphabet, and knowledge of letter names							
Use spelling approximations and some conventional spelling							
Common, phonetically regular words		•	•	•	•	•	•
Frequently used, irregular words		•	•	•	•	•	•
One-syllable words with consonant blends			•	•	•	•	•
Contractions, compounds, orthographic patterns, and common homophones				•	•	•	•
Greek and Latin roots, inflections, suffixes, prefixes, and syllable constructions					•	•	•
Use a variety of strategies and resources to spell words							

Listening and Speaking

Listening Skills and Strategies

	GR K	GR 1	GR 2	GR 3	GR 4	GR 5	GR 6
Listen to a variety of oral presentations such as stories, poems, skits, songs, personal accounts, or informational speeches							
Listen attentively to the speaker (make eye contact and demonstrate appropriate body language)							

Key

Shaded area   Explicit Instruction/Modeling/Practice and Application

•   Tested

Assessment resources include: Kindergarten Assessment Handbook; Placement and Diagnostic Assessments, Grades 1, 2, and 3–6; Reading and Language Skills Assessments, Grades 1–6; Holistic Assessments, Grades 1–6; End-of-Selection Tests, Grades 1–6; and Oral Reading Fluency Assessment, Grades 1–6

	GR K	GR 1	GR 2	GR 3	GR 4	GR 5	GR 6
Listen for a purpose							
Follow oral directions (one-, two-, three-, and multi-step)	■	■	■	■	■	■	■
For specific information	■	■	■	■	■	■	■
For enjoyment	■	■	■	■	■	■	■
To distinguish between the speaker's opinions and verifiable facts				■	■	■	■
To actively participate in class discussions				■	■	■	■
To expand and enhance personal interest and personal preferences							■
To identify, analyze, and critique persuasive techniques							■
To identify logical fallacies used in oral presentations and media messages						■	■
To make inferences or draw conclusions						■	■
To interpret a speaker's verbal and nonverbal messages, purposes, and perspectives						■	■
To identify the tone, mood, and emotion							■
To analyze the use of rhetorical devices for intent and effect							■
To evaluate classroom presentations							■
To respond to a variety of media and speakers		■	■	■	■	■	■
To paraphrase/summarize directions and information			■	■	■	■	■
For language reflecting regions and cultures					■	■	■
To recognize emotional and logical arguments						■	■
To identify the musical elements of language				■	■	■	■
Listen critically to relate the speaker's verbal communication to the nonverbal message							■
Speaking Skills and Strategies							
Speak clearly and audibly and use appropriate volume and pace in different settings	■	■	■	■	■	■	■
Use formal and informal English appropriately	■	■	■	■	■	■	■
Follow rules of conversation	■	■	■	■	■	■	■
Stay on the topic when speaking		■	■	■	■	■	■
Use descriptive words		■	■	■	■	■	■
Recount experiences in a logical sequence			■	■	■	■	■
Clarify and support spoken ideas with evidence and examples						■	■
Use eye contact, appropriate gestures, and props to enhance oral presentations and engage the audience				■	■	■	■
Give and follow two-, three-, and four-step directions		■	■	■	■	■	■
Recite poems, rhymes, songs, stories, soliloquies, or dramatic dialogues	■	■	■	■	■	■	■
Plan and present dramatic interpretations with clear diction, pitch, tempo, and tone				■	■	■	■
Organize presentations to maintain a clear focus			■	■	■	■	■
Use language appropriate to situation, purpose, and audience				■	■	■	■
Make/deliver							
Oral narrative, descriptive, informational, and persuasive presentations				■	■	■	■
Oral summaries of articles and books					■	■	■
Oral responses to literature						■	■
Presentations on problems and solutions							■
Presentation or speech for specific occasions, audiences, and purposes					■	■	■
Vary language according to situation, audience, and purpose					■	■	■
Select a focus, organizational structure, and point of view for an oral presentation						■	■
Participate in classroom activities and discussions	■	■	■	■	■	■	■

Key

Shaded area Explicit Instruction/Modeling/Practice and Application

• Tested

Assessment resources include: Kindergarten Assessment Handbook; Placement and Diagnostic Assessments, Grades 1, 2, and 3–6; Reading and Language Skills Assessments, Grades 1–6; Holistic Assessments, Grades 1–6; End-of-Selection Tests, Grades 1–6; and Oral Reading Fluency Assessment, Grades 1–6

Index

137K, 155K, 165K, 173I; **1-4:** 29J, 35I, 61J, 68-69, 97I, 119J, 145J, 153K, 156-157, 179J, 183I, 186-187, 209J, 215I, 218-219, 245J, 249K; **1-5:** 33J, 37K, 40-41, 59J, 67K, 93J, 123I, 149J, 155I, 181J, 185K, 211J, 217I, 247K, 253I

See also **Reaching All Learners.**

Advertisements, 1-4: 29B

See **Genre.**

Alphabet Cards, 1-1: I2, I4, I6, I8, I10, I11, I12, I14, I16, I17, I20, I21, I22, I23, I24, I26, I27, I28, I29, I30, 10I, 28I, 96I, 118I; **1-2:** 8I, 32E, 58I; **1-3:** 62–63; **1-4:** 35K, 36I, 66I, 98I, 124I, 154I, 184I, 245B; **1-5:** 8I, 38–39, 68–69, 124–125, 124I, 186I

Alphabetize.

See **Focus Skills.**

Alternative Teaching Strategies, 1-1: T2-T11; **1-2:** T2-T15; **1-3:** T2-T14; **1-4:** T2-T15; **1-5:** T2-T12

Antonyms.

See **Word Study.**

Apostrophe.

See **Mechanics.**

Art Activities.

See **Cross-Curricular Centers; Making Connections.**

Asking Sentences.

See **Grammar, Asking Sentences.**

Assessing Progress, 1-1: 69U, 141U; **1-2:** 161W; **1-4:** 249AA

Assessment

entry-level, **1-1:** 8F, 70F; **1-2:** 6F; **1-3:** 6I; **1-4:** 6H; **1-5:** 6I

formal

End-of-Selection Tests, **1-1:** 23A, 41A, 65A, 89A, 113A, 135A; **1-2:** 25A, 53A, 79A, 129A, 155A; **1-3:** 29A, 57A, 83A, 105A, 137A, 165A; **1-4:** 29A, 61A, 91A, 119A, 145A, 179A, 209A, 245A; **1-5:** 33A, 59A, 93A, 119A, 149A, 181A, 211A

Holistic Assessment, **1-1:** 8G; **1-2:** 6G; **1-3:** 6G; **1-4:** 6I; **1-5:** 6I

Oral Reading Fluency Assessment, **1-4:** 6H, 249AA; **1-5:** 6H, 253Y

Placement and Diagnostic Assessments, **1-1:** 8G, 70F; **1-2:** 6F; **1-3:** 6F; **1-4:** 6H; **1-5:** 6H

Reading and Language Skills Assessment, **1-1:** 8F-8G, 69U, 70F-70G, 141U; **1-2:** 6F-6G, 161W; **1-3:** 6F-6G; **1-4:** 6H-6I, 249AA; **1-5:** 253Y

informal

anecdotal records, **1-1:** 10L, 23B, 27A, 45A, 47C, 48L, 65B, 67A, 69A, 69K, 69U, 72L, 95A, 96L, 113B, 115A, 117C, 117M, 118L, 135B, 141A, 141K, 141U; **1-2:** 8L, 31A, 32L, 55A, 58L, 79B, 83C, 84L, 108L, 133A, 134L, 159A, 161A, 161K, 161W; **1-3:** 8L, 36L, 57B, 61A, 61K, 62L, 87A, 88L, 105B, 111A, 112L, 143C, 144L, 165B, 173A, 173K, 173W; **1-4:** 8L, 35K, 36L, 61B, 65A, 66L, 91B, 95A, 97A, 97K, 98L, 123A, 124L, 153C, 154L, 179B, 181A, 184L, 215A, 216L, 249C, 249AA; **1-5:** 8L, 38L, 68L, 97A, 98L, 123K, 124L, 155A, 156L, 181B, 185C, 186L, 217A, 218L, 253A, 253Y

checklists for evaluation

listening, **1-1:** R16; **1-2:** R16; **1-3:** R16; **1-4:** R16; **1-5:** R16

reading, **1-1:** R14-R15, R19-R21; **1-2:** R14-R15, R19-R21; **1-3:** R14-R15, R19-R21; **1-4:** R14-R15, R19-R21; **1-5:** R14-R15, R19-R21

speaking, **1-1:** R16; **1-2:** R16; **1-3:** R16; **1-4:** R16; **1-5:** R16

viewing, **1-1:** R16; **1-2:** R16; **1-3:** R16; **1-4:** R16; **1-5:** R16

writing, **1-1:** R15, R19-R21; **1-2:** R15, R19-R21; **1-3:** R15, R19-R21; **1-4:** R15, R19-R21; **1-5:** R15, R19-R21

comprehension skills, **1-1:** 69U, 141U; **1-2:** 161W, T15; **1-3:** 173W, T13-T14; **1-4:** 249AA, T15; **1-5:** 253Y, T11-T12

conferences, **1-1:** R5; **1-2:** R5; **1-3:** R5; **1-4:** R5; **1-5:** R5

Diagnostic Checks:

comprehension and skills, **1-1:** 20-21, 25I, 62-63, 67I, 86-87, 93I, 128-129, 139I; **1-2:** 18-19, 29I, 92-93, 105I, 114-115, 131I, 142-143, 159I; **1-3:** 44-45, 50-51, 59I,

66-67, 76-77, 85I, 94-95, 148-149, 171J; **1-4:** 44-45, 63I, 95I, 181I, 213I; **1-5:** 24-25, 35I, 52-53, 82-83, 86-87, 88-89, 95I, 102-103, 112-113, 136-137, 153I, 194-195, 200-201, 224-225, 242-243, 251I

high-frequency and vocabulary words, **1-1:** 32-33, 47B, 104-105, 117B; **1-2:** 36-37, 46-47, 57B, 66-67, 83B; **1-3:** 16-17, 35B, 143B; **1-4:** 16-17, 33H, 72-73, 74-75, 78-79, 84-85, 108-109, 121H, 138-139, 153B, 160-161, 172-173, 188-189, 192-193, 196-197, 220-221, 249B; **1-5:** 160-161, 168-169, 185B

phonemic awareness, **1-1:** 10P, 28P, 48P, 72P, 96P, 118P; **1-2:** 8P, 32P, 84P, 108P, 134P; **1-3:** 36P, 62P, 88P, 112P, 144P; **1-4:** 8P, 36P, 98P, 124P, 154P, 184P, 216P; **1-5:** 8P, 38P, 68P, 98P, 124P, 156P, 186P, 218P

phonics, **1-1:** 23G, 41G, 65G, 89G, 113G, 135G; **1-2:** 25G, 53G, 79G, 101G, 129G, 155G; **1-3:** 29G, 57G, 83G, 88R, 105G, 137G, 165G; **1-4:** 29G, 61G, 91G, 119G, 145G, 179G, 209G, 245G; **1-5:** 59G, 93G, 119G, 149G, 181G, 211G, 247G

phonics/decoding, **1-1:** 23G, 41G, 65G, 89G, 113G, 135G, 141U, T2, T4, T6, T8; **1-2:** 25G, 53G, 79G, 101G, 129G, 155G, 161W, T2, T3, T5, T7, T8, T11, T13; **1-3:** 29G, 57G, 83G, 105G, 137G, T2, T3, T5, T6, T7, T8, T10, T12; **1-4:** 29G, 61G, 91G, 119G, 145G, 179G, 209G, 245G, 249AA, T2, T3, T4, T7, T12; **1-5:** 33G, 59G, 93G, 119G, 149G, 181G, 211G, 247G, T2, T3, T4, T6, T8, T10

portfolio assessment, **1-1:** R5; **1-2:** R5; **1-3:** R5; **1-4:** R5; **1-5:** R5

record forms, student, **1-1:** R19-21; **1-2:** R19-21; **1-3:** R19-21; **1-4:** R19-21; **1-5:** R19-21

retell and summarize, **1-1:** 23A, 41A, 65A, 89A, 113A, 135A; **1-2:** 25A,

32H; **1-3:** 36H; **1-4:** 8H, 36H; **1-5:** 38H

Book Parts.

See **Research and Information Skills.**

Books for All Learners, 1-1: 27M-27P, 47L, 47O-47R, 69M-69P, 95J, 95M-96P, 117O-117R, 141J, 141M-141P, 141R; **1-2:** 31J, 31M-31P, 57L, 57O-57R, 83L, 83O-83R, 107J, 107M-107P, 133J, 133M-133P, 161J, 161M-161P; **1-3:** 35L, 61J, 61M-61P, 87J, 87M-87P, 111M-111P, 143L, 143O-143R, 173J, 173M-173P; **1-4:** 35J, 35M-35P, 65J, 65M-65P, 97J, 97M-97P, 123J, 123M-123P, 153L, 153O-153R, 183J, 183M-183P, 215J, 215M-215P, 249L, 249O-249R; **1-5:** 37J, 37M-37P, 67L, 67O-67R, 97J, 97M-97P, 123J, 123M-123P, 155J, 155M-155P, 185L, 185O-185R, 217M-217P, 253J, 253M-253P

Books on Tape.

See **Audiotexts.**

Brainstorming.

See **Writing Process, Prewrite.**

Build Spelling Words, 1-1: 10J, 10Q, 28J, 28Q, 48J, 48Q, 72J, 72Q, 96J, 96Q, 118J, 118Q; **1-2:** 32J, 32Q, 58J, 58Q, 83A, 84J, 84Q, 108J, 108Q, 134J, 134Q; **1-3:** 8Q, 36J, 36Q, 62J, 62Q, 88J, 88Q, 109G, 112J, 112Q, 144J, 144Q; **1-4:** 8J, 8Q, 36J, 36Q, 66J, 66Q, 98J, 98Q, 124J, 124Q, 154J, 154Q, 184J, 184Q, 216J, 216Q; **1-5:** 8J, 8Q, 38J, 38Q, 68J, 68Q, 98J, 124J, 124Q, 156Q, 186J, 186Q, 218J, 218Q

Building Background and Concepts, 1-1: 10S, 28S, 48S, 72S, 90-91, 96S, 118S; **1-2:** 8S, 26-27, 32S, 58S, 81D, 84S, 108S, 134S; **1-3:** 8S, 36S, 62S, 88S, 112S, 144S; **1-4:** 8S, 36S, 66S, 98S, 124S, 154S, 184S, 216S; **1-5:** 8S, 38S, 68S, 98S, 124S, 156S, 186S, 218S

Capitalization and Punctuation.

See **Mechanics.**

Categorizing/Classifying.

See **Comprehension, Classify/ Categorize.**

Cause and Effect, 1-1: 78-79; **1-2:** 33A, 34-35, 53A; **1-4:** 209A

See also **Comprehension, Cause/Effect.**

Center Icons, 1-1: T13-T18

Centers

designing a space, **1-1:** R2; **1-2:** R2; **1-3:** R2; **1-4:** R2; **1-5:** R2

introducing centers, **1-1:** R3; **1-2:** R3; **1-3:** R3; **1-4:** R3; **1-5:** R3

organizing materials, **1-1:** R3; **1-2:** R3; **1-3:** R3; **1-4:** R3; **1-5:** R3

suggestions for, **1-1:** R6; **1-2:** R6; **1-3:** R6; **1-4:** R6; **1-5:** R6

tracking progress, **1-1:** R5; **1-2:** R5; **1-3:** R5; **1-4:** R5; **1-5:** R5

work board, **1-1:** R4; **1-2:** R4; **1-3:** R4; **1-4:** R4; **1-5:** R4

work groups, **1-1:** R4; **1-2:** R4; **1-3:** R4; **1-4:** R4; **1-5:** R4

See also **Cross-Curricular Centers.**

Challenge.

See **Additional Support Activities; Books for All Learners; Reaching All Learners, Advanced.**

Character Cutouts, 1-1: 44-45, T19-T23; **1-2:** 57K, T18-T23; **1-3:** 61I, 105J, 105K, 165K, T17-22; **1-4:** 209K, T18-24; **1-5:** 37I, 59J, 155I, 181J, 247J, T17-22

Character's Feelings and Actions, 1-1: 10M; **1-2:** 36-37, 131I, 155E; **1-3:** 85I; **1-4:** 119A, 151A

Charts, Use and Interpret.

See **Research and Information Skills.**

Choosing Books, 1-1: 27J, 47L, 69J, 95J, 117L; **1-2:** 31J, 57L, 83L, 107J, 133J, 161J; **1-3:** 35L, 61J, 87J, 111J, 173J; **1-4:** 35J, 65J, 97J, 123J, 153L, 183J, 215J, 249J; **1-5:** 37J, 67L, 97J, 123J, 155J, 185L, 217J, 253J

Classifying/Categorizing, 1-2: 31D, 31K, 133B, 133E; **1-4:** 63I, 64-65, 67A, 95I, 96-97, 181I, 182-183

Classifying and Organizing Ideas.

See **Thinking, Organizing and Connecting Ideas.**

Classroom Library

Reading Center, **1-1:** 47L, 69J, 117L, R6; **1-2:** 8M, 31J, 50-51, 57L, 83L, 133J, R6; **1-3:** 111J, R6; **1-4:** 65J, 97J, 123J, 183J, R6; **1-5:** 37J, 67L, 97J, 123J, 155J, 185L, 217J, 253J, R6

See also **Trade Book.**

Classroom Library Book Lessons.

See **Library Book Lessons.**

Classroom Management, 1-1: xxviii-xxix; **1-2:** xxvii-xxix; **1-3:** xxvii-xxix; **1-4:** xxvii-xxix; **1-5:** xxviii-xxix

designing a space, **1-1:** R2; **1-2:** R2; **1-3:** R2; **1-4:** R2; **1-5:** R2

introducing centers, **1-1:** R3; **1-2:** R3; **1-3:** R3; **1-4:** R3; **1-5:** R3

managing small groups, **1-1:** 11A, 23J, 27I, 28L, 29A, 41J, 47K, 48L, 49A, 65J, 69I, 72L, 73A, 89J, 95I, 96L, 97A, 113J, 118L, 119A, 135J, 141I, 141N, 141P; **1-2:** 8L, 9A, 25J, 31I, 32L, 33A, 53J, 57K, 58L, 59A, 79J, 83K, 84L, 85A, 101J, 107I, 108L, 109A, 129J, 133I, 135A, 155J, 161I; **1-3:** 9A, 29J, 35K, 36L, 37A, 57J, 61I, 62L, 63A, 83J, 87I, 88L, 89A, 105J, 111I, 112L, 113A, 137J, 143K, 144L, 145A, 165J, 173I; **1-4:** 8L, 9A, 29J, 35I, 36L, 37A, 61J, 65I, 66L, 67A, 91J, 97I, 98L, 99A, 119J, 123I, 124L, 125A, 145J, 153K, 154L, 155A, 179J, 183I, 184L, 185A, 209J, 216L, 217A, 245J, 249K; **1-5:** 8L, 9A, 33J, 37I, 38L, 39A, 59J, 67K, 68L, 69A, 93J, 97I, 98L, 99A, 119J, 123I, 124L, 125A, 149J, 155I, 156L, 157A, 181J, 185K, 186L, 187A, 211J, 217I, 218L, 219A, 247J, 253I

organizing materials, **1-1:** R3; **1-2:** R3; **1-3:** R3; **1-4:** R3; **1-5:** R3

planning charts, **1-1:** 9C, 71C; **1-2:** 7C; **1-3:** 7C; **1-4:** 7C; **1-5:** 7C

tracking progress, **1-1:** R5; **1-2:** R5; **1-3:** R5; **1-4:** R5; **1-5:** R5

work board, **1-1:** R4; **1-2:** R4; **1-3:** R4; **1-4:** R4; **1-5:** R4

work groups, **1-1:** R4; **1-2:** R4; **1-3:** R4; **1-4:** R4; **1-5:** R4

See also **Cross-Curricular Centers, Reaching All Learners.**

Create Mental Images.

See **Strategies Good Readers Use.**

Critical Thinking.

See **Thinking.**

Cross-Curricular Activity Cards.

Cross-Curricular Centers

See also **Cross-Curricular Activity Cards; Making Connections.**

Cross-Curricular Connections.

See **Content Areas.**

Daily Language Practice, 1-1: 10M, 27K, 28M, 41B, 45A, 47C, 47M, 48M, 65B, 67A, 69A, 69K, 89B, 95A, 95K, 96M, 113B, 115A, 117C, 117M; **1-2:** 8B, 25B, 29A, 31A, 31K, 32M, 53B, 55A, 57C, 57M, 58M, 79B, 81A, 83C, 83M, 84M, 101B, 105A, 107A, 108M, 129B, 131A, 133A, 133K, 134M, 155B, 159A, 161A, 161K; **1-3:** 8M, 29B, 33A, 35C, 35M, 36M, 57B, 59A, 61A, 61K, 62M, 83B, 85A, 87A, 87K, 88M, 105B, 109A, 111A, 111K, 112M, 137B, 141A, 143C, 143M, 144M, 165B, 171B, 173A, 173K; **1-4:** 8M, 29B, 33A, 35A, 35K, 36M, 61B, 63A, 65A, 65K, 66M, 91B, 95A, 97A, 97K, 98M, 119B, 121A, 123A, 123K, 124M, 145B, 151B, 153C, 153M, 154M, 179B, 181A, 183A, 183K, 184M, 209B, 213A, 215A, 215K, 216M, 245B, 249C, 249M; **1-5:** 8M, 33B, 35A, 37A, 37K, 38M, 59B, 65B, 67C, 67M, 68M, 93B, 95A, 97A, 97K, 98M, 119B, 121A, 123K, 124M, 149B, 153A, 155A, 155K, 156M, 183A, 185C, 186M, 211B, 215A, 217A, 217K, 247B, 251A, 253A, 253K

Daily Routines, 1-1: 9C, 71C; **1-2:** 7C; **1-3:** 7C; **1-4:** 7C; **1-5:** 7C

warm up, **1-1:** 10G, 10O, 23D, 25C, 27C, 28G, 28O, 45C, 47E, 48G, 48O, 65D, 67C, 69C, 72G, 72O, 89D, 93C, 95C, 96G, 96O, 113D, 115C, 117E, 118G, 118O, 135D, 139C, 141C; **1-2:** 8G, 8O, 25D, 29C, 31C, 32G, 32O, 53D, 55C, 57E, 58G, 58O, 79D, 81C, 83E, 84G, 84O, 101D, 105C, 107C, 108G, 108O, 129D, 131C, 133C, 134G, 134O, 155D, 159C, 161C; **1-3:** 8G, 29D, 33C, 36G, 36O, 57D, 59C, 61C, 62G, 62O, 83D, 85C, 105D, 109C,

111C, 111K, 112G, 112O, 137D, 143E, 144G, 144O, 165D, 171D, 173C; **1-4:** 8G, 8O, 29D, 33C, 35C, 36G, 36O, 61D, 63C, 65C, 66G, 66O, 91D, 95C, 97C, 98G, 98O, 119D, 121C, 123C, 124G, 124O, 145D, 151D, 153E, 154G, 154O, 179D, 181C, 183C, 184O, 209D, 213C, 215C, 216G, 216O, 245D, 247C, 249E; **1-5:** 8G, 8O, 33D, 37C, 38G, 38O, 59D, 65D, 67E, 68O, 93D, 95C, 97C, 98G, 98O, 119D, 121C, 123C, 124G, 124O, 149D, 153C, 155C, 156G, 181D, 183C, 185E, 186G, 186O, 211D, 215C, 217C, 218G, 218O, 247D, 253C

Declarative Sentences.

See **Grammar, Telling Sentences.**

Decodable Books, 1-1: 10L, 23G, 27J, 28L, 41G, 47L, 48L, 65G, 69J, 72L, 89G, 95J, 96L, 113G, 117L, 118L, 135G, 141J; **1-2:** 8L, 25G, 31J, 32L, 53G, 57L, 58L, 79G, 83L, 84L, 101G, 107J, 108L, 129G, 133J, 134L, 155G, 161J; **1-3:** 8L, 29G, 35L, 36L, 57G, 61J, 62L, 83G, 87J, 88L, 105G, 111J, 112L, 137G, 143L, 144L, 165G, 173J; **1-4:** 8L, 29G, 35J, 36L, 61G, 65J, 66L, 91G, 97J, 98L, 119G, 123J, 124L, 145G, 153L, 154L, 179G, 183J, 184L, 209G, 215J, 216L, 245G, 249L; **1-5:** 8L, 33G, 37J, 38L, 59G, 67L, 68L, 93G, 97J, 98L, 119G, 123J, 124L, 149G, 155J, 156L, 181G, 185L, 186L, 211G, 217J, 218L, 247G, 253J

Take-Home Book Versions: **1-1:** 10L, 23G, 28L, 41G, 48L, 65G, 72L, 89G, 96L, 113G, 118L, 135G; **1-2:** 8L, 25G, 32L, 53G, 58L, 79G, 84L, 101G, 108L, 129G, 134L, 155G; **1-3:** 8L, 29G, 36L, 57G, 62L, 83G, 88L, 105G, 112L, 137G, 144L, 165G; **1-4:** 8L, 29G, 36L, 61G, 66L, 91G, 98L, 119G, 124L, 145G, 154L, 179G, 184L, 209G, 216L, 245G; **1-5:** 8L, 33G, 38L, 59G, 68L, 93G, 98L, 119G, 124L, 149G, 156L, 181G, 186L, 211G, 218L, 247G

Decodable Stories, 1-1: T60-T136; **1-4:** T76-T81

Decoding/Phonics.

See **Phonics/Decoding.**

Decoding Strategies.

See **Phonics/Decoding; Strategies Good Readers Use.**

Describing Words.

See **Grammar.**

Descriptive Words, 1-1: 27B, 67I; **1-2:** 8O, 55A

animal words, **1-3:** 165E; **1-4:** 8P; **1-5:** 121D

of art, **1-2:** 53B

color, size, and shape words, **1-4:** 124F, 145C, 153N

color words, **1-1:** 72N; **1-3:** 88H; **1-4:** 124F

direction words, **1-1:** 23I

family words, **1-3:** 62S

feeling words, **1-1:** 27D; **1-4:** 98M, 119C, 119J

games, **1-4:** 153N

house and home words, **1-4:** 66P, 66S

profession words, **1-3:** 141D

shape words, **1-1:** 25D

sound words, **1-2:** 131D; **1-5:** 59E

taste words, **1-4:** 247D

weather words, **1-1:** 10F, 10S, 93D; **1-4:** 66E, 216N, 245E, 247B; **1-5:** 124F

words for body parts, **1-3:** 29E, 35F, 112M

words that tell how many, **1-4:** 184N

See also **Writing; Writing, Purposes; Writing Activities.**

Diagnostic Checks, 1-5: 33G

comprehension and skills, **1-1:** 20-21, 25I, 62-63, 86-87, 93I, 128-129, 139I; **1-2:** 18-19, 29I, 92-93, 105I, 114-115, 131I, 142-143, 159I; **1-3:** 44-45, 50-51, 59I, 66-67, 76-77, 85I, 94-95, 109i, 148-149, 171J; **1-4:** 44-45, 63I, 95I, 181I, 213I; **1-5:** 24-25, 35I, 52-53, 84-85, 86-87, 95I, 102-103, 112-113, 121I, 136-137, 153I, 168-169, 185B, 194-195, 200-201, 215I, 224-225, 242-243, 251I

high-frequency words and vocabulary, **1-1:** 32-33, 47B, 104-105, 117B; **1-2:** 36-37, 46-47, 57B, 66-67, 83B; **1-3:** 16-17, 35B, 116-117, 143B; **1-4:** 16-17, 33H, 72-73, 74-75, 78-79, 84-85, 108-109, 121H, 138-139,

153B, 160-161, 172-173, 188-189, 192-193, 196-197, 220-221, 249B; **1-5:** 42-43, 67B, 160-161, 168-169, 185B

phonemic awareness, **1-1:** 10P, 28P, 48P, 72P, 96P, 118P, **1-2:** 8P, 32P, 84P, 108P, 134P, **1-3:** 36P, 62P, 88P, 112P, 144P, **1-4:** 8P, 36P, 66P, 98P, 124P, 154P, 184P, 216P, **1-5:** 8P, 38P, 68P, 98P, 124P, 156P, 186P, 218P

phonics, **1-1:** 23G, 41G, 65G, 89G, 113G, 135G; **1-2:** 25G, 53G, 79G, 101G, 129G, 155G; **1-3:** 29G, 57G, 83G, 105G, 137G, 165G; **1-4:** 29G, 61G, 91G, 119G,145G, 179G, 209G, 245G; **1-5:** 59G, 93G, 119G, 149G, 181G, 211G, 247G

Diagrams.

See **Thinking, Organizing and Connecting Ideas.**

Dialogue

reading, **1-1:** 113J; **1-2:** 25J, 25K, 57K, 83K, 129J, 133I; **1-3:** 57J, 83J, 87I, 111I, 165J, 173I; **1-4:** 29J, 29K, 119J, 209J, 215I; **1-5:** 33J, 37I, 67K, 185K, 247J

writing, **1-2:** 8M, 25B; **1-4:** 121A

Dictation

sentences, **1-3:** 85F, 109F; **1-4:** 33F, 95F, 181F, 213F; **1-5:** 34F, 35F, 95F, 153F, 186M

words, **1-1:** 10J, 10R, 25F, 28J, 28R, 48J, 48R, 67F, 72J, 72R, 93F, 96J, 96R, 113B, 118R, 139F; **1-2:** 8J, 8K, 8R, 29F, 32J, 32R, 58J, 58R, 83H, 84J, 84R, 105F, 108J, 108R, 131F, 134J, 134R, 159F; **1-3:** 8R, 36J, 36R, 59F, 62J, 62R, 88J, 88R, 112J, 112R, 144J, 144R; **1-4:** 8J, 8R, 36J, 36R, 63F, 66J, 66R, 98J, 98R, 121F, 124J, 124R, 154J, 154R, 184J, 184R, 216J, 216R; **1-5:** 8J, 8R, 38J, 38R, 68J, 68R, 98J, 98R, 121F, 124J, 124R, 156J, 156R, 186J, 186R, 218J, 218R

Dictionary.

See **Reference Sources.**

Differentiated Instruction.

See **Reaching All Learners; Universal Access.**

Digraphs.

See **Phonics/Decoding.**

Direct Instruction

comprehension, **1-1:** 25I, 67I, 93I; **1-2:** 29I, 105I, 131I, 159I; **1-3:** 59I, 85I, 109I, 171A, 171J; **1-4:** 33I, 63I, 95I, 151A, 181I; **1-5:** 35I, 65A, 95I

grammar, **1-1:** 10N, 28N, 48N, 72N, 96N, 135C; **1-2:** 32N, 58N, 108N, 134N; **1-3:** 36N, 62N, 88N, 112N, 144N; **1-4:** 8N, 36N, 66N, 98N, 154N, 184N; **1-5:** 8N, 38N, 68N, 98N, 124N, 156N, 186N

phonics, **1-1:** 10I, 28I, 48I, 72I; **1-2:** 8I, 58I, 83G, 84I, 108I, 133E, 134I; **1-3:** 36I, 62I, 112I, 144I; **1-4:** 8I, 36I, 98I, 124I, 154I; **1-5:** 8I, 37F, 98I, 124I, 156I, 181H, 215E-215F, 218I

phonics/spelling, **1-1:** 96I; **1-4:** 66I, 184I, 216I; **1-5:** 68I

spelling, **1-1:** 23H, 41H, 89H; **1-2:** 25H, 79H, 101H, 129H, 155H; **1-3:** 29H, 105H, 165H; **1-4:** 29H, 61H, 145H, 179H, 245H; **1-5:** 33H, 59H, 119H, 149H, 211H, 247H

writing, **1-1:** 141K; **1-2:** 161A; **1-4:** 183A; **1-5:** 98M

Directions, Follow.

See **Research and Information Skills, Following Directions; Writing; Writing Activities.**

Distinguishing Fact from Fiction, 1-3: 113A, 137A, 143F

Domains of Writing.

See **Writing Purposes.**

Double Consonants.

See **Phonics/Decoding.**

Draft.

See **Writing Process.**

Drama.

See **Genre, Play.**

Drama Activities.

See **Content Areas; Dramatic Interpretation.**

Dramatic Interpretation, 1-1: 10N, 23E, 28E, 41C, 65I, 69B, 84-85, 89E, 89I, 96N, S7, S31; **1-2:** 8P, 25C, 29D, 31B, 53C, 101C, 105D, 129I; **1-3:** 105C, 173B,

S18-19, S37; **1-4:** 61C, 95D, 98N, 145C, 179E, 184E, 209C, 213D; **1-5:** 68H, 121B, 124H, 149J, 206-207, 247C, 251D

See also **Pantomime.**

Draw Conclusions.

See also **Comprehension; Research and Information Skills.**

Editing.

See **Writing, Editing Skills; Writing Process, Respond and Revise.**

ELL.

See **Reaching All Learners, English-Language Learners.**

Encyclopedia.

See **Reference Sources; Research and Information Skills, Multiple Resources, Reference Sources.**

End Marks.

See **Mechanics.**

End-of-Selection Tests.

See **Assessment.**

English as a Second Language (ESL).

See **English-Language Learners, Activities for; Reaching All Learners.**

English-Language Learners, Activities for, 1-1: 23J, 27I, 41K, 47K, 65J, 69I, 89J, 135J; **1-2:** 8L, 25K, 53J, 57K, 60-61, 79J, 83K, 101K, 133I, 155K, 161I; **1-3:** 29K, 57J, 61I, 105J, 111I, 114-115, 137K, 143K, 165J, 173I; **1-4:** 29K, 35I, 61J, 65I, 68-69, 91J, 97I, 145J, 153K, 156-157, 186-187, 209J, 218-219, 249K; **1-5:** 33J, 37I, 40-41, 59K, 67K, 74-75, 93J, 97I, 123I, 149K, 155I, 181J, 211K, 247K, 253I

See also **English-Language Learners Resource Kit; Reaching All Learners.**

English-Language Learners Resource Kit, 1-1: 12-13, 30-31, 50-51, 74-75, 98-99; **1-2:** 34-35, 86-87, 136-137; **1-3:** 114-115, 146-147; **1-4:** 10-11, 38-39, 68-69, 100-101, 126-127, 156-157, 186-187; **1-5:** 70-71, 100-101, 126-127, 158-159, 188-189, 220-221

See also **English-Language Learners, Activities for; Reaching All Learners.**

Evaluation.

See **Assessment.**

Exact Words, 1-2: 25B

Exclamation Marks.

See **Mechanics.**

Explicit Instruction.

See **Direct Instructing.**

Expository Text.

See **Genre, Expository Nonfiction; Text Structure.**

Expository Writing.

See **Writing, Forms.**

Expressive Writing.

See **Writing Purposes.**

Extend Lessons.

See **Advanced Learners, Activities for; Reaching All Learners, Advanced.**

Extra Support, 1-1: 10-11, 10L, 10R, 25F, 26-27, 27F, 28-29, 28L, 28R, 46-47, 47H, 48-49, 48L, 48R, 67F, 68-69, 69F, 72-73, 72L, 72R, 93F, 94-95, 95F, 96-97, 96L, 96R, 116-117, 117H, 140-141, 141F; **1-2:** 8-9, 8L, 8R, 29F, 30-31, 31F, 32-33, 32L, 56-57, 57H, 58-59, 58L, 58R, 82-83, 83H, 84-85, 84L, 84R, 105F, 106-107, 107F, 108-109, 108L, 108R, 131F, 132-133, 133F, 134L, 134R, 159F, 160-161, 161F; **1-3:** 8-9, 8R, 34-35, 35H, 36-37, 36L, 59F, 60-61, 61F, 62-63, 62L, 62R, 85F, 86-87, 87F, 88-89, 88L, 90-91, 109F, 110-111, 111F, 112-113, 112L, 112R, 142-143, 143H, 144-145, 144L, 144R, 171G, 172-173, 173F; **1-4:** 8-9, 8L, 8R, 33F, 34-35, 35F, 36-37, 36L, 36R, 63F, 64-65, 65F, 66-67, 66L, 66R, 95F, 96-97, 97F, 98-99, 98L, 98R, 121F, 122-123, 123F, 124-125, 124L, 124R, 152-153, 153H, 154-155, 154L, 154R, 181F, 182-183, 183F, 184-185, 184L, 184R, 213F, 214-215, 215F, 216-217, 216L, 216R, 248-249, 249H; **1-5:** 8-9, 8L, 8R, 35F, 36-37, 37F, 38-39, 38L, 38R, 66-67, 67H, 68-69, 68L, 68R, 95F, 96-97, 97F, 98-99, 98L, 98R, 121F, 122-123, 123F, 124-125, 124L, 124R, 154-155, 155F, 156-157, 156L, 156R, 184-185, 185H, 186-187,

186L, 186R, 215F, 216-217, 217F, 218-219, 218L, 218R, 251F, 252-253, 253F

See also **Additional Support Activities; Below-Level Learners, Activities for; Books for All Learners; Intervention Resource Kit; Reaching All Learners.**

Fable, 1-3: 144S, 146-165

See also Genre.

Family Involvement.

See **School-Home Connection.**

Fantasy, 1-1: 74-89; **1-2:** 34-35, 34-53, 60-79; **1-3:** 90-91, 90-105; **1-4:** 125A, 186-187, 186-209; **1-5:** 10-33, 158-180, 158-181

compared to realistic fiction, **1-5:** 156M

distinguishing from reality, **1-2:** 34-35

See also **Genre.**

Fiction, 1-1: 30-41; **1-5:** 40-59, 68-93, 68N, 126-149

See also **Genre.**

Fiction from Nonfiction, Distinguish.

See **Literary Response and Analysis.**

Figurative Language.

See **Author's Craft; Vocabulary, figurative language.**

Finger Play

"Alone," **1-4:** 184P

"Going for a Walk," **1-1:** 113E, 115B

"Grandma's Glasses," **1-4:** 119E

"House, The," **1-4:** 66P, 91C

"Itsy, Bitsy Spider, The" **1-3:** 33D

"Mix a Pancake," **1-1:** 41E

"My Hat," **1-1:** 25D, 27B

"Ten Fingers," **1-2:** 55D

"Ten Fluffy Chickens," **1-2:** 25D, 25E

Fix-Up Strategies.

See **Guided Comprehension; Strategies Good Readers Use.**

Flowchart.

See **Research and Information Skills, Graphic Aids; Thinking, Organizing and Connecting Ideas.**

Fluency.

See **Assessment, Formal; Rereading for Fluency.**

Focus Skills

alphabetize, **1-4:** 33I, 121I

   introduce, **1-4:** 33I

   reteach, **1-4:** S42-43, T14

   test, **1-4:** T14

cause/effect, **1-2:** 59A, 79A; **1-4:** 209A, 215D, 217A; **1-5:** 38P, 39A, 59A

character, **1-2:** 109A; **1-3:** 63A, 83A, 85I, 87B, 87D, 145A, 165A, 171J, 173D

classify/categorize, **1-4:** 37A, 61A, 63I, 65D, 67A, 95I, 97B, 97D, 155A, 179A, 181I, 183D

distinguishing fact from fiction, **1-3:** 113A, 137A, 143F

distinguishing fantasy from reality, **1-4:** 125A, 145A, 153F

draw conclusions, **1-4:** 29A, 99A, 119A

main idea, **1-5:** 69A, 93A, 95I, 97D, 99A, 119A, 186H, 187A, 215I, 217D

main idea and details, **1-1:** 49A, 65A, 67D, 67I, 69L

note details, **1-2:** 85A, 105I, 107D, 135A, 155A; **1-3:** 171A

plot, **1-5:** 9A, 28-29, 33A, 35I, 37D, 125A, 149A, 153I, 155D, 251B, 251I

predict outcomes, **1-5:** 157A, 181A, 181E

sequence, **1-1:** 23A, 73A, 89A, 118H, 119A, 135A, 139I, T11

setting, **1-2:** 9A, 25A, 29I; **1-3:** 37A, 59I, 61D, 88H, 89A, 105A, 109I, 111B, 111D

Focus Skills/Phonics Skills, introduction,
1-1: xxxvi; **1-2:** xxxiv;
1-3: xxxiv; **1-4:** xxxiv; **1-5:** xxxiv

Focus Strategies

create mental images, **1-2:** 9A, 16-17; **1-4:** 98H, 99A, 104-105, 123L, 185A

look for word bits and parts, **1-2:** 85A; **1-3:** 9A; **1-4:** 66F, 67A, 76-77; **1-5:** 9A, 16-17, 26-27

main idea, **1-5:** 97B

make and confirm predictions, **1-1:** 73A, 80-81; **1-3:** 145A; **1-4:** 9A, 18-19

make inferences, **1-1:** 97A; **1-3:** 37A, 52-53; **1-5:** 125A, 128-129

read ahead, **1-3:** 98-99; **1-4:** 155A, 164-165, 174-175

reread, **1-2:** 59A, 64-65; **1-4:** 217A, 222-223, 228-229, 240-241; **1-5:** 39A, 54-55

reread aloud, **1-1:** 29A; **1-2:** 135A, 146-147; **1-3:** 113A; **1-4:** 125A, 134-135

self-correct, **1-1:** 119A; **1-2:** 109A; **1-5:** 69A, 80-81

sequence events/summarize, **1-2:** 33A; **1-3:** 63A, 72-73; **1-4:** 37A, 42-43; **1-5:** 219A, 228-229

use phonics/decoding, **1-1:** 11A, 49A; **1-5:** 157A

use picture clues to confirm meaning, **1-5:** 99A, 108-109

   See **Strategies Good Readers Use.**

Folktales, 1-2: 29B; **1-3:** 87B, 144S

   See also **Genre.**

Following Directions, 1-2: 57B; **1-4:** 154M; **1-5:** 153A, 217B

   See also **Research and Information Skills.**

Formal Assessment.

   See **Assessment.**

Forms of Texts.

   See **Genre; Text Structure.**

Games, 1-1: 10E, 47B, 47N, 69B, 93G, 117D, 141I, S25; **1-2:** 29B, 31B, 55D, 83D, 105H, 133B; **1-3:** 87B, 88E, 111G, 111H, 112E, 112P, 143D, 171C; **1-4:** 35H, 98E, 123B, 153G, 153N, 183B; **1-5:** 33I, 64-65, 67D, 93I, 95B, 97B, 121B, 124E, 124M, 153A, 155B, 156N, 185N, 217B

Genre

fiction, **1-1:** 30-31, 30-41; **1-4:** 100-101, 100-119; **1-5:** 10-11, 10-30, 68-69, 68-93, 126-127, 126-147

   fable, **1-3:** 146-147, 146-165

   fantasy, **1-1:** 74-75, 74-89; **1-2:** 34-35, 34-53, 60-61, 60-79; **1-3:** 90-91, 90-103; **1-4:** 125A, 186-187, 186-207; **1-5:** 158-159, 158-180

   folktale, **1-2:** 29B; **1-3:** 87B

   informational fiction, **1-5:** 220-221, 220-247

   play, **1-3:** 38-39, 38-57

   poetry, **1-1:** 42-43, 136-137;

1-2: 102-103, 156-157; **1-3:** 30-31, 102-103; **1-4:** 30-31, 210-211; **1-5:** 150-151, 212-213

   haiku, **1-5:** 98P

realistic fiction, **1-1:** 12-13, 12-23, 98-99, 98-111; **1-2:** 10-11, 10-25, 110-111, 110-129; **1-4:** 10-11, 10-29

science fiction, **1-4:** 126-127, 126-145

nonfiction, **1-2:** 86-67, 86-101; **1-3:** 10-11, 10-27, 114-115, 114-137; **1-4:** 38-39, 38-61, 68-69, 68-91; **1-5:** 70-71, 70-91, 100-101, 100-119, 188-189, 188-211

   advertisement, **1-4:** 29B

   biography/autobiography, **1-3:** 64-65, 64-83

   expository nonfiction, **1-1:** 50-51, 50-65; **1-2:** 136-137, 136-155; **1-4:** 156-157, 156-179

   informational article, **1-1:** 50-65, 90-91; **1-2:** 26-27

   magazine article, **1-4:** 92-93, 146-147; **1-5:** 60-63

   narrative nonfiction, **1-1:** 118-119, 118-135; **1-4:** 218-219, 218-244

   photo essay, **1-1:** 90-91

   See also **Comparing Texts; Comprehension Cards; Reading Across Texts; Real-Life Reading; Text Structure.**

Genre Study.

   See **Genre.**

Gifted and Talented Students.

   See **Additional Support Activities; Reaching All Learners, Advanced; Books for All Learners; Independent Reading.**

Glossary, 1-1: T140-T142; **1-2:** T58-T60; **1-3:** TT60-T62; **1-4:** T85-T87; **1-5:** T77-T79

Grammar, 1-1: 89D; **1-2:** 29C, 58O, 133C, 161C; **1-3:** 29D, 35E, 57D, 59C, 85C, 87C, 88O, 105D, 112G, 143E, 165D, 173C; **1-4:** 36G, 66O, 91D, 119D, 121C, 123C, 154G, 179D, 184G, 245D; **1-5:** 35C, 38O, 59D, 67E, 68O, 95C, 97C, 98G, 124G, 153C, 186O, 211D, 215C, 217C, 218O, 247D, 253C

Kinesthetic Teaching Modality, 1-1: T2-T11; **1-2:** T2-T15; **1-3:** T2-T14; **1-4:** T2-T15; **1-5:** T2-T12

    comprehension, **1-1:** T11; **1-2:** T15; **1-3:** T13, T14; **1-4:** T15; **1-5:** T11, T12

    grammar, **1-1:** T3, T5, T7, T9, T10; **1-2:** T4, T6, T9, T10, T12, T14; **1-3:** T4, T11; **1-4:** T5, T6, T8, T9, T10, T11, T13; **1-5:** T5, T6, T7, T8, T9

    other activities suitable for kinesthetic emphasis, **1-1:** 47F, 89E

    phonics/decoding, **1-5:** T3

    study skills, **1-4:** T14

    word structure, **1-3:** T6

K-W-L Strategy, 1-1: 92-93, 141Q, 141R, 141S, 141T, 141V; **1-2:** 57U, 84S

Language Arts

    Learning Support, *The Learning Site*, **1-1:** 27D, 65E, 69D; **1-2:** 53E, 84H,

101E, 107L; **1-3:** 59D, 88H, 109D, 141D; **1-4:** 8P, 61E, 63D, 91E, 119E, 121D, 181D, 184H, 245E, 247D; **1-5:** 65E, 95D, 121D, 183D, 218H

Shared Writing, 1-1: 10M, 23B, 27A, 72M; **1-2:** 105A, 108M; **1-3:** 111K, 112M; **1-4:** 35A, 36M, 98M, 145B, 213A; **1-5:** 8M, 37A, 38M, 119B, 124M, 186M, 247B

Writing, 1-2: 129B; **1-3:** 35M, 57B, 61K, 88M, 105B, 137B, 143M; **1-4:** 8M, 29B, 35K, 61B, 65K, 123A, 123K, 151B, 153M, 215A, 216M, 245B, 249M; **1-5:** 33B

Writing Across the Curriculum, 1-1: 93A; **1-2:** 57C, 84M, 107A, 131A, 133A; **1-3:** 61A, 111A, 141A; **1-4:** 33A, 63A, 121A, 124M, 184M, 247A; **1-5:** 35A, 67C, 98M, 149B

Writing Process, 1-1: 28M, 45A, 47M, 48M, 67A, 69A, 69K, 96M, 113B, 115A, 117C, 117M, 118M, 135B, 139A, 141A, 141K; **1-2:** 57C, 79B, 81A, 83C, 155B, 161A, 161K; **1-3:** 62M, 83B, 85A, 87A, 87K, 144M, 165B, 171B, 173A, 173K; **1-4:** 66M, 91B, 95A, 97A, 97K, 154M, 179B, 181A, 183A, 183K

Language Conventions.

    See **Grammar; Oral English Language Conventions; Spelling; Written English Language Conventions.**

Language Handbook, 1-1: 41C, 45B, 47D, 47N, 65C, 67B, 69B, 69L, 89C, 93B, 95B, 95L, 113C, 115B, 117D, 117N, 135C, 139B, 141B, 141L; **1-2:** 25C, 29B, 31B, 31L, 53C, 55B, 57D, 57N, 79C, 81B, 83D, 83N, 105B, 107B, 129C, 131B, 133B, 133L, 155C, 159B, 161B; **1-3:** 29C, 33B, 35D, 35N, 57C, 59B, 61B, 61L, 83C, 85B, 87B, 87L, 105C, 109B, 111B, 111L, 137C, 141B, 143D, 143N, 165C, 171C, 173B, 173L; **1-4:** 29C, 33B, 35B, 35L, 61C, 63B, 65B, 65L, 91C, 95B, 97B, 97L, 119C, 121B, 123B, 123L, 145C, 151C, 153D, 153N, 179C, 181B, 183B, 183L, 209C, 213B, 215B, 215L, 245C, 247B, 249D, 249N; **1-5:** 33C, 35B, 37B, 37L, 59C,

65C, 67D, 93C, 95B, 97B, 97L, 119C, 123B, 123L, 149C, 153B, 155B, 155L, 181C, 183B, 185D, 185N, 186N, 211C, 215B, 217B, 217L, 247C, 251B, 253B, 253L

Lesson Planners, 1-1: 10C-10D, 28C-28D, 48C-48D, 72C-72D, 96C-96D, 118C-118D; **1-2:** 8C-8D, 32C-32D, 58C-58D, 84C-84D, 108C-108D, 134C-134D; **1-3:** 8C-8D, 36C-36D, 62C-62D, 88C-88D, 112C-112D; **1-4:** 8C-8D, 36C-36D, 66C-66D, 98C-98D, 124C-124D, 154C-154D, 184C-184D, 216C-216D; **1-5:** 8C-8D, 38C-38D, 68C-68D, 98C-98D, 124C-124D, 156C-156D, 186C-186D, 218C-218D

Letter and Word Center, 1-3: 112I, 144I; **1-4:** 66I, 154I; **1-5:** 98I

Letter Patterns.

    See **Phonics/Decoding; Spelling.**

Letters, Writing, 1-4: 66M, 91B, 95A, 97A; **1-5:** 155K

    See also **Writing Activities.**

Letter-Sound Correspondences, Using.

    See **Phonics/Decoding.**

Leveled Activities.

    See **Reaching All Learners; Rereading for Fluency.**

Library Book Lessons, 1-1: 69S-69T, 141S-141T; **1-2:** 161S-161V; **1-3:** 173S-173V; **1-4:** 249U-249Z; **1-5:** 253S-253X

Library Books, 1-1: 8C, 69S-69T, 70C, 141S-141T; **1-2:** 6C, 161S-161V; **1-3:** 6C, 173S-173V; **1-4:** 6C, 249U-249Z; **1-5:** 6C, 253S-253X

Listen and Respond, 1-1: 10H, 10P, 23E, 28P, 45D, 48P, 72H, 72P, 96H, 96P, 118P, 139D; **1-2:** 8H, 8P, 29D, 32H, 81D, 84P, 129E, 134P, 159D; **1-3:** 33D, 36H, 36P, 61D, 62H, 83E, 88P, 105E, 112P, 137E, 144H, 165E, 173D; **1-4:** 8H, 35D, 36H, 95D, 98P, 145E, 151E, 154H, 154P, 179E, 184P, 213D, 216P; **1-5:** 8H, 8P, 33E, 38H, 38P, 68P, 97D, 98H, 98P, 124P, 153D, 156H, 156P, 211E, 215D, 247E, 251D

Listening.

    See **Listening and Speaking; Oral Language.**

Listening and Speaking

develop listening and speaking skills, **1-1:** 95B; **1-3:** 87B, 111B, 141B; **1-4:** 181B; **1-5:** 251B

listening, characteristics of a good listener, **1-2:** 55B, 57D, 57N, 133L; **1-3:** 35N, 61L, 87L, 173L; **1-4:** 65L, 121B, 145K, 215B, 216N; **1-5:** 35B, 67N, 95B, 97L, 123B, 218N, 253L

purposes for listening/speaking

listening critically, **1-2:** 57F; **1-3:** 87B, 111B, 141B; **1-4:** 181B; **1-5:** 251B

to ask and answer relevant questions, **1-1:** 95L; **1-2:** 107B, 108L, 129C, 133D, 133L, 134P, 155K, 159B, 161B; **1-3:** 29B, 33B, 35N, 87I, 111L, 143N, 171C; **1-4:** 65L, 98M, 121B, 183H; **1-5:** 35B, 37B, 67N, 95B

to evaluate, **1-1:** 48P, 95E; **1-2:** 32H, 32P, 53E, 105B, 107D, 129E, 131D, 131E; **1-3:** 36P, 37A, 57C, 87B, 88N, 111K, 137E, 165J; **1-4:** 29C, 29E, 36H, 95B

to follow directions, **1-3:** 112N

to interpret, **1-2:** 81B, 83F, 101I, 105H, 129I; **1-3:** 36S, 109I, 111I, 112P, 141B, 171C; **1-4:** 121D, 124N, 154N; **1-5:** 149C, 217E

musical elements of literary language, identify, **1-1:** 23C, 27B, 27E, 32E, 53B, 69E, 95E, 96H; **1-2:** 8H, 29B, 32H, 53C, 57F, 79C, 81B, 83D, 105D, 107B, 107E, 129C, 133B, 134N, 159B; **1-3:** 29C, 35N, 59B, 61B, 61E, 83C, 85B, 87L, 105C, 109B, 143D, 165C, 171C, 173B; **1-4:** 33B, 61C, 63B, 65B, 66N, 91C, 121B, 124N, 153N, 179C, 183B, 247B, 249D, 249N; **1-5:** 33C, 37B, 37L, 59C, 67G, 95B, 119C, 121B, 123L, 149C, 153B, 181C, 186N, 211C, 253B

onomatopoeia, **1-4:** 29E

oral activities, participate in discussions, **1-1:** 10M, 25A, 96S; **1-2:** 29D, 80-81, 108M, 155C; **1-3:** 36M, 36N, 109A; **1-4:** 33A, 91K, 98P, 145C, 151E, 154M, 154N, 245C, 249D; **1-5:** 38P, 65C, 68S, 93C, 94-95, 95D, 98S, 119A, 124N, 211E, 218H, 218S

See also **Morning Message.**

participant behavior during, **1-4:** 245C

speaking

ask and answer relevant questions, **1-1:** 117N; **1-2:** 31L, 108P, 155K, 161B; **1-3:** 29B

characteristics of good speaking, **1-2:** 31L, 57N; **1-3:** 35N, 61L, 87L, 111L, 173L; **1-4:** 151C; **1-5:** 67N, 123B, 183B

communication skills, demonstrate effectiveness in interviewing, reporting, requesting, and providing information, **1-1:** 41B, 41K, 96E, 113B, 117K, 118F; **1-2:** 79B, 155B, 161K; **1-3:** 83B-83C; **1-4:** 29K, 91B, 120-121, 123I, 153K, 154E, 179B; **1-5:** 211J

cooperative groups, **1-1:** 47M, 95B; **1-2:** 79J; **1-4:** 29J, 66F, 145J, 179J, 215I, 249K; **1-5:** 38L, 59J

description, giving, **1-2:** 84N, 101K, 155C; **1-5:** 121B

developing skill, **1-1:** 95B

developing vocabulary through, **1-2:** 84P

dramatic interpretations, present, **1-1:** 96N, S7, S31; **1-2:** 31B, 53C, 58N, 101C; **1-3:** 35D, 62N, 88N, 112E, 143D, 173K; **1-4:** 98N, 123B, 145C, 151E, 154E, 209C, 213D; **1-5:** 121B, 124P, 124S, 206-207, 247C, 251D

expressing feelings and personal experiences, **1-1:** 64-65, 88-89, 93A; **1-2:** 8G, 8M, 29B, 32S, 52-53, 105B, 108H; **1-3:** 33B, 36M, 36S, 165J, 171B; **1-4:** 36H; **1-5:** 33B, 37B, 68P, 98P

giving directions, **1-2:** 79B, 155B; **1-3:** 83B; **1-4:** 179B

giving positive feedback, **1-4:** 215B

group rereading, **1-4:** 215L

guidelines, **1-2:** 57K

intonation, **1-1:** 115C

oral book report, **1-4:** 119C

oral reading

accuracy, **1-1:** 29A, 89J, 117K; **1-2:** 8L, 32R, 55B, 101J, 108M, 133A, 133I, 134S, 135A, 146-147, 161B; **1-3:** 35K, 36N, 57B, 59A, 59D, 61I, 62F, 87F, 87I, 87K, 105J, 105K, 111I, 113A, 141A; **1-4:** 29G, 29K, 36S, 61J, 65A, 97I, 123B, 125A, 134-135, 145K, 151B, 151C, 183I, 183L, 215E, 216N; **1-5:** 37I, 38S, 59J, 59K, 65C, 67K, 94-95, 97L, 119C, 119J, 123B, 123H, 124N, 149B, 185K, 186M, 217I, 253I

expression and phrasing, **1-1:** 23J, 95I; **1-2:** 8N, 25J, 53C, 53J, 79C, 108N, 129C, 161I; **1-3:** 36F, 105K, 137C; **1-4:** 29J, 35B, 35D, 35I, 61C, 119J, 145J, 145K, 153C, 215I; **1-5:** 33J, 37D, 59J, 97I, 124S, 181J

rereading, **1-4:** 125A; **1-5:** 217I

presentations, **1-1:** 24-25, 25B; **1-2:** 57N, 107B, 129I, 133K, 161K; **1-4:** 65L; **1-5:** 120-121, 186F

reporting, **1-5:** 120-121

responding to questions, **1-3:** 29B, 62N, 85D, 87I, 165A; **1-4:** 33A, 124N, 154H; **1-5:** 97E, 98S, 119B

retelling, **1-1:** 41A, 65A, 113A; **1-2:** 25A, 53A, 79A, 101K, 108F, 129A, 155A; **1-3:** 29A, 35K, 57A, 58-59, 83A, 88P, 105A, 137A; **1-4:** 29A, 61A, 91A, 145A, 179A, 209A; **1-5:** 33A, 59A, 93A, 119A, 123I, 149A, 181A, 186N, 211A, 211K, 247A

distinguishing fact from fiction,
1-3: 113A, 137A

distinguishing fantasy from realistic stories, **1-4**: 125A, 145A, 153F

draw conclusions, **1-4**: 29A, 99A, 119A

main idea, **1-5**: 69A, 93A, 95I, 97B, 99A, 119A, 186H, 187A, 215I, 217D

narrative elements (setting, character, plot)

  character, **1-2**: 109A; **1-3**: 63A, 83A, 85I, 87B, 87D, 145A, 165A, 171J, 173D

  plot, **1-5**: 9A, 28-29, 33A, 35I, 37D, 125A, 149A, 153I, 155D, 247A, 251B, 251I

  setting, **1-2**: 9A, 25A, 29I; **1-3**: 37A, 59I, 61D, 88H, 89A, 105A, 109, 111B, 111D

note details, **1-2**: 85A, 105I, 107D, 133H, 135A, 155A; **1-3**: 171A

poetic devices (rhyme, rhythm)
  See **Author's Craft.**

responding to selections

  response activities
    See **Making Connections.**

sequence, **1-1**: 11A, 23A, 25I, 73A, 89A, 93I, 95D, 118H, 119A, 135A, 139I

Theme Connections, **1-1**: 9A, 71A; **1-2**: 7A; **1-3**: 7A; **1-4**: 7A; **1-5**: 7A

themes, identifying, **1-1**: 88-89

Think and Respond, **1-1**: 22-23, 40-41, 64-65, 88-89, 110-111, 134-135; **1-2**: 52-53, 76-77, 100-101, 126-127, 154-155; **1-3**: 28-29, 54-55, 80-81, 102-103, 136-137, 162-163; **1-4**: 26-27, 58-59, 90-91, 116-117, 142-143, 178-179, 206-207, 244-245; **1-5**: 30-31, 56-57, 116-117, 146-147, 178-179, 210-211, 244-245

  response activities
    See **Morning Message; Wrap Up.**

Literary Terms.
  See **Author's Craft; Genre; Literary Response and Analysis.**

Locating Information.
  See **Reference Sources; Research and Information Skills;**

Technology, Internet/World Wide Web.

Magazine Article, 1-4: 146-147; **1-5**: 60-63

  information sources, **1-3**: 35C
  See also **Genre.**

Main Idea, 1-1: 65A; **1-2**: 52-53; **1-5**: 97B
  See also **Comprehension, main idea and details; Text Structure.**

Make and Confirm Predictions.
  See **Comprehension, predict outcomes; Strategies Good Readers Use.**

Making Connections

  art, **1-1**: 24-25, 44-45; **1-2**: 104-105; **1-4**: 150-151; **1-5**: 120-121, 152-153, 182-183, 250-251

  Connect Across Texts, **1-1**: 45B

  health, **1-1**: 138-139; **1-2**: 158-159; **1-3**: 32-33, 108-109, 170-171; **1-4**: 246 247

  health/technology, **1-4**: 180-181

  listening and speaking, **1-1**: 24-25; **1-3**: 84-85

  math, **1-1**: 44-45, 114-115; **1-2**: 28-29, 54-55, 130-131; **1-3**: 58-59; **1-4**: 32-33, 180-181, 212-213; **1-5**: 34-35, 64-65, 94-95

  music, **1-2**: 28-29; **1-3**: 140-141; **1-5**: 152-153, 214-215

  science, **1-1**: 24-25, 92-93, 114-115; **1-2**: 80-81, 104-105, 158-159; **1-3**: 84-85, 100-101, 140-141; **1-4**: 32-33, 94-95, 246-247; **1-5**: 34-35, 120-121

  science/technology, **1-2**: 104-105; **1-3**: 32-33, 170-171; **1-4**: 120-121; **1-5**: 64-65, 250-251

  social studies, **1-1**: 36-37, 66-67, 92-93; **1-2**: 54-55, 68-69, 80-81, 130-131; **1-3**: 58-59, 68-69, 108-109; **1-4**: 120-121, 150-151, 212-213; **1-5**: 94-95, 182-183, 214-215

  technology, **1-1**: 66-67

writing, **1-1**: 44-45, 66-67, 92-93, 114-115, 138-139; **1-2**: 28-29, 54-55, 80-81, 104-105, 130-131, 158-159; **1-3**: 32-33, 58-59, 84-85, 108-109, 140-141, 170-171; **1-4**: 32-33, 150-151, 180-181, 212-213, 246-247; **1-5**: 34-35, 64-65, 94-95, 120-121, 152-153, 182-183, 214-215, 250-251
  See also **Cross-Curricular Centers.**

Managing the Classroom.
  See **Classroom Management.**

Math, 1-1: 10E, 28F, 44-45, 48F, 96E, 114-115; **1-2**: 8E, 28-29, 32E, 38-39, 54-55, 55D, 58E, 108E, 130-131; **1-3**: 8E, 36E, 58-59, 62E; **1-4**: 8E, 32-33, 66E, 180-181, 184E, 212-213, 216E; **1-5**: 8E, 34-35, 64-65, 68F, 94-95, 98E, 156E, 186E

Math Activities.
  See **Cross-Curricular Centers; Making Connections.**

Mechanics

  apostrophe, **1-2**: 107F; **1-5**: 123E

  capitalization
    months, **1-3**: 144N
    pronoun *I*, **1-2**: 8G
    proper nouns, **1-2**: 133D

  capitalization and end marks, sentences, **1-1**: 28N, 72N, 93B, 93C, 95B, 115B; **1-2**: 8G, 105B

  capitalization of proper nouns, **1-2**: 133D

  colons, **1-5**: 98O

  ellipses, **1-5**: 140-141

  end marks, **1-2**: 105B; **1-3**: 57J

  exclamation marks, **1-1**: 23J; **1-3**: 57J

  periods, **1-1**: 113D, 118G

  proofreading, **1-1**: 47C, 117C, 141A; **1-2**: 83C, 161A; **1-3**: 87A, 173A; **1-4**: 97A, 183A; **1-5**: 97A, 185C

  punctuation of special names and titles, **1-3**: 62N, 85B

  question marks, **1-1**: 96N, 115B; **1-3**: 57J; **1-5**: 123C

  quotation marks, **1-2**: 8O, 25B
  See also **Daily Language Practice.**

Media.

See **Oral and Media Communication.**

Meeting Individual Needs.

See **Reaching All Learners.**

Modalities of Learning.

See **Alternative Teaching Strategies.**

Modeling.

See **Guided Comprehension.**

Modified Instruction.

See **Reaching All Learners.**

Monitor Comprehension.

See **Guided Comprehension.**

Monitor Progress.

See **Assessment.**

Morning Message, 1-1: 10G, 10O, 23D, 25C, 27C, 28G, 28O, 45C, 47E, 48G, 65D, 67C, 69C, 72G, 72O, 89D, 93C, 95C, 96G, 96O, 113D, 115C, 117E, 118G, 118O, 139C, 141C; **1-2:** 8G, 8O, 25D, 29C, 31C, 32G, 32O, 53D, 55C, 57E, 58G, 58O, 79D, 81C, 83E, 84G, 84O, 101D, 105C, 107C, 108G, 108O, 129D, 131C, 133C, 134G, 134O, 155D, 159C, 161C; **1-3:** 8G, 8O, 29D, 33C, 36G, 36O, 57D, 59C, 61C, 62G, 62O, 83D, 85C, 87C, 88G, 88O, 105D, 109C, 111C, 112G, 112O, 137D, 141C, 143E, 144G, 144O, 165D, 171D, 173C; **1-4:** 8G, 8O, 29D, 33C, 35C, 36G, 36O, 61D, 63C, 65C, 66G, 66O, 91D, 95C, 97C, 98G, 98O, 119D, 121C, 123C, 124G, 124O, 145D, 151D, 153E, 154G, 154O, 179D, 181C, 183C, 184G, 184O, 209D, 213C, 215C, 216G, 216O, 245D, 247C, 249E; **1-5:** 8G, 8O, 33D, 35C, 37C, 38G, 38O, 59D, 65D, 67E, 68G, 68O, 93D, 95C, 97C, 98G, 98O, 119D, 121C, 123C, 124G, 124O, 149D, 153C, 155C, 156G, 156O, 181D, 183C, 185E, 186G, 186O, 211D, 215C, 217C, 218G, 218O, 247D, 251C, 253C

Multi-Age Classrooms.

See **Combination Classrooms.**

Multi-Leveled Practice, 1-1: 10-11, 10L, 10R, 25F, 26-27, 27F, 28-29, 28L, 28R, 46-47, 47G-47H, 48-49, 48L, 48R, 67F, 68-69, 69F, 72-73, 72L, 72R, 93F, 94-95, 95F, 96-97, 96L, 96R, 116-

117, 117H, 140-141, 141F; **1-2:** 8-9, 8L, 8R, 29F, 30-31, 31F, 32-33, 32L, 32R, 56-57, 57H, 58-59, 58L, 58R, 82-83, 83H, 84-85, 84L, 84R, 105F, 106-107, 107F, 108-109, 108L, 108R, 131F, 132-133, 133F, 134L, 134R, 134-135, 159F, 160-161, 161F; **1-3:** 8-9, 8R, 34-35, 35H, 36-37, 36L, 59F, 60-61, 61F, 62-63, 62L, 62R, 85F, 86-87, 87F, 88-89, 88L, 90-91, 109F, 110-111, 111F, 112-113, 112L, 112R, 142-143, 143H, 144-145, 144L, 144R, 171G, 172-173, 173F; **1-4:** 8-9, 8L, 8R, 33F, 34-35, 35F, 36-37, 36L, 36R, 63F, 64-65, 65F, 66-67, 66L, 66R, 95F, 96-97, 97F, 98-99, 98L, 98R, 100-101, 121F, 122-123, 123F, 124-125, 124L, 124R, 152-153, 154-155, 154L, 154R, 181F, 182-183, 183F, 184-185, 184L, 184R, 213F, 214-215, 215F, 216-217, 216L, 216R, 248-249; **1-5:** 8-9, 8L, 8R, 35F, 36-37, 37F, 38-39, 38L, 38R, 66-67, 67H, 68-69, 68L, 68R, 95F, 96-97, 97F, 98-99, 98L, 98R, 121F, 122-123, 123F, 124-125, 124L, 124R, 154-155, 155F, 156-157, 156L, 156R, 184-185, 185H, 186-187, 186L, 186R, 215F, 216-217, 217F, 218-219, 218L, 218R, 251F, 252-253, 253F

Multimedia.

See **Technology, multimedia.**

Music Activities.

See **Content Areas; Cross-Curricular Centers.**

My Reading Log, 1-1: R14; **1-2:** R14; **1-3:** R14; **1-4:** R14; **1-5:** R14

Narration.

See **Listening and Speaking, Speaking, Communication Skills.**

Narrative Elements

character, **1-2:** 109A; **1-3:** 63A, 83A, 85I, 87B, 87D, 145A, 165A, 171J, 173D

plot, **1-5:** 9A, 28-29, 33A, 35I, 37D, 125A, 149A, 153I, 155D, 247A, 251B, 251I

setting, **1-2:** 9A, 25A, 29I; **1-3:** 37A, 59I, 61D, 88H, 89A, 105A, 109I, 111B, 111D

See also **Comprehension; Literary Response and Analysis.**

Narrative Nonfiction.

See **Genre.**

Narrative Sentences, Writing.

See **Writing, Writing Forms.**

Narrative Text, Reading.

See **Genre.**

Neuro-Imprinting.

See **High-Frequency Words.**

Newspapers, 1-2: 58E; **1-3:** 36M, 105K; **1-5:** 121A

Nonfiction.

See **Genre.**

Note-Taking Strategies.

See **Research and Information Skills.**

Nouns.

See **Grammar.**

Observation Checklist, 1-1: 47M, 69K, 117M; **1-2:** 83M, 161K; **1-3:** 87K; **1-4:** 183K; **1-5:** 97K

Ongoing Assessment.

See **Assessment, Anecdotal Records.**

Onomatopoeia, 1-1: 139D; **1-4:** 29E, 151E

See also **Author's Craft; Listening and Speaking, Purposes for Listening/ Speaking, Musical Elements of Literary Language Identify**

Oo-pples and Boo-noo-noos: Songs and Activities for Phonemic Awareness

"Apples and Bananas," **1-1:** 41E; **1-3:** 112H; **1-4:** 29E, 119E

"Barnyard Song," **1-2:** 25E; **1-3:** 57E

"Clickety-Clack," **1-1:** 23F, 93D

"Corner Grocery Store," **1-2:** 79E, 129E

"Foo-Ba-Wooba John," **1-5:** 247E

"Fox, The," **1-1:** 96H; **1-3:** 165E

"Frog Went Courtin'," **1-4:** 98H

"Goin' to the Zoo," **1-5:** 181E

Writing Purposes

Written English Language Conventions

Acknowledgments

For permission to reprint copyrighted material, grateful acknowledgment is made to the following sources:

Kenneth C. Bennett: "When You Talk to a Monkey" by Rowena Bennett.

Ellen Cassedy: "Haiku" by Yayu from *Birds, Frogs, and Moonlight,* translated by Sylvia Cassedy and Kunihiro Suetake. Text copyright © 1967 by Doubleday & Co.

Dutton Children's Books, an imprint of Penguin Putnam Books for Young Readers, a division of Penguin Putnam Inc.: "Jump or Jiggle" by Evelyn Beyer from *Another Here and Now Storybook* by Lucy Sprague Mitchell. Text copyright 1937 by E. P. Dutton; renewed © 1965 by Lucy Sprague Mitchell.

Margo Ewart: "Footprints in the Snow" from *Like It or Not* by Gavin Ewart. Published by The Random House Group.

Handprint Books, Inc.: Untitled poem (Titled: "Chestnut Brown Is the Color") from *Colors* by Carol Diggory Shields. Text © 2000 by Carol Diggory Shields.

HarperCollins Publishers: "Wouldn't You?" from *You Read to Me, I'll Read to You* by John Ciardi. Text copyright © 1961 by John Ciardi.

Little, Brown and Company (Inc.): "To Walk in Warm Rain" from *Speak Up* by David McCord. Text copyright © 1979, 1980 by David McCord.

Oxford University Press: "The Ostrich Is a Silly Bird" by Mary E. Wilkins Freeman from *The Oxford Illustrated Book of American Children's Poems*, edited by Donald Hall. Text copyright © 1999 by Donald Hall.

Purple House Press: "This Little Pig Built a Spaceship" by Fredrick Winsor from *The Space Child's Mother Goose.*

Random House Children's Books, a division of Random House, Inc.: "The World" from *Christopher O!* by Barbara Young. Text copyright © 1947 by Barbara Young; text copyright renewed 1975 by Barbara Young.

Marian Reiner: "Keep a Poem in Your Pocket" from *Something Special* by Beatrice Schenk de Regniers. Text copyright © 1958, 1986 by Beatrice Schenk de Regniers.

S©ott Treimel New York: "River Winding" from *River Winding* by Charlotte Zolotow. Text copyright © 1970 by Charlotte Zolotow.

University of Virginia Library: "The Tree Frog" from *Cinnamon Seed* by John Travers Moore. Text copyright 1967 by John Travers Moore. Published by Houghton Mifflin Company.

Viking Penguin, an imprint of Penguin Putman Books for Young Readers, a division of Penguin Putnam Inc.: "In the Summer We Eat" from *Bits and Pieces* by Zhenya Gay. Text copyright © 1958 by Zhenga Gay; renewed © 1986 by Erika L. Hinchley.

Big Book of Rhymes

For permission to reprint copyrighted material, grateful acknowledgment is made to the following sources:

Curtis Brown, Ltd.: "Grandpa Bear's Lullaby" from *Dragon Night and Other Lullabies* by Jane Yolen. Text copyright © 1980 by Jane Yolen. Published by Methuen Children's Books Ltd.

Doubleday, a division of Random House, Inc.: "Mice" from *Fifty-One New Nursery Rhymes* by Rose Fyleman. Text copyright 1931, 1932 by Doubleday, a division of Bantam Doubleday Dell Publishing Group, Inc.

HarperCollins Publishers: "Cynthia in the Snow" from *Bronzeville Boys and Girls* by Gwendolyn Brooks. Text copyright © 1956 by Gwendolyn Brooks Blakely. From "The Yak" in *Zoo Doings* by Jack Prelutsky. Text copyright © 1983 by Jack Prelutsky.

Little, Brown and Company (Inc.): "To Walk in Warm Rain" from *Speak Up* by David McCord. Text copyright © 1979, 1980 by David McCord.

Spike Milligan Productions Ltd.: "Down the stream the swans all glide" by Spike Milligan from *Silly Verse for Kids*.

Marian Reiner, on behalf of Judith Thurman: "Lumps" from *Flashlight and Other Poems* by Judith Thurman. Text copyright © 1976 by Judith Thurman.

Acknowledgments

For permission to reprint copyrighted material, grateful acknowledgment is made to the following sources:

The Blue Sky Press, an imprint of Scholastic Inc.: From "The New Bed" in *Poppleton Everyday* by Cynthia Rylant, illustrated by Mark Teague. Text copyright © 1998 by Cynthia Rylant; illustrations copyright © 1998 by Mark Teague.

Farrar, Straus and Giroux, LLC: Baboon by Kate Banks, illustrated by Georg Hallensleben. Text copyright © 1997 by Kate Banks; illustrations copyright © 1997 by Georg Hallensleben. *The Story of a Blue Bird* by Tomek Bogacki. Copyright © 1998 by Tomek Bogacki. *The Puddle* by David McPhail. Copyright © 1998 by David McPhail.

Nikki Grimes: "Time to Play" by Nikki Grimes. Text copyright © 1991 by Nikki Grimes.

HarperCollins Publishers: "The Corner" from *Frog and Toad All Year* by Arnold Lobel. Copyright © 1976 by Arnold Lobel. From *How to Be a Nature Detective* by Millicent E. Selsam, illustrated by Marlene Hill Donnelly. Text copyright © 1958, 1963, 1995 by Millicent E. Selsam; text copyright renewed © 1991 by Millicent E. Selsam; illustrations copyright © 1995 Marlene Hill Donnelly. *Sleep Is for Everyone* by Paul Showers, illustrated by Wendy Watson. Text copyright © 1972 by Paul Showers; illustrations copyright © 1997 by Wendy Watson.

Bobbi Katz: "Pretending" by Bobbi Katz. Text copyright © 1973.

Lerner Publications, a Division of the Lerner Publishing Group: Fishing Bears by Ruth Berman, Photographs by Lynn M. Stone. Text copyright © 1998 by Ruth Berman; photographs copyright © 1998 by Lynn M. Stone.

National Wildlife Federation: "Piggyback Ride" from *Your Big Backyard Magazine,* February 1998. Text copyright 1998 by the National Wildlife Federation.

Scholastic Inc.: Illustration by Floyd Cooper from *Pass It On: African-American Poetry for Children,* selected by Wade Hudson. Illustration copyright © 1993 by Floyd Cooper. Published by arrangement with Just Us Books, Inc.

Mark Warner: "Frogs in Trees?" by Mark Warner from *U. S. Kids,* a *Weekly Reader Magazine,* April 1989.

Photo Credits

Key: (t)=top; (b)=bottom; (c)=center; (l)=left; (r)=right

Page 60-63(all), Mark Warner; 65, Joe McDonald / Animals Animals; 68(tl)-84, Lynn M. Stone; 85(t), Lynn M. Stone; 85,(inset), Glenn M. Oliver / Visuals Unlimited; 85(b), 86-87, Lynn M. Stone; 88, Rick McIntyre; 89-92, Lynn M. Stone; 93(t), Robin Buckely, courtesy Ruth Berman; 93(c), Brittany Stone / Lynn M. Stone; 93(b), Lynn M. Stone; 94, Rick McIntyre; 95, 96(both), Lynn M. Stone; 118, courtesy, HarperCollins; 121, Harcourt School Publishers; 149, Rick Friedman / Black Star; 180, Carlo Ontal; 181, 246-247, Black Star; 248(t), Tony Dawson; 248(b), Don Enger/Animals Animals; 249(t), Micheal Fogden / DRK Photos; 249(b), Wolfgang Kaehler; 265(t), Will & Deni McIntyre / Photo Researchers, Inc.; 265(b), Chip Henderson / Index Stock; 266(t), Benelux Press / Index Stock; 266(b), Catherine Lender / Stone; 267(t), Ken Kinzie / Harcourt; 267(b), Ron Chapple/FPG International; 268(t), Harcourt School Publishers; 268(b), Diaphor Agency / Index Stock; 269(t), Lawrence Migdale / Photo Researchers, Inc.; 269(b), Corbis.

Illustration Credits

Richard Cowdrey, Cover Art; Doug Bowles, 4-7; Tomek Bogacki, 8, 33, 36; Christine Mau, 34, 121, 214; C. D. Hullinger, 35; Liz Callen, 37, 250; Arnold Lobel, 38-59; Steve Björkman, 64, 95; Eldon Doty, 65 ,67, 253; Ethan Long, 97; Marlene Hill Donnely, 98-119, 122; Dona Turner, 120-121; Jo Lynn Alcorn, 123; David McPhail, 124-149, 152-154; Floyd Cooper, 150-151; Taia Morley, 155, 217; Mark Teague, 156-182, 184; Stacy Peterson, 185; Wendy Watson, 186-211, 215-216; Melissa Iwai, 212-213; Georg Hallensleben, 218-247, 252; Clare Schaumann, 251.

Pupil Edition Acknowledgments